Academic Initiatives in Total Quality for Higher Education

Also available from ASQC Quality Press

Orchestrating Learning with Quality
David P. Langford and Barbara A. Cleary, Ph.D.

Using Quality to Redesign School Systems: The Cutting Edge of Common Sense
Penny Siegel and Sandra Byrne

Public Schools Should Learn to Ski: A Systems Approach to Education
Stephen E. Rubin

Kidgets: and other insightful stories about quality in education
Maury Cotter and Daniel Seymour

Total Quality for Schools: A Suggestion for American Education
Joseph C. Fields

Total Quality for Schools: A Guide for Implementation
Joseph C. Fields

Quality Education
Gray Rinehart

To request a complimentary catalog of publications, call 800-248-1946.

Academic Initiatives in Total Quality for Higher Education

Harry V. Roberts, editor

ASQC Quality Press
Milwaukee, Wisconsin

Academic Initiatives in Total Quality for Higher Education
Harry V. Roberts, editor

Library of Congress Cataloging-in-Publication Data

Academic initiatives in total quality for higher education / Harry
   V. Roberts, editor.
      p.   cm.
   Includes bibliographical references and index.
   ISBN 0-87389-326-3 (alk. paper)
      1. College teaching—United States—Case studies.   2. Total
quality management—United States—Case studies.   I. Roberts, Harry
V.
   LB2331.A28   1995
   378.1'25'0973—dc20   95-18839
                                                             CIP

10 9 8 7 6 5 4 3 2

ISBN 0-87389-326-3

Acquisitions Editor: Susan Westergard
Project Editor: Kelley Cardinal

ASQC Mission: To facilitate continuous improvement and increase customer satisfaction by identifying, communicating, and promoting the use of quality principles, concepts, and technologies; and thereby be recognized throughout the world as the leading authority on, and champion for, quality.

Attention: Schools and Corporations
ASQC Quality Press books, audio, video, and software are available at quantity discounts with bulk purchases for business, educational, or instructional use. For information, please contact ASQC Quality Press at 800-248-1946, or write to ASQC Quality Press, P.O. Box 3005, Milwaukee, WI 53201-3005.

For a free copy of the ASQC Quality Press Publications Catalog, including ASQC membership information, call 800-248-1946.

Printed in the United States of America

 Printed on acid-free paper

 ASQC
Quality Press
611 East Wisconsin Avenue
Milwaukee, Wisconsin 53202

Contents

Introduction

Harry V. Roberts

University of Chicago Graduate School of Business

Faculty Involvement in Total Quality

The papers in *Academic Initiatives in Total Quality for Higher Education* suggest many ways in which total quality can be used effectively by college and university faculty to improve academic quality.

Many people feel that it is hard to get the faculty involved in total quality. An unpublished survey of deans of business and engineering schools was conducted in connection with Total Quality Forum VI, hosted by Texas Instruments in the fall of 1994. Almost all responding deans felt that total quality was very important for teaching and research as well as for university administration, but they also felt that their own faculty were much less convinced than they were that this was so.

From assembling the papers for this book and reflecting on my own experiences in total quality for higher education, I think that I am in a good position to offer some useful suggestions about how to get faculty interested and involved in total quality. Setting down these suggestions in this introduction also serves to provide an overview of the book. The papers in the book fill in the picture that I sketch here.

Myron Tribus said, "Do total quality in the classroom or don't do it at all." He had two main points in mind.

- The academic side of education is the main arena, and total quality must reach that arena to bear real fruit.

- Improving the administrative side of education can be wasteful if, as sometimes happens, it is directed to administrative processes that are not needed.

I am more sanguine than Tribus about improving administrative processes. Many of them are needed to support essential academic processes, but we should not stop with administrative improvements, nor defer academic improvements to the indefinite future. We should look to the faculty—and students—to draw on the ideas and tools of total quality.

Academic Initiatives in Total Quality for Higher Education is about the faculty and student side of total quality. A central theme of the book is that total quality can be in the faculty's self-interest in a number of ways.

- Administrative successes in total quality usually make faculty life better. It's nice when the bookstore has the textbooks available when they are needed.

- Total quality can make the direct administrative activities of professors less unpleasant and more rewarding. Businesslike faculty meetings would be a major advance.

- Most professors would like to be better teachers and could benefit from the help total quality offers toward achieving that goal—if it doesn't take too much time.

- Most professors wish they had more time for research and scholarship. The personal brand of total quality—*personal quality*—can be of genuine help in finding that time.

Total quality advocates often follow the strategy of preaching to professors about students as customers or urging them to take training in team problem-solving procedures. I think that it is better, though not easy, to convince faculty by an appeal to self-interest. The argument is as follows.

The potential gains from total quality come not from working harder, but from rooting out the wastes that pervade organizational and individual work processes, *including teaching and research processes*. Waste includes process flaws and mistakes, and process steps that are unnecessary.

These wastes are pervasive, but not obvious until faculty start learning how to look for them. Once faculty catch on to the idea of waste elimination, they will find that the potential improvement is much greater than they would have imagined.

In short, it is possible for professors not only to do their jobs a little better, but a lot better. And the improvement can be never ending. This, to me, is what makes total quality exciting. I've seen it happen in the best companies, like Motorola. I've seen foreshadowing of it in a few universities, colleges, and community colleges, many of which are reported in this book. And I've experienced it in a small way myself by exploring two concrete routes to improvement that can be applied by individual faculty members, regardless of whether their colleges or universities have total quality initiatives. The two routes are two-way fast feedback in teaching and personal quality. Next I'll summarize highlights of these two routes, both of which are discussed at length in this volume.

Two-Way Fast Feedback Leads to Improvement of Teaching

The key idea of this concept is that the professor uses simple questionnaires to get fast feedback from students at all or most class meetings and then gives the students prompt, detailed feedback, oral or written, on their feedback. Two-way fast feedback leads to continuing improvement of teaching and learning via correction of teaching flaws (such as unreadable overheads or difficulties in being heard) reported by students and deeper problems such as muddy explanations, failure to build enthusiasm for the subject, or tension between students who are well prepared and those who are not. It also opens up a second channel of communication between professor and students. For example, muddy points in one lecture can be cleared up quickly in written feedback from professor to student, without taking more class time in the next session. Students read and value written fast feedback from the professor. Through time, the frequency of flaws and muddy points is gradually reduced, and the professor learns general lessons about teaching. For example,

- Students can never get too many concrete examples to illustrate theory.

- Students are frustrated by course reading packets that contain vastly more material than they can possibly read.

- Students often are inherently skeptical about the value of course material, and a little "marketing" by the professor can reduce this skepticism.

- Tension between better- and poorer-prepared students is inevitable, but it can be managed if the professor has current information on the problems faced by each group.

Two-way fast feedback is springing up at business schools and on campuses more generally all over the country. This observation is based on my own direct experience in visiting a number of universities in the last few years and on reactions that I have received to a paper by George Bateman and me, "Total Quality for Professors and Students," which is included in this book. Several other examples are included in this book.

Many professors use a "minute paper" that asks only one or two questions such as "What was the muddiest point in the lecture?" and "What was the most important thing you learned?", while Bateman and I use a formal one-page feedback questionnaire. Many provide somewhat less extensive reverse feedback—professor to students—than we do. (If they provide too little reverse feedback, students cease cooperating and the effort dies.) But regardless of details of methodology, the results are usually gratifying.[1]

These successes suggest the possibility that faculty may gain from application of other total quality ideas and tools as well, not just fast feedback.

Personal Quality for Improvement of Research

There are also potential applications of total quality for research. Total quality relies on down-to-earth application of scientific method. This creates possibilities, such as

- Freed-up time for research by application of principles of personal quality: total quality applied to ordinary job duties. The amount of time is not trivial. For many faculty members, I would suggest two hours per day as a reasonably attainable gain within a relatively short time.

- Improvement of research processes, especially by waste reduction.

- Reduction of wasteful faculty administrative activities with consequent freeing of time for actual research.

- Facilitation of team research by application of total quality experiences with effective use of teams.

Since personal quality is one way to make more time available for research, I'll turn now to a brief discussion of personal quality. One approach to improved personal quality is to use a personal quality checklist.

- Choose one or a few processes that you employ in doing your daily work or in your personal life.

- Set customer-based performance standards that define flaws or defects in these processes.

- Count and record defects by days, weeks, or months.

- Treat defects as friends who are giving you hints as to underlying root causes that you can correct and thus reduce the frequency of defects in the future.

- Use the desire to avoid defects as a psychological boost to improvement.

- Keep improving, including improving your checklist by adding new standards.

Examples of useful performance standards for your checklist follow.

- Arrive on time to appointments and meetings and promptly reply to phone, fax, e-mail, and other messages.

- If you are going to do a small task eventually, do it when it first presents itself.
- Every day you work in your office, make some improvement in its organization or functioning.
- Don't let interruptions fluster you and throw you off stride.
- Don't ever put anything down other than in the place it belongs. (This may force you to think about where it belongs!)
- Plan a realistic, congenial fitness program and count defects on failure to conform to it.

Some tips on personal quality checklists include the following.

- Take the idea seriously, give it a chance. It may liberate you from job discouragement!
- Standards need to be well-defined.
- Standards are not New Year's resolutions. Most people are already trying hard, and resolution to try harder is pretty futile.
- Standards should be focused on time saving and waste reduction.
- Activity-expanding standards (for example, "Spend twice as much time on research as I am currently doing") should be used sparingly, if at all. Expansion of time comes from waste reduction.

The personal quality checklist is a simple and practical example of the application of quality ideas to improve personal quality. But personal quality approaches other than checklists are also available. For example, improvement can often be achieved by a special effort, or project, directed to a perceived improvement opportunity. For a simple illustration, in a very short time I applied simple total quality concepts to reduce my shaving time from 6 minutes to 3 minutes. With further effort, I reduced 3 minutes to less than two. I did not hurry up, but I did cut out waste. The improvement sounds small, but it is impressive in the aggregate—roughly three working days a year—and it suggests the potential for further improvement in many other personal processes.

Recently, for the first time, I had the opportunity to supervise a substantial number of personal quality improvement projects by students in an executive MBA class. It has turned out that my shaving example may be just the tip of an iceberg for possible improvements. Students have easily and quickly found ways of making similar percentage reductions in cycle time—half to two-thirds—but much bigger absolute time savings—typically 15–45 minutes a day—in a variety of routine personal processes, such as getting started with work in the morning. Similar improvements are obtained in job processes, such as the quality of meetings or the use of communications. I think that faculty could do at least as well as my executive students, if only because faculty have fewer deadlines to constrain their activity. Moreover, as a result of conversations with Duncan Neuhauser of Case Western Reserve University, I realize that there is very substantial room for improvement in the research processes themselves, if quality principles are applied. Here are possibilities.

• It is usually assumed that time sheltered from other activities, such as teaching, is necessary for research. Yet we are usually limited in the amount of time that we can shelter for research, so we must learn to make good use of nonsheltered time. Fast changeover is the quality idea that is applicable here. For example, fast changes of die on an assembly line can make it possible to switch quickly from production of one model of motorcycle to another. The analogue for the assembly line of research is the capability of making quick mental transitions from a non-research task to a research task. My personal experience suggests that this capability can be influenced by one's own attitude: once we realize that there will never be enough unbroken time for all the research we want to do, and that some broken time can be used for research, then it's not hard to extend our research to fill some of the broken time.

• We can concentrate on reducing the cycle time of research projects to the extent possible. For example, we can try always to have one priority research or writing project continually in background mode, which can be activated promptly whenever a small block of time opens up. Neuhauser's work shows that many faculty have substantial interruptions in which they are diverted from a research project for days or weeks, during which they can easily lose momentum.

• In writing projects, it is especially important to press for fast cycle time in producing "drafts" of articles or chapters of books. Completion of a draft, however rough, is often an occasion for which interruption of further work at that time is actually desirable, however much room for improvement there may be. For after the manuscript has been set aside for a while, it is much easier to see opportunities for further improvement. This leads to the continuing improvement that is so stressed by total quality.

• On the other hand, incomplete drafts that are set aside defeat the aim of fast cycle time. It has been found repeatedly in manufacturing that having too many incomplete assemblies in various stages of completion can greatly reduce throughput. Research implication: don't try to do too many research projects in parallel, lest bottlenecks arise that will delay or defeat your entire research program.

Curriculum: The Galvin Challenge

The Galvin challenge is a response by Bob Galvin, then chairman of the board of Motorola, to a faculty member who asked in 1989 at the Xerox Quality Forum what courses should be given up in order to make room for total quality in business school curricula.

> What do you give up? I wonder if it's fair to ask of you, as we in industry have been obliged to ask of ourselves, "How efficient are you? Why can't you teach 50 percent more in a year than you're now teaching?" Not one percent. It's this big step-function phenomenon. Why can't you in two or three years change your curricula? Decide that you're going to add all these things in two or three years, and do it. That is what we in industry are having to do to serve our customers.

Stretch goals, such as "50 percent more in a year," are common in industry. Motorola has made great advances by setting outrageous stretch goals and then making major progress toward them. Currently its corporate goal for all processes is to achieve a tenfold reduction in cycle time every five years. Brenda Sumberg of Motorola University says, in a paper in this book, "The company's stress on the importance of reduction of cycle time applies to training and education just as to any other process. We are thinking of how to reduce the time it takes for students to learn a given amount of materials. The company goal of a tenfold decrease in cycle time every five years means that we would have to provide as much learning in four hours as we now do in forty hours. We don't know if it's possible or not. But that's certainly the direction we need to look."

Potential Contributions of Total Quality

Applied, for example, to the teaching of a course, total quality suggests

- The possibility of teaching more in a given course (or the same course in less time).
- Cutting out unnecessary topics that contribute little or nothing to the course, or unifying concepts that are now treated separately.
- Continually making the course content more up-to-date and valuable.
- Continually removing obstacles to student understanding while finding better ways of helping students reinforce learning by doing.

- Several papers in this book show that total quality lends itself to doing this by means of real-world, real-time student quality improvement projects.

For applications to curricula, total quality suggests possibilities like these.

- Current curricula could be shortened.

- Some engineering deans say that the advertised four-year undergraduate program has become a de facto five-year program. Why not a de facto four-year program, or even three?

- Why can't two-year MBA programs be done in a single, intense year with no summer internships?

Further, radical revisions of curricula might be contemplated. Unified, team-taught curricula could replace traditional courses that are individually taught and imperfectly integrated. This has been done in the business school at the University of Tennessee, reported in this book. Some other examples of encouraging progress also reported are Babson College, the University of Maryland, the University of Kansas, Rochester Institute of Technology, Arizona State University, Oregon State University, and the Keller School of Management.

Signs of Progress: The Total Quality Forums and the University Challenges

There have been two major initiatives from the business sector toward the effective use of total quality in higher education. Beginning in 1989, several leading companies including, among others, Xerox, Procter & Gamble, Motorola, and Texas Instruments, have sponsored a series of annual Total Quality Forums for colleges and universities, with two primary aims.

- To encourage the application of total quality to teaching, curriculum, and research, with major initial emphasis on colleges of business and engineering

- To encourage the application of total quality in running colleges and universities

The forums have been addressed mainly to senior academic leaders—presidents, vice presidents, provosts, and deans. This focus is based on the belief that total quality implementation in higher education must have the informed support and the active participation of its senior leadership. Two of the leaders of the first forum—Bob Galvin of Motorola and David Kearns of Xerox—provided outstanding examples of senior leadership in their own companies, and it seemed natural to address the Total Quality Forums to their potential counterparts in higher education.

Sponsors of the Total Quality Forums and other interested companies have undertaken what is called a TQM University Challenge. This idea was pioneered in 1991 by Bob Galvin of Motorola at the Total Quality Forum of that year. In most cases the challenge starts with a visit to the company by about 100 faculty members and administrators. Several days of training are then followed up by continuing company–university partnerships to apply total quality ideas and tools to higher education. About 22 companies and over 40 universities were involved in these partnerships as of fall 1994. Several of the case histories reported in this book were stimulated by such partnerships.

Finally, the Total Quality Forums have worked with the business community and the National Science Foundation (NSF) to set up an NSF program for research in total quality. The first awards were made in early 1995. This program not only encourages research in total quality, but legitimizes total quality as a field in which academic research is possible.

Signs of Progress

A number of schools have tied major changes in important courses, even the whole academic program, to total quality. Hence, although total quality has not yet become a top priority at more than a handful of colleges and universities, there are encouraging case histories to report. Here are examples that I have learned about in the process of editing this book, which contains the stories of most of them.

Major curricular changes in MBA and/or undergraduate business programs happened at the following institutions.

- Rochester Institute of Technology
- Babson College
- The University of Kansas
- Oregon State University
- Portland State University
- The University of Tennessee
- Arizona State University
- The Keller School of Management
- The University of Chicago

Major curricular changes in other programs occurred at these schools.

- The engineering schools at the Georgia Institute of Technology, the University of Wisconsin-Madison, and Rochester Institute of Technology

- The entire University of Maryland
- Classroom instruction at Pennsylvania State University, Rio Salado Community College, and Belmont University
- Undergraduate statistics or quantitative methods teaching at the University of Kansas, the University of Nevada-Las Vegas, Valparaiso University, and Florida State University
- Graduate statistics teaching at Baruch College, CUNY, and the University of Chicago

Student Involvement in Quality Improvement Projects

Courses have been developed in which business students (individually or in teams) do successful real-life quality improvement projects. By successful I mean not just a valuable educational experience for the students, though these courses certainly provide that. I mean that substantial practical quality improvements can be made by students in real organizations during a few weeks or months. Cost savings from these improvements are sometimes very substantial, running up into six or even seven digits. Examples (not an exhaustive listing!) include

- University of Chicago
- Columbia University (Peter Kolesar)
- University of Wisconsin-Madison (Mark Finster)
- University of Nevada-Las Vegas
- Portland State University

As Willard Zangwill of the University of Chicago has pointed out, these student successes have implications not only for student training in quality, but for the implementation of quality. Perhaps there should be more emphasis on speed and quick improvement, on the reduction in cycle time for key processes. This can be surprisingly easy to do if the students know a little about process analysis and just-in-time production. The improvements achieved by students need not be small. But small or large, their cumulative impact can be enormous. Moreover, in the context of higher education, college and university students can be engaged in the total quality efforts at their own schools and can make substantial contributions to it. This is an example of what can be called grass-roots total quality: students can be shock troops for improvement at their own schools.

Grassroots Total Quality

In implementation of total quality, it is desirable to have strong leadership from the top. It is also desirable to have quality initiatives at the grassroots of the college or university to reinforce the top-down efforts. Susan Engelkemeyer of Babson College calls this "top-down, bubble-up." However, it may not always be feasible for top administrators to play an active leadership role. The experience of the University of Chicago and others suggests that quiet support and encouragement from the top may suffice, so long as the organizational culture is favorable to innovation. Faculty members need not roll over and play dead with respect to total quality just because the boss is not pushing them to do it!

A key success factor is the point I made at the outset: total quality can be in the strong self-interest of faculty. At the same time, most faculty members have a strong tendency to ignore or to resist total quality efforts in higher education. The balance of this Introduction is a discussion of faculty resistance and ways of dealing with it.

Faculty Resistance and Ways of Dealing with It

We all think that our own organizations present unique obstacles to implementation of total quality. Higher education is no exception. The obstacles in higher education, however, are somewhat different from those in business organizations, and these obstacles need to be understood. Before I get into the obstacles and their corresponding challenges, some general suggestions.

- Beware of semantic traps. Total quality, TQM, and the many other names and acronyms for quality can easily be tarnished by poor attempts at implementation or by association of quality improvement with the business world, with no applicability to education.

- Stress what you're hoping to do, and how; don't give it a name or acronym.

- Beware the term *customer* as applied to students: don't hassle the faculty about that.

- The key idea behind "student as customer" is that faculty should assume some degree of responsibility for student success and avoid the rationalization that poor student performance is beyond faculty control. This can come as a by-product of trying to improve one's teaching, as in two-way fast feedback. Notice that students can't tell much about *what* to teach, but they can tell very accurately when they are confused, bored, or skeptical about the value of the course.

Incentives for improvement are needed. Public course evaluations can be strong incentives for improvement of teaching. I believe, for example, that teaching at my business school at the University of Chicago is very good. I believe that a major reason for that success is one that would be abhorrent to W. Edwards Deming: for a quarter-century Chicago has had public course evaluations. The ratings are widely read by students, faculty, and administrators. Faculty accept them as valid and respond to the incentive they create. Faculty want to be good at anything they do that can be measured! The Kellogg School at Northwestern reports a similar experience. Public course evaluations are not always pleasant. Even good teachers have occasional lapses. But they are accepted by the faculties both at Northwestern and Chicago.

Faculty Apathy Toward Total Quality

Faculty resistance to total quality is one thing. Faculty apathy is a deeper problem. Many faculty members see nothing bad or threatening about total quality, but they are happy in their own work and don't want to take time for an activity such as total quality that seems to be of low priority. As I argued at the outset, total quality can be in faculty self-interest, and self-interest should be the central theme of any effort to sell total quality to faculty.

To do this effectively, we first must understand that for most professors, the total quality notion of never ending process improvements—large and small—is simply not believable. Maybe continuous improvement applies to automotive manufacturing, say faculty, but it certainly does not apply to teaching! Professors think (rightly) that they are pretty good teachers. They think (wrongly) that only fine-tuning of teaching is possible. I believe that more than fine-tuning is possible even when teaching is already very good by usual standards. Remember the Galvin challenge!

Superficially, there appears to be both convincing evidence and sound reasoning to support these faculty views. For reasonably successful teachers, their student course evaluations or general reputations are near the top of the scale and can't go very much higher. Student test scores—a common measure of teaching success—could, in principle, go much higher, but they seem to be bounded by ceilings that are difficult to break through. It may even be that as teaching generally improves, student aspiration levels rise, so that keeping close to the top of the course evaluation scale or retaining a reputation for good teaching becomes a sufficient challenge for most professors.

The incentive to try major teaching innovations is relatively weak. If the innovation succeeds, the measured improvement may be small. If it fails, there is lots of room on the downside of the evaluation scale.

As to student improvement, we usually measure what students have learned (though not what they can do with what they have learned) by paper-and-pencil tests administered at the time a course is taken. Faculty are often disappointed at test performance, but they accept tests as necessary. As an example, consider Ph.D. preliminaries. Faculty often deplore doctoral student performance, yet the faculty who are deploring today's doctoral students were themselves deplored in the past. It never seems to occur to them that the measurement instrument, the preliminary exam itself, may be at fault!

I am skeptical about the assumptions of paper-and-pencil tests: that tests measure knowledge; that knowledge is storable in a general form, so that we can draw on it for application at the time of need; and that we apply knowledge without quite being aware of what particular knowledge we are drawing on. There is something to be said for these assumptions: our ability to function effectively in life is a tribute to the knowledge we have picked up in school.

But in the total quality view of learning, these traditional assumptions represent "just-in-case" learning, as opposed to "just-in-time." Experience in total quality suggests that knowledge not applied quickly is quickly lost. The idea that specific learning should lead to specific action is axiomatic in training for total quality. The student quality-improvement projects described earlier suggest that learning can lead to specific and highly desirable action. I regard this as a major victory for the just-in-time philosophy, one that challenges the just-in-case philosophy.

In some academic fields—specifically business and engineering—we need not rely on paper-and-pencil tests. As suggested, we can evaluate students based on their performance on practical projects that require them to apply what they are learning. If we do this, the ceilings on student performance need not be fixed. The successes of student quality-improvement projects support this view. I do not know how widely the project approach is feasible in other educational areas, but I would presume that improvement projects are always worth consideration, even in the liberal arts.

Academic Culture and Total Quality

The faculty culture—and university culture in general—does not make it easy to convince faculty that never ending improvements—both small and large, but always large in cumulative impact—are possible. I now sketch some salient features of academic culture that must be taken into consideration when attempting to apply total quality. The tone of this sketch is pessimistic because I want to convey the root causes of difficulty in reaching faculty with the message of total quality. Difficulties can be surmounted only when they are well understood.

In many fields, elementary textbooks differ only in minor respects and evolve very slowly through time. Modalities of teaching lag behind current best practice and available technology. Lecture and blackboard are still the dominant mode.

More broadly, universities seldom formulate vision, mission, and values statements or do effective strategic planning. According to conventional academic wisdom, presidents and deans can have only very limited impact on academic processes at their institutions. Faculties are thought to be too independent, too powerful, and too stubborn to heed directions from the top.

For most faculty, there is almost nothing in all prior experience to help them to conceive what total quality might accomplish. They can't imagine, for example, how much waste there is in the work processes they use for teaching and research. Most faculty seek very ambitious outcomes—home run articles, Nobel prizes, outstanding textbooks, and spectacularly good teaching. They think hard and work hard in hopes of doing so. It does not occur to them that aggressive improvement of the processes of research and teaching might help to reach these desired outcomes.

If pressed, most faculty would concede that existing processes of teaching and research are not perfect and that they could be modestly improved if faculty worked a little harder, had better administrative and budgetary support, or were freed from some of the unpleasant chores of academic citizenship. But Bob Galvin's concept of "teaching 50 percent more in a year" comes from another world that has little in common with colleges and universities.

Faculty research, in practice, is usually much more cautious than would be expected from total quality ideas. The possibility for never ending and substantial improvement in current processes of research is not perceived. Even though they aspire to do pioneering research and to hit home runs in their own publications, many faculty members are conservative in the kinds of research they actually do. Much academic research is done within narrow paradigms, specialization is extreme, and one's main customers are tiny bands of workers in one's own field. Major changes in research paradigms are infrequent, and even when they occur, most researchers tend to stick with the old paradigms.

Faculty members often are involved, at least part-time, in administration. They often serve on quasi-administrative committees, such as curriculum committees, hiring committees, promotion committees, and governance bodies. Much of the time, committee members try to persuade each other of the correctness of their own views, not to obtain a group synthesis. For example, curriculum committees often are concerned mainly with the allocation of turf to the component academic disciplines represented by their members and with argumentation about philosophical views. Even when committees try to work as teams, they don't know how to do it.

The total quality idea that opinions should be supported by facts is largely absent. Protocols for efficient meetings are all but unknown in universities. If suggested, such protocols might meet resistance, or even contempt or ridicule, as being incompatible with thoughtful exploration of important ideas.

The faculty culture is strongly individualistic. Even in fields like medicine where journal articles have long lists of coauthors, faculty research and teaching is dominated by individuals, not teams. Collaborations involve mostly pairs and occasional threesomes. Total quality does not insist on teamwork in all circumstances, but it emphasizes the great potential value of teamwork on cross-functional problems.

There has been little or no team "new product development" for new educational programs, research, or teaching. Research grant applications aside, faculty are rarely involved in fund-raising or in lobbying for public funding. There may be major advantages in the encouragement of greater faculty involvement in fund-raising.

Summary Suggestions for Appealing to Faculty Self-Interest

The generally discouraging picture just painted has its bright side. *If faculty can be convinced—especially by demonstration—that total quality is in their self-interest, they are much more likely to be interested in total quality.* So we are back to the starting point of self-interest. Here are summary suggestions.

- Faculty have a great deal of freedom in deciding on the research they will undertake and how they will do it, and they have a very strong interest in being highly regarded researchers.

- At the very least, total quality principles may free additional time for doing research, and they may suggest how to do more effective and efficient research.

- Faculty have at least some freedom in deciding what they teach and how, and they have an obvious self-interest in being more highly regarded as teachers.

- Application of total quality principles to the classroom offers potential help in achieving this goal.

- Total quality principles can be applied to curriculum development. Some universities and colleges are already doing it. Will they be tomorrow's leaders?

Note

1. One caution is in order: when quality improves, the aspirations of the customers are raised, whether in business or in education. A sensational improvement in customer satisfaction today will be taken for granted tomorrow.

Total Quality Management in Schools of Business and Engineering

Myron Tribus

Exergy, Inc.

Introduction

Total quality management (TQM)* has been proven successful in many different enterprises around the world. Applications in engineering and business management have also been clearly advantageous in commerce, especially in the design and manufacture of automobiles and consumer products. The interest in total quality management is now worldwide. In North and South America, England and Europe, Australia and Asia, conferences and seminars on TQM occur, almost daily, with large attendance and testimonials to its success.

As we all know, although educators are among the first to write about new ideas, they are almost always the last to apply them to their own activities. Schools of business are not famous for being well managed. Schools of engineering do not apply engineering methods to their own operations. Thus it has happened that the quality movement has been active in the United States for over a decade, and, yet, it has been only in the last year or two that we have heard of schools making a definite attempt to apply TQM to their own activities.

In presenting this paper, I begin by assuming that the reader already knows what TQM is. The reader is presumed to have read books such as Deming's *Out of the Crisis*,[1] and other related works. My objective is to discuss how to apply TQM to education, especially higher education, in schools of engineering and schools of

---

*Editor's note: *Total quality management* is a synonym for *total quality*, the term used in most papers in this book.

17

business administration. Because there are no examples of schools that have done this to my knowledge, my examples will be taken from isolated instances of work done in education by myself and others, in an environment in which TQM has not been established for the institution as a whole.

What Is the Product?

To begin, let us agree that *the student is not a product.* The product is *the education of the student.* In the manufacture of this product, as with any other product, it is essential that the worker (student) be an active participant in the design and creation of the product. The student, who is the person who stays with the learning process longest, should learn to become the comanager of his or her education. This means, according to the tenets of TQM, that the student should be involved, consciously and with skill, in the continuous improvement of the processes that create the product.

Who Are the Customers for the Product?

The customers for the education of the student are several. They are, in order of importance,

1. *The student,* who must live with the product for the rest of his or her life. The student must become the comanager of the production of the education and, having such a personal stake, must be considered first when attempting to define what it means to have quality in education.

2. *The student's parents and immediate family,* who, in many instances, are paying for the product and must also live with the results for the rest of their lives.

3. *Potential employers,* who will rely on the education of the student after graduation to achieve the purposes of their enterprises.

4. *Society at large,* which pays a substantial proportion of the cost of the education and requires the future participation of the student as a citizen in the operation of government, as a contributor to the general welfare of society, and as a taxpayer who will support the education of future generations of students.

Within the educational enterprise, at the K–12 level, we have recognized the existence of a number of supplier–customer relations, as pictured in Table 1.[2] I have not yet seen a similar table for engineering or management schools. That is a challenge I leave to you.

Table 1. Customer–supplier relations in K–12 education.

Customer	Supplier	Services
Students	Teachers	System management Curriculum design Counseling Leadership Materials and equipment
	Administrators	Systems development and analysis Materials and equipment
	School boards	Policy
Teachers	Administrators	Materials and equipment
Parents	School system	Knowledge, wisdom, know-how, and character of their children
Industry	School system	Knowledge, wisdom, know-how, and character of graduates

What Should We Expect from Education?

I propose that we examine any educational offering by analyzing its content in four categories.

1. *Knowledge*, which enables us to understand what we learn in relation to what we already know. Knowledge is both practical and theoretical. Theoretical knowledge provides us with the ability to generalize from unique instances. With theoretical knowledge, we can accumulate 30 years of experience. Otherwise, with only practical knowledge, we will have only one year repeated 30 times.

2. *Know-how*, which enables us to *do*. Know-how takes us past merely understanding. Know-how enables us to put knowledge to work. Know-how differs significantly from knowledge. Knowledge can be organized into intellectually tight compartments, and these compartments may be taught as a subject unto themselves. Know-how, on the other hand, requires the purposeful organization of knowledge from many different areas of learning. As know-how is extended to higher and higher levels of accomplishment, it requires extension to more and more areas of knowledge. When teaching know-how, it is impossible to put bounds on the areas of knowledge which will be encompassed.

3. *Wisdom* is the ability to distinguish what is important from what is not. Wisdom enables us to set priorities on how to use our resources of time, energy, and emotion.

4. *Character,* as Stephen Covey has said, is a combination of knowledge, know-how, and wisdom coupled with motivation.[3] We often recognize the development of character by certain character traits, among which we might list

Honesty	Initiative	Curiosity
Truthfulness	Integrity	Cooperativeness
Ability to work alone	Ability to work in groups	Self-esteem

It is up each educational enterprise to identify what to include in each of these four categories. It appears that in higher education, attention is given only to the first of the four categories, with the last two not even given lip service.

Professors often believe, as I once did, that at the university level their sole duty is to develop knowledge and pass it on to the next generation. The development of the student's character is none of their business. President Robert Gordon Sproul used to say to the students, "The university sets a bountiful table, but it guarantees neither the appetite nor the digestion." Only the football coach seems to care about the development of character.

The typical professor in the university would consider it beneath a professor's calling to actually teach people to apply their knowledge in a practical way. I recall my professor of mathematics when asked, "Sir, what good is the hypergeometric equation?" replying, in all seriousness, "Some people may use it to put two cars in every garage or two chickens in every pot. I, for one, do not give a damn!"

Professional schools, such as schools of business and schools of engineering, usually attempt to provide more than knowledge and understanding. They claim to provide the competence to actually do something, but because they are imbedded in a university setting, they find themselves struggling to maintain status while they depart from the norms of the university. The result is that while they may often move to include the second category, for example, teaching effective presentation skills or the ability to design, they are often on the defensive, trying to justify these objectives to other faculties.

Faculties seldom make an overt effort to include the third and fourth categories. Indeed, I have had more than one professor say to me, "How could I possibly teach wisdom, when I have so little of it myself?"

What Do Future Employers Want from Education?

The list of knowledge that students are expected to acquire is usually a composite of what is required for accreditation and what the school decides itself. The list of know-hows is usually less specific, except for vocational schools. In general, the accrediting authorities pay no attention to the development of either wisdom or character. For example, the U.S. Department of Education, in laying out the goals for education in the year 2000, is silent on these matters. On the other hand, when the secretary of labor of the United States appointed a commission from industry to say what was wanted of the graduates of our schools, it identified five competencies and a three-part foundation of skills and personal qualities needed for solid job performance.[4] Figure 1 is taken directly from the Secretary's Commission on Achieving Necessary Skills (SCANS) report.

Defining Quality in Education

What do I mean by quality in education? *Quality in education is what makes learning a pleasure and a joy.* Some measures of student performance may be increased by threats, by competitions for grades, or by prizes, but the attachment to learning will be unhealthy. It takes a quality experience to create an independent learner.

Joy is ever changing. What is thrilling at one age is infantile at another. Teachers must be ever alert to engage the students in a discussion of what constitutes a quality experience. The negotiations and discussions are never done. It takes constant engagement to wed a student to learning.

You know you are providing quality in education when you find your students working diligently with enjoyment in independent study and discussing what they have learned, in an animated way, eager to engage you in debate or to show you what they have discovered for themselves. This is the kind of joy I have in mind. It is based on doing a quality job because a quality job feels good.

If you are a teacher, imagine how it would feel if after giving a lecture and asking, "Are there any questions?" the students didn't ask, "Will this material be on the exam?"

The Difference Between Features and Quality

In the application of quality principles, it is important to distinguish between the concepts of *features* and *quality.*

Features are what you put into the product to distinguish it from other products and to appeal to the people for whom the product is intended. Thus, the kinds of knowledge and know-how that are included in the curriculum represent the features of the educational program. A school of engineering may boast, for example, of the excellent laboratories and shop facilities it has for student use. A business school may tout its computer facilities and internship program with industry. These are features.

WORKPLACE KNOW-HOW

The know-how identified by SCANS is made up of five competencies and a three-part foundation of skills and personal qualities that are needed for solid job performance. These include

COMPETENCIES—Effective workers can productively use

- *Resources*—allocating time, money, materials, space, and staff
- *Interpersonal skills*—working on teams, teaching others, serving customers, leading, negotiating, and working well with people from culturally diverse backgrounds
- *Information*—acquiring and evaluating data, organizing and maintaining files, interpreting and communicating, and using computers to process information
- *Systems*—understanding social, organizational, and technological systems; monitoring and correcting performance; and designing or improving systems
- *Technology*—selecting equipment and tools, applying technology to specific tasks and maintaining and troubleshooting technologies

THE FOUNDATION—Competence requires

- *Basic skills*—reading, writing, arithmetic and mathematics, speaking, and listening
- *Thinking skills*—thinking creatively, making decisions, solving problems, seeing things in the mind's eye, knowing how to learn, and reasoning
- *Personal qualities*—individual responsibility, self-esteem, sociability, self-management, and integrity

---

Figure 1. The suggested competencies and foundation of skills and personal qualities necessary for a solid job performance.

Quality, on the other hand, has to do with the way the features are delivered. Laboratories may be unkempt, equipment may not always work, the instructions may be poor. The internship in industry may be just an excuse to send the students away for a time and allow them to earn some money while the faculty consults.

The Difference Between Teaching and Learning

Teaching occurs when I show you how I solve a problem. *Learning* occurs when you figure out how to solve your problem. Quality management in education should be concerned with the improvement of both processes, teaching and learning.

Learning, of course, can never be separated from the motivation to learn. One of the most powerful principles of learning is this.

People learn best when they feel the need to know.

Teachers, therefore, should pay great attention to creating a healthy situation in which the students feel a need to know.

A common mistake in teaching is to create a need to know through fear, for example, announcing an important test to be given in the near future and emphasizing that grades will be strongly dependent upon the results. This is the aspect of education that made Einstein say that it was only after his education that he could begin to learn! W. Edwards Deming is explicit on this point: Eliminate fear! Fear is destructive of education. At best it produces conditioned reflexes. At worst, it generates cynicism and disgust with education.

There are many possible relations between teacher and learner. They may be put in a spectrum, as indicated in Figure 2.[5]

The Role of Tests and Examinations

Just as quality leaders in world commerce have eliminated the need for final inspection, so should the aim of academia be to eliminate the need for final examinations in education. Final inspection used to be the method whereby a manufacturer attempted to assure the company and its customers that the product was fit for use. It seemed like a reasonable approach, and, for most educators, the concept of a final examination seems rational. It isn't.

In industry we have found that reliance on final inspection increases cost, produces inferior products, and masks the inefficiencies of the process.

As one who has been an executive and has had to rely on the education of my employees to produce better, more competitive products, I can testify to what every engineering executive will tell you: most of our employees do not know how to make use of the materials they studied in school. Most use only a very small fraction of what they have been taught. The efficiency of the teaching/learning process is low. Education, for most students, is getting past the next examination. As I mentioned

Teacher	Do to	Do for	Do with	Enable
Learner	No choice Captive Antagonist	Captive Passive Dependent	Dependent Accepting Follower	Independent Investigator Seeker of knowledge
Attitude	Let me out	I'll tough it out	I'm OK, you're OK	Joy in learning
Motivation	Extrinsic	Extrinsic	Extrinsic	Intrinsic

Figure 2. A spectrum of possible relationships.

earlier, the teacher asks, "Are there any questions?" and the first question is always, "Is this material going to be on the test?"

Many educators are beginning to understand the following principle with regard to examinations.

> The only legitimate purpose of an examination is to enable the teacher and learner to decide what to do next.

What is implied in this principle is that the learning process should be a process of constant improvement in the acquisition of knowledge, know-how, wisdom, and character. The assessments should be designed to provide feedback to both the student and the teacher as a means to improve the processes of teaching and learning.

The student should use the feedback to improve the learning process. The teacher can use the information to help the student improve the way the student learns. Since each student may have a different style, students should be encouraged to perform tests and to measure the results of different approaches. (Does background music help or hinder learning? Try it both ways and see.)

The teacher should use the feedback from all students to assess the effectiveness of the teaching process and to improve it. (Do the class notes really help? Did the text provide a better result? Divide the class in half and see if you and the students can tell.)

Competency-Based Education

At the beginning of the semester, the teacher should discuss with the entire class the list of competencies and the level of mastery expected for each competency. The students should participate in the discussion of each competency; how they, themselves, will know their level of competency; how they will demonstrate it; how the teacher will assess it; and what the teacher will do to help them achieve it. An example of what can be done, at the high school level, is given in the appendix. I look forward to some day seeing a similar example at the college and graduate school level.

The Purposes of Schools of Engineering and Business

Questions of purpose in the professions of engineering and business are not new. They have been discussed for at least a century. Statements of purpose of schools of engineering and business are important. If students, faculty, and administration are to cooperate, they need a common goal. They need to share a common vision of how this goal will be achieved. They need to know how well they are achieving it, and they need to be able to discover, for themselves, what they can do to achieve it better. Setting goals and developing visions begins with a sense of purpose. What should be the purpose of a school of business or a school of engineering?

I have examined a number of statements of purpose of different schools. Most consist of lofty phrases with nary a testable proposition among them. I do recall, however, the dean of a prestigious business school telling the spouses of his students, "We teach our students how to get next to the money." Another dean of another prestigious school told me, "We prepare the leaders of business." That conversation, by the way, was part of a discussion in which he explained to me why he did not want his school of business to be too close to a school of engineering. He believed the engineering schools were not intent on the preparation of leaders, but intended to prepare journeymen in their trade.

The best definition of a proper goal for a business school came from Tomas Bata who said in 1924: "The purpose of the business colleges is to teach their students to create values by honest work."[6] Today, I would modify that only by saying

> The purpose of a school of business is to teach students how to organize and lead the efforts of others in the improvement of processes that create value for customers by honest work.

I would modify this statement for schools of engineering only insofar as the objective would emphasize the skill and ability to design and to work with physical systems. Thus, for engineering I would write

> The purpose of a school of engineering is to teach students how to create value through the design of high-quality products and systems of production and services, and to organize and lead people in the continuous improvement of these designs.

In this statement of purpose, management is considered a part of, not apart from, engineering.

We should recognize, of course, that the statements of purpose of business schools and engineering schools cannot be totally inconsistent with the views of business and other enterprises outside the school system. If they are to be professional schools, they need to play a role in reshaping these views. The question of the purpose of our enterprises is now undergoing a healthy review, thanks in no small part to the quality movement. A decade ago, if I asked a CEO, chosen at random, "What is the purpose of your business?" he or she would probably have immediately shot back, "To make a profit!" and turned away, thinking I was hopelessly naive. Today I no longer meet very many CEOs like that. The managers of successful companies in today's markets know that profit is a result of achieving a purpose that attracts the hearts and minds of customers and employees. Making a profit is essential to survival, but it is not a purpose of successful companies. Breathing is essential to living, but it is not a purpose. Eating is essential to survival, but it is not a purpose. Profit is essential, but it is not a viable purpose.

The Vision

I have a vision of how education should be conducted in schools of business and engineering. The features, that is, the topic included in the education, will differ, of course, but the approaches to quality will be the same. I visualize a process of change, with the following steps.

1. The administration and faculty of the school meet and develop a statement of purpose of the school. That purpose will make the development of the ability to lead others in the creation of value central to the mission of the school.

2. The faculty and administration will develop goals for themselves and their students. These goals will include learning objectives for the administration, faculty, and students. The goals will each be stated in such a way that an assessment is possible. The assessment should be planned to be continuous, not periodic, and designed to improve, not rank students and faculty.

3. The students, faculty, and administration develop policies with respect to how the education should be presented. These policies describe the responsibilities of all three parties. In many of the transactions of the school the different parties are, at one time or another, customers and suppliers of one another. A teacher giving an assignment is a supplier for a student. A student turning in a report is a supplier to the teacher.

Policy statements should be based on the quality first principle, that is, every supplier should aim to provide customers with the highest possible quality goods and services.*

4. Faculty and administration should develop a list of competencies as a way of defining the content of the educational offering of the school. Each competency should be described by giving both the level of competency and the method of assessment. Descriptions of level of competency and methods of assessment are given in the appendix. These lists cannot be developed by faculty alone because each item on the list has resource implications that the faculty cannot meet without administrative support.

---

*At Mt. Edgecumbe High School, in Sitka, Alaska, the students developed two policy statements: "If it isn't perfect, it isn't done" and "No excuses."

5. Faculty and administration should develop their own approaches to the development of wisdom and character. Specific methods for developing wisdom and character are given in a later section. These, too, have resource implications.*

The main tool for teaching wisdom and character is the group project. Experiences with group activities, in which the members of the group are required to exhibit honesty, integrity, perseverance, creativity, and cooperation, provide the basis for critical review by both students and teachers. Teachers will need to learn to function more as coaches and resources and less as givers of knowledge.

6. All teaching/learning situations will be under constant review by faculty, students, and administration seeking to find ways to improve their quality. There will be a new division of labor.

Students will monitor their own learning activities and, with the guidance of teachers, develop measures of quality and productivity (such as amount learned as a function of time spent in different ways to learn). The students will each be seeking to improve the quality of their own learning processes.

Faculty will monitor the effectiveness of the teaching/learning process and the statistical distribution of various measures of effectiveness among the students as a guide to improvement of the teaching process.

Administration and faculty will develop measures for and monitor the development of wisdom and character among the students. Since this will often require cross-functional cooperation, the administration should provide leadership in breaking down barriers between departments and among subjects.

Quality Management Methods Adaptable to Education

Many special tools and techniques have been developed for TQM. These range from new graphical representations to methods appropriate for group problem solving. The various tools and techniques may be readily adapted to education. In the remainder of this paper I will touch on only a few of the techniques.[7]

Nominal Group Technique

When I began to teach quality management methods at the graduate level at MIT eight years ago, I introduced TQM into the teaching/learning process in several

---

*My experience in education, over a period of 40 years, has taught me that when the objectives of education are set high enough and carried out with integrity, the resources can be found. We should not look on education as a zero-sum game, to be played out with limited financial resources, even in the public sector. When they have reason to believe in it, citizens will tax themselves to support education.

ways. On the first day of the class, I used nominal group technique (NGT) to explore the question: "What do we want to gain from attending this class?" NGT is akin to brainstorming, but much more productive in developing a consensus on objectives.[8] In the process the students and I defined and voted on the priorities of our objectives. Note that I included myself as a participant in the voting, for while I invited the students to participate, I did not abdicate my responsibility as a teacher. The results of the prioritization of interests guided me in the preparation of the remainder of the semester's work.

Deployment Flowcharting

One of the principles of quality management requires a focus on the processes that produce a product, instead of looking only at the product itself. Therefore, I introduced the students to flowcharting, using their own work, as indicated in Figure 3, showing only the starting phases of their work. The students were required to complete the diagram, making it specific to their own project.

We found these flow diagrams, which were revised as the semester went along, very useful as a means of charting progress and testing the students' understanding of what they were doing. Within the teams, the students were encouraged to develop more detailed flowcharts showing assignments of team members and how the work was expected to flow. Today I would give this much more emphasis than I did then, for the charts display customer–supplier relationships, in which students need to supply information to one another, and such relationships can be used to advantage in studying not only how attention to quality reduces the need for rework, but also how students need to cooperate with one another if the job is to be done on time, in budget, and with high quality.

If I were teaching the course again, I would spend much more time discussing with the teams the way they set their own priorities and the way their understanding of quality influenced this setting of priorities. Flowcharting is a useful tool in helping students to become aware of their own group process.[9]

The student projects were selected in cooperation with industry and involved a search for a way to improve an ongoing process. Eight years ago all of the companies we met were at the very beginnings of their quality journey (or had not even started, even if they said they had), so each of the projects turned out to have a dual purpose.

1. We applied quality management processes to the organization of the work done by the students, as part of their education.

2. We applied quality management processes to the work of the company we were trying to improve and introduced some of them to the advantages of TQM.

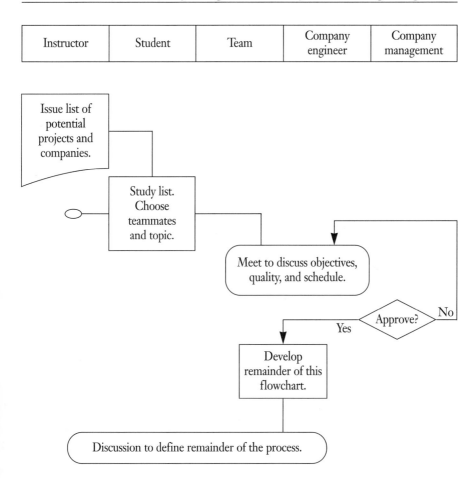

Figure 3. An example of a deployment flowchart.

The biggest barrier to our efforts was the need to assign grades to individual students. MIT was (and is) the same as most schools in regard to grading. Most faculties believe that competitiveness is essential to the maintenance of the reputation of their school. They often create a highly competitive environment for both students and faculty, despite the evidence to the contrary.[10]

Quality Characteristics Evolution Diagram

Teamwork is essential to quality management. This teamwork should extend not only sideways in the enterprise, allowing people to break down barriers between departments, but also upward and downward, transcending historical patterns of human behavior in a hierarchical structure. A method to transcend the vertical barriers is to develop flowcharts and quality evolution diagrams in a layered fashion. Figure 4, for example, shows how the major topic Quality management might appear from a high level. Each of the boxes on the right of the diagram is marked with a drop shadow, which indicates that more information is to be found on another sheet. The box labeled Statistics is expanded in Figure 5. A curriculum planning committee might develop the first figure, while the staff teaching statistics might develop the second.

Figure 5 shows a greater level of detail. Once Figure 5 has been completed, the faculty, with some input from students and potential employers, should consider the level of competency to be attained by the students for each topic, and how it will be developed, self-monitored by students, assessed, and demonstrated. (See the appendix for an example.)

Quality Function Deployment
Once the desired core knowledge and know-how are identified and there is general agreement on the attributes the faculty would like to see in the students, quality

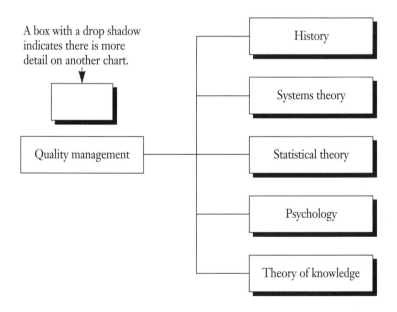

Figure 4. A quality characteristics evolution diagram has a tree structure in which each branch leads to a finer and finer detailed description of what is meant by the phrases to the left.

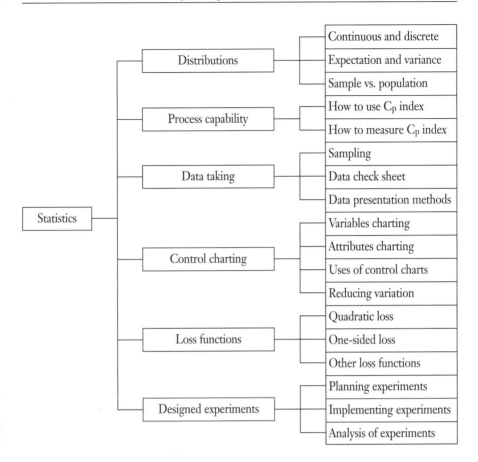

Figure 5. Second-level quality evolution diagram.

function deployment (QFD) may be used to see how the institution is deploying its resources against its professed objectives. An example of a QFD matrix is shown in Figure 6.

The numbers in the matrix of Figure 6 indicate the teaching/learning objectives in each of the topics, as agreed on by the faculty, including input from students from previous years.

The actual work can be done by a small committee. Software for the detailed work has already been developed by GOAL/QPC. Figure 6 indicates how faculty teaching different courses may examine whether the desired objectives (as developed in the quality characteristics evolution diagram) can be attained with the courses in the curriculum.[11] Figure 6 is not complete. At the right end of each row, faculty

		Courses			
		Introductory statistics (Stat 101)	Manufacturing laboratory (ML103)	Intermediate statistics (Stat 121)	Engineering laboratory (EL37)
Statistics	Continuous and discrete	2			
	Expectation and variance	2			
	Sample vs. population	1			
	Use of C_p index	1			
	Measurement of C_p index	1			
	Sampling data				2
	Data check sheets		2		
	Data presentation methods		2		3
	Control charts, variables		3		
	Control charts, attributes		3		
	Uses of control charts		2		
	Reducing variation		2		
	Quadratic loss function			2	
	One-sided loss functions			2	
	Other loss functions				
	Planning of designed experiments		2	2	
	Conducting designed experiments		2		
	Analysis of designed experiments		2	3	

Figure 6. A portion of a quality function deployment matrix.

should provide a reference to the definition of competency required for successful completion of the course, using the format shown in the appendix.

A diagram such as the one shown in Figure 7 may be prepared and distributed to the students with a request for them to fill it out by giving their subjective evaluation of how much the specified experiences contributed to the capabilities desired. Many schools use instructor evaluation forms, which serve to grade the teachers. My experience with these forms has been that they are nearly useless. If I rated high (and I often did) or if I rated low, there was nothing in the forms that guided me to improvement. The QFD matrix is readily adapted to become a tool for the improvement of teaching and learning, but only if the instructor wants to improve and the reward structure encourages improvement.

Through the use of a list of competencies, developed in detail in a tree diagram, the instructors may use the details in the branches of the tree as the inputs to a QFD matrix. The QFD matrix may be used for student evaluation of the teaching process in a form that will guide the instructor to continuous improvement. If the students are made aware of the competencies to be developed and how they are to be evaluated, they will be *responsible* because they have been made *response-able*.

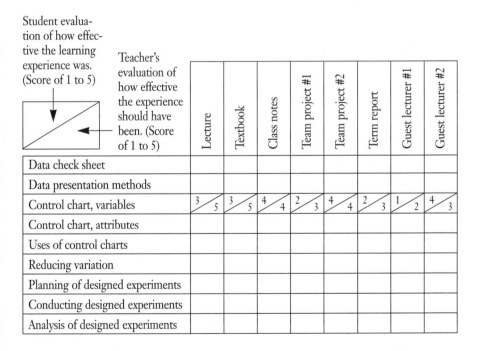

Figure 7. Using the QFD matrix for evaluation by students and faculty.

Where to Begin?

Quality management methods may be introduced into a school in three distinct, but not exclusive, ways.

1. *Apply quality methods to administrative practices.* This approach is the least threatening to the faculties and, therefore, may be expected to be the first step universities take. Because so many of the administrative practices are similar to those that occur in industry, it will be easy to find consultants and to obtain guidance from friends in industry. Proceeding along this line, however, will have but marginal effect on education. It can make life better for the officers of the institution. It probably will save money. The support staff will become happier.

2. *Introduce courses in quality management.* This approach will have an immediate effect on the students in the classes and the faculty who are teaching the subject. This approach has two potential consequences, both of them positive.

If the students engage in improvement projects that involve processes in the school itself, many people outside the class will become aware of what quality methods can accomplish.

If, and this is a big if, the teacher is truly a practitioner in quality, he or she will conduct the class using quality management methods. The resulting change in student behavior and performance will, most likely, be very dramatic, and, therefore, the behavior and competence of the students may be used to help persuade other faculty members to do likewise. For example, student projects can be presented to faculty meetings.

If the class is conducted using quality techniques, the students will become evangelists for the new way to teach and learn. They will become the shock troops in the transformation of the school.

3. *Use quality management as the way of life in the school.* This means bringing the philosophy and methodologies of quality to bear upon all aspects of the enterprise. In a school of engineering this implies that continuous improvement will occur not only in the offices, the support functions, and the classroom, but it will affect all parts of the school, including research, student advising, sports, student activities, and extracurricular activities.

I am not too sanguine about how quality methods will appear in universities. Discussions with personnel at all levels, from university presidents to students and secretaries, make it clear that universities are hard nuts to crack. The more prestigious the institution, the more likely it will resist the paradigm shift. A case in point is MIT, which recently announced that it will reengineer its administrative processes. When I inquired whether this meant that the committee assigned to the task would employ quality management tools and techniques, I was told that MIT wasn't ready for that yet.

Conclusion

This paper merely scratches the surface of our topic. The literature in the field of education is rich in information dealing with each and every topic discussed in this paper. What is necessary is the will and determination of the leaders in engineering and business education to apply this knowledge.

As all of you are aware, changing a curriculum is no easy task. I know. In my teaching career, spanning 45 years, I have been involved in three fundamental changes of curriculum. I agree with the statement, "It is easier to move a graveyard than to change a curriculum." Yet, change we must. The change will not take place overnight. We are talking about changing the way we educate our youth and ourselves from preschool through grade school, high school, the undergraduate years in the university, and even graduate school. It is not a task for those of tender skins or faint hearts.

The current system of education must be reformed. It must be changed from one that sorts, ranks, and winnows the youth of the nation to one that develops them into quality performers, at whatever level and in whatever field they choose to work. The quality methodologies provide the tools and techniques to do the job. For the sake of the future of this nation, I hope you will learn to use them and apply them well.

Appendix

Levels of Competence*

LEVEL 1. KNOWING (Remembering)

◄──────── HOW STUDENT ────────►			◄── HOW TEACHER ──►	
Self-tests	**Learns**	**Shows**	**Assesses**	**Teaches**
Can I recall? Bring to mind right material at right time? Have I been exposed to the information? Can I answer questions?	Reading material. Listening to lectures, watching videos, taking notes, taking a written test	Name? List? Tell. Define. Who? Where? What? When? Did . . . ? Was . . . ? Is . . . ? How many? How much? What did book say? Meaning of key words?	Asks questions that may be answered by simple recall	Directs, tells, shows, examines information necessary to this level

---

*This material was prepared by David Langford and his students at Mt. Edgecumbe High Schools, Sitka, Alaska. Used with permission from Mt. Edgecumbe High School.

LEVEL 2. COMPREHENSION (Understanding)

◄——— HOW STUDENT ———►			◄— HOW TEACHER —►	
Self-tests	**Learns**	**Shows**	**Assesses**	**Teaches**
Comprehend and understand what is said. Make use of the ideas by relating them to other material. Able to participate in the conversation on the subject.	Explaining the idea in written or oral form. Translating idea to own words. Providing an example. Doing textbook type problems. Recognizing and extracting relevant information.	Give an example of. . . . What is most important idea? What caused this? Compare. . . . Contrast. . . . Why do you say that? Give idea in own words? What does . . . mean?	Asks "Give the idea in your own words." Gives tests that require material to be organized in student's own words.	Demonstrates, listens, questions, compares, contrasts, examines information and student's knowledge.

LEVEL 3a. THINKING (Applying, solving a problem)

◄——— HOW STUDENT ———►			◄— HOW TEACHER —►	
Self-tests	**Learns**	**Shows**	**Assesses**	**Teaches**
Tests ability to use ideas, methods, concepts, principles, and theories in new situations. Recognize limits of own knowledge and ability.	Applying in a new situation. Solving problems unaided, adding other techniques to one being tested. Recognizing new situations and developing useful tools. Evaluating utility of tools.	Solving, finding answer to. . . . Applying the generalization to. . . .	Observes student involved in problem and solving new situations with minimum of prompting. Asks application questions. Uses tools appropriate to question.	Shows, facilitates, observes, criticizes work being done by the student.

LEVEL 3b. THINKING (Analysis, logical ordering)

◄——————— HOW STUDENT ———————►		◄— HOW TEACHER —►				
Self-tests	**Learns**	**Shows**	**Assesses**	**Teaches**
Examines methodically ideas, concepts, writing and separates into parts or basic principles. Break down information into component parts to make the organization clearer. Use previous knowledge, comprehension and application.	Analyzing how knowledge is applied. Explaining rationale for each step. Discussing why steps are in given order and how they might be changed. Dissecting the basic logic of the process.	Gives reason for conclusions. Uses logical method to convince teacher of correctness of results. By consciously filtering out words that are biased or emotional. Organizes evidence in support of conclusion.	Ability to break idea into component parts for logical analysis. Ability to identify assumptions, facts, opinions, logical conclusions. Ability to demonstrate a logical ordering to process, identify causes and effects.	Probes, guides, observes, acts as a resource.

LEVEL 3c. THINKING (Synthesizing, creating)

◀——— HOW STUDENT ———▶			◀— HOW TEACHER —▶	
Self-tests	**Learns**	**Shows**	**Assesses**	**Teaches**
Can recognize new problems and develop tools to solve them. Create own plan, thought model, hypotheses for finding solutions to problems. Can put together the parts and elements in a unified whole. Create a self-consistent design.	Creating something: Physical object, a communication, a set of abstract but related concepts. Discussing, generalizing, relating, comparing, formulating.	By developing a plan, developing a thought model, combining parts to create a new whole.	Examines statements, plans, products that are new to the student. Ability to extract good ideas from one application and apply in another.	Reflects, extends, analyzes, evaluates.

LEVEL 4. APPRECIATION (Evaluation)

◀——— HOW STUDENT ———▶			◀— HOW TEACHER —▶	
Self-tests	**Learns**	**Shows**	**Assesses**	**Teaches**
Explicitly develops criteria and applies them to judge and appreciate the value of ideas and methods.	Evaluating works, ideas, presentations for utility, aesthetics, and logic. Judges theories for consistency and utility.	By demonstrating ability to write about or discuss a work, theory, process, method, or treatise and exercise judgment.	Written or oral presentations, formal and informal with respect to applying judgment with respect to criteria.	Clarifies, accepts, harmonizes, and guides.

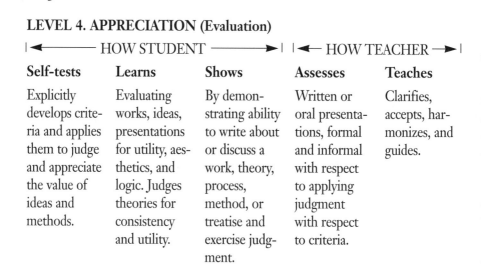

Notes

1. W. Edwards Deming, *Out of the Crisis* (Cambridge, Mass.: MIT Center for Advanced Engineering Study, 1986).

2. This table was supplied by David Langford and his students at Mt. Edgecumbe High School, Sitka, Alaska. Used with permission of Mt. Edgecumbe High School. The last entry, Industry, was added by the students in Theresa Hick's class of second graders!

3. Stephen R. Covey, *The 7 Habits of Highly Effective People* (New York: Simon and Schuster, 1989).

4. U.S. Department of Labor, *What Work Requires of Schools—A SCANS Report for America 2000* (Washington, D.C.: GPO, 1991).

5. This diagram was given to me by students at Mt. Edgecumbe High School, Sitka, Alaska. Used with permission from Mt. Edgecumbe High School.

6. Tomas Bata, *Knowledge in Action* (Amsterdam: IOS Press, 1992), 106.

7. The tools and techniques are described in many publications. A concise summary of the most important may be found in *The Memory Jogger II* and *The Memory Jogger Plus* available from GOAL/QPC, 13 Branch Street, Methuen, Mass., 01844.

8. Peter R. Scholtes, *The Team Handbook* (Madison, Wis.: Joiner Associates, 1988).

9. Ibid.

10. Alfie Kohn, *No Contest*, rev. ed. (Boston: Houghton Mifflin, 1992).

11. For a more detailed discussion of QFD, see Robert King, *Better Designs in Half the Time* (Methuen, Mass.: GOAL/QPC, 1987).

Bibliography

Bloom, Benjamin S., editor, et al., *Taxonomy of Educational Objectives: The Classification of Education Goals. Handbook I, Cognitive Domain.* New York: McKay, 1956.

Clark, Barbara, *Growing Up Gifted.* Columbus, Ohio: Merrill Publishing Company, 1988.

Gallagher, J. J., and Mary Jane Aschner. "A Preliminary Report: Analysis of Classroom Interaction." *Merril-Palmer Quarterly of Behavior and Development* 9 (1963): 183–194.

Wiles, Jon, and Joseph Bondi. *Supervision: A Guide to Practice.* Columbus, Ohio: Charles E. Merrill Publishing Company, 1980.

Using Total Quality Education to Prepare Globally Competitive Citizens: The Perspective of Motorola University

Brenda B. Sumberg

Editor's note: For readers who are unaware of Motorola's eminent company stature in total quality, in 1988 Motorola won the first corporatewide Malcolm Baldrige National Quality Award and has not rested on its laurels since that time.

In this paper, Brenda Sumberg describes Motorola University as an "industrial university" in transition to a "lifelong learning institution." Motorola University is inevitably in close contact with the educational needs and requirements of its students. It is, so to speak, in the front lines of education and training for business and engineering. From her frontline position, the author gives invaluable depth and breadth of perspective on the connections between total quality and higher education. She makes a fascinating distinction between education that is just-in-case, which we in universities mainly do, and education that is just-in-time, which is what Motorola University aims at doing.

I believe that all of us in higher education have a lot to learn from Motorola. This paper conveys the scope of educational and training activities at Motorola University, activities that embrace many of the functions of traditional colleges and universities and much more besides, all carried out from multiple locations around the world. Motorola has given much thought to defining who its customers are. They include not only all the business units of Motorola, but all current Motorola employees, customers, and suppliers. They even include potential employees and customers and suppliers.

Sumberg begins with Motorola University's vision for the new millennium. That breathtaking vision presents significant challenges for all colleges and universities.

She brings out these challenges by a series of explicit queries that are interspersed throughout the paper. These queries were originally addressed to the academic members of an audience who were attending Total Quality Forum VI at Dallas, Texas, in October 1994. These academicians included primarily deans of engineering and business, provosts, presidents, and other top academic administrators. (See the introduction to this book for background on the Total Quality Forums.) Readers of this volume from academia will want to give thoughtful consideration to these queries.

Introduction to Motorola University

Motorola University began in 1981 as the Motorola Training and Education Center. It was created as a result of an analysis of Motorola's training needs and established as a corporate department in the human resources functions.

During the 1980s, Motorola University's charter was to help the corporation build a quality culture. To meet this challenge, an internal training design system and implementation process were developed. The 1980s also saw the establishment of corporatewide training plans and training investment policies.

By the end of the decade, Motorola University had expanded its operations both in the United States and abroad. The opening of the Galvin Center for Continuing Education in 1986 and the Singapore Training Design Center in 1989 brought new educational opportunities to employees around the world. Motorola University was also offering new and more comprehensive services such as applications consulting.

Since 1990, Motorola University has diversified further, establishing academic partnerships with institutions of higher learning around the world. Motorola University has also implemented cultural design and translation services. This has become especially important as Motorola moves into new and emerging markets in Eastern Europe, South America, and the Asia-Pacific region.

As a resource for change within Motorola, Motorola University works best when business objectives are clear. The organization regularly seeks guidance and input from its board of trustees, made up of general managers of Motorola businesses, and many others in the Motorola community.

The university's instructional design and development efforts are divided into competency centers. The centers include technical experts, researchers, and course developers who produce courses, videos, books, and software. The centers are technology, market development, executive education, product and software engineering, quality, and management education. Other Motorola University services include evaluation, alternative learning, supplier customer training, and the transformation of public education. The university manages numerous training facilities around the world. In general, the facilities include classrooms, break-out rooms, training laboratories, and conference planning and management.

In preparing our 1994 long-range plan for Motorola University, we had to consider our responses to the changing requirements presented to us by Motorola's business units. We recognized that instead of doing the usual update to our five-year plan, it was important to identify some major shifts that we would have to make over the next several years and then develop our strategic plan from these. We really began to create a new vision for ourselves of what the future was going to look like. We recognized at the outset that even though we were not sure we had adequately defined what an industrial university is, we had to contemplate the shift from an industrial university to a lifelong learning institution.

In this paper, I shall discuss changes we are facing, our contemplated reaction to them, and the implications of these changes for colleges and universities.

We knew that our training and education had to continue to support

- Motorola's key business initiatives. These include continuous improvement of products, processes, services, and people.
- Motorola's emphasis on becoming a premier employer.
- Motorola's emphasis on good corporate citizenship.

In addition, we recognized that we needed to continue to identify, create, and lead the changes at Motorola. In other words, Motorola University's responsibility is not only to continue the role of change agent traditionally played by training organizations, but to use our contacts in the business world and our alliances with universities around the world to identify needed changes and create those changes and lead them.

Finally, we recognized that our responsibilities included the training and education needs not only of current Motorola employees, customers, and suppliers, but of potential employees, customers, and suppliers. These considerations are driving a vision of Motorola University for the new millennium, in making the transition from industrial university to lifelong learning institution.

I now turn to a detailed consideration of specific issues enumerated earlier. I shall draw attention to possible implications for colleges and universities by specific queries interspersed through my discussion.

Business Issues

Three pervasive business issues are cycle-time reduction, global expansion, and optimization of creativity and innovation.

Cycle-Time Reduction

As a part of striving for quality and continuous improvement, Motorola has the following goal for all its processes.

> Whatever the initial cycle time, achieve a tenfold reduction in cycle time every five years.*

A number of companies are introducing an average of a new product once a day. Reduction of cycle time of new product introduction is critical. In today's world, with its rapidly increasing rates of change and its imperative of quickly meeting market demands, fast cycle time is critical for global competitiveness.

> *Query to those in colleges and universities:* Are you conveying to your students the urgency of speedy new product introduction and finding ways to achieve it?

A key component of new-product cycle time is design cycle time. Motorola has benchmarked a number of companies both in the United States and overseas to find ways of reducing design cycle time. Because it was determined that training and education can impact the goal, in the last two years Motorola University has trained 2500 people in concepts of design cycle-time reduction. These trainees not only learn engineering concepts, but also other functions that can impact design cycle time, such as manufacturing, quality, human resources, finance, and marketing.

> *Queries:* When you teach design to engineers, is the ability to manufacture a design given consideration? When you teach marketing majors, do you stress the cycle time of gathering design requirements? Of getting the marketing information to appropriate design people? Within your own institution, are you modeling the importance of cycle-time reduction and conveying the sense of urgency required to be globally competitive?

Global Expansion

If Motorola is to remain globally competitive, we must expand our employee base and marketplaces around the world. As of November 1994, Motorola had hired over 40,000 new employees in the last 21 months, about equally divided between the United States and overseas.

---

*Cycle time is the total time for one execution of a process. For example, the cycle time for order filling is the time from receipt of the order to shipment of the product.

In China, we had 100 employees in 1991, and we had about 4000 by the end of 1994. We expect to have 20,000 by the year 2000. There is no middle management population within China, yet we predict that by the year 2000, we will need at least 700 middle managers in China. Therefore, one of the current initiatives of Motorola University is to put together a process that will allow us to train Chinese middle managers within a 2.5-year period, as opposed to the 10 years it would normally take. Reduction of cycle time must be achieved in training and education as well as in business processes!

> *Queries:* Are you making your students aware of the kinds of global expansion occurring in major companies today? The shifts of employee populations from domestic to outside the United States? How to communicate, work with, and manage a worldwide employee population? How to maintain company focus and culture in the face of global expansion? To achieve product acceptance in different countries?

Optimization of Creativity and Innovation

As an extension of our programs for design cycle time, Motorola is offering a program on innovation in design that gives engineers specific tools to help them to work toward innovative and creative designs. In the face of global competition we believe that it is very important to help people to understand how to think "outside the box."

> *Query:* Are you stressing innovation and creativity in product design, or are you encouraging only conventional thinking "within the box?"

Premier Employer

For Motorola to maintain its status as a premier employer, we strive toward two specific initiatives: a diverse workforce and participation/empowerment.

Diverse Workforce

One of the ways for Motorola to become a premier employer is to develop a truly diverse workforce in which employees are drawn from all ethnic, racial, and cultural groups. Motorola also attempts to help them all to work together, to understand the strengths and benefits of diversity, and to appreciate what diversity means both to them and to Motorola.

Motorola employees in Israel, Wiesbaden, Germany, and Schaumburg, Illinois, may all be part of a single team working on the same product design and having to communicate with each other in order to achieve their goal. These teams bring different cultures to the way they approach that design. They can benefit from these differences and draw strength from them, or they can see them simply as obstacles.

> *Queries:* Are your students learning to work with a diverse population? Do they experience a diverse population at your college or university? Are they encouraged to learn the benefits of working with people who may have different approaches to problem solving and different ways of thinking and relating to issues?

Participation/Empowerment

Another aspect of becoming a premier employer is recognizing and respecting the capabilities of all employees. Taking full advantage of the contributions of all Motorolans is an essential element of global competitiveness. Proactive encouragement of the participation of all employees in goal setting, problem solving, and decision making has been part of the culture literally for decades. In recent years, decision making has been constantly driven further down in the organization to the people who have hands-on involvement in the situation. Motorola University's role in the creation of this culture has been to help teach people the skills required for an environment of participation and empowerment.

> *Queries:* Are your students' problem-solving and decision-making skills being honed? Are they learning to participate actively and to not only allow but encourage the participation of others? Will they be able to handle empowerment or be able to provide appropriate leadership to an empowered workforce?

Good Corporate Citizenship

Good corporate citizenship is important for global success. One element of citizenship is ethics—simple business ethics. One of Motorola's key, never changing values is uncompromising integrity in everything we do. This was pretty easy as long as we operated mainly within the United States, but it is much harder as we begin to operate globally. How, for example, can a Motorola employee succeed in a country where a normal part of doing business is what would be called bribery in the United States? What does Motorola tell that employee?

Queries: How well do your students understand different cultures and different meanings of ethics around the world? How well do they understand the importance of ethical behavior to the success of a globally competitive company?

Protection of the environment is another facet of corporate citizenship. The importance of environmental protection depends, of course, on the nature of company products, but it can be very important.

Queries: Are your engineering students learning to design for protection of the environment? Are your engineering and business students learning to consider the environment as they manage and make decisions about the kinds of processes to use. Are they sensitive to the dangers of making short-term decisions that will adversely impact the environment and the good citizenship of the company?

Identify, Create, and Lead Change Efforts at Motorola

We proactively attempt to notice and identify trends, important things that are happening in other places, so that Motorola University can begin to help senior leaders in Motorola identify those that are potentially relevant to us and to introduce them to Motorola. There are several ways of doing this. For example,

- Alliances throughout the world with other corporations and with universities
- Facilitation of interactions within the corporation: all the businesses and all the regions

Motorola University may see something happening in one small part of the company that is promising for transfer to the entire company, so it then facilitates the transfer to the entire company.

Queries: Are you identifying changes occurring in institutions of higher learning around the world that might be appropriate for your own institution? Can you help to bring these changes into your institution?

Change As a Way of Life

Motorola can no longer be complacent about its success. We can no longer assume that what we are doing today is the right thing for us to do tomorrow. In our globally competitive world, change is not just occasional chaotic shocks separated by periods of smooth sailing. Rather, significant change is occurring constantly and the growth rate of change is itself increasing. Two examples convey the impact of such change.

- We have mentioned that in the last 21 months, Motorola has hired over 40,000 new employees. This brought the total to 140,000. Yet only a couple of years ago, it was assumed that the Motorola employee base would remain indefinitely at 100,000.

- In the Motorola University five-year plan of 1992, it was forecast that Motorola University would have 13 regions by the end of 1995. It turned out that Motorola University had 13 regions by the end of 1993.

Change and Cycle-Time Issues

After we began to incorporate quality into the Motorola culture, it took us about 12–14 years to get even to the first step we wanted to reach. When we later aimed at quality improvements in software that would bring us up to the best-in-class status that we had achieved in hardware, we knew that we couldn't afford to take 12–14 years to do that. We felt that we would have to do it in a maximum of 7 years or, if possible, more quickly. The increasing rate of change and the increasing cycle-time pressures are closely related.

> *Queries:* Are your students sensitive to the environment of change, or are they living in an environment that is status quo? Are they living in an environment where change and the need for appropriate response to change is obvious, or are they coming out into the business world expecting that what they are seeing today is what they're going to see tomorrow?

Lifelong Learning

When Motorola University talks about becoming a lifelong learning institution, we are recognizing that if Motorola is going to grow at its current rate, we must identify our potential leaders earlier and earlier. To make the point by an extreme position, we would like to identify future leaders by the time they are 14 years old. In fact, we are already working with children of Motorola employees from the age of nine into the early teens by offering summer technology classes to intrigue them with the notion that math and science can be exciting and to encourage them to consider technology in their future education and careers.

One of my colleagues—a technologist with a Ph.D. in physics—had a young son go through the Motorola summer technology camp. This son intends to go to law school. My colleague feels that the technology camp may be the only experience in his son's lifetime where he is immersed in technology, whereas students who plan to go into science and mathematics will have many other experiences with technology. This experience may impact his son's entire lifetime response to technology, even though he won't be a technologist. He may end up helping to make laws that impact technology, making decisions in corporations as they purchase technology, or using technology himself in many ways.

> *Query:* Are you giving students who may not become technologists these same kinds of experiences and an awareness of how technology can impact their lives?

It is not far-fetched to think that as we are beginning to build day-care centers around the world, our employees aren't going to be happy with minimum care and nurturing. Before long, they are going to expect well-designed educational programs. So it seems likely that Motorola University is going to become involved, in one form or another, in the business of educating the children of Motorola employees. These children are potential employees.

From education of children of Motorola employees it is only a short step to start thinking of education for our customers and our suppliers. Motorola products are becoming more and more dependent on technology. Our customers and suppliers will have to be more and more sophisticated in technology. Therefore it becomes increasingly more important for us to become involved with current and future customers and suppliers and their education.

It's for reasons like these that we have become involved with school districts from prekindergarten through high school in areas where Motorola has a significant employee base. Even if children in those school districts do not become Motorola employees, they are going to become customers or potential customers, and some of them may become suppliers. It is important to us that the quality of their education be improved.

> *Queries:* Institutions of higher learning are also customers of local school districts from prekindergarten through high school. Are you making it clear to those school systems what your requirements are? Are you working with your schools of education to train the teachers who can help to develop the kinds of students you are looking for? Are you reaching out and helping your supply

line to improve? Are you helping your own students, who may not go to work for Motorola, but who may become Motorola customers or work for Motorola suppliers, to understand technology and how it impacts their lives?

Five Shifts Needed at Motorola University

To become a lifelong learning institution, Motorola University must make five shifts.

* From funded operations to a not-for-profit business
* From limited systems to integrated systems
* From a loose federation of educators to a league of innovators
* From a global institution to a transnational institution
* From instructor-based learning to multilearning formats

I will emphasize the last two shifts, but I will first touch briefly on the first three.

From Funded Operations to a Not-for-Profit Business

Motorola University was originally funded primarily through a corporate tax. We decided that the corporate tax should grow at only half the growth rate of the corporation. Since we wanted to be able to respond to added requirements assigned to us by the corporation, we needed to obtain funding from other sources. These funds could be applied to our efforts within the corporation while keeping the corporate tax at a relatively flat rate. This is our counterpart of the funding restrictions and cuts placed on colleges and universities.

> *Query:* Do your students have a realistic view of the constraints that exist within corporations, or are they encouraged to believe that corporations have deep pockets and unlimited funds to spend?

From Limited Systems to Integrated Systems

As Motorola University has grown and expanded around the world, we have developed stand-alone processes and systems that are geographically dependent, functionally independent, but not necessarily integrated either globally or functionally. We now know that if we are to meet the expansion and cycle-time needs of

Motorola, we must have integrated systems designed so that we can move these systems into a new area in the world and have them operational very quickly. For example, as we opened our training center in China, we needed immediately to bring up registration systems, scheduling systems, and instructor systems that we did not have.

> *Query:* Do you have effective and efficient systems that allow you to reduce your cycle times and that can support the changes you need to make?

From a Loose Federation of Educators to a League of Innovators

Within Motorola, there are multiple training organizations. Motorola University is only one among many of these. Some years ago the Motorola University Board of Trustees requested that we put together a federation of all the training and education professionals within the company. The aim was to reduce redundancy and increase efficiency and effectiveness by bringing all the people with similar interests to the same table. Some were very willing to come, some were less willing. After a few years, we had a number of successes.

We realized, however, that by confining our scope to training professionals, we were leaving out a lot of people in the company who were very interested in training and education and who could contribute good ideas. We recognized also that there were training and education professionals from outside Motorola from whom we could learn. So we decided that we must invite other people to the table, to move to a broader group that we call a League of Innovators, which brings people of all kinds from many places who are interested in studying the ideas of training and education. We borrowed the group's title from a group of community colleges because it so clearly conveyed what we were trying to accomplish by gathering people who have ideas that can help us continuously improve our training and education.

> *Queries:* Are you in colleges and universities looking only internally to yourselves, or are you looking at what's going on in the outside world and bringing in outsiders and trying to learn from them? (I know that many college and university people are indeed looking to industry and alumni to get ideas, but this notion can be expanded, for example to students.) Do you understand the benefits of bringing together people with different mindsets and perceptions in order to get good ideas for improvement and innovation?

From a Global Institution to a Transnational Institution

Not very long ago Motorola University was creating a product in the United States and, when necessary, was shipping it overseas. We then began to recognize that the product needed translation to make it more useful overseas. Ultimately we recognized that the processes being used for translation were not guaranteeing the quality of the product. Hence we began to define new processes for translation that would guarantee product quality.

At the next stage, we recognized that the product needed not only to be translated, but to be adapted culturally. Translated programs needed to retain the Motorola corporate culture, which was essential to the program, but they also needed to be appropriate and learnable by the ethnic or geographic cultures to which they were directed. This can entail a balancing act.

We also had to contend with the cycle-time problem discussed earlier, which applies to all Motorola processes. There was a very long cycle time between the introduction of a program in the United States and the time the program reached our international participants. We have now put a process in place for reducing that cycle time.

At the time we were pressing these initiatives, we also came to realize that the end result of training is not that all Motorola employees would think and act in exactly the same way, nor conform to a single profile. There is a great benefit to maintaining the natural differences between employees.

This has helped me to understand the difference between *global* and *transnational*. One of my colleagues says that being global is like an American stew where you put all the ingredients into a pot, cook them very slowly for a long time, and obtain a tasty end result in which most of the ingredients of the stew have a similar consistency and a similar taste. Being transnational, he says, is much more like a stir fry. You put varying ingredients into the same pan, but cook them very quickly so that each of the main ingredients maintains its own flavor and consistency, while blending together in a harmonious way. That's what we are trying to accomplish in moving from a global to a transnational institution.

This leads us again to diversity. A workforce with diversity permits the company to benefit from the differences among the employees and to better respond to customers around the world by understanding those differences. Diversity also has implications for the careers of students coming out of colleges and universities. Will they be able to have a career in a globally competitive company, yet spend their entire working lives in a single location or region? It may be possible to do that if they are willing to make certain tradeoffs or limit their potential for advancement within that company. But if they want to achieve their potential for advancement, they are probably going to have to work overseas, and they certainly will be working with people who live in some other region of the world.

> *Queries:* Are your students going to be prepared to do these things? Do they have the thinking patterns, the openness of mind, the ability to relate to people who may be very different? Are you on campus giving them some sampling of these kinds of experiences? Are you taking advantage of the ethnic mixtures on your campuses as opportunities rather than obstacles?

From Instructor-Based Learning to Multilearning Formats

Motorola University has traditionally been very dependent on instructor-based learning. A number of reasons have led us to begin to use varying learning formats.

• The company's stress on the importance of reduction of cycle time applies to training and education just as to any other process. We are thinking of how to reduce the time it takes for students to learn a given amount of material. The company goal of a tenfold decrease in cycle time every five years might be interpreted to mean that we would have to provide as much learning in four hours as we now do in 40 hours. We don't know how to do that. We don't know if it's possible or not. But that's certainly the direction we need to look. So one of the reasons for looking at multiple learning formats is that they may help to reduce the cycle time of learning.

> *Query:* Are you thinking of trying to reduce cycle time in your college or university? Or, to put it differently, are you trying to increase the amount of learning in the same time?*

• People's learning styles point toward new learning formats. Instructor-based formats use a variety of audio/visual modes that attempt to deal with different learning styles, but we are not at all certain that we are taking full advantage of existing knowledge on the different ways that people learn. We do not know if we are addressing the whole range of learning styles of our students. We are wondering if by using various formats of learning, we can do a better job of helping people to learn by appealing to their particular learning preferences.

• With the increasing rate of change that I addressed earlier, there is a corresponding increase in the need for information and skills. People need to understand

---

*****Editor's note:** See the quotation by Bob Galvin, formerly chairman of the board of Motorola, in Bateman and Roberts, "Total Quality for Professors and Students," page 242.

what they have to learn, to take responsibility for looking for ways to learn it, and to find specific sources of the needed information. As an example, the half-life of a software engineer's knowledge is about 2.5 years. That is, if we employ a fresh-out-of-college software engineer who knows everything that will be needed at Motorola, within 2.5 years 50 percent of that knowledge will no longer be of value to us. The engineer must take some responsibility for identifying what new knowledge needs to be learned and what sources may be able to provide it.

For another example, we estimate that in a 40-year worklife from age 25 to age 65, an average individual will change jobs 8 to 10 times. For any one of these jobs, there will be substantial changes in job requirements. What needs for retraining will there be, and how do individuals identify what they need to learn and where they need to go to learn it? People need to be able to direct their own learning: to understand what they need to learn and to be able to source it for themselves.

• If Motorola is going to remain globally competitive, our employees must be adept at taking the concepts and theory they learn and applying them to what they have to accomplish.

> *Queries:* Are your students becoming adept at applying what they are learning? I've heard it said that universities give just-in-case training while companies give just-in-time training. If you're giving just-in-case training, if you're stressing concepts and theories, are you also helping students to understand how they're going to apply these concepts and theories to the work they will do in order to obtain the outcomes they will be expected to produce? I don't believe that students can walk into a company and hit the road in a cycle time that is quick enough for the company to remain competitive if they can't apply the concepts and theories they've learned to specific situations.

• There is a need for definition of learning. Learning occurs every day, all around us.

> *Queries:* Do your students know how to continue to learn? Are you simply hand-holding, pouring in the information, structuring the learning for the students so that they never really learn how to learn? Are you giving them a sense that learning occurs every day, all around us, not just when students are sitting in lecture halls, working in laboratories, or reading textbooks? Do your students understand that every experience they have, every interaction they

have, offers an opportunity to learn and to apply that learning to their world?

Are your students thinking in these ways? That's the only way they're going to be successful in a globally competitive company. If they wait to move into a classroom or to have a structured learning situation, they will never find enough opportunities to remain competitive in today's global workforce. You must help them see their total experience as a continuing opportunity for learning and for application of that learning to the things they need to do.

Final Queries

Is your institution

- Providing the required knowledge base and the opportunities for your students to become globally competitive citizens?
- Modeling globally competitive citizenship?

These two queries sum up my message.

Georgia Tech's Continuous Quality Improvement Journey

Jane C. Ammons and Joseph E. Gilmour
Georgia Institute of Technology

Introduction

Georgia Institute of Technology is in the initial phase of its continuous quality improvement (CQI)* journey, which began in the early part of this decade. Located in the midtown area of Atlanta, Georgia, Georgia Tech is a public institution of nearly 13,000 students and 1500 faculty. CQI is an important element in our vision to become a premier technological university. Meanwhile, we are hard at work preparing our campus to serve as the Athletes' Village of the 1996 Centennial Olympics and also as the setting of two major sports venues—swimming and boxing.

Background on CQI Initiation

Like many U.S. higher education institutions, Georgia Tech's quality journey has been stimulated and influenced by quality leaders in business and industry. Connections were made at the individual level during the 1980s, leading to a one-day quality orientation trip in 1991 for top Georgia Tech administrators to Milliken & Company headquarters in Spartanburg, South Carolina. This trip exposed key institute leadership to the promise and concepts of quality management and initiated the development of quality awareness in our culture.

In 1992, Georgia Tech was selected as one of the original participants in the Business/Education Total Quality Challenge. Our partner, Milliken & Company,

---

*Editor's note: *Continuous quality improvement* is synonymous with *total quality*, the term used in most papers in this book.

hosted 50 of our faculty and administrators at an excellent week-long on-site learning and sharing session. A follow-on program, QualTech, was held on our campus later in the year, so that additional faculty could be exposed to continuous improvement principles. During the QualTech meeting we were informed that IBM had selected Georgia Tech to receive one of eight Total Quality Management University Competition Awards. This $1 million grant to our institution is focused on the objective of implementing CQI within university operations, curricula, and research. Our proposal to IBM contained the heart of our strategic plan for implementing CQI at Georgia Tech. The award added enormous impetus and focus to all of our CQI efforts, whether they were funded directly from the IBM grant or not.[1]

Overview

We have reported CQI plans, progress, and results in both administrative and research areas in other places;[2] this article will focus on the academic side of CQI at Georgia Tech. We center our attention on engineering since we are a technological institution with a majority of students and faculty in that field. In the upcoming sections, our activities and lessons learned are described as we have endeavored to establish structure, curriculum development processes, course delivery improvements, innovation processes, and partnerships.

Academic Progress

Structure

Georgia Tech's CQI strategic plan designed an organizational structure for leading our implementation. The Georgia Tech Quality Council was constituted in September of 1992; regular meetings have been held since. The composition of the quality council includes the president, key vice presidents and deans, selected faculty, and leaders of student organizations. The quality council has had limited impact on the adoption of CQI by the academic portion of the Georgia Tech community. There are several reasons.

- The quality council has struggled with its own effectiveness in the face of a transition in top leadership and uneven understanding/commitment of its members.

- The quality council does not effectively touch many of the campus academic processes.

- The quality council has focused its attention on institute-wide efforts in training, improvements in administrative processes, and overall strategic planning, assessment, accreditation, and operational issues.

We have relied on the critiques of our visiting committee, which has met annually to review CQI progress and strategy. On June 29, 1993, reviewers included Ben Bethell, senior vice president of Procter & Gamble; Chip Caldwell, CEO of West Paces Ferry Hospital; Pat Bowie, vice president quality, Milliken & Co.; Mike Flanagan (business manager) and Jim Sweitzer of IBM-Charlotte; and Steve Ward of IBM-Atlanta. A second review meeting was held August 4, 1994, and included Bethell, Bowie, and Ward. In each of these review sessions, deans of engineering and management explained CQI curriculum development plans and progress and received valuable feedback.

We have established the Office of Continuous Improvement and Assessment to facilitate CQI implementation efforts on campus. Led by Facilitator Hal Irvin, who came on board in January 1994, this office has developed training programs tailored to Georgia Tech's needs. Initial efforts are being focused on unit champions rather than attempting a comprehensive cascade implementation. Unit champions include Human Resources, the College of Engineering, the School of Management, Georgia Tech Research Institute, and the Office of Minority Educational Development.

Georgia Tech has also established the Institute Continuous Improvement Curriculum Committee, chaired by the dean of engineering, John White, and cochaired by the dean of management, Arthur Kraft. Faculty representatives include the chair of the campus Undergraduate Curriculum Committee, chair of the campus Graduate Curriculum Committee, and faculty representatives from engineering and management. This committee has assumed leadership for CQI curriculum development from four faculty teams that were formed in 1993 to develop a freshman CQI course, structured CQI cooperative education experience, a capstone design program, and a certificate program. Little progress was made by these faculty committees. Insights into causes include

- Faculty had pressing commitments to other endeavors and little in their reward/recognition system to encourage commitment.

- Unforeseen changes occurred in the strategic directions of our curriculum efforts; for example, replacement of the need for the freshman course with the freshman preseason pilot (to be explained).

- Disincentives to the faculty caused by general leadership transition issues were significant.

We have been on a steep learning curve as we develop organizational structures to lead our CQI implementation. In spite of setbacks and slow progress, however, we are able to report progress in several academic areas.

Curriculum Development

For our academic programs, Georgia Tech's objective is to develop a customer-driven process for continuous curriculum development. There are several activities that support this objective. Processes that more directly connect curriculum development to customers include

- Twenty of our academic programs receive input from corporate advisory boards on a regular basis.

- Fifteen of these programs conduct periodic surveys of alumni.

- Focus groups and a quality function deployment (QFD) process were used by the Computer Integrated Manufacturing Systems (CIMS) program to assess "industry needs to successfully generate the CIMS continuing education curriculum."

Leading the continuous improvement of the overall undergraduate education program at Georgia Tech is the Undergraduate Education Assessment Seminar. Modeled after the Harvard Assessment Seminar, it is undertaking several studies, including student and alumni input, to improve undergraduate instruction and is charged with the continuous improvement of Georgia Tech's general education program following Georgia University System assessment guidelines.

Assessment is becoming an increasing part of our culture and reality, not only for general education, but also for specific degree programs. Assessment will be conducted for every academic major following the Georgia University System guidelines. Measurable outcomes are defined for every undergraduate major, and data collection plans are under development.

We are learning how to use benchmarking as an effective improvement tool. For example, we have been doing informal benchmarking with other IBM TQM Grant recipients and are participating in the Academic Quality Consortium (25 universities) benchmarking efforts. At the college of engineering level, the systematic approach began with comparative benchmarking of 10 peer institutions analyzing input/output variables. Best-practice process benchmarking visits are now planned to four universities: Michigan, Illinois, California-Berkeley, and Texas.

Perhaps the most publicized CQI success at Georgia Tech is the improvement obtained by the Office of Minority Educational Development (OMED).[3] This academic service unit at Georgia Tech is charged with facilitating the success of African-American, Hispanic, and Native American students. In 1991 and 1992, the OMED team members enrolled in our regular undergraduate quality management course to look for ways to apply what they learned to OMED operations. The OMED team rewrote its mission statement to focus on its customers' needs and reorganized its structure around the identified needs of its "client–students." It collected and analyzed data and initiated decision making by fact.

One of the outcomes was the reengineering of the traditional OMED Challenge Program from a social worker approach to one driven by the customers' needs. The OMED Challenge Program assists minority students with the transition from high school to Georgia Tech. The overhauled program was designed and is operated using CQI principles and tools, includes a CQI instruction module, and is aimed to give the students success skills not only for their studies at Georgia Tech, but for all of their lifelong endeavors. OMED is measuring the impact of its improvements, attempting to learn and continuously improve each cycle. Thus far the results have been impressive: significant improvement in retention and grade point average data for the minority students at Georgia Tech. In the spirit of continuous improvement, OMED has served as a role model for other innovations not only at Georgia Tech, but at other universities.

The undergraduate quality management class taken by the OMED team was developed within the engineering program and has been a fertile development ground for Georgia Tech students and several other key people. In the past two years, over 500 students and 150 Georgia Tech faculty, staff, and administrators have taken the course. One of the unique features of the course is that students team with faculty, staff, and administrators to tackle improvement projects within the Georgia Tech system, allowing us to use Georgia Tech itself as a quality improvement laboratory.

In addition to these training opportunities, we have sought other ways to develop CQI understanding and usage in our faculty and administrators. Many have attended national meetings and seminars. We have invested over $45,000 for materials for programs and courses and for a quality resource center established at the reserve desk in the library. We have held a series of brown bag lunch seminars, and our speakers have included Tom Smith, vice president for the southern region of IBM, Ben Bethell, Chip Caldwell, and Pat Bowie.

An especially important development opportunity is provided by the Center for the Enhancement of Teaching and Learning. The Class of 1969 Teaching Fellows Program pairs junior and senior faculty and provides a forum for improving teaching skills of newly hired faculty. The center also provides workshops, consulting advice based on videotaped lectures, evaluation, and discussion with faculty at all stages of development—a true model for continuous teaching improvement.

Inside the Classroom

Delivery of course materials at Georgia Tech is in very mixed stages of improvement and is extremely instructor dependent. The concept that has been most widely adopted in the past five years is based on the principles of fast-feedback systems, where professors obtain frequent feedback from students and report what they have learned back to the students with real-time teaching adjustments. Faculty in engineering have implemented this concept in a number of simple ways, for example, by

- Giving the students red and green slips of paper and asking them to silently hold up the red one when the lecture is going too fast and losing the student or the green one when the lecture is beginning to drag. The instructor can respond immediately by clarifying the topic or moving onto the additional points.

- Passing out index cards at the end of class and asking the student to answer two questions. (1) "What was the main point in today's lecture?" and (2) "What concept needs further explanation at the beginning of next period's class?" The lecturer can analyze the answers to make sure the material is coming across appropriately, and clear up any misunderstandings at the beginning of the very next class.

Being a technological institution, some of our Georgia Tech instructors and students were driven to explore a novel technological implementation of the fast-feedback concept. Exploiting the ease of the electronic mail system and adding an anonymity cloak for the students, a project team of students in the computer science class CS4351 developed an automated class-feedback system, which they call BuzzBack. (Georgia Tech's symbol is the yellow jacket wasp, and our mascot is called Buzz.) Pilot testing of the system was conducted in summer 1993, and full installation is underway this year.

Other initiatives are underway that are focused on significantly improving our core business process of learning. For example, Georgia Tech has a large-scale research endeavor, EduTech, composed of a large and diverse team of cognitive scientists, multimedia technology experts, and engineers to use technology to enhance and facilitate the way people learn. Funded at the level of $1 million annually by the Woodruff Foundation, EduTech has a number of promising research efforts underway that we hope will have significant impact on engineering education for the 21st century.

Building on Lessons Learned

Georgia Tech would not be faithful to the practice of CQI if we were not exploiting the power of the third and fourth steps in the plan-do-check-act cycle. In addition to having learned some things that do not work well for us, we are trying to innovate based on our successes. For example, the OMED Challenge Program opened our eyes to potential improvement opportunities for all of our students. We have extended the OMED concepts and developed an initiative, Freshman Preseason, with a pilot session for 100 incoming students in September 1994. The new program provides the general student population with an introduction to CQI principles and tools, an improvement project, and a CQI-oriented visit to Milliken. The students use CQI tools in a quality improvement project that involves assessing segments of the Preseason Program. The Preseason pilot will be improved/enhanced based on the fall 1994 experience. Enhancing this innovation are CQI-content fine tunings applied to a course in which two-thirds of the freshman class enroll: Psych 1010, an interactive, team-based course designed to enhance skills that will help freshmen successfully transition into Georgia Tech.

Partnering with Suppliers

CQI principles have fostered better partnering with our suppliers, specifically kindergarten–12th grade education systems. Several activities are reported in this area. First, we have included 20 area K–12 school administrators in the engineering undergraduate CQI course, which provided them with training and teams of Georgia Tech students involved in improvement projects on their sites. Additional on-site training sessions have been held at two of the major school systems in the area. Also, free CQI consulting and facilitation has been provided to some of the school systems' educational improvement proposal teams.

At the university level, we have been partnering and sharing at both the individual school level and in several consortia, including the Academic Quality Consortium and the Oak Ridge Associated Universities. For example, North Carolina State University has adopted the program of summer TQM internships that we developed out of our TQM challenge interaction with Milliken. Similarly, the OMED Challenge Program has been extended to other universities.

One of our most outstanding partnership efforts has been led by the Center for Education Integrating Science, Mathematics, and Computing (CEISMC), funded by the National Science Foundation. CEISMC has developed several programs for our K–12 suppliers to meet Georgia Tech's special responsibility for statewide leadership in K–12 math and science education. Teacher-focused initiatives include the Georgia Industrial Fellowships for Teachers, Science Workshops for Elementary School Teachers, and The Science of Sporting Events. Innovative K–8 student focused programs include SummerScape, Space Science and Environmental Camps, and KIDS Club, which are all designed to build interest in math and science. High school students can take Georgia Tech calculus and chemistry courses in selected Gwinnett, DeKalb, and Fulton County schools. Georgia Tech students can now obtain teacher certification in several math and science areas on campus through CEISMC, even though Georgia Tech does not have a school of education.

Lessons Learned

In all parts of CQI, and especially for the academic side, we are learning that as we improve, the more we see that needs improvement. Changing our culture is not easy; we have a long way to go. The academic environment, with a centuries-old scholastic heritage and a span of many campuses within specific disciplines, has a strong drive to preserve its legacies. There is tremendous resistance to many kinds of change, including the paradigm shifts required for CQI implementation. We are convinced that the system for faculty rewards and recognition is a critical driver in the change process and therefore *must* be addressed for long-term success. We are committed to our CQI journey for the long term, because we know that there is much to be gained with CQI deployment. Our challenge is to exploit its power.

Summary and Conclusions

CQI implementation is underway at Georgia Tech. Here we have reported on some of our academic side activities that have led to progress to date along with some of the insights we have gained.

- We are still learning how to configure the structures in our systems that will provide the most efficient leadership for our journey.

- Our curriculum development is becoming more strongly influenced by inputs from our industry customers.

- Assessment is becoming part of the way we close the loop in the plan-do-check-act cycle.

- Several efforts, including the OMED Challenge reengineering, have resulted in better learning outcomes for our students as measured by retention and grade point average data.

- Classroom learning is being improved by fast-feedback methods, although their adoption at this time is still very instructor-dependent.

- We are excited about the EduTech research effort: there is great potential to exploit technology to enhance learning, especially for technological subjects.

- The Freshman Preseason Pilot Program this fall demonstrates Georgia Tech's capacity for innovation based on lessons learned.

- Partnering with our K–12 suppliers is providing opportunity to make both those systems and our own more efficient.

We cannot emphasize enough that we think that Georgia Tech still has a long way to go on its CQI journey. The same can be said for higher education in general, where the metaphor glacial speed seems to apply to its adoption of change. Our challenge is to learn from our initial efforts and begin to exploit the true power of CQI.

Notes

1. J. C. Ammons and J. E. Gilmour, "Continuous Quality Improvement at the Georgia Institute of Technology," *Journal of Quality and Productivity Management* 10, no. 2 (January 1993): 41–50.

2. J. C. Ammons and J. E. Gilmour, "Implementation of Continuous Quality Improvement in American Higher Education Institutions," in *Proceedings of the 38th EOQ Annual Conference*, Vol. 2, ed. Isabel Almeida (Lisbon, Portugal: European Organization for Quality, 1994), 203–210; Jane Ammons, "Total Quality Management Research at Georgia Tech," white paper, July 1993.

3. R. Hume, et al., "Improving the Success of Traditionally Underrepresented Students at Georgia Tech," in *Proceedings of the Second International Symposium on Productivity and Quality Improvement with a Focus on Government* (Norcross, Ga.: Industrial Engineering and Management Press, 1993), 298–307; Daniel Seymour, "Quality on Campus: Three Institutions, Three Beginnings," *Change* (May/June 1993), 14–19.

Total Quality and the Academy: Continuously Improving the University of Maryland

Arjang A. Assad and Judy D. Olian
The University of Maryland at College Park

The Maryland Total Quality Experience

Total quality embraces all parts of the University of Maryland at College Park. Without the contributions of total quality team members, from the president on down, there would be no story to tell in this chapter.

The University of Maryland's journey in total quality began in 1990, when the president took an initial interest in the potential application of total quality to the university. From this interest, he has evolved into the role of leader in driving cultural change through the total quality framework in both academic and administrative support functions. As with other universities, there has been significant investment in bringing total quality processes and thinking into the service operations of the University of Maryland at College Park. Perhaps in contrast to most other universities, however, we have also focused heavily on advancing pedagogy, viewing the contributions of faculty through the lens of total quality.

This chapter concentrates primarily on the academic component of the total quality efforts of the university. After a brief account of the evolution of total quality at Maryland, we discuss the three areas that have received the lion's share of our attention and resource expenditures: addressing total quality principles in the context of the values of academia, applying total quality to classroom teaching and learning processes, and using information technologies to support continuous improvement in the classroom. We end with our personal views on the challenges and opportunities in changing the culture of universities through the framework of total quality. In our descriptions, we have not shied away from reflecting frustrations and discouragements alongside our predominantly uplifting experiences with total quality. We believe that in implementing total quality, just as in any other major reengineering effort, successes and setbacks both offer potential lessons that should not be ignored.

The Chronology of Total Quality at the University of Maryland
Why Change?

The university's pursuit of total quality was driven by necessity as well as by the desire to excel. From the president's perspective, three key factors motivated a serious look at total quality: the uneven quality of services provided by the university, the financial realities besetting the university as a state institution, and the extent to which industry was embracing the total quality framework.

The unevenness of the university's operations was a constant source of frustration to the president. On any single day, he might receive mail that included letters vociferously condemning the shortcomings of the university's services along with letters praising a unit or an individual for exceeding the writer's wildest expectations for service. How could a university simultaneously exemplify excellent and very poor quality? What could be done to even out the level of academic and administrative services so that all were at least satisfactory, if not excellent? In the president's view, the framework and tools of total quality offered a systematic means for understanding and responding consistently to the requirements of clients.

From late 1990, for a period of approximately two years, the state of Maryland experienced its most severe financial crisis since World War II. This crisis brought the university eight rounds of budget cuts, reducing its state support by 20 percent. Enrollment declines further exacerbated the crisis. The university was forced to resort to extreme measures, including layoffs and program shutdowns; no activity or program remained unscathed. Pressured by declining state revenues and the prospects of growing entitlement programs, the state legislature had to plan for long-term cuts in its funding. This led to more stringent accountability requirements for funded state organizations, including the university. Pure and simple, business could *not* go on as usual. More had to be done with fewer people and less resources. In the eyes of the president, the only solution was to radically reengineer, to eliminate the many unnecessary bureaucratic blockers that introduced non-value-added work, wasted resources, and slowed customer service.

The final reason for the president's adoption of total quality is (admittedly) more prosaic. There was a buzz in the air about total quality: the chief executives the president mingled with spoke enthusiastically of culture changes emerging from total quality efforts. They cited service excellence and financial improvements that, if not directly attributable to total quality, were at least advanced through the implementation of total quality and changes in management thinking. Sufficiently intrigued by these reports, the president decided to explore the promise of total quality in the context of the academic environment.

The Process of Introducing Total Quality

The chronology of total quality at the University of Maryland is summarized in Figure 1. Between 1990 and 1991, the president and the top management team spent over 30 hours in formal training to learn about total quality and to develop an understanding of the extent of its compatibility with the university's values and goals. In 1991, the president appointed a broadly representative planning committee including faculty, staff, and students to develop a strategy for total quality implementation. For input into its planning process, the committee solicited information from a variety of customer focus groups. Unlike most other universities that have initially set the academic side of the house aside, the committee's plan also focused on the quality of delivery of academic and pedagogical processes. Fully cognizant of the unique position it was taking, the committee argued that exclusion or delayed integration of the academic core of the institution from the total quality implementation plan risked creating a destructive cleavage in the university's process of culture change. The deliberate choice of the dean of engineering as chair of the committee was meant to lure the academic side of the university into the fold. Had the committee been chaired by a pure administrator, no matter how senior, many academics would have inferred that the total quality plan applies to "them," not "us." The plan was endorsed by the university's top management team in early 1992, and the president came out publicly, though cautiously, to lead the university along its total quality journey.

The champions of quality on campus felt that it was important to commit to a few carefully chosen but realizable goals. Unrealistic or vague expectations would only deflate enthusiasm. The committee therefore adopted the following initial plan of implementation.

- Units initially sign up for continuous improvement training and support on a voluntary basis.

- The implementation is copied at the top with projects undertaken by the president.

- Vice presidents will be increasingly accountable for measurable improvements in key results areas within their divisions.

Selected events:	CQI	IBM-TQ project
1990	• UMCP president initiates campus interest in TQ	
1991	• Executive on loan from Xerox to support TQ	
3/91	• UMCP president hosts a day of learning on TQ in higher education with 400 participants	
12/91	• First CQI plan for campus presented to the president	• Cross-disciplinary team formed to plan for IBM-TQ grant
1/92	• AT&T awards grant to propagate TQ	
2/92	• Office of CQI formed	
4/92		• IBM-TQ grant application submitted by UMCP
5/92	• Overview of campus TQ approach for deans and department heads in TQ	
6/92	• CQI initiatives formed by UMCP VPs	
10/92		• IBM-TQ grant awarded to UMCP
11/92		• UMCP hosts first IBM-TQ sharing conference
2/93	• Two-day training in CQI for deans and selected staff	
4/93		• First cohort of 40 IBM-TQ students admitted
6/93		• Construction of electronic classroom begun
8/93	• TQ Challenge, 120 faculty and senior administrators trained in TQ by Westinghouse	
9/93		• Orientation for IBM-TQ students
		• First course of IBM-TQ core sequence started

Figure 1. Chronology of total quality at the University of Maryland.

Selected events:	CQI	IBM-TQ project
9/93 (continued)		• Electronic classroom completed for use
11/93	• Four major cross-divisional CQI projects initiated	• Dean of business school speaks at IBM Leadership Forum
1/94		• Second IBM-TQ core course started
		• Experiential learning module on TQ piloted for MBA students
2/94	• Teams for four CQI projects launched	• Electronic classroom demonstration-teleconference with IBM
3/94	• President and IBM-TQ project director keynote Higher Education Forum for the state of New Jersey	• Student representatives of IBM-TQ cohort participate in second IBM sharing conference
5/94		• Second cohort of 40 IBM-TQ students admitted
7/94	• Teams for CQI projects complete recommendations	• Two-year self-assessment of IBM-TQ project conducted
8/94		• Begin strategic planning for IBM-TQ project with core process owners

Figure 1. (continued).

- Over time, the campus would mature into cross-functional continuous improvement efforts.

- The executive body for the campus continuous improvement effort would be the Continuous Quality Improvement (CQI) Council, chaired by the president.

"How will we know if we have progressed toward our goals two or five years down the road?" The top management team asked this crucial question in the process of adopting the preceding plan. In order to provide metrics for gauging continuous improvement, the team crafted indicators of quality for each of the university's goals.

Continuous Quality Improvement in Administrative Areas

Our local term for *total quality* is *continuous quality improvement* (CQI). CQI activities in administrative areas were coordinated in the early stages by the Office of Continuous Improvement, formed in December 1991. This office acted as both a clearinghouse and a source of training and expertise. With the formation of the CQI Council in June 1993, a focal point for the programmatic deployment of CQI activities on campus was established.

Initially, CQI pilot projects targeting administrative processes were established in service units such as the graduate school, health center, registrar, bursar's office, payroll department, and communications center. Each unit was supported with training from campus resources, with the critical help of corporate partners who donated their consulting expertise. Some of the pilot processes were highly successful along conventional quality measures of customer satisfaction (in the communications group), or wait or cycle time (financial approval in the bursar's office; on-line electronic registration, faculty appointments, or wait times in the health center). Other pilot processes withered away without achieving significant results, largely because team members and their leaders became too discouraged with the initial setbacks to bounce back for a second-wave effort.

The implementation strategy for total quality had to reckon with staffing issues. To fuel the total quality process in the absence of a large training staff, change agents were identified within each implementation unit to receive total quality facilitator training. They would serve, in turn, as the unit facilitators who kept the total quality process moving. Periodically, facilitators received assistance from the CQI office. There are now close to 30 CQI teams on campus, some focused on problem solving within their own units and others, broader in scope, that reach across units, or even divisions, in their improvement goals.

The most ambitious CQI activities to date are four wide-reaching cross-functional projects operating in the four divisions of the university (see Figure 2). By design, these projects span the strategic priorities of both academic and administrative divisions. For example, the project on student employment can enrich the student's academic experience by strengthening the link between the academic and employment interests or qualifications of the student. The projects were all selected based on evidence of problems ("pain points") drawn from seven sources of student satisfaction data. This selection was particularly sensitive to student retention and the quality of the first-year experience on campus, issues identified by the president as strategically important.

As outlined in Figure 2, each project is sponsored by one of the four vice presidents who is accountable to the CQI Council for results. In each project, the team

Project title	Problem indicators	Project scope	Project sponsor/team leader
Large classes	• First-year students find adjustment to large classes difficult • 53% of nonreturning students dissatisfied with class size • Large classes impede access to faculty • Large classes adversely affect retention	• Improve learning in large classes • Develop new techniques for faculty • Improve lecture hall facilities • Help students to adapt to large class environment	Provost/VP-academic affairs
University climate	• Campus lacks holistic view of student needs • Campus climate considered impersonal • 61% of nonreturning students dissatisfied with support for academic needs • Cold and unfriendly bureaucracy	• Inform every campus employee about basic academic needs of students • Identify essential information faculty and staff should know • Improve access to specific information and answers • Eliminate misinformation	VP-institutional advancement Director of communications and business services
Student employment	• Amount of hours employed adversely impacts progress toward graduation • Employment interferes with academic requirements, causes some students to leave • Upward trend of employment on campus expected	• Assess steps for locating on-campus student employment • Improve linkages between employment and student's academic program • Induce students to work on campus rather than off campus	VP-student affairs Director of physical plant
Student financing process	• Financing problems are a source of major delay in degree completion • Improvement in financing will help retention • Graduating seniors dissatisfied with money management decisions they made while on campus	• Assess current steps in student financing and associated communication and coordination issues • Respond to student requirements for performance of financing process • Improve financial decision making of students • Anticipate external changes requiring response from finance department	VP-administrative affairs University bursar

Figure 2. Outline of four divisional campus projects on CQI.

leader coordinates a cross-divisional action team from multiple campus units. The projects share several common features. All project teams were given a fixed project duration of 120 days, at the end of which they were expected to report to the CQI Council. The teams used the language and tools of total quality to arrive at their recommendations and frequently sought supporting data or additional feedback. In the course of each project, the teams had to grapple with process issues such as team composition, and make interim adjustments in the size and composition of the teams. Most importantly, the projects have been instrumental in opening multiple channels for the voice of the student to be heard. Examples of diverse sources of feedback data include: surveys of first-month impressions from student hall residents, Nielsen-type residential-based groups surveyed several times during the academic year, mini-surveys incorporated into the (remote) telephonic registration process, systematic surveys of seniors to assess global satisfaction with the educational experience, and focus groups conducted in the electronic classroom.

The project on large classes is an intriguing example of the use of CQI to impact a pervasive teaching/learning issue. In this project, a large class was defined as a class with over 100 students. It turned out that most large classes are concentrated in a small number of colleges. Based on surveys of students and faculty who teach in large classes, the team found the following problem issues in order of importance: unsatisfactory contact with professor, lack of feedback, classroom facilities (acoustics, heating), and lack of student preparedness in dealing with large classes. The initial solutions recommended on the basis of these data were pilot-tested by 40 instructors of large classes. A resource team was designed to visit colleges with the greatest incidence of large classes. Along the way, the team encountered a number of college-specific issues in the way large classes are handled. The final recommendations include a variety of different measures, among them an improved set of guidelines for selecting instructors to teach large classes.

At this writing, the initial phase of all four projects is drawing to a close. In keeping with the guiding theme of CQI, an assessment of the four projects has been launched to obtain feedback on the success factors and possible problem areas in the operations of the cross-divisional teams, in order to plan for the next cycle targeted for improvement.

Critical Milestones in the CQI Journey

Two additional milestones have critically shaped our CQI journey. The most important event has been the IBM-TQ award for which the university competed with over 200 universities nationwide. IBM challenged U.S. universities to act as total quality role models for their students and to deliver graduates who are better prepared to add value in a total quality culture, think cross-functionally (especially across engineering and business), and thrive in a team environment. This, according to IBM, would enhance the competitiveness of U.S. products and services by supplying more productive graduates to American businesses. The attraction of the IBM grant was that it emphasized the academic side of total quality—an area traditionally neglected in most total quality change processes—and that it provided a framework for accountability as we progressed along our CQI journey.

The Total Quality Challenge was the other significant event in the seduction of the academic side of the house into total quality. Our corporate partner in this event—Westinghouse Corporation—generously hosted a three-day total quality orientation and training program for over 120 faculty and administrators from business, engineering, computer sciences education, and central administration. This created a core of quality-trained change agents from a variety of academic programs. Faculty talked formally and informally about the implications of the total quality message in their teaching activities and took the first steps in contemplating implementation issues. The Total Quality Challenge also triggered some interest among faculty in conducting interdisciplinary research on total quality. We attribute subsequent responses to internal university and National Science Foundation requests for research proposals on total quality, at least in part, to the interest sparked during this event.

Introducing Total Quality into the Academic Core

As mentioned before, the decision that uniquely defines Maryland's experience with total quality is the deliberate strategy to apply change principles to core academic processes such as teaching and academic decision making. While many implementation questions are common to academic and industry settings, some thorny issues arise in applying total quality to the academic environment, and specifically when classroom learning and teaching processes are targeted. In this section, we discuss in general terms our experience with the challenge of introducing cultural change in the academic setting.

In recent years, there have been many calls to reengineer the academy.[1] Given the pride academics take in the values of intellectual freedom, shared governance, critical and original thinking, and job security through tenure, can the university respond to these oft-stated demands for change? Our experience indicates the importance of certain features—success factors—in enhancing the participation of the academic core in the total quality culture. Not only will the absence of these features reduce the probability of effecting culture change, it may induce wholesale dismissal of total quality ideas as soon as they are introduced. What follows is our compilation of these success factors.

Fitting the Terminology of Total Quality to the Task

Much sensitivity and effort is needed to fit the terminology of total quality within the university's traditions and academic discourse. Among faculty in particular, questions abound as soon as the standard terminology of total quality is introduced. Is the notion of customer too passive a label for the student who is partner to the creation of the product (knowledge and personal development) through collaborative learning? Does student involvement in defining academic requirements undermine the role of the teacher? Does the adjective *total* in total quality reflect an impossible search for the Holy Grail? Is the goal of consistency of service quality across the institution anathema to the academic ideal of creative diversity and intellectual freedom?

An interesting example of the total quality language barrier relates to the notion of the customer. Consider the diversity of customers laying claims to universities' services: students, parents, prospective students and their families, alumni, employers, faculty and staff, researchers at peer institutions, granting agencies and donors, industrial and business partners of the university, accrediting bodies, citizens in surrounding communities, the legislature and tax paying public, community groups, athletic program supporters and fans, and so forth. Given the rarity of alignment among the manifold interests of these diverse customer groups, the needs of these customers must be balanced against one another.

The many-customers syndrome was vividly demonstrated in an exercise the top management team conducted in the president's house. The team covered an entire wall with notes as each member added his or her view of the customer to the university. After much debate, the group finally converged on the student as the primary recipient (directly or indirectly) of most of the university's core academic and administrative services. Nevertheless, we still find it prudent to use the term *student* as the designation for our primary customer group to avoid the occasionally vitriolic opposition the generic terminology of customers and suppliers may evoke in an educational setting. Similarly, the use of the terms *continuous improvement*, and later *CQI*, for campus efforts in total quality reflected a compromise in diction over the total quality label.

Opting for Incremental Culture Change

Challenges to total quality culture changes are sometimes posed by the very sources of universities' traditional strength and distinctiveness. Universities are not hierarchical and faculty can be expected to respond negatively (at times, violently) to edicts from above. The tenure system flattens the organizational pyramid and empowers the faculty to "just say no." The participatory structure of academic governance, defended as key to the creative flow of ideas, removes the pressure to conform. The institution tolerates determined resistance to change and congratulates itself for promoting diversity of opinion and actions. Culture change is not easily advanced within such traditions.

Sudden change from above is a frontal assault on the cultural traditions of shared decision making. It invites opposition from the skeptics and may lead them to announce defeat of total quality in the face of occasional setbacks. Our approach has been to introduce total quality slowly and incrementally, picking off the "low-hanging fruit" first. We invited the initial participation of a few champions who were already exemplifying service excellence and continuous improvement without calling it total quality. The intention was to build on these successes in expanding into less committed environments.

Guru-Less Total Quality

At Maryland, despite frequent examples to the contrary, we chose *not* to adhere to a particular dogma or guru model. Implementation frameworks may follow the models of Deming or Crosby; that of such benchmark organizations as Xerox, IBM, or AT&T; or the favored approach of a particular consulting firm. We were, however, sensitive to the translation difficulties in adopting models developed in entirely different settings. Many institutions and corporations also devise a structured rule book when implementing total quality and use a systematic, tool-based sequence of steps. We elected to do neither and, undoubtedly, some total quality observers will find fault with our loose strategy, especially since the ultimate goal is to achieve consistent, organization-wide culture change.

Our decision was guided by both pragmatic and philosophic considerations. We felt that any appearance of evangelism or dogmatic adherence to a guru model could be counterproductive. Given our approach of disseminating total quality through inducements and voluntary buy-in, it was important that the initial implementors of total quality own their process and adapt it around their local needs. Force-fitting a precise total quality model or set of tools might have hindered pilot teams' progress efforts and adjustment of total quality processes around their own needs. Our corporate partnerships raised another pragmatic concern. Each of our corporate partners—Xerox, Westinghouse, IBM, and AT&T—was trained under a different guru model and brought a slightly different set of tools to support our total quality pilot teams. Moving ahead with the appropriate support outweighed the concerns over slight differences in implementation strategies, as long as the university's overarching continuous improvement values and goals were being furthered.

The absence of a guru model or rule book should not be interpreted as anything goes. There is a university framework for implementation of total quality (the campus planning committee document) and team facilitators receive common total quality training and resource materials. Moreover, much of the value-added of total quality stems from the availability of proven problem-solving tools that are effective and efficient. We recognize the potential diminution of the benefits of total quality if systematic processes are ignored. As we mature and the knowledge and practice of total quality are more broadly shared, there is reason to codify *the* total quality approach for the university. This need becomes more obvious as teams increasingly span multiple functions or divisions, and one team's local application of total quality may no longer generalize everywhere.

Rewards and Incentives for Change

Is total quality in conflict with the traditional reward structure of research-oriented institutions that recognize, first and foremost, research winners? This value system is reflected in the stronger allegiance paid by most faculty to their academic disciplines over their university or department.[2] The greater portability of research recognition provides economic reinforcement of this system on a national level.

How can the contributions of teaching and service champions receive recognition on a par with star-quality research? The importance of research contributions will not, and should not, be downgraded in order to accelerate total quality implementation. Instead, the second-class status of quality-based pedagogical innovators and champions must be elevated in ways that compare with the prizes given to excellent researchers. These ideas parallel Ernest Boyer's thesis in *Scholarship Reconsidered* in which he exhorts leaders of universities to nurture alternative, but equally valued, forms of scholarly contributions to student lives (discovery, integration, application, and teaching).[3]

Debate on these issues is both necessary and inevitable, but should not induce paralysis. For example, despite the standard incentives and pressures of promotion and tenure, given the proper leadership, many faculty members (and tenured faculty in particular) devote significant energy to effecting change in both teaching and service. The recent experience of business schools in revamping MBA programs shows that such time-consuming design changes are, in fact, undertaken and executed seriously. The challenge for total quality in academia is to muster some of the same energies for other process changes—small and large—consonant with the overarching goals of total quality process changes.

The President's Role

The president has been the loudest voice on campus articulating the compelling reasons for the culture change and has risked significant personal capital in driving the change process. This is a tall order for any leader of a complex and dynamic institution. It has required focus on a lean agenda and constancy of purpose over an extended period despite the daily, and sometimes hourly, distractions that compete—in time and resources—with the culture change efforts.

Recognizing the importance of his personal involvement, the president has acted periodically to refocus and reenergize the institution around the total quality goals and processes. This happens through the president's role in chairing the CQI Council, participation in campus recognition events, quality-related op-ed pieces in the student and campus newspapers, total quality training that the president attends with faculty groups, or quality-focused speeches in the business community that are reported back through the campus and popular press.

Total Quality in the Classroom

As shown in our chronology, CQI was already making initial inroads into the administrative side of the campus when the IBM-TQ competition was announced. The attraction of the IBM competition was expansion opportunity into the academic side of total quality.

At Maryland, as with the other award recipients, the IBM-TQ grant has galvanized the implementation of total quality principles in academic programs, pedagogy, and administrative support processes. The objective of our project is to develop a prototype educational process that provides students with cross-functional and team skills, and pedagogical experiences built on an application of total quality principles to teaching and learning. This prototype, developed initially across business and engineering, develops learning and teaching models that are slowly perfected and then exported to increasingly larger academic spheres on campus. In this section, we use our experience to date with the IBM-TQ grant as a vehicle for discussing the pedagogical application of total quality principles. The subsequent section focuses more specifically on the use of the electronic classroom as an enabler of quality in the classroom.

In general, the presence of total quality in the classroom can be felt along the two parallel and interacting dimensions of *curriculum content* and *delivery processes*. We are attempting to apply total quality in a programmatic fashion along both dimensions. Accordingly, after a brief overview of the IBM-TQ Program, we review the curriculum component of the grant that targets a cohort representing an equal mix of business and engineering students. We then analyze the program delivery throughout the lens of total quality principles.

The IBM-TQ Program

In responding to the IBM-TQ competition, the design objective of the curriculum was to enable students to operate in, and contribute to, the culture of total quality in their future workplaces. Rather than sponsoring the development of a new total quality major, whose graduates would specialize in total quality, the intent was to develop in graduates a capacity for incorporating the framework of total quality into daily tasks. Going beyond the letter of the IBM requirements, we also strove for embodiment of total quality principles in the actual design of the IBM-TQ Program. First, by highlighting and appreciating the importance of processes and skills that are most likely to contribute to the effectiveness of our graduates in the workplace of the twenty-first century, the program focuses on one of the key customer groups of the university—employers. Second, it attaches due importance to delivery processes as well as content. Third, it reaffirms the traditional academic values of the core disciplines by retaining the requirements of proficiency in a given discipline. Thus, a graduate of the engineering school, for example, is expected to join the workforce in that capacity, armed with the appropriate technical expertise traditionally required in that field. Thus, business and engineering students would graduate in their normal majors without sacrificing the rigors of their established major areas, although they have the additional skills and knowledge acquired during their total quality curriculum.

It is natural for faculty to focus the design of curricula around issues of content. This is, after all, their traditional domain of expertise. Exciting opportunities for innovation and engaging intellectual debate have long centered on this topic in the academy. In the design of the IBM-TQ core, the added issues of delivery and learning processes, learning environment, and climate presented us with a different set of challenges. How could we weave certain thematic strands illustrating the principles of total quality into the fabric of the core program? After some thought, we adopted the following themes as our guiding principles in delivering total quality in the classroom.

- Customer-driven orientation
- Feedback-driven design and improvement
- Empowerment of students as coproducers
- Integrative view of problem solving
- Extracting value through teamwork and diversity
- Mutual respect in the classroom

These themes underlie the methods and the practices of the program. We found that, broadly interpreted, these principles can be used as seeds for clusters of activities and decisions, particularly in process-oriented features of the program. In charting our course through both the longer term design and the day-to-day administration of the program, we repeatedly asked ourselves how these principles could be applied or illustrated. Fortunately, the fluid boundaries of these concepts allow considerable latitude compared to a more rigid, guru-driven implementation framework, and appear better suited to the adaptation needs of faculty. Later in this section, we describe how various components and elements of the program illustrate these principles.

The IBM-TQ Core Curriculum

The core curriculum for the IBM-TQ Program consists of a sequence of four courses offered to a cohort of approximately 40 students. Students are recruited in their freshman year on campus for enrollment in the fall semester of their sophomore year and stay with the program through the spring semester of their senior year. Each cohort has a balanced mix of engineering and business students (see Figure 3). The four required courses of the core are outlined in Figure 4. All courses are team-taught in an electronic classroom. The instructor teams for the first two courses are from engineering and business. In addition to the courses, the students are encouraged to engage in a host of other activities such as an orientation retreat, quality teams, company visits, campus events, internships, and outreach activities. Several features of this core program deserve comment.

1. It is a prototype. Just as with a prototype in a design laboratory, we hope that our experience with this core program will trigger new thinking in both content and processes for deployment on a much larger scale on campus. In fact, while some positive experience with the use of total quality in the administration of university affairs has been published, next to nothing had appeared on the integration

1993 Students		1994 Students	
Females:	14	Females:	19
Males:	26	Males:	20
Business:	21	Business:	19
Engineering:	19	Engineering:	20
Female engineers:	2	Female engineers:	7

Figure 3. The IBM-TQ Four-Course Program: student demographics.

Year	Semester	Course description
Sophomore	Fall	**Introduction to Design and Quality** Dimensions of product and service quality Principles of engineering design Quality function deployment Introduction to manufacturing organization Foundations of manufacturing systems
Sophomore	Spring	**Strategies for Measuring Quality** Outline of descriptive statistics Common distributions (normal, etc.) Design of experiments—the Taguchi method Full and partial designs Statistical process control
Junior	Spring	**Competing Globally on Quality** The strategic role of quality Customer satisfaction—measurement and use The globalized market and its implications Introduction to cultural differences Importance of cultural determinants in the global market
Senior	Spring	**The Total Quality Practicum** Team projects exploring quality management and continuous improvement in industry

Figure 4. The IBM-TQ Four-Course Program design.

of total quality in core teaching and learning activities when we faced this issue early in 1992.[4] A test bed for developing and trying out new ideas was needed. The intent, however, was to export successful elements of the prototype to the regular slate of course offerings within both engineering and business schools, and perhaps other colleges as well.

2. Since the students admitted into the IBM-TQ Program ultimately graduate with business or engineering degrees, the core courses are carefully integrated into their existing degree programs to avoid an overload of extra credits. Certainly, lengthening the cycle time to graduation was not desirable to the students or to us. This consideration further constrained the design. In the more constrained engineering curriculum, the IBM-TQ core resulted in a one-course overload. Because of these constraints, the program had to seek and attract highly motivated students who were willing to take on the challenges of a demanding program.

3. The design of the core sequence drew on a rich history of collaboration between the schools of business and engineering. Established contacts centered on such areas as manufacturing and telecommunications (rather than quality per se), with the goal of offering more integrated programs in response to industry needs. Correspondingly, the two schools were ripe candidates for the launching of collaborative and integrative courses. Moreover, the theme of quality provided an effective and convenient framework for fleshing out areas of conceptual or practical overlap. This initial fit expedited the startup of the core program.

4. Multiple objectives drove the design of the four courses in the sequence. First, the core had to provide basic grounding in the principles of total quality and in the techniques associated with measuring quality. Second, we wanted the courses to stimulate and hold the interest of both engineering and business students. Thus, the inclusion of design in the first course provides a natural meeting ground for the two disciplines (from mapping the needs of the customer into product features, through such business decisions as pricing or marketing strategy associated with full deployment). More opportunistically, we expected this course to directly dovetail into the first-semester experience of engineering majors who take the engineering design class, a project-driven course guided by just-in-time learning principles. Third, we wanted students to develop an appreciation of the business environment they would enter. The coverage of strategic decisions and the globalized business environment in the third course and the practicum contribute to this objective.

Alignment with Total Quality Delivery Principles

Earlier in this section, we mentioned several guiding themes for the integration of total quality practices into the curriculum portion of the IBM-TQ Program. We now illustrate the themes in relation to total quality delivery processes.

1. *Customer-driven orientation.* A keen awareness of its various customer groups has lent focus to the IBM-TQ Program. Clearly, the student is viewed as the foremost customer, but due attention is also given to the needs of industry as future employers.[5] At our request, the Office of Institutional Studies conducted interviews with focus groups of employers in the area to assess the desired profile of their future recruits. As one outcome of this process, we expect to integrate employer needs into the set of metrics that track program success. In keeping with this industry orientation, students are exposed to corporate practices during class time earmarked for speakers from industry, and they also participate in less formal company-of-the-month events, where small groups of students and a faculty member take field trips to examine the quality management practices of companies on site.

An internal customer group for our program is the faculty teaching the core sequence. We obtain frequent feedback from this group using both traditional instruments and detailed one-on-one and small-group discussions. These discussions range from more general topics as evaluation mechanisms and grading, to specific requests for resources and support. Meetings of faculty as a team were crucial in the early design stages of the program: it was important not to make commitments on behalf of the faculty that they later could not live with or deliver. As experience accumulates, the regular team faculty meetings increasingly focus on issues of improvement.

2. *Feedback-driven design and improvement.* Bateman and Roberts have emphasized the need for frequent and fast feedback as a cornerstone of quality in the classroom.[6] An important use of the electronic classroom is to easily capture and collect this feedback using several tools. For example, a one-minute paper is routinely completed after each class, and groupware is used during presentations and assessment sessions to solicit and collect group input from both students and faculty teams (see Section 4 for other examples).

As expected, students are quite appreciative when they observe that the feedback is operating two-ways. Instructors who go to the trouble of starting a class with a summary of the feedback from the last class are repeatedly praised in the student evaluations. On the other hand, instructors who systematically ignore students' comments are roundly criticized. The underlying notion of fast feedback pervades routine aspects of the course as well. Driven by the overall orientation of the course, instructors make every effort to return graded examinations and papers as soon as possible, reducing cycle times compared to other courses.

The program as a whole uses multiple channels of feedback. A detailed evaluation is conducted several times a year and recorded longitudinally for an assessment of the program over time. Pizza nights are held to allow students to comment on the program informally with both faculty and program administrators. Students often visit the administrators to volunteer comments on the program or ideas for improvement. In the case of the few students who withdrew from the program for various reasons, the program director personally conducted detailed exit interviews.

3. *Empowerment of students as coproducers.* Anyone who has gone through the ordeal of a faculty meeting where the notion of "student as customer" is hotly debated, can imagine the resistance elicited by the idea of student empowerment. While the implementation of such empowerment in the academic setting is naturally delicate, it also holds the key to the most far-reaching paradigm shift in educational processes.[7] This redefinition of the boundaries of the teacher–learner relationship presents challenges on both sides. The challenge for faculty is to make the difficult transition from "sage on the stage" to "guide on the side," without a feeling of loss or

resentment. The challenge for students is to accept certain (possibly evolving) limits to the extent of empowerment. While the student is empowered to participate in designing and changing many features of the ongoing learning experience (for example through fast feedback), the students' initiatives and changes must conform to established ground rules and stop short of setting the academic rules. Moreover, empowerment does not imply an immediate adoption of all suggestions from students. Some may require further discussion in the students' quality team, and some may be tabled because they are in conflict with an instructor's values or teaching style.

As a step in the direction of empowering the students in the IBM-TQ Program, we have tried to encourage a sense of ownership of the program among the students. Students have formed quality teams, ad hoc committees, and a student chapter of ASQC, and offered various concrete suggestions to enrich the program. The first cohort designed the official logo for the program. At the recent sharing conference attended by all eight IBM grant winners, the bulk of our presentation was delivered by two student speakers elected by their peers to represent the program at the meeting. We similarly rely on the help and advice of our students in marketing the program to prospective students and in screening incoming applications. In a few meetings, our commitment to empowerment meant acceding to the students' wishes even when this challenged the initial plan for accomplishing a programmatic element. While each occasion for student participation and leadership may be viewed as small in itself, the cumulative message indicates genuine respect for students and their ability to coproduce the program.

4. *Extracting value through teamwork and diversity.* The central importance of teamwork to the IBM-TQ Program objectives was realized early on. Not only was facility in teamwork an important consideration in employers' minds, the design of cross-functional class assignments necessitated the honing of team skills. Convinced that team processes should be facilitated from the start, we require all students to attend an orientation program for team skill development. This intensive three-day program goes a long way toward creating team spirit and bonding, and is reinforced immediately thereafter through the assignment of a team project. The composition of each team is deliberately diverse, including both engineering and business students, males and females. By the end of the first course, students are quite advanced in negotiating roles and responsibilities within the teams and derive considerable satisfaction from the work performed in the teams. Indeed, when we broached the issue of reconstituting the teams, students were quite resistant to any proposals to alter team composition.

5. *Integrative view of problem solving.* Total quality involves an integrated, horizontal view of organizations. To prepare students for a total quality culture in the workplace, the university has to address horizontal linkages among disciplines and courses

as well.[8] As mentioned earlier, a project-based approach has been implemented in the introductory engineering design course. Engineering students work in teams to design and produce an assigned product. The just-in-time learning philosophy of this course dispenses with regular class lectures in favor of problem-driven acquisition of information on an as-needed basis. Naturally, this approach moves the delivery mechanisms of engineering expertise away from preset discipline-oriented (vertical) channels.

Knowing that the engineering students in the IBM-TQ cohort had already experienced horizontal learning and teamwork in connection with this course, our goal in the first IBM-TQ course was to extend the boundaries of learning to encompass traditional business functions and operations management as well. The projects assigned in the first and second courses both required integration at this level. In the first course, students must design a new product (such as a hairdryer) and prepare a complete manufacturing and business plan for its deployment. Completed projects are presented to and judged by a cross-functional team of faculty members from different disciplines. Some business students were initially apprehensive about these project requirements since they were not scheduled to take courses in the functional areas (accounting, marketing, operations, and so forth) until their junior year. Students were encouraged to act proactively and to contact faculty to seek the necessary information. Indeed, two students remarked that they felt as if they had already learned all that a business education can offer them in the next 2.5 years! To us, this comment is an indication of the power of an integrated project to facilitate and dramatically accelerate learning. In fact, subsequent course evaluations showed that the students associated the greatest amount of learning with the project components of the course, and observed that their effectiveness in teams enabled them to accomplish much more learning than in a regular course.

Another telling remark came from a business student who commented that working with engineering students had increased her appreciation and respect for the role and contributions of engineers in the workplace. Remarks such as these, though anecdotal, signal that the program is on track in facilitating integrative thinking and operational skills. Students' attitudes such as these are likely to carry forward into the workplace.

Working in teams is a nontrivial learning experience for the faculty as well. In addition to adapting to each others' teaching styles, the two instructors of the course from business and engineering must build a level of trust, mutual respect, and meeting of the minds that carries well beyond the classroom. They have also commented on the new insights gained from listening to a colleague from another discipline present a known concept from a different angle.

6. *Mutual respect in the classroom.* All of the preceding points require a healthy environment, unadulterated by the trappings of dominance and power play. This applies to faculty respect of students, students' respect of faculty, and students' respect for each other. Significant maturity is expected from the students who, in turn, require caring respect from their instructors and the program administrators. We know from experience that all bets are off when the foundation of mutual respect is found to be shaky.

7. *Extending the prototype.* In keeping with the role of the IBM-TQ curriculum as a pedagogical prototype, the transfer and porting of ideas and course elements first tried out in the IBM-TQ core sequence is already under way. The MBA curriculum within the College of Business and Management now includes a week-long module in total quality, required of all students, that incorporates some of the pedagogical approaches and methods tested in the IBM-TQ Program. Individual courses in the business school have expanded their coverage of total quality as well. Building directly on the working relationships and exposure to the student mix developed in the IBM program, faculty from business and engineering are collaborating to incorporate principles of design, operations, quality, and statistical tools for quality management into a new engineering curriculum implemented under a major curriculum transformation grant.

Initiatives for much wider coverage of the student body on campus (beyond the two colleges of business and engineering) have been undertaken. Experience with the IBM-TQ students suggests that training in team processes and the use of cross-functional thinking can form the basis for generic skill building to benefit the undergraduate student body at large. The Honors Program (1600 students) is a natural initial target group for such training and an implementation strategy for this initiative is being developed.

Using Technology for Continuous Improvement

One of the goals in designing the IBM-TQ Program was to marry the concepts of total quality with the improvement opportunities offered through information technologies. The primary arena for this confluence is the IBM-TQ electronic classroom, although several other CQI projects have been enhanced by information technology as well.

The IBM-TQ Theater includes 20 computers, linked to each other and to the instructor's computers. With each pair of students sharing a computer that recognizes the individual students' inputs, the capacity of the classroom is 40 students. The information technology architecture includes multiple software applications including shared graphics, word processing, courseware specific to various classes, groupware, as well as software developed explicitly to support class note taking and feedback processes. Two large projection screens display the information generated on computers by the students. Alternatively the screens can be used to display instructor-designed information or input provided by any one of the students in the class. The theater also serves as a true virtual classroom. It is equipped as a teleconferencing facility, enabling the integration of corporate boardrooms or factory back rooms into the learning experience, as long as our counterparts have similar teleconferencing capabilities. Classes conducted in this environment range from Chinese literature and art history, to physics, information systems, and measurement for quality.

There are several pedagogical advantages that are uniquely facilitated by this electronic architecture: (1) It provides equal opportunity for student involvement in ongoing classroom activities, regardless of the student's learning and communication styles; (2) It enables multidirectional communication and feedback processes among students or between professors and students; (3) Cycle time for all processes is dramatically reduced, allowing the use of more frequent and diverse learning and feedback activities in any given class.

The classroom is not simply a bunch of boxes in search of applications. Total quality principles guide the pedagogical innovations in the theater, and the computers are mere enablers of these innovations. Some examples of total quality-based learning and teaching processes and tools, facilitated through the electronic classroom environment, include

1. One-minute, anonymous papers at the end of each class, in which students take a few minutes to articulate the key points learned in class and the points that remain muddy. This provides teachers with immediate knowledge of teaching and learning effectiveness, and they respond via electronic or regular mail, or during the next class period, as warranted by the feedback.

2. A student feedback meter that acts as an ongoing pulse taker for teachers. This feedback is also anonymous. Students can hit a key signaling that they got it or didn't get it. The tally is displayed on the instructor's screen as a bar graph in two colors, green for "got it," red otherwise. This meter informs the instructor, in real time, about the pace and success of the teaching and learning, and allows for immediate corrections to be made.

3. Complete group involvement in class design and learning processes via group-based interactive software. The tools are very fast and can be used to involve students in establishing class agenda ("Which of the topics for today reflect your top learning priorities?"), in uncovering difficulties in understanding the material

("What are the most important questions remaining in your mind from the material for today"?), in processing cases ("How would you solve this problem?"; "what questions would you ask this client?"), in gauging class opinion around a controversial topic or issue ("Do you agree or disagree with this legislative decision, company policy, suggested design strategy?"), and in designing facets of the course ("Assign suggested weights to the exams and papers for this course"). Every student provides input, and input can be displayed piecemeal (for example, every idea during a brainstorming exercise arrayed on the screens) or in the aggregate (rankings or means displayed).

4. Facilitation of student learning by providing electronic outlines and notes from the instructor, which the students can augment with their own electronic notes. Not only does this facilitate organized learning, it also maintains student attention during the class.

5. Collaborative learning, since students are involved in delivery of the material, and their input is readily shared (via electronic sharing devices) with all other students and with the instructor.

6. Ongoing measurement of learning and teaching processes, facilitated through immediate display of results of the data collection. Results can be discussed as soon as the last person has input his or her ratings.

7. Team teaching to reflect multiple perspectives on a given topic, facilitated through electronic communication between the faculty jointly teaching courses.

It is important to emphasize that the IBM-TQ Teaching Theater is not, by itself, the embodiment of total quality in teaching and learning processes. The teaching environment is merely a tool (albeit an efficient and readily available tool) to enable total quality–based processes. The faculty must still decide on the nature of the systematic linkages between total quality principles and teaching applications, and exploit the tools of the classroom to this end. Untrained or unwilling faculty thrust into this environment can continue to teach their classes as before, leaving untouched the possibilities inherent in the classroom architecture.

Our evaluation of this marriage of total quality principles with the tools of information technology has demonstrated that

- The range of pedagogical approaches used by an instructor can be enlarged through this learning architecture.

- Real-time involvement of the entire class greatly adds to the excitement of the learning process.

- Ongoing student feedback enables the teacher(s) to stay in touch with student reactions, and to improve classroom processes immediately.

- This is the classroom and the pedagogy of the year 2000. Faculty using these processes are ahead of the curve.

Nonetheless, a note of caution is appropriate. Electronic classrooms have bugs—both hardware and software. Some (though fewer and fewer) students lack keyboard skills. There is a learning curve that must be built into each course, until both instructors and students overcome the initial trouble spots that are almost inevitable in this environment. If perfection is expected from the outset, the environment will be disappointing and quickly dismissed. In addition, these tools raise the expectations of students. Students want to observe, and participate in, use of the electronic tools if they are learning in an environment that offers these possibilities. They also want to see obvious results flowing from their input and feedback. Students become quickly disillusioned when the tools remain unused or when they perceive little effects to their involvement in class improvement efforts.

The IBM-TQ Teaching Theater is a dramatic example of the enhancement of the CQI process through information technology. There are, however, other illustrations. Technology has enabled on-line student registration and billing using Touch-Tone telephones, thereby providing students with 24-hour access to this instant service from anywhere in the world, cutting down on long lines and wait times, and freeing personnel to engage in more value-added activities. As another illustration, we are also now in the process of introducing customer feedback surveys via our fiber optic (data linked) telephone system. At the end of a service call after the service provider has signed off, a random sample of customers will receive an on-line customer service survey, delivered and instantly coded via the voice-based digital telephone system.

Lessons Learned and Future Challenges
The chronology in Figure 1 shows that, at Maryland, only three years have passed since the beginning of programmatic efforts in total quality. Even by industry standards, this is far from maturity in the process of evolving into a changed culture. Nevertheless, in this period we have learned some lessons that provide a firmer foundation for charting our future course. The following briefly lists the main insights we take away from the experiences to date with the IBM-TQ Program and the campus CQI initiatives.

Empowerment of Students As Coproducers Works
Students are energized by the sense of ownership and the challenge presented by the program. Students will tolerate a certain level of experimentation and will forgive

unintended errors that arise from trying novel processes. They strictly require, however, that faculty walk the talk. Students' heightened expectations make shortfalls from the stated commitments particularly painful and disappointing.

Cross-Functional Learning Enriches Both Learning and Teaching

There is no substitute for hands-on cross-functional application of principles learned. Issues that make for dry class lectures come to life in teams and in the course of working on specific projects. With the appropriate structuring and guidance from faculty, this dimension can significantly enhance the value of the educational experience. Similarly, even faculty who have benefited from years of teaching in an area report new insights from the experience of coteaching with a peer from a different discipline.

Team Teaching Is Only the Start

Team teaching is often a first response to the call for integrative course content. As a source of cross-pollination and exchange of ideas, this first step has worked well in our core program. Students, however, expect the teaching team to add value beyond simple division of labor between the instructors. Team teaching elevates expectations by drawing the student's attention to the interplay of the ideas and perspectives of the two instructors. Students appreciate a true dialogue between their teachers and are disappointed if the teachers act as ships passing in the night. More pragmatically, as few teamed instructors are completely evenly matched, coteaching may inevitably invite the students to compare the two teachers to the detriment of the less-skilled teacher.

Time Management Is Crucial for Program Successes

The high expectations created by the message of total quality principles is bound to conflict with other commitments of the students. And yet, additional activities scheduled outside of the classroom are important contributors to the overall experience of students and faculty in the program. Ambitious courses similarly compete for students' time. The ultimate responsibility for managing the burden of the requirements rests with the faculty. Faculty must also deal with significant added demands on their own time imposed by new course design and delivery, and by the necessity of interacting with other faculty as an important source of innovation and learning.

Faculty Development Must Parallel Infusion of Total Quality

Buy-in of faculty into total quality programmatic goals is crucial. Inevitably, some faculty will ask, "What is in it for me?" Certain individuals who associate ideal instruction with a perfect set of reusable notes will be threatened by changes that must be introduced into courses. Ultimately, faculty will be convinced through examples, seminars, new tools, and resources that change can be liberating and that unintended outcomes can hold many pleasant surprises as well.

Electronic Classroom Requires Instructor Readiness
The rich learning environment of the electronic classroom is ideally suited to experimentation with total quality principles. However, we caution against its introduction before faculty are ready to live with the consequences. Total quality learning technologies change the balance of power in the classroom. The electronic environment serves as an equalizer given the comprehensiveness, multidirectionality, and anonymity of inputs into ongoing classroom activities. Many professors are not ready for this and have to be acculturated slowly.

Final Observations
The IBM-TQ Program is approaching its third year. It has already accounted for numerous radical teaching and learning innovations, albeit focused in a few classes. In the colleges of engineering and business, most of the faculty are aware of the existence of certain total quality–based innovations in teaching, although far fewer have actually changed their teaching processes accordingly.

Looking to the future, the experiences with the IBM-TQ Program and CQI on campus have clearly thawed the status quo and even initiated the process of culture change. The broad-based CQI projects have gone a long way toward disseminating the language of total quality and gaining acceptance for its tools. These projects have also exemplified productive use of teams and team processes, management by data, and the use of feedback. As mentioned before, the campus has seen an unprecedented expansion in the number of channels and mechanisms for hearing the student voice.

Some deans have used continuous improvement as a springboard for advancing their own strategic priorities. For example, the dean of the College of Education is using total quality as the diagnostic framework for his faculty's outreach efforts in helping K–12 schools understand the sources of success and failure in their delivery of education. Our future steps must focus on expanding this sphere of influence into other colleges on campus. To determine our course in the face of these questions, we are currently conducting a sequence of strategic planning events with the goal of formally incorporating total quality into the overall strategic course of the university.

Critical to these expansion plans is the senior leadership's ability to remain uncharacteristically preoccupied with the total quality effort and to translate this into gains that matter to faculty. The president and top leadership must repeatedly model total quality behaviors and keep reminding the deans and faculty that continuous improvement is part of our mission. This is easier done in the first three months of a total quality effort. What about in the second or fifth years? Is the leadership able to remain committed in words as well as actions? Is the insistence on total quality as a priority consistent with the stringent resource allocations on campus, particularly when these resources seem to be shrinking? Are deans—the most direct channel for influencing continuous improvement among faculty—reflecting the same reward and resource allocation priorities as those articulated by the president? Have the deans and chairpersons of departments used continuous improvement to advance the agenda of their own colleges and departments with regard to priorities that are meaningful to faculty? If not, faculty will remain focused primarily on advancing their personal career priorities that thrive on the status quo, rather than risk investing in an uncertain and effort-consuming change process.

The total quality journey for a large and nonhierarchical culture such as a university's is sometimes difficult, but often gratifying. We look to the future with optimism. Continuous improvements are occurring, and they provide the motivational boost and energy to forge on. The example of the IBM-TQ grant also shows how industry can significantly fuel the movement toward quality in higher education and keep it on course with demanding but fair accountability requirements. As Theodore Marchese has argued, an even broader link between assessment and CQI is needed.[9]

The impressions articulated in this paper should be regarded as an effort to freeze temporarily a moving target as we continue traveling on this never ending road. Nevertheless, in looking back, we see numerous points of light along the way that justify an underlying current of enthusiasm in this account.

Notes

1. E. L. Boyer, *Scholarship Reconsidered: Priorities of the Professoriate* (Princeton, N.J.: The Carnegie Foundation, 1990).

2. Ibid.

3. Ibid.

4. Ellen Earle Chaffee and Lawrence A. Sherr, *Quality: Transforming Postsecondary Education, Report Three* (Washington, D.C.: ASHE-ERIC Higher Education Reports, 1992); Daniel T. Seymour, *On Q: Causing Quality in Higher Education* (New York: Macmillan, 1991).

5. See as examples, John P. Evans, et al., *Report of the Total Quality Leadership Steering Committee and Working Councils* (Cincinnati, Ohio: Procter & Gamble, 1992) and Brian O'Reilly, "Reengineering the MBA," *Fortune*, 24 January, 1994.

6. George R. Bateman and Harry V. Roberts, *TQM for Professors and Students* (Chicago: University of Chicago Graduate School of Business, 1993). A revised version of this paper, "Total Quality for Professors and Students," appears in this book.

7. Judy D. Olian, "TQ and the Academy, Problems, and Opportunities," in *The Quality Approach to Higher Education*, ed. B. Ruben (New Brunswick, N.J.: Transaction Books, 1994).

8. O'Reilly, "Reengineering the MBA."

9. Theodore J. Marchese, "Assessment, Quality, and Undergraduate Improvement," *Assessment Update* 6 (May–June 1994): 1–14.

Integrating Principles of Total Quality into Teaching and Learning

Gary Bonvillian, Ph.D.
William Nowlin, Ph.D.

Introduction

The College of Business at Rochester Institute of Technology (RIT) has been committed to the principles and application of total quality since 1990. With the arrival of a new dean, Richard Rosett, the college seized an opportunity to assume a leadership role in this important movement, which has since influenced a transformation at many other academic organizations. Neither the administration nor the faculty accepted this new direction lightly, as it was quickly recognized that such an initiative would challenge the very nature of traditional academic thinking on organizational structure, leadership, faculty responsibilities, and relationships with constituencies.

During the 1990–1991 academic year, the faculty and staff were introduced to the tools and techniques of total quality through a series of industry-sponsored workshops, seminars, and training sessions. They provided a foundation on which to consider application of these principles in an academic environment. A tremendous amount of support was obtained from industry partners such as Xerox Corporation, IBM, Eastman Kodak, and Motorola. These early relationships were invaluable in providing the most current and relevant training available at that time.

In the fall of 1991, the faculty unanimously approved a formal resolution to proceed with the transformation of the college. The college committed itself to the integration of total quality into both the curriculum and operations, resulting in an aggressive transition plan and workload for faculty and staff. With few exceptions, they accepted and met the challenge.

In 1992 the college abandoned the traditional departmental structure found in most colleges, adopting instead a flat organization with decentralized decision making. Program teams of faculty, staff, and even central support personnel, oversee many of the current initiatives in the college.

The challenge of additional work entailed by this aggressive initiative was somewhat eased by the national recognition the college received when awarded two industry prizes. The first was the Motorola University Challenge, which involved a full week of comprehensive training in total quality. Twenty-nine universities competed; only seven were awarded the training opportunity. The second award was an IBM grant of $1 million to advance the principles of total quality in the academic community. Two hundred and four schools competed for eight grants.

These awards were not only a welcomed acknowledgment of the hard work of the faculty and staff in the college, they also provided additional training and financial support for curriculum development, research, and other specific discipline related and collegewide projects.

Important Early Initiatives

Vision and Values Statement

Several important steps were taken early in the transition period that reinforced and clarified the implications of total quality on the future of the college. First, through the collective efforts of faculty, staff, administrators, and external advisory groups, vision and values statements were crafted that clearly articulate the college's commitment to total quality (see Figure 1). This document continues to provide the guiding total quality principles for the college.

Promotion and Tenure Norms

Another step taken early in the transition period—considered by many to be the most important—was a revision of the promotion and tenure norms. The existing norms, while appropriate for the expectations of an AACSB accredited school, did not express and consequently support the college's resolve to become a total quality organization.

The transition to a total quality organization began with the faculty resolution of 1991; it continues to be dependent on faculty commitment. Current literature on total quality in colleges and universities suggests that few schools have taken this important step in assuring longevity of the movement. The College of Business recognized that it is the faculty, not the administration, who must carry out the changes. Faculty are at the center of the most important functions of any school—teaching, research, and service.

College of Business
VISION

The College of Business will distinguish itself nationally and internationally as the premier source of graduates fully prepared for employment by organizations committed to total quality management.

- We will adhere faithfully to the philosophy and practice of total quality management in serving our customers, both internal and external.

- Our customers include students, employers of our students and graduates, students' parents, alumni, coworkers within the College of Business and other colleges, and administrative units within RIT.

- Total quality management practices, principles, and concepts will be integral to our curriculum.

- We will encourage, support, and reward research directed toward understanding, explaining, and enhancing the management practices associated with total quality management.

- We will pioneer the application of total quality management to the teaching process. In retention of students, in their mastery of our curriculum, and in their satisfaction with the quality and delivery of their education, we will set an example for all of higher education.

College of Business
VALUES

Our conduct must command respect for its integrity. We must set an example for our students and for all our colleagues in higher education. These are the values to which we commit ourselves.

Continuous improvement is everyone's responsibility. We must constantly encourage change and strive for improvement, setting new standards for excellence in everything that we do.

Teamwork is integral to everything we do. In teaching, in serving our students and their future employers, and in fulfilling the requirements of our coworkers, we promote the involvement of everyone who can contribute to continuous improvement.

Openness and mutual trust are imperative in our dealings with one another and with our customers.

Frequent two-way communication throughout the college is critical in our challenging environment.

Immediate action is essential. We have chosen to lead in a rapidly changing educational environment. We cannot wait for someone else to show us the way.

Forthright dealing with our colleagues, our students and their future employers, our alumni, and the schools on whom we depend for students is required for long-term success.

Figure 1. RIT's vision and values statement.

Consequently, the promotion and tenure norms express teaching as the central mission of the college. The norms further state that the college goal is to be "recognized as a total quality management based teaching school offering quality management education." The three dimensions of good teaching are

1. An effective learning environment

2. Professional competence/expertise

3. Service to organizations whose missions are to enhance education and to disseminate the subject matter, that is, educational and professional organizations

The new norms also provided a broader definition for faculty professionalism and competency. Influenced in part by E. L. Boyer's *Scholarship Reconsidered: Priorities of the Professoriate*,[1] the college sought to capitalize on the full range of contributions faculty are capable of making, provided that the primary function of quality teaching remains paramount.

Excellence in Teaching . . . A Long-Standing Tradition

A reputation for excellence in teaching was not something the College of Business earned from its total quality initiative. The college has a long history of outstanding teachers and has been recognized accordingly by the number of individuals who have won RIT's prestigious award in this area of faculty performance. In 1965, RIT established an annual award to recognize excellence in teaching. With an emphasis on teaching effectiveness, the award acknowledges those individuals who have been selected by their students and peers for this honor. The College of Business currently has six winners on the faculty.

To take advantage of the collective wisdom of these outstanding teachers, to begin working as a team, and to improve the learning environment, a task force was formed early in 1991. Among other things, this task force was responsible for compiling a set of techniques for improving teaching performance in the classroom. (See appendix.) The document was widely distributed and has since served as a valuable guide for new faculty as well as for veterans who are striving to improve their own teaching performance.

A Design for Continuous Improvement in Teaching

Appreciating the Uniqueness of Academia

The total quality movement has challenged all organizations to begin considering entirely different and innovative ways to encourage and support a high degree of interaction among group members, to foster a climate of open and forthright communication, and to measure individual as well as collective performance. Although many of our business and industry partners have embraced models of total quality to advance their own organizations, the academic community has been faced with a much more profound challenge.

Ours is not an environment in which a sense of order and control often prevails. Major corporations that have embraced total quality and implemented it from the top down have insisted that everyone be involved or else! Faculty, by nature and professional character, act as near independent entrepreneurs in their organizations. Each faculty member has considerable latitude in controlling not only his or her fate but also that of students, the organization's primary customer.

Consequently, it is rash to assume that total quality models, which have been predominantly designed for and by business and industry, will work without modification in a college or university environment. A more promising approach is to seek out customized quality principles that can most easily be adapted to academia and to develop a model from them. This same idea can be applied to the behavior of individual faculty in the classroom, as will be illustrated later in this paper.

Unlike most service activities, teaching requires the full participation of the customer. If a student does not study, review, question, and seek help when it is needed, the best efforts of the teacher will fail. Any plan for achieving continuous improvement in teaching must include provision for involving students in the process.

Similarly, more than almost any other service activity, teaching tempts—and permits—the seller to blame the customer for failure to achieve the objective. Any plan for achieving continuous improvement in teaching must include provision for discovering the causes and defects so they can be eliminated.

Teaching can be viewed as the process of instruction and facilitation of learning. Students are excellent judges of the quality of the teaching process since they are the immediate customers of that process. They can provide feedback on the quality of the delivery of instruction and facilitation of learning. Students can tell us whether they are learning, whether our processes do what they purport to do, and whether we are meeting their expectations.

It should be noted that many faculty in the College of Business believe that there should be a clear distinction between the quality of the service and process (teaching) from that of the product (what students know or are able to do). Students can judge the delivery process—how we do it—but employers are the best judge of the quality of the product.

Establishing Expectations

In teaching, we should seek to meet the expectations of students. The best way to know what they expect is to ask them. Asking students in just one course is not sufficient because they will have different expectations depending on the subject matter. How do we get the real expectations to surface?

- Ask students, on the first day of class, what are their expectations. Some faculty in the College of Business ask students to

  —List three things about previous courses that you liked and would like to have repeated in this course.

  —List three things about previous courses that you did not like and that you would like not to have repeated in this course.

- Compile the responses.

- Calculate frequencies.

- Considering the items and their frequencies, place the items in the following categories.

  —Things that you already plan to do

  —Things that you did not plan to do, but will because it seems important to several students

  —Things that seem important to students that you cannot or will not do

  —Other (usually the unreasonable or the low frequency items)

- At the start of the next class give the students feedback on their input, your analysis, and what is likely to happen based on the input. If it is in written form, it tends to make a greater impact. It also establishes a framework for feedback during the term and for the post-term ratings.

Learning Process

Variation occurs in the learning process and can be measured by what students know or are able to do upon completion of a course, possibly using an exam for measurement. The primary measure is still the grade.

There are many causes of variation in learning. Some due to students themselves, others due to a poorly designed system for helping professors understand the nature of the process. In higher education, professors are hired because of their subject matter expertise and research potential. Few are hired because they are good teachers.

Some students do not perform well in particular courses because they are ill-prepared from the start. This can be due to their own inability and performance or to poor preparation in foundation courses. The lack of standardization in the design and delivery of college courses is clearly a contributor to this problem. This is further compounded by the fact that students are operating within the framework of six stages of learning: knowledge, comprehension, application, analysis, synthesis, and evaluation.[2] Consider this scenario.

Imagine, for example, two sections of a statistics course. In Section A, the professor teaches in a way that students learn how to calculate and remember formulas and rules. Students are tested using multiple choice exams or they are asked to define items, recall, and/or list items. In Section B, the professor teaches in a way that students are required to comprehend what they learn and apply it to solving problems.

Jane was in Section A (learned statistics at the knowledge stage), and she earned a grade of A. Sally was in Section B (learned statistics at the application stage), and she also earned a grade of A. For what was required in the respective statistics courses, both students performed well. They earned equal grades. But, are they equally prepared for subsequent courses that will require them to apply what they know about statistics?

In the ensuing academic term both students enrolled in the same section of a course in financial management. In the design of the course, the finance professor had assumed (and correctly so) that all students had completed a course in statistics. The professor also assumed (incorrectly) that students entering the course were equal in their ability and preparation to apply statistics to business financial problems.

At the end of the term, Jane (who learned statistics at the knowledge stage) earned a C in financial management, while Sally (who learned statistics at the application stage) earned an A.

The variation in learning and in performance was caused by the absence of a standard format and standardized objectives for the statistics course. Professors, based on their experience and preferences, develop different course objectives. Even with similar learning objectives, courses still differ in how they are delivered.

An important question the college needs to ask itself in this situation is: who is the customer of the statistics course? There are several. A very important one, however, is the professor who is teaching financial management. These kinds of variations in learning and performance could be reduced by developing objectives and outcomes for each course. The outcomes should be driven by the needs of the next customer in the process. Course objectives should specify the stage of learning (knowledge, comprehension, application) a student is required to achieve before finishing the course.

Bloom's Taxonomy of Learning is an excellent tool to minimize variation in the learning process.[3] The Learning Stages Matrix describes the six stages of learning, how to teach consistently with each stage, and how to measure learning at each stage. Within the College of Business we do not systematically use this model and consequently suffer from the same inconsistencies that result in a poorly established process.

Feedback As a Prerequisite to Continuous Improvement

Continuous improvement should be sought by every employee in an organization in pursuit of total quality. Professors are no exception. In order to improve, a professor must ask for and receive feedback from students on the progress of the course and on the teaching process. Students have varying concerns that they do not communicate to the professor because of the absence of an adequate feedback system. Some professors have such a rapport with students that regular dialogue yields frequent feedback on their teaching performance. The concept of fast feedback, as pioneered by Harry Roberts, a professor at the University of Chicago and a total quality advocate, is intended to provide students with frequent opportunities for this exchange.

There are several relatively simple ways in which feedback can be collected—on 3 × 5 cards, a short questionnaire, or just plain paper.

• *Data collection.* Questions can be open-ended, such as: What is the most important point of today's lesson? What suggestions do you have to improve the course? What concerns do you have about the course so far?

Questions can also be asked so that responses are given on a Likert scale. The feedback you receive will vary. It may be about a point that was not explained to a student's satisfaction, the readability of overhead transparencies or photocopies, or confusion about the relationship between something said today and something said two days earlier.

• *Analysis of the data.* After collecting the data, analyze them to determine which items you will do something about and which items you cannot or will not address. If Likert scales are used, consider asking a volunteer student team to take the data and prepare charts so that students can track improvement.

• *Feedback to students.* At the next class, give students some feedback on the data. If they do not believe that you are being responsive to their feedback, they will simply stop giving it.

A common error made by some professors who use this feedback mechanism is that they ignore the data and do not make any adjustments in their own behavior. Another error is a failure to inform students how the data were used.

College of Business Models for Applying Total Quality in the Classroom

Business Concepts for Freshmen and Sophomores

In the 1989–1990 academic year, another early initiative was a response to the retention level of freshman and sophomore students. In studying the issue, it became obvious that lower division students did not feel connected to the college. Indeed, most of their coursework in the college occurred in the junior and senior years. Prior to fully launching the total quality initiatives in the College of Business, a problem had been identified with respect to the integration of freshmen into the mainstream of undergraduate studies at RIT. Retention levels were relatively low.

A plan was presented by a select group of faculty to develop a sequence of six credit courses entitled Business Concepts. These six courses, then spanning the freshman and sophomore years, were designed to provide students with a basic understanding of the principles of total quality as well as to develop specific personal skills to ensure they could function effectively in small work teams and organizational units. Although the Business Concepts sections were, and continue to be, taught by individuals, these faculty are a cross-disciplinary team committed to the continual refinement of their courses. The team meets regularly to ensure standardization across the sections and a continuity in the sequence of courses.

The Business Concepts series, as it is currently designed, enables students to incrementally develop their topics and personal knowledge and skills. The subject areas include

- Use of the computer network for communication with faculty and fellow students

- Application skills

- RIT's instructional resources

- Career exploration

- Interactive skills, effective communication, empowerment, group decision making, and teamwork

- History of the total quality movement and applications in business and industry

- Problem-solving tools

Due to the number of credit hours committed to this series, faculty have ample time to teach theoretical frameworks as well as to have students experience and apply what they learned. This initiative has successfully demonstrated the effectiveness of a cross-functional team in development of courses and in delivery of instruction. It has also contributed to an improved student retention rate, one of the highest at RIT. Finally, it provided an excellent forum in which to introduce the key principles of total quality to an impressionable group of students early in their academic experience.

Business Concepts for Transfers . . . A Primer in Total Quality

The college was faced with an even greater challenge in ensuring that its entering class of transfers—predominantly at the junior level—were also delivered the same principles and concepts as the freshman and sophomores. This group typically constitutes approximately 40 percent of the student body in the College of Business and could not be ignored.

From a curricular perspective, the problem is that only two credit hours could be devoted to the course. A five-hour seminar in interactive skills and teaming was required as a supplemental experience and conducted just prior to the beginning of formal classes. Recognizing it was an impossible task to replicate the material from the freshman and sophomore series, the instructor considered alternative delivery methods in which the students themselves would become more active participants in their own learning. In doing so, he was able to capitalize on the students' basic knowledge of total quality and to create a forum for them to share this information with their classmates. The following describes the framework and design for this primer in total quality and illustrates the potential to introduce an otherwise complex set of material in relatively little class time.

The instructor determined that the most expedient way students would begin to grasp the principles of quality was to personalize the material. In effect, he challenged them to think in terms of what quality means to them, as consumers and perhaps even as providers of goods and services. From personal experience, he recognized the importance of developing a conceptual framework in which the total quality principles would fit and have a succinct purpose rather than being merely a set of ideas. Accordingly, the course description and objectives were stated as follows:

> This course is required for incoming transfer students. The purpose of this course is to expose students to the current total quality movement and consider its implications on personal, academic, and career goals. Emphasis will be placed on understanding the

history and underlying principles of total quality. At the completion of this course, students should

- Recognize those factors that created the need for change in American business practices.
- Be capable of identifying and articulating the underlying principles of the current total quality movement.
- Demonstrate an ability to analyze the impact the total quality movement may have on personal academic and career decisions.

The entire Business Concepts faculty team continuously reviews current total quality literature to be used for these special courses. For many classes, supplemental reading material is often provided to students when covering specific material. Transfers, in particular, were not held to a rigid schedule of readings. Rather, they were expected to be prepared to discuss the topic of the day and were encouraged to search the current periodical literature for relevant subject matter.

Topically, the course covered the following.

- Interactive skills, teaming, and effective communication
- History and evolution of the quality movement
- Quality assessments through the Malcolm Baldrige National Quality Award
- Meeting customer expectations and requirements
- Transformational leadership in quality organizations
- Participatory management and empowerment
- Process management/problem-solving process
- Tools of quality/measuring quality
- Total quality and career decisions

All students were required, within the first week of classes, to activate their personal account on RIT's VAX network and be prepared to communicate with the entire class via electronic mail. Even the most timid users of technology recognized the potential of this powerful and efficient communication tool, and, within a relatively short period of time, the entire class was functioning on the system. This initiative not only allowed for a continuous dialogue with students outside of the formal class period, it eased their own communication with the instructor on personal matters as well as within their small work teams.

More importantly, electronic mail allowed the instructor to introduce a requirement in the course for sharing total quality experiences, enabling students to express their views and analysis as either consumers or providers of goods and services. This experience was extremely valuable in providing a means for students to internalize their own total quality experiences, while also providing material for discussion in classes. The instructor's role was to keep the students focused on the core principles of total quality as they examined and reported their experiences. As the students matured in their own understanding of total quality, the dialogue gradually transformed from criticism of organizations with poor quality practices to a genuine analysis of what could be introduced to improve performance. Many students discovered they knew a great deal more about total quality than they realized and were anxious to share their knowledge over the electronic mail.

The instructor used other opportunities to internalize total quality by challenging the students to think in terms of their expectations as consumers of education. For this exercise, much of the session was conducted by the students themselves. In addition to discovering the organizational challenges of customer relations, students were asked to further consider individual responsibilities. For example, what are the customers' (students') responsibilities in a relationship with providers (faculty) of educational services?

This session helped the students recognize the complexities of customer relations. The students defined a set of personal responsibilities that placed the burden for learning squarely on themselves and that of teaching on the instructor. The session also illustrated the importance of establishing expectations and clearly articulated responsibilities in the relationship between providers and customers.

One such responsibility was determining how peer evaluation would occur in the team project. The instructor allowed the students to determine the criteria by which they would be measured for their performance. Borrowing from the scholarship of RIT lecturer Robert Slavin on cooperative learning techniques, the instructor established a two-tiered grading scheme for this assignment. One grade would be given to the group as a whole and another for individual performance, which was entirely based on the students' own feedback. As Slavin has suggested, the individual grade should never be lower than the one awarded the group as a whole. This is an effective technique for rewarding outstanding individual performance, and the students are good judges of who is most deserving.

This course not only teaches total quality, it is designed to demonstrate the responsibilities both faculty and students have in their mutually dependent relationship. Consequently, performance expectations, which are largely defined as the students discover the meaning of total quality, are high for all parties.

Summary

When RIT's College of Business launched its total quality initiative in 1990, it was among a small number of colleges and universities that recognized the changing conditions in higher education. Today the demand for increased quality in goods and services in the United States is reaching a fever pitch. The not-for-profit sector, including higher education, cannot ignore the resulting market implications. Since 1990, increasing numbers of schools have adapted total quality principles in their own environments. This is evidence that impending changes are expected to have a lasting effect on the manner in which we all operate in the future.

Although the jargon may sometimes seem to outdistance the substance, total quality as a business and industry movement has been labeled a revolution. If there is to be a parallel revolution in colleges and universities, it will be a result of the changes at the center of activity for any college or university—the classroom. This places the challenge of change squarely on the shoulders of faculty. It is commonly accepted that leadership must facilitate and support the process; faculty must be willing to accept and meet the challenge.

Appendix

Techniques to Improve Teaching and Interaction with
Students in the College of Business

Teaching Effectiveness Task Force

June 7, 1991

Richard Rosett, Dean, Chairman

Gary Bonvillian	Terry Dennis
Mary Hope	Francis Kearns
Erhan Mergen	Joann Middleton
William Nowlin	Thomas Pray
Franklin Russell	William Stevenson
Philip Tyler	Donald Wilson

Introduction

Teaching effectiveness is essential to our mission in the College of Business. Teaching effectiveness will be emphasized as we continuously improve the products (curriculum, majors, courses) that we offer our external customers (students and employers) and the process (teaching, advising, administration) by which the products are delivered.

Crucial in this endeavor are techniques to improve our individual and collective effectiveness as teachers. This document is not the exclusive aid to improvement, but it can make a difference. We ask that you embrace the items with which you are comfortable, and set aside the others, perhaps for reconsideration at another time. There is not a teacher in the college who does, has done, is trying to do, or should try to do everything listed in this document.

The use of this document is voluntary. It focuses exclusively on the *process* of teaching and interacting with students. It is not policy, procedure, or a set of rules. It is not provided for peer or administrative review for annual evaluation, tenure, promotion, or for awarding successive contracts to nontenured faculty.

Although we recognize the need to measure teaching effectiveness as well as to improve measures of teaching effectiveness, this document is not designed to satisfy either objective.

You will note the conspicuous absence of discipline-specific techniques. We began this task with the full knowledge and confidence that the faculty have the academic, experiential, and scholarly credentials in their disciplines. Accordingly, we focused on the process of teaching, not the substance.

Improvement in most processes occur on an incremental basis. These techniques will aid in the improvement of the teaching process as well as our individual and collective interaction with students.

Course Preparation and Organization

Think through the course before it begins.

Prepare a syllabus in accordance with college guidelines.

Be ready for the students who do not perform as well as your best students.

Use Bloom's Levels of Cognition to write learning objectives for each class session. As a result of each session, which objective(s) should the student achieve?

- *Recognition or recall.* Students should remember or recognize appropriate terminology, facts, ideas, trends, sequences, and principles.

- *Comprehension.* Students should understand written communications, reports, tables, diagrams, directions, and regulations.

- *Application.* Students should be able to apply ideas, rules, procedures, formulas, principles, and theories in job-related situations.

- *Analysis.* Students should be able to break down materials or information into parts, detecting relationships or the parts and how they are organized.

- *Synthesis.* Students should be able to put together elements and parts to form a whole, combining to form a pattern or structure not previously obvious.

- *Evaluation.* Students should be able to make a judgment about the value of ideas, works, solutions, methods, or material using prescribed criteria or standards for estimating the extent to which they are accurate, effective, and economical.

First Day of Class

Welcome students, introduce yourself, and tell them what you prefer to be called (Dr., Mr., Ms., first name).

Have students introduce themselves.

Introduce sign language interpreter.

Have an informal discussion about the course. Ask students to relate experiences within the framework of course topics.

Inform them how they will be evaluated, weights for each item, dates for exams, types of exams, and due dates for projects.

Institute a system that will enable you to know students by name. Consider the use of a seating chart, name tags or placards, or photographs.

Inform students of the days and times that you will be available for office hours.

Adjunct professors should provide times they can be reached.

Demand Their Best

Tell students that you expect them to work hard.

Emphasize the importance of holding high standards for academic and personal achievement.

Being customer/student focused does not mean lower standards or expectations.

Outline each session on the white board, a transparency, or in a handout.

Summarize main points before class ends. Give a 1–3 minute summary of the last class at the start of each class.

Use visuals to supplement lectures and provide copies when possible.

Consider whether instructional methods used for day sections are suitable for evening students.

Choose strategies to fit the level of students and learning objectives.

Have clear and readable handouts.

Write legibly on white board, transparencies, and on exams and papers.

Use Real-World Examples

Encourage students to seek outside materials. Recommend books and articles from the library.

Provide applications as often as possible.

Give students real-life situations to analyze.

Let students share and examine learning derived from their cooperative education experiences.

Show Interest and Respect for Students

Respect students as adults.

Address students by name and encourage them to do the same with each other.

Students may show more interest if you show interest in their learning.

Ask questions and encourage class participation.

Show that you care about them, whether they do A work or C work.

Use appropriate humor.

Respond respectfully to questions.

Let them know that you know when they are absent.

Be Flexible

Be fair to students who have missed a class or an assignment for a good reason.

Acknowledge when you don't know the answer to a question. Get the answer and report back at next class.

If an emergency causes your absence from a class, arrange for an explanatory note to be posted on the classroom.

If you miss a class, make it up. Provide alternatives for students who have conflicts at your planned make-up time.

Care about factors in students' lives beyond the classroom; for example, be aware that most students are enrolled in other courses in addition to yours.

Show Concern for Their Learning

Speak at a pace that students can take good notes.

Listen to their questions and comments.

Avoid rushing through material that students do not understand.

Ensure understanding, especially students who have a hearing or visual impairment or a learning disability.

Avoid excessive discussion of material not related to learning objectives.

Encourage students to speak up when they don't understand.

Be patient with students who are struggling.

Provide extra material for students who lack essential background or knowledge or skills.

Avoid giving exams on the last day of class.

Refer students who need special assistance to the Office of Special Services (College Union), Learning Development Center (George Eastman Building), or to the College NTID Support Team (Max Lowenthal Building).

Be Aware of Student Uniqueness

Know that students are unique in intellect, motivation, and drive, as well as gender, race, ethnicity, sexual orientation, country of origin, disability, and social class. Avoid making comparisons of cultures unless based on empirical evidence. Discourage stereotypical comments that leave students with incorrect data about other groups.

Be aware of how remarks may contribute to one's view of an educational environment hostile to minority cultures.

Discourage snide remarks, sarcasm, kidding, and other behaviors that embarrass students.

Use a Variety of Instructional Methods

Use an appropriate mix of the following methods: case studies, role plays, guest lecturers (industry professional colleague), media such as film strips, demonstrations, class discussion, small-group discussion, exercises, simulations, and video recording.

Try a Mix of Learning Projects

Use an appropriate mix of learning projects, such as term papers; case analysis, critical analysis; individual or group presentation research project that requires either a survey or interviews, or other methods; site visits and tours; and problem solving and field activities.

Use Available Equipment

Make use of available instructional equipment, such as the white board, flip charts, overhead projector, slide projector, VCR, movie projectors, data show projector, PC, VAX, and other equipment.

Advocate Teamwork and Cooperation

On the first day of class, ask students to tell each other about themselves.

Encourage students to prepare together for class.

Encourage students to do projects together.

Ask students to praise the accomplishments of others.

Create study groups or project teams.

Set aside class time for some work to be done in groups or teams.

Encourage students to join at least one campus organization.

Students Learn Best by Doing

If you tell students something, they may forget it. If you show them something, they may remember it. If you involve them in learning, they may understand it.

Ask students to present their work to the class. Give guidance on presentation skills.

Ask students to summarize similarities and differences among theorists, formulae, methods, models, research findings, procedures, and processes.

Ask student to relate outside events or activities to course topics.

Encourage students to respectfully challenge ideas of others.

Use simulations, role-plays, or labs.

Encourage students to challenge old ways.

Get Frequent Feedback from Students

Ask students periodically if they are keeping up with the material.

Ask what they learned in class, such as, "What was the most important thing you learned?" and "What didn't you understand?"

Respond to feedback in a way that encourages students to freely and frequently give it.

Listen intently to student comments and opinions. Add to their ideas.

At the end of class, summarize the main points. Announce that everyone who does not understand should see you after class.

Either in week 3 and 6, or in week 5, ask students to write on a piece of paper any comments about the course and to anonymously submit them. Consider making appropriate adjustments in the course.

At the end of the quarter, as they complete course rating forms, ask students to use the reverse side to comment on all aspects of the course.

Seek Feedback from Colleagues

Initiate dialogue with colleagues about teaching problems and challenges, as well as techniques that tend to be successful.

Ask a colleague to observe two to three of your classes and give you a confidential evaluation of his or her thoughts and any suggestions for improvement.

Ask a colleague if you can visit two to three of his or her classes to gather ideas.

Ask a colleague to review your syllabi, instructional materials, exams, and projects, and to provide appropriate feedback.

Seek opportunities for standardization in objectives and requirements in courses taught by more than one teacher.

Give Students Constructive Feedback

Provide positive reinforcement and constructive criticism. Students can better measure their progress in a course if they are graded on three to four items (an appropriate mix of papers, exams, projects, and participation) and if the items are evenly spaced during the quarter.

As they approach the final week of class and exam week, students would like to know their grade on all other items.

Return examinations and papers at the next class or as soon as possible.

Rather than award participation grades (or scores) only at the end of the quarter, consider awarding a grade for the first half and another for the second half. Inform students of their status.

Use instructional strategies that give students immediate feedback on their performance.

Ask students to visit you to discuss their progress, especially students who are not doing well.

Give students written comments on strengths and weaknesses of exams, papers, and problems.

Call students periodically to make sure they are okay when absent from class one or more days.

Issue a mid-term grade.

Be Accessible and Approachable

Include office hours in the course syllabus. Also, post hours outside of your office.

Be in your office during scheduled hours. If an unavoidable conflict arises, have a notice posted to apologize for your absence and to set alternative hours. Consider offering a telephone number and times at which you can be reached. Respond to messages left on your answering machine or with the department secretary as soon as possible (within 24 hours).

Give students your home telephone number (with hours that they may call).

Encourage students to visit your office. Once they arrive, make them feel welcome.

Speak directly to hearing impaired students, not their interpreter.

Encourage Student–Faculty Interaction

Attend and participate in college social events designed for students.

Create opportunities to interact with students outside of the classroom.

Consider leading periodic informal study groups or group discussions outside of class time.

Invite students to professional meetings or other events.

Occasionally attend student club meetings.

Be a Good Advisor

Know your advisees and know the curriculum.

Listen to their comments, questions, and concerns.

Write or call each advisee in the fall to welcome him or her back to school.

Extend personal invitations to college social events.

Give careful and thoughtful advice on academic, career, and professional questions.

Contact advisees who are on probation to encourage them.

Encourage students to visit you.

Notes

1. Ernest L. Boyer, *Scholarship Reconsidered: Priorities of the Professoriate* (Princeton, N.J.: The Carnegie Foundation for the Advancement of Teaching, 1990).

2. Benjamin S. Bloom, *The Classification of Education Goals: Cognitive Domain* (New York: McKay, 1956).

3. Ibid.

Additional Reading

Bentley, Kathleen, and Donald Zrebiec. "Creation of a Freshman/Sophomore Curriculum as a Component of Transforming a College of Business" (paper presented at the annual meeting of the Production and Operations Management Society, Orlando, Fla., October 1992).

Bonvillian, Gary. "Transforming a Business College into a Total Quality College" (paper presented at the annual meeting of the Association of Business Simulation and Experiential Learning, Las Vegas, Nev., March 1992).

———. "An Academic Approach to the Introduction of Total Quality Management" (paper presented at the annual meeting of the Production and Operations Management Society, Orlando, Fla., October 1992).

Chickering, Arthur. *Education and Identity*. San Francisco: Jossey-Bass, 1972.

A Faculty Guide to the Learning Disabled Postsecondary Student. Rochester, N.Y.: Office of Learning Disabilities at RIT, 1988.

55 Practical Suggestions for Improving Student-Faculty Interactions at RIT. Rochester, N.Y.: Faculty Council at RIT, 1987.

A Guide for Disability Accessibility at RIT Handbook. Rochester, N.Y.: Subcommittee of the Disabled Students Advisory Group at RIT, 1990.

Hunt, V. Daniel. *Quality in America*. Homewood, Ill.: Business One Irwin, 1992.

La Francois. *Psychological Theories and Human Learning*. Monterey, Calif.: Brooks/Cole Publishing Company, 1982.

Lowenthal Group: An Undergraduate Volunteer Service Group in the College of Business that supports a variety of initiatives, including the advancement of total quality management.

Nowlin, William. "Teaching/Learning Methodologies." In *Total Quality Forum V Proceedings*. Chicago: Motorola, 1993.

Rogers, Carl. *Freedom to Learn*. Columbus, Ohio: Charles Merrill Publishing Company, 1969.

7 Principles for Good Practice in Undergraduate Education. Racine, Wis.: The Johnson Foundation, 1989.

Taylor, Vernon. *How to Hold Students*. Chatam, Ill.: Key Productions, 1983.

Tips for Communicating With Deaf People. Rochester, N.Y.: NTID at RIT, 1990.

Total Quality Management and the Integrative Curriculum of the University of Tennessee MBA Program

Michael C. Ehrhardt
University of Tennessee

During the last decade, the business community has become increasingly critical of graduate management education. Many contend that typical MBA graduates are not prepared to contribute value to the corporation. They do not write or speak effectively, do not work well in teams, and do not understand the cross-functional processes necessary in an organization.

In response to these criticisms, many business schools are making substantial changes. This paper describes the changes in the MBA program at the University of Tennessee (UT).[1] Reflecting my observations as a member both of the university's finance department and of the team that developed and now delivers the first year of the MBA curriculum, this paper describes that curriculum, particularly in finance, as well as the process of changing it.

The first section explains our rationale for making a nonincremental change in the curriculum, one that led to much more integration. The section also describes our process, which follows many total quality management (TQM)* guidelines. The next section describes the new curriculum, which contains many TQM concepts. Section three discusses administrative issues: grading, textbooks, and cost. The fourth section describes the finance components of the new curriculum, and at the end is a brief summary.

---

*Editor's note: *Total quality management* (TQM) is a synonym for *total quality.*

Deciding to Make Nonincremental Changes: The Rationale and the Process

In August 1991, the University of Tennessee implemented an integrative core curriculum for its MBA program; the story, however, begins much earlier. For most of the 1980s, observers of business flooded the media with scathing critiques of American management and management education. Roger Jenkins, then the associate dean of the UT College of Business, passed copies of these indictments to the MBA faculty, loosely defined as anyone who had ever taught an MBA course. By the time of an MBA faculty retreat in May of 1990, my accumulated stack of such articles was about 12 inches high.

MBA faculty, former MBA students, and managers from Procter & Gamble, Texas Instruments, and Xerox attended the retreat, which was a psychological turning point for many of us. It was one thing to read criticisms of MBA education, but another thing entirely to hear in person that our profession wasn't doing a satisfactory job, as these managers and students told us.

From our subsequent experiences, I believe such a transforming event is a prerequisite for making nonincremental curriculum changes. Without it, faculty have little incentive to pursue difficult and often painful change.

The outcome of the retreat was the formation of an ad hoc committee for the summer of 1990 with about 10 faculty members, of whom I was one. The stinging criticisms of managerial education from our customers (our students and the firms that hire them) had convinced us to work on this problem even though it was summer; of course, the small stipend we received also encouraged us.

I suspect that none of us anticipated radical changes in our MBA program; however, our first meeting set us on a path of revolution rather than evolution. The chairman, another nonadministrative faculty member, instructed us to split into small groups to work on particular problems and directed us to develop a list of about 70 recommended changes that he would present to the dean. Most faculty members don't particularly like being told what to do, as I am sure administrators will agree, and we were no exception. We rebelled and refused to engage in "incrementalism." Instead, we decided to present a proposal for a fundamentally different MBA program.

We met regularly (a four-hour weekly meeting) during the summer and agreed to a few guiding principles, many of which are consistent with TQM. In retrospect, I believe that some formal training in team dynamics and group interaction would have helped the committee. Professors are a self-selected group whose common characteristics include an extremely high capability for working independently without much experience or natural aptitude for teamwork. One principle was to make decisions by consensus. This meant that we accepted no decision unless *all* members of the group were at least partially comfortable with the decision. That is very different from accepting a proposal if the majority vote yes. In an elective process, the minority voters may strongly oppose the decision, and their opposition can often hamper the successful implementation of the proposal.

In contrast to the elective process, which chooses one of several mutually exclusive alternatives, consensus requires finding one position acceptable to all team members. It frequently took enormous time and effort to do that. The effort was worthwhile, since it ensured that every member of the group supported each decision. The value of a consensus decision is that with no dissenting minority opinions, implementation of the decision is much easier.

The committee began by identifying eight desired outcomes of MBA education.

1. Strong functional skills, but also a grasp of the firm's integrative framework, so skills can be applied to cross-functional problems

2. Awareness of current issues and a commitment to lifelong, hands-on learning

3. Analytical skills, particularly those of systematic problem prevention in contrast to "fire brigade" problem solving

4. A global perspective

5. Adaptability to changing technology

6. A sense of social responsibility and environmental stewardship

7. Ability to handle organizational politics

8. Interpersonal skills and persuasive leadership

The committee next examined the existing MBA curriculum and decided that it posed barriers to achieving the desired outcomes. Topics are batched in a traditional curriculum, much as manufacturers run large batches of a single product. For example, all statistics topics are batched together into a single statistics course. Just as large batches can cause problems in manufacturing, they also can in education. Courses that emphasize tools, such as statistics and management science, are subject to "spoilage." Students often do not use a tool in other courses until months after they learned it, and by then many have forgotten how to use it.

Independent three-hour courses lead to "excess inventory." We found that many techniques from the "tool" courses are never used again in the core curriculum. Similarly, when functional disciplines such as finance are batched into a single core course, certain topics are not used in any other core courses, but only in other elective finance courses. In other words, the fixed class hours of a three-hour core course may lead to inclusion of topics essential for only those students with concentrations in that discipline. The result is excess inventory of topics not required by many of the "customers."

Besides covering topics essential only for majors in their discipline, faculty tend to create excess inventory by covering too much theory. Obviously, the relationship between student needs and the appropriate balance of theory and application is complicated. I believe that the objective of an undergraduate education should be to develop the student's mind and expand the student's awareness of the world; specific career training is the icing on the cake. Thus, an undergraduate education in finance should have a strong theoretical component. The MBA, however, is a terminal professional degree, whose primary objective is to make the student a successful manager and, particularly, to assist the student's early career. To accomplish this goal in the relatively short time of an MBA program, application must take precedence over theory.

Large batches in a manufacturing process limit a company's flexibility in responding to customers' needs. A similar problem occurs when functional disciplines are batched into independent courses. In each traditional course, problems are usually limited to a specific discipline. Yet most problems that companies face are cross-functional, not calling on only a single discipline. Managers must be able to integrate different functional skills to solve these problems. For example, solving real-world capital budgeting problems draws not only on finance, but also on market forecasts, product costing, and production methods. Most of the chapter problem sets used in a traditional course focus on problems specific to topics of that particular discipline. Such problems teach fundamentals, but do not help students learn to solve cross-functional problems. Even the use of cases does not resolve the dilemma, since most cases fit a specific functional course.

The committee presented a white paper to the dean in September 1990, recommending that the core curriculum of the university's MBA program abandon traditional three-hour independent courses. In their place, we recommended an integrative curriculum that would pursue the eight objectives described earlier.

The ad hoc committee was then disbanded, and a call went out for a new team to design and teach the new curriculum. But an odd thing happened: no one rushed to answer the call.

It was one thing to recommend sweeping changes, but it was another thing entirely to implement the changes. In retrospect, we learned that it is important not to have one group design the curriculum and then have a different group teach it. The group that teaches the new curriculum should be the same group that designed it. During the fall of 1990, the original committee members enacted something like an elaborate mating ritual. A told B that he would be on the new team if B and C were members. But C would be on the team only if D, who hadn't been on the original committee, joined the new team. B said he would be on the team only if the team members received a stipend for the summer of 1991. Finally, after several months of iterations and negotiations, 12 faculty members agreed to be on the MBA Core Team. They included some, but not all, of the faculty who had been on the ad hoc committee and several additional faculty members. The team members represented a cross-section of various disciplines, but had several common characteristics. They did receive a stipend for their work over the summer.

The first characteristic was that all members had tenure and most were full professors. We did not believe untenured faculty members could devote the time and effort required, because the traditional reward system at most universities, including UT, places a high priority on the publication of articles in discipline-specific academic journals. In contrast, the new UT MBA program requires more effort and time in teaching than does a traditional curriculum; it also fosters a faculty perspective that lends itself to cross-functional research and practitioner-oriented research. Even if the UT reward system were to fully recognize and reward the efforts consistent with participation in the new MBA program, our team believed it would be unwise for a nontenured faculty member to participate until most other universities also changed their reward systems. Their perceptions of the current reward system have led the MBA team members to maintain their previous research agendas and to conform to the traditional reward system. Since they therefore spend the same amount of time on research as before but have added time to teaching and curriculum maintenance, the time available for their families and personal lives has diminished.

A second characteristic was that most of the members had taught in executive education programs at UT. This was important because those programs have several common themes (which also are common to most definitions of TQM): (1) creating value for customers, (2) improving quality, often through statistical process control, and (3) the recognition that companies must improve all processes and systems, not just those on the manufacturing floor. From their participation in executive education programs, the team members had a shared vision of corporate problems and a recognition that they cross functional boundaries. Thus, team members viewed curricular issues from a broader perspective than just those of their respective departments.

Designing the New Curriculum: Content and Process

As in most MBA programs, the original curriculum at the University of Tennessee had two components: the core curriculum, in which all students take the same coursework, and the elective curriculum, in which students choose different functional areas.

The first step in the MBA Core Team's process was to define the task, which we limited to revision of the core curriculum, deferring revision of the elective curriculum. The task was to design an integrative core curriculum that would help students acquire the eight previously identified skills of a successful manager. The team began meeting once a week, with subgroup meetings during the week.

During this period, the core team communicated regularly with the rest of the faculty. In addition to several semi-formal collegewide "town meetings" and several departmental briefings, individual team members regularly spoke with other members of their respective departments. In retrospect, however, it would have been better to have had more involvement from the faculty who teach the elective MBA courses. It would also have been better to develop revisions in the elective curriculum during the first year of implementation of the new core curriculum, so that the revised elective curriculum would be in place when the students completed the first year of the new core curriculum. (As it was, the revised elective curriculum was not in place until the fall of 1993, which meant that the students who took the new core in the academic year 1991–1992 ended up choosing from the old electives in 1992–1993.)

The MBA Core Team debated how long the core curriculum should last. One view was that the core should last as long as needed, even if it spilled over into the second year. After exhaustive discussions, we agreed to limit the core to one academic year, believing that suboptimization from fixing the length of the core was more than compensated by the easier logistics of a one-year core. The team decided on a core curriculum with two student class sessions per day, each counting as 1.5 semester hours. A five-day week and a 14-week semester results in 280 sessions in the academic year. The team designed and currently teaches a curriculum for these 280 sessions.

Although viewing the entire core curriculum as a single course, for administrative reasons, we divided it into two courses, each counting for 15 semester hours. Thus, the new core curriculum contains a total of 30 semester hours of coursework. The old core contained a total of 36 semester hours (12 three-hour courses).

We matriculate between 80 and 100 full-time MBA students each year who are distributed into two sections. Thus, UT offers two sections of the core course BA 504 in the fall semester, and two sections of BA 505 in the spring semester. The same faculty deliver both sections of both courses. In essence, these two courses have replaced 10 three-hour courses in the previous curriculum, one of which was an introductory finance course.

Our next two decisions were to decide what material the core should include and how it should be covered. As the following sections make clear, these are not independent issues.

A Framework for the New Curriculum

Since all students take the core curriculum, the team agreed it should include only topics required by all managers. Although in retrospect it seems simple, arriving at consensus on this point was time-consuming and painful. It did provide, however, a relatively unambiguous criterion for deciding which topics to include in the core curriculum.

But how should the topics be covered to provide students with the eight required attributes? Having rejected the traditional structure, we needed an organizing framework for the 280 sessions in the new curriculum. This was a major issue, since the framework is a critical element in an integrative curriculum.

After much discussion, we decided to organize many of the sessions around the problems faced by a single hypothetical firm, Volunteer Vegetables (VV), a canner of vegetables and beans. (Although the major projects are associated with this single firm, class discussions and other individual and team assignments often are based on other firms and industries.) We chose this type of firm for several reasons: (1) Students are familiar with the product; (2) The production process is simple enough that students can understand it, but complicated enough to provide realistic examples of such production/logistic problems as quality, on-time delivery, supplier relationships, and inventory build-up; (3) Seasonality of production process is a rich source of illustrations of such issues in financial accounting and financial planning as fluctuations in inventory and accounts receivables; and (4) The distribution channel is sufficiently complicated to illustrate many marketing and logistics issues.

During the course of the year, Volunteer Vegetables faces four major problems: (1) It is losing sales because it doesn't understand what its ultimate consumers (that is, those who eat the vegetables) value and how they decide what to buy; (2) It must apply for a line of credit to finance its seasonal buildup of accounts receivables and inventory; (3) It faces the loss of a major customer due to the product's deteriorating quality and excessive delays in filling orders; and (4) It must decide whether or not to expand into a new product line. The students face these problems in this sequence. The first problem revolves around understanding the customer, which we believe is fundamental for almost all business decisions. Managers should understand how the different parts of a financial statement articulate and how to do pro forma statements. These skills, addressed in the second problem, are also required for the fourth problem. In fact, analysis of the fourth problem requires most of the skills learned in the first three. Although it might be possible to present these problems in a different order, we believe that this sequence allows students to address problems of increasing complexity.

In choosing the problems for VV, we followed a somewhat circular process. First, a subgroup consisting of team members from accounting, finance, marketing, and production met and discussed the learning objectives and typical topics covered by each discipline. Then we brainstormed to imagine company problems that would trigger sessions on typical topics. For some problems, we realized we would need to add sessions not covered in a typical curriculum. For example, the typical finance core course does not cover monthly pro forma statements in enough detail for the line of credit application, nor does the typical production course cover statistical process control thoroughly enough for the third VV problem. This process caused us also to reevaluate the topics that we had first listed. If we could not create a problem that triggered a topic, it made us wonder whether that topic was truly relevant for every manager. (For example, we have virtually no coverage of linear programming in the new curriculum.) After several iterations, we agreed on a set of problems that triggered an appropriate set of topics.

In the core curriculum, we form teams consisting of five students. The students stay in their team for about one semester and then are reassigned to new teams for the second semester. We reassign students into a final team for the last two weeks of the second semester, during which they engage in a comprehensive business simulation. We try to balance each team with respect to academic ability, work experience, and minority/gender representation.

For each of the four problems, each team produces a major written report addressing the problem and presents the report's recommendations to a committee consisting of MBA Core Team faculty, other college faculty, and members of the business community. The presentations occur in boardrooms of local businesses, creating a realistic and nonacademic atmosphere.

The presentations raise several logistical problems. For each of the four major reports (which are spaced out during the academic year, with the first report due in mid-October and the fourth in early April), each team makes a presentation. For each report date, we run four sessions in parallel with four teams presenting in each session. (There are 16 teams.) Each presentation lasts one hour; the first presentation starts at 1:00 P.M. and the last ends at 5:00 P.M. This format requires that we have four rooms available on each presentation date, and local businesses have been very supportive in supplying them. We usually ask a business to provide only one room, and we do not ask the same four businesses each time we have presentations. In other words, we spread out our requests for favors.

Because the four sessions are scheduled simultaneously, each member of the core faculty does not view each presentation. Usually we have four core faculty per room. (There are four presentations in each room during the afternoon.) We also have one or two noncore faculty in each room; for example, noncore finance faculty members view the application for the line of credit, while noncore marketing faculty view the customer analysis. We schedule one or two members of the business community in each room, varying participants depending on the nature of the presentation. For example, we have commercial lending officers at the line of credit application, but they do not attend the other presentations. Again, we spread out our requests for favors from noncore faculty and business participants. It is easier to get a larger total number of participants if their commitments are relatively small. Almost all participants have been enthusiastic and very helpful.

This curriculum framework is consistent with our concept of just-in-time learning. Having determined the skills students need to solve the major problems, we schedule sessions with appropriate faculty members prior to the date of the presentation. For example, the first presentation requires sessions devoted to the importance of creating value for customers, the theory of consumer choice, distribution channels, field research in marketing, written communication skills, oral communication skills, and interpersonal skills within the context of team dynamics. Note that many of these sessions fall outside the normal definition of a single functional discipline; in other words, the VV problems trigger a wide variety of topics and not just functional fundamentals. Note also that prereport class sessions with more than one faculty member are needed. Due to the complication of scheduling multiple faculty and the requirement that certain sessions occur prior to the reports, we use PERT/CPM software to schedule sessions, with sessions having interlinked dependencies.

Many class sessions are linked directly to the VV problems, for example, the sessions on market research. Other sessions are indirectly linked; for example, sessions on team dynamics may not address the problems of VV directly, but the students must apply these concepts in their own teams when they work on a problem for VV. Other sessions, such as those on radioactive waste disposal, are completely independent of VV.

In addition to the track of sessions directly related to VV, the framework for the new curriculum has three other tracks: interpersonal skills, the role of the firm, and off-line activities.

The interpersonal skills track sessions cover negotiation, team building, organizational behavior, and communications. The role of the firm track sessions cover business law, macroeconomics, and environmental management. As mentioned, however, many of these topics come into play as students work on the VV problems.

We call the fourth track off-line to indicate it is outside the regularly scheduled 280 class sessions. Some of these off-line sessions are mandatory, such as plant trips (usually four manufacturing facility tours per year), others are optional, such as Q&A sessions before the major presentations. We also feature outside speakers and special seminars. One series prepares students for job interviews.

The final element in our framework is a business simulation, the marketplace, during the last two weeks of the first year, no other classes are scheduled then. Teams of students manage either a manufacturer or a retailer. In addition to decisions involving the allocation of funds to market research, advertising, and production, the teams must also design the product by choosing certain features and attributes. They also conduct face-to-face negotiation as manufacturers develop relationships and contracts with the retailers. The firms must secure financing from venture capitalists, roles played by the Core Team faculty.

The new curriculum has no separate capstone course in policy. We do have sessions devoted to corporate strategy, but they are integrated within the curriculum rather than batched in a single course. The objective of such a course, as indicated by the AACSB accrediting board, is for students to integrate functional knowledge in solving a comprehensive cross-functional problem. Such a traditional capstone policy course seems similar to rework in manufacturing. That is, its objective is to correct a problem that should have been addressed earlier. The new MBA curriculum satisfies the AACSB requirement during the first year with a combination of the integrative curriculum itself and a comprehensive case analysis at the end of the year.

Topics in the New Curriculum: Process and Content

We used the following question to determine whether a topic should be in the core or deferred to the elective curriculum: "Is the material something that every manager needs?" The following discussion describes how we applied this criterion.

While one subcommittee was meeting to decide on the major deliverables for the VV track, two other subcommittees were meeting to put together a preliminary set of topics and exercises for the interpersonal skills and role of the firm tracks. Then the full team met and discussed these preliminary plans. We reached an agreement on the general framework of the program and the tentative sets of major problems for VV, other exercises, and topics.

Next, each faculty member was asked to estimate how many sessions he or she would need to accomplish the learning objectives of the agreed-upon sets of problems, exercises, and topics. He or she was also asked to describe each block of one to three sessions with respect to topic and pedagogy.

When we met again, our first discovery was that the total number of sessions proposed exceeded 280. We then began the ordeal that we called the pit, so named because we met in a tiered, horseshoe-shaped room. Each member had to sit in the center, the pit, and explain to the other faculty members what topic he or she wanted to cover, how it would be covered, and how many sessions would be needed. In extensive give-and-take, faculty questioned the necessity of a particular topic, the depth and scope of its coverage, or the use of other pedagogy. Eventually, agreement on the topics that a professor would cover was achieved.

As painful as this process was, it had positive results. First, it eliminated redundancies. For example, we realized that the marketing, economics, and accounting faculty each addressed different aspects of product pricing/costing. We grouped these sessions, replacing a segmented treatment with a unified and consistent one. Second, each faculty member learned in much more detail than ever before what others were teaching. Third, the discipline of a fixed number of sessions really helped put issues into perspective. For example, is a fourth session on corporate control more important than a second session on quality function deployment?

The exercise of the pit succeeded because the team shared many viewpoints and experiences from teaching in executive development programs and could view problems from outside their respective departments. Also, the team had worked together long enough to trust one another. Although team members were not shy about suggesting changes in another member's proposed sessions, we also trusted the judgment of a member proposing a session. This trust did not occur immediately. For many months, team meetings were characterized by conflict. We certainly went through the storming phase of group formation.

Although the new core curriculum is only a little shorter than the old core (30 semester hours vs. 36 semester hours), the content is much different. The criterion of including material only if it is required by every manager caused us to delete substantial portions of the old curriculum. (For example, linear programming is not in the new curriculum.) There is also much new material, particularly material related to SPC, the quality movement, and interpersonal skills. The resulting set of topics addresses our previously defined eight skills.

1. For the problems associated with VV, students immediately apply the tools and functional knowledge gained in class to realistic integrative cross-functional problems.

2. We weave current issues into the required projects (for example, the impact of NAFTA on the possible location of a VV facility in Mexico, which is part of the fourth major problem). Certain issues we deliberately do not cover thoroughly in

class so that teammates must help one another. The major problems also are intentionally somewhat ambiguous; we do not spell out for the students exactly what is required. The students must take responsibility for much of their own learning, which we hope forms learning habits useful for a lifetime.

3. We teach traditional analytical skills, such as regression analysis, which the students subsequently apply to the various projects. But we also emphasize problem prevention in numerous sessions on statistical process control and the management of business systems. The students apply these problem prevention skills, as well, to the major problems of VV.

4. As in most other curricula, we devote certain sessions to global issues and also incorporate global examples in the other sessions. We have a major global component in one of the VV problems, that is, building a manufacturing facility in Mexico.

5. We have tried to focus on technology changes within the context of specific problems. For example, a number of class sessions (and off-line sessions with outside speakers) cover environmental management—not only stewardship, but also the technical aspects of the problem.

6. We devote sessions to ethics and business law. (See also the fifth topic.)

7. Specific class sessions cover topics in organizational behavior, but we also have several simulations to demonstrate the sometimes gritty reality of organizations.

8. In addition to specific sessions devoted to interpersonal skills (communication, negotiation, and team dynamics), during the first weeks of the year we put the students through an assessment of managerial competencies, including the Briggs-Meyers Indicator and role playing. We videotape each major presentation for the VV deliverables and have these tapes critiqued by speech coaches from the College of Communications. In general, we give students opportunities to practice their interpersonal skills.

Administrative Issues

Grading, Evaluation, and Feedback

During their first year, students receive only two grades, one for each of the two 15-hour core courses. First-year grades are pass, probation, or fail, with all but a few students receiving a pass. Despite a potential free-rider problem, this has several advantages. Students can concentrate on learning, rather than on working the system to get a good grade. When they know that they are not competing with one another for a grade, they are willing to cooperate with one another. Faculty need not waste time and effort ranking students to assign them different grades.

We are still experimenting with the grading system within the confines of the university's existing system of letter grades. For example, one year we defined pass as an A, and another year we defined pass as a B+. We plan to initiate university procedures to actually assign pass, probation, or fail, as soon as we are sure that is what we want. Grading for the elective curriculum in the second year remains the traditional letter grade system.

We emphasize feedback, treating assignments as a chance to learn. If the assignment is not well done, we suggest ways to improve. If the assignment is well done, we congratulate the student, but we still point out ways in which the assignment could be done even better. I often have students ask, "I know it won't count for a grade, but if I do the assignment again, will you read it?" I have never had this happen in any other course.

In addition to the four major VV problems, students are evaluated on other group projects, individual projects, and individual essay exams. The students also evaluate the other members of their team in peer reviews. For the presentations of the VV problems, we ask participants (core faculty, other college faculty, and members of the business community) to fill out evaluations. Each of the four problems has an owner in the core who evaluates the student teams' reports for that problem.

Individual essay exam questions are written and administered by the core faculty. Individual faculty members also assign and grade individual and team exercises and projects.

We record all evaluations in a centralized database. We identify any students having problems and intervene as early as possible. When we meet to decide whether any students should be assigned a semester grade other than pass, we use no formal criteria, such as a weight for each assignment, but look for a pattern of performance and behavior.

We have been extremely pleased with the students' effort and the quality of their work. In fact, they often exceed our expectations. Under a traditional grading system, students may ease up when they believe their work is sufficient for an A. With no well-defined upper limit, our students work harder than we intend. Very few students attempt to free ride. Through counseling and through assigning a grade less than a pass (which is quite serious, since it is for 15 semester credit hours), we have modified the behavior of these few free riders. Some have dropped out of the program, and others have begun working harder.

Textbooks and Class Materials

Most faculty members have overhead transparencies of their class notes and make printed copies available to the students. As described, we have developed numerous assignments and projects. Most, but not all, of the core faculty still assign readings from traditional textbooks, although the outline of a typical textbook does not match well with our curriculum. We also use extensive readings from journals and business publications. Finally, we are now creating custom readings for specific topics.

Faculty Workload and the Cost of the New Curriculum

The development costs were primarily the stipends for the 10 faculty members on the ad hoc committee during the summer of 1990 and the stipends for the 12 faculty during the summer of 1991. I estimate the total cost was approximately $130,000 to $150,000.

There are few direct costs in administering the new program. One cost is for hiring, part-time, speech and writing coaches from the College of Communications. Small expenses occur irregularly, such as renting a bus to take students on a field trip to a manufacturing facility. The total of these costs ranges from $20,000 to $40,000 per year.

Some core faculty teach fewer than 15 sessions, others teach as many as 28. The rule of thumb is that 14 or fewer sessions are equivalent to one regular course. Since we deliver each session in the new curriculum twice, once to each section of students, a 14-session count is actually 28 contact sessions. Therefore, it is roughly equivalent in contact sessions to one traditional class. A team member who has more than 20 sessions (which is more than 40 contact class sessions) receives credit for teaching two traditional courses.

For some departments, the new curriculum has had no effect on teaching resources. For example, the net change in teaching resources for the finance department is zero. Some departments have actually experienced a net decrease in teaching resources committed to the new curriculum (for example, business law), while other departments have had a slight increase (for example, the management department, which houses organizational behavior, strategic management, and production). The net result for the college is a small increase in the teaching resources devoted to the new program.

There are a number of time-consuming activities associated with this program that are not present in a traditional program, such as regular faculty meetings, attending all major presentations, meeting regularly with a student team (each student team is assigned a member of the core faculty to act as an advisor and to help with any student team conflicts), and attending many of the off-line sessions. A significant nonfinancial cost of the program is the extra burden on the core faculty.

Finance in an Integrative Curriculum

What are the finance topics, and where do they fit in an integrative curriculum? The following section describes the topics in the fall and spring semesters of the integrative first-year core curriculum. It also describes the elective curriculum.

Fall Semester Topics

The first finance topics of the fall semester are triggered by the line of credit application of the second major VV problem. The ability to forecast monthly the rate of draw and the rate of repayment on the line of credit requires an in-depth understanding of the way in which the components of financial statements articulate. That is, how do changes in certain elements of a financial statement affect other elements? An accounting professor, Jim Reeve, and I jointly produced a multistage assignment to develop this knowledge. The students begin with a simple model and progress to creating monthly pro forma statements. This entire assignment is done by individual students, although I do encourage team members to discuss the project because they are valuable teaching resources for the less experienced students.

This milestone also triggers sessions in financial accounting, which are taught by an accounting professor. For example, in order to construct the pro formas, the students must have first learned about financial statements. Therefore, there are financial accounting sessions prior to the finance sessions, which are themselves prior to the actual line-of-credit application.

Eleven finance sessions in the fall cover these topics: financial statement analysis, ratio analysis, financial planning, and banking relationships. The assignments of the semester prepare the students for the task, and the task requires that the students apply their skills on a realistic problem. The culmination is each team's presentation of the loan request for VV, which is attended by a commercial loan officer as well as by college faculty.

There are an additional five sessions in the fall devoted to time value of money, dividend growth models for stock valuation, and term structure of interest rate issues, including bond valuation. These topics are required by subsequent projects in the spring semester.

Spring Semester Topics

Most of the finance topics in the spring semester are triggered by the last major VV problem, the evaluation of an expansion into a new product line. This deliverable requires knowledge of capital budgeting techniques and methods of acquiring funds from the capital markets. There are about 10 sessions devoted to capital budgeting concepts and applications (risk measurement, the cost of capital, estimation of cash flows, project evaluation, and real options). There are about six sessions devoted to capital market topics (issuing securities, choosing a capital structure, setting dividend policy, agency conflicts, and the market for corporate control).

The Elective Curriculum

During their second year in the program, students must take at least 24 hours of elective coursework; no specific courses are required. Students choose at least one area in which to concentrate during their second year, with many students choosing two concentrations. Approximately 40 students select a concentration in finance. In the fall of their second year, all of these majors take a six-hour finance course, taught by a team of four finance faculty members, that covers a variety of topics from the areas of investments, corporate finance, and financial markets. Students complete their concentration in finance by taking at least two more three-hour finance courses in the spring of their second year, covering specialized topics such as derivative securities, real estate, and financial institutions.

For finance majors, the first 30 hours in the core provide the basics required by all managers, the next six hours provide the fundamentals required in any finance career, and the final two three-hour courses provide knowledge about particular specializations within the field of finance. Finance majors also take at least 12 additional hours of nonfinance coursework during their second year.

Summary

The new curriculum was put in place during the fall of 1991. At the time this was written, we have had three groups of students from the new program work in summer internships (the summers of 1992–1994), and two groups have graduated and accepted job offers (May 1993, May 1994). Following are a preliminary assessment and my own observations on teaching in an integrative program.

A Preliminary Assessment of the New Program

Perhaps the best way to measure the success of a program is to track the success of graduates, but that is not yet possible for us since the changes in our program are recent.

Another important criterion in evaluating a program is the success in placing students. Since we implemented our new program, the number of companies interviewing at the University of Tennessee has increased. In the spring of 1993 (the first year graduates of the new program were on the market), 22 new companies interviewed on campus that had not interviewed in 1992. The number of job offers increased from just a little over one per student in 1992 to almost three per student in 1993. The average salary offer increased from $40,284 per student in 1992 to $45,212 in 1993. Obviously, caution should be used in interpreting these numbers, since they represent the change for only one year and the economic outlook was somewhat better in 1993.

Compared to our previous MBA program, we now have 60 percent more companies offering our students internships for the summer after they have completed the first year of the program. Ninety-two percent of all firms hiring our students for summer internships stated that they would like to continue hiring our students for internships. By the end of their internships, 20 percent of our students had received firm offers for permanent employment; previously, only 2 percent of our students received such offers. These results for our new program compare favorably to the national average, which is only 5 percent for summer internees receiving permanent job offers.

Another measure is the quality of the incoming students. The class matriculating in the fall of 1994 is larger, has a higher average number of years work experience, a higher average GMAT score, and a higher average GPA than previous classes.

Since the planning process for the new program was relatively short, we made many mistakes. The biggest was our tardiness in changing the elective curriculum. For those programs contemplating change, I urge changing the elective curriculum while making changes in the core. Most of our other mistakes have been less significant, and many could be corrected during the course of the year. For example, students wanted all handouts to be on three-hole paper, so we did that. Other mistakes could not be corrected immediately, but we corrected them in the next year. For example, some students felt they needed an introduction to accounting prior to the start of the program, so we now have a one-week optional "boot camp" for students who want a little extra preparation. Trying for continuous improvement, we regularly seek and get feedback from students, faculty, and the firms that hire our students. We identify problems and attempt to address them. Our process of curriculum reform will never be finished.

The Experience of Teaching in an Integrative Program

Teaching finance in an integrative curriculum is unlike any other teaching I have ever done. One major difference is that my class sessions focus on preparing the students for a realistic cross-functional problem that they must shortly solve. This provides very clear objectives for each session and makes it easier for me to create individual assignments that foster them. It also highly motivates the students. For example, knowing that they soon will be questioned sharply by a loan officer in the boardroom of a downtown bank causes the students to be very attentive during my class discussion on cash-flow forecasting.

A second major difference is the reduction in my academic freedom. In teaching a traditional course, a faculty member has enormous latitude with respect to the topics, the pedagogy, and the exam formats. The MBA Core Team faculty gave up most of that. The number of sessions that I teach, the topics covered, and the pedagogy (to a certain extent) must be approved by the team of core faculty. Although I can make individual assignments, I no longer design and administer my own separate exams; the team designs the exams. I no longer have sole responsibility for assigning a grade to a student; the team decides on one grade for each 15-hour core course.

A third major difference is the need to understand what the other faculty are teaching and when they teach it. Without this knowledge, it is impossible to mesh the finance sessions into the fabric of the curriculum. True integration of material also requires that several faculty members codevelop and administer assignments that cut across their respective disciplines.

In summary, I am positive that teaching in an integrative curriculum is more difficult and time-consuming than teaching in a traditional curriculum, but it is more intrinsically rewarding. The students are more highly motivated and that makes the class sessions more fun. Most importantly, I firmly believe that an integrative curriculum produces a better manager, which, after all, is the reason for the existence of a professional program such as the MBA.

Note

1. A previous version of this paper appeared as "An Integrative Curriculum: The University of Tennessee MBA Experience," *Financial Practice and Education* 4, no. 2 (fall/winter 1994): 25–34.

Total Quality: A Mechanism for Institutional Change and Curriculum Reform

Susan West Engelkemeyer, Ph.D.
Director of Quality and Assistant Professor of Management
Babson College

In recent years the quality, relevance, and cost of higher education has come under increasing scrutiny and criticism. I believe that higher education must follow the example of U.S. industry in improving competitiveness by increased responsiveness to customer needs. This means better meeting the needs of today's students and the organizations they will be working for tomorrow. Experimentation, creativity, and change will be required; there are few models to follow.

Many colleges and universities will choose to do nothing. They will continue to struggle with declining enrollments, student dissatisfaction, disenfranchised alumni, and public criticism. Well-known institutions of higher education—sleeping giants that have never had to worry about competition in the past—will diminish in prestige due to lethargy. New leadership institutions will emerge. Some of these new leaders may not even be in the business of higher education at this time.

There is demand for programs and services that are different, sometimes very different, from those being currently delivered. Now is the time to reevaluate what we are doing in order to develop and deliver programs that meet these new demands. The needed primary focus is not on educational administration, as important as that is, rather it is education in and out of the classroom. There are three imperatives.

- Focus on learning, not on teaching or on research of questionable usefulness.

- Determine student outcome measures to develop, monitor, and assess student performance in relation to desired competencies.

- Assess organizational performance to ensure it clearly demonstrates effectiveness in meeting customer requirements.

Criticisms of Higher Education Today

Higher education is accused of many shortcomings. Some common ones are

- Poor teaching. Many institutions focus so heavily on research that there is little emphasis on the quality of teaching.

- Anachronistic programs. Many programs today are not sufficiently up-to-date or comprehensive enough to fully meet the needs of today's organizations.

- Incoherent curricula. Students must often navigate a curriculum that appears illogical and poorly articulated, with overlaps, omissions, and unnecessary redundancy.

- Excessive price. Between 1980 and 1992, the cost of tuition, room, and board increased, on average, 9.2 percent per year, twice the average rate of inflation. Even health care costs have been better contained.

- Growing and inefficient administrative bureaucracies. Between 1975 and 1985, nonteaching professional staff at colleges and universities expanded by 61 percent, while the number of faculty grew by only 6 percent.[1] In fairness, some of the increase may be ascribed to increasing regulation of higher education, but it is doubtful that students are receiving comparable increases in the services they receive.

The Crisis in Higher Education

A crisis in higher education is reflected in

- Declining enrollments. The number of college-bound students has decreased over the past several years, and the number of students electing some majors (such as business) has declined sharply.

- Changing demographics. As higher education pursues a more diverse student body and more nontraditional students, there is increasing challenge in meeting student needs.

- Mounting financial pressure. Families are finding it increasingly difficult to bear the costs of higher education, and the demand for financial aid is growing rapidly.[2]

- Diminishing public confidence. Organizations that hire graduates say that students are underprepared to meet the requirements and demands of the workplace.

- Rising tuition/spiraling costs. Institutions have neglected to contain costs, dismantle weak programs, and streamline inefficient operations.

- Increasing government intervention. Pressure is mounting to provide more evidence of value received for the investment in higher education and of accountability for program costs.

Time to Focus on the Customer

Change is required, soon, but where should it begin? One possibility is to focus on the customer. Who is the customer of higher education? Many in higher education are reluctant to consider students as customers. We see ourselves as the masters who pour knowledge and wisdom into students. It is easy for us to rationalize poor student performance: they are poorly prepared for college, they are not motivated, they don't listen carefully.

Sometimes we use the term *constituents*, assuming that we are the experts who know what is best for them. If our constituents want something we approve of, then perhaps we'll do it. If we consider state legislators or congress members as a model, it seems that constituent needs are not clearly considered and met.

Sometimes we use the term *clients*, assuming again that we are the experts providing a necessary service, though perhaps doing so with a greater sense of obligation to clients than to constituents.

Sometimes we use the term *customers*, but with quotation marks. To think of students as "customers" usually means that we consider them quasi-customers. We resist the notion that students can be considered full-fledged customers, even though this does not have to mean that they are always right, nor that we must deliver to specifications set by the customer alone. In any customer–supplier relationship, expectations must be communicated, negotiated, and agreed-upon.

In a mutual learning environment such as higher education, we have to clearly state what we can and cannot deliver. We should be able to provide our students with a rationale for the content and structure of the curriculum and related support services, and we should obtain their feedback. Students are good at letting us know if we're effective at attaining our stated goals. They should not dictate what is taught in an individual class, but they are able to provide reliable feedback about how the goals of the class are being met.

Higher education has other customer groups. Employers of our graduates are primary external customers, and we have an obligation to provide them with high performers who are prepared for the challenges and demands of the workplace. We also must serve parents, prospective students, and alumni. Parents, who often provide financial resources, are customers with specific requirements of various kinds, including safety and information about student progress and placement rates. Prospective students need to understand how our own institution's programs and services match their needs and expectations, so they can make informed choices of a college to attend. Alumni need to be cultivated so that they value their experiences and are willing to give something back to their alma mater. Finally, society as a whole is our ultimate customer. Figure 1 depicts customers of higher education.

Total Quality in Higher Education

How will we enable ourselves to address the criticisms and manage the crisis in higher education? Total quality under various names—for example, total quality management (TQM) and continuous quality improvement (CQI)—has gradually taken hold over the past decade and is demonstrating a positive influence on the competitive position of a number of American industrial companies. In a letter to the *Harvard Business Review*, CEOs from six major U.S. corporations stated they "are absolutely convinced that TQM is a fundamentally better way to conduct business and is necessary for the economic well-being of America."[3] They also state that "business and academia have a shared responsibility to learn, to teach, and to practice total quality management." Higher education is nearly a decade behind industry

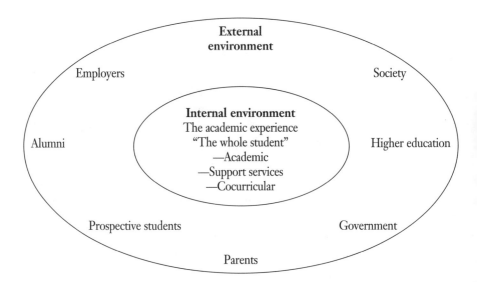

Figure 1. Who is the customer of higher education?

in the application of total quality principles to their organizations. Other service industries, particularly professional service providers, have been slow to draw upon quality principles.

Health care providers are beginning to show interest, but they are probably not far ahead of higher education where schools of business, engineering, and others are increasingly using quality principles in managing their organizations. Involvement, however, is still at an early stage of development.[4]

Why are total quality activities necessary? Their successful implementation will enable institutions of higher education to

- React quickly to customer needs. By determining customer expectations and surveying satisfaction, we can become more responsive to the needs of our customers.

- Focus limited resources on activities that truly satisfy customer needs. With data and information regarding customer satisfaction areas we can eliminate services that are not key drivers of customer satisfaction.

- Make improvements in a systematic way. Engaging in the problem-solving process will enable us to analyze facts and base actions on facts and test results, thereby becoming more effective organizations.

- Engage and use the creative abilities of all organization members. An effective quality implementation strategy in higher education will involve all community members in the continuous improvement and change process.

- Focus on improving processes. When results are unacceptable we can flowchart, troubleshoot, and modify the processes that deliver those results.

In industry, a focus on the product is perhaps the most straightforward application of total quality because product characteristics are relatively easy to measure, monitor, and improve. Support services are slower to adopt quality management principles. In higher education, we see progression in the opposite direction. The product of education is delivered in the curriculum. Curriculum is the domain of the faculty, who may resist change. Results can be difficult to measure. Administrative support services, not curriculum, have been the primary focus of most quality initiatives in higher education.

As Figure 2 details, what is required is a twofold quality process, one that addresses not only our basic offerings (curricula), but encompasses administrative processes as well. By understanding how we can deliver enhanced service (by determining what our customers would like to see in the future), we can be one of the first to offer it. Eventually, what was initially an enhanced service will become part of either the basic offering or support service in order to yield higher levels of customer

Three rings of perceived value

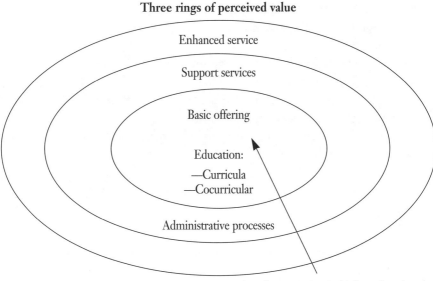

Most total quality initiatives in higher education do
not address the core education products/processes.

Figure 2. A two-fold total quality focus.

satisfaction. This also will enable the institution to provide products or services that
competitor institutions do not currently offer, which yields competitive advantage.

Will adopting total quality necessitate giving up ownership of the curriculum by
the faculty? No, but it will require consideration and accommodation of the needs of
multiple customer groups. No longer can we simply say the curriculum is the exclusive domain of the faculty. Faculty will need to develop and modify curricula according to input, data, and information from customer segments, including students,
employers, and parents. In addition, faculty will need to be cognizant of the connection between the classroom and cocurricular student development opportunities.

Implementation Strategy for Total Quality

Professional service providers (like health care and higher education) must develop
more effective strategies to engage the professionals—doctors and faculty—in the
adoption and implementation of total quality. The classic implementation strategy
in industry is a top-down approach. With this strategy there is typically a full-scale,
organization-wide total quality launch. Training is conducted, teams are launched,
and all employees are expected to be involved within a relatively short period of time.

In higher education, however, a top-down strategy is difficult to implement because there are few mechanisms to compel faculty to become involved. Instead a strategy must be devised to effectively engage and involve faculty in the initiative. A strategy that allows interest and enthusiasm to bubble-up from faculty is needed to support, or even to make possible, a top-down approach applied to other areas of the college.

The strategy used at Babson has been a combination top-down and bubble-up approach. We made a deliberate effort to implement a differentiated strategy across the campus. With administrative and staff personnel, quality training is required. Involvement in continuous improvement initiatives will eventually be part of all performance evaluations; however, the faculty have been approached more cautiously. The approach has been to involve them in issues they deem important, and to highlight existing practice that is consonant with the tenets of total quality. Although every opportunity to engage faculty is explored, training and involvement is voluntary for faculty.

Total Quality at Babson College

Business schools have been criticized for producing graduates unaware of total quality principles, unable to integrate across functional disciplines, and lacking leadership and problem-solving skills—knowledge and skills that are essential within globally competitive organizations. At the same time, business schools have been criticized for not adopting methods for continuous improvement and change within their own organization. Even schools that teach total quality often are criticized for not practicing what they preach.

At Babson, we realized we needed to do a lot more than just teach total quality. We needed to use total quality tools and principles to manage our college in both the academic and administrative areas. We believe total quality will help us to realize our vision of becoming an international leader in management education. Our journey has just begun. We realize we have a long way to go, but we have acknowledged the challenges and criticisms faced by higher education and have taken action. We are completing a five-year strategic plan for quality that articulates the phases of total quality as we continue our journey, as shown in Figure 3.

Babson College now integrates total quality philosophy throughout the curriculum at both the undergraduate and graduate levels, has developed an innovative MBA curriculum that is integrative by nature and focuses heavily on teamwork and problem-solving skills, and has embraced total quality philosophy as a method for running the institution.

Phase 1 (1992–1993): Awareness and enthusiasm

  • Voluntary participation
  • Demonstrate pilot project results
  • Build on faculty interests

Phase 2 (1994–1995): Understanding and transition

  • Formal strategic total quality plan published
  • Organization structures modified
  • Key drivers of customer satisfaction measured

Phase 3 (1996–1997): Transformation and emerging results

  • Recognition and reward systems modified to incorporate total quality
  • Significant improvements in customer satisfaction
  • Total quality is a way of life at Babson College

Figure 3. Total quality at Babson College.

In 1989 Xerox Corporation hosted the first Quality Forum, a gathering of academic and business leaders, in which total quality and its role on U.S. campuses (particularly at business and engineering schools) was discussed. Academia was charged with the challenge not only of teaching the concepts of total quality, but also of using quality as a way to run their organizations. We at Babson College listened to what industry leaders were telling us and have responded accordingly. Within the last four years we have made substantial changes in the following four areas.

1. Teaching total quality management

2. Research in the area of total quality

3. Curriculum development

4. Using total quality in running the institution

Since 1991, we have offered full-semester courses on total quality at both the graduate (MBA) and undergraduate (BSBA) level. While we were developing the total quality courses, we also integrated quality topics throughout the curriculum. At least 15 courses throughout the curriculum contain 10 percent to 50 percent total quality content.

In addition to introducing students to tools and techniques of total quality, courses are also designed to enhance the communication skills of our students, further develop group interaction skills, and provide field experience—key factors deemed important by the employers of our graduates. Most courses in the curriculum evaluate student class participation as a component of the course grade, with as much as 40 percent of the course grade based on the quality of class participation. A majority of courses require students to work in teams for written case analyses and/or field-based projects, which range from 15 percent to 60 percent of the course grade.

In addition to field-based work as a component of individual courses, Babson also offers course credit for group experiential work. The Management Consulting Field Experience (MCFE) Program recommends solutions to the business problems of sponsoring companies and provides Babson students with valuable, practical work experience.

Teams of undergraduate or MBA students have been consulting with Boston-area businesses since 1976 through MCFE projects, analyzing and responding to a wide range of problems. Project teams consist of three to five students and at least one faculty adviser. At the conclusion of a project, the MCFE team's findings and recommendations are presented to the sponsoring company in a detailed written report and oral presentation. Last year the MCFE office organized 22 graduate and 26 undergraduate projects in a wide variety of organizations, from Fortune 500 companies to nonprofit organizations.

Babson has a commitment to create an environment on campus that is as close as possible to the environment our students will be in after they graduate. In addition to extensive fieldwork, most courses within the business component of the curriculum contain some element of field-based cases. Case teaching places students in the position of a practicing manager and allows them to see the challenges managers face every day in the workplace. The realism inherent in a case allows students to see the wide range of problems that exist, realize that problems are interrelated, that the solution to a problem in one area of the company could have implications in other areas, and that identification of the problem and distilling the most important information can sometimes be a struggle. Having been introduced to the problems managers face in the workplace and involving them in solving real problems, students better understand and appreciate the complexity of today's workplace.

Academic Research

Academic research is often criticized for placing too much emphasis on research that has minimal application to practice, is too narrowly focused, or outdated. Babson has a cultural tradition of encouraging applied research that is of value to our external customer—the business community that employs our graduates. Babson believes that faculty competence is enhanced by research that will eventually find expression in the courses taught and in books, articles, cases, simulations, and speeches delivered.

In defining research, many traditional colleges and universities primarily consider articles that appear in peer-reviewed journals whose readership consists mostly of other academics. At Babson, communications that influence managerial decision making are given equivalent status with articles that appear in peer review journals. Professional competence as well as traditional research is considered essential for the growth and development of faculty members. Professional competence entails involvement in professional organizations, the presentation of papers and speeches, enrollment in relevant courses and seminars, and participation in business and consulting activities.

MBA Curriculum Development

At the initial Xerox Quality Forum in 1989, one of the implications for management education was that quality will require rethinking of the MBA curriculum— management as a total system and process, versus function and disciplinary views. Porter and McKibbin's landmark study *Management Education: Drift or Thrust into the Twenty-First Century?* identified several developments to guide graduate management education, including the need to deliver management education in a cross-disciplinary manner rather than in functional areas.[5]

After much input from our customers, including students and companies that employ our graduates, the Babson faculty curriculum committee for the graduate program discarded the traditional functional course program concept and developed a revolutionary curriculum that would meet the needs of tomorrow's managers. This curriculum not only addresses the concerns raised by the corporate world, but also enables students to learn in situations similar to the work environment they will encounter after graduation—business in a globally competitive environment.

Babson's revised two-year MBA curriculum was implemented in September 1993. The first year of the program is divided into four thematic modules under the unifying concept of Entrepreneurial Management in a Changing Global Environment. The four themes are shown in Figure 4. The four modules in the first year are detailed as follows.

• *Module I: Creative Management in Dynamic Organizations.* This introduction encourages students to develop new ways of thinking about managerial behavior. Students explore leadership, ethics, innovation, and creative problem solving. Individually and in groups, students apply these standards to managerial problems. Work in this module strengthens business skills in computers, written and oral

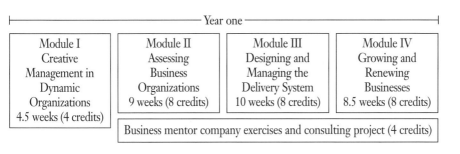

Figure 4. Babson's two-year MBA program.

communication, economics, and mathematics. Through activities ranging from outdoor team-building exercises to assisting with a community-based project, Module I lays the intellectual and motivational foundations for the Babson MBA.

• *Module II: Assessing Business Opportunities.* Module II introduces students to the analytical tools necessary to master industry analysis and assess a company's competitive position. Through the understanding of market segmentation, product positioning, pricing, and financial data analysis, students see the differences among types of organizations, from entrepreneurial start-ups to multinational corporations. In this module, students are assigned exercises to be completed in conjunction with their business mentor company.

• *Module III: Designing and Managing the Delivery System.* This module builds on the preceding theme of opportunity assessment and focuses on the integration of operations, accounting, financial, marketing, and organizational systems within an organization that are consistent with the chosen strategy. In this module, students develop the skills needed to design and manage the system that turns an opportunity into reality. The classes examine the ability of existing and new delivery systems to support company strategy. Students also look at processes from an operations perspective: how they work, how much they cost, and how they affect customer value. As an important component of this module, students recommend the design or redesign of a delivery system to their business mentor company.

Two themes help create cross-functional cohesion in this module: total quality and strategic fit. Presenting total quality as the driver of competitive advantage emphasizes how all areas of the business contribute to high-quality products and services. Strategic fit stresses the critical importance of making every element of the delivery system consistent with the strategy of the organization and with each other.

• *Module IV: Growing and Renewing Businesses.* This module reinforces concepts from previous modules and introduces concepts needed to manage effectively in the short and long term. Managing for effectiveness requires that leaders be aware of, adjust for, and anticipate changing competitive conditions. This module takes a broad perspective of the range of forces that might impinge on the business and helps students develop skills to diagnose, plan, and implement management activities. Students assess management of large and small organizations under conditions of growth or adversity, examine internal and external forces driving change, develop a complex set of strategies to lead an adaptive organization, and evaluate the operation of global enterprises.

With this new curriculum, functional discipline topic areas are delivered in units within modules. Therefore, students are exposed to accounting, finance, marketing, operations, organizational behavior, and other traditional functional areas, but coverage is integrated within the context of each module while addressing complex and interrelated business problems throughout the first year.

During the first year, teams of five students are also assigned to area corporations—mentor companies—to complete a series of projects and assignments. This provides an opportunity for students to further develop and apply their teamwork and problem-solving skills within the corporate environment. Teams work directly with executives to react to business challenges and take advantage of opportunities. During the year, students complete three projects for their mentor companies.

1. During Module II, the groups prepare a financial analysis and a competitor analysis.

2. During Modules III and IV, the teams evaluate an internal system of the mentor company's choice and identify its fit with the company's strategic objectives.

3. The students then recommend the design or redesign of a delivery system.

Total quality is integrated as a major theme occurring across the entire first year curriculum. Other themes include innovation as a strategic tool, entrepreneurial thinking, the importance of a global perspective, and the value of leadership.

The second year of the new MBA program builds on the student's integrated exposure to management education to develop expertise in a specific area by focusing on an elective concentration. Included in the second year is a required cross-cultural experience and a full-year course on global strategy, which includes a computer simulation game that parallels the course work.

How will we evaluate curricula development and assess the program once implemented? Representatives from the corporate community will serve on a curriculum development team, a measurement system for customer requirements will be developed, and ongoing assessment of student capabilities throughout the program and following graduation will be developed.

Undergraduate Curricular Reform

Undergraduate curricular reform began with a three-day retreat on the undergraduate program in August 1993. This was a result of a business–education partnership with The New England (a Boston-based insurance and financial services organization). The New England hosted the event and provided expertise in strategic planning for the goal of the retreat—launch of undergraduate curricular reform. All customer groups were represented as participants in the retreat: faculty, administration, staff, students, alumni, employers, governance, and parents.

Throughout the retreat we made a point of focusing on the customer by actively involving customers as participants and presenters in the retreat. In addition, data from surveys of primary customers were shared in order to establish a compelling need for change. Customer panels were also used to highlight opinions of program strengths and weaknesses. Resulting from the retreat was the formation of a vision for Curriculum 2000. The intent is to have a reformed undergraduate curriculum in place for students entering fall 1996, in order that they will graduate in the new millennium from a revised, up-to-date, and world-class curriculum.

Task forces were launched in order to develop Curriculum 2000 and involve faculty, administrators, and students (with input and representation from other customer groups where appropriate). The task forces are core competencies, curriculum integration, field-based learning, and academic regulations, as shown in Figure 5. We have committed to development of a competency-based curriculum, to be integrated where appropriate, and to involve a four-year field-based experience component. Academic policies and procedures will be reviewed and modified as appropriate in order to further the goals of the undergraduate program and move us toward Curriculum 2000.

• *Core Competencies.* This task force was charged with determining the core competencies that should be expected of all Babson graduates. This includes recommending a flexible curriculum that will allow multiple pathways to graduation to exist (competency), and enabling students to participate in foreign language study and to study abroad.

In May 1994, the Core Competencies Task Force proposed a statement of core competencies. These high-level competencies are now being used to identify those competencies that must be defined by divisions and those competencies that cut across the curriculum.

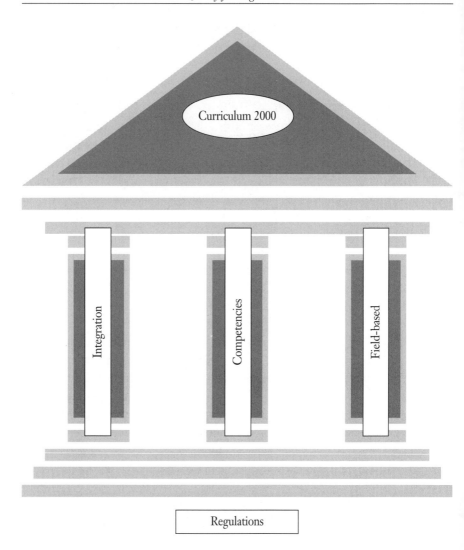

Figure 5. Curriculum 2000.

• *Curriculum Integration.* The faculty have reached consensus that some of the competencies might best be developed in courses that are integrated with one another. This task force was charged with exploring ways to integrate the functional areas of the management disciplines. In addition, the task force is exploring ways to integrate the general education courses and/or disciplines. In order to achieve this, the task force will assess current integration mechanisms, including the cluster program and the freshman management experience integrated course. In addition, the task force will explore how to infuse rhetoric into all areas of the curriculum, a major goal established due to feedback from employers as well as input from faculty.

Based on the recommendation of the integration task force, a Management Core Design Team was established to look at the current required business core courses and to attempt to integrate these into a three-semester sequence that would take fewer credit hours.

• *Field-Based Learning.* This task force emerged primarily due to feedback from employers and alumni. The group was charged with recommending a four-year, flexible, coordinated program of field study that cuts across both general education and business and that builds on existing programs. The intent is to enable students to test and apply theory learned in the classroom through a variety of planned field experiences. In addition, field study is expected to enhance development of competencies that are valuable in students' initial job placements, their careers, and throughout their lives.

In May 1994, the task force recommended a four-year, competency-based, coordinated program of field study. This program identifies specific opportunities for field-based learning in three time frames: The first year, sophomore and junior years, and senior year. Students will also be required to provide documentation by which to assess their achievement (for example, a portfolio developed over time).

• *Academic Regulations.* This group is charged with reaffirming or recommending academic policy regulations on a variety of issues, such as off-campus course credit, class attendance, academic good standing, and course credit criteria. The intent is to ensure that college policies are consistent and flexible during curriculum change and that they are consistent with the goals of the undergraduate program.

A number of recommendations were made and approved, including a change in the policies on academic good standing and class attendance policy. Many other policy areas are under review or recommendation for change at this time.

The Academic Role in Total Quality and Curriculum Reform

At this time, over 50 percent of our faculty are actively involved in curriculum reform initiatives. They are practicing total quality in our core business area, the curriculum. What was the key to engaging faculty and overcoming resistance? The following are several mechanisms that were instrumental in involving faculty. These include

• *Establish a compelling need for change.* Customer survey data, enrollment trends, cost factors, and demographic and competitive information are all mechanisms to motivate faculty to realize that doing things the way they have always been done may not be sufficient to sustain us in the future.

- *Provide opportunities for issue-based involvement.* Create interest and enthusiasm among the faculty by providing opportunities to become involved in a true change effort. Allow faculty to identify priority areas for change.

- *Focus on QUALITY, not quality.* Concentrate on the goal—education and a well-structured curriculum that supports the institutional mission. Do not focus on the process (application of tools and techniques). Provide opportunities for the application of tools and techniques to particular issues as the need arises.

- *Deliver tools and techniques just-in-time.* Provide opportunities for learning and applying tools and techniques to particular issues on an as-needed basis. Abstract training of tools is not sufficient; application is essential.

- *Be flexible.* It is necessary to accommodate the faculty need for discussion and dialogue, and to be sensitive to possible resistance to tight structure. Allow faculty to dictate the pace, but be willing to sense when there is a need to back off and when there is a need to firmly encourage structure and consensus.

- *Provide opportunities for frequent two-way communication.* Continually invite feedback, act on it, and communicate changes made due to faculty input. Inform faculty of the status of the total quality initiative, and invite input and involvement.

- *Involve other constituents in the change process.* Allow the voice of the customer to be heard directly. Involve students on task forces to allow them to be heard and to be active participants in the improvement process. Train students in the use of quality tools and allow them to serve as role models for the use of quality principles, tools, and techniques.

The academic deans and chairs of the college participated in a total quality retreat in September 1992, where they were introduced to quality philosophy, tools, and techniques. One of the quality techniques they engaged in for problem solving was performing KJ (affinity diagram) analysis on determining and evaluating faculty load, an issue they had been working on for some time. In a multiprogram institution such as Babson, faculty may be involved in a broad range of academic pursuits, including undergraduate, graduate, and executive education, as well as program development and administrative service to the college. A primary challenge of the deans and chairs group was to develop a system for determining and evaluating faculty load as they trade off between various teaching-related activities.

The problems with the old load evaluation system included a lack of flexibility, changing course structure, the need to address individualized plans, and allowing for multitrack development. A new system to determine faculty load was the result of a project initiating in the retreat. The objectives of the new faculty load system, GuideProf, include

- To provide a flexible tool for planning each year's teaching, research, professional development, and service activities

- To provide a system that is equitable despite variation in the individual mix of activities

- To recognize the many ways that faculty members contribute to the college

The deans and chairs group agreed that a basic 60/30/10 formula is appropriate (60 percent teaching, 30 percent intellectual vitality, and 10 percent college service). The load evaluation system assigns unit value to various activities. For example, teaching one section of a traditional course would be eight units; four MBA module sessions would be two units, and a major college committee would be four to seven units. This new system, which is being used experimentally at this time, allows flexibility in assessing faculty time and provides adequate credit for the many components of academic endeavor. Therefore, it encourages faculty to dedicate time to the institution in several ways, including curriculum reform and preparation of new course material.

Using Total Quality As a Way to Manage the Institution

Utilizing a total quality philosophy at Babson can be traced to the development of the *Strategic Plan 1991–95*. The development of the plan involved over 130 members of the Babson community, including faculty, administrators, students, alumni, and trustees. The planning process translated major college goals into specific objectives, with timetables and methods for evaluating results. In a letter to the Babson community dated February 27, 1992, President William Glavin stated that "in order to be successful, we need to coordinate the adoption and implementation of the principles of total quality in the classroom as well as in the way we operate the college to help us achieve the mission and goals we all agreed to in our strategic plan. To that end, we will establish an Office of Quality to oversee all our quality efforts. That office will be responsible for the management and coordination of our training and implementation programs. The Office of Quality will be structured in such a way that both the academic and administrative efforts are integrated."

In June of 1992, Babson College established the Office of Quality, which includes one full-time administrator, whose primary responsibility is to oversee the training and implementation of the total quality process in the administrative sector, and one faculty member, who was released from one-half time of her full-time teaching responsibilities to work with the faculty on quality training and the implementation of total quality principles in the academic community.

A main goal of the Office of Quality is development of an organizational infrastructure to facilitate total quality implementation. (See Figure 6.) The model, to be detailed, was developed using the Shiba model.[6] Specific elements of each of the infrastructure areas are as follows.

1. *Goal setting* involves articulating what we want to achieve with respect to total quality. This includes results as well as process-related goals. At Babson, this was achieved through the incorporation of quality goals into the current evaluation system and preparation of a strategic plan for quality that includes specific goals for the next five years.

2. *Organization setting* involves deploying the necessary resources for implementation. This could involve setting up an Office of Quality or deploying a champion in the organization who reports to the highest level in the organization (president, dean). This individual will own the initiative. The individual in charge should be a strategic thinker, well-respected, a good communicator (and listener), and have hands-on capability (a doer). At Babson, we have two directors of quality: one from the administrative ranks and one tenure-track faculty member. This ensures that both perspectives are accounted for as the implementation strategy proceeds.

3. *Training and education* involves enabling people with tools and techniques. Decisions must be made regarding the content and length of training based upon the individual needs of the institution. At Babson, our basic training involves a heavy focus on the tools and techniques of quality management, with a specific focus on work process analysis. A significant proportion of the training is dedicated to effective meeting skills, in order to enable a more disciplined and effective process for meetings.

4. *Promotion* involves flyers, newsletters, and other written materials as well as visual displays and promotional events to pique interest and enthusiasm. At Babson, we host two open houses a year, where we celebrate our progress and recognize team efforts. We also submit information on our quality initiative to the student and employee newsletters on a regular basis.

5. *Diffusion of success stories* is a mechanism to learn from others and includes communication of specific means and results, the methodology applied by particular teams, and so forth. At Babson, we profile team initiatives, approaches, and results during quality open houses, and teams make presentations to other work groups

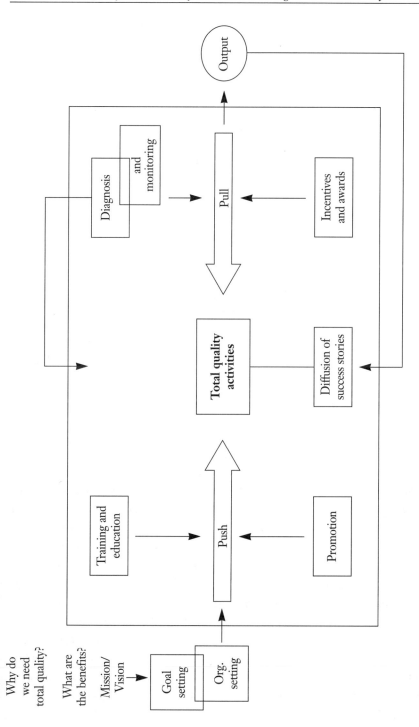

Figure 6. Total quality organizational infrastructure.

on their progress, results, challenges, and key learnings. In addition, we have two storyboards placed in strategic locations on the campus that profile the methodology and results from the quality initiatives of specific teams.

6. *Incentives and awards* includes incentives for teamwork and involvement in total quality, and recognition and reward systems that encourage involvement. This is perhaps one of the most important areas for higher education, particularly with regard to faculty. Modification of the reward and recognition system needs very careful consideration in order to facilitate involvement. At Babson, we have modified the faculty load system in order to encourage participation in activities that further the goals of the institution. In our administrative areas, modification of the performance management system is placing importance on involvement in team-based improvement efforts. Monetary rewards are perhaps not appropriate to non-profit organizations, but there is much we are doing to recognize participation via certificates, notes, announcements, special luncheons, and the like.

7. *Diagnosis and monitoring* involves a plan-do-check-act (PDCA) cycle of the overall total quality initiative, which allows modification if necessary. As a result of our initial PDCA we started working more closely with the cabinet on inspecting the process and furthering team motivation. We developed additional training opportunities in response to employee needs. In the future we plan to do a self-evaluation with the Baldrige criteria in order to understand where our strengths and opportunity areas exist. A long-term goal of the Office of Quality is to ensure that key processes have been identified within all divisions. This involves identifying the outputs of all processes, determining customer requirements, flowcharting the work processes, and determining if work processes are capable of consistently meeting customer requirements. Once processes have been identified and measured, a quality cost review will be conducted in order to determine the costs associated with not meeting customer requirements in the most efficient and effective manner, and to identify improvement opportunities.

Corporate models might suggest moving linearly in development of the organizational infrastructure. In higher education it is probably important to initially obtain buy-in before setting goals and objectives and driving the process. Starting with promotion, limited training and education are mechanisms to pique interest and prove the value of involvement and the resulting benefits that can be obtained. Highlighting the results of pilot projects can add support for institutional commitment to total quality. Without a conscientious effort to mobilize an organization infrastructure for quality, it is doubtful that the initiative will be successful because all elements are necessary in order to enable a systemwide integrated, comprehensive, and compatible initiative.

Babson's top management (cabinet) participated in total quality training in 1992 and have been involved in a number of quality-related retreats. They have been involved in several projects in order to showcase the quality tools and concepts they learned and serve as a model for senior and mid-level managers. One project was a comprehensive review of the college's goal and objective-setting process. The cabinet as a whole documented the current process using a flowchart. Looking at senior and mid-level managers as customers, interviews were held to confirm customer requirements. The team then generated a problem statement, worked out a potential solution that was tested with the managers who were interviewed, and then implemented a modified solution collegewide.

As part of our total quality efforts, we have committed to train all employees in quality management tools and techniques. To date, approximately 85 percent of all administrative employees have completed a three-day quality training session. In order to accelerate the initial rate of training and develop internal expertise in quality, ten quality specialists were trained. These individuals volunteered to dedicate approximately 25 percent of their time to Babson's total quality initiative, including

1. Delivering the three-day workshops to other employees

2. Assisting in follow-up training of employees

3. Assisting managers and employees in planning the implementation of total quality in their teams and departments and in the development of quality objectives, standards, and measures

4. Facilitating the identification, management, and achievement of quality improvement teams by serving as process coach and/or facilitator for team meetings

5. Serving on the Steering Committee for Administrative Services

As part of initial total quality training, groups select a particular project and tackle it utilizing quality tools and techniques. For example, the graduate admissions office decided to examine the enrollment process. The staffers discovered eight mailings were being sent to accepted students over the summer, involving many different kinds of information and forms. After flowcharting the process, they used the problem-solving process to combine these separate mailings into one acceptance packet. The new packet eliminated 220 staff hours formerly used in producing and coordinating the separate mailings, plus additional time that was spent tracking missing forms. Results of a survey administered to new students during orientation indicate that the new acceptance packet had a significant impact on the decision to enroll at Babson for 22 students. The survey (now included in the packet) has also provided detailed information on the clarity and usefulness of components of the new packet so that the continuous improvement process can roll on.

Currently we have numerous completed projects that addressed such diverse issues as the student loan process (examining the process from the time eligibility is determined until the check is endorsed at accounting) and the assessment of graduates with respect to level of preparation for their chosen careers (a survey of employers of graduates). Other completed projects to date have resulted in a better distribution of materials to incoming students and major changes to the freshman advisory program and daily operations of the Information Technology Services Division of the college.

Since our total quality journey formally began just two years ago, we have encountered some challenges and fully realize that as we continue on that we will be faced with additional challenges in the future. Some of the key challenges we have experienced and the methods we have chosen to address the issues include

1. *Teams lose motivation and/or get stalled in some stage of the problem-solving cycle.* As our initial teams got underway, we realized that many tried to take on too much and became overwhelmed by the enormity of the issue they were attempting to resolve. Others team efforts fizzled due to lack of coordination and direction. And, in general, there was not a concerted effort to monitor the progress of quality improvement teams. In order to address these issues we initiated the Quality Specialist Program to train individuals as key resources that can be called on to provide necessary assistance to teams and trained cabinet members on how to inspect the quality improvement team process.

2. *Determining the best method to engage faculty in total quality and identify how total quality can be implemented in the academic area.* We mobilized a core group of faculty to identify and initiate projects in the academic area, relied on information from the academic deans and chairs, and launched undergraduate curricular reform as a mechanism to involve faculty in continuous improvement and change efforts.

3. *Total quality orientation training for senior managers.* Initially, we encouraged senior managers in our organization to undertake quality training, but did not specify a common program. Although the varied experiences were no doubt beneficial to all, we decided that common tools and language were necessary in order to operate from a common base of knowledge and further facilitate total quality practice. As a result, a three-day quality training program was developed and launched. Senior managers now attend training with their staff and are also able to participate in other related and follow-up quality-related training.

4. *How to facilitate the paradigm shift for managers.* In a total quality environment, managers need to transition from the role of the one who has the answers to the one who asks the right questions. To address this, numerous workshops have been developed, including The Role of the Manager in a Quality Organization.

5. *Tackling issues that cross organizational boundaries.* Initial teams at the college consisted of people who work within a particular department or division of the college. We felt it was most logical to train individuals in family groups so they could practice applying the tools and techniques they learned to familiar territory. We now must help groups think toward larger problems that cross divisional boundaries and have the potential for greater benefits to the institution. One major undertaking involves reengineering all administrative areas that affect a student from inquiry through graduation. This involves analysis and redesign of the processes that deliver various administrative services to the student.

Obstacles to total quality implementation that seem to plague numerous schools as well as possible mechanisms to overcome them are identified in this table.

Obstacles to total quality implementation in higher education	Mechanisms deployed to overcome implementation obstacles
• Translating corporate models and jargon	• Modification of models and methods to adapt to the needs and culture of higher education
• Determining the best method to engage faculty	• Providing opportunities for issue-based involvement
• Teams losing motivation or getting stalled	• Providing resources for coaching and facilitation via trained quality specialists
• Thinking and problem solving across boundaries (crossing artificial functional boundaries)	• Flowcharting processes, using customer data and information
• Management by intuition	• Using customer satisfaction data and facts for decision making
• Lack of strategic planning	• Articulating a vision, mission statement, and specific goals for the institution and total quality

We realize our journey has just begun. However, we have a clear vision of who we want to be: an international leader in management education. We have a measurement system in place to monitor progress toward our goals and objectives. We have trained our employees to use quality management tools and techniques in order to make incremental changes in the way we undertake our daily activities. We also listened to our multiple customers and mobilized our efforts to make revolutionary changes in our MBA curriculum and launch undergraduate curricular reform in order to better prepare our graduates for business organizations of the future.

We are doing our best to enable our students to understand the complexity, challenge, aspects, and functional interrelationships of a total quality system. In addition, we have embraced total quality as a way to manage our organization in order to improve what we do today and redesign our organization for the twenty-first century. We know, however, that we have a long way to go to ensure our graduates leave our institution fully prepared for the business environment and to fully engage the creative energies of all the members of our community.

Notes

1. Christopher Farrell, "Time to Prune the Ivy," *Business Week*, 24 May 1993, 112–118.

2. Ibid.

3. J. D. Robinson, III, H. A. Poling, J. F. Akers, R. W. Galvin, E. L. Artz, and P. A. Allaire, "An Open Letter: TQM on the Campus," *Harvard Business Review* (November–December 1991): 94–95.

4. S. Axland, "Looking for a Quality Education?" *Quality Progress* (October 1991): 61–66.

5. Lyman W. Porter and Lawrence E. McKibbin, *Management Education: Drift or Thrust into the Twenty-First Century?* (New York: McGraw-Hill, 1988).

6. Shoji Shiba, Alan Graham, and David Walden, *A New American TQM: Four Practical Revolutions in Management* (Portland, Ore.: Productivity Press, 1993).

Applying Quality Function Deployment to Improve an MBA Education

Steven C. Hillmer, Professor, University of Kansas
Barbara Hoehn Hillmer, Graduate Student, University of Kansas
Beverley Wilson, Assistant Professor, University of Kansas
Jordan Yochim, Quality Engineer, Bausch & Lomb

Introduction

Many organizations are realizing that to be competitive they must focus on their customers. They must know and listen to their customers, develop products and services to meet customer requirements, and work to improve their products and services. Though simple in principle, achieving a customer focus is frequently difficult in practice. Some organizations have turned to quality function deployment (QFD) for help in accomplishing this task. In this paper we explore the application of QFD to the design and continuous improvement of a service, a master of business administration (MBA) education program.

Our purpose is to describe the QFD process in general and to illustrate the stages in some detail of its application, providing an overview of the steps involved and enough details to help others wanting to use quality function deployment. It is important to note that successful application of QFD requires an appreciation of its underlying philosophy and sufficient flexibility to modify its stages to fit particular circumstances. In this paper, we first review the history of QFD and the reasons why organizations have found it useful. We summarize the major steps involved in the QFD process. We then illustrate these steps by describing how data were gathered on customer needs and perceptions of the current MBA program. We describe how to organize these data into useful information, how to develop measurable characteristics, and how to correlate these characteristics with demanded customer attributes. Finally, we discuss how to use this information to improve the delivery of an MBA program and how to evaluate the success of the process undertaken.

Quality Function Deployment Reviewed

QFD is an approach to operationalizing the concept of customer focus for an entire product or service line in an organization. The QFD process ensures that customers' needs, expressed in customers' own language, become the basis for definition of a product or service. These needs are translated into operationally defined characteristics, with target values and detailed plans for achieving those values. QFD's purpose is to ensure that quality, as demanded by the customer, is incorporated into each stage from definition to delivery of the product or service.

Introduced by Yoji Akao in the late 1960s, QFD was used in Japan in the early 1970s by Mitsubishi and Toyota to improve the quality of their products. Because of its success in Japan, American companies recently have shown a growing interest in QFD. A number of books and articles have appeared, the majority of which have focused on the use of QFD in the design and improvement of manufactured products. (See the suggested reading list for examples.)

The success of QFD requires that the entire organization understand how the work of every department is linked to meeting customer needs. In a manufacturing organization, for example, marketing, research, design, production, sales, and service people must work as teams to ensure that customer-demanded quality is incorporated systematically through the definition, design, and improvement of a product. Teamwork and a constant focus on customer demands can substantially reduce the time and cost associated with the delivery of a quality product. When more time is spent defining the product, typically less time is required to design the product, and the need to redesign is minimal. The use of QFD shortens the entire process by helping to focus priorities, providing better documentation, and facilitating communication among team members.

In contrast to the earlier focus on manufactured products, in this paper we describe the use of this systematic customer-driven process in a service organization, a university. Unlike a manufactured product, a service is not a material object with easily measured properties, but rather it is the result of interactions between provider and user. In our example of an MBA program, the number of direct interactions with each customer is large, making the dimensions of quality numerous. With so many opportunities to fall short, the importance of a systematic approach to achieving a customer focus and satisfying a customer's demands is clear.

In our illustration, we describe an approach to the design and continuous improvement of a service that combines the concepts of QFD (see Figure 1) together with some of the seven management tools that have been used to support QFD. The MBA program is offered by a state-supported university and has a target market of

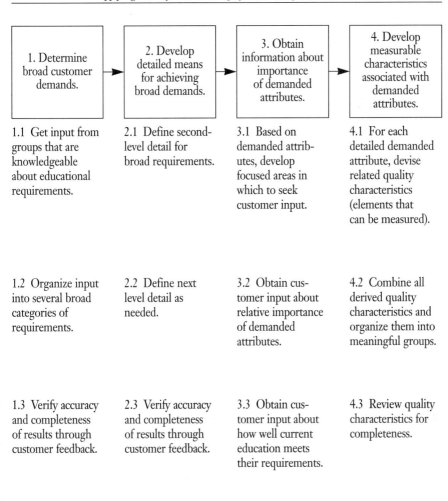

Figure 1. Top-down flowchart of the QFD process.

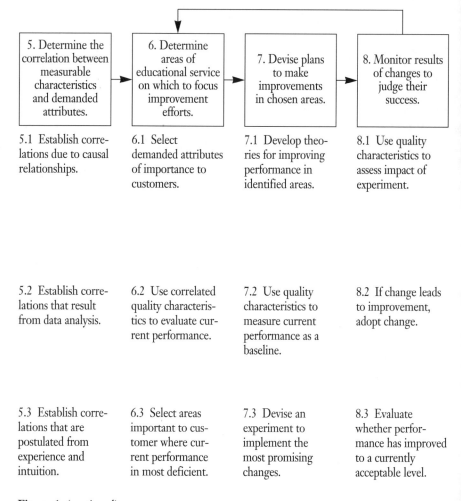

Figure 1. (continued).

students in the surrounding geographic region. Throughout the paper, *we* refers to a team with student, faculty, and administrator members.

QFD Illustrated: Designing an Improved MBA Education

The top-down flowchart in Figure 1 outlines an approach to the use of QFD in the education environment. It begins with the very important, often difficult, step of listening to the customer. This involves asking the question: "Who is the customer, and how should we listen?" There may be several groups of customers and many ways to listen, including customer surveys, focus groups, customer interviews, customer complaints, and third-party reports.

We identified current full-time, on-campus students as one group of customers of the MBA program. Other groups of customers included alumni of the program and recruiters of current students. Finally, we sought input from faculty teaching in the program.

Determine the Broad Customer Demands

Our initial action (step 1.1 in Figure 1) was to listen to our customers by asking approximately 50 students to respond in writing to the question: "As customers of the School of Business, what are your needs?" Their responses centered on the logistics of obtaining their education and their perceptions of the educational content needed to be a successful manager. In order to obtain information about the type of education needed from the perspective of people more familiar with business, about 60 faculty, alumni, and recruiters were asked to respond to the question: "What general characteristics do business students need to have successful business careers?" Recruiters were asked a second question: "What characteristics do you look for in students you hire from business schools?"

Finally, information concerning current trends in MBA programs was obtained from Graduate Management Admission Council (GMAC) publications. Specific expressions of need sometimes were reinterpreted by the authors to reflect a more general concept. For example, a recruiter's statement that MBA students need a working knowledge of a particular software package was reinterpreted: MBA students need a familiarity with, and a basic understanding of, software alternatives. Sample responses are presented in Figure 2. The collective customer responses, combined with the GMAC information, revealed a wide range of needs and demanded characteristics of an MBA program.

The question addressed to the students was designed to solicit input regarding their needs while obtaining their education. Their answers reflected the fact that many students, because of their limited work experience, do not realize the full range of qualities and skills they will need to be successful in the future. The questions addressed to the other groups of customers were designed to gather this information. In our analysis we handle the student responses separately from those of all other customers.

Upon completion of this stage of QFD, we had a large volume of information related to needs that an MBA program could meet. The information consisted of many seemingly unrelated responses and needed to be organized. To accomplish this

Good knowledge of international competitive forces

Graduates able to mentor, teach, and coach

Graduates exposed to the humanities

Graduates have some idea of how a real company operates

Graduates sensitive to other cultures

Graduates that are computer literate

Graduates value cooperative behavior

Graduates who understand the principles of competing on quality and business speed

Graduates with a high energy level

Graduates with common sense and general knowledge of the business environment and culture

Graduates with good communication skills

Graduates with realistic expectations about their future careers

Graduates with the ability to recognize what is not known

Have the facility to organize and characterize information

Knowledge of the basic subjects from the liberal arts that are relevant to business analysis

Knowledge of the relationship between business and society through history

People who can work across organizational boundaries

Skills at collecting data, prioritizing, and hypothesizing

Skills at conceptualizing problems that are presented in messy, confusing ways

Skills at hiring, firing, evaluating others, and working with difficult people

The ability to listen effectively

The ability to observe an activity and to understand why it is being done

The ability to understand how organizations and groups work

The capacity to shift focus from the microlevel to the big picture

Willingness of graduates to share power

Figure 2. A partial list of customer responses to questions.

task (step 1.2 of Figure 1), affinity diagrams were constructed from the responses for each of the two groups. The procedure consisted of transferring the responses to index cards, randomly scattering them on a large table, and regrouping them according to their perceived affinity for one another. For each group an underlying theme was identified and written on an index card to be placed on the top of that group of cards. Subsequently, the each group was treated as a single card with the response being the underlying theme. The process of grouping responses by their affinity for one another and determining a theme for each group was repeated until seven to 10 groups were formed. Construction of an affinity diagram is expected to reveal the broad underlying themes in the original verbal data. (For more information on affinity diagrams and other management tools used here, see Brassard 1989 in the suggested reading list.) The resulting broad categories of demand are shown in Figures 3 and 4.

1. Ability to recognize and solve problems

2. Ability to analyze and synthesize

3. Sound business skills

4. Knowledge of competitive business strategies

5. Understanding of issues facing business people in the real world

6. Ability to enable people

7. Good interpersonal skills

8. Personal attributes

9. Attributes associated with renaissance people

Figure 3. Broad demanded characteristics of students as expressed by recruiters, alumni, faculty, and publications.

1. Better delivery of information about the education

2. Better delivery of the education

3. Fewer hassles in obtaining the education the students need

4. Facilities more conducive to learning

5. An expanded curriculum

6. More exposure to real-world issues

7. More cohesiveness within the school-of-business community

8. Better services for placement of graduates

9. Better reputation for the school of business

Figure 4. Demanded characteristics of an MBA program as expressed by students.

As expected, demands differed with perspective. Figure 3 makes apparent the curriculum-related concerns of faculty, alumni, and recruiters. In contrast, Figure 4 reflects students' concerns with administration and delivery of the MBA program as well as curriculum. Clearly, both views would require attention in the subsequent design process.

Before proceeding, results were shared with key alumni to verify that all the important dimensions of an MBA program had been identified (step 1.3 in Figure 1). This group affirmed the broad dimensions in Figure 3. In general, it is important to the QFD process that an attempt be made to verify the accuracy of the interpretation of customer-expressed needs and to reinterpret if necessary (step 1.4 in Figure 1).

At this point, we decided to focus our attention on one of the broadly defined customer demands, realizing the effort required to address each demand would be significant. Although it is important to eventually attempt to address all customer-identified demands, initially one or two priority demands should be targeted for immediate additional analysis (step 1.5 in Figure 1). In setting priorities, consider the relative importance of each demand to the customer, the degree to which the organization currently is succeeding in meeting the demands, and the interrelationships among demands. The goal is to focus first on the one or two customer demands that will result in the greatest perceived and actual improvement in service.

To assist in setting priorities, it is useful to consider relationships among the broad groups of demands identified. One way to understand these relationships is to construct an interrelationship digraph. For our illustration, we considered the customer demands in Figure 3. For each broad category of demands we asked the question: "Will addressing the needs in this category address at the same time needs in other categories?" If so, an arrow was drawn to indicate a causal relationship between demand categories. The result was the interrelationship digraph in Figure 5.

Notice the category "understanding of real-world issues" has four arrows pointing to other categories. This suggests that if changes could be made to improve this category, these changes would affect four other categories: "ability to analyze and synthesize," "ability to recognize and solve problems," "knowledge of competitive strategies," and "renaissance people." Thus, based on its relationships with other customer demands, "understanding of real-world issues" was assigned a high priority. The interrelationship digraph in Figure 6 was derived from the student demand categories in Figure 4. The two digraphs, considered in light of organizational core competencies, lead to the final priorities and a selection of the customer demand for understanding of real-world issues for further study. It appeared on both customer demand lists and was prominent in both digraphs.

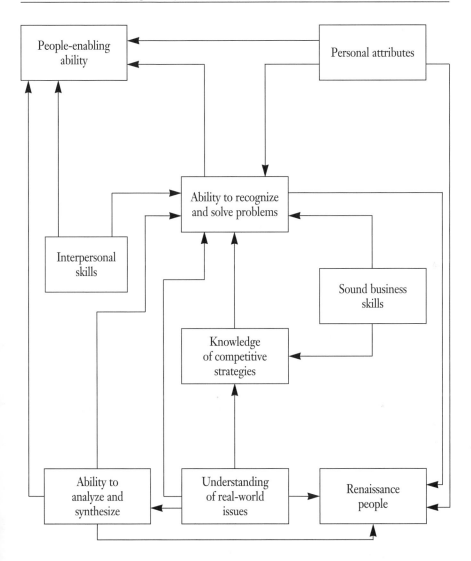

Figure 5. Interrelationship digraph for broad demanded student characteristics.

Develop Detailed Means for Achieving Broad Demands

The first series of steps helped clarify the broad categories needing attention and resulted in the selection of one category for further analysis. The next series of steps would yield the details necessary for achieving this broad demand. One tool that is useful in developing the required level of detail is the tree diagram. We constructed

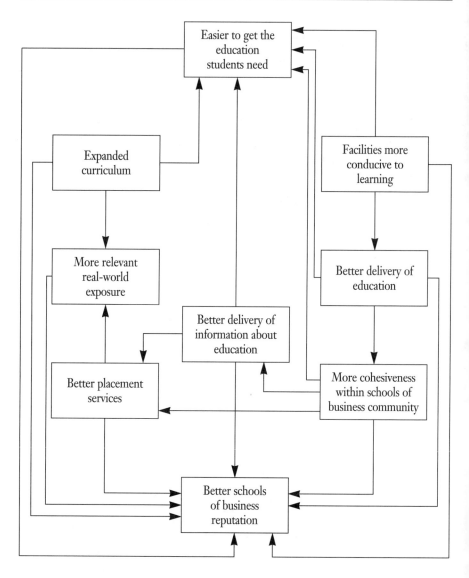

Figure 6. Interrelationship digraph of characteristics of education demanded by students.

a tree diagram for the characteristic "understanding issues facing business people in the real world."

To begin construction of this tree diagram, we asked: "What needs to occur in order for students to have an increased understanding of real-world issues?"

Answers, which became branches of the tree, were based on original customer responses coupled with the knowledge and experience of team members. The first-level answers to this question are shown in Figure 7. (This is an example of the output of step 2.1 in Figure 1). Notice that while these answers provide detail about the dimensions of understanding the real-world environment, they are still quite broad. To achieve an even greater level of detail, for each branch in Figure 7 the question was asked: "What needs to occur in order for this (answer) to be achieved?" The answers provided in greater detail the means for achieving the original broad customer demands. The process was continued until a sufficient level of detail was achieved to enable a complete listing of demanded attributes. As an illustration, detailed tree diagrams for the branches "ethical dimensions of business" and "real-world work experience" are shown in Figures 8 and 9. (This illustrates step 2.2 in Figure 1).

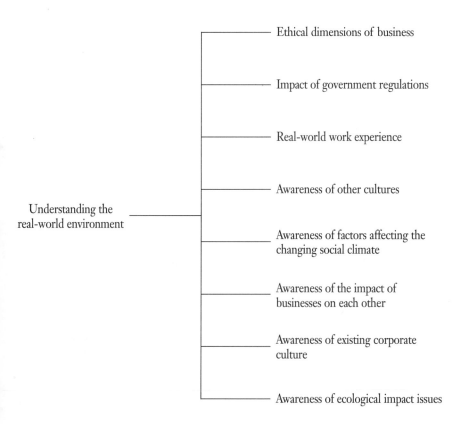

Figure 7. First-level means to understanding the real-world environment.

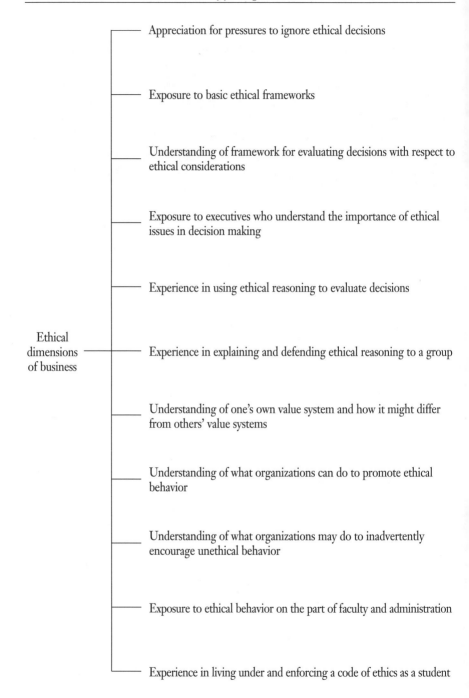

Appreciation for pressures to ignore ethical decisions

Exposure to basic ethical frameworks

Understanding of framework for evaluating decisions with respect to ethical considerations

Exposure to executives who understand the importance of ethical issues in decision making

Experience in using ethical reasoning to evaluate decisions

Ethical dimensions of business

Experience in explaining and defending ethical reasoning to a group

Understanding of one's own value system and how it might differ from others' value systems

Understanding of what organizations can do to promote ethical behavior

Understanding of what organizations may do to inadvertently encourage unethical behavior

Exposure to ethical behavior on the part of faculty and administration

Experience in living under and enforcing a code of ethics as a student

Figure 8. Second-level means to understanding ethical dimensions of business.

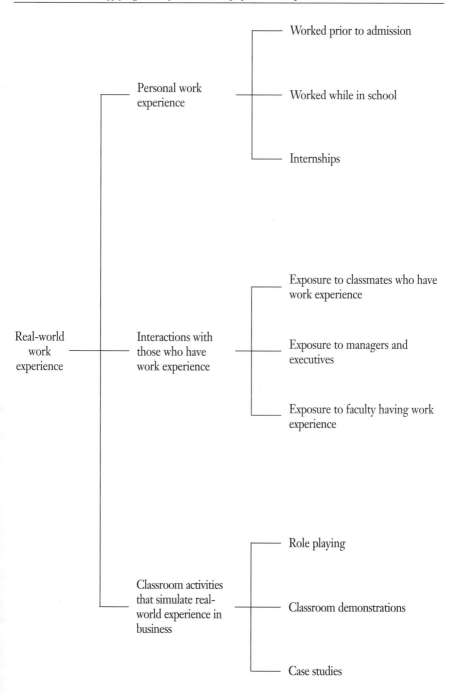

Figure 9. Second-level means to real-world experience.

Following the drafting of any tree diagram, one should work backward from the end branches to ensure that implementation of lower-level details actually will lead to the accomplishment of next-higher-level objectives. For example, (see Figure 9) the only means for students to obtain "personal work experience" are "worked prior to admission," or "work while in school," or work in "internships." Since these possibilities are all included in the branches, this aspect of the diagram is complete. This step in the construction of a tree diagram should help to ensure its completeness and the soundness of its logic.

Steps 2.3 and 2.4 of Figure 1 involve verifying the accuracy and completeness of the demanded attributes by obtaining feedback from customers. Because of time constraints, we did not obtain a formal customer evaluation of the resulting attributes. We did share the results with several people who provided input in the data gathering stages—they verified our results.

Obtain Information About the Importance of Demanded Attributes

The full set of demanded attributes for "understanding the real-world environment" consisted of branches like Figures 8 and 9, one for each of the items listed in Figure 7. The sheer volume again forced the setting of priorities. For any given MBA program, some of the attributes identified will be strengths of the current program while others will be weaknesses. Some of the attributes will be very important to customers; others will be less important. In addition, the characteristics of competing MBA programs will affect customers' perceptions of the quality of the subject program. Thus information on the perceived strengths and weaknesses of a program, the felt importance of related attributes, and the attributes of competing programs together will aid in the process of setting priorities regarding customer demands.

In the example being described, we lacked the ability to obtain much of this information. Nevertheless the importance of attempting to gather as much information as possible should not be overlooked. Information could be obtained by querying selected customers. Earlier results should help with the development of a focused questionnaire. For instance, with respect to the issue of students' understanding of "ethical dimensions of business" (see Figure 8), a questionnaire to alumni and recruiters could be used to discover which of the attributes listed are of highest priority and how well graduates of our program compare with graduates of other programs for the attributes listed. In addition, questionnaires to students could provide information on the extent to which the current program addresses each demanded attribute. (These efforts are steps 3.1, 3.2, and 3.3 of Figure 1).

Initially there is no reason to focus on strong attributes of the current program. Likewise, there is little reason to spend time and effort to improve attributes that customers deem relatively unimportant. The greatest benefits will be derived from efforts focused on attributes judged by customers to be important, but that are perceived to be deficient in the current program.

Develop Measurable Characteristics Associated with Demanded Attributes

To improve a product or service, it is helpful to be able to measure the attributes demanded by customers. Experience has shown that it is easier to plan for and monitor progress if measurements related to customer demands can be devised. In QFD measurable attributes are called *quality characteristics*. Quality characteristics help operationalize needed improvements. For example, one demanded attribute of an MBA program in Figure 8 is "experience in using ethical reasoning to evaluate decisions." This attribute is not directly measurable, but it is related to the measurable characteristic, the number of times students analyze cases involving ethical decisions. Thus, one way to increase the attribute and improve this aspect of an MBA program would be to use more cases involving ethical issues in decision making. As another example, the Figure 8 attribute "exposure to ethical frameworks" is related to the measurable characteristic, class lecture time devoted to the subject ethical frameworks. An increase in this measurable characteristic would indicate improvement in the attribute.

The development of quality characteristics may seem inherently more difficult for service applications than for product applications. However, careful attention in the early stages of the QFD process usually results in a sufficient level of detail to mitigate the problem. For our MBA illustration, we developed quality characteristics for a set of attributes in the following way. For each customer demand, we listed variables that were measurable and correlated with the demand (step 4.1 in Figure 1). For example, we decided the measurable quantities work experience of the student body, amount of time students were exposed to real managers discussing ethical decisions, number of cases concerned with ethical pressures, and number of role playing situations dealing with ethical pressures were related to the customer demand, "appreciation for pressures to ignore ethical decisions." The combined lists of measurable quantities consisted of a large number of items. To organize the items and develop general categories of measurable characteristics, we constructed an affinity diagram. The results are shown in Figure 10 (step 4.2 in Figure 1). We reviewed the list to ensure that obvious measurable quantities had not been omitted (step 4.3 in Figure 1).

1. Characteristics of the incoming student body

    1.1 Related work experience

    1.2 Related cultural experience

    1.3 Previous formal educational experience

2. Characteristics of the curriculum taken by all students

    2.1 Faculty lecture delivered

    2.2 External manager lecture delivered

    2.3 Case delivered

    2.4 Delivered by demonstration

    2.5 Delivered through role playing

    2.6 Delivered through structural self-assessment

3. Characteristics of faculty

    3.1 Experience in the business world

    3.2 Cultural experiences

4. Characteristics of student body

    4.1 Subject matter knowledge upon course completion

    4.2 Subject matter knowledge upon program completion

5. Feedback related to the quality of the program

    5.1 Student feedback related to curriculum delivery

    5.2 External customer feedback related to quality of graduates

    5.3 External customer feedback related to curriculum quality

Figure 10. Measurable quality characteristics for understanding the real-world environment.

Determine the Correlation Between Measurable Characteristics and Demanded Attributes

The demanded attributes indicate what is desired, while the quality-characteristics measures provide a means for determining whether what is desired has been accomplished. For planning, it is important to understand the relationships between the demanded attributes and the quality characteristics. In many instances, quality characteristics will be related to more than one attribute. One tool used to represent these relationships is the matrix diagram, a two-by-two display of attribute-characteristic correlations. With demanded attributes on the vertical axis and quality characteristics on the horizontal axis, the matrix represents, with symbols, the correlations between attributes and characteristics. Figure 11 shows part of the matrix diagram for demanded attributes associated with "ethical dimensions of business." In the diagram, symbols SP, MP, WP, SN, MN, and WN describe relationships as strong, moderate, or weak, and positive or negative. A blank indicates no relationship.

As indicated in steps 5.1, 5.2, and 5.3 in Figure 1, assessments of the strength and direction of correlations were based on our knowledge of causal relationships, data that suggested relationships, or simply our experience. When the matrix was complete, it was checked for blank columns and rows. A blank column indicated, for the quality characteristic heading it, a lack of correlation with any demanded attribute. That quality characteristic was dropped. A blank row indicated a lack of quality characteristics for a demanded attribute. Additional effort was made to discover some way to measure the attribute. While the resulting categorization may seem coarse, the process of completing the matrix diagram forces consideration of the correlations in a systematic manner and displays this information in a concise format.

Determine Areas of the Educational Service on Which to Focus Improvement Efforts

To determine where to focus efforts to improve, the two-by-two matrix described can be augmented with the following information: (1) customer ratings of the relative importance of each demanded attribute; (2) customer ratings of the service to be improved (current service); and (3) customer ratings of competitors' services. This information can be gathered through customer questionnaires. A simplified example of a matrix augmented with this information is shown in Figure 12. It is similar to the house of quality, a tool used frequently in QFD applications (see Hauser and Clausing 1988 in the suggested reading list). Organizing the MBA program information in this way enables the setting of priorities for improving quality characteristics and ultimately improving the program.

A common approach to setting priorities for the quality characteristics involves the use of a simple weighting scheme. In our illustration, Figure 12 correlations are assigned values of 1, 3, or 9 according to whether they are weak, moderate, or strong. The sign of the value is + if the correlation is positive and – if the correlation is negative. Customer ratings are represented on a scale from 1 to 5, 1 representing the lowest and 5 the highest rating.

As an illustration of how the ratings of customer attributes are translated into ratings for quality characteristics, consider the measurable characteristic "cultural experience" in Figure 12. This is moderately positively correlated with both "appreciation for pressures to ignore the ethical component of decisions" and "exposure to

Characteristics

	Work experience	Cultural experience	Previous educational experience	Faculty lecture	External manager lecture	Case studies	Demonstrations	Structured experiences	Structured self-assessment	Discussion	Retention of knowledge on course completion	Ability to apply knowledge on course completion	Retention of knowledge on program completion	Ability to apply knowledge on program completion
Appreciation for pressures to ignore the ethical component of decisions	MP	MP		MP		SP	MP	SP	MP	SP				
Exposure to basic ethical frameworks		MP		SP		MP		MP				SP	SP	
Understanding of frameworks for evaluating decisions with respect to ethical considerations				SP		MP				MP		SP	SP	
Exposure to executives who understand the importance of ethical decision making					MN	SP								
Experience in using ethical reasoning to evaluate decisions	MP	MP			MN		SP		SP		MP			
Experience in explaining and defending ethical reasoning to a group		MP	MP	SN		MP		SP		SP		SP		SP
Understanding of one's own value system and how it might differ from others' value systems	MP	SP	MP			MP	MP	MP	SP	SP				
Understanding of what organizations can do to promote ethical behavior						MP	SP	MP	MP	SP		MP	SP	SP
Understanding what organizations may do to inadvertently encourage unethical behavior	MP					MP	MP	MP	MP	SP		MP	SP	SP
Exposure to ethical behavior on the part of faculty and administration			MP	MP										
Experience in living under and enforcing a code of ethics as a student			MP											

Legend: SP = Strongly positive, MP = Moderately positive, MN = Moderately negative

Figure 11. Partial matrix of relationships between demanded attributes and quality.

Quality characteristics

Demanded customer attributes	Work experience	Cultural experience	Previous educational experience	Faculty lecture	Customer rating: importance of attribute to customers (scale 1–5)	Customer rating: our service (scale 1–5)	Customer rating: competitor service (scale 1–5)
Appreciation for pressures to ignore the ethical component of decisions	MP	MP		MP	4	2	2
Exposure to basic ethical frameworks		MP		SP	3	3	4
Understanding of framework for evaluating decisions with respect to ethical considerations				SP	3	2	3
Composite rating: importance—quality characteristics		21					
Composite rating: our service		15					
Composite rating: competitor service		18					

Legend: SP = Strongly positive, MP = Moderately positive

Figure 12. Simplified house of quality.

basic ethical frameworks." In order to compute an importance rating for "cultural experience," the rating for "appreciation for pressures to ignore the ethical component of decisions" is multiplied by a value +3, the weight associated with a moderately positive correlation (this is denoted by MP in Figure 12). Similarly, the rating for "exposure to basic ethical frameworks" is multiplied by +3. These two values are then added to obtain the importance rating of 21 ($3 \times 4 + 3 \times 3$) for "cultural experience."

The correlation-weighted ratings provide information that is useful in choosing characteristics on which to focus improvement efforts. One approach to making a choice would be to focus on those characteristics rated as important by customers that have current service ratings that are below the ratings of competitors' services. What is important to observe is that this house-of-quality tool brings together, in a coherent way, a large body of information relevant to decisions to improve a product or service. It can be used to select demanded attributes that are important to customers (step 6.1 in Figure 1), to evaluate current service with respect to the correlated quality characteristics (step 6.2 in Figure 1), and to identify areas where performance is most deficient (step 6.3 in Figure 1).

Plan, Implement, and Monitor Changes

What has been described is a method for gathering information from customers and using this information to understand where to focus efforts to improve a product or service. What is needed now are specific plans for changes (step 7 in Figure 1). Current levels of performance could serve as baseline quality-characteristic measures, providing a basis for systematically and unambiguously evaluating the planned changes. In some cases a trial implementation is advisable, with adoption of the change coming only after evidence of desired improvement is observed. Finally, the attribute-related measures should be used to assess the degree to which changes actually have resulted in improvements (step 8 in Figure 1). The information that has been gathered and organized is the basis upon which to take action on steps 7 and 8 in Figure 1. All of this is part of a continuous cycle of planning, implementing, and monitoring activities.

Conclusion

QFD is a process by which customer requirements are translated into design features, specifications, and operational targets. Customer-perceived value drives the process from beginning to end. In this paper we have described the application of QFD to the design/redesign of an MBA program.

In this paper we have illustrated how to determine broad customer demands and how to use these broad demands as a basis to derive more detailed requirements. We have shown how to develop measurable characteristics that are correlated with the detailed demands and how to summarize the correlations between the derived measurable values and the customer demands. Finally, we have indicated how to summarize all this information in a manner that is useful for development of improvement plans. This is only the beginning of a process of continuous improvement. Each subsequent contact with the customer is another opportunity for the supplier to reexamine the product or service in light of customer requirements and to make changes as needed.

The strength of QFD comes from its ability to capture a customer's needs and to make them drivers of all processes, from design to delivery of a product or service. By its nature, QFD involves the entire organization seeking to bring about change, enabling individual members to discover ways to contribute to the improvement of a product or service. Of course there are cautions. For QFD to be effective, sufficient and accurate market research data must be precede it. QFD, as a framework for analysis and implementation, must have employee involvement to succeed. Finally, it must be viewed as a continuous process. Customer needs and perceptions of quality change, requiring the supplier to inquire and listen, again and again.

Suggested Reading

Bossert, James L. *Quality Function Deployment: A Practitioners Approach*. Milwaukee, Wis.: ASQC Quality Press, 1991.

Brassard, Michael. *The Memory Jogger Plus*. Methuen, Mass.: Goal/QPC, 1989.

Eureka, William E., and Nancy E. Ryan. *The Customer-Driven Company: Managerial Perspectives on QFD*. Dearborn, Mich.: ASI Press, 1988.

Hauser, John R. "How Puritan-Bennett Used the House of Quality." *Sloan Management Review* 34 (Spring 1993): 61–70.

Hauser, John R., and Don Clausing. "The House of Quality." *Harvard Business Review* 66 (May/June 1988): 63–73.

Hosotani, Yoshinobu, ed. *TQC Solutions: The 14-Step Process Volume I: The Problem Solving Process*. Cambridge, Mass.: Productivity Press, 1991.

Hunter, Michael R., and Richard D. Van Landingham. "Listening to the Customer Using QFD." *Quality Progress* 27 (April 1994): 55–59.

Jones, Ken. "High Performance Manufacturing (Part 4): A Break with Tradition." *Industrial Management* 12 (June 1988): 30–32.

Kane, Victor E. *Defect Prevention*. New York: Marcel Dekker, 1989.

King, Robert. *Better Designs in Half the Time*. Methuen, Mass.: Goal/QPC, 1987.

———. "Listening to the Voice of the Customer: Using the Quality Function Deployment System." *National Productivity Review* 6 (Summer 1987): 277–281.

Maduri, Omnamasivaya. "Understanding and Applying QFD in Heavy Industry." *Journal for Quality & Participation* 15 (January/February 1992): 64–69.

Mizuno, Shigeru, and Yoji Akao, eds. *Quality Function Deployment: Approach to Total Quality Control.* Tokyo: Japanese Union of Scientists and Engineers, 1978.

Vasilash, Gary S. "Hearing the Voice of the Customer." *Production* 101 (February 1989): 66–68.

System-Supported Teaching and Learning to Improve Student Performance, Satisfaction, and Retention

Pat Mayers, Vice President, Academic Affairs;
Tim Ricordati, Director of Operations;
Don Carter, Director of Institutional Research; and
Tim Hohmeier, Director of Curriculum
Keller Graduate School of Management

Introduction

Keller Graduate School of Management is using total quality management (TQM), referred to as total quality in this paper, in the classroom to increase student performance, satisfaction, and retention (the proportion of students graduating from the program). Our strategy is to combine two elements.

- A proven educational theory and methodology, mastery learning, for improving teaching and learning in individual classrooms

- Total quality, a proven business theory and methodology, that permits distribution of the benefits of mastery learning to multiple sections, courses, and locations

This paper provides operational definitions and examples of a new instructional process that combines mastery learning and total quality in the classroom, and a status report on the outcomes of these efforts at this time.

The new instructional process includes frequent feedback and correctives using quizzes and retests. It is supported by

- Faculty-developed and shared item banks keyed to course objectives

- Software for generating parallel tests and answer keys

- Well-defined administrative procedures and support

- Additional compensation for the faculty

The process is outcomes-driven. It is applied to the 20 percent of courses in which 80 percent of attrition occurs (an application of the Pareto principle).

The mission of Keller Graduate School of Management is to provide high-quality, practitioner-oriented graduate management degree programs with an emphasis on excellence in teaching and service to working adults. The school now has approximately 3000 students at 17 educational centers distributed across six states. In 1987, Keller Graduate School of Management acquired and merged with the DeVry Institutes of Technology, which have approximately 26,000 students in undergraduate programs in business and technology at 13 schools in the United States and Canada.

Keller is different from many traditional schools in three important ways.

- Its primary reliance on practitioner faculty

- Its focus on teaching excellence and service to working adults

- Its multicenter distribution system

Like traditional schools, the Keller School offers its core, or foundation, courses across multiple sections and terms of the year.

Theoretical Underpinnings

Although the present work draws on numerous concepts and tools of total quality, the primary theoretical grounding lies in applying to students (and faculty) Juran's concept of "worker self-control," and Deming's complementary emphasis on providing workers (students and faculty) with operational definitions and examples.

On self-control, Juran says

> Creating a state of self-control for a human being requires that we meet several essential criteria. We must provide people with the means for:
>
> 1. Knowing what they are supposed to do.
>
> 2. Knowing what they are actually doing.
>
> 3. Taking regulatory action.
>
> These criteria for self-control make possible a separation of defects into various categories of "controllability," of which the most important are
>
> 1. *Operator-controllable.* A defect is operator-controllable if all three criteria for self-control have been met.

2. *Management-controllable.* A defect is management-controllable if any one or more of the criteria for self-control have not been met.

The theory behind these categories is that only the management can provide the means for meeting the criteria for self-control. . . .[1]

And from Deming:

In response to a problem in quality and productivity: "What could management do? The consultants made the suggestion, based on experience, that possibly the people on the job, and the inspector also, did not understand well enough what kind of work is acceptable and what is not. The manager and two supervisors eventually accepted this possibility and went to work on the matter. With trial and error they came up in seven weeks with operational definitions, with examples of conforming items and of nonconforming items, posted for everyone to see. A new set of data showed that the proportion defective had dropped to 5 per cent (from 11 per cent). . . . Gains: quality up, production of good product up 6 per cent, capacity up 6 per cent, lower cost per unit of good product, profit improved, customer happier, everybody happier. . . . This is an example of gain in productivity accomplished by a change in the system, namely, improvement in definitions, effected by the management, to help people to work smarter, not harder. . . .[2]

The new instructional process described in this paper applies these concepts of Juran and Deming to focus on the responsibility of academic managers to provide system supports for teaching and learning, and hence to improve student academic achievement, satisfaction, and retention.

Keller's Instructional Infrastructure

Before presenting the new instructional process, we briefly describe the instructional infrastructure at Keller Graduate School.

Each term, in every class, the course objectives are handed out in class the first night as a part of the syllabus. For each objective, there are one or more problem types, which are the specific processes that we want the students to master. Within each problem type, there are variations, which are the relatively minor changes in certain elements or conditions of the problem. The distinction between problem types and variations is a matter of judgment, which is best exercised in collaboration by faculty teaching the course.

Instruction includes a demonstration of each of the discrete problem types and variations, which together constitute the operational definitions and examples of the course objectives.

Homework is then assigned. The homework is parallel in content and level to the material presented in class. It includes the opportunity for the students to practice the required problem types and their variations. The homework is reviewed in class the following week, during which the instructor provides feedback and correctives based on his or her knowledge and experience.

Outcomes assessment in various forms is applied, including some combination of quizzes, midterm and final exams, projects, papers, and presentations.

In week nine of the 10-week term, all classes are evaluated by the students. They are asked to evaluate the instructor, the course, the administrative support, and the accomplishment of course objectives.

The new instructional process builds on this infrastructure through the introduction of additional feedback and correctives, to help students and faculty better understand what is expected of them, how they are doing, and how to get from where they are to where they need to be. The theory and methodology for doing this in individual classrooms already exists, and is known as *mastery learning*.

Mastery Learning in Individual Classrooms

Mastery learning was developed by Benjamin Bloom at the University of Chicago in the 1960s and has been applied by his students and many others in the following years.[3] In essence, mastery learning focuses on providing feedback and correctives to students in individual classrooms to bring the majority of the students up to a predetermined standard. In general, students, faculty, and researchers report that mastery learning, appropriately applied, results in increased learning, more positive feelings, about the school and about one's self as a learner, and improved retention.

Although mastery learning was developed independently of total quality, it is entirely consistent with total quality. In fact, mastery learning provides an excellent example of total quality applied to individual classrooms. Both mastery learning and total quality are grounded in Shewhart's plan-do-check-act cycle, which itself is based on the work of the educational philosopher John Dewey.[4] In the present context of teaching and learning, the course objectives and the instructor's lesson plans reflect the "plan." The instruction and homework provide the "do." The homework review and the quizzes and answer keys are the "check." The students' and teachers' efforts to correct the deficiencies and improve their respective learning and teaching, so as to prevent problems in the future, are the "act."

In 1991, two Keller faculty members began experimenting with mastery learning in their statistics classes. Based on their positive experiences, three additional instructors, two in accounting and one in economics, adopted the mastery learning approach in their classes. All five instructors have experienced directly both the positive results and the administrative difficulties described in the literature; these will be discussed later.

Keller's Variant of Mastery Learning

There are many acceptable variations of mastery learning, all centered around feedback and correctives. The two initial instructors developed the following variant at Keller. The first night of class, students are informed that they are not in competition with each other for grades: all can earn an A, and all are encouraged to work cooperatively. From cooperative work, both givers and receivers of help will derive great benefits that will help them in the workplace, where the ability to continuously teach and learn with others is increasingly critical.

The previously used midterm exam has been replaced by four quizzes, each lasting 45–60 minutes of a class that meets for 3½ hours once a week. The four quizzes together take no more in total time than the midterm exam. (Instructors in other courses have settled on three quizzes as more appropriate for the content of their courses.) One instructor uses quizzes in weeks 2, 4, 6, 8, in a 10-week term, and the other instructor prefers weeks 3, 5, 7, 9. (Of course, each instructor is convinced of having the better method.)

Prior to a quiz, both instructors demonstrate specific examples of a problem type and the variations that occur. They assign homework that allows the students to practice on problems of this type and its variations. The instructors review in class the homework undertaken by the students, and they supply feedback and correctives to the students.

On the night of the quiz, the homework is reviewed prior to the quiz. (Other instructors prefer a week's lag between the homework review and the quiz.) As each student finishes his or her quiz and turns it in, the instructor hands the student a copy of the quiz with the stepwise solutions. This simple device was introduced by one instructor, Arunas Dagys, and has been so positively received by the students that all faculty employing mastery learning have adopted it. With the answer keys in hand, the students are actively and cooperatively analyzing their mistakes in the hall outside the classroom, which fosters collaborative learning.

Class resumes five minutes after the stated time limit of the quiz, and the instructor asks for and answers any questions about the quiz, although generally there are very few remaining questions.

Students now have the opportunity to retest on the quiz. Each student is entitled to one retest on each quiz. The highest grade earned is the grade recorded for the quiz. This opportunity encourages students to continuously improve. Retests are done Friday evenings at the school from 6:30–7:30 P.M., when no other classes are scheduled.

For any given quiz, there are two administrations of the retest, using parallel forms of the quiz. The first retest is the Friday evening of the week the quiz was first administered. At this point the quizzes have not been graded, but, because of the provision of the answer key, students have a good idea of how they did. The second retest is scheduled the Friday evening of the following week, after the graded quizzes have been returned by the instructor. The Friday evening retests are proctored by the school and expressed to the instructor's home or work, whichever is preferable to the instructor, and are graded by the instructor prior to the next class.

Students who miss the in-class quiz may take both of the Friday evening quizzes, but students who miss the class quiz and a make-up quiz have only one opportunity and no retest. The few students who are in this situation are offered the prior quizzes and solutions for additional study support. (At the first meeting of the class, it is explained to the students that in order to make the retesting option available to the class, certain limits have to be set on the retest option. In general, the students have been very understanding of these limits on the retesting.)

In a further experiment to reduce the rework of retests, several instructors are now including a parallel practice quiz and answer key as a part of the homework. The taking of the practice quiz is voluntary, but most students report liking it as a simulation of the actual quiz they will take in class. It has resulted in a reduction in the number of retests.

The final exam is comprehensive, covering the content of the entire course. The first night of class the students are told that the quizzes will not necessarily include all of the content that will be covered on the final exam, but that everything included on the final will have been demonstrated in class with homework and homework review. There is no retest option on the final exam, and this is explained at the first class meeting; it is presented as a system constraint. The instructor who uses practice quizzes, however, is also experimenting with a practice final exam, which the students can take at home, and which is a part of the review in week 9 for the final exam in week 10. This has also been very well received.

The instructors are paid an additional 15 percent per course (approximately $250) for the extra time spent grading retests. The additional compensation is in no way tied to student grades at the end of the term or to student retention.

Instructors using mastery learning have found that about one-third of the students retest on any given quiz, which includes students performing at all levels, including A–, on the first testing of a given quiz.

Reactions of Students and Faculty to Mastery Learning

The process just described is the variant of mastery learning now being applied in core courses in statistics, accounting, and economics at Keller Graduate School. What are the results? In Figure 1, we show the form used each term to gather student feedback on their mastery learning experience. The students, in general, have responded very favorably. Here are some representative positive comments. "Takes a lot of stress out of exams . . . provides immediate feedback on learning . . . ability to learn from mistakes . . . helps focus on important concepts . . . concepts learned are retained better . . . it encourages learning rather than competition . . . helps as we juggle school, work, and home . . . as a student coming back from a 10-year break from undergrad school, it has helped me regain my confidence . . . I have had to be out of town and this approach has allowed me to catch up."

Negative student reactions are very much in the minority, but they include the following representative comments. "If there's competition between students for grades, or because the instructor curves the class grades, the student who takes it a second time receives an advantage over the student who does well on the first quiz . . . people tend to 'relax' on the first attempt on a quiz, because they have a second chance . . . too easy to fall behind in current assignments while studying weaknesses in attempt to retake quiz . . . even though we can retake quizzes, final accounts for 45 percent of grade and we cannot retake the final . . . the instructor must be in tune to this approach, this instructor was great in understanding student questions and anxiety and making students feel good about themselves, not all instructors may be able to do this."

What do the faculty, all of whom are experienced teachers, think about mastery learning? Faculty using mastery learning are asked to fill out a variant of the student feedback form. On the positive side, here are some representative comments. "It pushes the students to stay on pace . . . it gives them some flexibility, and lots of feedback at regular intervals . . . bottom line, student achievement is clearly better with this method . . . they work harder and they like it . . . eliminates quiz anxiety . . . I knew who cared and who didn't . . . lets the student try to continuously improve if

End of Term Evaluation

As you know, the school is in the process of evaluating mastery learning as a way of better serving working adult students. This approach is based on feedback and correctives, which are intended to help both the student and the faculty continuously improve. We would very much appreciate your input.

I. For each of the following variables, please mark the *single rating* that most closely summarizes your evaluation.

	Excellent	Good	Fair	Poor
Use of quizzes	☐	☐	☐	☐
Provision of answer keys	☐	☐	☐	☐
Opportunity to retest	☐	☐	☐	☐
Overall mastery learning rating	☐	☐	☐	☐

II. What do you feel are the strengths and weaknesses of the mastery learning approach?

III. One of the purposes of mastery learning is to enable working adult students to continue in school and be successful by providing feedback, correctives, and flexibility in meeting course objectives. To what extent is this true for you, and why?

IV. We are considering expanding the mastery learning approach to include all core courses. What do you think of this idea, and why?

V. After this course, I will have completed _____ courses at Keller Graduate School.

Figure 1. Keller Graduate School of Management mastery learning approach.

he or she wishes to put out the additional effort . . . we've given them a pathway for success, a 'road map' if you will."

On the negative side, the faculty expressed the following kinds of feelings. "In a large class situation, the retest grading could put a burden on the instructor . . . there is a significant increase in time spent in grading and in the preparation of exams and solutions (this varied from 30 percent to 100 percent) . . . the creation of multiple quizzes caused anxiety (in the faculty member) and schedule juggling (to get all the quizzes prepared)."

In terms of performance, the instructors all felt that the learning and achievement of the students were higher under mastery learning than under the traditional format, with which all had extensive experience. For example, one instructor who has used mastery learning in seven sections calculated the students' grades with and without the retest option. Without the retest option, the mean grade of the students was 3.23 (on a four-point scale in which A = 4.0). With the retest option, the mean grade of the students was 3.49. Since the retests used items that were parallel but not identical, the instructor believes the increase in the mean reflects increased student learning.

As widely reported in the literature, under mastery learning the distribution of student performance shifts to the high end with a concomitant reduction in variability among the students.[5] All the instructors commented that the students overwhelmingly liked the approach. The central issue for the faculty was the additional time demand on them due to the preparation of quizzes and answer keys and the grading of retests. These faculty comments, both positive and negative, are consistent with those of many other faculty who have used mastery learning over the past 30 years.

The TQM Challenge: Distributing the Benefits of Mastery Learning Across Multiple Sections, Courses, and Locations

The experience of the two initial instructors and the reactions of their students were so positive that a team of three administrator-teachers was constituted to think through the challenge and the opportunity of applying mastery learning to multiple sections, courses, and schools. The major focus of the team was on using mastery learning to improve retention. The challenge was to figure out why mastery learning has not worked in other schools when attempts have been made to extend it beyond individual classrooms and to design and implement a new and more effective instructional process.

The Crux of the Problem: Overloading of Teachers and Staff, and a Lack of System Supports

The team examined data and input from Keller students, faculty, administrative staff, and senior management, as well as faculty from other schools where attempts had been made to widely deploy mastery learning.

Clearly, a major barrier was the generation of multiple quizzes and answer keys. Keller had been very fortunate in the statistics class because one of the instructors had developed a fairly deep item pool that he was willing to share. Other instructors in other courses did not have the depth of items needed. Textbooks and publisher-supplied text banks have nowhere near the number of parallel items needed, namely, a minimum of 15 parallel problems for each problem type. This number is based on the sense of experienced faculty of the number of items needed to "break the float" of quizzes circulating among students.

Moreover, even with the availability of items, the production and management of the quizzes and retests presents a real challenge. For example, in the statistics class, we needed four alternate forms for each quiz (the pretest, the in-class quiz, and two make-up quizzes) times four quizzes, times two formats (to provide both a quiz and an answer key). There are, therefore, $4 \times 4 \times 2 = 32$ discrete documents to be generated and managed for the quizzes, plus the final exam and an alternate final exam for regular make-ups, with answer keys ($2 \times 2 = 4$), for a total of $32 + 4 = 36$ discrete documents, for one section of one course.

Add to this volume of documents the burden and expense to the school of duplicating the quizzes in appropriate numbers, proctoring the make-up quizzes, getting the make-up quizzes to the faculty in a timely manner, and having the faculty grade them in time for the next class: there is a major problem. Small wonder that attempts to implement mastery learning across multiple sections, courses, and schools have failed.

A Strategic Opportunity for Schools

Herein lies a central and strategic challenge for schools (and, we believe, for American industry, which faces the same problem in the training of its workforce). Students (and workers) want and need feedback and correctives in order to accomplish objectives and to feel good about their own learning and the learning environment. But providing the feedback and correctives on a systemwide basis is a complex and difficult activity. It requires that management assume its appropriate responsibility for creating and sustaining the climate, culture, and specifics of feedback and correctives.

Management's failure to provide leadership in this vital area creates such a burden on individual teachers and students that, except for isolated pockets of teachers and students, inaction engulfs the school. The result is that students don't learn as much as they can and need to, teachers don't get the results they need and want, and employers and society don't get the motivated, trained, and constantly improving workforce that they require. Teaching and learning continues as usual, and students don't know what is expected of them, don't know how they are doing, and don't know how to get from where they are to where they are expected to be.

In confronting this strategic challenge, the team concluded that releasing the enormous potential of mastery learning required a total quality approach that focused on management's responsibility for the system. As Juran, Deming, and many others have pointed out, 85 percent to 95 percent of problems in quality and productivity are due to the system, which is the responsibility of management. With this in mind, the team hypothesized that mastery learning may fail in systemwide implementations because of a failure of management to assume its responsibility for leadership and operational support of the system.

In short, administrators may have to give faculty the responsibility for implementing mastery learning. Where individual faculty were sufficiently motivated to create the needed infrastructure, there were successes. But most faculty didn't have the same commitment and had other pressures on their time. For them, the directive from the top to implement mastery learning, without the needed support, only led to overwhelming paperwork, increasing frustration, and, ultimately, to the rejection of this very promising educational innovation.

With this hypothesis in mind, the team analyzed the system requirements and came to the following conclusions about the responsibility of educational management.

• It clearly seemed a system responsibility to develop the item pools that would be the basis for the feedback and correctives. Faculty needed to be involved, but the burden should not be thrown onto them, as has happened in other attempts to introduce mastery learning in a school. Faculty contributions to the item banks needed to be collegial, and, where substantial incremental time was involved, compensated for. The greatest value from faculty involvement would come in the opportunity to use the item pool as a basis for faculty discussions of the course objectives and the operationalizing of those objectives in the items used to assess their accomplishment. The school, in other words, the system, needed to provide the resources to define the needed problem types, develop items and stepwise solutions, with a minimum of 15 parallel problems for each problem type, load them into a database, edit the items and solutions, and manage the item bank over time.

• The team concluded that there was a need for software that would reduce the drudgery of quiz and answer key generation, and that the creation and support of this software was a system responsibility. From our teaching experience we knew that exam construction is a highly repetitive process, which is very time-consuming and prone to error. The software needed the capability to generate questions, step-wise solutions, and cover sheets. Moreover, the software had to be responsive to the needs of individual faculty to set their own unique requirements for points (open or closed book and notes, time, calculator use, and handouts). Perhaps most importantly, the software had to enable faculty and secretaries to easily add, change, or delete parts of items to meet the needs of individual faculty.

• The team did a Pareto analysis of student attrition and determined that approximately 80 percent of the attrition occurred in 20 percent, or 11, of the courses in the curriculum. In addition, the 20 percent of courses, because they are core courses, account for approximately 60 percent of all the sections offered. Further, the 11 courses divide almost evenly between quantitative, or problem-based, and qualitative courses. Mastery learning applies equally to both kinds of courses, but the team decided to work initially with the six quantitative courses in part because there are greater numbers of items already available from which to draw, and in part because the quantitative courses are often perceived to be the more difficult by students.

• There had to be a process for tightly managing the production and flow of quizzes, from the faculty member's selection of items to quiz creation, duplication, storage, and delivery on the appropriate evening to the make-up exam proctor and the faculty member.

• There needed to be an operations handbook that would provide guidelines for staff and faculty at the centers. The handbook would spell out the responsibilities for each person involved, including the students, faculty, secretary, center administrator, proctor, and curriculum manager (who would be managing the item pool).

• The implementation should be staged. The first step would be the shift from a midterm exam to quizzes without retests. This would require current faculty to adjust their syllabi and would take some time. Since student data indicated that the students prefer quizzes, this seemed like a reasonable step. Once the transition to quizzes was in place, the next step would involve the use of the item bank and the software to generate quizzes and answer keys. Finally, it would then be a relatively small step to incorporate the use of retests.

• The school needed to compensate the faculty for their additional time spent in contributing to the item pools and grading retests. Also, additional clerical support would be needed at the center, so as not to overload the center secretary.

The team concluded that, although there was complexity in this interrelated set of demands, they were facing a well-defined problem that was amenable to solution. Moreover, the team judged that any school (or company) that managed to design and implement the new instructional process would not only release the enormous potential of increased student/worker productivity and satisfaction, but would also have a competitive advantage. This advantage would be gained because, although the underlying logic of feedback and correctives is easy to understand, institutions of higher education (and most companies) are not well organized to undertake such cooperative efforts among faculty, students, and administrators.

The Economics of Improvements in Retention

We need to consider the economics of improvements in retention and the role that quality plays. Deming is especially cogent on the interrelationships of quality, productivity, and competitive position. As applied to retention, the argument is that retaining students through the quality of the education and supporting services—including the maintenance of academic standards to protect students' long-term investment—leads to increased revenue for the school; happier students, faculty, and staff; and greater usefulness to employers and society as a whole.

This reasoning is plausible, even compelling, to those directly involved in quality. Juran has pointed out that money is the language of top management and that managers interested in quality have a responsibility to translate opportunities for quality improvements into their dollar impact on the organization, both short-term and long-term. The present discussion will be limited to introducing a few of the possibilities and elements for consideration.

Historically, Keller Graduate School has a graduation rate of 36 percent. This is typical of programs serving working adults. It reflects the difficulty of balancing work, family, and school. Those of us who have been working adult students or who have had the pleasure of teaching them, marvel at the courage and determination that makes working adults able to successfully complete a program in higher education.

Faculty with substantial experience teaching the core courses believe that 85 percent to 90 percent of admitted students are capable of meeting the demands of individual courses and the overall program. This leaves a very large and enticing gap between the 85 percent to 90 percent of admitted students who are capable of graduating and the 36 percent who are actually graduating.

Consider further the school's historical experience.

- Students who drop out of the program complete, on average, four courses.

- Approximately 80 percent of the attrition occurs in the first eight courses. That is, if students successfully complete the first eight courses, the probability that they will go on to complete their degrees (requiring a total of 13–16 courses, depending on the program) is four times larger than the probability that entering students will complete the first eight courses.

Here is a brief exploration of the possibilities for translating this opportunity into dollars. Readers—especially readers who are administrators—will readily develop other ways of figuring the economic potential in increasing retention.

- Approximately 2000 new students are admitted to Keller Graduate School each year. To simplify the arithmetic, we shall assume that all students take 16 courses to graduate because the largest program takes 16 courses. With a 36 percent graduation rate, this means that $.36 \times 2000 = 720$ students take 16 courses and graduate. The remaining $2000 - 720 = 1280$ students do not graduate. They take, on average, four courses before dropping out. With tuition of approximately $1000 per course, if each of the 1280 students took on average one more course, the increased revenue to the school would be $1280 \times 1000 = \$1,280,000$ for each year's cohort of new students.

- Another way of viewing the economic potential of increasing retention is to hypothesize an increase in the graduation rate, say 10 percent. If Keller's graduation rate increased from 36 percent to 46 percent, the number graduating from each year's cohort of new students would rise from $2000 \times .36 = 720$ to $2000 \times .46 = 920$, for an increase of 200 students graduating. Since students dropping out complete on average four courses, and students graduating complete 16 courses, each additional student graduating adds 12 additional courses. In terms of revenue, 200 additional students $\times$ 12 additional courses each $\times$ $1000 per course $= \$2,400,000$ in additional revenue for each year's cohort of new students.

As we will see, the costs are relatively low and the benefits of even modest improvements in retention are fairly sizable and certainly interesting in a time when budgets in higher education are under severe pressure.

The team prepared a proposal for the president and dean, including the elements just discussed, that focused on a pilot project to be conducted at one center (each developed Keller center has between 150 and 300 students).

Included in the proposal were the following cost considerations. Instructors using mastery learning are paid an additional $250 per section to compensate them for the additional time spent grading retests.

- $250 $\times$ 6 courses targeted for mastery learning $= \$1500$ per center per term

- + $1800 per center per term for additional administrative support, including proctors, overnight mailing charges, and additional clerical support = $3300 per center per term

- × 5 terms per year = $16,500 per center per year

In addition to these costs, the team estimated that the software would cost $4000 to create, and the six item banks would cost approximately $5000 each, for a total of $30,000, to create and load them into the computer. Although this is a substantial sum of money, once the software and item banks are developed, they can be used at all 17 centers.

Approval of the Pilot Project

The president and the dean were cautiously supportive. They agreed that the proposed new approach has potential for improving student performance, satisfaction, and retention, and for these reasons they approved the funds for the pilot. But they also made it clear that the school has other priorities, namely, maintaining current levels of productivity and continuing current improvement initiatives in cost containment, marketing, facility expansion, and academic quality.

They also specified four requirements for the pilot project.

- The team needed to demonstrate that the new instructional process actually improves retention significantly and substantially.

- The team had to ensure that academic standards and student performance are not compromised.

- The team had to satisfy local administrators (center directors and directors of operations) that the new process can be effectively implemented at the center level with no disruption of ongoing operations. A corollary of this requirement was that the new instructional process had to be robust enough that any faculty member or administrator could successfully implement it, with appropriate training, which the team would be responsible for incorporating into the process.

- The team needed to accomplish all of this without any team member jeopardizing any other responsibilities, all of which are viewed as critical to the overall success of the school.

The team was pleased with the response to the proposal and has been working for the past year to accomplish the objectives of the pilot project. The optimism of the team was grounded in the positive feedback term by term from the students and the faculty, confidence in the team's analysis of past failures in implementing mastery learning in a system, and the simplicity of the proposed design for the new instructional process. The team also had a number of anxieties.

- They knew there was substantial resistance among some of the staff. Some felt the proposed approach would make things too easy for students and that retesting would diminish the reputation of the school. Others felt that the new instructional process would be an administrative nightmare, that it would be impossible to get faculty cooperation, or that the new process could only be done by exceptional teachers.

- The development of software and the building of item banks, with a minimum of 15 parallel problems and stepwise solutions all keyed to course objectives, were daunting tasks.

- The team members feared that they would not have enough time to meet the demands of their regular assignments and do justice to the pilot project.

We now describe developments over the past year, and the outlook on remaining challenges.

The Present Level of Implementation

At present, the pilot is running at one center with four courses, plus selected statistics sections at other centers. At the one center, the following sections are using mastery learning: applied managerial statistics, principles of accounting and finance, managerial accounting, and business economics.

In each of these courses, item development and quiz construction are being done by the individual instructor, with support from the center staff. The item banks and software, to be described, are not yet in use. Retests are being employed in all sections, and the faculty are being compensated an additional 15 percent for their added grading. For the entire center, the four courses require approximately 110 discrete documents to prepare and manage each term.

Very tight procedural controls have been put in place and are working well. The center secretary has a spreadsheet that lists all courses, whether or not they are using mastery learning, and, if so, on what night of what weeks the quizzes are being offered. She uses the spreadsheet to control the preparation, copying, storing, and distribution of the quizzes and answer keys. For the Friday night retests, the proctor has been trained on the needed procedures for managing different time requirements and other individual specifications by individual faculty. Also, the proctor takes responsibility for overnight mailing the retest quizzes to the faculty at work or home. The faculty have responsibility for grading the retests by the next class meeting. Overall, the pilot has demonstrated that the process of using mastery learning in multiple sections can be well defined and managed effectively.

The drawbacks are that the preparation of quizzes and answer keys is still very laborious, and the faculty still have limited sources of items from which to draw for the quizzes and retests.

The positive reactions of the students were presented earlier, and they are significant. Each term the students tell us how much they like and appreciate the increased feedback and correctives. But the effort, even with four courses, is enormous and the prospect of adding additional courses at the one center, or trying to get faculty and staff at another of the 17 centers, let alone all of them, to undertake the same challenge is intimidating and risky. This is what makes the additional system supports of item banks and software so appealing, and necessary, if the potential in mastery learning is to be made available more broadly. The substantial progress being made in the development of these capabilities will be described.

Before doing so, however, we will present the limited data that are presently available for assessing the impact of mastery learning.

Assessing the Impact of Mastery Learning

We began tracking outcomes from the September 1992 term (Keller has five 10-week terms per year—September, November, February, April, and June). For each term, starting with the September 1992 term, we developed a cohort of all new students who started in that term. To date, we have accumulated data for four cohorts, including 1136 new students who started in the September 1992, November 1992, February 1993, and April 1993 terms. For these students, we divided them into two groups, mastery learning students and non–mastery learning students, and we tracked their retention in the program through four courses.

Of the 1136 starting students, 1056 completed the first course and 80 did not complete the first course, for an attrition of 7 percent. Of the 1136 starting students, 856 completed a second course and 280 did not complete a second course, for an attrition of 24.6 percent. From the original group, 750 completed a third course, and 665 completed a fourth course, for attrition levels of 34 percent and 41.5 percent respectively.

We then repeated this analysis for the mastery learning students versus the non–mastery learning students. A mastery learning student was defined as a student who had one or more courses using the mastery learning approach. In the first course, if the course was taught using the mastery learning approach, the student was considered a mastery learning student, whether or not the student finished the course.

The data are provided in Table 1. At the level of four courses completed, it shows that the mastery learning students' attrition was 18.8 percent, compared to attrition of 46.1 percent for the non–mastery learning students.

Although the team is obviously pleased with the data, team members are treating them cautiously. Clearly, we need to continue the analyses over more time. Also, this is not a true experiment in that students self-selected which center to attend and which course to take. There may be a halo effect with a new approach that won't hold up over time. The observed differences may be a function of particularly dedicated faculty using the mastery learning approach. Or, the mastery learning students may have a lower level of attrition for a reason not related to the treatment. And so on. The critical point is that the basic data, from the team's perspective, are the consistent positive feedback from the students term after term and the conviction of the faculty that the students learn more under mastery learning. These data are congruent with this perspective, and our analyses of the data, from various perspectives and over time, will continue.

Finally, the full implementation of the pilot project is not yet complete, since the critical components of the item banks and the software have not been fully integrated. It is to these elements of the project that we turn next.

Item Banks

The creation, editing, testing, maintaining, and changing of an item bank is a major undertaking. It should not be entered into lightly. On the other hand, as we hope the earlier discussion indicates, there are enormous potential benefits to be derived. What is so intriguing about the item banks is the simple recognition of the obvious: we teach the same basic courses over and over and over. By carefully specifying and operationalizing the outcomes in a bank of items and answer keys, we open up opportunities for continuous process improvement through sharing among faculty, students, and administrators. This apparently simple observation is a cornerstone of total quality: mutually agreed-upon data and operational definitions are essential to make quality happen in an organization.

The development of the item banks begins with the course objectives, which are operationalized in the questions and answers used to measure their accomplishment. The answers in particular reflect what it is that we as teachers want the students to be able to do. Each course objective will have one or more problem types associated with it, reflecting both distinctive ways of measuring an objective and distinctive competencies within an objective.

The new instructional process requires a minimum of 15 parallel problems, with solutions, for each problem type. It should be noted that the item banks do not

Table 1. Attrition data from mastery learning pilot.

Number of courses completed	Number of students completing the designated number of courses	Number of students not completing the designated number of courses	Cumulative percent of students not completing the designated number of courses	Number of ML students completing the designated number of courses	Number of ML students not completing the designated number of courses	Cumulative percent of ML students not completing the designated number of courses	Number of non-ML students completing the designated number of courses	Number of non-ML students not completing the designated number of courses	Cumulative percent of non-ML students not completing the designated number of courses
1	1056	80	7.0%	60	0	0.0%	996	80	7.4%
2	856	280	24.6%	116	10	7.9%	740	270	26.7%
3	750	386	34.0%	141	18	11.3%	609	368	37.7%
4	665	471	41.5%	156	36	18.8%	509	435	46.1%

• Combined cohorts September 1992, November 1992, February 1993, and April 1993.
• Number of new students starting = 1136.

use multiple choice items but, rather, problems and stepwise solutions. Since the individual items are mixed and matched for individual quizzes, 15 parallel items for each problem type make possible a large number of unique quizzes. Any student who goes to the trouble to collect all 15 variations and memorize them is likely to either know the material, or will find it easier to learn the material than just memorize the answers.

Each of the six targeted courses has approximately 20 problem types, and therefore each of the six item banks will require a minimum of $20 \times 15 = 300$ items with answers. Over time, we expect to continue to broaden the item banks, as other faculty contribute new problem types, and to deepen them, as other faculty contribute items of their own. Each of the items is coded by objective, by problem type within objective, and by parallel item within a problem type.

The problem types were defined by the curriculum manager and two or three senior faculty with specific examples of each problem and its solution. Once this was accomplished, the critical question was how were we going to get the depth of items required. At present, all six item banks are under development and four different, but overlapping, approaches are being used to develop the items.

• *Individual faculty members share their items.* In the statistics class, as described earlier, we had the benefit of an individual faculty member's hard work and generosity. Another statistics teacher helped by adding a few items where the pool was a little thin.

• *A team of faculty works together to develop an item bank.* In the managerial accounting course three senior faculty members, one of whom is also the director of curriculum, met weekly over a period of three months to talk about the items and then create them along with the solutions.

• *A publisher is investing in a long-term relationship with the school.* Following Deming's advice to reduce the number of suppliers and develop long-term relationships, two years ago Keller Graduate School entered into discussion and, subsequently, an informal agreement to develop a new kind of relationship between a school and a publisher.

We agreed to use the publisher's texts in the core courses wherever the publisher had a functionally equivalent text. The definition of functionally equivalent was left entirely up to the school. Although not all core course texts are being purchased from the one publisher, we went from one adoption to five, which are used across all 17 Keller centers. This represents approximately $200,000 in additional business per year for the publisher. In return, Keller wanted an improved discount, increased cooperation between the publisher's writers and editors and Keller's faculty and curriculum managers, and, most germane to the present discussion, we wanted its support in the development of item banks and software.

It turned out that it was too costly for the publisher to modify its software to meet our requirements. The publisher has, however, been very forthcoming in providing assistance in the development of the item banks for economics, foundations of managerial mathematics, and principles of accounting and finance.

• *Another publisher works with us around a single text.* A variant of the previous arrangement, in the managerial finance course where there was not a functionally equivalent text, is underway with another publisher. In this case, a Keller senior faculty member is defining the problem types and identifying appropriate items from the test banks of five texts published by the publisher. Once the problems have been identified, the publisher has committed to developing the stepwise solutions and loading questions and solutions into WordPerfect, which the school needs for its software. Moreover, the publisher has committed to developing additional items to bring the database up to the needed depth of 15 items for each problem type.

The six targeted courses are at the following stages of development.

Course	Percent completed
Statistics	90
Math foundations	90
Principles of accounting and finance	90
Economics	90
Managerial accounting	75
Managerial finance	50

We anticipate completion of all six item banks by November 1994. Once the items and solutions are edited and loaded, we will open them up for faculty discussion. This will inevitably lead to further adjustments before the item banks are ready for distribution to the centers. The use of the item banks will also depend on the availability of software for the generation of quizzes.

Software Development

Software is necessary for accessing, arranging, formatting, and printing items in the bank. We designed the software and then contracted with Nick Barbatano, a gifted software consultant with whom the school has a long-term relationship, to develop it for us. It is built on a WordPerfect platform and essentially it is a macro attached to WordPerfect, which accesses the word processing files that contain the items and solutions. The items and solutions are coded with what are called *tokens*, which the macro uses for accessing and assembling the items into quizzes. In addition, the software includes a user interface, which is a screen that walks the user through the entering of the information needed to identify the particular course, instructor, center, and specific requirements of the instructor. The items can be generated by random selection or by specifying individual problems, depending on the wishes of the faculty.

The software has been developed and tested, and it is everything we hoped for. It is very easy to use, and it generates quizzes within WordPerfect, which makes it easy to modify and tailor any particular quiz to meet the needs of individual instructors. Quizzes and answer keys have their own cover sheets, and the answer keys include the questions. As simple as it sounds, everyone who has seen a demonstration of the software working in conjunction with an item bank who has been involved in the production of quizzes and exams in a school setting, including faculty, secretaries, and center administrators, is awed by the production within five minutes of four alternate and parallel quizzes, with their respective answer keys, cover sheets, and labels for the packets of duplicated quizzes.

Next Steps in Implementing System-Supported Teaching and Learning

Our present plan calls for a two-pronged implementation strategy. As the item banks are finished, we will implement them at the pilot center, and we will bring to six the number of courses using mastery learning at the pilot center. In addition, we will select one of the courses for implementation at all 17 centers. In preparation for this systemwide implementation, we are taking several critical steps.

• Before using the item banks or mastery learning, it is necessary that the faculty convert from a midterm examination to quizzes. Since quizzes are much preferred by students, this transition is well underway already.

• Once this is accomplished, the software with the selected item bank will be installed at all centers, and the staff will be trained in the use of the software and the procedures developed at the test center for the implementation of mastery learning.

• Once a center has been checked out, the adoption of additional item banks will depend on the readiness of the center staff and faculty to take them on. We do not anticipate great difficulties at this stage, because faculty and staff who have seen the software and item banks used to generate quizzes and answer keys see them as making their work easier. They have been eager to have them available as soon as possible.

• The final step is the inclusion of retests. With the above groundwork, this will be a relatively small step, but it will require careful training and support of faculty and center staff, as has been done at the pilot center. Once the six item banks for the problem-based courses are completed, we will begin work on the following components of the overall plan.

• Development of the qualitative courses will begin. Conceptually this has already begun, and our discussions with faculty and curriculum managers suggest that feedback and correctives, which are at the heart of mastery learning, can best be incorporated through class projects and team exercises. For example, in the marketing course, the integrating activity of the course is a marketing plan, which can be submitted in stages. The students would benefit from feedback and correctives from the instructor.

• We plan to deepen the feedback and correctives provided by the answer keys by designing more instruction into them. At present we are focused on providing stepwise solutions. But we envisage additional improvements to this in the form of expanded explanations, direct access via computers for students to retests, references to the text pages where the content is discussed and examples are provided, and references to videos of superior teachers demonstrating the particular problem type.

Quality and the Convergence of Interrelated Problems and Solutions

One of the most powerful dimensions of total quality is the recognition that improvements in quality tend to solve multiple problems. Improved quality reduces scrap and rework; which increases productivity and competitive position; which frees resources for price cutting, added features, research and development, or some combination thereof; which leads to happier customers, who spread the word, and happier workers, who have less absenteeism and turnover.

In education the same dynamic is at work. System-supported teaching and learning increases student performance, satisfaction, and retention, which creates increased faculty satisfaction and student referrals to potential students, and facilitates outcomes assessment and new faculty training. System-supported teaching also stimulates discussion among faculty around course and program objectives. The increased revenue to schools can be used for increased faculty compensation, reductions in tuition, additional services for students, research and development, or some combination thereof.

Conclusion

Keller Graduate School has formulated and is in the process of implementing a new instructional process that combines total quality and mastery learning to provide system supports for teaching and learning to improve student performance, satisfaction, and retention. The classroom has long been held to be the private preserve of individual faculty, free to play out their brilliance or mediocrity without interference or support from the outside. One of the unpleasant secrets of education at all levels has been the agreement, largely unspoken, between teachers and administrators that teachers will get no real support from the system and in return the system will not interfere with the individual teacher's control of his or her classroom. This is why, in our view, total quality has heretofore been applied to almost everything in the university except the classroom. Now the relationship between the classroom, the school, and the larger society is changing under the stimulus of larger social and economic forces.

Our greatest hope is that our work, and that of others working to apply total quality in the classroom, will contribute in some measure to the creation of conditions of true self-control for teachers. In such an environment, educational management will provide appropriate leadership in communicating objectives for teachers, providing feedback on how they are doing relative to the objectives, and ensuring that teachers have the resources they need to accomplish the objectives. Then, and only then, will teachers be able to assume the role of honor and dignity in our society that they so much deserve, but have been so long denied.

Notes

1. J. Juran and F. Gryna, *Quality Planning and Analysis* (New York: McGraw-Hill, 1980).

2. W. E. Deming, *Out of the Crisis* (Cambridge, Mass.: MIT Press, 1986).

3. B. Bloom, *Human Characteristics and School Learning* (New York: McGraw-Hill, 1976); B. Bloom, G. Madous, and J. Hastings, *Evaluation to Improve Learning* (New York: McGraw-Hill, 1981).

4. J. Dewey, *How We Think* (Boston: Heath, 1933).

5. T. Guskey, *Implementing Mastery Learning* (Belmont, Calif.: Wadsworth, 1985).

Incorporating Total Quality into a College of Business

Donald F. Parker, Professor of Management and
Sara Hart Kimball Dean of Business;
Daniel J. Brown, Associate Professor of Marketing;
and Dennis O. Kaldenberg, Research Associate;
College of Business, Oregon State University

Introduction

The purpose of this article is to provide a description of the infusion of total quality management through the administrative processes of an academic college and into the classroom and curriculum. The paper begins with a brief description of the conditions that preceded and led to change. It introduces some of the total quality initiatives carried out; discusses what the college has gained; and reviews lessons learned from both successes and failures. Finally, it identifies the work that remains to be completed.

Because each academic unit is a product of its history and organizational constraints, we do not presume that these efforts should be used as a blueprint for other colleges. We do hope, however, that something can be learned from examining the early stages of our total quality management experiment.

Setting the Stage

The College of Business at Oregon State University is part of a land, sea, and space grant university located in a medium-sized town 90 miles from the state's only metropolitan area. Accredited by the American Assembly of Collegiate Schools of Business (AACSB) at the undergraduate and MBA levels, the college offers both undergraduate degrees and the master of business administration. The undergraduate program is the largest offering. All undergraduate business students complete a nonbusiness minor; this is regarded as a strength by many employers. Compared to other accredited business schools, the college has a relatively small budget, which means fewer frills. Due to state and university constraints, the college exercises limited control over the selection of students compared to similar units in private universities.

Total quality management efforts in the college came about as part of a university-wide initiative. Total quality was first used in 1990 by the vice president for finance and administration to improve operations in the physical plant. Using this success as a springboard, numerous administrative units began to apply total quality principles. Ultimately, in an effort to diffuse the spirit of continuous improvement throughout the institution, the university president gave his endorsement and encouraged faculty and staff to learn and apply principles of total quality.

The introduction of total quality principles into the college occurred more recently. It was accelerated by fortuitous enablers and environmental demands. There were four enablers: strong support from the top management of the university; a new dean not invested in the status quo; assistance from industry in the form of financial resources, technical support, and training; and a core group of faculty eager to test the promise of total quality.

Environmental demands had a greater effect than the enablers. The first pressure originated with the college accrediting agency. In 1988, the AACSB significantly altered its accreditation standards for the first time in more than 30 years. The new standards emphasize the college mission and processes to a much greater extent than the preceding ones and, consequently, make total quality an almost ideal approach to satisfy accreditation expectations and to identify and eliminate deficiencies.

Other pressures were imposed within the state of Oregon. Faced with a dramatic decrease in state appropriations to higher education as a consequence of a statewide ballot initiative to reduce property taxes, the college was required to do more with fewer resources and ultimately had to provide justification for its continued existence.

Questioning the need for six publicly funded business programs during a budget crisis, senior officials in the state system of higher education suggested that each business program should develop a distinctive niche. The college leadership hoped that the effective use of total quality principles would not only reduce costs, but also provide the college with a competitive advantage to the extent that this approach was not duplicated in other state-supported business schools.

Finally, and perhaps most importantly, doubts expressed by the public about the cost and effectiveness of higher education increased the need to focus on stakeholder concerns. In this setting, what better management framework could an organization select than one designed specifically to delight customers?

Getting Started

If total quality is to take hold in higher education, faculty, staff, and administration must understand what it is and how it may be used. Therefore, one of the first steps in our implementation process was training, and in this regard, the college and the university benefited greatly from industry support. Companies that used total quality widely had a vested interest in bringing it to higher education because they see universities as suppliers of future managers and want graduates to understand total quality. Hewlett-Packard, Xerox, Motorola, and IBM sent trainers to educate faculty and administrators and an E & J Gallo Winery executive was the first to provide funding for activities designed to integrate total quality into the business curriculum.

Formal training began with an invitation from Hewlett-Packard to attend one of the company's internal 10-week total quality courses. The university president, some vice presidents, and three College of Business faculty participated in the program. Later, Hewlett-Packard offered two-day total quality seminars for business and engineering faculty on campus.

In the fall of 1992, all business faculty and a cross-section of engineering professors attended a two-day program presented by Xerox and Motorola. This seminar provided information on how total quality principles had been used to improve operations in these two organizations and at a number of universities with whom the firms had worked previously. One goal of the event was to provide faculty with a common quality framework and a shared vision for the future of the colleges. Most faculty found the training thought-provoking. Others viewed it as an attempt to undermine faculty autonomy or an administrative fiat. Some hostility resulted.

IBM created a national program to award grants of $1 million cash or $3 million in equipment to universities and colleges that could demonstrate that they were in a position to integrate total quality into their curricula and research. More than 200 universities applied, and in 1992 IBM notified Oregon State that the colleges of business and engineering would share one of the eight grants awarded. Trainers were sent to Oregon State to describe IBM's perspective on how to apply total quality principles, and Oregon State was teamed with an IBM facility for joint total quality learning and research.

What Is Total Quality in the College of Business?

Mentor companies demonstrated that total quality is different in every organization. We developed an approach based upon our definition of total quality, our choice of a customer, and our belief about the best way to improve the quality of our students' education. The following section briefly reviews our approach.

We view total quality as a general management philosophy that includes theory, principles, procedures, and tools. The theory comes from Deming, Juran, and other pioneers. Simply stated, the idea is that improved quality will satisfy customers and make organizations more successful. Although numerous principles are embedded in total quality, proponents in the college find the following to be particularly relevant to accomplishing our mission. They are loosely arranged in order of importance to the college.

- *Customer orientation.* A customer orientation requires us to behave as if we are here to serve customers. We focus on our customers' needs, and customer satisfaction drives our decisions. Mechanisms to gather specific customer information assist in decision making.

- *Participation/teams.* A team approach requires everyone involved in educating students—faculty, administrators, businesses, and students themselves—to participate. All team members need to understand how their work fits into the whole effort.

- *Continuous improvement.* The general idea is that organizations must unceasingly strive to become better and better. In the past we revised programs primarily through intuition, and we did not gather feedback. Thus, we were unable to ensure that an intervention actually brought lasting improvement.

- *Process orientation.* Total quality literature describes a process as a series of activities that lead to a result. Every process can be mapped, measured, and improved to produce desired results. However, a process can only be improved if it is understood. (The appendix is an example of a process that faculty recently created and improved.)

- *Data-based decisions.* In the past, the faculty made decisions based primarily on debate about academic theories regarding education. As a basis for decisions we now attempt to collect data systematically about customer needs.

- *Benchmarking.* It is useful to know how much improvement is possible. Data from the best business schools or businesses can provide one measure; time-lapse measures of internal progress supply another.

- *Support from the top.* Daniel Seymour and other experts postulate that total quality will never succeed without support from the top. For the college, this means that the dean must advocate and support total quality experimentation in teaching, research, and administration. From the beginning of his tenure, the dean has encouraged faculty members to experiment with total quality. Still, we believe that few, if any, faculty members would report that total quality has been imposed by the administration.

Total quality procedures include training, quality planning, design and redesign, and process improvement. As noted in the previous section, training is essential in getting faculty and successive classes of students to work as a coordinated team. Plans, perhaps in the form of a hoshin framework, address the organization and its market, product, and objectives. Design and redesign of quality educational programs are accomplished by process definition and improvement based on customer data. Unlike the past, however, we have no illusions that a particular improvement will make us as good as we can be; continuous improvement goes on indefinitely.

Total quality tools include specific techniques that aid in the improvement of quality. Statistical process control techniques such as Pareto charts would fall into this category, as would the house of quality matrix and affinity diagrams. We try to use these as a set of useful tools rather than as dogma.

Adopting a Customer Orientation

Historically, the college made instructional changes to satisfy the demands of the AACSB and the university administration or the interests of the faculty. We relied on our own academic training and our peers or responded to criticism and praise from particularly outspoken individuals. Until recently, we did not ask our students what their needs were or how satisfied they were with the education we provided. We had not even profiled them. We suspected that our student population had changed over the years, but we never accurately measured the changes or investigated how they affected the students' needs. As a result, our first customer research efforts were admittedly primitive.

In order to define educational objectives in terms of quality as perceived by customers, the college had to increase market research dramatically and had to confront very difficult issues. Some are broad: "What is quality education?" Others are very specific: "What educational outcomes do we need to measure and improve?" and "Who is our customer?" This was a definite change of direction for the college. One of our former students wrote a comment in response to a recent survey: "This is the first time in 30 years you have asked my opinion. During my undergraduate years I can tell you that Oregon State certainly did not view me as a customer."

Defining the Customer

For some, the implicit view that the academy exists for the faculty will die hard. We now recognize, however, that many groups have a stake in how well we develop students' talents. Critical incidents can make any one of the following groups seem more important than the others at a particular moment; however, the list reflects a more or less stable array.

- Students

- Employers

- Other colleges in the university

- Taxpayers

Our students are very important customers, and we are concerned about their satisfaction. However, we recognize that many of them when they enter the college, often in their late teens, do not have a good understanding of what is best for their professional preparation.

Gathering Customer Information

The college has used a number of methods to obtain customer input with each successive approach building on the others. Based on lessons learned from our total quality mentor organizations, we gathered data to answer four basic questions.

- What do our customers expect from us?

- How do they evaluate our performance?

- How well do they think we are doing?

- What suggestions do they have to help us to improve?

Basic research about business students began with a transcript analysis of the previous year's graduates. To determine who our students are and what they do, we collected data on entrance point (freshman, sophomore, and so on), entrance channel (high school, other colleges on campus, community colleges, and so on), and measures of the students' progress through the program (how many times they retake classes, how long their program takes, and so on).

We completed two surveys of former students. College alumni are familiar with the entire educational process, and, after a suitable time lapse, they are in a position to evaluate how well their education has served them in the business world. A telephone survey focused on recent graduates to determine their starting salaries, experiences when entering the job market, and, if applicable, their graduate school experience. A mail survey was sent to all College of Business alumni for whom we have a current address. Since the majority of our graduates seek employment in Oregon, we also conducted a small probability survey of manufacturers in the state.

Based on previous surveys, interested faculty designed a student exit survey using an innovative computer-based questionnaire program. Graduating MBAs and seniors, students with firsthand knowledge about our programs, were asked to answer the four customer expectation questions and to evaluate specific experiences in the college and the university and their own current skills and abilities, to provide sociodemographic data (age, sex, place of origin), and to indicate employment offers and aspirations.

The first focus groups were conducted by the accounting faculty. Twenty accountants, half from industry and half from the public sector were invited to participate. They were asked to give opinions about the skills, competencies, and experiences that graduates in accounting should possess. In addition they were asked to evaluate the extent to which deficiencies or duplication existed in the accounting curriculum based on information provided, such as a list of the courses accounting students take, the topics covered in each course, and the amount of time spent on each topic. Subsequent research collected data from three other groups: employers from companies with formal total quality programs, alumni, and businesses represented on the college advisory council.

Preliminary Findings

Although these studies left us awash in data, we have come to a number of generalizations about students and potential employers. Most undergraduates come from Oregon, many from small towns. The majority transfer into the college, many from community colleges. An increasing proportion is "older than average," and many have to work while attending school. Our primarily regional student market is mixed with international students. In the MBA program, their proportion, especially from Asian countries, is nearly 40 percent.

We found that measures of career success used by other universities may not apply to our students. Few of our recent graduates seek advanced degrees outside the state. Most domestic students go to work in Oregon, and as a result, about half take positions in companies with 500 or fewer employees.

Students rated the college highest on "how much you learned" and "quality of teaching." Lower ratings were given to "getting placed in jobs" and "exposure to the real world." Correlation analysis shows that former students' satisfaction with their college experience is associated with their subsequent experience in professional life. When students reflected on their skills, they generally gave themselves the highest grades for "ability to work in groups" and lower grades for "knowledge of total quality management."

To our dismay, many employers in Oregon have little awareness of, let alone opinions about, what we do in the college. They have a pragmatic view of the service they expect: "the role of the business school is to prepare students for the 'real world' so that they can obtain jobs in their chosen fields and achieve their professional goals."

Our customers in industry want the college to provide more than a traditional academic education. In addition to knowledge, communication, interpersonal, computer, problem-solving, and decision-making skills are important to them. Further, they want students to have "real-world" experience and practical career preparation. This last demand is a jarring one since the college had heretofore regarded the finding of a job as outside our zone of responsibility.

Although not all do, some companies want students to have total quality–related abilities, not necessarily theories, but basic skills such as the ability to work in groups and an understanding of how to approach messy problems.

Disseminating Customer Data

The data gathered have been reported to the faculty. Focused on data, faculty are beginning to ask deeper questions about customers. Because we want other potential team members (students, alumni, and other interested parties) to know that we are a total quality organization, we include highlights of our total quality activities in our alumni newsletter. We have been astonished by the responses from graduates who themselves have become total quality experts in various professions.

Specific Initiatives

At first many faculty felt that total quality was a good idea for someone else (in other words, the college administration) to use to improve support processes like the faculty expenditure approval process. After a while, faculty turned to improving processes over which they have control, like teaching and curriculum design.

In this section, we review specific total quality implementation examples in the college. Many changes are a direct result of the customer data we discussed previously. We have taken to heart the frequently stated maxim that we must "walk the talk" in order to achieve successful implementation of continuous improvement. To begin, we had to experiment with the best way to implement total quality in management education.

Classroom Experiments

One way to implement total quality is on a class-by-class basis. The faculty have taken two approaches in this direction. Some utilize a small quality team of students who function together for a term. The team gathers data from fellow student customers about problems relating to a particular aspect of the class. The group then analyzes the problem and, using total quality tools, designs an improvement plan. This approach was used in management, accounting, and business law.

Other faculty use surveys to define student needs, identify problems as perceived by students, and monitor satisfaction levels. Exploratory surveys typically employ open-ended questionnaires that ask customers to indicate their needs, expectations, evaluations, and suggestions for improvement. Answers are distilled and analyzed. Simple problems are resolved. Notions about deeper problems can be developed and explored further in future surveys. Later, these faculty employ questionnaires with fixed rating scales. Numerical trends are tracked by means of repeated measures during or between terms.

Experimenting with Curricula

Although classroom experiments provide interesting insights, the college's overall total quality objective is to enhance the quality of all business classes. This required us to look also at processes that extend beyond individual classes. First, we want to design a program that delivers a quality education and prepares graduates in terms of knowledge, skills, and attitudes, consistent with the needs of employers.

Second, we want to design a curriculum that guarantees a solid knowledge of basic total quality principles, skills (such as teamwork and decision making), and attitudes (such as customer orientation). Coordination among classes will ensure that there is sufficient total quality content in each business student's program and that every class does not repeat the same lessons. In the initial enthusiasm for total quality, the same videos popped up in many classes; students had to sit through them over and over.

Third, we want to teach by example, showing students that the college is a total quality organization, that their needs as customers are important, and that they are part of the management team. If we provide a quality education that uses total quality principles, we believe our students will be more likely to understand and internalize this approach to management.

Improving the accounting curriculum. The first curriculum review was completed by the accounting team. In addition to examining the content of the three courses that serve as an introduction to accounting for all business students and the basis for all other courses for future accountants, the team studied its delivery. The group constructed an activity inventory that identified the number and types of papers, projects, presentations, case discussions, and computer assignments in the program. A number of changes resulted from customer input and total faculty involvement.

- The accounting faculty agreed to spend more time on certain topics and less on others.

- Activities were modified to create a balance of experiences for program participants.

- The faculty created an integrated project set that carries across classes during the entire sophomore year.

- An introduction to total quality concepts and tools was incorporated into the accounting program.

- All faculty members left with a view of the big picture.

- The process improved external (employers) and internal (faculty who have earlier accounting courses as prerequisites for their classes) customer relations.

- The basic accounting core was reduced from three courses to two.

Improving the core curriculum. Early in our total quality journey we discovered that a number of faculty did not understand the college's curriculum review process. Therefore, the faculty decided to design a new process using total quality principles (see the appendix). It would be used not only for the present goal of integrating total quality content, but also to modify the curriculum in the future. Over time, the process will be evaluated and streamlined to make curricular changes more straightforward and less time-consuming.

A team of faculty examined to what extent total quality content should be integrated into core classes and as part of which discipline's offerings. Customer focus groups provided information on the types of skills business graduates should have. Data from these groups suggest that, while basic total quality principles are important and should be taught in some form, employers are equally concerned about fundamental business knowledge and job-related practical skills. A number of changes are being made in curriculum, pedagogy, and administration.

- Total quality principles will be included as a major topic in an introduction to business course.

- Although team efforts have appeared in classes for some time, more team activities have been adopted across disciplines to help students practice and learn group skills.

- A new course is being offered covering basic total quality procedures and tools such as planning, process improvement, and introduction to quality function deployment. Students examine several companies and complete individual improvement projects using these tools.

- The responsibility to teach communication skills was assigned to the introduction to marketing course, which is part of the core curriculum.

- When making class size recommendations to the college Executive Committee, the Undergraduate Program Committee focused on skill building. To ensure that all students have an opportunity to learn written and oral communication skills, introduction to marketing classes were given small sections. Team skills were the justification for recommending smaller sections of a basic management class.

- To cover career planning in the program, although not in the classroom, the college hired an advisor to provide additional career counseling. The counselor helps students prepare and evaluate their resumes, create strategies for the job search, and evaluate career alternatives.

- A much broader, faculty-taught career preparation curriculum crossing all four undergraduate years is in the proposal stage.

- A new course was designed to teach fundamentals of management from a systems perspective, using the Deming management method as a theme and core concept. Quality topics comprise three weeks of the course. New teaching techniques, including computerized instruction and other multimedia approaches, will be utilized and improved during subsequent offerings of this course.

- An advanced-level quality management course was developed as part of the revised management option. The course includes computerized learning modules addressing quality function deployment and hoshin planning.

- Total quality was incorporated into the marketing policy class, and a new class, marketing and technology, will introduce total quality applied to the product development process.

- The Deming library of films and tapes has been procured for faculty and student use.

Improving teaching beyond the College of Business. Due to chronic overcrowding, the college historically resisted requests from other colleges on campus for a business minor. Partly because of the recognition that other campus units are customers, this approach was reconsidered. Representatives from other colleges were interviewed by a faculty team, and their input was used to design a transcript-visible business minor.

Similarly, a new course teaching concurrent engineering jointly to teams of engineering and business students is offered for the first time this year by a team of business and engineering faculty. This course will better prepare both types of students to function in technology-based organizations. It includes developing computerized design information networks and new teaching methodologies that integrate the key aspects of concurrent engineering: design process, business planning process, design information system, manufacturing process design, and teamwork. There may be value in using cross-functional teams to teach other classes as well, but this is a radical change for us. Movement in this direction is admittedly slow, and much work remains if this area is to be developed.

Experimenting with a Team Approach

Our total quality efforts emphasize a team approach and broad participation. A cross-functional Total Quality Council consisting of four College of Business professors was appointed by the dean; they represent accounting, management, management science, and marketing. The council advises the college leadership on overall total quality efforts and attempts to serve as a source of encouragement for new initiatives. Each member has written and published articles on total quality, contracted research, and participated in quality training programs. In addition, a number of ad hoc cross-functional committees (tiger teams) have emerged. Some were appointed by the dean, others volunteered. These groups championed particular causes, for example, designing a total quality elective class, incorporating total quality into the curriculum, and gathering data on customer needs and satisfaction.

Students are also part of the total quality team. They have responsibilities in their own learning process and in that of others and provide customer feedback. Regular feedback sessions with groups of students are chaired by the dean. Students also serve as focus group members and advisors on student recruitment efforts.

Taking a team approach was risky. In order to work together and to teach a complete and coordinated business curriculum, faculty had to overcome well-defined boundaries based on discipline and research specialties. This required trust, respect, and an ability to communicate with people from different backgrounds. Prospects for interdisciplinary sharing and cross-functional teams seemed to contradict the specialization and autonomy to which faculty were accustomed. By tradition, faculty members often are successful as the result of their entrepreneurial (and sometimes competitive) activities, and they work alone in determining the content of the courses they teach. The classroom was seen as a protected domain that others would not intrude.

The existing administrative structure of the college also seemed to conflict with the cross-functional team approach. Although it had been supplemented by a few standing committees, the structure had always operated along functional lines (accounting, finance, marketing, and so on) headed by department chairs. What would be the effect of using functional and cross-functional organizational structures simultaneously?

Embracing Total Quality: A Process of Learning and Unlearning

We are learning through experimentation. Our experiments generally have followed a plan-do-check-act (PDCA) cycle, and not all tests succeeded. Some tools were tried and dropped, such as K-J analysis, and others were altered or combined to fit the unique needs of the college. We have learned from both successes and failures.

Total quality is a radical management innovation that takes time to diffuse through traditional American business. In a university, its evolution is likely to be even more prolonged. For the ripples to spread, attitudes must be changed, knowledge must be gained, skills must be learned, and old practices must be replaced. This section attempts to inventory what we have learned.

Attitudes

Much of the effectiveness of total quality is based on a change of attitude. After one has personally internalized the theory and principles, one can easily understand why the procedures and tools are necessary. On the other hand, focusing on any particular tool, or even the entire array of Baldrige Award criteria, can distract from what is important.

Early on, some faculty resisted total quality. A year ago faculty skepticism was reflected in the volume of anti–total quality articles that appeared on the faculty mail room door. One common question was: "Why use the term 'total quality' for principles we have always taught?" From a practical standpoint, nonbelievers argued that there was insufficient evidence in the literature to demonstrate that total quality is effective in improving higher education. They also pointed out that the literature showed that adopting total quality takes a lot of time and that the immediate outcomes of such efforts are not necessarily superior to those obtained using traditional methods.

The most acrimonious debates involved a threat to academic freedom. Many faculty are innovators/entrepreneurs who have been rewarded for making autonomous decisions about both the generation of knowledge (research) and its dissemination (teaching). Many believed that truth is the customer. The profession and the individual faculty member, they argued, are always the best judges of classroom needs. After experimenting with total quality as a tool kit of ideas and techniques and realizing that the focus is on improvement rather than on following a set of rigid rules of total quality, more faculty have become comfortable with it. Of course, skepticism has not been entirely obliterated, nor should it be in a learning environment.

To varying degrees, the attitudes of the business faculty have changed. Some faculty have become true believers. For example, consider the following testimonial.

> Winter term of 1991 was the last term I approached teaching with an "inspect and reject" psychology. I entered the classroom well prepared, dispensed knowledge, and tested to see how much students knew . . . A few brave souls brought complaints to me. I wasn't receptive because I knew I was working hard to deliver quality instruction. Besides, I was supposed to be the expert, the professor, the one in control.
>
> During spring break, I decided things had to change. I am a teacher because I want to help people learn. Fortunately, hardly anyone questioned the substance of what I was teaching. The assignments and readings were generally good. So I turned my attention to the tone and style of my interactions with the students and the assumptions I brought to the teaching process. I concluded that if I couldn't improve things during spring term 1991, I would leave Oregon State. In the last three years, my ideas about teaching have changed dramatically, and I expect the process of change to continue.

Many of our faculty are coming to believe that a customer-oriented team approach to continuous improvement is legitimate for higher education. One very significant change has been the switch from an input orientation (preparation, lecturing, testing, and so on) to an output orientation. There is more agreement among the faculty that the college's value-added product is the preparation of students for their professional lives.

As a faculty we came to the conclusion that we *wanted* to satisfy the needs of students and departments across campus with a business minor. This was our first customer-oriented consensus.

Knowledge

The knowledge base of the college has grown. We have learned about total quality and about our customers. In the beginning there was uncertainty about basic questions: "What is total quality?" "Who is our customer?" After training and subsequent discourse, most faculty have developed answers to these questions. Now there is a shared base of general understanding of total quality.

To establish this base, we looked for information about the experiences of other colleges and universities, and we assembled a bibliography of publications on total quality inside and outside higher education. The investigation of quality in education also took us into the outcomes-assessment literature. We found Internet discussion groups that link faculty members interested in total quality around the world. Here are some realizations about the total quality process.

- Gathering data takes time and adds to faculty workloads.

- Asking for customer feedback requires confidence and a thick skin; some criticism is not intended to be constructive.

- Students, for understandable reasons, are jealous of their time. Until they see a clear linkage between furnishing data to achieve needed improvement, we must expect many to ignore our requests for feedback.

- Continuous improvement requires constant changes, leaving instructors always on the edge.

- As a practical matter, it is simply easier to teach total quality now than it was earlier because many textbooks now have total quality content.

- We have learned that if we prepare our students better, we will see grade inflation. Achievement becomes the responsibility of the instructor as well as the students.

- Although skills are considered more important outcomes, faculty find it difficult to give up traditional context-oriented exams completely. They seem to gravitate to using them to generate about 50 percent of a student's grade.

About student quality teams, we have learned a little.

- Students work better if a trained facilitator is added to the group.

- Students can use encouragement to join a total quality team, in other words, course credit incentives for participating.

- It is not easy to complete a quality project with inexperienced team members in the confines of a 10-week academic quarter.

- When setting up student discussion groups, faculty find that three members is about right; diverse opinions can be expressed while classroom noise and freeloading are minimized.

- A total quality philosophy is not immediately compatible with everyone's administrative leadership or teaching style.

We now know something about the needs, satisfaction, and skill levels of our customers, and for the first time we have baseline data on quality measures. We developed a database that tracks former students and follows their future career. We know how to gather customer data through PC-based questionnaires and focus groups.

To date, we have found that the greatest benefit of classroom experiments is the identification of what student customers do not like or want rather than what satisfies them. For example, a management professor realized that students thought the furniture configuration in the assigned classroom was wrong for the class; a business law professor found that students were dissatisfied with the legal brief format; and an accounting professor changed assignment instructions that students perceived to be ambiguous. In addition, customer-oriented activities are usually appreciated by the students as a sign of sensitivity to their needs, and there is a general belief that midterm evaluations have a positive effect on course evaluations at the end of the term.

Some say that the room for improvement is "the world's largest room." Our experience is that an indication to customers that one is prepared to listen and respond to complaints increases the number of complaints and suggestions. Moreover, the provider can expect results and steadily increasing responsiveness. But one is ill-advised to seek customer feedback unless it will be used.

Skills

In order to teach skills to students, the instructors themselves must have skills. Ad hoc teams have provided an opportunity for many faculty to practice team skills. Not only are faculty working together more efficiently on curricular matters, they are also engaged in collaborative research and consulting activities. A spin-off from team interaction is the ability to run better meetings. Our belief is that faculty are now more focused on goals, and agendas are more likely to be accomplished within time limits.

A total quality skill base is developing among the faculty. The ability to conduct focus groups has increased significantly. Members of the faculty have acquired expertise as total quality trainers (for example by helping others complete the Hewlett-Packard seminar) and as facilitators of total quality teams on campus.

Culture

The culture of an organization becomes apparent in the shared values of its members. Although it is too early to be certain, the authors believe that values in the college are changing. Politics are less frequently the basis for decision making. Instead, decisions are, to a greater extent, based on data.

Perhaps the biggest change can be seen in the level of teamwork and communication through cross-functional networks. Functional walls in the college have started to come down. The faculty recommended almost unanimously that the college be reorganized on a program basis that would replace functional departments. This radical request would never have emerged in the earlier environment, not even two years ago.

General Observations

The total quality journey bears some resemblance to a spiritual quest. The process is difficult, it takes a long time to learn what you need to know, and there is frequent cause to wonder about the ultimate outcome.

On average, most of the business faculty are still total quality beginners. It may take years before diffusion is complete among all faculty and students, but the process of becoming a quality organization, embracing the principles presented at the beginning of this paper, is underway.

One of the first observations regarding the use of total quality to improve instructional and administrative processes is that change does not come quickly or easily. Any attempt to force faculty to adopt total quality would undoubtedly have failed. In our college, total quality approaches were implemented gradually and often parallel to existing structures and processes. Even though implementation efforts are encouraged, the use of total quality remains voluntary.

What of the Future?

We acknowledge the criticism of total quality that has appeared in the press. We are convinced, however, that customer-based and systems approaches are too powerful to ignore. We feel that pressure to adopt total quality and systems perspectives, under whatever name, will continue. Even if we do not improve, our overall success will be measured in terms of maintaining quality with fewer resources. The push will be both internal, from colleagues and administrators, and external, from business. Examples already exist in new textbooks expounding total quality ideas and new journals that publish related research.

Measuring Quality As Educational Outcomes

The quality of education is measured in terms of outcomes as perceived by customers. We have assessed customer satisfaction with our classes and programs. We have examined students' career experiences and their own skills assessments. These measures have been useful in identifying areas for improvement. However, they do not seem to capture completely the essence of the product. We are currently struggling with ways to monitor many variables.

- Business knowledge
- Critical skills
- Essential attitudes
- Employers' perceptions of our graduates
- Effects of our management education on graduates' careers

The curricular review process is still underway. The faculty recently began to develop a set of measurable teaching objectives relative to the principles of total quality and continuous improvement. They asked, for example

- Will our graduates choose to take a customer-oriented approach to solving business problems?
- Are they able to make data-based decisions?
- Are they able to influence group decisions?

Although we have generated some baseline information, we need true benchmark data. Eventually we will need to share outcome measures with other business schools. We need to design more standardized exit survey questions to facilitate benchmarking with other institutions.

Understanding College Processes

Measuring performance may only reveal symptoms. While exploring total quality we have found that we need to understand underlying processes. Although we depicted some existing processes in terms of Deming flow diagrams and flowcharts, and although we designed an improved curriculum review process, not much real progress has been made in this area. Processes in higher education are hard to define. For example, we have found that alumni satisfaction is related to getting and keeping the first job, but we do not thoroughly understand that process.

One of the extensions of a process approach is that processes rather than people are usually responsible for suboptimal performance. Yet, the inspect and reject mentality still reigns in academia. It is used in the performance evaluations of both students and faculty. New approaches must be designed to help all students acquire the fundamental business skills a graduate needs.

Processes must also be designed to assist those faculty who are not effective in satisfying student needs. Besides total quality training opportunities, more general faculty development programs, including teaching effectiveness seminars and conferences should be developed. The faculty proposed peer evaluation of teaching as a method of sharing and improving instructional technique, instead of an inspect and reject method; and many of us see an urgent need for a mentoring process for new faculty.

Systems View

It has been noted that the term *total quality* may not persist into the future. A few of our more innovative faculty believe that a systems approach will be the next wave beyond total quality and that expansion of the theory will help make the quality perspective more relevant. Innovators remind us that we need to look at educational outcomes in terms of all forces in the system that affect them. Only then can we hope to break out of the circle and come up with better solutions.

No business class operates in a vacuum. Many exogenous forces affect the quality of teaching. Administrators determine teaching loads, class sizes, class times, term lengths, and classroom equipment configurations. Other faculty determine the extent to which students know prerequisite material and possess basic skills. Librarians determine the quality of library collections and access. Campus recruiters determine the quality of the student raw material. For the college, the high quality of computing facilities depends on the generosity of corporate donors. And so on. . . .

Systems content has been incorporated into the curriculum.

- Systems theory is introduced in the basic management class.

- We have created an elective class in systems management for those with a special interest in this area.

Total quality has helped us look outside the classroom to larger processes like curriculum design.

Expanding Participation

The college is part of a university team. In the past we did not work very closely with some of our colleagues on campus, and the symptoms are visible. For example, our students are not satisfied with the career planning and placement in the university, and some believe that a resume format they have learned elsewhere in the university does not provide employers with the information they require.

Relationships must be improved with departments and colleges that serve as suppliers and partners in educating students, such as the faculties of the English and speech departments to ensure that business students receive the training required by future employers.

One proposed collaboration is a joint total quality minor with the College of Engineering. The concurrent engineering course is one step in this direction, as are the new design and the quality management design courses. In addition, some spin-off from the college effort to add total quality to the business curriculum can be expected, since this effort should contribute to our understanding of appropriate total quality content for non–business students.

The university is presently not organized to encourage or recognize group efforts. Awards are given to individuals, and current performance reviews do not emphasize group contributions. In order to enhance cooperation, recognition of group efforts needs to be encouraged. According to our friends at Hewlett-Packard, "What is measured is what changes." Thus our reward and evaluation systems need to be improved. Indeed, we must ask, is there true wisdom in Deming's untiring admonition to eliminate employee evaluation systems? If so, what will serve in their stead? Perhaps more critically, if evaluation systems are not appropriate for faculty, why do we maintain grades for students?

Reorganizing the College

One final and highly perplexing question remains for the college. In our exploration of total quality, we have largely abandoned our former management structure. We once had a dean, an MBA program director, six department chairs, and a number of standing faculty committees. We have evolved to the point that executive decisions are now made by an executive committee consisting of the dean and two department chairs (who also serve respectively as undergraduate and graduate program directors). Many new policies arise from ad hoc committees or standing committees whose membership has been supplemented through appointments. Some are comfortable with the ad hoc structure. The question is, in an organization that is improving continuously and trying something new all the time, what is the correct balance between stability and evolution?

Summary and Conclusion

This paper, written by a team comprised of one administrator and two faculty members, has attempted to report the status of total quality in the College of Business at Oregon State University. Others in the college were asked to review conclusions. For example, when asked to assess how well the total quality principles listed at the beginning of this paper have been adopted by the college, the members of the Quality Council agreed that customer orientation had come the furthest and that benchmarking and process orientation have further to go.

Compiling this report has benefited us by making us aware of where we stand and what remains to be done; we will use the document for internal purposes. The diffusion of total quality has progressed in our organization. Total quality topics have been incorporated into the business curriculum, total quality principles are practiced by many of the faculty, and a core of the faculty are working very hard to turn the college into a total quality organization. Unintended consequences of total quality analysis include the realization that we really have a long way to go and that we may have to go beyond continuous improvement to effect the type of changes required to achieve our objectives with future resources.

Appendix: Curriculum Development and Evaluation Process

(This process was designed by a cross-functional team of 10 faculty led by Associate Professor Ilene Kleinsorge.)

Objectives

- Ascertain if elements of total quality and continuous improvement should be incorporated systematically in the business curriculum.

- If so, identify elements and decide whether they should be taught to all students (in the core) or made available only to interested students (as electives).

- Ascertain how to teach or present elements identified above.

Development Process

Step 1: Identify customers of College of Business education.

Step 2: Review existing information about and from customers regarding total quality principles and continuous improvement concepts. Determine whether additional (internal and external) customer information is needed and how to obtain it.

- Review information from college surveys.

- Review business education literature regarding vision for the future of business careers and educational needs.

- Review total quality literature for common body of knowledge.

- Consider Professor Gobeli's "Quality Constellation."

- Study critiques of total quality, weaknesses, and the distinction between goods and services applications.

- Review the Baldrige 1993 Award Book.

Step 3: Collect data from internal and external customers.

- Conduct focus groups of professionals from companies with and without formal total quality programs.

- Interview college faculty teaching at the senior level regarding quality principles they expect as prerequisites for their students.

Step 4:   Analyze all customer information and set objectives for business curriculum regarding total quality principles and continuous improvement concepts for different customer groups.

- Consider the political, educational, and promotional ramifications of the objectives set.

Step 5:   Present progress-to-date to faculty.

- Solicit cooperation and participation for next two steps.

- Maintain close liaison with Undergraduate Program Committee on remaining steps.

Step 6:   Diagram existing curriculum content regarding total quality principles and continuous improvement concepts and determine if objectives for the business curriculum are currently being met in the most efficient and effective way possible.

- Use data collected from faculty in fall 1992 on current total quality teaching to identify courses in which total quality concepts and principles are addressed and confirm whether this is still being done. If not, document the changes.

    If *yes*, skip to step 9. If no, proceed.

Step 7:   Cross-functional teams evaluate existing curriculum content and propose strategies for closing identified gaps.

- Provide team training for team members.

- Provide faculty development.

Step 8:   Faculty approval of suggested curriculum changes.

Evaluation Process

Step 9:   Develop performance measures to ensure that objectives continue to be relevant and are being met. Include both process indicators and outcome indicators.

Step 10:   Measure feedback. Change if necessary.

Step 11:   Benchmarking, feedback. Change if necessary.

Acknowledgments

The authors wish to acknowledge the members of the College of Business Quality Council, Professors Ilene Kleinsorge, Stefan Bloomfield, and David Gobeli, for reviewing the article and providing information on total quality initiatives in the college. Thanks also to the college faculty for discussing their individual total quality projects and to Ute Vergin for her editorial assistance.

Bibliography

Bergquist, William H., and Jack L. Armstrong. *Planning Effectively for Educational Quality: An Outcomes-Based Approach for Colleges Committed to Excellence.* San Francisco: Jossey Bass, 1986. (See chapters on outcomes and assessment.)

Brocka, Bruce, and Suzanne Brocka. *Quality Management: Implementing the Best Ideas of the Masters.* Homewood, Ill.: Business-One Irwin, 1992.

Brown, Daniel J., and David H. Gobeli. "Improving the Quality of Business Education." *Enhancing Knowledge Development in Marketing.* Edited by David W. Cravens and Peter R. Dickson. New York: AMA Educators' Proceedings, 1993. 36–41.

Deming, Edward W. *Out of the Crisis.* Cambridge, Mass.: MIT Center for Advanced Engineering Study, 1986. (Statement of 14 points for management)

———. *The New Economics.* Cambridge, Mass.: MIT Press, 1993.

Juran, Joseph M. *Juran on Quality by Design: The New Steps for Planning Quality into Goods and Services.* New York: Free Press, 1992. (Process design, planning, and improvement)

———, ed. *Juran's Quality Control Handbook.* 4th ed. Toronto: McGraw-Hill, 1988. (General reference)

Meller, Richard L., ed. *Applying the Deming Method to Higher Education for More Effective Human Resource Management.* Washington, D.C.: College and Personnel Association, 1991.

Seymour, Daniel T. *Developing Academic Programs: The Climate for Innovation, ASHE-ERIC Higher Education Report #3.* Washington, D.C.: Association for the Study of Higher Education, 1988.

———. *On Q: Causing Quality in Higher Education.* New York: Macmillan, 1992; Phoenix: Oryx Press, 1993.

Walton, Mary. *The Deming Management Method.* New York: G.P. Putnam, 1986.

The Business College at Arizona State University: Taking Quality to Heart

Mimi Wolverton

Background

Each year, the College of Business at Arizona State University enrolls more than 8000 students (20 percent of the university's total enrollment). Of these, about 7000 are undergraduates. Twenty-five percent of all university graduates in any given year come from the College of Business, but available persistence data show attrition rates of 86 percent among college freshman and 68 percent within its lower-division transfer students. Although Arizona State serves an ethnically diverse region, students of color currently constitute less than 15 percent of the business college's baccalaureate graduates.

In the past few years, efforts to improve the quality of the college's programs at both the undergraduate and graduate levels can be linked to total quality. For instance, the college redesigned its day, evening, and executive MBA programs based entirely on market and customer needs. A lockstep format and a trimester system during the first year increased core course availability by 50 percent. Faculty work collaboratively within the trimester offerings to coordinate student work and projects. Part of the first-year experience includes community service. A flexible second year allows students to engage in elective course work, field projects, and international studies. These graduate programs continuously benchmark their offerings against those of their peers, and regularly survey current students and alumni.

About the Author: Mimi Wolverton holds an MBA and a Ph.D. in educational leadership and policy studies from Arizona State University, has 20 years of administrative experience in private enterprise, and is currently a postdoctoral research scholar at Arizona State University.

At the undergraduate level, class size in most core courses runs from 250 to 400 students. Six courses—two accounting, one computer, two economics, and one statistics—make up the preprofessional core. The professional core includes courses in finance, law, management, organizational behavior, marketing, and operations and logistics. Prior to the college's total quality efforts, lectures dominated course delivery; homework consisted of working hypothetical textbook problems; and successful test taking amounted essentially to the regurgitation of definitions and mathematical rules.

This paper looks at the total quality attempts of the College of Business in undergraduate education. Here, the college not only tried to improve student academic success, but to enhance the applicability of its undergraduate preprofessional (freshman and sophomore) and professional (junior and senior) programs.

The Movement Toward Total Quality

Like most professional schools, the College of Business maintains close ties with the local business community. In fall 1991, the college, under the guidance of the Dean's Council of 100—a group of influential Phoenix-area business executives—entered into a planning process called ASU Business Partners. The college's mission was redefined; and the college began to strategically reorient itself to meet the needs of its environment. The dean, Larry Penley, developed a preliminary vision for the college. The Business Partners' steering committee (13 high-level business executives, three faculty, and two students) designed a process for collecting data to assess the college's current education quality relative to that of its peers.

Customer surveys and focused interviews targeted four groups—current students, recent graduates, recruiters, and employers. Data consistently pointed to four weaknesses in the college's current preprofessional and professional programs.

- Students noted their inability to solve unstructured, real-world problems and to manage people and the business environment.

- Employers singled out poor written communication skills and poor student transition into the workplace as their biggest concerns.

Using this information, five task forces—each comprising eight faculty members, one or two students, one staff person, and three business executives—formulated strategies for fulfilling the mission. The mission statement reads

> The mission of the College of Business is to expand knowledge
> and educate men and women for managerial leadership in a world
> characterized by demands for continuous improvements in quality;

rapid advancements in technology; a workforce of ethnic, cultural and gender diversity; the need for employees with practical skills and an understanding of global markets.

From a practical standpoint, the college's commitment to quality and the total quality process translates into five key areas: globalization, information technology, total quality management, diversity, and communication skills. Working from the Business Partners strategic plan, several groups—college administrators, the task force groups, individual departments, and the undergraduate committee of the faculty council—addressed these concerns with respect to curriculum, classroom technique, and the college's support systems.

Curriculum Revision
Accountancy

A Big Eight white paper provided the initial impetus for change. It suggested that undergraduate accounting education hindered the development of critical thinking, communication, and team skills among accounting program graduates. Based on these admonitions, Arizona State's School of Accountancy took the lead in curriculum revision.

Simply put, the faculty no longer wanted to teach accounting using conventional methods. By fall 1992, the school had recreated its preprofessional program and introduced a series of three courses—two three-credit classes and a third one-hour course. In Accounting 230 and 240, students, individually and in teams, explore feasible approaches to solving accounting problems, and then select and defend their plans of action. Faculty use exercises like one-minute papers, which call for short, concise explanations, to discern whether students have a clear understanding of accounting principles as they apply to real-world situations. As Steven Happel, the associate dean for undergraduate education, put it, "The idea is to make students think like accountants without having them actually do the accounting work."

The complementary one-hour, computerized course, which is required for accounting majors, but optional for other business students, provides students with exposure to, and practice in, the more traditional accounting realms of debits and credits. Schoolwide revisions should be completed by 1996, but already upper division core courses, as well as electives, depend heavily on computerization. In the end, about one-third of the program revisions impact course content; more than one-half deal directly with pedagogy, format, and delivery.

Arizona State's curricular approach to accounting education provides such a radical departure from traditional programming that in the first few months of its commercial availability through McGraw-Hill, 700 demonstration packets have been requested. Results from formal testing in 25 programs across the country have also been very positive. Patrick McKenzie, the project director, observed, "We have made some wonderful changes, but we have a long way to go. I keep thinking about where we could be, if everybody was on board." In the estimation of one high-level administrator, one-third of the faculty actively participated in the change process; another 15 percent to 20 percent have been somewhat active; one-half have done nothing at all. Similar faculty-involvement scenarios now seem to be playing themselves out in other departments across the college.

Other Preprofessional Areas

Following the School of Accountancy's example, decision systems' faculty realigned the content of the preprofessional statistics core course. Students generate statistical information using computerized applications and then work through simulations that reflect everyday business circumstances. The intent is to have students focus on the interpretation of the results they produce rather than on rote memorization of statistical formulas and equations. As equipment becomes available, the finance department plans to use a similar approach.

At-Risk Preprofessionals

To address severe attrition rates among minority students in the business preprofessional core courses, the college initiated the Business Enrichment Program. Participants are ethnic minorities who enroll as freshmen or sophomores in a three-course block, which includes an introduction to business, microeconomics principles, and a humanities class called contemporary issues in humanities.

Within the business course, students form study partnerships for the other courses, practice college survival skills, gain a better understanding of the college's academic requirements and policies, explore opportunities provided by campus organizations, and learn how to seek out and apply for internships and scholarships. The emphasis throughout this early intervention is on teamwork.

Professional Program

The undergraduate committee's 1994 recommendations for the professional program touch on three key points—the need for an integrated core curriculum in which students can see the links between courses and can grow in their understanding of business organizations as integrated systems, the expansion of the college's five themes with special emphasis on international issues, and the importance of changing the delivery of core courses to enhance student learning and skills development.

The committee's recommendations changed the configuration of the program. They led to

1. Inclusion of an administrative communication course as a first-semester requirement

2. Establishment of a new standing committee (the core committee) to coordinate the upper-division core and to address inconsistencies in the program's noncore electives

3. Addition of one elective international course to the core requirements

4. Incorporation of international issues into all core classes

5. Creation of two new required classes

The new required classes. Students encounter both new courses in their junior year. The first is an integrative introduction to the college's professional program. A cross-functional faculty team exposes students to the complexities of business by employing such techniques as business simulations, comprehensive cases, business audits, historical and current readings, and computer-based analysis. Topics covered include the basic nature of the business environment, the nature of managerial work, organizational dynamics, alternative decision-making models, the use of information and statistics in decision making, total quality management in service and manufacturing contexts, quality management from a global perspective, and business ethics. In addition, emphasis is placed on diversity, information technology, service quality, and learning organizations. Specially designed exercises link this course to the required communications course.

The second required course provides a practical bridge between student life and employment life. This one-credit class pays attention to the practical aspects of entering the job market. Sessions deal with proper table etiquette, professional appearance, resume preparation, and how to interview with and make presentations for potential employers.

Revision of the capstone course. The undergraduate committee also suggested the revision of Management 463 (strategic management) to create a more integrated capstone experience that connects closely with the core. One faculty member experimented with a three-hour, weekly session, which focused on presentation skills, decision making, and collaboration. In its first offering, class enrollment was restricted to honors students.

Other core areas. With the aid of accountancy faculty and the support of the college's dean, other core areas such as marketing, operations and logistics, management, and finance are moving toward similar course revision especially in delivery and format. One professor, however, spoke of the challenge of incorporating active learning into large classes. "It's a matter of logistics. It's relatively easy to break a class of 50 into groups for team exercises. But, when it comes to 250 students, it takes at least 10 minutes to break into groups and hand out the exercise, and another 10 minutes to collect it. For a 10-minute exercise, you probably have 30 minutes taken up by logistics. We have to figure out how to cut down on that wasted time."

Decision systems electives. Within the last two years, the department of decision and information systems deemphasized the focus of its upper-division courses on theory and the application of quantitative techniques to managerial problems. Instead, students devote considerable time to the analysis of quality problems that are related to operations, process analysis, and the design and improvement of processes. In addition to a major in decision sciences, the department now also offers a certificate in quality analysis.

Real estate electives. Changes in the upper-division real estate program are also under way. Beginning in 1994, real estate majors will encounter a seamless program consisting of four modules—analysis, finance, development, and brokerage/management. Students meet in three-hour sessions, three days per week. Presentations on related topics, such as international business, strategic planning, geographic information systems, and ethics, supplement the required classes. A team-generated market analysis project ties the first two modules together, and a land parcel development plan helps students synthesize the course work in the second two segments.

Curriculum Revision Impact

Preliminary results from these curriculum revisions are heartening. The drop rate in preprofessional core accounting courses declined from close to 40 percent to 3 percent. Test results in the core statistics class show higher median scores than in the past. The experimental managerial capstone course showed enough promise to suggest that the approach be expanded to all students. And students who participated in the Business Enrichment Program achieved a higher grade point average than did all other College of Business freshmen and, on average, completed more credit hours.

Classroom Techniques

Through the initial customer surveys, the college learned that one of the major shortcomings of its undergraduate program is the large class size of many of its core courses. To overcome a tendency toward one-way instructional communication, student passivity, and recognition-oriented multiple choice testing, faculty began focusing on the use of cooperative and active learning techniques that stress oral and written communication, teamwork, and the use of analytical skills.

Business Law

In some instances, course content remained relatively intact, but the methods used by faculty in the classroom changed. For instance, two business administration faculty, one who specializes in law and the other in communication, realigned a course on the legal and regulatory environment of business. By incorporating short writing assignments, the instructor makes writing a relevant component of the class. To encourage collaboration, she divides the class into groups of five. Using electronic mail, students within the teams and the instructor read and critique each others' writing samples. The electronic format makes team participation easier and more convenient than exchanging papers, and writing skills seem to improve.

Economics

The economics department took a multifaceted approach to improving both student success and student diversity in its lower-division micro- and macroprinciples classes. These courses serve as gatekeepers for the professional program, and faculty believe that increasing the success rate among all students will ultimately improve the diversity of the college. Seven faculty used one of 11 approaches in classes that ranged in size from 51 to 449 students. In all, more than 2200 students participated in either micro- or macroeconomics pilot programs. Pilot treatments included mandatory graded homework, required computer tutorial assignments, targeted review sessions, voluntary group study sessions with a professor or a tutor, and optional study guides, review packets, and computer tutorials.

The experience of one instructor bears closer scrutiny because she taught the same courses using the same texts in the previous year, but without the pilot modifications. In addition, she employed different instructional options in the two microeconomics pilot sections under her supervision. In one, she required five homework assignments, which students turned in at an economics study lab. The lab was offered at regularly scheduled times 10 hours a week with teams of graduate students and undergraduate majors providing the tutoring service. The homework constituted 20 percent of the students' grades. At first, students only turned in their assignments; but by midsemester, an average of 100 students per week attended the lab sessions.

In her second section, the instructor announced that at the beginning of the semester 10 pop quizzes would comprise 20 percent of each student's grade. The quizzes covered previous lectures and reading assignments, and students were encouraged, but not required, to attend the study lab. For the most part, these students did not use the lab.

When the instructor compared the grade distribution of the minority students in the two classes, in the section that required homework, the percentage of those receiving a grade of C or better rose 15 points over the previous year. In the section in which pop quizzes had been given, the percentage of minority students who received a grade of either D, E, or W remained unchanged from the previous year.

In all, the results of more than 2200 micro- and macroeconomics students indicate that grade distribution did increase in students at large as well as in minority students, particularly in sections that required either homework or computer tutorials, or offered targeted review sessions.

Support for Change

Educational changes inspired by a desire for improved quality can be sustained only when efforts are properly rewarded, student supports are in place, an adequate financial base underlies such endeavors, the organization's structure promotes rather than hinders total quality efforts, and leadership values and encourages change. To some extent these crucial building blocks seem to exist or are being developed by the college.

Faculty Rewards and Incentives

The associate dean for undergraduate education says, "The college is sending out signals that good teaching matters. Faculty can prepare portfolios to highlight their strengths, but student evaluations are the bottom line even when it comes to decisions about tenure and promotion. On the one hand, yes, we reward research, but a good researcher who is a poor teacher will not be rewarded to the same degree as he or she was in the past. On the other hand, excellent teachers with relatively modest research records will be rewarded. This was not the case in the past." Although merit pay seems to be allotted based on teaching expertise, evidence to substantiate whether the college follows through in its pledge to grant tenure using similar criteria may take time to manifest itself.

To encourage teaching excellence, the dean of the college has initiated a procedure for identifying faculty with particular performance problems. The process targets faculty who, over time, receive below average student evaluations. These faculty meet with the associate dean for undergraduate education and the department chair to develop a plan for improvement.

Monetary incentives, in the form of teaching and travel grants and teaching awards, exist as well. For example, the college funds summer teaching grants that allow faculty to pursue new and innovative teaching techniques and curriculum revisions. The guidelines for these awards are straightforward—concentrate on incorporating technology, active learning, and continuous quality into classroom efforts. Typically, 10 undergraduate grants are given out each year. Travel grants are divided between those attending professional meetings and those participating in training programs in quality and in cooperative and active learning. In addition, the college has organized in-house training for cooperative and active learning. The college also recognizes outstanding teachers. Two awards, in particular, pertain to undergraduate education—one for a faculty member, the other for the best teaching assistant. Each receives a plaque and a $1000 savings bond from the Business Alumni Association.

Student Support

Based on student and alumni feedback, the undergraduate advisement center revamped its operations and initiated new access and admissions policies. As part of its minority-targeted Business Enrichment Program, the center offers DESKLAB, which requires that students spend a minimum of 10 hours per semester working on either skill improvement, if remediation is needed, or on computer-related activities, if college preparatory work is not required.

Financial Resources

External funding eased the financial pain of transition for the college. The Dean's Council of 100 generated the initial funds for Business Partners process and continues to raise funds for summer teaching grants. A $250,000 grant (one of 10) from the Accounting Education Change Commission enabled the development of the accounting undergraduate teaching program. Initially, money was dispersed over a four-year period and matched by the college. Ultimately, the project's director estimates that, over a five-year period, the accounting school had between $500,000 and $1 million at its disposal.

Most recently, Hewlett-Packard awarded a $100,000 computer grant that allowed the college to convert from mainframe and DOS-based processing to UNIX-based workstation networks. With these technological changes in place the college is developing a state-of-the-art undergraduate decision information systems curriculum.

Organizational Structure

Besides the Business Partners, two other groups that affect undergraduate education came into existence as the college embraced total quality management. The Dean's

Board of Excellence, a group of relatively new Phoenix-area business leaders, works closely with students in the undergraduate honors program. Through focused interviews, the board and honors students gathered information for the faculty council's undergraduate education committee. The second group, the Business College Council, gives undergraduate students a voice in college developments.

Leadership

The college's dean regularly communicates and reinforces his commitment to quality and a customer focus through meetings, speeches, and written communiques. Internally, he meets each semester with the faculty and staff to advise them of the college's accomplishments, the goals that remain unaddressed, the opportunities he sees for improvement, and new goals for the college. He conducts monthly meetings with faculty, semimonthly meetings with department chairs, and holds regular meetings with staff, students, and the Business College Council. Externally, he meets on an ongoing basis with advisory committees, contributes to college publications, and emphasizes the college's commitment to total quality in presentations and speeches.

Operationally, the dean, associate deans, department heads, and center directors function in a manner that resembles a quality council. The group's main concerns center on education quality, program improvement and design, program accessibility and advisement effectiveness, process streamlining, resource allocation, continuous internal quality measurement (for example, through customer audits, senior exit interviews, and by tracking persistence rates and the time from entry to graduation), and external benchmarking against peer institutions.

Closing Comments

The college's dean commented, "At first, I never mentioned total quality management or used the words *students* and *customers* in the same sentence. Now, I can speak of students as customers without the faculty visibly flinching." The associate dean (who is a member of the economics faculty) says, "The college has moved away from believing that students are inputs to be transformed by us into outputs. Today, students are our customers. We listen to them. Of course, we're aware of quality principles, but we don't dwell on them. In fact, I'm not so sure it's total quality management as much as being market-driven. If faculty don't change, their ratings go down, courses don't fill, and consequences set in. To me, that's pure economics." Call it what you may, the end result, an attempt to achieve continuous quality, seems more important than the name.

Bibliography

Blakemore, A. "Undergraduate Initiative: Improving Success and Diversity." Tempe, Ariz.: Arizona State University, March 1994.

College of Business. *Arizona State University MBA Programs.* Tempe, Ariz.: Arizona State University, 1993.

———. "Strategic Plan for the College of Business." Tempe, Ariz.: Arizona State University, May 1993.

———. "Application for the Pioneer Award." Tempe, Ariz.: Arizona State University, 1994.

———. A *Strategic Plan for the Future.* Tempe, Ariz.: Arizona State University, 1994.

Hershauer, J. "College of Business Undergraduate Committee Proposed Business Core Improvements." Tempe, Ariz.: Arizona State University, 1994.

General Catalog 1994–95/1995–96. Tempe, Ariz.: Arizona State University, 1994.

Graduate Catalog 1992–1993 with 1993–1994 Supplement. Tempe, Ariz.: Arizona State University, 1992.

Graduate Catalog 1994–95/1995–96. Tempe, Ariz.: Arizona State University, 1994.

Lomeli, R. "Business Enrichment Program Evaluation." Tempe, Ariz.: Arizona State University, 1993.

Smith, G. "Being a Business Student in the '90s Is Not Like You Remember." *Business* (Winter 1994).

Total Quality for Professors and Students

George R. Bateman and Harry V. Roberts

Total Quality and Higher Education

We begin with a 21-word definition that, for us, catches the essence of total quality: "Continually serve customers better and more economically, using scientific method and teamwork, and concentrating on removal of all forms of waste."

Total quality has not bypassed universities, colleges, and community colleges. Many colleges are now exploring the potential of total quality, and some have begun to attempt its implementation. In most initial efforts, the major emphasis has been on improvement of administrative rather than academic functioning. Professors are not felt to be receptive to improvement ideas coming from the business world. But note these points.

- Administrative improvement is not necessarily a soft target. College and university administrators are often in much the same position as politically appointed heads of government agencies who have great difficulty when they try to change rigid bureaucracies.

- Myron Tribus has argued that many administrative processes are actually counterproductive for the central academic functions; that counterproductive processes should be eliminated, not improved; and that counterproductive processes can be identified reliably only after the academic processes have been improved.[1]

- On the other hand, college professors have a strong self-interest in improving teaching, and individual professors often have substantial freedom to act on their own.

We therefore suggest high priority for the application of total quality to the improvement of teaching, and we report on some interesting explorations in that direction.

The Galvin Challenge

Our theme comes from Bob Galvin's challenge to professors at the Xerox Quality Forum of 1989, where the attending deans and professors in business schools agreed on the desirability of including total quality courses in MBA programs. But they saw formidable obstacles: MBA curricula were already packed full, they said. Several other new areas were contending for inclusion: international business, business ethics, environment, diversity, regulation, leadership, innovation, creativity, and so on. How could they possibly make room for total quality? What would they have to give up? Galvin, then chairman of the board of Motorola, replied as follows.

> What do you give up? I wonder if it's fair to ask of you, as we in industry have been obliged to ask of ourselves, "How efficient are you? Why can't you teach 50 percent more in a year than you're now teaching?" Not one percent. It's this big step-function phenomenon. Why can't you in two or three years change your curricula? Decide that you're going to add all these things in two or three years, and do it. That is what we in industry are having to do to serve our customers.
>
> How do you do it? I don't know. That's not my business. But I do know that for our business, we have to accept the challenge. You have to have the mindset that it can be accomplished. Once you start looking for the solution, you'll come close. Maybe you'll only improve it 40 percent instead of 50, but you can put out a lot more information!

Galvin challenged us to change our curricula in two or three years. His challenge was unconventional in that he suggested the possibility of major improvement, not minor refinement.

Another way to express the challenge would be in terms of reducing educational cycle time. The following example from the training within industry (TWI) of World War II suggests that dramatic reductions in cycle time may sometimes be possible.

> An early success of the TWI service was its role in eliminating the nation's critical shortage of skilled lens grinders. In late 1940, a government search for 350 such specialists for use in bombsights,

periscopes, and other optical equipment, had turned up no qualified people. Unfortunately, under the existing system it took five years to train a master lens grinder. TWI was asked to study the problem. It was found that a master lens grinder was expected to be able to perform twenty jobs, of which only a few were highly skilled. The unskilled jobs could be assigned to less skilled workers. When these tasks were reassigned according to TWI recommendations, the problem eased tremendously. What is more, TWI specialists, using the methods from the JIT (Job Instruction Training) course, redesigned the program for new lens grinders and managed to reduce the training time from five years down to two months.[2]

The example of the lens grinders suggests that the potential for improvement of education can be much greater than at first appears possible. But how could a 97 percent reduction of training time—five years to two months—have been possible?

We do not know the details, but total quality suggests that one key is waste reduction. All processes in all organizations entail waste, often substantial and seldom obvious. Total quality has especially emphasized waste due to poor quality, which leads to defects that require rework. In education, for example, students may misunderstand and have to be corrected, possibly repeatedly. Another important form of waste is the waste of doing things that are unnecessary or counterproductive, even though they do not result in defects. For example, teachers may emphasize topics and concepts that do not contribute to the objectives of their courses.

How to Respond to Galvin's Challenge?

In 1989 when we heard it, we were inspired by Galvin's challenge, but we had very little idea as to how we could respond to it. Like many others, we could easily see how to apply total quality to other people's problems, but our own work seemed different. In this paper, we shall explain a partial but satisfying response, a response that is occurring very widely and seemingly spontaneously in many sectors of higher education today.

Professorial Freedom and Students As Customers

To develop an approach to Galvin's challenge, we begin by noting

- Professors are relatively free to change the way they teach.

- Professors want to be good teachers, and there are ways—even for college presidents, deans, and department heads—to encourage good teaching.

- One key total quality idea is customer satisfaction. We contend that in some important respects, it is useful to think of students as customers.

- The total quality movement has already led many professors to begin to think of students as customers.

The view of students as customers is not universal; it is often resisted, even resented, by professors. It can be construed much too narrowly. Students are not customers in the sense of customers of Honda or Chrysler, where the customer must always be assumed to be right. Nor are students the only customers of professors. And students play other roles than that of customer. For example, it is sometimes useful to regard them as raw materials or coproducers.

But the idea of students as customers is a healthy offset to the paternalistic assumption that many professors have traditionally made, namely that the professors know what is best for students, and that students cannot judge their own long-term self-interest and have to be given lots of medicine that they don't want to take. This professorial paternalism can lead to complacency, stagnation, failure to check how much is really being learned and retained, and the working hypothesis that students' needs coincide with professors' interests. Worst, it can lead to fatalistic acceptance of poor student performance.

By contrast, the idea of students as customers encourages professors to take responsibility for success of teaching, and therefore to become interested in methods of improving teaching. We can testify from personal experience that teaching looks very different when one thinks of students as customers. Professors begin to try to figure out *why* students perform poorly or challenge the relevance of the subject matter for their needs, and they begin to think about getting relevant data. *Our thesis is that professors need much more data than they usually get, and they need it in a more timely fashion.*

The Role of Course Evaluations in Improving Teaching

We begin with the topic of performance appraisal, which is heretical to many total quality gurus. We believe that if a customer focus is to be achieved, some information about customer satisfaction is essential. Since the late 1960s, the Graduate School of Business, University of Chicago, where the authors teach, has used student course evaluation questionnaires in all courses, with systematic public reporting of results. The Kellogg Management School at Northwestern University also makes use of public course evaluations and regards them as essential for maintenance and enhancement of high teaching standards.

Just as grading often make students uncomfortable, course evaluations often make professors uncomfortable. Even the best teachers occasionally stumble, and consistently poor teachers are known to all, students and faculty. But, in spite of minor technical reservations, almost all Chicago faculty believe that the course evaluations provide the best generally available information we have about teaching effectiveness. Faculty members do not believe that the evaluations are mere popularity ratings or that they can be manipulated to achieve high ratings by debasing content and emphasizing entertainment and showmanship. In promotion decisions, a summary of course evaluations always is included in reports and discussions of the Appointments Committee, and this encourages good teaching. Both at Chicago and Northwestern, the course evaluations are taken into serious account by the deans in programs to improve teaching.

Further, although we cannot prove it, we believe that teaching at Chicago is much better than it would have been in the absence of public course evaluations because evaluations encourage the faculty to treat students as if they are customers, whether or not the word *customer* is used.

The Teaching Laboratory at the Chicago Business School

Unfortunately, course evaluations are not very helpful in suggesting specific things to do in order to improve. They are available only after the course has ended. They use general-purpose questions that apply to all courses; by their nature they cannot include course-specific questions. Their numerically scaled questions tell almost nothing about what worked and what didn't. Some information can be gleaned from tabulation of free response comments to see which themes occurred most frequently, but these tell mainly about pervasive problems rather than specific difficulties.

There have been many attempts at many colleges extending over many years to employ very simple feedback questionnaires at the end of class sessions, usually informal but focused on the particular class session, not the course as a whole. The questionnaire might be as simple as the question, "What was the muddiest point in today's lecture?"

At Chicago, two developments led some of us to systematic experimentation in the use of feedback questionnaires and other total quality methodology. This experimentation led to our first concrete response to Galvin's challenge. These were the key developments.

In the fall of 1990, Ian Hau was teaching a large undergraduate statistics course at the University of Wisconsin-Madison. From the students in his class, Hau formed a small quality improvement team to help him improve the course while he was teaching it. (We did not know it at the time, but similar use of student teams was being made at Samford University.)[3]

In March 1991, Andrew Appel, a Chicago MBA student suggested that we use the Chicago laboratory course format to help Chicago faculty members to apply ideas and tools of total quality to improvement of their teaching, curriculum development, and research. The idea of a laboratory course was originated by Deputy Dean Harry Davis about 15 years ago. In its original format, it was a "new product laboratory," in which teams of students work with client companies to develop and implement ideas for new products. The students are coached by faculty and by executives from client companies. The laboratory format has been extended to other kinds of applications, such as implementation of total quality. Thus was born Business 712, The Laboratory to Achieve Organizational Excellence: Improvement of Teaching, Curriculum, and Research (Teaching Lab, for short). In the Teaching Lab, clients are usually faculty members, and most student activity during the first year (1991–1992) was focused on helping these clients. For example,

- Eleven faculty members worked with lab course students or student teams on the improvement of ongoing courses.

- A team of five students worked with the behavioral science group as a unit on the design of a new required course in behavioral science.

- Two students worked with marketing faculty on curriculum issues in introductory marketing courses.

- A student worked with a faculty member in development of a course on high-tech marketing.

- One student in the lab benchmarked the performance of two of the school's most outstanding case teachers.

These student efforts were generally very successful. With respect to ongoing courses, the students developed feedback mechanisms that tell the instructor continually and quickly what is and what is not working—both in class and in the readings—so that, when necessary, appropriate adjustments can be made, usually very quickly. Various tools were used, including focus groups, videotaping, and broader surveys, but the key tool turned out to be a simple fast-feedback questionnaire, used at all or almost all class sessions. The feedback questionnaire evolved from lengthy to streamlined, and, as we shall explain later, the process was simplified to the point that faculty members could do it themselves, and many are now doing so. They design simple questionnaires of their own (often confined to one side of one page), administered and interpreted by the professors themselves. The use of fast feedback has become widespread, though far from universal.

Once it became apparent that professors could apply the techniques themselves, students in the second year of the lab turned to broader issues of curriculum development (for example, developing a proposal for entrepreneurship as a new area in the curriculum), management education (for example, benchmarking business efforts in general management training), and administrative facilitation of education (for example, the use of information technology in MBA education). In the third year, the emphasis was enlarged to broader issues of management education, and in the fourth year there was further expansion to take on general quality improvement projects in educational and professional organizations.

Our experiences in the lab in 1991–1992, when the development of fast-feedback questionnaires was explored systematically, led to several conclusions and hypotheses about ways of improving teaching by fast feedback.

It is essential for students in the class to be sold on the feedback questionnaire. The most important thing is to emphasize at the start that responses will benefit the current class, not just future classes. Use of feedback questionnaires can be damaging to professorial egos because there are sometimes very negative, even hostile, student reactions, even when a course is going well overall. It is extremely helpful, however, to learn about problems while something can be done to address them, rather than to encounter them in full force on the course evaluation questionnaire at the end of the course.

Ordinarily, instructors must rely on subjective impressions as to what works and what doesn't work in the classroom. Experiences in the lab suggested that these impressions are often untrustworthy and that they tell almost nothing about variations in reactions by individual students or subgroups of students. Often student feedback suggested problems that were not obvious to the professor. For example,

- In almost every class, there were problems with hearing or understanding the professor, reading the writing on the board, or seeing the visuals.

- Almost always, students wanted more examples and applications to illustrate abstract concepts.

- Students were impatient with fellow students who try to dominate class discussion.

- It was very hard for the professor to judge whether the pace of the class is too fast or too slow for most students, and casual, volunteered student comments were not a reliable guide.

The feedback questionnaires can probe into deeper problems, such as understanding of basic ideas, student motivation to put effort into course preparation, or reactions to outside readings. We found, for example, that most students tended to skip readings that could have no impact on the course grade.

Probing into these deeper problems, however, requires intense involvement by the professor in the feedback process: *the professor must provide reverse feedback.* Reverse feedback can be oral or written, or both. It can take the form of modifications of the course, answers to specific questions, elaboration of obscure points, clarification of the grading system, fuller comments on student papers or cases, additional references, or bringing in outside speakers.

The process of feedback and reverse feedback tends to draw students and professors more closely together in the improvement of the learning experience. Written reverse feedback from professor to student can literally open a second channel of communication. For example, the professor can provide explanations of points singled out by the fast-feedback questionnaires, even answer specific questions asked on the questionnaires by the students. Reverse feedback can require mean substantial time and effort by the professor, but the payback in avoidance of rework is large for students and professors alike. Rework limits what can be covered in a course, thus limiting our ability to respond to Galvin's challenge.

When we first started to give written reverse feedback to student feedback, we were not sure whether it would be appreciated or even read. From a question on a later fast-feedback questionnaire, however, we learned that our reverse feedback was both read and appreciated.

To emphasize the essential role of reverse feedback, we have begun to use the term *two-way fast feedback* for the combination of fast-feedback questionnaires for students and fast written response from the professor.

Students want professors to provide feedback, preferably fast, not only on the feedback questionnaires, but on all work that they hand in. Students are not happy, say, with a grade on a returned case or other written assignment that is unaccompanied by comments. On the other hand, there is much to be gained by use of technology to speed up feedback on student work. For example, if students send project progress reports by fax, so that these reports come in a steady stream rather than a surge, it is possible to give very fast turnaround by return fax. The authors have found that this is entirely practicable and makes supervision of student projects much easier.

Ground rules for courses should be made explicit: students should understand what is expected of them and what the instructor expects to teach them. It may even be desirable to discuss the ground rules and possibly modify them with the aim of a mutual understanding that is sometimes called a *course contract.*

Examinations and grades play a major role, not always positive, in student responses to courses. Many students seem to lack Deming's "constancy of purpose" in pursuing their own long-term best interests. Motivation is often extrinsic rather than intrinsic; it is a challenge to professors to create intrinsic motivation.

Major improvements can be gained by helping students to make better use of their study time. The fast-feedback questionnaires can obtain information on how the students are actually using their study time. This is a first step for the professor to provide guidance in how to improve study effort.

Another useful total quality aid to students may be the Personal Quality Checklist, developed by Bernard F. Sergesketter of AT&T. This is a simple application of total quality to personal work processes, which turns out to be adaptable to student work processes.[4]

Students need continued guidance—no matter what type of class or class level. There should be some structured instruction even in courses where the faculty are primarily coaches and facilitators, including laboratory courses.

Lastly, we have learned that instructors should devote some time to marketing their courses, including the outside readings, both in advance and during the course itself. If instructors speak enthusiastically about a course, they are "selling" students on the class and will probably find greater student participation.

Experiences and Suggestions

In 1991–1992, the authors not only facilitated and coached lab students who help other faculty, but began to apply some of the lessons learned in the Teaching Lab to their own teaching in statistics and quality management. For example, observing what was being learned from the lab, we made some immediate changes in our own courses.

- Put a copy of the course syllabus and a short student background questionnaire into student mail folders before the first class meeting of a term.

- Reduce the number of course readings and include only highly relevant material.

- Provide a clear idea of what each reading is to accomplish, not just a general feeling that it will be interesting for the students or "good for them."

- Try to "sell" the readings.

- Use short fast-feedback questionnaires ourselves.

All these steps proved to be helpful, but the last one was the most important. We make no claim for novelty, but the experience of the lab helped us to develop a more systematic and intensive approach than many other feedback approaches that we know of. We use a formal one-page questionnaire and do so after *every* class meeting. (Our classes are typically three-hour classes that meet once a week.) We ask all students to respond and make a major effort to achieve a near–100 percent response rate, and we analyze the questionnaires and plan appropriate adjustments almost immediately after the class.

There are, of course, many ways for professors to seek out feedback. The time-honored approach is to evaluate quizzes and homework. An increasingly common approach at our business school and others is to require real-life projects in which concepts of the course are actually applied. Since the authors mainly teach statistics, we assign projects that require real-world application of statistical tools. Student progress reports on these projects provide excellent feedback, especially on pervasive misunderstandings of statistical ideas that are somehow acquired before reaching our courses. For example, students often believe that the size of the R-square coefficient is the only important indication of the success of a regression study; that statistical significance means practical importance; that haphazard sampling is the same as random sampling; that numerical computations make graphical analysis unnecessary; and that correlation means causation.

Professors can do other things. They can ask for a showing of hands on student experiences or problems, institute a suggestion system, and administer (often to only a few students) very short questionnaires, such as Mosteller's famous, "What was the muddiest point in this lecture?" But the formal fast-feedback questionnaire goes one step further: it is systematic, frequent, and focused on learning about specific problems that students may be experiencing.

Feedback Questionnaires

The feedback questionnaires developed in the lab have varied from class to class, but the questions have generally asked both for scaled responses (five-, seven-, or nine-point scales) and free-response comments. Some questions are the same from week to week; others vary according to the structure of individual classes. Questions may refer to such issues as

- Clarity of lectures, quality of discussion, and so on, which can be broken down into specific topics for each class session.

- Presentation effectiveness, such as use of overhead projectors, flip charts, the blackboard, or microphones.

- Student preparation outside of class, including how much time is spent on readings, problems, and cases, and how helpful each reading, case, or problem is perceived to be.

- Free-response comments on what students feel to be the most important ideas, the most unclear or difficult ideas, strengths and weaknesses of the instructor, the quality of discussion, suggestions for improvement, and so forth.

Because of the constraint to limit questionnaires to a single page, which seems to most students to be reasonable, one cannot ask about everything at every session. Certain specific, high-priority questions tend to suggest themselves by the way the course is developing. A few general questions are almost always useful. Example: (five-point scale) "How much did you get out of today's class?"; (free response) "What was the muddiest point in today's class?"

It may be useful to stratify answers according to students' backgrounds. For example, in an elementary statistics course ask

- Quantitative emphasis (engineering, math, science: yes/no)

- One or more prior courses in statistics: yes/no

Then sort the questionnaires into four groups for tabulation.

Feedback questionnaires have usually been anonymous, which means that comparisons through time for the same individuals are not possible. Lab students have experimented with pseudonyms and code numbers in order to be able to make such comparisons, but this has proven cumbersome. The anonymous questionnaires do permit systematic comparison of changes through time for the class as a whole when response rates are high. However, response rates may not remain high if the questionnaire is lengthy or if the instructor gets lazy about reverse feedback.

In summarizing fast-feedback questionnaires for faculty clients, lab students initially did fairly elaborate analyses, including generous use of graphics. Simpler ways kept commending themselves. For example, on questions requiring scaled responses, percentages can be typed onto blank questionnaires; graphs may not be needed except for showing changes through time. Comments can be typed out verbatim or classified into major categories for which numerical counts are given, so that Pareto analysis can be applied to focus on priority concerns.

When the faculty member is doing the whole job, even simpler procedures can suffice: simple tabulations of marginal distributions on scale-response questions and listings of free-response comments. Both can be included in the reverse feedback, with written responses from the instructor on all questions raised by students.

We have never found an urgent need to use the computer in questionnaire analysis. Simple hand sorts and counts can be finished in less time than would be needed for data entry.

Do It Yourself

In designing feedback questionnaires, one must take into account both response burden on students and time available to tabulate and analyze the results, which means that the questionnaires should be as clear and short as possible. Each question should be aimed at specific information that may be useful. Not all questions have to be asked at every class session, even though this means loss of a complete time series over the course of a term.

Whether the questionnaires are administered by lab students, teaching assistants, or the professor, it is essential that students in the class be sold on the process. Typically, students will see benefits quickly as the professor clears up misunderstandings or deals with other problems revealed by the questionnaires.

A Five-Minute, Two-Page, Fast-Feedback Questionnaire

The questionnaire in Figure 1, prepared by Roberts for the first meeting of a course called Statistics and Quality Management, fits on two sides of a single sheet of paper. The instructor hand-tabulated each of the scaled responses, entered the resulting counts on a blank copy of the questionnaire, and simply read through the free-response comments. In about an hour he quickly read through 80 questionnaires to conclude that

- Some students had trouble hearing the instructor, a problem that had never been uncovered by informal processes. (The instructor used a portable microphone in subsequent classes.)

- Students preferred that the classroom be fully lighted when overhead slides are used, and the overhead slides needed to be printed in larger type.

- Most of the students had actually done an advance reading assignment on total quality, found it useful, and felt that the instructor's total quality lecture had too much repetition of material in the book.[5] (Further feedback showed that general ideas about total quality could largely be acquired by reading and that the major emphasis in class should be placed on the more difficult statistical material. Students were able to consolidate their reading background by actually doing two required quality improvement projects, one personal and one organizational. Thus in class, the instructor focused on data analysis; out of class, he focused on project supervision.)

- The students wanted more examples. (The use of examples was accelerated throughout the balance of the course.)

The questionnaire was so designed that the process of actually filling it in—and anticipation of filling it in—can be valuable for the student. The questions focused

FAST-FEEDBACK QUESTIONNAIRE FOR BUS. 520-88, CLASS OF WEEK ____, WINTER, 1992
TODAY'S CLASS

	Little or nothing	A fair amount		A great deal	
Overall, how much did you get out of today's class?	1	2	3	4	5

What was the most important thing you learned?

What was the muddiest point?

What single change by the instructor would have most improved this class?

Please comment briefly on the helpfulness of the advance reading assignments for today's class.

YOUR PREPARATION FOR TODAY'S CLASS

	Little or nothing	A fair amount		A great deal	
Overall, how much did you get out of your preparation for today's class?	1	2	3	4	5

What one thing can the instructor do to help you to improve your future class preparations?

What one thing can you do to help improve your future class preparations?

YOUR PROGRESS ON QUALITY IMPROVEMENT PROJECTS

	Behind schedule		On schedule		Ahead of schedule
On balance, how are you doing on your quality improvement projects?					
Project 1	1	2	3	4	5
Project 2	1	2	3	4	5

What one thing can the instructor do to help you make better progress on the projects?

What one thing can you do to help you to make better progress on the projects?

GENERAL
Is there any other feedback about any aspect of the course, including use of computing or topics, that you would like to hear more about?

Are you having problems unrelated to this course that the instructor should be aware of?

Figure 1. Sample fast-feedback questionnaire (top is side 1, bottom is side 2).

on facts about performance and specific ways to improve performance. The questionnaire also tried to pinpoint difficulties encountered on the course projects and to problems outside class that might adversely affect performance. The questionnaire can easily be adapted to other courses. It should be simple and short.

By the third class meeting, the questionnaire was down to a single page, and all subsequent questionnaires were held to this length. It takes substantially less than five minutes to complete such a questionnaire unless comments are very extensive. Longer, more complicated questionnaires risk a lower response rate.

The questions common to all remaining classes were these.

	Little or nothing		A fair amount		A great deal
Overall, how much did you get out of today's class?	1	2	3	4	5
What was the muddiest point?					

Here, as an example, are the questions unique to the fourth class.

	Not yet in action		Hanging in there		Quite confident
How would you assess your ability to handle the computing in this course?	1	2	3	4	5
	Hardly at all		A fair amount		A great deal
Is project 1 helping you to improve your job performance?	1	2	3	4	5
	Not at all		Getting started		Encouraging progress
On balance, how are TQM ideas being applied in your own company?	1	2	3	4	5
Comments on TQM in your own company?					

Finally, Figure 2 is the one-page questionnaire used at the final class session, the session at which the course evaluation questionnaire was also administered. The question "How much did you get out of the course" also appears on the course evaluation questionnaire. But this last feedback questionnaire obtains a comparative

FAST-FEEDBACK QUESTIONNAIRE FOR BUS. 520-88, CLASS OF WEEK 11, WINTER, 1992

	Little or nothing		A fair amount		A great deal
Overall, how much did you get out of today's class?	1	2	3	4	5

Comments on today's class?

	Little or nothing		A fair amount		A great deal
Overall, how much did you get out of your reading in *Curing Health Care?*	1	2	3	4	5
Overall, how much did you get out of your reading in Schonberger?	1	2	3	4	5
Overall, how much did you get out of your reading in DAFM?	1	2	3	4	5
Overall, how much did you get out of the packet readings?	1	2	3	4	5
Overall, how much did you get out of project 1?	1	2	3	4	5
Overall, how much did you get out of project 2?	1	2	3	4	5
Overall, how much did you get out of the course?	1	2	3	4	5

Any other feedback about any aspect of the course?

Figure 2. Final fast-feedback questionnaire.

reaction to all major components of the class. It turned out that the two class projects—one an individual quality improvement project, the other an organizational quality project—were the most successful of these components.

Reverse Feedback: An Example

To illustrate written reverse feedback, we include Figure 3, a recent feedback questionnaire for the second meeting of a course in the winter of 1994, which is followed by a sample of the reverse feedback provided to students. (See Figure 4.) The student feedback from the first meeting had clearly indicated that the instructor's pace had been too slow (see the bottom of Figure 4). The reverse feedback shows that the pace had been well adjusted at the second meeting. (The question on pace of the class was repeated for the next few meetings to make sure that the gain would be maintained.)

A sample of reverse feedback comments by the instructor is also given. Typically the written fast feedback for a three-hour class meeting of a class of 80 students takes about 3–5 pages, since our rule is that no muddy point, comment, or question goes unanswered. (Of course if several students raise the same issue, only one response is needed.) Note that some instructor comments are simply specific references to readings.

The responses to this question for the first two weeks provide a clear demonstration of the value of prompt customer information in suggesting needed adjustments in the product: the pace at class one was too slow! (The instructor speeded up largely by skipping some of the details on the overheads and concentrating on the essentials.)

Selected Specific Feedback by the Instructor

The following text is an example of reverse feedback. The first two paragraphs are summaries from the instructor. The student questions and comments are in quotation marks; the instructor's response immediately follows.

A frequent muddy point was the specification "–3.25 0.5" in obtaining the histogram of standardized or centered SCORE in the target application, and also what standardization accomplishes. Standardization expresses data in relative terms: deviations from the mean (whatever the mean happens to be for your application) in units of the standard deviation (whatever that happens to be for your application). Hence we can compare distributions from any application on a common scaling. Thus 1 means "one standard deviation above the mean; –2 means "two standard deviations below the mean"; and so on.

The three intuitive ideas of statistical control are listed explicitly and amplified on pages 8–9 of chapter 2 of the text.

FAST-FEEDBACK QUESTIONNAIRE FOR BUS. 520-88, CLASS OF WEEK TWO, WINTER, 1994

	Little or nothing		A fair amount		A great deal
Overall, how much did you get out of today's statistical material?	1	2	3	4	5

What was the muddiest point?

	Little or nothing		A fair amount		A great deal
Overall, how much did you get out of today's quality management material?	1	2	3	4	5

What was the muddiest point?

	Much too slow		About right		Much too fast
On balance how did you find the pace of today's class?	1	2	3	4	5

Comments?

	Little or nothing		A fair amount		A great deal
Overall, how much did you get out of the readings for today's class?	1	2	3	4	5

Comments, overall or on individual readings?

Do you have any questions that you would like the instructor to address in reverse feedback?

What single change by the instructor would have most improved this class?

Any other feedback about any aspect of the course, including questions about where we're going or topics that you would like to hear more about?

Figure 3. Recent fast-feedback questionnaire.

	Pace of Class				
	Much too slow		About right		Much too fast
On balance how did you find the pace of today's class?	1	2	3	4	5
	0	7	62	5	0
(Week One	3	25	43	2	0)

Figure 4. Student feedback on pace of class, week two.

"Copies of overheads are useful for post-class review."

"The interpretation of data is extremely valuable (and can be very damaging if done improperly!). How can we share our knowledge of statistics and quality with others in our organization?" Personal quality gives a good route for explaining general quality concepts. Data analysis is tougher: simple, pertinent graphs are the best route to communicate data analysis.

"Reading is the right way to handle the quality management material."

"Have class submit examples of quality/statistics from their companies." In the past we've had excellent student presentations at the final class.

"I'd like to hear about ISO 9000." There just isn't room for this. To really learn about it, find a member of the class whose company is going through it! If you want my opinion about it, speak to me privately.

"Where does the 3 per 1000 come from?" It's a mathematical fact about the normal distribution. It's useful when the normal distribution is a good model for the data, which often happens.

"Your outline package was great. Thanks for putting it out in advance, too." I hope I can keep doing so.

"RUNS was muddy until it was clarified." Others found it still muddy. Try reviewing carefully pages 10–12 of chapter 2 of the text.

Fast Feedback for Short Courses and Seminars

The authors have also had the opportunity to apply fast-feedback questionnaires at short courses and seminars. In an all-day short course, for example, we have used a fast-feedback questionnaire at the end of the morning session to make adjustments in plans for the afternoon session.

Moreover, we almost always ask questions about audience background, answerable by a show of hands, at the beginning of a presentation, even a short presentation, to *any* new audience. Our experience in the Teaching Lab has convinced us that *detailed information about each specific audience is essential.* Approaches that work spectacularly for one audience can completely fail for another, apparently similar, audience. Each audience presents a unique challenge.

Warning: Student Feedback May Not Always Be Pleasant

Our experience suggests that fast feedback is invaluable for improvement of teaching, but, as we have mentioned earlier, instructors will not enjoy some of the feedback. Individual students may be very cutting in their criticisms. (One of the authors once received the following suggestion for improving his class: "Get a new instructor.")

Moreover, as the current course improves, the students will continue to find things to criticize. The instructor may be happy that the course is enormously better than it was a year ago, but students will want it to be better than it was last week. Instructors are always battling rising student expectations and can never relax with the feeling that the course is well in hand and that it will go smoothly with only minor updating until they retire.

Criticisms of Fast Feedback

Our experience and that of many others at Chicago and elsewhere suggests the value of two-way fast feedback. We know of no other easy way to tell what is working and what is not. Not all faculty members, however, are receptive to two-way fast feedback. Here are some common criticisms and our comments on the criticisms.

- "Fast feedback is time-consuming." This is true, but there is at least a partial offset: fast feedback reduces the time spent in rework, both for faculty and students.

- "After initial enthusiasm, students seem to lose interest." This has not been our experience. Possible problems: the questionnaire is too long or the instructor has neglected reverse feedback.

- "My course evaluations were poor and did not improve with fast feedback." Most experience we know of is otherwise, but we can suggest two possibilities.

  —Remember that fast feedback can lead to rising student aspirations and more exacting evaluations. The same thing happens with purchasers of cars or personal computers.

—The sources of low course evaluations may lie in the instructor's attitudes and personality, as perceived by students. Careful reading of responses to free-response questions can provide clues. For example, student comments may reflect a feeling that the instructor is arrogant, has no interest in students, is inaccessible to students, or is bored with having to teach.

• "Fast feedback lets the students dictate what they are taught, yet they are incompetent to judge." In our view, this reflects a misunderstanding of the rationale for fast feedback. Students have only a limited ability to evaluate the importance of subject matter, but they can tell with high reliability if they are confused, bored, or skeptical about the value of the material. It is essential for instructors to deal with confusion, boredom, or skepticism. Instructors who attempt to deal with these problems are rewarded by enhanced sensitivity to obstacles to learning.

• "Fast feedback is too late. We need real-time fast feedback in electronic classrooms in which students can signal problems as they arise and instructors can deal with the problems in real time." We concur. Improved technology offers the potential of even faster feedback. As this technology becomes available, it should be used. However, the technology is expensive and still not widely available. Moreover, fast feedback on paper can obtain some kinds of information that cannot be captured in real-time in class.

• "Students in my classes have such diverse backgrounds that I can't possibly meet all their needs. I'm sure I'd get bimodal distributions on all the questions if I tried fast feedback." Maybe you would, but in our experience, all distributions have been unimodal, and we haven't had to make heroic tradeoffs in the attempt to cope with student diversity. For example, we have found it possible to adjust class presentations so that virtually all students feel that the pace of the course is reasonable, either about right or, at worst, a little too fast or a little too slow.

How Does the Fast-Feedback Approach Relate to Research on Teaching Methodology?

Have we discovered things that we should have known all along? Could we have learned what we are learning from fast feedback from study of the research literature in education? After all, teaching methods have been studied systematically for decades by professionals in colleges of education. We and some of our students have searched this literature enough to be discouraged. We have the impression that the total quality approach of improving specific courses offers much that is not captured in any general principles of pedagogy emerging from the research literature.

Both research and total quality rely on the scientific method, but there is an interesting difference in emphasis. Successful research leads to principles of varying generality, but it may not be obvious how to apply these principles to make specific improvements. Successful total quality leads to quick, specific improvements of the things one is doing. General principles are likely to emerge from combination and synthesis of what is learned from individual total quality projects.

After starting our work with the Teaching Lab at Chicago, we learned of educational research that is closely related to what we have been doing.[6] Thomas Angelo in *Classroom Research* explains the background thus.

> Despite fifty years of inquiry into teaching and learning in college, the gap between research and teaching is still a chasm that is rarely bridged. Why has this large body of research, much of it good, had so little effect on the practice of college teaching?
>
> Faculty often accuse educational researchers of failing to address the practical day-to-day needs of classroom teachers. . . . Researchers counter that their job is to seek verifiable answers to general questions, not to figure out the specific applications of their findings to particular classrooms. . . .
>
> . . . the critical questions remain unanswered. How can the strengths of research and teaching be joined to improve learning in the classroom? . . .
>
> In 1986, in an effort to narrow this long-standing gap between research and practice, K. Patricia Cross proposed a novel way to engage faculty in the systematic, disciplined study of teaching and learning in their own classrooms. She called this approach Classroom Research. . . . Cross . . . envisions Classroom Research as a way to "reduce the distance between researchers and practitioners to zero . . . by encouraging faculty to investigate questions that arise in their own teaching. . . . Researcher and teacher are one and the same person, and the research-practice gap disappears."

Classroom research entails feedback questionnaires and might be described as "feedback in depth." It is typically focused on a specific pedagogical problem such as failure of students to focus on the main points the instructor intended to convey. This problem may be addressed repeatedly during a course as the instructor experiments with ways of emphasizing the main points more forcibly.

Fast feedback, as described in this paper, is broader. It is designed to unearth and fix problems of any kind that turn up from student feedback. In our experience, most of these problems can be fixed quickly once one knows what they are. Classroom research could be used to follow up in depth on more pervasive and difficult problems.

Beyond Two-Way Fast Feedback

The full scope of the Teaching Lab includes not only teaching and curriculum, but research as well. We have had some experience in the design of individual courses and in exploring areas of potential relevance to MBA curricula such as entrepreneurship and globalization. Even at the individual course level, however, we have focused more on tactics than strategy, and the lab has not had an opportunity to address broader questions of curriculum design (as opposed to course design). Nor has it had an opportunity to address application of total quality ideas to research.

We can still offer a few useful suggestions on course strategy. The usefulness of feedback tools stems from the fact that students know when they can't see or hear the instructor, or when they are confused or unclear about content. They can tell an instructor when a particular topic seems irrelevant to their interests. Instructors must interpret such information in light of all their knowledge and experience. Usually some changes are indicated, if only in devoting more time to marketing the ideas of the course.

Ideas for basic improvements of course strategy, by contrast, must come largely from the instructor. One major source of improvement may come from improved understanding *by the instructor* of the subject matter of the course and of its connections with other subject matter. For example,

- Which topics are essential, and which topics can be left out or deemphasized?
- How can I better exploit what students already know?
- What new topics are needed to keep the course up-to-date?
- Are there simpler and better frameworks for understanding the subject matter? Can, say, one general idea unify several specific ideas, which can then be seen as special cases of the general idea?
- Can process mapping and flowcharting be effectively used to improve course strategy?
- Can the students' own study time be better guided? Can more individual attention to student problems be achieved?

Total quality can make contributions to course strategy. For example, total quality's insistence on continual and substantial improvement is essential to combat the tendency toward very slow evolution—often amounting to stagnation—of textbooks and courses. Total quality encourages widening of horizons beyond minor issues, such as, "Should we teach the median before we teach the mean?" Moreover, total quality tools such as benchmarking, concurrent engineering, brainstorming, and focus groups can bring out new opportunities in course strategy and in curriculum design.

A Personal Postscript on the Galvin Challenge

The preparation of this paper has given the authors a chance to reflect on what progress we personally have made in responding to the Galvin challenge. Most of our teaching relates to statistics and quality management. One area reinforces the other. Exploiting this potential synergy and drawing on the waste reduction achieved from fast feedback, we believe that we are teaching at least 50 percent more than we were five years ago. We are covering as much statistics and have added substantial coverage of total quality. Student performance on quality-improvement projects and applied statistical projects, which is our main measure of success, is substantially better. Course evaluations, reasonably good before, have improved.

A key challenge was posed to one of us during the summer of 1993. The director of our Executive MBA Program had been experimenting with the introduction of new material from business law in two of the 11 weeks dedicated to his own course in operations and management science. The business law material was so well received that he asked us if we would be willing to make available two of the 11 weeks dedicated to our course in statistics and quality management for a further expansion of the law material. Our first impulse was to say, "We're already teaching much more than before in 11 weeks, but going from 11 weeks to nine is simply out of the question. You just don't understand what we're trying to do." Our actual response was, "We're not sure we can do it, but we think we can, and we welcome the chance to try." In planning for this effort, we were stimulated to make a number of improvements, including better guidance of students in hands-on computer data analysis; preparation of special overheads on the salient points of each lecture; and a complete rewrite of the text on data analysis used for the course. The need for all of these changes had been suggested by past fast feedback.

The nine-week experiment is now complete. It was successful in most respects; in particular, about the same material was covered and learned in nine weeks as had been done the year before in 11 weeks. The one problem was completion of the students' quality projects aimed at improvement of organizational performance. Some students needed short time extensions beyond the nine-week period in order to complete their projects, and this work left them less time for business law during the two weeks following our course. On the other hand, all projects were completed at the end of 11 weeks, and this was a better performance than had been achieved the year before.

Notes

1. Myron Tribus, "Do It in the Classroom or Don't Pretend to Do It at All!" (paper presented at the National Quality & Education Conference, Denver, Colo., November 1993).

2. Alan Robinson, *Continuous Improvement in Operations: A Systematic Approach to Waste Reduction* (Cambridge, Mass.: Productivity Press, 1991), 14–15.

3. Kathryn H. Baugher, "Applications of Quality Improvement for the Classroom: Using the LEARN Process for Assessment," National Quality and Education Conference, Denver, Colorado, November 8, 1993.

4. Harry V. Roberts and Bernard F. Sergesketter, *Quality Is Personal: A Foundation for Total Quality Management* (San Francisco: Jossey-Bass, 1993); Harry V. Roberts, "Using Personal Checklists to Facilitate TQM," *Quality Progress* (June 1993): 51–56.

5. A. Blanton Godfrey, Donald Berwick, and Jane Roessner, *Curing Health Care* (New York: Free Press, 1990).

6. Thomas A. Angelo, ed., *Classroom Research: Early Lessons from Success* (San Francisco: Jossey-Bass, 1991). A revised and greatly expanded edition became available in March 1993.

Listening to Our Coworkers: Using the LEARN Process to Improve Teaching and Learning

Dr. Kathryn H. Baugher

A team of students in a vocal performance class leads a discussion that allows class members to express differences of opinion with the instructor over the direction of the ensemble. They focus on what the meaning of *performance* could be and spend hours in class and during the remainder of the day coming to an agreement about the intent of the course. The instructor is thrilled. Never has a class taken such interest in its own direction.

Elsewhere, a team of students designs a survey to determine which testing styles classmates prefer and which type of test helps them learn best. The class identifies a combination test—short answer and essay—as the preferred type. The instructor, agreeing that this type accurately measures the elements of the course, uses it and grade averages rise 68 percent.

A team of students in a philosophy course determines that the greatest barrier to classroom learning is the lack of preparation by some classmates. The team undertakes a pilot project to call these students and ask them questions about the assignment on the evening before class. Class discussion rises to record levels. Everyone is pleased with the outcome.

These are just a few examples of the types of projects LEARN teams are undertaking to systematically improve the learning in their classrooms. Many improvements are on a smaller scale, some larger, but the intent is the same—to improve classroom teaching and learning.

For years there has been ongoing debate about ways to measure and improve classroom instruction. Institutions of higher education have frequently used end-of-course evaluations for this purpose. These evaluations are typically pencil and paper questionnaires administered by some proctor at the end of a course, often at the conclusion of the final examination. These questionnaires cover topics ranging from "fairness of grading" to "subject knowledge of the instructor." Instructors and students alike are very skeptical about the ability or desire of students to rate such course characteristics. Similarly, most are convinced that the primary purpose of these evaluations has nothing to do with improving learning.

Students, instructors, and administrators encourage the search for tools that provide feedback as a course progresses, allowing midcourse correction, as necessary, and allowing professors to adjust teaching styles and assignments to the distinct needs of a particular class. A growing body of work in this area is that of K. Patricia Cross and Thomas Angelo's classroom assessment and classroom research. Many examples are developing as instructors seek to find means of obtaining formative, on-going classroom assessment. Although there are many different tools for conducting classroom assessment, they are generally of short duration, administered and evaluated by the instructor, and helpful in determining where students stand in relationship to course content.

The LEARN team process is one form of classroom assessment. It differs slightly from the previously given description in that it utilizes a team of students to design, administer, and evaluate feedback measures as well as to implement suggestions. The focus of LEARN is the improvement of the classroom teaching and learning process. This difference in focus is at the heart of the LEARN process—to help students and instructors begin to focus on continuous improvement of processes rather than to seek out and solve problems.

Goals and Purposes

The purpose of LEARN is to help students and faculty members work together to improve teaching and learning. This is accomplished by using a team of students who gather formative data from the class and work with the instructor to provide an optimal learning environment and experience for students. Students in this process become responsible for their own learning and for communicating their concerns.

As I began this project in 1992, there were a few basic goals for the design of the process itself.

1. The process would be set forth clearly and would be easy to follow.

2. The process would be nonintrusive to the academic setting.

3. The process would give formative feedback so that instructor and students could adapt the class for better learning.

The first goal was primarily aimed at the design of the process and accompanying materials. I had no desire to make this a complicated process with very specialized materials that instructors had to attend seminars to learn to use. Since this material was using total quality principles, it was also important that the same process used to improve nonacademic processes be used with the model.

The second goal was to make the process nonintrusive to the academic setting—in other words, students attend history class to learn about history, not to learn about process improvement. It is important for students to be able to improve their learning without invading the classroom and actually taking time away from the class. This is a difficult goal; one that still plagues any improvement process.

The third goal was to design a process that would give formative rather than summative feedback to instructors and students. So many of the problems with end-of-course evaluations surround the summary nature of these instruments and the inability of students to benefit from the feedback they give. It became very apparent that improving classroom teaching and learning needed to benefit currently enrolled students.

The first pilots of this process began in the summer and fall semesters of 1992. There were five goals for these pilots.

1. To enhance learning in the classroom

2. To improve student awareness of the university's concern for their learning

3. To raise awareness of the quality movement

4. To discover new ways to improve learning

5. To discover applications of this tool to various disciplines and environments

Results of the Pilot Studies
Enhancement of Learning

To measure the success of the first goal was problematic. It was very difficult to determine what appropriate measures were for "enhancing learning in the classroom." The instructors and I agreed that no single measure could tell us if learning was enhanced. Improvement in grades, increased interest levels among students, better quality course assignments, and improved end-of-course evaluations could all be signs and parts of the larger picture, but we chose not to have one single element determine the outcome. The primary measurement of the achievement of this goal was done through focus group evaluations with faculty and students.

I am very pleased with the results we achieved with the first pilots and continue to get with the ongoing classes who use LEARN. Students and faculty members report improved learning and participation as outcomes. Faculty members continue to participate in subsequent terms and encourage colleagues to do so. Students continue to volunteer for teams. They also encourage other instructors to begin teams. Administrators are pleased with the involvement of faculty and students and have provided additional support voluntarily and upon request.

Student Awareness of University Concern

The second goal was expected to be a by-product of involvement with the project. From focus group evaluations with students, they have become more aware of the importance the university places on their learning. Students have been pleased to see the university make an effort toward improving the classroom experience.

Awareness of Quality

The third goal was also expected to be a by-product of the process. The intent of this goal was to make students more aware of TQM and what part it was playing in their world and the working world. Student focus groups have provided substantial feedback regarding their new awareness levels. Many students have also reported increased interest in prospective employers due to their involvement with TQM.

Discovery of New Ways to Improve Learning

Faculty can and should be involved in numerous activities to enhance their teaching skills. Among these activities should be involvement in classroom research. The aim of this goal, however, is different. The aim here was to involve students in the improvement process in order to tap new ideas and discover ways to improve which occurred to them. Many of the improvements undertaken by our LEARN teams could not have been done by a lone instructor. This approach also fosters student responsibility for learning, which has surfaced as a primary by-product of this process.

Applications

The final goal for the initial pilots of LEARN was to discover the application of this tool to various disciplines and environments. Initial questions about the applicability of this process to humanities, music, and remedial courses as well as courses in math, science, and business have been answered now many times. This process is not linked to particular subject matter or course-related skills. In fact, this process is now being used in a local high school. So, it is apparent that college students have the needed ability to work through this process.

The Codependent Nature of Learning

The codependent nature of teaching/learning has been a significant lesson for me that has arisen somewhat unexpectedly from the implementation of LEARN. Combining a focus on process improvement (rather than problem solving) with the joint responsibility for this improvement on the part of both the student and the instructor helps both to see learning as a shared responsibility. See Figure 1.

Classroom learning generally flows from "points of learning." These points are the intersection of faculty and student engagement. They are the points at which learning occurs. Occasionally students will acquire knowledge through independent sources, but in the classroom, the primary source is the point where student and faculty engage one another in mutual learning.

Barriers to learning exist, however. Problems may also arise in the teaching process. The purpose of LEARN is to enlist students and faculty as a team, working together to remove barriers to learning and, thus, to continually improve the teaching/ learning process. The ultimate goal of this continuous improvement process is to create not points of learning, but channels of learning—to have students and faculty engaged so often that the points simply flow together in a stream of learning. See Figure 2.

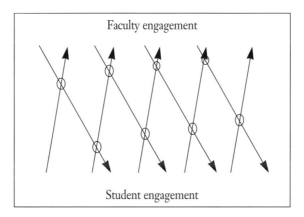

Figure 1. Points of learning.

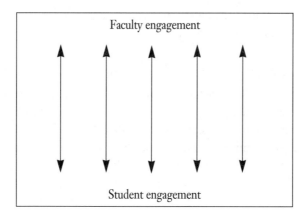

Figure 2. Channels of learning.

Channels of learning occur only when barriers to learning are removed and both instructor and student understand the needs of the other in the teaching/learning process. When a channel is opened, there is a sense that the learning that has occurred is beyond the simple addition of the two inputs—the learning is exponential.

The LEARN Process

LEARN is a team process designed to assist students and instructors in working together to improve the classroom teaching/learning process. The quality team uses the LEARN acronym to work through a basic quality improvement model. The steps are

L   Locate an opportunity for improvement.

E   Establish a team to work on the process.

A   Assess the current process.

R   Research root causes.

N   Nominate an improvement and enter the plan-do-study-act (PDSA) cycle.

The team works through this process several times during the course, identifying improvements and implementing suggestions.

Synopsis of the Process

An instructor determines that one or several of the courses he or she is teaching might be improved by using a LEARN team. This is the L phase. It is the buy-in phase of the instructor. The instructor decides to either investigate the possibility of course improvement through this model, or, if that determination has already occurred, to further improve a course.

During an early class session, the instructor should discuss the LEARN process briefly (5 to 10 minutes) with the students and detail the reasons for forming a LEARN team. The instructor may pass around one of the manuals if the students have an interest in previewing the materials. The method for obtaining team members should be discussed with the class. Generally, volunteers are used. Election by the class and appointment by the instructor are also possibilities. The means of selection should be determined by the anticipated task of the team.

Once the team has been selected, roles should be assigned, and the manual should be reviewed so that team members are familiar with the tools and worksheets available to help them work through the process. Team selection and introduction are parts of the E phase. At this point the team and instructor should evaluate their previous experience with LEARN and other continuous improvement processes in order to determine if there is a need for a facilitator. If so, someone with experience on the university campus should be contacted to meet with the team regularly or on an as-needed basis.

I will address this issue in greater detail in subsequent sections of this paper, but it is of such significance, I feel I must address it here also. Most instructors (nine out of 10) believe that they should not be a member of the team, at least not the leader. This, however, is an erroneous assumption, and our experience with LEARN has proven that it is almost always detrimental to the team. Instructors believe that their presence might stifle or inhibit the team. This is simply not the case. Students will see that an instructor is committed to this process when he or she commits time and energy to its success. The team feels empowered to make changes by the owner of the process. All of the great successes of student teams have occurred when the instructor was a contributing team member or leader. The teams that have faltered have done so because of ineffective leadership.

The A phase—assess the current process—involves using the LEARN team as a focus group of the class. Using simple brainstorming techniques, the team identifies opportunities for improvement within the course. The team attempts to brainstorm all opportunities, making no attempt to exclude options it feels are beyond its scope. Once these opportunities are identified, the team surveys the class to determine which issues are most significant. (See Figure 3 for a sample survey.) The team is looking for issues that present the greatest opportunity for improving the learning in the class. The team is responsible for designing, administering, and evaluating the survey. If the instructor is not a member of the team, he or she should be kept informed of these results. (See Figure 4.)

Oratorio LEARN Team Survey

Our student quality team is undertaking improvements in the teaching and learning of our class. Please rate the following items as they apply to your experience in this class. The rating scale is 1 to 5 with 1 being best (least troublesome) and 5 being the worst (most troublesome).

Classroom environment	1	2	3	4	5	NA
Energy level	1	2	3	4	5	NA
Musicianship	1	2	3	4	5	NA
Background (history) of the music	1	2	3	4	5	NA
Professionalism (of students)	1	2	3	4	5	NA
Unity of the group	1	2	3	4	5	NA

On a scale of 1 to 5, rate the improvement the following changes would make in Oratorio— 1 being most beneficial and 5 being least beneficial.

Mix seating	1	2	3	4	5	NA
Sing to one another (Sections face to face)	1	2	3	4	5	NA
Give back rubs during rehearsal	1	2	3	4	5	NA
Provide history of the music	1	2	3	4	5	NA
Stay on one piece until perfect	1	2	3	4	5	NA
Serve hot coffee	1	2	3	4	5	NA
Distribute pencils to take notes	1	2	3	4	5	NA
Use warm-ups that get class energized	1	2	3	4	5	NA
Other _____	1	2	3	4	5	NA

What about Oratorio pleases you? _____

_____

_____

_____

What about Oratorio displeases you? _____

_____

_____

_____

Figure 3. Sample classroom survey.

Oratorio LEARN Team Survey

Our student quality team is undertaking improvements in the teaching and learning of our class. Please rate the following items as they apply to your experience in this class. The rating scale is 1 to 5 with 1 being best (least troublesome) and 5 being the worst (most troublesome).

Classroom environment	(1.89)
Energy level	(3.09)
Musicianship	(2.21)
History of the music	(2.59)
Professionalism (of students)	(2.8)
Unity of the group	(2.77)

On a scale of 1 to 5, rate the improvement the following changes would make in Oratorio—1 being most beneficial and 5 being least beneficial.

Mix seating	(2.6)
Sing to one another (Sections face to face)	(3.09)
Give back rubs during rehearsal	(2.77)
Provide history of the music	(3.02)
Stay on one piece until perfect	(3.92)
Serve hot coffee	(3.68)
Distribute pencils to take notes	(2.04)
Use warm-ups that get class energized	(1.89)

Figure 4. Sample survey results.

Once the current process has been assessed and the team has identified the issues of greatest importance to the class, the R phase begins. The team uses a cause-and-effect diagram to research the causes of the barriers that have been uncovered or what might be used to effect some particular improvement. (See Figure 5 for a sample fishbone diagram.) Again the team uses a brainstorming mode in order to discover all the possible causes. The team may use a second cause-and-effect diagram to brainstorm possible solutions or courses of action.

With this data in hand, the N phase begins. The team must reach consensus on an improvement and undertake a pilot using the PDSA cycle. I have listed some improvements undertaken by LEARN teams in Figure 6.

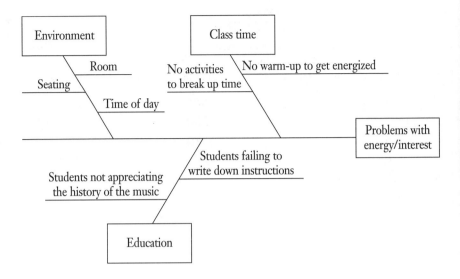

Figure 5. Sample fishbone diagram of discussion.

1. Obtaining enough left-handed desks for students.
2. Better organization of class material for improved retention.
3. Reassigning grade values to assignments to more accurately reflect the work required and the contribution of the assignment to learning.
4. Changing dates of tests/assignments to provide for better feedback to students.
5. Organizing study sessions and study groups.
6. Working with the computer center to provide training to lab assistants on all programs used by students within particular labs.
7. "Buddy" assignments for students to check with each other to improve class preparation and participation.

Figure 6. Improvements undertaken by some LEARN teams.

Recently, we have begun development of a method for LEARN teams to identify barriers to their classroom learning that are system problems across the university. For example, one LEARN team uncovered a problem with computer facilities. This problem is not unique to that single class. Some communication tool would allow this team to provide feedback to the university system and bring about an improvement for many students.

This basic synopsis provides a background of the substance of the LEARN process. The following section details some of the distinctive traits of LEARN.

What the LEARN Team Does

The LEARN team

• *Acts as quality team.* It provides its own insights and suggestions as well as designs and administers surveys to the class. This distinctive trait of the LEARN process enables it to be more effective than end-of-course evaluations or even teacher-administered questions and papers during the course because the students interpret their own answers with the instructor. The LEARN process seeks root causes for course improvement rather than simple statements from students about their own individual difficulties.

• *Focuses on process improvement rather than problem solving.* This enables even the most competent, well-respected faculty member to use a LEARN team because the team is not looking for problems, it is looking for the barriers to learning within an individual course that might improve the learning for that particular set of students.

• *Implements its own improvements.* Rather than merely dropping its suggestions in the lap of the instructor, the team takes action. This characteristic is one of the elements of the LEARN process that brings the sense of responsibility for one's own learning home to students. It is not simply the instructor who is responsible for the learning in the classroom. A wonderful synergistic blend of forces must be present for real learning. Students begin to accept their own part in this process as they seek to implement improvements. They also come to understand other barriers of the total university system that prohibit maximization of instruction.

What the LEARN Team Does Not Do

The LEARN team does not

• *Dictate course content to the instructor.* The LEARN team's responsibility is to design improvements in the teaching and learning process. The team asks questions such as: What are the opportunities for improvement that exist in this course?

What exists in the university system that prohibits the optimal teaching and learning experience in this course? It is the instructor's responsibility to know what needs to be taught in terms of content, and students expect research and preparation on the part of the instructor to stay current. Where the LEARN team is most helpful is in identifying barriers to learning and implementing improvements that result in improved learning on the part of the students.

• *Deal with individual student grievances.* There are university procedures in place to deal with these issues. The purpose of the LEARN team is to uncover barriers to learning that exist because the process needs improvement. It is not the purpose of LEARN to champion the causes or concerns of individual students.

• *Equate improvement with responding to student whims.* One of the greatest concerns and criticisms I hear from instructors (and, believe it or not, students) is that this type of involvement from students in assessment is nothing short of selling out to the customer-is-always-right mentality. That is an incorrect assumption about this process. Students and instructors must work together in order to improve the process. Only by working together can the areas of improvement be correctly identified. Remember, the focus of LEARN is a team approach to process improvement. Once the LEARN process has been in operation about half the term, students begin to dialogue about what are the serious issues that must be uncovered and addressed.

What We Have Learned by Using LEARN

The pilot for LEARN was conducted during the summer term of 1992 at Samford University. The following fall semester over 30 classes used the process at Samford and Belmont Universities. It is currently in use in over 50 courses in a variety of institutions. These attempts to use and refine the process have yielded the following issues, many of which are being designed or implemented at the present time.

1. It is very important, if not imperative, that the instructor be a member of the LEARN team. When it is possible, the instructor should serve as the team leader.

2. This system takes time outside of class to accomplish. There needs to be commitment to this process in order to persist through the entire process. We continue to look for ways to streamline the process and help take less time.

3. The current American educational system spends at least 12 years telling students that they can sit in class and the teacher will give them learning.

They don't see the process as codependent at all. Being involved with a LEARN team really awakens this sense of responsibility for learning in students, and they begin to distinguish their own preferences from barriers to learning.

4. A communication mechanism should be available (whether a university tool or a part of LEARN) to provide feedback to the system from student quality teams. This feedback will prevent improvement, which should occur system-wide, from occurring in isolated areas. In other words, it allows our system to learn.

5. Students become very interested in continuing this program and spreading it to other classes. They also become interested in learning more about continuous improvement. It is now important to develop some means for providing education to students about TQM and to develop a university-wide support structure for LEARN teams.

As we continue to use and track the LEARN process, new opportunities for improvement continue to surface. Students and instructors are helping address these issues and design more useful tools and methods. Beginning in the fall of 1994, four pilot courses began in a local high school setting. Additionally, we hope to have additional training materials developed for use with LEARN and a pilot program for students to earn certification in continuous improvement theory and techniques.

The LEARN process is one method of continuous improvement in teaching and learning. Many others exist. I encourage you to join us in this journey of discovery. It is an exciting adventure to take together.

Bibliography

Baugher, Kathryn H. "Student Quality Teams: Adapting Deming at Samford University." Ph.D. diss., Peabody College of Vanderbilt University, 1992.

———. "LEARN: The Student Quality Team Process for Improving Teaching and Learning." In *Continuous Quality Improvement: Making the Transition to Education.* Dean L. Hubbard, ed. Maryville, Miss.: Prescott Publishing, 1993.

———. "TQM in the Classroom: Using Student Teams to Improve Teaching and Learning." *TQM in Higher Education* 2, no. 11 (November 1993): 2–6.

Three Classroom Experiments on the Use of Quick Feedback

John A. Flueck

College of Business and Economics

University of Nevada-Las Vegas

Introduction

The transfer of knowledge from instructor to student—teaching—should be a straightforward process. One must decide what topics to teach, determine how to teach them, teach them, evaluate how well they were understood, and finally assess how the teaching process can be improved for the next iteration of the course. These steps can be visualized in terms of the Shewhart/Deming cycle.[1]

- *Plan.* Select the topics to teach and how to teach them.

- *Do.* Implement the teaching of the topics.

- *Check.* Evaluate how well the topics were understood.

- *Act.* Institutionalize the new teaching process subject to improvement.

When the teaching process and its steps are examined more closely, however, it becomes apparent that the process is more complex than first imagined. New results and theories keep appearing, budget constraints have doubled the size of the general introductory courses, you no longer have a grader, the course is scheduled just after lunch time, and finally you learn that the incoming students are quantitatively less well-prepared than expected.

These are changing times in the education industry, and instructors will need to review and renew teaching processes in order to remain relevant and competitive.

Total quality (under any of its names) offers a formal approach to systematically improving the teaching processes, and a few colleges and universities already are trying this methodology, as is apparent from many of the papers in this volume. To explore the usefulness of total quality in improving the teaching process in the quantitative areas of a business school, three classroom experiments on the use of written and/or oral quick feedback were conducted in the College of Business and Economics, University of Nevada-Las Vegas, in the summer and fall of 1993. This paper presents the results of these experiments.

The Three Experiments

The background and design of each of the three experiments are as follows.

Experiment 1: Introduction to Management Information Systems (MIS)

This is an undergraduate introductory course covering the topics of DOS, WordPerfect, Lotus, dBase, and Windows. It was taught as a five-week evening summer school course meeting for $2\frac{1}{2}$ hours twice weekly in July and August 1993. The instructor was a mid-30-year-old male with a bachelor's degree in mechanical engineering and an MBA with concentration in MIS. He had a few years of experience in manufacturing and had taught these topics at least 12 times in the past three years. I worked with the instructor on the feedback experiment.

The instructor assigned five paperback texts, each covering one of the five main course topics. He used real-time computer displays, computerized assignments, and optional but recommended laboratory sessions for the delivery of the course material. He had a prespecified set of office hours just prior to the course meeting. The approximately 50 class members were largely first-year business students who worked full-time in the Las Vegas area. The students were encouraged to work together, and there was no grading on a curve or forced distribution of letter grades.

At the opening session of the class, I informed the students that they were an important customer of the instructor (there being other customers, such as the MIS curriculum committee, the department chair, and potential employers). Hence student comments and suggestions were sought to improve the transfer of knowledge from instructor to students. Three feedback questions were asked.

- What topics went well today?
- What topics did not go well?
- What additional comments do you have?

Each student's answers were written on a blank $3'' \times 5''$ card at the end of each class session.

To enhance the motivation to participate, I mentioned that a similar quick-feedback study had been tried at Harvard for an introductory statistics course, and it appeared to have been helpful to both the students and the instructor.[2] I also mentioned the more recent University of Chicago Graduate School of Business experience (Bateman and Roberts, "Total Quality for Professors and Students," in this volume) in using quick or fast-feedback reporting to improve teaching. The instructor's feedback to the students—reverse feedback—was oral. It attempted to briefly clarify some of the points of the previous lecture and to reemphasize the need to use the optional but strongly recommended laboratory sessions.

In an effort to assess how well a teacher can anticipate the student's reception of a lecture, I asked the instructor to predict which topics in the lecture would go well and which would not.

Experiment 2: Introduction to Management Science

This is an undergraduate introductory, applications-oriented operations research course covering the topics of linear programming, transportation and assignments, nonlinear programming, decision theory, critical path analysis, Markov analysis, and queuing theory. The course was taught as a semester-long, twice-weekly course, with 75-minute class sessions, in the fall 1993.

The instructor—the author—was an older (over 50) male with a bachelor's degree in physics, an MBA, and a Ph.D. from a graduate school of business. Although he had extensive experience in teaching and research in quantitative areas, he had not taught the topics of this course in over 12 years.

The instructor was required to teach from a popular management science hardback textbook. He supplemented the textbook with numerous handouts, assigned homework problems, and gave answers to both assigned and unassigned problems. He held office hours immediately following the course and maintained an open-door policy. Student grades were largely based on two exams and a term paper employing at least one of the operations research topics covered in the class.

The 22-member class was composed of junior and senior business students, over half of whom were currently working part- or full-time in the Las Vegas area. There was no grading on a curve or forced distribution of grades.

At the opening session, and periodically throughout the course, the students were reminded of their customer status and the importance of providing quick feedback to the instructor about the course. This experiment's reporting form was slightly modified based on the experience gained from experiment 1 and the reading of a prior version of Bateman and Roberts, "Total Quality for Professors and Students." The quick-feedback report form was changed to a $5'' \times 7''$ card with preprinted headings.

- "Date."
- "List topics that were well understood."

- "List topics not well understood."
- "Hours spent on class preparation."
- "Further feedback."

To increase the reporting motivation, the instructor told the students about the Harvard and Chicago research on the use of quick-feedback reporting to improve the delivery and understanding of the teaching points.

The instructor's feedback to the students included

- Over 15 handouts delivered both before and after class presentations of the topics
- Additional suggested problems with fully worked answers
- Two student-requested review sessions
- A complete review of a draft of each student's term paper

Experiment 3: Introduction to Management Science

This is a graduate MBA operations research techniques course, taught one night a week in the fall 1993 semester. The instructor, the course topics, and the general assignments were the same as experiment 2, except that the operations research material was more intensive, and the feedback from the students was oral rather than written.

The instructor was required to teach from a new hardback textbook covering the standard management science topics. Unfortunately, this text was not very popular with the class, the instructor, and, ultimately, with the textbook selection committee. Thus, the instructor freely supplemented the text's material with numerous handouts and assigned homework problems, and distributed fully worked answers to both the assigned and additional textbook problems.

All 26 students were in the MBA program and over 90 percent were holding full-time jobs in the Las Vegas area.

At the opening session, after informing the class of its customer status, the instructor asked the class to keep him orally informed, typically at the end of each evening's session, as to what topics were going well and what topics were not. This request was periodically repeated throughout the course. Again, there was no grading on a curve or forced distribution of grades.

As before, the feedback to the students included numerous handouts (now over 20), assigned problems and their fully worked answers, two additional student-requested sessions, and a complete review of their term paper before final submission.

Results

These three experiments primarily requested qualitative information from the students. In experiments 1 and 2, this information was processed as follows: the morning after the collection of the written quick-feedback reports, I would classify each student's feedback report into one of three categories: "all went well," "some went well," and "I'm lost." If there was doubt as to which category applied, it was placed in the least favorable category. After constructing the three groups, the instructor and I, or just I in experiment 2, would read the additional comments for further insights.

Experiment 1

Table 1 presents the tabulated results for the three performance categories in the first quick-feedback experiment.

One result is that the student response rate tended to decline throughout the course: the first class meeting yielded 82 percent, the last lecture meeting, only 18 percent. The decline probably reflects a number of factors, including diminishing student interest, their perception of the instructor's interest in the quick-feedback report, my failure to closely monitor the data collection process, the use of only oral reverse feedback (in other words, handouts were not used to reply to the students' comments), and, toward the end of the course, the increasing pressure felt by the instructor to use the full three and one-half hours for the lecture topics.

Table 1. Quantified quick feedback percentage results for experiment 1.

Date	Number (percent)	All went well	Some went well	I'm lost	Total
7/12	41 (82*)	29	59	12	(100)
7/14	26 (52)	46	54	0	(100)
7/19	28 (56)	50	46	4	(100)
7/21	27 (54)	41	59	0	(100)
7/26	16 (32)	63	31	6	(100)
7/28	—Forgot to give out the feedback cards—				
8/2	24 (48)	88	12	0	(100)
8/4	18 (36)	50	39	11	(100)
8/9	9 (18)	22	56	22	(100)
8/11	—Final exam—				

*These percentages are based on a class of 50 students.

A second result is that the "all went well" category substantially improved during the period of July 12 to August 2—from 29 percent to 88 percent—and then dropped substantially in the last two lecture sessions of the class—50 percent on August 4 and 22 percent on August 9. See Figure 1. Correspondingly, the "I'm lost" category was highest at the start of the class (12 percent on July 12) and at the end of the class (22 percent on August 9).

The instructor may have been rushing to finish the required material or tired of this condensed course. In light of the down trend in response rate, there may have been other factors at work. Whatever the causes, it does not appear to be a good ending for the students.

Although the instructor had taught this same course at least 12 times in the past three years, he often was not able to predict which topics would go well and which would not. In addition, upon seeing the first two days' quick-feedback results, and

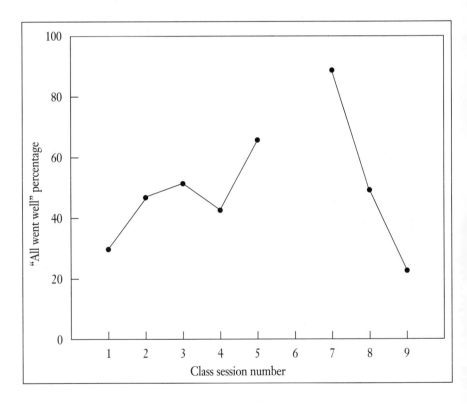

Figure 1. Run chart of "all went well" percentages for experiment 1.

reading the additional comments, he began taking notes on adjustments he would make in the next lecture and changes he would make in the next presentation of the course. Thus, the information in the quick-feedback reports already was having an effect on his teaching process.

The additional/open comments were very revealing in both their breadth and depth.

• *"I won't comment, you can't make me. [Instructor] is doing well, get off his back."* I clearly failed in describing the reasons for the experiment to this student, and perhaps he/she was feeling uneasy and uncertain about the student's role as a customer.

• *"My brain went dead" or "slow down . . . give us more time to do our assignments."* There were a number of comments along these lines throughout the course. They suggest that condensed third summer session courses may be hard on both the instructor and the student. There is little time for replication and digestion.

• *"[Instructor] is entertaining on an otherwise dry subject."* This comment illustrates the problem of keeping students interested in a course that is required but not necessarily desired. Jokes or interesting stories that reinforce the subject matter seem to be appreciated by the class.

• *"Highly skeptical that I can convert lecture to computer!"* There is a difference between seeing someone demonstrate operations on a computer and being able to perform them yourself. It appears that a course of this type should be taught in a computer laboratory where the students can get immediate experience. This approach certainly is easier now with the numerous computer laboratories found at most universities and colleges.

• *"I'm learning, thank you!"* It is rewarding to an instructor to hear from a student that the course's education process is working well. Students need to feel comfortable in using a quick-feedback report for favorable as well as unfavorable comments.

• *"I understand everything, but it will take some time to KNOW!"* This comment succinctly summarizes the problem of a course's goals. One can understand the mechanics of a topic but not really understand the topic.

Experiment 2

The initiation of the quick feedback reporting was delayed until the second week of the class, in the hopes that some of the initial anxieties would be reduced and the class's wishes would be more clear.

After the first few weeks of written feedback, a number of the students suggested that they give the instructor their feedback comments orally in order to save time. After some discussion, the instructor and the class agreed that this change would be made. Thus at the end of each Thursday's lecture, provided there was sufficient time (I sometimes failed to allow time), the class provided oral comments on the week's lecture content and delivery. Unfortunately, this feedback time degenerated into something of a gripe session, and thus the instructor reinstated the written quick-feedback report late in the course, with no student resistance.

The tabulated results for the brief period of written responses is presented in Table 2. Although the initial experiment had a substantial interruption, a few results are worth mentioning.

• Even though repeated emphasis was placed on getting a 100 percent response rate from the students, it did not occur in either of the two written feedback periods; for example, 73 percent responded in September and 70 percent in November. Some students indicated that they were not interested in the feedback experiment because they believed it would have little effect on the material that the instructor was required to present.

• The "I'm lost" category was zero in both of the written quick feedback reporting periods. This was encouraging in that the instructor had prepared over 15 handouts in order to provide the class with explanations and worked examples of the use of various operations research tools. Some of the handouts were preventive, but many were in response to student comments.

• Even during the oral reporting period, there were no "I'm lost" comments, and comments favorable to the handouts were given.

• My impression is that the form of the feedback, written or oral, may not be important provided the instructor addresses the comments in a structured and timely manner.

Table 2. Quantified quick-feedback percentage results for experiment 2.

Date	Number (percent)	All went well	Some went well	I'm lost	Total
9/2	16 (73*)	50	50	0	(100)
9/9	13 (59)	31	69	0	(100)
		—Oral feedback was given in this period—			
11/11	14 (70)	57	43	0	(100)

*These percentages are based initially on 22 students, and after November 4, 20 students.

On this experiment's quick-feedback forms, "further comments" were diverse and included the following:

- *"Can you put examples more to the middle of the board or should I just change seats? Also, overheads are not dark enough to really see. Red felt pens should be make extinct!"* Comments such as these quickly resulted in the instructor becoming more focused and careful with the mechanics of presenting the lectures. Two overhead projectors, properly adjusted, became the standard.

- *"I think class time would be more effectively used if you just taught the best way to do problems instead of going through trial and error examples!"* The instructor presented some of the theory and alternative approaches to solving operations research–type problems. Many of these undergraduate students wanted more of a cookbook approach that would simply show them how to plug in the numbers, and they only wanted to be held responsible for cookbook-type questions on the exams.

The instructor held to his teaching plan, however, and eventually basic theory and word problem applications won the battle. Toward the end of the course, the students even asked for more word problems so they could better prepare for the tests.

- *"Hard to follow along with transparencies and the constant flipping from one to another. . . . if problems were done on the whiteboard in . . . step-by-step manner it would be easier to follow and understand!"* By the third week of the class, the two overhead projectors resulted in less flipping of overheads. There still was the choice between using transparencies with fully worked answers and working problems step-by-step on the board in class. Clearly, the latter is more time-consuming and will reduce the amount of material covered in the class. For me, the choice was quickly dictated by the following comment.

- *"Football coaches who can lift as much weight as their players usually get more respect from their players. If you worked these problems out on the board like you expect us to do on a test, not only would it help us to learn it better, but students would proba-bly have more respect for you!"* As a former high school and college athlete, this comment went right to the heart. I quickly decided to view the teaching process as a team sport with the instructor/coach having the responsibility of preparing the students/players for an excellent performance in the forthcoming conTESTS.

I initiated a playbook: a number of handouts supporting and supplementing the textbook material with fully worked answers for the assigned problems. The play-book grew as each new topic was presented. As instructor/coach I tended to address those items that the team found more difficult to master and worked on them in class.

This last experience led me to rely more heavily on the Socratic approach to teaching, posing questions like: "Why do we need these resource values? Can you graph this solution? What are the values of the optimum solution?"[3]

I extended the sports analogy to the homework/practice sessions; the practice results were counted toward a final course grade only if the performance was outstanding. The star team members, those with B+ and above, were identified when the homework was returned, and the other team members were encouraged to talk to and learn from them. Small study teams also were encouraged, and these seemed to form around some of the star players. All tests were open-notes, closed-book, so the student players could use their playbooks, any last-minute preparation notes, and the practice results for support in the conTESTS.

The students also began to become more aware of their responsibilities for class preparation and mastery of assigned material. This sports team approach clearly clashed with the idea that students were customers of the instructor. Now they were players in whom the coach/instructor had a responsibility for their development. Hence, there was an implicit contract between the instructor/coach and the students/players to teach and learn to the best of their respective abilities. This became the general model within which all subsequent teaching in the course took place.

By the end of the course, the instructor had made a number of substantial changes in the teaching process, and the written student comments also had changed. Now the strongest recommendation for change was: "Need more homework and extra sessions." The instructor scheduled extra practice sessions, and these were attended by over half of the class.

Even in these extra practice sessions, the instructor had the students/players going to the board and working problems selected by the class/team. The instructor and the other students served as coaches, and if all failed the instructor/coach went to the board and relied on the Socratic method and the student coaches to guide him in solving the problem. This team learning approach seemed to work well for most participants.

Experiment 3

Recall that this experiment took place in a graduate, one-evening-a-week, MBA class, and that only oral comments were solicited at the end of the each evening's lecture. I tried the sports team analogy from experiment 2, but, to my disappointment, the class initially did not warm to the team idea. Over time students became more interested, and by the end of the course they too were requesting additional sessions and handouts.

Initially the only comments of any type were typical of evening courses.

- "Too much too quickly."

- "I've forgotten much of my past mathematics. Will we really need it?"

"Too much too quickly" well illustrates the difficulty with once-a-week evening courses of two and one-half hours duration and typically one break. The students arrive at the classroom from a full day's work, and possibly a late night the prior evening doing the required course work. Work problems are still on their minds, and now they must weather two and one-quarter hours of lecturing.

Once a week provides only 13 lecture sessions to cover what is covered in 26 or 27 class sessions for a course that meets twice a week. To cover a week's material in one evening's lecture, instructors must hold to a tight time schedule (breaks tend to last longer than planned), and question and answer periods must be limited. Further, it is not easy to provide a through and stimulating lecture when students disappear at the break, and many of the remaining students are beginning to sport blank stares and drooping eyelids by the last half-hour of the session.

This raises the question as to whether the once-a-week offerings are what the students want or what is convenient for instructors. I find it heartening that our twice-a-week early evening MBA classes have become popular. Clearly, however, we need student data about which is preferred and by whom.

The second comment, forgetting of past mathematical skills, raises questions of what we should teach MBA students, and how a review of needed skills should be conducted. My view is that shared learning implies that both instructor and student are responsible for refurbishing the mathematical skills; hence class time, special sessions, and handouts are needed. It is not consistent with total quality to say to students, "That's your problem; go review your past math courses."

As the course progressed, the "quick oral feedback" period at the end of the lecture became a release valve for more than the course and its presentation. Students questioned such things as the graduate grading policy, the need for mathematics in the MBA program, and the sequence of various courses. I found that my liberated "customers" wanted to let "top management" know that they had a number of suggestions for changing both the current MBA program and the business school itself. I decided to let the "genie out of the bottle," and tried to provide thoughtful answers to student concerns. Over time the vigor of the comments waned.

Lessons Learned

Total quality in higher education makes it natural to address many basic questions, such as

- What topics should be taught?
- How should they be taught?
- When should they be taught?

- How well are the students receiving the transferred knowledge?

These are as important today as in the past.[4]

The three classroom experiments reported in this paper are only first efforts to see how total quality philosophy, concepts, and tools might be applied to improve classroom teaching. These initial efforts have indicated to me that total quality has an important role to play in improving both our teaching and students' learning. Some of the initial lessons that I have learned from this effort are as follows.

- *The opportunity to be heard, orally or in writing, appears to have positive effects on student attitudes toward a course. It is presumed that improved attitudes will lead to improved comprehension.*

All three experiments indicated that students appreciate being able to provide quick feedback, either orally or written, to the instructor. Even when the instructor did not change the course topics or teaching process in response to student feedback, the students still seemed to feel better about the course.

Students can, at times, be very blunt and negative, and this can be quite upsetting to the instructor who thought he or she was giving a great educational performance. I believe that it is better to get these reactions in a timely fashion when there is still a chance to deal with them, than to meet them later in the student's course evaluations, or worse, in the department chair's office.

- *The quick feedback report provides timely student data about all steps of the teaching process. I find that these data are vital for improving the planning, contents, and delivery of a course.*

The quick feedback report can provide both aggregate and individual information in real-time. The data can be analyzed by total quality tools such as run charts, control charts, Pareto charts, or even a sequence of Pareto charts giving a week-by-week account of the teaching problems, as illustrated in Figure 2.

- *Handouts in support of the course, either before or after the class presentation of the assigned material, are highly valued by the students.*

These handouts—reverse feedback—often become the written translators of the course material, and it was not unusual to see students with their three-ring notebook of handouts and worked homework problems studying for an exam. At times the instructor's handout workload was sizeable, particularly when there obviously was need for support beyond that provided by textbook and class presentation. There were many sessions in which the handouts were three or more pages, and the handout on the review of mathematical techniques was over 14 pages. By the end of the course there was a loose-leaf notebook full of handouts, which could serve as the start of a formal set of classroom notes for students in future classes. Also, handouts

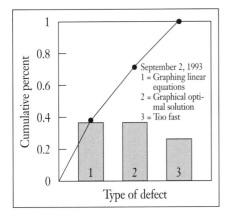 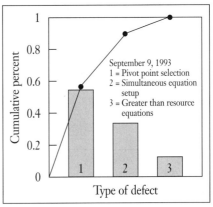

Figure 2. Weekly Pareto charts for the two before periods of experiment 2.

are an important part of the two-way student–instructor teaching system for fixing the learning. See "The Use of Two Active Teaching Methods to 'Fix the Learning'" in this volume.

• *Some students are not comfortable, or not interested, in supplying feedback to the instructor.*

The quick-feedback report response rates never reached 100 percent of the attendees, no matter what the instructor said or did. Names were never requested on the feedback report, so confidentiality did not appear to be a barrier. I doubt that attempting to make reporting mandatory would be effective. Perhaps the free-rider problem is present: some students may be willing to let the others do the work of responding. Elsewhere in this volume, Bateman and Roberts suggest that response rates can be kept high if instructors can convince students, by use of reverse feedback, that it is in the student's self-interest to respond.

• *The sports team approach to a shared responsibility for learning eventually became successful, but initially it was not well-received by a number of the students.*

There is much merit in the concept of joint responsibilities that are shared by instructor and students. The use of quick, two-way, feedback is important in making this concept work. Initially many students were not comfortable with this shared learning responsibility. They indicated a preference for a top-down military approach to teaching: "Tell me what to memorize for the exam, and I will regurgitate upon command."

As the two management science courses progressed, however, and both students and the instructor learned how to better perform their respective roles in this shared learning process, the atmosphere changed. A number of students showed improvement in both attitude (for example, there were oral and written compliments on the shared learning approach), class attendance, and course performance (for example, from F on the first exam to A on the second exam).

• *Students should not be viewed as customers: they are academic clients and should be treated accordingly.*

My experience with the sports team approach to a shared responsibility for learning has convinced me that students should not be viewed as customers of an instructor. When a faculty member accepts the concept of a shared responsibility for learning, which entails two-way quick feedback, he or she consequently accepts the responsibility for attempting to educate the student. This instructor–student relationship is a professor–client one, and hence there is little question in my mind that students are best viewed as clients of the school in which they are enrolled.[5]

Surprisingly, this research on quick feedback has led me to change my view of the student's role in the educational process. I now view students as academic clients, and I treat them thusly.

Concluding Comments

A traditional approach to teaching an academic course is to create an artificial barrier or wall between the instructor and the students in the name of impartiality. In essence, the instructor decides what to teach and how to teach it, and then he or she broadcasts those lessons over the wall. The students on the other side of the wall have the responsibility for receiving, translating, and understanding the lesson's messages.

Unfortunately, this traditional approach does not address important teaching questions, such as what is the best way to teach the course for the particular set of students, what topics are difficult for the students, and how effective are the lectures in transferring the knowledge to the student.

The ideas and tools of total quality provide a methodology for addressing these questions and providing useful answers and improved processes. The three simple experiments on the use of quick feedback are examples of how total quality, and the Shewhart/Deming improvement cycle, in particular, can be used within an educational setting to improve the transfer of knowledge from the teacher to the students.

Acknowledgments

The author thanks David Charron for trying quick feedback in his class and is especially indebted to the students in the three classes for their willingness to try the quick-feedback reports.

Notes

1. W. E. Deming, *Out of the Crisis* (Cambridge, Mass.: MIT Center for Advanced Engineering Studies, 1986).

2. F. Mosteller, "The 'Muddiest Point in the Lecture' as a Feedback Device," *On Teaching and Learning* 3 (April 1989): 10–21.

3. J. A. Flueck, "Some Thoughts on Methodology and Training," *Las Vegas ASQC Section Newsletter* 1, no. 5 (1994).

4. G. Highet, *The Art of Teaching* (New York: Vintage Books, 1950).

5. *Client* is defined as, "One that is under the protection of another, a person who engages the professional advice or services of another." *Webster's New Collegiate Dictionary*, 9th ed., s.v. *client*.

The Use of Active Teaching Methods to 'Fix the Learning'

John A. Flueck
College of Business and Economics
University of Nevada-Las Vegas

Introduction

For centuries, humans have learned by repeatedly performing a task under the guidance of a master, and this approach to learning still applies today, whether it be the plumber's apprentice, the bank teller's new trainee, the store manager's assistant, or the golf pro's aspiring player. In higher education, guided learning is often reduced to the traditional lecturing or broadcasting of the instructor's selected course material, with midterm and final exams used to assess the student's progress. Even if assigned homework is graded, there still is little effort devoted to showing the usefulness and excitement of the subject, the principal concepts and their importance, and the need for guided practice to fully appreciate and understand the subject. These elements are vital to "fixing the learning," however, and the instructor, as master or coach, has this responsibility.

The concepts and tools of total quality offer an additional opportunity to systematically fix the learning through the use of student-led quality and productivity improvement teams. These team projects, under the guidance of an instructor, allow students to try out their classroom learning on real-world problems and to create an active learning experience like the use of laboratory sessions in the physical and biological sciences. In fact, the improvement team projects are better than laboratory sessions because they provide the challenge to find solutions to real-world problems for which, unlike many laboratory applications, answers are not known.

This report focuses on two types of active learning projects, student book reviews and student-led quality and productivity improvement teams, to fix the learning in a senior-level management course on quality, productivity, and competitiveness at the College of Business and Economics, University of Nevada-Las Vegas.

Background

In the spring semester of 1994, I taught a total quality course under the auspices of a required seminar for senior management majors. Two sections of the course were taught: Tuesday and Thursday, 75-minute morning session (17 students) and Thursday evening 2½-hour sessions (24 students). Over three-quarters of the students were working part- or full-time in the Las Vegas area.

This 15-week course used a number of teaching resources to enhance the learning process.

- A recent textbook on total quality
- Videos (for example, *Quality or Else*)
- Weekly lectures, including some guest speakers
- Problem sets with answers
- Numerous class handouts

In an effort to fix the learning, the students were required to provide two written reports.

- A book review of a total quality publication or one that applied it
- A report on a team quality and productivity improvement project

The course sequence started with videos, which were followed by lectures, some quick-feedback reports, and problem-solving homework for an initial assessment of the learning. Then the book reviews were due; the team improvement project presentations and written reports concluded the course. Student grades were largely based on the book review and the team quality and productivity improvement report.

Book Review

The goals of the book review were

- To rapidly immerse the students in the total quality literature
- To develop a student's ability to critique, especially in regard to total quality models used in managing quality, productivity, and competitiveness
- To ensure that these students could write a report whose grammar and composition would be acceptable in the business community

I handed out an outline of the topics and sections that I desired to see in the book review report (see Figure 1), and in keeping with the concept of continued improvement, I promised to critique the initial draft of the book review for structure and coverage in order to enhance the final product.

The book review had not been planned at the outset; I had scheduled a midterm exam. By week two of the class, however, written quick feedback from students prompted me to review this decision: "Why is this class called a seminar in management? I thought this was supposed to be more of a hands-on class with student involvement—not just lectures."

I found the feedback persuasive, and in week three I replaced the midterm exam with a book review. I allotted the next five weeks for each student to select an appropriate book, read it, and write an initial draft review.

Team Improvement Project

The team improvement project was announced in the course syllabus, and a handout in the first week of the course gave the project requirements (see Figure 2).

This suggested outline for the book review of a total quality model is presented to guide the student in the review process and the written report. The emphasis of the review should be on specifying the underlying philosophy, structure, methods, and results that are obtained from the use of the particular total quality model. The book review report should include the following sections.

1. Cover page
2. One-page overview of the book
3. Introduction to the book review
4. General philosophy behind the total quality model
5. Author's definitions of key terms including *quality, productivity,* and *competitiveness*
6. The structure and components of the total quality management model
7. Results of the applications of the model
8. The strength and weaknesses of the model
9. References

The report should be no longer than eight pages, excluding appendices, and a summary of the report will be presented to the class.

Figure 1. Outline of the total quality model book review.

1. Each improvement team should at least outline the problem, identify the underlying process(es) to be investigated, collect data to understand and baseline the process, provide a potentially improved solution, design a statistical study to evaluate the performance of the new versus old process, and select the best of the possible solutions.

2. Each team will produce a typed final report, present a synopsis of it to the class, and support its improvement recommendations.

3. The report will have the following structure and sections.

- Cover page
- Table of contents
- One-page executive summary
- Introduction to the problem and process
- Causes of the problem(s) and baseline results
- Suggested changes in the process
- Pilot study and its comparative results
- Recommendations and expected improvements
- References
- Appendices

4. The investigation and improvement of the process should follow the steps in the Statistical Thinking handout, and thus it should at least contain the following graphs and quantitative results.

- Flowchart of old process
- Cause-and-effect diagram
- Pareto chart
- Baseline results of old process
- Flowchart of new process
- Results of comparative analyses of old to new solution

Figure 2. Requirements for Q&P&C improvement team report.

Students were required to voluntarily form teams of two or three students, select a sponsoring organization from their work experience or the list assembled by the instructor, and select a problem that both the instructor and the sponsoring organization agreed would be suitable for an improvement team. The resulting 15 teams were reinforced by two or three additional members from the sponsoring organization. These teams looked at improving business processes[1] in a wide range of settings from an undergraduate student advising center, a plastic extrusion plant, and a casino's video games and rides arcade, to the Las Vegas valley water district.

As the course progressed, additional handouts were distributed with more detailed information on the required subtasks of the improvement project (see Figure 3).

Statistical thinking is a methodology for problem recognition and solution, and it can be performed by using the following six steps.

1. Recognize the problem and define the associated process.
   a. What is the problem and the related process?
   b. Who has ownership and what are the objectives?
   c. Diagram the current process.
2. Investigate the problem and its underlying process.
   a. Identify causes of the problem.
   b. Define key process measures.
   c. Baseline the current process using the selected key measures.
3. Formulate solutions to the problem and select the best one.
   a. Propose various solutions to the problem.
   b. Prioritize the solutions in the solution set.
   c. Select the best of the available solutions.
4. Try the best solutions in a comparative pilot study.
   a. Identify opportunities for testing solutions.
   b. Try the selected solutions in a small study.
   c. Compare the new with the old solution.
5. If warranted, install the new solution and process.
   a. If a new process clearly is better, change processes.
   b. Incorporate the new solution into the training.
   c. If the new solution is not better, return to step 1 and reassess.
6. Prepare a report on the problem, process, results, and final decision.
   a. What was the problem and the process of interest?
   b. What was done to eliminate the problem and improve the process?
   c. How much was the process improved?
   d. What problems still remain to be investigated?

Figure 3. A statistical thinking methodology.

During each of the last six weeks of the course, I used a questions and answer—Socratic—approach to fixing the learning by requiring each team to present an in-class stand-up report of its current status. I would question and comment on their progress and problems much like the clinical training of third- and fourth-year medical students.[2] Typical issues raised in these sessions included the framing of the problem, the proclivity to jump from problem to solution, the importance of quantitatively baselining the investigated process, the lack of planning for pilot testing of the solutions, and the need to provide clear quantitative results on the before and after investigated process. Thus, all teams got substantial feedback each week.

The final team report included both a 30-minute presentation of the report to officers of the sponsoring organization, invited guests, and the instructor, and the delivery of a typed team improvement project report. Because the presentation preceded the delivery of the final project report, each team also had the opportunity to fine-tune its written report based on comments offered at the presentation.

Results

Book Reviews

The first drafts of the book reviews were an unpleasant surprise in terms of organization, content, and, particularly, spelling, grammar, and overall composition; most of the students simply could not write. To handle this setback, I quickly took three remedial measures.

• To indicate that this problem probably was university-wide and required immediate attention, I handed out copies of a *Las Vegas Sun* newspaper editorial by city editor Geoff Schumacher who decried the lack of English composition skills by college juniors and seniors.

> I taught a writing course at UNLV this fall, and it was quite an eye-opener. . . . Their spelling was atrocious. Their grammar was abysmal. Their organization was poor. Run-on sentences, bizarre capitalizations and mistaken homonyms popped up everywhere. Further, many of them had considerable trouble organizing their thoughts on paper.[3]

• I strongly recommended each student review past English composition texts, and I passed out examination copies of *The Elements of Style* by W. Strunk Jr. and E. B. White, indicating it was my favorite book on English composition style and that I still used it.

• In keeping with the total quality concepts of quick-feedback and continued improvement, the students were allowed to rework their book reviews in light of my detailed comments. This report and critique cycle was repeated two more times beyond the promised original cycle. At the end, I felt there had been substantial improvement in the book reviews and that the marginal benefits of further rework did not seem to be worth my marginal costs of another critique.

Improvement Team Presentations and Reports

There was a high variability among the 15 improvement team presentations.

• Three of the teams were quite professional with team members sharing the presentation, using both handouts and overheads, responding with thoughtful answers to questions, providing all of the required charts, graphs, and comparative results, presenting clear recommendations for improvement, and having their sponsor attend the presentation.

• At the other extreme was one team with a dominant speaker, no handouts and very few overheads, apparent errors in the results, very limited coverage of the required graphical and tabular results, no strong recommendations for improvement, and no attending sponsor.

• The remaining 11 teams had some strong points, but also problems, such as reading from a script, no mention of comparative pilot study results, too little use of handouts or overheads, and failure to emphasize and prioritize the recommendations.

Table 1 presents the list of the 15 improvement teams—the initial five teams were from the morning class and the last 10 teams were from the evening class—with the sponsor's type of business, the process that was investigated, and whether or not the team's recommendations were implemented. In spite of the variability of presentations, it was gratifying to hear that 10 of the 15 (67 percent) sponsors stated they had, or were ready to, partially or fully implement the improvement team's recommendations.

With one exception, those seven sponsors who undertook full implementation of the team's recommendations had at least one employee in the class, and the employee coordinated the improvement team. Alternatively, also with one exception, those five sponsors who did not implement any of the recommendations had no employees in the class. The first exception was the disposable cups team that apparently gained the confidence of the plant quality assurance officer through its diligent, thorough, and quantitative investigations of the cup forming process. (The team worked evenings and weekends in the plant, conducting small experiments on cup brittleness.) Also, this team's presentation was excellent and the project report was detailed, well-written, and utilized both the recommended (see Figure 2) and additional statistical tools.

Table 1. Improvement team projects.

Sponsor's business	Investigated process	Implementation results
Gaming resort	Hiring arcade workers	Partial
Local water supply	Property easements	Full
Perfume retailer	Sales performance	Full
University advising center	Student advising	None
University facility management	Work order system	Partial
Credit cards	Lost credit card	Full
Gaming resort	Arcade promotion	None
Interstate banking	Teller services	Full
Local credit union	Market penetration	Partial
Local credit union	ATM card service	None
Office supplies	Inventory system	None
Plastic extrusion	Print setup time	None
Realty office	Agent satisfaction	Full
Disposable cups	Cup quality control	Full
Time-share resort	Visitor survey	Full

The second exception was the office supplies team whose coordinator was a company employee who was separated just before completion of the project. The team's criticism of the current inventory system, for example, finding unacceptable levels of inventory shrinkage, and its proposal for major changes in the current inventory system, for example, a centralized distribution system employing cross-docking, may have been a factor in this separation. Thus, the implementation of an improvement team's recommendation may depend not only on the quality of the project report, but also on the status of the team's coordinator, the closeness of the team to the owner of the investigated process, and the magnitude of change inherent in the recommendation.

Student Evaluations and Suggested Improvements

In the interest of getting specific student/client feedback to improve the teaching of the course, I asked each student to fill out a one-page feedback form concerning the usefulness of the types of teaching materials, the relative time commitment spent on the book review and the improvement team projects, the preferred team size, and the team collaboration. It typically took a student 3 to 5 minutes to answer the 13 questions and to provide some additional comments. Table 2 and the following discussion are based on the responses of the 41 student feedback reports.

The students perceived great differences in the usefulness of the four types of instruction. The handouts and lectures were indicated to be the most useful teaching techniques. The handouts provided specific explanation and applications concerning the teaching points, and the lectures both encouraged and posed questions to the students. Hence, both teaching techniques were active in that they used either an oral or written student-question-instructor-answer system.

The handouts were a response to student feedback. Their top rank in student-perceived usefulness is not a surprise given some of the experiences in classroom two-way quick-feedback reporting, as is shown in several of the papers in this volume. Also Mosteller has found that handouts of "concrete real-life problems" are very useful for illustrating a specific technique and reviving the students.[4]

The relatively low ranking of the usefulness of videos in the teaching process is surprising, but this finding is consistent with recent research on the appropriate role for video in the new multimedia instructional system.[5] At best, the video appears to be a complementary teaching resource and thus should be used to enhance, not replace, other modes of teaching. It is heartening to see that, contrary to some predictions, there still is an important role for a live teacher in the classroom.

As mentioned earlier, in response to student feedback, I changed my plans from a conventional midterm exam to a student book review. About two-thirds of the students preferred the book review, even though it was much more time-consuming. The students reported that their median study time commitment for a typical senior midterm exam was 6 hours versus the median time of 18 hours reported for

Table 2. Student-perceived usefulness of four types of information transfer, in percents.

Type	None	Little	Moderate	Substantial	Total
Videos	17	25	46	12	100
Textbook	0	19	59	22	100
Lectures	0	2	61	37	100
Handouts	0	0	41	59	100

the book review. This latter time included the time needed to rework their reviews in response to my critiques. Their reasons for preferring the book review included

- "More interesting;" "Allows more room for creativity."

- "I would rather learn than memorize."

- "It forced outside reading in current material on important topics. . . . Also I need practice writing."

- "Gained better understanding of quality process by more in-depth research than from textbook."

These and other student comments suggest there is considerable student preference for active, as opposed to passive, learning.

Students preferring a midterm exam had their reasons, including

- "I prefer the objectivity of the exam."

- "Book review was too vague. I like to know exactly what's needed."

- "Textbook information was better learned and used in case study."

- "[I] just like tests."

The third comment raises a question that is worthy of classroom investigation in its own right. What type of midcourse evaluation best prepares a student for a subsequent active learning project?

I asked for a similar comparison between a final exam and a team improvement project, and now 90 percent of the 41 students preferred the active learning—the improvement team project. Again, this was in spite of the substantial difference between the two student estimated time commitments: a median of 8 hours for a final exam and 55 hours for the improvement project. The students' reasons for preferring the improvement project included

- "Learn more from first-hand work."

- "Able to tie together everything that you have learned."

- "I've learned more with this project than I have learned on any exam."

- "Although it takes more time, there's more learning than the typical 'memorize and regurgitate' processes of examinations."

The four students who preferred a final exam gave two types of reasons.

- "Simply in the interest of time"

- "Easier during finals week"

With regard to number of students on improvement teams, only one of the 33 students who served on a three-student team would have preferred a larger student contingent. On the other hand, of the eight students who served on a two-student team, seven would have preferred a three-student team. The remaining student, a real estate agent, preferred to work alone—not because her team was dysfunctional—because she valued her time highly.

The collaboration among team members was rated as good or better by 39 of the 41 students. The two students who rated collaboration fair and poor were a two-student dysfunctional team; they were no longer speaking to each other. I insisted that they at least make the presentation to the sponsor as a team, and then they could write separate reports if so desired. Their presentation was well-coordinated and went smoothly, but they still wrote separate improvement reports. The sponsor was surprised to receive two reports.

Students' additional comments generally focused on the improvement team project and the enjoyment they got out of active learning. One student summed it up well: "A very neat experience and a chance to taste the real world."

Lessons Learned

In the rest of the 1990s, educational systems at all levels will be under increasing financial and performance pressures. This will result in the reexamination of many of the basic questions related to effective and efficient teaching including how to go beyond mere rote memorization to develop real understanding of a subject in the relatively short period allotted to the teaching. Highet has termed this step "fixing the impression."[6] Total quality provides a philosophy, methodology, and tools for accepting this challenge. This study used two active learning techniques—book reviews and quality and productivity improvement teams—to examine the issue of "fixing the impression" or "fixing the learning." Although the results are based on only 41 students, it is instructive to summarize the lessons I have learned from this study.

• The students have a clear preference for what I term *active*, as opposed to *passive*, teaching techniques. The students found the lectures and handouts—both used interactively between the instructor and the student in this study—more useful than the videos or the required textbook.

• A strong preference was exhibited by the students for real-world fixing-the-learning activities—the book review and improvement team projects—as opposed to written examinations.

• The students strongly preferred to work as members of a three-student component team on the quality and productivity improvement team projects.

• The use of student-led quality and productivity improvement teams to solve real-world problems is a very promising technique for fixing classroom learning.

• I found it surprising that 67 percent of the sponsors already were making changes in their manufacturing or service processes based on the relatively brief student investigations and the resulting reports. I believe that this success primarily was due to three factors: (1) The front-end screening I and the student-employee team coordinator put in discussing the proposed project with the potential sponsor; (2) the trust that student-employees had already built up with their employers; and (3) the fact many of the selected processes appeared to be ripe for change.

• Both the book review and the improvement team project require vastly more work for the instructor than do examinations. To attract sponsors, guide and monitor improvement teams' efforts, and ensure a useful project report requires the instructor to take on numerous roles including salesperson, coach, business consultant, English composition teacher, and so on. There were weeks in which preparing for the two sessions of the course, teaching the interactive course, dealing with team problems, and keeping the projects moving in order to finish on time became more than a full-time job. However, the students' and sponsors' comments made it seem worthwhile.

• Given my experience in this course, I have become a strong advocate of "writing across the curriculum."[7] This means that effective communication is essential in every discipline, and thus specific emphasis is placed on writing in all courses. Also, some universities now are offering specialized writing courses for various disciplines.[8]

Concluding Comments

The traditional approach to teaching a course is to (1) select a textbook whose topics and coverage you like (a departmental committee may have done this for you); (2) use some traditional methods to teach the course, for example, the textbook, lecture notes, chalk and blackboard, a few exams; and (3) wait a few months for the summary of the student evaluation forms.

Unfortunately, none of these steps focuses directly on the most important teaching task: fixing the learning. The goal of fixing the learning is to make permanent the subject matter through understanding the concepts and related material so that even some years later one can still recall the major points of the subject.

The discipline of total quality, through the use of quality productivity improvement teams, provides a methodology for quantitatively addressing this problem. The use of two active learning techniques—book reviews and improvement teams—

are examples of how one can both improve a teaching process and provide the students with better methods for fixing the learning.

Finally, one can add a fourth method, the quality productivity improvement team project, to Highet's three chief methods of fixing the impression in the minds of the students—end-of-course review, open question and answer sessions, and discussion of yet-to-be-solved problems. In turn, the improvement team project can use all three of Highet's suggested techniques.

Lastly, it should be remembered that whatever one's profession, we all at one time or other become teachers, and we have a responsibility to teach well and to make sure that we fix the learning so that future generations can build on our present knowledge.

Acknowledgments

The author thanks the project sponsors, the guest speakers, and most importantly the students in the two classes for their willingness to participate in this new teaching venture. He also thanks the United States Department of Energy, YMPO, Nevada, for its support during the write-up phase of the project.

Notes

1. H. J. Harrington, *Business Process Improvement* (New York: McGraw-Hill, 1991).

2. J. A. Flueck, "Some Thoughts on Methodology and Training," *ASQC Newsletter* 1, no. 5 (1994).

3. G. Schumacher, "Students Lack Fundamental Skills," *Las Vegas Sun*, 1 January 1994.

4. F. Mosteller, "Classroom and Platform Performance," *American Statistician* 34, no. 1 (1980).

5. D. Moore, "The Place of Video in New Styles of Teaching and Learning Statistics," *American Statistician* 47, no. 3 (1993).

6. G. Highet, *The Art of Teaching* (New York: Vintage Books, 1950).

7. G. D. Gopen and J. A. Swan, "The Science of Scientific Writing," *American Scientist* 78 (1991): 550–558.

8. G. Samsa and E. Z. Oddone, "Integrating Scientific Writing into a Statistics Curriculum," *American Statistician* 48, no. 2 (1994).

Total Quality in Instruction: A Systems Approach

Laura Helminski and
Sharon Koberna

Rio Salado Community College, one of the Maricopa Community Colleges in Phoenix, Arizona, is committed to total quality management in its vision, mission, and across its culture. Since 1991, the faculty and staff have worked hard to understand quality improvement. Recent discussions focus on a key point in the quality improvement philosophies of Dr. W. Edwards Deming, Dr. Joseph Juran, and Philip Crosby: "More can be accomplished by working together to improve the system than by having individual contributors working around the system."

As of fall semester 1994, we have worked for almost three years at piloting applications of total quality in the classroom, which we now call TQM in instruction. When we talk about total quality management (TQM) in instruction, we have come to realize that we must work together to improve the entire system that we work in. The larger issues of process improvement, meeting long-term goals, enabling students to be the kind of learners the community wants and needs, and meeting our mission and vision, cannot be the sole work of individual contributors. Therefore, we can no longer talk about total quality only in the classroom; we must spend time discussing and thinking about the entire system. The teaching and learning that goes on in a classroom are part of the larger system—whether we view this as a school, school district, or college. Teachers and students in their classes and the staff and the administrators all operate in a larger system.

Systems Thinking

Understanding a systems approach to total quality in instruction is very important to us. Peter Senge, director of the Organizational Learning Center at MIT and author of *The Fifth Discipline*, states that "systems thinking is a discipline for seeing wholes, recognizing patterns and interrelationships and learning how to structure them in more efficient ways."[1] Everyone, therefore, needs to have a grasp of the big picture, understand the overall goals of the system, know the vision, be aware of the budget, and know the effects of decision making and related actions.

Total quality certainly gives us a way to discuss improvement and, therefore, explore systems and processes. This discussion is very complex. It is not as simple as using new tools and a model for process improvement. There must be new conversations about the system. To give us a common starting point, consider three scenarios.

Family System

One scenario to consider is the family system, which includes everyone in the extended family. A specific example of the process of decision making in systems thinking comes to mind for the holiday season. My immediate family had made specific plans, and each side of our family's relatives also had plans. In essence, there were three family groups involved. Each group had its own needs and methods of operating. As a part of a larger system, I was trying to balance and blend all requests. My brother wanted the celebration at his house at a specific time that conflicted with the time I wanted the celebration at my house and the celebration at my mother-in-law's house. Without communication across the system, there would be hurt feelings, misunderstandings, and confusing information. Through discussions that went across the system, as well as within each group, however, we achieved a solution that did not neglect any one part of the system. This is *system-down thinking*. What occurs or is chosen as the goal for the large system must be clearly communicated and understood down through each level and process so that it can become part of the frame of reference for the most specific process. (See Figure 1.) These spirals can represent the critical levels in the college system. Each spiral has three rings. The center represents the classroom, the second ring is the department level, and the outer ring is the college, or larger system. The shading in the spirals represents the focus of the communication, and where there is no shading, no communication is built in.

Grading Process

Another scenario has us looking at the grading process. The student completes the work, and then the individual teacher records the grade and turns it in to a department

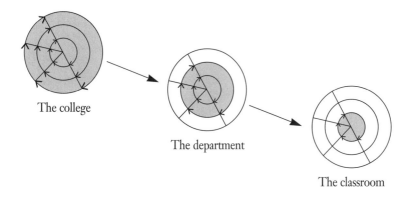

The college

The department

The classroom

Figure 1. System-down thinking.

or program. The staff checks in the roster and turns it in to the Admissions and Records department. Grades are posted to the college transcript and mailers processed. This is an example of *system-up thinking*. The smallest or most specific process must be clearly communicated and understood up through each level and process until it becomes part of the larger system. (See Figure 2.)

No System Thinking

Finally, let's consider a scenario where there may be no system thinking in operation. Getting different medications often is a process without regard for a system. Your primary care physician has prescribed a specific medication, but you may need a prescription from your dentist for dental work, and you may also ask your friend for something for a headache. There may be no information exchanged between these three sources even though you are part of all three processes. In this case, none of the processes is clearly communicating and none is clearly understanding any of the other processes, or the larger system—which is your overall state of health. (See Figure 3.)

In each of these three scenarios we need to consider the impact as well as the necessity of system thinking. The system that we work in may never really become clear to us. Many of us have a job description that focuses almost entirely on a single process, even though it is part of the whole system. Or, instead, we work in departments that are set up to implement some process. Although we realize that we are impacted by others, still we engage in *we* and *they* discussions. In the classroom, department meetings, reports, and side conversations, we believe that *we* are working as hard as *we* can to meet our goals, and we place blame for problems on other

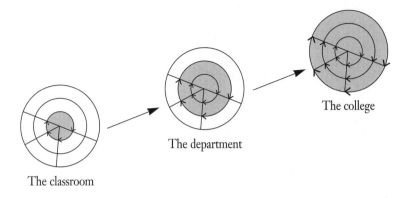

The college

The department

The classroom

Figure 2. System-up thinking.

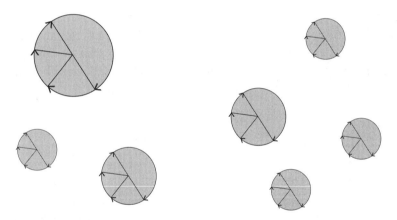

Figure 3. No system.

people responsible for other processes. *They* must be causing the lower student achievement, the lack of resources, or the rework.

Focusing on Process

The entire system we are involved in is made up of processes, each of which is a complete series of actions that produce a specific result. Many of these are fairly standard processes—hiring, scheduling, requisitions—that in the past could be displayed on an organizational chart. However, this organizational chart did not address the communication and teamwork needed to create a learning organization and to enable systemwide efforts and change. Therefore, the continuous improvement that we may want cannot occur. The philosophy of system thinking reminds us that the interrelationships are key for long-term change to occur.

It has become relatively easy to have a cause-and-effect discussion when considering a single process such as teaching a class or hiring a faculty member. Such a discussion usually considers the causes of the effect or considers the effect of several causes. For example, we discuss what could cause an increased student dropout rate or what the effects of an across-the-board budget cut might be. Educators who have these discussions often think they are making progress on improving the process, but because they do not have the larger picture/system in mind, they are not usually making any long-term improvement and may even be making matters worse. Therefore, we need to develop skills in systems thinking before we act on too many cause-and-effect discussions.

One way to develop systems thinking and get a handle on the big picture is to consider how major processes interact. Major instructional processes in the college might include budget, scheduling, marketing, admissions, hiring, and securing facilities and materials; processes in the classroom might be instructional decision making, delivery, assessing, and keeping grades/records. As indicated, we tend to focus on the process we are involved in because it is most immediate to us. Unfortunately, we could spend a lot of time and energy making a change that, while it makes sense in the process, will not work or have the intended effect across the system.

For example, one department might initiate a program to improve student retention. The staff could work directly with the instructors who teach in this program. Advisors and tutors, however, may not be aware of the changes and some of these teachers may also teach in other programs where these changes may have different effects. The bookstore might need to purchase increased numbers of textbooks for students who are now going into higher level courses in increased numbers. The impact of the change would be felt across the system where resources are not ready to accommodate it.

When we are having discussions about our system and processes we need to ask three important questions.

- Are our processes getting better, getting worse, or staying the same?
- How do we know?
- If our processes are changing, how are they impacting the total system?

At the same time we need to ask the most important question: If we want to improve one process, do we know how this change will affect the entire system? An institution that dares to ask these questions must seek out a methodology to answer them. We have found that total quality enables us to move forward, to frame our discussions, and to work toward a common vision.

Implementation Across the System: Operations and Instruction

Rio Salado began exploring total quality as a possible management style in spring of 1991. The president of the college called together members from each constituent group—administration, management, faculty, and support staff—to participate in learning and exploring the principles, philosophy, and techniques of total quality management. This group decided that the college would adopt the quality philosophy in both the operational and instructional sides. A steering team was established to develop and oversee an implementation strategy. All parties—administration, faculty, and support staff—have an equal voice on this team. Our implementation has been based on teamwork within the entire college. After extensive training—an average of 88 hours for all full-time employees—continuous improvement teams were started on the operational side. These teams made improvements in areas such as the requisition process, developing the college schedule, and reducing student bad debt. In October 1993, Rio Salado Community College was awarded the Arizona Governor's Award for Quality 1993 Pioneer Award for implementation of total quality throughout the college.

Instruction

Our efforts for TQM in the classroom were never really just in the classroom. We started the improvement of instruction processes by looking at teaching and learning. Because of accreditation requirements, we had to develop a plan for assessing and increasing student achievement. We used the plan-do-check-act (PDCA) model for continuous improvement as the conceptual framework for our plan, and total quality tools to brainstorm collegewide goals. The Student Achievement Committee uses total quality data collection tools and processes to analyze grade and retention data across the college. Faculty, administrators, and staff brainstormed and developed a list of collegewide expectations of quality instructors and shared these with our adjunct faculty. Feedback from adjunct faculty enabled us to develop expectations of a quality college. Most intriguing and valuable were the conversations that we had and are continuing to have. We spent a great deal of time discussing the old paradigms in which the college operated, trying to envision and work toward the new paradigms. Often we had heated discussions that we called "new conversations in the old paradigms," as we found ourselves starting to look at our system and processes in different ways.

We have come to realize that "continuous improvement of instruction" means that we must be able to communicate and enable change system-down and system-up. What we learn about process improvement from assessment data across the college leads to improvement in programs and departments and then leads to improvement in teaching and learning in the classroom. This is system-down thinking.

Moving from College Level to Program Level

The Student Achievement Committee is using the PDCA cycle to improve the process of teaching our collegewide goals. This committee is a cross-functional, vertically integrated team that includes four faculty, the dean of instruction, the coordinator of institutional research, the director of the Learning Assistance Center, the associate dean of academic studies, the director of admissions and records, and the director of the Media Center. The current pilot project for this committee has focused on a portfolio for student achievement of the collegewide goals in one major program of study. Faculty in this program used several of the total quality tools to brainstorm the concept and process of the portfolio. The Student Achievement Plan has become a critical process at the college. While not one of the traditional existing processes at most institutions, the plan was created because it is critical to meeting our mission and vision. Other programs and departments are working on their own mission statements and goals to ensure alignment with college-level work.

Moving into the Classroom

When implementing total quality in a classroom, several aspects and approaches can be investigated. It has been helpful to lay the following elements on a grid, or matrix, for clarification of areas for improvement: curriculum competencies, teaching processes, and learning processes. (See Figure 4.) Total quality principles, tools, and processes are methods for improving these areas.

This matrix can be filled in a variety of ways as a faculty member explores classroom applications. An example of a tool used to improve a curriculum competency is the cause-and-effect diagram. Using the cause-and-effect diagram can increase comprehension of content (plot, historical event, and so on) with increased student participation. Faculty and students can initiate the use of such a discussion tool for in-depth analysis. We are finding increased comprehension through the use of these tools.

Another approach is to apply the principles of total quality for the purpose of increasing student achievement. We have found we can improve teaching processes by forming a student quality team to provide feedback to faculty during the course.

	Curriculum competencies	Teaching processes	Learning processes
Principles		Student quality team	Student quality team
Tools	Cause/effect diagram		
Process (PDCA)			Improving homework assignments

Figure 4. Sample matrix to determine areas for improvement.

A student quality team is a small group of students who have volunteered, or are taking their turn, to give feedback to the teacher and to the rest of the class on the teaching and learning in the class. They are involved in data collection and analysis. They discuss and suggest possible improvements for the teacher *and* their classmates. This team may meet during class time or before or after the class. Another application that can appear in the matrix is using the PDCA cycle for researching and implementing a change in homework assignments that were perceived as not being helpful, thus improving the learning process.

First Class Session

Instructors can immediately begin to discuss quality improvement with their students. At the beginning of each new class, the instructor normally distributes a class syllabus containing the instructor's expectations of the students. Items include course objectives, homework policy, grading criteria, timelines, and class participation expectations. These expectations should be very clear and specific. After discussing the syllabus, students should be given an opportunity to express their expectations of the instructor and course. For many students this is the first time they have been asked what expectations they have of an instructor. This is also a great opportunity to discuss the teaching/learning relationship and explore the quality principles of learning. We have been surprised almost every time we ask the students about their specific expectations. Expectations we have heard include

- Return my paper by the next class (class meets once a week).
- No trick questions on the test.
- Be a fair grader.
- Be patient if I get frustrated or don't understand.
- Try and keep the material as interesting as possible.

A great deal of time had been spent at Rio Salado developing general principles for quality learning based on the work of Deming, Juran, and Crosby. The intent was for teachers to introduce these in their first class session to set the tone and climate for the semester. Our principles are

1. Quality learning is defined as the continuous process of meeting or exceeding the standards of the teacher, the discipline, and the educational institution (grading criteria, competency-based curriculum, syllabus, and so on) balanced with the expectations of the students (the learning environment, teaching methods, grading, testing, and personal and professional growth).

2. Quality learning is everyone's responsibility; therefore the teachers and the students form teams to make decisions with a focus on measuring and increasing the student's achievement of the competencies.

3. Students want to be involved, are knowledgeable about their own learning, and are able to make decisions that increase the quality of their own learning.

4. Through the use of a structured problem-solving process, teachers and students improve the critical processes of quality learning.

5. An attitude of continuous improvement and a climate of trust promote increased student achievement.

Discussing these principles the first night of class encourages a free exchange of ideas and sets the stage for open discussions. Students are asked to consider what each principle means to them personally and how they can work with the instructor to ensure that the principles are followed. In the first principle, the quality standards of the discipline, college, and instructor are ensured. Principles two and three encourage students to become involved and take responsibility for their learning. This is not always easy for the students. Many of them are used to passive roles and situations that must be accepted as out of their control.

Ground rules is another tool that is introduced the first night. The draft version is first distributed as a starting point for the group. Discussion is held on each rule and agreement is reached on whether to keep it as is, modify it, or leave it out. In this way each group develops its own custom-made version. Ground rules are posted at each class and can be modified at any time. It is important that they become a living document for the group. The following is an example of ground rules commonly used.

- This is an environment of continuous improvement.
- It is OK to make mistakes.
- There is no rank in the room during process improvement.

- Everyone participates, no one dominates.
- Help each other stay on track.
- Be an active and objective listener.
- Respect each other and maintain confidentiality.
- Ask questions.
- Know the lesson's objectives, and use the +/Δ (plus/delta). (This is explained later.)
- Make our needs and expectations clear.
- Collect and analyze data to determine problems and successes.
- Our goal is student achievement.
- Have fun!

Tools

The tools of continuous improvement are utilized in a variety of ways in the classroom. Brainstorming techniques are used to develop the initial thought for a critical thinking essay. The affinity diagram, in particular, can enable students to look at specific processes they are involved in and engage in conversations that give them great insight. Figure 5 is a finished affinity diagram that students generated to start their discussion on increasing learning on homework assignments.

The cause-and-effect diagram can be used to identify the possible causes of low test grades. Data collection tools such as check sheets can be employed to track how many times a student asks questions during a lecture. Numerous classroom assessment techniques can be used by both students and teachers to gather immediate feedback on the learning process.

The cause-and-effect diagram in Figure 6 was completed by a class looking at the possible causes of students not following directions. Using this tool enabled the class to look at many possible causes rather than engage in blaming. The discussion pointed out that there is seldom one cause for one given effect, and that the teacher and the students must carefully consider areas for improvement.

Students were also asked to construct a deployment flowchart of the steps they followed when taking a test. The students and the teacher discussed individual flowcharts in comparison with ideal test-taking habits. Analysis discussions focused on improving each student's approach to taking a test. Figure 7 illustrates one student's test-taking process. This student quickly realized that he had several steps that were missing or not carefully thought through. Analysis of the chart indicated that there

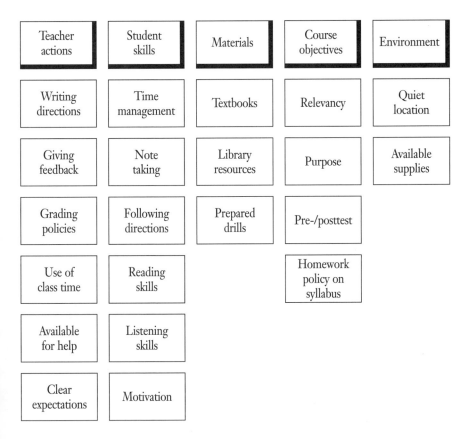

Figure 5. Sample affinity diagram. "What are all the factors in the homework process?"

are several areas where he could improve his efforts. Students often work in groups to discuss possible improvement strategies in their own learning habits.

Improvement Projects

It is valuable to show students that learning is a process and as such can be improved. There are several process improvement projects that we have conducted in different classes. Samples of our process improvements projects include the following.

- To improve the process of students completing independent learning projects so that the students decreased their total time, but still successfully—a grade of A or B—completed the assignment.

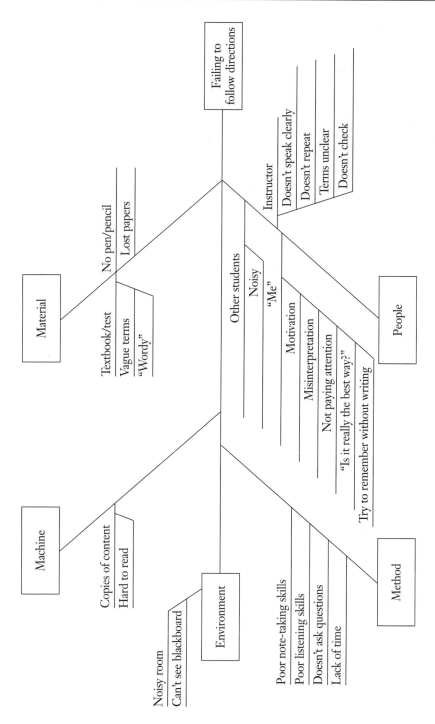

Figure 6. Cause-and-effect diagram of students not following directions.

Time	Student	Instructor	Quality issues

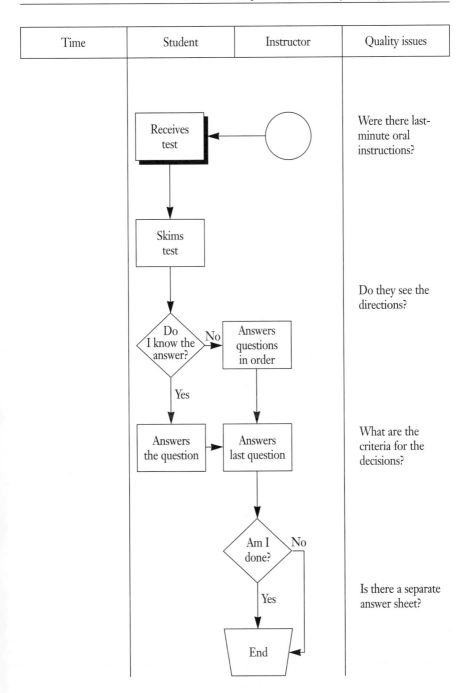

Figure 7. One student's view of following written test directions.

- To improve the process of choosing appropriate test-taking strategies by the student so that test scores are increased (and more accurately reflect students' knowledge without the usual effects of test anxiety).

- To improve the process of studying for tests so that time spent studying decreases and test scores increase.

All process improvement projects begin with a standard statement: "Improve the process of . . . so that. . . ." This allows more consistent discussion and improvement across the college.

After a process improvement project is identified, the class goes through the PDCA cycle to identify possible causes, collects data, analyzes the data, develops a possible change/improvement, and implements the change. Data are collected again to determine the effectiveness of the change and the students determine how to integrate this new information into their existing learning processes.

Issue Bin and Plus/Delta

Two other tools used regularly in classes are the issue bin and plus/delta. The issue bin is a useful tool to help the class stay on track. When topics or questions come up that are important, but not related to the topic at hand, they are placed in the issue bin. At the end of class the group decides what action will be taken on each item in the issue bin.

The plus/delta, often called plus/change, is used as an evaluation tool at the close of each class session. The instructor and the students list the things that went well and they want to keep on the plus side and things that need to be changed on the delta side. (See Figure 8.) Students, usually eager to give the instructor feedback on how the class went, make an important contribution to improvement. Of equal importance is the opportunity for students to evaluate their own behavior for the class session and be aware of areas that may need improvement.

Students' Responses to Total Quality in Instruction

Students definitely feel a change in the climate of the classroom when the teacher introduces total quality principles, tools, and process improvement. They like the emphasis on teams for improving processes, whether these teams work during, before, or after classes. It is interesting to note that often the teacher's role is that of a member of the team when the focus is on process improvement. Student comments indicate they like seeing that they have more responsibility because it gives them more power and control and ultimately increases their own learning.

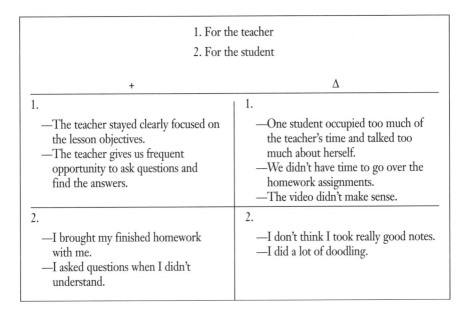

Figure 8. Sample plus/delta evaluating feedback on teaching/learning in a class session.

The use of total quality tools for content analysis and process improvement generates many good discussions, gives variety to the classroom activities, and provides opportunity for physical movement. The biggest advantage of the use of total quality tools is that productive conversations can come to closure with everyone feeling that learning was achieved. The structure of the tools, having a beginning, a middle, and an end, enables this productivity to happen. It is particularly interesting to watch students initiate the use of the tools. While the initial teaching of the tool does take additional time, any resulting problems would be alleviated when the skill is integrated into the system. Not having the same discussion regurgitated over and over again because there wasn't a sense of closure saves time overall.

In-depth total quality implementation in instruction focuses on process improvement: improving a teaching or learning process with our students during the semester we are teaching them. It is also important that communication of this improvement must take place across the system, so that the teachers in subsequent classes know about and can build on the work that has already been done. In a class on critical and evaluative reading, one student wrote, "I know that if the next teacher that we have will use the plus/delta, we would participate more because we saw how you considered our suggestions, made changes, and improved the learning process."

Students always comment on the surprising insight they gain on how other students learn. A strong comment reflected this: "I was very surprised that one person in my group said she just sat the night before the ILP (independent learning project) was due and wrote it. She took notes of what we did, implemented the changes for the next ILP, and as a result, she got a perfect paper." A final comment was very encouraging: "I'm glad that I decided to take this class because it showed me how total quality in the classroom works. If this is the way that it is going to be taught under total quality, I hope that it is here to stay and that you guys can spread it fast." In another class, an introduction to psychology, the comments were also encouraging. One student commented, "It's not just a teacher lecturing to a class. I like the fact that we can all participate and put in our ideas." Another students' comment reflects the improvement in the learning process, "Total quality is cool because it helped me to shut up and listen to someone else's opinion and to get something from the group and to find value in others' opinions and ideas."

Pitfalls/Cautions

When working toward systemwide change, reactions often appear that may cause major concern to those leading the new conversations. We have experienced the stress that change causes and would caution others to work harder than ever at clear and open-minded communication.

In discussing possible pitfalls that accompany a systemwide change, it is important to realize that the old paradigm has encouraged a person to be a single player who gets his or her own job done and knows that his or her own perceptions are the "real" story. Common reactions that need to be dealt with include these comments.

- People don't like you any more; you become an outcast, a rabblerouser.
- There are many misunderstandings because of different perceptions and hidden agendas.
- People who have worked in "lone ranger" professions now must be team players.
- Consensus means backing off.
- Systemwide changes take more time.
- Some people, students and staff don't want increased responsibility.
- Some people don't want their work to be measured or affected by work completed by other team members.
- There is often a sense of not doing something fast enough.

- Never-before-collected data can be overwhelming and depressing; it is easy to have a knee-jerk reaction to symptoms rather than finding the root causes.

Benefits

There are great advantages to working toward systemwide change. These benefits can be felt by the individual and by everyone throughout the system. Common benefits include

- Results are long-term.
- There is more buy-in because of the teamwork.
- There is less sabotage or ignoring of changes and improvements.
- There are less wasted resources.
- Students get the course content and process improvement skills, and the ability to apply both.
- The dynamic of the class is different; it takes the burden off the instructor to make sure everyone is learning.
- There is increased student achievement.
- You are actually moving toward your vision.
- You are becoming a learning organization.

Implementing total quality in instruction means improving teaching and learning processes *and* learning new ways of thinking and interacting in order to understand the system in which we work.

It is apparent to us now that a key word in Senge's definition of systems thinking is *discipline*. A discipline has content and requires time and conscious effort to master. The long-term results will certainly be worth it.

Note

1. Peter Senge, *The Fifth Discipline* (New York: Doubleday, 1990).

Using Minute Papers in an Executive MBA Program: Listening to the Voice of the Customer

David M. Levine
Bernard M. Baruch College (CUNY)

Introduction and Background

One of the interesting dilemmas for a faculty member who is professionally interested in the area of quality improvement is determining how the principles that are central to the quality improvement philosophy can be applied to improve the quality of one's own classes. Without a doubt, one aspect of any course relates to what students are actually learning, and, in particular, what subject areas of the course are the students having the most difficulty with. This is something that a traditional student evaluation form is unable to measure, particularly on an ongoing basis. One useful instrument that has been developed to enable a faculty member to receive continuous feedback is the minute paper.[1] This evaluation instrument (see Figure 1 for a sample form) can provide an immediate feedback to the instructor concerning what topic was most important, most difficult, and most confusing, along with suggestions for what the instructor and the student could have done to improve the quality of the class. In addition, the use of the minute paper approach sends a message to the students that this class will be different from traditional ones in that the input of the student (as a customer of the course) will be considered.

The course in which the minute paper was used was part of an Executive MBA Program at Baruch College. The Executive MBA Program differs from traditional programs in that students (who are typically working full-time in managerial positions in a variety of organizations) attend classes as full-time students, taking three courses per semester (on alternative Fridays and Saturdays) for three semesters per year for a period of two years. It is an intensive program, with students as a cohort

Minute Paper

Course _____   Date _____   Prof. D. Levine

1. What was the most important topic in today's class?

2. What was the most difficult topic in today's class?

3. What was the "muddiest" point of today's class?

4. Did you get what you came for in today's class?
   Yes _____   No _____
   If you answered yes, what did you get? If no, what was missing?

5. Was the pace of today's class
   Too slow   Just right   Too fast

6. What could the instructor have done to improve the quality of today's class?

7. What could you have done to improve the quality of today's class?

Figure 1. Sample form for the minute paper.

group. Students in this program exhibit a strong desire to receive a more practical, nonacademic approach to course material. Their attitude is "How can we use this Monday morning when we go back to work?" Teaching these students is demanding, challenging, but also very rewarding, although clearly not something that many academics would be interested in or able to successfully deal with.

The need to listen closely to the voice of the customer in the course that I was teaching was even more critical due to the restructuring of the MBA curriculum. The quantitative elective course in the new curriculum was selected to be regression and time series forecasting for the executive program. In addition, the introductory statistics course, which was part of the core requirements in the old curriculum, became part of the preliminary requirements in the new curriculum. This created a specific dilemma for the executive program, since this preliminary material had to be fit into an already intensive cohort program. After much discussion between the program director and me, we decided that six classes would be taught to the students on weeknights early in the fall 1993 semester in preparation for the regression and time series forecasting course, which would be taken in the spring 1994 semester.

Using Minute Papers in the Regression and Time Series Forecasting Course

This reorganization of the curriculum made it even more important to obtain immediate feedback from the students in this course before a situation developed in which students were not able to keep up with course material. My intention, when I began the course, was to spend one week reviewing basic material prior to beginning coverage of regression analysis. On the basis of feedback obtained during the class and in the minute papers filled out at the end of class, it was obvious to me that I had to reevaluate my plans. Two things had occurred that impeded a smooth transition into the course. First and foremost, it was clear that the retention of the basic statistical review material was not what I had expected. I realized that part of the problem was that this material should have been presented just prior to the spring semester on a just-in-time basis, rather than six months before it was to be used. Second, due to the nature of the executive program, some students did not enter the program until after some of the review sessions had taken place and were able to get only minimal benefit from them. These deficiencies would have been much more difficult to uncover had I not used the minute paper approach.

The minute papers also provided a transition into each subsequent class since I decided that before beginning any new material, I would address the issues raised in the comments contained in the minute papers. Here, I noticed that an interesting phenomenon occurred. Once the students realized that I was taking their comments seriously and adjusting the course accordingly, a different atmosphere, one of greater cooperation, became apparent. The use of the minute papers was especially appreciated by executive students, who unlike traditional students, consider themselves much more of an academic customer.

After the second class, I found that 16 of the 18 students had judged the pace of the class just right. However, there still seemed to be a need to use one additional class for further review. This suspicion was confirmed by the minute papers of this third class that included comments such as "I have a clearer understanding of the basics," "I have a foundation that I can build on," "Great review. Thanks for caring," "Excellent broad brush of the forest," and "All the parts fit, great overview."

In the next three classes the basic elements of the linear regression model were developed, the data sets for the regression term project were introduced, and the use of the STATISTIX statistical software package was explained. Each class began with a discussion of the muddiest point from the previous class. Among the topics that were reviewed based on the minute papers were the standard error of the estimate and patterns in residual plots. Perhaps the most valuable comments for me as the instructor were those in response to the questions "What was missing from today's class?" and "What could the instructor have done to improve the quality of today's class?" Among the responses were: "Give layperson examples of the jargon," "More case studies," "Need a better overview," "Present a case and have us work through it in class," "As a businessperson I really want to understand practical applications of the material," "More cases to discuss in class and build on," "Show me when the flags go up," and "Take one case from beginning to end."

These comments made me realize that the use of a regression case study was needed to tie together the material from several classes. Fortunately I had access to several case studies from a forthcoming text that combined both managerial and statistical issues in a set of cases that ran throughout the text as well as a chapter of case studies.[2] I selected a portion of a case entitled the Whitney Gourmet Cat Food Company Case and gave it to the class as a homework assignment for the following class. At the beginning of that subsequent class, we spent about one hour discussing both the interpretation of the statistical results and their managerial implications. I then distributed annotated copies of computer output obtained from the STATIS-TIX package for the data contained in the case, along with a detailed statistical analysis and interpretation of the results. The response from the class when we finished the case was highly positive and enthusiastic. This was reinforced when I read the minute papers. Among the responses were the following: "The class provided a transition from theory to practice," "Going over the case was extremely helpful," "Case was great," "I obtained a practical understanding because of the case," "The case was extremely important. It tied the various statistics together, and gave meaning to what we have been doing thus far," and "The case was realistic and helped me to understand how to apply the concepts we have learned so far."

Since the reaction to the case was so positive and with several students asking for additional cases, I decided that the main part of the midterm exam should consist of a case analysis. In fact, I took a portion of another case involving the *Lacey County Courier* newspaper, provided the students with relevant computer output, and gave an exam that contained absolutely no computations.

The last experience that I would like to report concerning the minute papers occurred in response to the first class in which I discussed multiple regression. More than half the class reported that the pace of that class was too fast. One even responded "Don't turn off the flow of questions—in TQM talk, aren't we the customers?" I realized, in retrospect, that I had unconsciously felt a pressure to try to cover too much material too soon and quickly adjusted my style in subsequent classes.

Conclusions and Epilogue

I found that the minute papers made me more sensitive to how I was presenting material in my classes. It was an interesting, although sometimes a sobering, experience to get some immediate feedback on what was the most important, most difficult, and muddiest topic of the class, along with whether the pace of the class was just right and what both the students and I could have done to make the class better. It truly enabled me to get much closer to the voice of my student customer than I had previously been able to. Finally, it created more of a bond between the professor and the group of students. If fact, on the last day the class, much to my surprise, the class presented me with a thank you card signed by the entire class and a small gift. Although quite rewarding to me, this could be rather threatening to instructors who are used to the "sage on stage" teaching style.

Notes

1. F. Mosteller, "Broadening the Scope of Statistics and Statistical Education," *American Statistician* 42, no. 1 (1988): 93–99; D. A. Zahn, "Notes on the Use of Minute Papers in Teaching Statistics," in *Proceedings of the Statistical Education Section of the American Statistical Association* (Alexandria, Va.: American Statistical Association, 1992).

2. D. M. Levine, P. P. Ramsey, and M. L. Berenson, *Business Statistics for Quality and Productivity* (Englewood Cliffs, N.J.: Prentice Hall, 1995).

Instantaneous Feedback

Terence Reilly
Department of Decision Sciences
University of Oregon-Eugene

In my teaching, I have been using a variation on the theme of fast feedback that may be of interest to readers of this volume. The impetus for this method came from a workshop given by Harvey Brightman.

The title, "Instantaneous Feedback," is at most a slight exaggeration. At a point late in a lecture—usually with 10 to 15 minutes remaining—I ask my students to do the following:

- For one minute, sit and reflect on the lecture. Think of a question you wished that you had asked during the lecture. For example, were there any points that you do not understand, or do you have any question concerning the examples?

- Take one minute, write down your question(s). Pass them to the front. (No names.)

Note that this takes only two minutes. The time limit is important: it sets a structure within which the students feel more comfortable. Two minutes are ample for serious students. Longer than two minutes opens the door to possible distractions. The deadline helps the students stay focused.

With the remaining few minutes of class time, I answer these questions. In a class of 50 students, there are usually about 20 questions, and many of these questions are essentially duplicates.

Benefits for the Students

I have found the students are very receptive to this process. They see that I care about their understanding of the material. Their questions are answered immediately when the concepts are still fresh in their minds. In addition, this process allows the opportunity for follow-up questions.

When the students know I will ask them for questions, many of them pay closer attention and start to mentally catalogue possible questions.

Benefits for the Teacher

This procedure takes very little of my time, but it provides me with immediate and useful information.

- It leads to dialogue between the students and me.

- There are times when I do not fully understand their questions, which gives both students and me insight into their difficulties. It could be that the question is not well formulated, but it could also be that they think they are asking something different from what they actually wrote.

- I can start the next lecture with a tie-in from the previous one. I start by referencing a previous question.

It may seem that this method should take more than 10 to 15 minutes, but my experience is that 15 minutes is sufficient. When it occasionally turns out that I do not answer all the questions, I deal with these unanswered questions in my office immediately following the lecture, or, at the latest, at the beginning of the next class period.

I do not follow this process in every class, but I do it about 70 percent of the time. My students tell me that they wish I would do it in every class.

I would like to acknowledge Harvey Brightman and Bob Clemen for introducing me to cooperative learning techniques and would like to give a special thanks to Harry Roberts.

From the Front Lines: Improving Quality in the Classroom at Penn State

Larry D. Spence, Associate Professor, Political Science, and
Louise Sandmeyer, Executive Director, Continuous Quality
Improvement Center, Penn State University

The Need for Total Quality in Higher Education

We believe that the time has come for serious application of total quality principles to higher education. Surveys show that faculty and administrators alike recognize an imbalance between teaching and research. Most support the view that more universities should reemphasize the mission of undergraduate instruction. The emphasis of total quality on feedback, teamwork, intrinsic student motivation, and process improvement could help faculty to seek, apply, and document the outcomes of superior teaching practices.

Yet for all of its promise—and for all the encouragement from leading corporations—total quality has thus far had limited impact on the core processes of higher education. In particular, the principles and tools of quality improvement have not blossomed in the classroom. There are many reasons why this is so. The explosion of funded research since World War II has diverted effort, creativity, and resources from undergraduate teaching. Even before the war, educators complained of an academic culture that weakly supported teaching improvement. That culture has promoted these conditions.

- Most university teachers operate with only crude theories of how to teach and of how students learn.

- Faculty are without the benefits of careful teaching evaluations and assessments of learning outcomes.

- Faculty regard teaching practices as private and individual, and rarely discuss what goes on the classroom.

Although Clara Lovett has noted that no culture may be more receptive to the idea of continuous improvement than higher education,[1] the culture of higher education is hostile to the language of quality management and especially total quality management. Most faculty members don't like the vernacular of manufacturing processes or consumer services.

In fact, however, industry has historically provided models for undergraduate education. In the early decades of this century, universities applied the Taylor model to mass produce education; employing rigid course schedules, uniform teaching units, standardized classrooms, and inflexible academic calendars. Hence a discussion must end at 2:15 P.M. or a subject must be taught three hours per week for 15 weeks because the scheduling bureaucracy has ordained it. Having adopted the older industrial model of teaching, universities today must deal with its inefficiencies and rising costs. Modern corporations may have much to tell faculty and administrators about quality improvement, but the alien jargon of the business world keeps many from listening.

Professors operate like entrepreneurs, within a management-by-objectives structure. That structure emphasizes short-term objectives—research publications, especially articles in peer-reviewed journals—over long-term accomplishments—the creation of new knowledge or improvements in teaching and learning. Research publications enhance the reputation of the institution, at least among peer educators, but they have fewer benefits for students or the public. Many administrators and faculty members recognize the need to change this, but no one knows how. So the emphasis on research publications bleeds faculty time and leaves little for classroom innovation efforts.

Many faculty members believe that administrators rarely set clear priorities or give them the resources to redesign and improve undergraduate instruction. They also believe that there are few rewards for faculty who take seriously their obligations to students in their own classrooms or in classrooms upstream or downstream from their own.

Discussions of applying the outlook and tools of total quality to higher education tend to get bogged in verbal disputes, but there is some good news. Professors still must teach, and pressure grows for them to teach more and better. Every day instructors face the issues of how to improve the quality of undergraduate education. Many seek and use what principles and practices they can find and adapt to enhance their teaching.

We survey here several efforts to raise the quality of the undergraduate classroom at Penn State in the hope of expanding the conversation about quality and education. We write as participant/observers, not aspiring consultants; we try to minimize jargon and missionary zeal; and we do not push a particular quality approach. We seek promising initiatives, but we also report conflicts and apparent failures. We do not offer a how-to manual, but suggest some promising routes to improve teaching and learning in higher education.

Total Quality Classroom Initiatives at Penn State

Of the more than 20 Penn State faculty members who expressed some interest in applying quality techniques in the classroom during the last year, we interviewed nine in May and June of 1994. These faculty members were

- Larry D. Spence, associate professor, political science

- Gren Yuill, professor, architectural engineering

- Robert Melton, associate professor, aerospace engineering

- Mary Kendall, director of instructional services, College of Engineering

- Jack Matson, professor, civil engineering, and director of the Leonhard Center for the Enhancement of Engineering Education

- Michael Dooris, research and planning associate, Office of the Vice Provost and Dean for Undergraduate Education

- Robert Novack, associate professor, business logistics

- Frederick Eisele, professor and head of the Department of Health Policy and Administration

- Kathryn Dansky, assistant professor, Department of Health Policy and Administration

Note that four of these are from fields other than engineering and business, the fields that have received the greatest attention by advocates of total quality in higher education.

We first asked them to tell us, in their own words, how they were using the principles and tools of total quality to improve classroom teaching and learning. (At Penn State we use the term *continuous quality improvement* (CQI). In keeping with the terminology of this book, we use the phrase *total quality* in this paper.) We followed up this initial approach with more specific, but open-ended questions. Based on these interviews, we found that the total quality movement has encouraged three important practices in the classroom.

- Frequent feedback from students on instructional delivery

- Teamwork among students in various collaborative learning projects

- The use of students as focus groups to reflect student attitudes back to instructors and as quality teams to survey student satisfaction with course conduct and to suggest improvements

Another practice frequently mentioned was "classroom assessment," an idea not usually labeled as a part of total quality. Assessment refers to systematic attempts to find out what students are actually learning as opposed to what they can memorize and regurgitate. Concern with total quality has promoted interest in Cross and Angelo's ideas about classroom research on learning outcomes. Concern with classroom research likewise promoted interest in total quality. The American Association of Higher Education currently sponsors an annual meeting devoted to assessment and total quality.[2]

A few of the professors mentioned the usefulness of the idea of variation and the use of quality tools in plotting and analyzing data and generating improvements. Larry Spence, coauthor of this paper and an associate professor of political science, has experimented in this area, and we include a brief report on his results.

We found some faculty exploring the best teaching practices established through research and practice over the last decades. Quick summaries are found in the *Seven Principles for Good Practice in Undergraduate Education* and Thomas Angelo's "teacher's dozen" of research-based principles for improving teaching.[3] This literature suggests that

- Listening to students may be the quickest way to improvement.

- Student participation is central to the teaching/learning process.

- Assessment, feedback, and other ways to find out what students have learned should be part of the training of all faculty and students.

- Formative evaluation to improve teaching and learning is key to pedagogical development.

(Had we surveyed faculty working in this area we could have generated a larger list of classroom improvement efforts at Penn State.)

We found a few professors beginning to think about the idea of seeking and surveying the outside customers of higher education—corporations, governments, and communities—to find what they need by way of skills and knowledge in university graduates. An account of two institutional efforts in this direction at Penn State concludes this paper.

In summary, we found many toes in the waters of quality improvement in the classroom, with a few instructors ready to plunge, but most were content to wade in deeper over the next few years.

Student Feedback

Initial discussions on campus about total quality in higher education have made instructors more sensitive to student feedback. Instructors want to know what students think of their course design and presentation. Every instructor we talked to employed some way of eliciting student views on how they were conducting their courses. Sometimes these were elaborate.

- Robert Novack, in his business logistics course, uses a six-person total quality management team of current and former members of the class. This team designs and conducts surveys of student satisfaction every two weeks. Students are asked about the legibility of overhead projections, effectiveness of instructor's communication, accessibility of the team, fairness of the grading system, and quality of the course. The team plots the data using run charts for each item and brainstorms ways to improve student satisfaction when student responses point to problems. Novack says his next step is to find some ways of assessing teaching and learning.

- Jack Matson uses a quality team to conduct weekly surveys of his class in environmental engineering. He asks, "How is the course going so far?" and students answer on a scale of 0 to 10, meaning from very poorly to very well.

- Gren Yuill in his course in the fundamentals of heating, ventilation, and air conditioning, surveys students' satisfaction with the quality of his presentations, course notes, and teaching assistant two or three times a semester. He reports that student input was helpful in improving presentations. He gives extra credit for suggested improvements in the course notes.

  Yuill reports that he has difficulty maintaining enthusiasm for using quality techniques in his course, although students show higher satisfaction. He says either his course is now perfect or he hasn't made any real difference. Total quality needs to go beyond improving teaching to improving students' skills as learners, Yuill thinks.

- Mike Dooris solicited student expectations of his course in organizational behavior, offered his expectations of students, and, at the end of the course, used a questionnaire to find out if the expectations were met.

- Some faculty employed less formal techniques. Mary Kendall comes to class one-half hour before and stays one-half hour after class to build relationships with students in her graduate course in teaching for graduate engineering students. Several instructors employed student E-mail accounts to get comments on assignments, lectures, and examinations.

- Larry Spence, who teaches a political science honors course in critical reasoning, says customer satisfaction questionnaires are limited in their usefulness. He finds they are a useful way to explore the quality perspective in the classroom for both students and instructors. "But if you get stuck there," he adds, "You won't get any quantum leaps in the quality of instruction or learning. I try to assess what students learn and how I can improve that."

Student Teams

Everyone we interviewed made some use of student teams. Five of the nine employed quality teams that served as focus groups, reflecting student responses and suggestions to the instructor; as collectors of data on student attitudes; or as partners in monitoring and improving classroom quality.

- Matson reported that his team (with an outside facilitator) gave him unique insights and caused him to look more closely at the teaching/learning process.

- Novack's teams are responsible for everything that goes on in his class except what is taught and how it is taught. The quality team creates the syllabus, drafts examinations to be edited, schedules exams, conducts exam reviews, administers exams, and holds office hours to help students.   .

- Spence formed a total quality team according to university guidelines with three students, a faculty member, a statistician/facilitator, and an outside member from a local school board. That team examined what the instructor had to do to provide a learning context and what students had to do to learn and to become self-directed in his honors course.

All the instructors who worked with quality teams employed some form of team training or training in the tools of total quality. Nearly all thought more training in both areas was necessary to better performance. Eisele said that students working in teams needed "handrails" and that meant more training in total quality skills and more training in team building and teamwork skills.

Because of the growing demand for training in quality efforts, the Continuous Quality Improvement Center at Penn State is sponsoring a one-credit course in total quality tools especially designed for undergraduates who are or want to be involved in quality projects.

- Kathryn Dansky, who teaches an undergraduate course in human resource management in health care organizations, has devoted much thought and effort to using student teams as a focus of learning. Her formula for building successful student teams is

Training

Constant feedback to and from teams

Stating and keeping deadlines and giving recognition and reward to team outputs.

She has devised a four-level developmental classification of workplace groups: (1) committees, (2) task forces, (3) cross-functional teams, and (4) self-directed work teams. In the classroom, she translates these levels into types of student group assignments in collaborative learning. The committee can be simulated by assigning group exercises in class; the task force, by assigning group research papers; and cross-functional teams, by a group term project in which students meet regularly and develop specific team roles. Dansky hasn't yet tried self-directed work teams.

Using Dansky's classification we found that eight instructors employed committees and task forces. Several used cross-functional teams, and one had students collaborate in self-directed work teams.

• Kendall emphasizes the role of relationships in learning, the effectiveness of collaborative learning, and the empowerment of students. She uses teams to help students take responsibility for their learning and to change classroom focus from teaching-centered to learning-centered. Her group assignments range from pairs in class who explain to each other how they solved homework problems to teams of four students who undertake the redesign of undergraduate engineering courses to involve collaborative learning.

Kendall is an example of an instructor who employs collaborative learning techniques, but does not explicitly use the language or tools of total quality.

• Matson designs his class to involve cross-functional student teams. During the first five weeks of the course he assigns each student to a team of four. Each team's task is to master the knowledge content of the course. He gives the class 50 questions and the notes to the course. At the end of five weeks he administers an oral exam to the teams. Each student answers one question, and the team must achieve the same mastery as previous classes. Teams pass or fail as a whole and can retake the exam up to three times. Matson dismisses failed teams from the course.

During the second five-week segment, students form new teams of four by selecting an interest group that will participate at the end of the segment in a mock hearing on locating a nuclear waste disposal site in Nevada. A panel of experts and student peers evaluate the team performances. Matson says this exercise requires students to be both teachers and learners.

During the last five weeks, student teams design and carry out a project to improve some environmental condition so students can employ their knowledge to guide actions.

• Melton assigns students to cross-functional teams the first day of his two-semester course. He trains them in team building and maintenance with tasks such as building the tallest structure possible with uncooked spaghetti and masking tape. Teams undertake a one-year design project that results in a presentation to NASA officials. Team members evaluate their peers at midterm and at the end of term, and Melton shares these evaluations with each student.

• Spence's teams of four to five students function as something approaching autonomous work groups. Their task is to help each other prepare weekly home-work assignments. He gives them a general procedure and they modify it to fit their abilities and learning strategies. Students discuss and work on problems together, but hand in individual assignments. In addition, each team prepares a policy brief for presentation at the end of the semester.

• In Eisele's course, students work in teams on similar policy briefs.

A Broader Initiative

At least one cross-functional team has been formed to look at courses from a broader institutional standpoint. In November 1991 the deans of two colleges (science and engineering) appointed a team to identify ways to improve the basic physics prepa-ration of undergraduate engineering majors. The team included faculty from both colleges, undergraduate and graduate students, and administrators. This was the first total quality team to look at the teaching/learning process and to measure how well a sequence of courses met curricular goals.

Mike Dooris, team facilitator, reports that the team has used a variety of feedback mechanisms such as surveys, tests, and interviews to learn about faculty perceptions, student levels of satisfaction, and student learning.

Some improvements implemented by the team include

• Revising homework, grading, and quiz policies to encourage out-of-class study

• Introducing an alternative course structure to the large lecture

• Adding more laboratory opportunities

• Enhancing teaching assistants' training

• Giving a study strategies guide to all students in the introductory course

- Offering a one-credit physics preparation course to students who have been identified as at risk

- Employing CD and video production capabilities in the lecture hall setting

Dooris says that members of the team see the total quality framework as an imperfect but useful fit with the complexity of teaching and learning. They view the quality perspective as a useful catalyst for a systematic and constructive effort to improve the learning of physics by engineering majors. Students can be seen as customers, but are also understood as the workforce and the product. The team thinks there are many other customers besides students. It concluded that grades are an incomplete measure of student learning.

One of the team reports states that its task has been and will continue to be stimulating better teaching and learning. The team wants to address the issue of how to better motivate today's students and make them want to learn rather than threaten them into memorizing formulas. Team members want to find out how to keep faculty motivated to enhance their teaching without detracting from their research activities. Finally, the team wants to convey the message to faculty that effective teaching is much more than telling and that effective learning is more than listening.

Classroom Assessment

The use of teams to introduce collaborative learning in classes shifts the focus from instructors and teaching to students and learning. A complement to this shift are the classroom assessment techniques devised by Patricia Cross and Thomas Angelo.[4] Their approach to the improvement of undergraduate education is based on the assumption that the quality of student learning is determined by the quality of classroom teaching, although not exclusively. Thus the best way to improve learning is to improve teaching.

Improvement of teaching, in turn, depends on instructors creating explicit objectives and devising ways to get specific feedback on the extent to which these objectives are met. The improvement of teaching and learning requires classroom research—the attempt by instructors to find answers to questions they have formulated in response to the problems encountered in their classroom. The major question to be answered by classroom research is: what are the students learning?

At Penn State, classroom research has attracted many instructors in the last years. The Instructional Development Program has offered two faculty workshops on the subject, and the Office of Undergraduate Education has distributed copies of Cross and Angelo's book to every academic unit.

Cross and Angelo offer a smorgasbord of techniques to find out what students learn from and/or how they respond to assignments and exercises, but none is more popular than the one-minute paper. Four faculty members interviewed use this device. First formulated and widely used at Harvard, the one-minute paper is designed to elicit timely specific student responses to lectures, discussion, and assignments.

Typically the instructor stops the class a few minutes early, tells students to fold a sheet of paper in half, and answer one question on each half. The questions usually ask about the most important or interesting thing learned today, issues that remain unanswered, or things that were most unclear.

- Melton assigns two one-minute papers per week in his class and asks students not only what they learned and what remained murky, but what is most/least helpful about the course and lessons.

- Yuill assigns the exercise at the end of every class and writes a reply to the class's comments that he distributes at the next class.

- Spence employs the device occasionally, but also experiments with other Cross and Angelo techniques including background knowledge probes, concept maps, assignment evaluations, and memory matrices. He argues that what is important about assessment is how the data generated can be used to improve the teaching/learning process.

The temptation of one-minute papers and similar devices is to correct only an immediate problem by discussing it more fully in the next class, offering additional examples, reviewing problem sets, or giving additional assignments. In other words, they help instructors put out fires, but may not help them improve the process. Of course fires may have similar origins and putting out one fire may teach something about preventing others. (This view underlies the paper by Bateman and Roberts in this book.)

Classroom assessment techniques (or *CATs* as they are fondly called) have real promise for classroom improvement. Their generated data require analysis with elementary tools of statistical process control, particularly run charts and control charts. This helps instructors to find out what differences in teaching—in terms of assignments, texts, discussions, and so on—make a difference in learning. Several instructors are beginning to use these tools, using quiz and examination scores as indicators of what students learn.

- Yuill gives one examination a week, thus using one-third of his class time on testing. Although he does not believe that he can compare data from year to year with great precision, he does report that his text and quiz scores keep getting better.

- Dansky plots individual and class quiz performances on run charts and then has the class brainstorm improvements to raise the mean on quiz scores.

- Melton agrees with Yuill that historical data comparing class performances from year to year aren't useful because the content and methods of his course change each year.

Variation and Statistical Process Control in the Classroom

Despite the limited precision of year-to-year comparisons, Spence has applied the techniques of statistical process control to the homework results of his critical reasoning course. He has taught this honors seminar in how to think better for more than 10 years to a class of 10 to 25 students. Based on the work of Eugene Meehan, he calls the 300H course "applied epistemology."[5] Students call it "300 Hell."

Spence began teaching it in the traditional way: lectures, reading assignments, memorization, and regurgitation. He says that his homework assignments asked always the burning question: "Did you read and understand the text?" But he found that when he assigned something like real problems to the students—problems that citizens, legislators, or policy analysts try to solve—most of the students failed miserably.

There were always one or two bright students who came up with respectable solutions, however. He asked them how they did it. They said they tried to apply what they were reading to their everyday lives. And they argued that the homework assignments contradicted the whole point of the course. The students insisted that memorizing the text was not thinking. Spence discovered that his assignments didn't prepare students to frame or solve problems; they even dampened performance.

As a result, he modified the homework assignments to require students to apply what they read. Since these assignments were novel, he paid close attention to students' performance and began to keep better records from year to year. If he found a poor class average on an assignment, he revised it, eliminating problems like vagueness and ambiguity; or he revised the way he prepared students for the assignment through class discussion and exercises.

After several years Spence saw some improvement and some puzzling failures. Sometimes he could not tell if he was making improvements. Then he says, "I discovered Deming and the ideas of variation."[6] Ignorance of variation leads professors into dubious practices, Spence says. Beginning instructors are very sensitive to student criticism and failures. In response, they innovate. Each time there are many failures on a quiz or many snores in the classroom, they try something new—a new set of questions, examples, approaches, textbooks, or seating arrangements.

This behavior lasts for about five years. Then instructors discover that nothing works! None of the changes seem to make any particular difference over time, although sometimes they work spectacularly or fail horribly. So most professors quit paying much attention to student responses and learn to teach to please themselves. When bored, they make changes; but the failure of students to learn no longer spurs them to try to improve. Often the students are blamed.

Spence says something like this happens to every professor. By responding too frequently to variations in learning, instructors drive the classroom process out of control. (Deming called this behavior tampering.) Once they see that students' performance gets worse over time, they give up on improvement and often turn to research or other pursuits to satisfy their instincts of workmanship.

Variation plagues faculty relations with students in a more insidious way. When a student achieves a high score on an assignment, the most probable score on the next assignment is a lower score. Conversely when a student scores poorly, the most probable next score will be higher. (This is an example of what statisticians call the regression phenomenon.) Combine these probabilities with the usual professorial techniques of motivation—chew tail if the score is low, praise if the score is high—and the consequence is that instructors learn that praising students spoils performance and yelling and blaming spurs improvement.

Spence concludes that professors need to understand variation and the processes of teaching and learning so well that they can predict the quality of their output. Once they understand how they contribute to variation they can work toward improvement. The goal becomes the design of learning exercises with measurable outcomes that give students the opportunity to master knowledge and attain intellectual skills. They try to change assignments from drills that make students memorize and regurgitate into practice sessions requiring students to think—to acquire, apply, assess, and, as necessary, correct the new knowledge.

The major question becomes: How can instructors change grading assignments from a means to motivate to a means to measure the effectiveness of pedagogical designs? Spence attempted to answer that question by applying the principles and tools of continuous quality to his classes. With the help of former students he developed a procedure for reading the assigned text, reviewing it in work teams, doing class application exercises, and completing the homework in the same teams. With student assistants, he then grades, returns, and reviews the homework. The class then analyzes the entire process in the light of results.

This procedure reduced cycle time from one week to 48 hours on graded homework and from two days to 15 minutes on graded class exercises. "Once you see how prompt feedback helps improve student learning, then grading assignments becomes less drudgery and more of a useful task," Spence says.

Spence also changed the grading system to account for variation. All students whose scores were within the normal distribution of the class and don't show consistent improvement or consistent below-average performance receive the same grade. Students outside the distribution on the high side receive higher grades provided they can document and explain their improved techniques to the class. Students outside the distribution on the low side receive lower grades. Spence taught students how to keep their own control charts. At first, the students reacted by calling Spence's new performance evaluation socialism. He told them that the source was actually the Ford Motor Company.

Spence's results are promising, but preliminary. Based on the data he has analyzed and charted over the last four years, there has been smaller variation as measured either by the range or standard deviation of scores. See Figures 1 and 2 for examples.

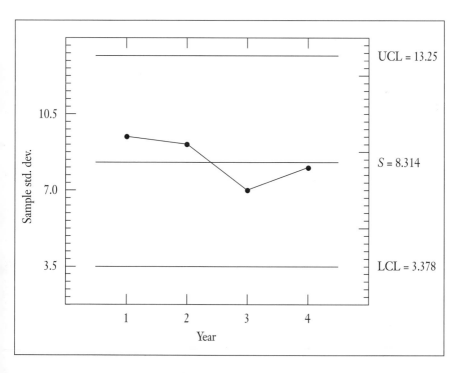

Figure 1. *S* chart for score.

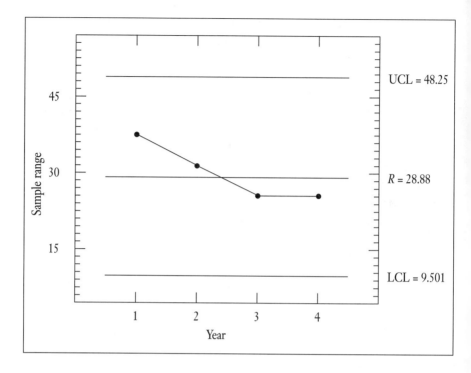

Figure 2. *R* chart for score.

With the help of Beth Meteer of the Continuous Quality Center and Sue Cross of the University Testing Center, Spence has established control limits and process capabilities. The average class score has improved and the upward trend in class averages is significant and shows a rate of change of .22. See Figures 3 and 4.

These data help Spence focus improvement efforts, but he is not satisfied with them as good measures of how well students are learning. The data from year to year are not exactly comparable since Spence and his student assistants keep trying to improve the assignments. The quality team working on improving the class is trying to devise better measures. Specifically the team is looking more closely at individual questions and at clusters of questions defined by the central knowledge and skill objectives of the course. "What we have learned by trying to measure teaching/learning effectiveness is not just how hard it is, but that it can be done better." Spence finds it more rewarding to work on improving measures than to create arguments that conclude the assessment of teaching effectiveness is impossible.

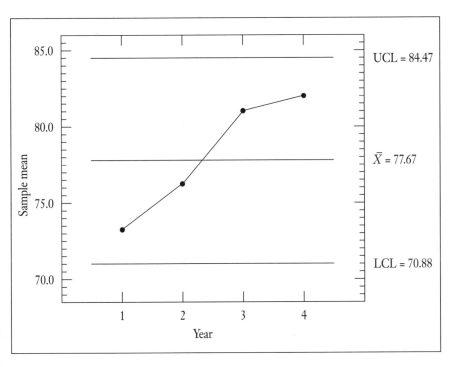

Figure 3. $\bar{X}$ chart for score.

Barriers to Quality Improvement in the Classroom

Why hasn't quality improvement made better headway in the classroom? Most of our interviewees said it was the extra time and energy required. Eisele remarked that it was easier to teach in the old talk-and-test way. Dooris saw time and energy as a barrier because faculty don't see a problem or anticipate any reward for improvement. Continuous quality improvement is time-consuming and not easy if you have been teaching one way for a long time, says Matson. He points out that instructors have to learn to deal with student feedback, which creates vulnerability. That can make professors uneasy as they try to deal with students as coworkers and without resorts to power to achieve results.

Melton cites the jargon of total quality and the lack of explanations of how the tools and concepts of total quality for manufacturing relate to the work of teaching.

Novack says that the culture of higher education doesn't accept the importance of student feedback and that the academic reward structure discourages faculty from

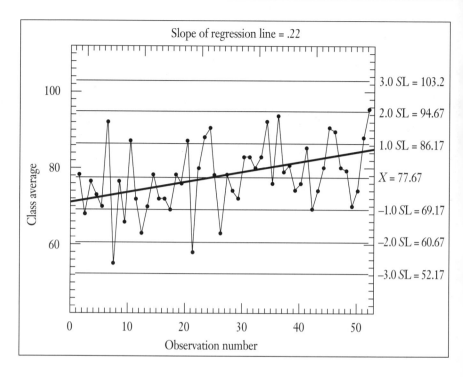

Figure 4. *I* chart for score.

investing their time. Professors who adapt quality principles to their classroom are probably the ones who least need to use them, according to him. Since the real need, he believes, is to open communication lines between faculty and students, then it is not so important that you do it with a quality vocabulary, but that you do it at all.

Spence thinks the biggest barrier may be the insistence that quality improvement in the classroom requires that the customer metaphor be applied to students. "Customers consuming" conveys too passive an image of what students do to learn. "As long as you think professors are dispensing and students are absorbing, you're missing the basic process of teaching and learning," he claims.

We asked our informants what metaphor or metaphors best applied to students: were they most like customers, workers, or products? Almost everyone thought that all of the metaphors applied. Novack said students are customers, workers, and products, but so are faculty. Melton thought that students were customers because they or someone else was paying for their education. In the first day of class, Dooris establishes the financial investment that students have in his course to help them understand that they are customers.

Matson declared that students are "learning partners." Spence said students are only slightly like customers, but more like producers and workers. The product, according to him, is the knowledge and the skills that graduates take with them into their careers and lives. He agrees that by treating students as customers and listening to their evaluations you can locate barriers to learning, but he maintains that insistence on the customer metaphor obscures the work that students must do to learn. As the saying goes, learning is not a spectator sport, nor is it a matter of just purchasing the right instructors, courses, majors, and institutions.

We think that the biggest barrier to quality improvement in the classroom is the lack of profound knowledge into the teaching/learning process itself. Most professors lack training in pedagogy. Few professors examine the literature or follow the research in teaching effectiveness. Many, if not nearly all, instructors in higher education operate with crude theories of learning and crude techniques of instruction.

Some 40 years of research on how students learn have created a knowledge base for instructors to adapt to their classrooms. For a quick summary see Chickering and Gamson's "Seven Principles for Good Practice in Undergraduate Education" or Thomas Angelo's "A 'Teacher's Dozen': Fourteen General Research-Based Principles for Improving Higher Learning in Our Classrooms."[7] The challenge to faculty is to see if they can adapt these principles to their own classes and see if they can apply them well enough to improve learning.

But many faculty members remain unchallenged by this knowledge base of best teaching practices. For example, surveys at Penn State suggest that 80 percent of the teaching is lecturing. Lecturing is not a bad technique for transmitting knowledge—it works. But it does not work as well as some other techniques that engage students more actively and cooperatively in classroom learning.

The problem with lecturing is that it fosters a false image of teaching. Instructors work to formulate knowledge into concise and clear statements. They repeat those statements to classes. Then they test students to see if they have memorized them. Instructors see their own work and effort, but not the students'. Students either get it or they don't, depending on their background, abilities, motivation, and effort. Thus the instructor's job is to communicate clearly and to motivate through fear or demonstrations of enthusiasm.

All this promotes what Marshall Gregory has called the most powerful, widespread, and worst metaphor in education: learning is storage.[8] According to the metaphor, minds are boxes or buckets. Teaching is stuffing or pouring. Learning is storing as much of the stuff taught as possible. Evidence of learning is recall or taking stuff out of the bucket to show that it is still there and in good shape. The result is that memory is the major mechanism of modern education. As Gregory writes, "Students memorize and teachers test." Most college and university professors are great memorizers. But memory is not the instrument for making knowledge, for solving problems, or for choosing courses of action. All these require critical reasoning skills and creativity.

After all, it isn't memorized facts that solve our problems. It takes judgment and creativity to come up with a possible solution supported by available evidence. This, however, is an opinion, even if well-justified. The more difficult the problem, the more the reliance on opinions and the more opinions there will be. We have to decide which opinions, if any, are best under the circumstances, given the evidence we have or can obtain with reasonable costs. If we wait around for all the facts to come in, we will decide too late. For most of the big issues of modern life we don't have and never will have enough facts to automatically choose the best course of action.

What students need, then, is not a dose of facts, but the skills of making and evaluating arguments and evidence plus the ability to formulate the most defensible opinions. That is what the customers outside the university are telling us today. They say that they don't want heads stuffed with facts that will be obsolete tomorrow; they want thinking minds that can frame and solve problems using the best knowledge of the day.

As long as instructors slumber in the cocoon of the storage metaphor, real breakthroughs in teaching and learning efficiency are not likely. When instructors begin to elicit and listen to student comments, criticisms, and suggestions about their courses they gain an opportunity to get out of the cocoon and get a real understanding of classroom processes.

Next Steps for Application of Total Quality

A promising next step in applying the principles of quality improvement to undergraduate education is to introduce larger projects beyond the confines of a course, a professor, or even the university itself. One attempt to get beyond the walls of the academy and connect the intellectual requirements of work and politics to the inner sanctum of the classroom is the Leonhard Center for the Enhancement of Engineering Education. The center was established in 1990 through a deferred gift by Penn State alumni William Leonhard and his wife, Wyllis. Several of the nation's largest corporations contribute to the project. Its vision is to, "Illuminate new paths to student excellence through innovative partnerships with students, faculty, industry and society." The center promotes curiosity-based student learning that emphasizes components of design, active learning, and cooperative projects in engineering courses.

One-third of the program's funds are disbursed on faculty projects selected by students. Recruited undergraduates form partnerships with faculty fellows to undertake projects in classroom innovations. They review and select faculty projects aimed at involving students in active learning experiences in which students apply knowledge as they would as professionals. Students also work to create partnerships with industrial practitioners to get them involved in the educational process. An advisory board, consisting of engineering CEOs, reviews and comments on the center's projects. Engineers in residence, on leave from corporate or public institutions, participate in the projects.

Center director Jack Matson says that the center is dedicated to revolutionizing engineering education by moving beyond the model of dogmatically presenting today's knowledge to passive students who may someday use it and may even have new ideas themselves. He encourages faculty to incorporate problem- and curiosity-based learning in their classrooms. The center provides a place where faculty and students can meet to explore new ways to teach and learn the core arts of engineering. Matson hopes that one-third of the courses in the College of Engineering will have design and active learning components in the next five years.

Thus the Leonhard Center has reached outside to discover what skills and knowledge graduates need in the new environment of business today, and it has reached inside the classroom to break the talk/regurgitate syndrome. The center's initiative has inspired an even more ambitious university-wide project.

In October 1993, a team of professors and staff, including Provost John Brighton, was established to create a new classroom culture at Penn State. This team has proposed an Institute of Active and Collaborative Learning, borrowing some of the successful practices of the Leonhard Center for university-wide application.

This proposal would bring together the best undergraduate teachers to display and share their successful practices with the academic community. The institute will be a gathering of faculty members who wish to investigate, improve, or apply the best pedagogical practices of interactive and collaborative learning in their classrooms. It will be a highly visible, centrally located laboratory where faculty can enter an ongoing, scholarly conversation about teaching and learning, and where students and teachers can participate in innovative learning projects. Its goal is to transform Penn State's culture of teaching and learning to meet the rigorous demands of intellectual competence required by the workplaces and communities of the twenty-first century.

The proposed institute is designed to be a workshop and showplace of Penn State's efforts to raise the level of teaching and learning to new standards of distinction. Among its functions will be to showcase current faculty projects that engage students in active learning and teamwork, to recruit the most motivated students to become partners in those projects, and to train and support new faculty in adopting active learning projects in their courses.

The team justified the need for the institute this way.

> The days of the passive employee who does what she is told and the passive citizen who lets others decide for him are numbered. The employees and citizens of the new century face problems of such magnitude and complexity that they must participate intellectually, morally and emotionally in producing acceptable solutions. That means they must be able to frame and reframe problems to try to fit solutions to environmental and social limits. They must understand the kinds of information and intellectual instruments needed to solve particular problems. They need to have the drive to ferret out data and create new conceptual frameworks. The emotional maturity and commitment to decide what they love and what they will do is also needed. They must be able and willing to test what they know, confirm what they feel, and discriminate between the true and the false. Finally they must have the confidence to seize the opportunities of failure, to learn from mistakes and to reflect upon the smash of human hopes against an often harsh and unfathomable reality.

The team hopes to recruit a highly prestigious advisory committee made up of exemplary alumni and backers of the university and include distinguished academics from other universities. Team members hope that such a board will be a source of ideas for bringing the concerns of stakeholders outside the university into conversations about teaching and learning. The team envisions a central, conspicuous, and unique setting that facilitates a variety of activities. It should be a separate building where people work together or, at least, the entire floor of a building that includes classrooms, meeting rooms, and a lounge/workshop for participating students. The team hopes to begin recruiting faculty and student volunteers in the 1994–95 academic year.

Conclusion

We see a three-step progression in applying total quality in the classroom. The steps reflect three levels of feedback that try to get at different learning results.

• Basic feedback is the attempt to find out if students receive the information conveyed by the instructor. It is elicited by instruments that ask in various ways: "Are you getting it?" Examples of this feedback from the interviews are student satisfaction surveys, student focus groups, and one-minute papers.

• Secondary feedback is the attempt to find out what students have learned in the sense of understanding material well enough to evaluate it and use it on classroom problems. Examples from the interviews are the assignment of problems as mock trials, issue briefs, design projects, and team reports.

• Tertiary feedback is the attempt to find out how well graduates can employ and improve the knowledge they have learned and the skills they have gained to frame and solve the problems of the real world. Preliminary examples are Penn State's efforts to establish units like the Leonhard Center and the Institute for Active and Collaborative Learning to satisfy outside customers.

Figure 5 shows the way we view the levels of feedback. Notice that treating students as customers only keeps feedback efforts at the basic level. Seeing students as learning partners enables instructors to attempt to elicit secondary feedback or learning assessment. Seeing the knowledge and skills of graduating students as a product spurs faculty to attempt to gain feedback at the third level.

Our model of quality improvement in the classroom sees students accomplishing the kind of things employees accomplish in a quality-driven organization. That

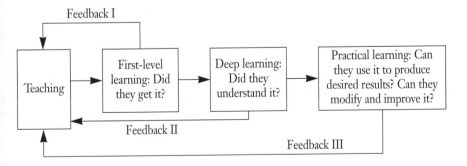

Figure 5. Levels of feedback.

requires student empowerment, and if we see them as customers only, it makes no sense. In business, customers are powerful. That is why firms must attend to customers' needs or cease to stay in business. To attend to customer needs, a firm needs empowered workers. That model holds for education.

Indeed its power for reforming education is exciting and frightening because we have become so jaded in our disregard of the customers—parents, legislatures, industries, and citizens—who pay our bills. So the customer metaphor, if we stick to it dogmatically, retards the necessary investigation of our real customers' needs and satisfaction.

Deming was ingenious in using the idea of customers and their needs to get corporate leaders to see the ethical implications of their actions and to make the point that without a stated purpose, we cannot evaluate performance. The philosophical background of his position lies in Dewey's pragmatism. Because of the limitations of the human sensory and neural systems, we cannot evaluate our knowledge by comparing it to something called reality. Evaluation of our knowledge can proceed indirectly by comparing the results we achieve against the purposes we desire. That way we can get an approximate, but useful, sense of the quality of the knowledge that directed our actions.

Further we can only evaluate those purposes by comparing our satisfaction in their achievement against what we thought our satisfaction would be. Eugene Meehan concludes that we must assume that the purpose of all human knowledge is the improvement or maintenance of the conditions of life of some human population.[9] If we don't make that assumption then we can't systematically criticize or continuously improve our knowledge.

If we restate the definition of quality management in the language of higher education it becomes: A philosophy of work based on the belief that all organized human effort should improve the conditions of human life through the analysis and assessment of processes, the encouragement of cooperation, the removal of waste, and the elimination of fear. We offer this definition to promote an ongoing conversation about total quality in higher education.

Ultimately, the movement for quality is trying to continually improve the conditions of human life efficiently by creating, applying, and correcting the knowledge that guides our actions. Surely that project cannot succeed without the help of higher education, even as higher education cannot help without embracing the principles of total quality.

Notes

1. Clara Lovett, "Assessment, CQI, and Faculty Culture," in *CQI 101: A First Reader for Higher Education*, ed. Steve Brigham (Washington, D.C.: American Association of Higher Education, 1994), 5.

2. K. Patricia Cross and Thomas A. Angelo, *Classroom Assessment Techniques: A Handbook for Faculty* (Ann Arbor, Mich.: National Center for Research to Improve Postsecondary Teaching and Learning, 1988). A revised and greatly expanded edition became available in March 1993. See also, Thomas A. Angelo, ed., *Classroom Research: Early Lessons from Success* (San Francisco: Jossey-Bass, 1991); K. Patricia Cross, "Involving Faculty in TQM," *ACCC Journal* (February/March 1993): 15–20.

3. A. W. Chickering and L. M. Barsi, *Seven Principles for Good Practice in Undergraduate Education: Faculty Inventory and Institutional Inventory* (Milwaukee, Wis.: Johnson Foundation, 1989); Z. Gamson and A. Chickering, "Seven Principles for Good Practice in Undergraduate Education," *AAHE Bulletin* 39, no. 7 (1987): 3–7; Thomas Angelo, "A 'Teacher's Dozen': Fourteen General, Research-Based Principles for Improving Higher Learning in Our Classroom," *AAHE Bulletin* 45, no. 8 (1993): 3–7; W. J. McKeachie, P. R. Pinrich, Y-G Lin, and D. A. F. Smith, *Teaching and Learning in the College Classroom* (Ann Arbor, Mich.: National Center for Research to Improving Postsecondary Teaching and Learning, 1986).

4. Cross and Angelo, *Classroom Assessment Techniques*.

5. Eugene J. Meehan, *Social Inquiry: Needs, Possibilities, Limits* (Chatham, N.J.: Chatham House, 1994); Eugene J. Meehan, *Cognitive Education and Testing: A Methodological Approach* (New York: Greenwood Press, 1991).

6. W. Edwards Deming, *Out of the Crisis* (Cambridge, Mass.: MIT Center for Advanced Engineering Technology, 1986).

7. Gamson and Chickering, "Seven Principles for Good Practice"; Angelo, " A 'Teacher's Dozen.'"

8. Marshall Gregory, "If Education Is a Feast, Why Do We Restrict the Menu? A Critique of Pedagogical Metaphors," *College Teaching* 35, no. 3 (1987): 102.

9. Eugene Meehan, *Ethics for Policymaking* (New York: Greenwood Press, 1990).

E-Mail Minutes: The Marriage of E-Mail and the One-Minute Paper

Sandra E. Strasser
College of Business Administration
Valparaiso University

Introduction

The one-minute paper and E-mail, both innovative forms of communication, encourage feedback between students and instructors. By combining both techniques and calling it E-mail minutes, an instructor can give students the opportunity to comment or ask questions about a topic, and the instructor can respond quickly and efficiently to these comments. The marriage of the one-minute paper and the use of E-mail allows for immediate feedback for both instructor and student without requiring an inordinate amount of time from either participant. This innovative combination of two communication formats takes advantage of available technology to maximize student–instructor contact beyond the confines of the classroom.

To illustrate and explain this innovation, the next two sections of this paper address the one-minute paper and E-mail separately, describing the benefits of each technique. The third section provides a procedural analysis of the combination of the two formats. Illustrations and preliminary results based on the author's experience are included in this section. Conclusions, limitations, and ideas for future research are discussed in the last section of the paper.

The One-Minute Paper

The one-minute paper is a fast and relatively simple method of obtaining feedback from students.[1] During the last few minutes of class, students are asked to respond to one or two questions on index cards or small sheets of paper. To encourage honest responses, students are advised to respond anonymously. The cards are then collected, read, and summarized by the instructor. Instructors can address a number of issues through the use of these questions and responses.

The one-minute paper can be used to assess the lecture in general. How was the pace? Were the examples clear? Were individual topics covered sufficiently? Asking what the students believe to be the most important point of the lecture provides a check on the organization and focus of the lecture. This technique can also be used to determine what the students may want to know more about. What specific questions do students have about a particular topic or concept? To assess how well the material was understood, students can be asked what they believe to be the "muddiest point of the lecture."[2] The muddiest-point question not only zeros in on any unclear or confusing portions of the lecture, it also encourages students to ask what they want to know more about. These suggestions and comments are usually very specific and can aid the instructor in further explanations.

The index cards can also gather data from the class to be used in a future lecture or demonstration. Asking students to supply their height, weight, and shoe size is a fast and easy way to build a database to be used in a regression demonstration in the future.

Once the cards have been gathered and read by the instructor, they can be summarized in a report form for the students or for the instructor's information alone. It is often helpful to address some of these issues at the beginning of the next lecture or to hand out summary reports so that students know how others feel about the class.

E-Mail

The use of E-mail to encourage communication and improve telecommunications skills is well documented in the education and communication literature. (See References.) The wide use of computer networks provides class members an efficient and effective method of communicating. Not only can the instructor answer questions and post information via E-mail, but students can correspond with each other as well. Students can communicate with fellow class members regarding questions or comments about the class. Often students have friends in other schools throughout the country and enjoy corresponding electronically through bitnet. Whether working on an assignment or discussing last night's basketball game, the availability of E-mail can encourage communication and improve telecommunication skills.

The convenience of E-mail also helps to encourage communication. A key feature of E-mail is the ability to send one message to multiple addresses simultaneously. Information regarding an upcoming exam can be sent to every student in the class as easily as it can be sent to only one student. Messages can be sent and/or read at the participant's convenience, a major advantage for commuting students who are only on campus a small portion of the day. If time is critical, E-mail messages can be sent and answered within minutes.

Shy students who might be too timid to ask a question or comment in class are encouraged to communicate using E-mail. These students have personal access to the instructor and all class members without the fear of face-to-face communication.

Improved writing skills can also be a benefit of using E-mail. Lacking facial or tonal cues to help interpret meaning, the computer medium requires explicit communication to be clearly understood. These demands force students to write more clearly and concisely, improving their writing skills. The original text for a message can be written on a word processor and then uploaded to a mainframe and sent through E-mail, affording the student practice in writing and telecommunication.

The use of E-mail is often more effective and accurate than phone messages or face-to-face communication. Messages sent on E-mail lack spontaneity and, therefore, can be more thought out. Because computer communication can be edited, it is often free of the confusion contained in oral messages. Messages can be copied and retained, avoiding the problem of inaccurately repeated messages.

Perhaps one of the most important advantages of E-mail is the increased student–instructor contact made possible through electronic communication. Office hours are essentially extended, allowing for communication at the convenience of both student and instructor. Based on a research report of students' study preferences, over half of the sampled students studied between 6 and 10 P.M., a time when instructors are not usually on campus.[3] The use of E-mail allows for communication between student and instructor, regardless of individual time schedules. Knowledge can be delivered in a cost-effective manner, any time throughout the day or night.

Procedure

The one-minute paper was designed to elicit feedback from the students for the instructor. The drawback is that students must wait at least until the next class to gain feedback from the instructor. This method of communication appears one-sided at best. Should students have a pressing question, by the time they receive an answer or explanation, it may be too late. Timely feedback should occur for the students, as well as for the instructor. Using E-mail to answer questions and address comments collected on the one-minute papers seems to solve this problem. By sending responses electronically, instructors can take advantage of all of the benefits of E-mail and at the same time provide important information quickly and efficiently to students. This innovation is the E-mail minute.

The E-mail minute works as follows. The last two or three minutes of each lecture should be set aside for students to fill out index cards in response to one or two carefully thought out questions. Immediately after class, the instructor should read through the cards and sort them into two groups, those that require a response and those that do not. This process usually takes about 10 to 15 minutes depending on class size and depth of the questions/answers. At this time, while the questions are fresh in the mind of the instructor and the students, responses to individual questions or comments should be sent via E-mail to the entire class.

Using the class address, the instructor needs to type only one message; the message then goes to everyone signed up on the class account. Because students usually do not sign their names to the cards, responses must be sent to the entire class. This gives the students an idea of what others are asking about and answers questions that many students may have wanted to ask, but didn't know how to phrase. The time required to send responses is usually about 15 minutes. Within 30 minutes of the end of class, students have all of their concerns addressed and waiting to be retrieved at their convenience.

Once the instructor takes the first step toward electronic communication, students usually continue the correspondence either in the form of a comment or as a request for further clarification. The instructor gains important information with which to assess the class and the lecture. The student gains important information, perhaps a clearer understanding of the subject, increased contact with the instructor, and has the potential to improve telecommunication skills. A 30-minute investment does not appear to be too costly for all of these benefits.

Conclusions and Future Directions

My own experience with E-mail minutes in introductory statistics classes have produced several interesting side effects. Although one of the purported benefits of E-mail is the extension of office hours, I feel that more students frequent my office in person now. A possible explanation for this effect could be that increased communication makes students feel more comfortable. Perhaps communication in one medium transfers easily to another and students who communicate with me using electronic mail also feel more comfortable coming into my office.

Student evaluations of my performance as a teacher have greatly improved. Nothing else about the course has changed, and I believe that the use of E-mail minutes has affected the evaluations. Students seem to appreciate the fact that I am interested in improving the class and that I am willing to listen to them. Perhaps students also appreciate receiving my responses to their comments and questions. I hope that students understand that my goal is to help them learn and that E-mail minutes are a method for achieving that goal.

I also believe that most students actually enjoy electronic communication. Figure 1 contains the results of a survey of 63 introductory statistics students who were asked how they feel about E-mail minutes. Seventy-six percent of the students communicate with me through E-mail and find that the E-mail minutes are of benefit.

A cautionary note must be included. The only way to promote acceptance of this innovation is to make certain that the index cards are read and answered promptly and with interest. If the students believe that this system is only a gesture, the entire process will fail. At the beginning of the semester, the first several attempts at using E-mail minutes are never well received on the part of the students. Their responses are usually very brief, appearing to resist my efforts at honest communication. During these first sessions it is imperative that the instructor read all comments and make every effort to address all questions and concerns immediately. I try to let the students know through my actions that I am putting a lot of trust in the honesty of their feedback.

Once the students are convinced that I believe strongly in E-mail minutes and that I am willing to make changes based on their feedback, the replies become longer

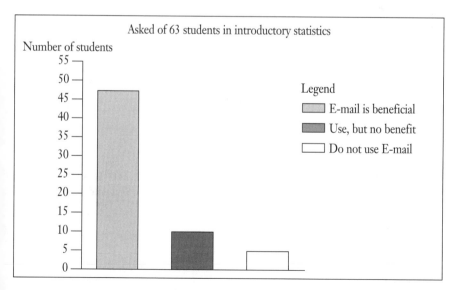

Figure 1. E-mail minutes survey.

and the comments more honest. After the first few lectures, most students don't even have to be reminded about the cards; they automatically pull them out at the end of the lecture.

As the data supporting this technique are primarily anecdotal, it is important that quantitative results be gathered and analyzed to further understand the benefits and costs of this innovation. Future research is needed to measure the effects of E-mail minutes and to suggest improvements in the procedure.

To truly take advantage of new computer capabilities, educators should not just use the computer as a substitute for the telephone or the typewriter. The classroom should be redesigned around the new technology to allow for the greatest benefit. E-mail minutes takes advantage of new computer technology, not by replicating an existing process, but by designing an entirely new process. Future directions in innovative education should be in the creation and analysis of technologically advanced systems to gain the most benefit from new technology.

There is one limitation on the applicability of E-mail minutes (and on the applicability of E-mail for any purpose). The method assumes that there is a user-friendly E-mail system universally accessible to faculty and students, the campus culture encourages its use, and it is, in fact, widely used. These conditions are met at Valparaiso University; they are not met universally.*

Summary

The one-minute paper was designed to elicit feedback from the students for the instructor. This method of communication appears one-sided at best. Timely feedback should occur for the students and the instructor. E-mail minutes, the use of E-mail to answer questions and address comments collected on the one-minute papers, seems to solve this problem. The marriage of the one-minute paper and the use of E-mail allows for immediate feedback for both instructor and student without

---

*Editor's note: At the Graduate School of Business, University of Chicago, there was widespread and effective student use of E-mail until the mid-1980s. At that time students were required to own or have ready access to their own personal computers, and personal computer ownership among students became nearly universal. Although students were urged to acquire modems and communication software, they found that they were virtually self-sufficient and had no strong reason to use features of the central computer, including E-mail. Instructors had to exert great pressure to get students to log in to the central computer for any purpose. I decided that it was a losing battle to try. In recent years, fax has performed some of the same functions, but I cannot obtain all the advantages of Professor Strasser's E-mail minutes because I cannot broadcast my feedback to the class as soon as I have prepared it. See Bateman and Roberts, "Total Quality for Faculty and Students," in this volume.

requiring an inordinate amount of time from either participant. The benefits of this innovation include convenience for both instructor and student, improved telecommunication skills, increased contact between student and instructor, extended office hours, and more timely feedback. The cost of this innovation in terms of time is about 30 minutes per lecture for the instructor and about three minutes for the students.

Notes

1. Frederick Mosteller, "Broadening the Scope of Statistics and Statistical Education," *The American Statistician* 42, no. 2 (1988); Patricia K. Cross and Thomas A. Angelo, "Classroom Assessment Techniques," prepared for the National Center for Research to Improve Postsecondary Teaching and Learning, 1988.

2. Mosteller, "Broadening the Scope."

3. Barbara Wolf, Todd Schmitz, and Marilyn Ellis, "How Students Study: Views from Bloomington Campus Undergraduates" (report, University of Indiana Office for Academic Affairs and Dean of the Faculties, 1991).

Bibliography

For more information about E-mail use in the classroom, see these references.

Beals, Diane E. "Computer Networks as a New Data Base." Paper presented at the American Educational Research Association, April 1990.

Callahan, Elias R. "Survey, Implementation and Utilization of Instructional Technology Tools." Paper presented at the 1992 annual DSI meeting, November 1992.

Cotlar, Morton, and James N. Shimabukuro. "Stimulating Learning with Electronic Guest Lecturing." *Interpersonal Computing and Technology: An Electronic Journal for the 21st Century* 1, no. 1. (1993).

Harasim, L. M. "Online Education: An Environment for Collaboration and Intellectual Amplification." *Online Education: Perspectives on a New Environment.* (1990): 39–64.

Hiltz, Starr Roxanne. "Collaborative Learning in a Virtual Classroom: Highlights of Findings." Paper presented at the Computer Supported Cooperative Work Conference, June 1988.

———. "The 'Virtual Classroom': Using Computer-Mediated Communication for University Teaching." *Journal of Communication* 36, no. 2 (1986).

Kuehn, Scott A. "Discovering All the Available Means for Computer Assisted Instruction: Adapting Available University Facilities for the Small to Medium-Sized Course." Paper presented at the Eastern Communication Association Convention, Baltimore, April 1988.

Lyness, Ann L., Susan A. Albrecht, and Jean A. Raimond. "Social Learning and Electronic Communication: Development of a Conceptual Framework." Paper presented at the Annual Convention of the Association for Educational Communications and Technology, Showcase of Achievement, Washington, D.C., February 1992.

Phillips, A. F., and P. S. Pease. "Computer Conferencing and Education: Complementary or Contradictory Concepts?" Paper presented at the annual meeting of the International Communication Association, Honolulu, HI, May 1985.

Phillips, Gerald M., and Gerald M. Santoro. "Teaching Group Discussion Via Computer-Mediated Communication." *Communication Education* 38, no. 2 (1989).

Showalter, R. G. "Educational Teleconferencing: Continuing Professional Education in Speech-Language Pathology and Audiology." Paper presented at the Congress of the International Association of Logopaedics and Phoniatrics, Edinburgh, Scotland, August 1983.

Smith, K. L. "Collaborative and Interactive Writing for Increasing Communication Skills." *Hispania* 73, no. 1 (1990): 77–87.

Statistics: From Stumbling Block to Stepping Stone

Douglas A. Zahn
Department of Statistics
Florida State University

Introduction

Each semester approximately 60 percent of the students taught by the Florida State University Department of Statistics are enrolled in an undergraduate course, Statistics 3014: Fundamental Business Statistics. This course is taught in large lecture sections of 250 students each. It and comparable courses at other universities are either the only statistics course or one of two statistics courses taken by probably 90 percent of undergraduate business students.

Large introductory courses offer an opportunity to introduce the power of statistics and statistical thinking to future business leaders. Unfortunately, it appears that this opportunity has often been missed. Some even suggest that these courses contribute to the public's negative attitude toward statistics and statisticians. The challenge to teachers of statistics is clear.

Several factors led me to confront this challenge.

• *Teaching statistical consulting.* In 1980 I formed a partnership with Dan Boroto, a professor in the psychology department at Florida State to develop a process that statistical consultants could use to improve the quality of their services. Then we built a course to teach this process to graduate students in statistics and related areas.[1]

A key part of the course was videotape-based coaching. Developing this part of the course gave me several opportunities to be videotaped while consulting and then be coached in front of the consulting class by Dan using these videotapes. Not surprisingly, there was eventually a session that did not go well.

My explanation for the session was, in essence, that the client was a bad client. Dan gently, but firmly, invited me to consider whether I made any contribution to how the session ended. I resisted his coaching, but finally I saw that I was part of the problem. I saw that I had not liked to work with this client and hadn't had the courage to be honest about it. The lessons I learned from this incident helped to toughen me for the challenges I would encounter in the large undergraduate course.

In developing the consulting course, I often asked statistical consultants about problems they encountered in their work. One problem was that many clients came to them very late; they had already taken off and were in danger of a crash landing. Often these clients had taken an undergraduate statistics course and had decided either that statistics was worthless or that they were terrified of the subject, or both, so they avoided statistical issues whenever possible. The quality improvement principle of moving upstream to remove causes of problems suggested to me that I consider teaching one of these large undergraduate courses.

• *Dissatisfaction with the current course.* I heard repeated complaints from all participants in the current course.

—Faculty were displeased with student mathematical skills, level of effort, and attitude.

—Teaching assistants were displeased with student mathematical skills, level of effort, and attitude, and also with the fact that they, the teaching assistants, were being asked to do something for which they were given no training.

—Students were displeased with the attitudes of both faculty and teaching assistants. In addition, students could not see applications for the tools covered in class, and they had little confidence in their ability to use them anyway.

I also heard from a wide variety of former students that "Statistics was the worst course I ever took." I was led to think that the current course would lead to this evaluation of statistics in yet another generation of students.

• *The quality revolution in Japan.* The third factor was of a different kind. As I learned more about the quality revolution in Japan, I discovered that the backbone of the effort is widespread knowledge and use of simple tools of quality improvement. This led to a shift in my objectives for the course: previously I had thought it was enough to help students become better "consumers" of published statistics. Now I shifted to also wanting to help them be able to do at least simple statistical studies using sound statistical practice.

• *An important personal consideration.* A fourth factor was that I remarried in 1984, and in the process of doing that, rethought my life vision. After some months of reflection, my vision emerged as "a world in which statistics is a stepping stone empowering people to reach their visions and not a stumbling block to their progress."

After considering these factors for some time, as well as concerns about lecturing to a large group twice a week and managing all the awesome details associated with such a large class, I volunteered in 1985 to teach one of the sections of Statistics 3014. In this paper I report on my experiences in grappling with the challenge of improving the quality of this course.

I will first sketch the environment in which I have been working.

- The Florida State University Statistics Department has a primary commitment to research and scholarly activity, particularly in theoretical areas of mathematical statistics and probability.

- It has a secondary commitment to graduate training in statistics.

- It has a lower-level commitment to service teaching at graduate and undergraduate levels.

- Statistics 3014: Fundamental Business Statistics, is taught in two sections of 250 students each in the fall and spring semesters.

- Each section has a lecturer who delivers two 50-minute lectures a week and is supported by three teaching assistants (TAs).

- Each TA meets once a week for 50 minutes with three different recitation sections, each of which contains about 30 students.

- There is generally a departmental final examination.

Since 1985 I have implemented both on-line and off-line quality improvement procedures in this course. In this article, as in the course, I use Joiner's triangle as a guide for discussing this process.[2] This triangle (Figure 1) represents three critical elements of quality improvement in any organization: commitment to quality, teamwork, and use of the scientific method. Upcoming sections in this chapter discuss actions taken and barriers encountered relating to commitment to quality, teamwork, and use of the scientific method, respectively. I discuss findings from my quality improvement efforts, and close with some thoughts on where to go from here.

Commitment to Quality

I approach quality improvement in Statistics 3014 by regarding myself as chief executive officer (CEO) of my company, FBS, Inc. The main activity of my company is to teach my section of Statistics 3014. This approach comes from the suggestion

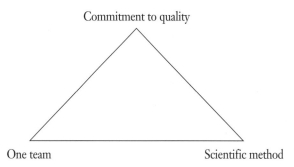

Used with permission from Joiner Associates Inc., *The Team Handbook*, Peter R. Scholtes, 1988.

Figure 1. The Joiner triangle.

of an executive of Florida Power & Light who listened to me complain about a lack of a clear commitment by my senior management to quality improvement in large lecture courses. He pointed out that, regardless of this, I could view myself as the CEO of my own class, and, as CEO, state the company's commitment to quality. In my capacity as CEO, I therefore declare publicly in each new class that I am committed to the systematic improvement of the quality of the services rendered by the firm.

This firm, like any other, delivers its service using a process that has inputs, a value-added step, and output. There are suppliers, workers, and customers. The students are both input and suppliers. There are other suppliers: the prerequisite algebra course, high school, middle school, primary school, families, churches, peer groups, and so on. The contributions of these suppliers are filtered through and delivered as input to the course by the student.

The TAs and I are workers. Also, no value will be added by the course unless the students also do part of the work. Thus, they are also coworkers.

Further reflection led me to see that the students are hiring me: they (or their parents) are paying part of my salary. Society as a whole, as determined by the legislature, pays the rest. Thus, the students are customers. There are four other generations of customers.

- Current students

- Faculty in subsequent courses

- Eventual employers of the students

- Society at large

I came to realize that my course can contribute to subsequent customers, including society at large, only if the student uses learning from the course in his or her profession or personal life.

Motivation is critical if students are to carry forth the value of the course into the world. Motivation is not something that we do to students; it is not something that you will find if you dissect a student. Rather, motivation is a word that we use to describe a set of behaviors that appear when a student sees a link between what we are teaching and the results this student is committed to producing in his or her lifetime. Thus, the primary focus of the course is to help students see this link by giving them an opportunity to experience how statistics will help them realize their goals. I think of the students as the first-generation suppliers and the first-generation customers of the course. See Figure 2.

Another essential step in quality improvement is deciding on an operational definition of high quality. Building on Boroto's description of an effective consultation, I propose that a high-quality course is one in which

- The material delivered is correct.

- The students learn an implementable plan for using the material.

- The plan is implemented.

- The results stand up to external scrutiny.[3]

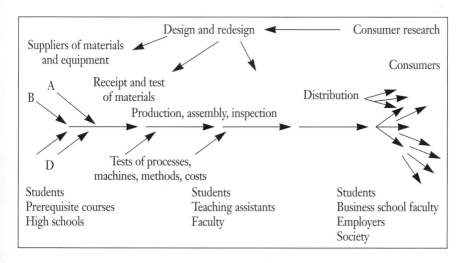

Figure 2. A diagram of the course process.

More specifically, here are dimensions of quality.

- Students are participants in the creation of the course, not spectators at a performance.

- The course provides an opportunity for the students to see the usefulness of statistics.

- Students can use and interpret tools and concepts set forth in the course syllabus.

- The syllabus reflects the outcomes desired by various customers: students, faculty teaching subsequent courses, future employers, and society at large.

- Students do not encounter hassles during the course.

- Students are regarded with dignity and treated with respect.

- Students do a term project from start to finish in which they identify a business question to study, gather and analyze data relevant to it, and present oral and written results on their study.

These dimensions can be measured during or at the end of the course. I describe instruments I have developed to do this and later some results of using them.

Perhaps the most critical dimensions of quality are those that cannot be measured until 5 or 10 years later when the student is on the job and in a situation in which the course concepts and tools could be used. Faculty in all areas have been reluctant to tackle longer-term assessment. Yet, addressing this challenge is a way we can be proactive in meeting increasingly strong societal pressures for accountability.

Barriers

All participants in large lecture courses—faculty, TAs, and students—tend to share the view that this course cannot work well and that they would rather be somewhere else. (Students, in particular, feel that they are lost in a nameless crowd.) So all put in their time, suffer through the course, and then at the end of the term, check off the accomplishment of an unpleasant duty. All feel that "there is no solution," an attitude that serves as an insidious barrier to making an attempt to improve the quality of the course and runs counter to the central theme of total quality that quality can always be improved.

A variant on the theme "there is no solution" is the view that we just do not have the resources to do this course well, an attitude that runs counter to the total quality idea that we should strive to do more with less.

My strategy for addressing this barrier has been to keep making data-based improvements in the course each semester I teach it so that the course now works well for 70 percent to 90 percent of the students, depending on the criterion employed. This necessitates a change in the conversation from "There is no solution," to "Well, Zahn (and others) have produced a partial solution, *but* they are different." This is a major shift in the conversation.

All on One Team

My work with statistical consultants has convinced me that a professional, before beginning to work with customers, should establish what services the customers hope to receive. The first step in a successful consultation is to determine what the client wants and needs so that the consultant and client will be on one team working toward a shared goal.[4] The challenge in Statistics 3014 is to adapt this idea to a course with 250 students. There are several key groups here: teaching assistants, students, and customers. I consider each in turn.

Teaching Assistants

In August 1989 and 1990 I held a half-day workshop before the fall semester started to prepare my TAs. Prior to the workshop, I asked the TAs to fill out the questionnaire shown in Figure 3 to tell me what they wanted and needed from their work as TA. I gave them my teaching assistant job description to tell them what I expected from them. Discussing these items gave us all a better idea of each others' expectations. It helped to make us one team.

I share the power in the course with the TAs by having structured weekly staff meetings with them as full voting partners in the production of the course. This reduces stress on me (once I got over my fears about loss of control and became aware of the paradox that the more power one gives away, the more power one has) and helps prepare them for the many nontechnical aspects of teaching. I distribute an agenda to everyone the day before the meeting using the form in Figure 4. I chair the meeting and one TA serves as timekeeper and another as scribe. The meeting ends with a five-minute review of action items and decisions made. Then we all participate in a five-minute critique of the process of the meeting to see where there is room for improvement.

The careful structure in this meeting may seem overdone to some, given that there are only four people present. In my experience, it helps to keep the meetings on track and dealing with the highest priority items, thereby avoiding scrap and frenzy at the end of the meeting. It also helps us to manage the multitude of details present in running a large course. It frees my concentration to focus on the matters at hand, knowing that someone else is keeping track of the time and of the activities to be done. It reduces the rework resulting from unclear assignment of duties.

The Florida State University
Tallahassee, Florida 32306-3033

Department of Statistics and
Statistical Consulting Center "B-167"
(904) 644-3218

August 4, 1989

MEMORANDUM

TO: STA 3014 TAs and potential STA 3014 TAs

FROM: Doug Zahn

SUBJECT: Questionnaire for the STA 3014 TA Workshop; Friday, August 25, 1989; 9:00 A.M. to 12:00 noon; Location: 205 OSB

PURPOSE OF
WORKSHOP: 1. Clarify STA 3014 TA and STA 3014 faculty understandings of their own and each other's jobs.

               2. Lay a foundation for ongoing quality improvements in STA 3014.

   To improve our chances of achieving these purposes and to increase the probability that this workshop will be of value to you, please thoughtfully consider the following questions and give me your current answers to them by Tuesday noon, August 22, 1989.

QUESTIONNAIRE

1. What did you want from your TA when you were an undergraduate student in a TA's recitation section?

2. Do you have any questions about the attached TA job description? If so, what are they? Please suggest any additions or deletions that occur to you.

3. What would you suggest we include in a STA 3014 faculty job description?

4. If you have previously been a STA 3014 TA, what are the roughest situations you have encountered on the job?

5. What would have to happen in STA 3014 this fall so that you would be satisfied on December 15, 1989, with the time and effort you have expended as a TA?

6. If you operated optimally as a TA in an ideal course

   a. What would be happening then that is not happening now?

   b. What is happening now that would not be happening then?

7. What do you plan to be doing five years from now?

8. What could you learn as an STA 3014 TA that could enhance your chances of achieving this goal?

9. What do you want to gain, learn, or discover in this workshop?

Figure 3. TA workshop questionnaire.

Group _____	Date _____	Timekeeper _____
Meeting type _____	Time _____	Scribe _____
	Place _____	Chairperson _____

Time spent	Began at	Time est'd	Priority	Potential agenda items
___	___	___	1	Start
___	___	___	2	Set agenda, priorities, time estimates
___	___	___	___	Report on action items
___	___	___	___	Policy questions, decisions
___	___	___	___	_____
___	___	___	___	_____
___	___	___	___	_____
___	___	___	___	_____
___	___	___	___	_____
___	___	5	___	Review of action items and decisions
___	___	5	___	Critique of process of meeting
	___			End

ACTION ITEM SUMMARY

Activity	By whom	By when
_____	_____	_____
_____	_____	_____
_____	_____	_____

Decisions made:

_____

_____

_____

_____

Figure 4. Staff meeting agenda.

Three years ago my TAs and I decided to have all jobs, including chairing the meeting, circulate among those present. This idea, suggested by one of the TAs, worked out very well, as the TAs ably took on the responsibility of chairing the meeting. I noticed that when I was not chairing the meeting, I was able to concentrate more on the business of the meeting and make more creative suggestions.

Students

Identifying what 250 students want and need from Statistics 3014 is challenging. I approach this task using the General Information Handout, assignment 1, and minute papers. My General Information Handout tells students what is available in the course and what I expect from them. The last page is assignment 1 (Figure 5) in which they tell me what they expect of me, my TAs, and the course. The minute paper (Figure 6) offers a random sample of the students an opportunity each lecture to tell me whether they got what they came for and what parts of the lecture were unclear.

A key part of creating the sense of teamwork with the students is the term project, which is done by teams of three to five students.[5] The project gives students a chance to discover for themselves that the material in this course can be used to address business questions of interest to them. This is the most powerful tool I have found for getting the students to be participants in the course rather than spectators.

Each team selects the quality improvement question it wishes to study. The team then constructs a proposal for how it will conduct the study. This proposal is presented orally to the other students in the team's recitation section and in writing to the instructor. Then data are gathered, analyzed, and the final report is prepared. This report is also presented orally and in writing. The appendix gives two executive summaries of recent projects, along with letters written by managers at the businesses where the projects were done.

In the past, I have had trouble creating an all-on-one-team attitude during the lectures. Spring semester 1990 (my tenth time teaching this course) was the first time that I felt some satisfaction with my crowd control activities and the creation of a team in the lecture. Here are the steps I took.

• When discussing Joiner's triangle, I indicated that for me all-on-one-team spirit includes the lecture and that each of us has a job to do to produce a high-quality lecture. The students' job includes being prepared by reading the assigned reading, asking questions when anything is unclear, being at class on time, staying to the end, not moving around during lecture, and not talking, except to me. My job includes being prepared, being sure that content is clear to them, managing the crowd, and starting and ending on time.

Name _____   FSU STATISTICS
                          Quiz 1 Assignment   STA 3014 (21-29)
                                                       Spring 1990; Zahn
Recitation section _____

Due in your recitation section on January 12, 1990.

Note: There is no "right answer" to Questions 1–10. You will earn 10 of the 30 points on quiz 1 for your effort in considering and answering the questions clearly. Use the back of this page if necessary.

1. What do you want to gain, learn, or discover in this course? Please be specific.

2. What grade are you working for? _____

3. What do you think your job is in this course? Please be specific.

4. What do you think Dr. Zahn's job is in this course? Please be specific.

5. What do you think your TA's job is in this course? Please be specific.

6. In lecture we will often work through a particular type of problem. Then I will ask, "Are you confident you can do a problem of this type on this week's quiz?" What percent of the students in attendance would you like to see say "Yes" before we move on to the next topic?

7. Topics I would like to see used in class examples to illustrate the use of statistics are

8. For the course project you will be working on a team that you have formed.
   a. If you operated optimally in an ideal team, how would this team function?
   b. What concerns do you have about working on a team on the course project? (In the Team Working Agreement due on February 9, 1990, you and your teammates will have the opportunity to develop a strategy for addressing these concerns.)

9. What can your course project team count on you for during the team? Please be specific.

10. Any other comments, questions, or concerns?

11. By my signature below, I certify that I have read the General Information Handout and choose to be in this course under these terms.

Figure 5. Assignment 1.

Please take a minute at the end of class to answer these questions to help me plan for tomorrow.

1. Did you get what you came for today? If yes, what did you get? If no, what was missing?

2. What was the muddiest point in the lecture?

3. In your own words, what did you learn today?

4. Any other comments?

If you have a specific request or question, please put your name on your minute paper so I may give you a response. Otherwise, names are optional on minute papers.

(For background information on minute papers and related ideas in statistical education, see the article "Broadening the scope of statistics and statistical education," by Frederick Mosteller, which appeared in *The American Statistician*, pp. 93–99, Vol. 42, no. 2, May 1988).

Figure 6. Minute paper questions.

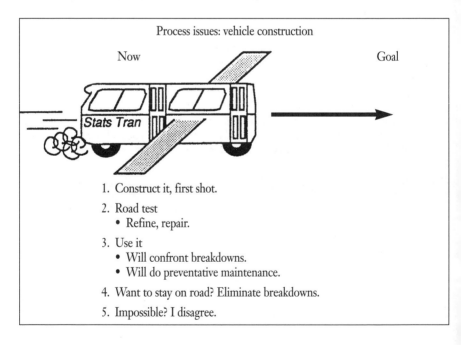

Figure 7. Vehicle construction.

• I described our work environment as one in which we would go slow so that we could go fast later. I likened the process to that of building a vehicle for a trip and summarized the discussion by the illustration in Figure 7.

• Whenever I noticed a student violating an aspect of company policy, I would ask for his or her name and section number and ask him or her to see me after class. I then gave the form shown in Figure 8 to the student. A typed response to this assignment was the student's entry ticket to the next lecture.

Subsequent to these steps, there was less movement during lecture, virtually no late arrivals or early leavers, and a much quieter class time than during any of my nine previous semesters in the course, which reduced greatly my feelings of exasperation. The few students who were cited for violations of company policy responded well. I noticed that after the first two citations, all I had to do when I noticed talking was to pause and look around. Silence returned in less than five seconds and then I would resume. I also noticed that when I felt tired, I would sometimes not hold the students accountable for being late. How well I managed the quality of the lecture had a lot to do with how well I was managing my well-being. All in all, this system worked well enough that I used it again.

After using it a second time, I became dissatisfied with the atmosphere this system created in class. I felt like I was treating the students like middle schoolers, rather than professional colleagues. Now I tend to stop and ask if there is a question for me when I become aware of people talking. Also, I have noticed that side conversations are common among faculty at colloquia and professional meetings, and that sometimes they serve a useful, nondisruptive function. So I decided not to assume that a student side conversation was an affront and to work more collaboratively with the students in dealing with this problem.

Customers

To achieve the all-on-one-team spirit with the executives of those companies that will be hiring the graduates of the business school, I use every opportunity to ask them what they would like to see students learn in their first statistics course. On the basis of these conversations, I have incorporated topics and activities relating to quality improvement in the course: Ishikawa's Seven Tools, the comparison of analytic and enumerative studies, and the term project, which is done in teams of three to five students.[6]

FBS, Inc.
Department of Statistics
Florida State University
Tallahassee, FL 32306

MEMORANDUM

TO:

Someone   arriving late and sitting in the middle of the class
           leaving early from the middle of the class
           reading a newspaper
           talking

FROM: Douglas A. Zahn, CEO of FBS, Inc.

DATE:

SUBJECT: Your behavior and the quality of the company's services

You have engaged in a behavior that does not contribute to improving the overall quality of the services provided by FBS, Inc. In fact, by your signature on assignment 1, you have previously agreed to not do this.

As a consequence of this incident, your job is to give me a typed response to the three questions below prior to the next lecture as your entry ticket to that lecture.

1. If you were managing a company, had set a company policy, and had a worker who agreed to this policy and then broke it, how would you deal with this worker?

2. How did today's incident occur?

3. In the rest of the term, what can I count on you for relative to the behavior at issue today?

Figure 8. Assignment for policy breaker.

Barriers

A barrier to creating all-on-one-team spirit is the traditionally adversarial relationship of faculty and students. Fifteen years in the U.S. school system have left many students skeptical of students and faculty playing on the same team. I seek to convince them of my commitment to being on one team with them by

- Being clear as to what the course requirements are

- Being clear about what will be on quizzes and tests

- Giving sample projects to indicate what I am looking for on that assignment

- Having a stated policy on excused absences

- Having clear deadlines, announced well in advance

- Considering all student complaints about any aspect of the course (I respond in writing to each written complaint.)

Over the years, lessening adversarial tension has been hard for me. My efforts seemed to lead students to blame me for any aspects of the course that are not going well, and I reacted by thinking that it is the fault of the students. There was an unhappy standoff with anger, discomfort, anxiety, discouragement, conflict, and blame seething just below the surface and sometimes bubbling up into view. I came to realize that my course quality improvement plan should embrace improvement of the process of dealing with complaints.

I now see my job as CEO as including the responsibility to take the first step toward addressing the impasses that tend to occur when complaints arise. My goal is, first, to stay present, open, honest, compassionate, and clear in the face of the students' complaints, and, second, to keep talking with the students, even when all of us are upset, gathering information that can be used to sort out what are often conflicting or competing priorities or values. With the help of my coaches, I am slowly and with difficulty progressing toward this goal. I think often of a statement made by W. Edwards Deming: "Long-term commitment to new learning and new philosophy is required of any management that seeks transformation. The timid and the fainthearted, and people that expect quick results, are doomed to disappointment."[7]

I see a paradox: the more effectively I create the sense of all-on-one-team attitude with my TAs and students, the more intensely they look at the quality of all aspects of the course. They begin to question, even to criticize, aspects of the course that I had never questioned before.*

---

*Editor's note:** This is an example of the phenomenon of rising customer expectations. As improvements are made in any product or service, customer aspiration levels rise, so that what would have been accepted gratefully this year is taken for granted next year.

Use of the Scientific Method

A traditional source of data on the quality of the course is the gradebook. The weekly quizzes, term project, and final exam reflect how well the students perform on those tasks. Other data collection activities include the following.

- The statistics student survey gathers attitudinal data on students as they enter and exit the course.

- Assignment 1 gathers data on the students' expectations as they enter the course.

- The minute papers gather data from a 10 percent sample (those whose social security numbers end in a randomly chosen digit) at the end of each lecture on the quality of the lecture.

- Attendance is taken each day.

- The midterm course evaluation assesses how well the students are being served at midterm.

- A poll on day 26 (Fall 1989) identified the highest and lowest quality aspects of the course from the students' perspective.

- A working group meeting during the last week of class in fall 1989 produced a cause-and-effect diagram for the quality problems of low quiz scores and 60 percent lecture attendance at the end of the term.

- The course evaluation questionnaire gives a summary evaluation of many aspects of the course.

- Each examination and quiz contains an item at the end asking a student to list any defective questions and the asserted defect.

I have also observed and videotaped the TAs in their recitation sections, guiding my coaching by using a form contained in the Teaching Assistant Job Description, which tells the TAs what I expect of them. I have also videotaped most of my own lectures in recent years.

Barriers

The first barrier encountered was resistance to gathering data on oneself. The resistance I had noticed to videotaping my own consulting sessions showed up again. No one likes to stand in front of the mirror. This was a difficult barrier for me. It also shows up whenever I invite others to gather these data on their own courses.

After getting some data collected, I ran into a second barrier: finding the time to analyze the data. I have gathered an enormous amount of data and analyzed only a small part of it. I have not yet figured out a way to find enough time on the job to do these analyses.

Then, as I get some data analyzed and they suggest a need for modifying some aspect of the course, there is a third barrier: resistance to change! My approach to addressing these barriers has been to surround myself with coaches who share my goals and who promise to treat me with respect, while being honest with me whenever they see me allowing myself to be diverted by these barriers.

Findings

Traditional Measures of Course Quality

The most traditional and the easiest, though not necessarily the most useful, measures of course quality are the course grades and the final exam grades. For the early years—fall 1985 through spring 1990—I made careful tabulations, but the variations from class to class were generally small. (The average final exam grades for the other instructors were within 5 percent of my averages.) During those years, I tried many strategies to improve exam and course grades: making previous final exams and solutions available, making the quizzes similar to the final exam, holding additional review sessions, reducing the amount of material in the course, and reserving lecture time at the end of the semester to teach students how to diagnose what tool to use in word problems). At least as reflected in these data, I apparently had little success; in fact, the grades declined slightly from fall 1987 to fall 1989, a period in which the students in the course shifted from being primarily juniors to primarily sophomores.

Another traditional measure is the Florida State University Student Instructional Rating System (SIRS) done by the 60 percent to 70 percent of the students attending class at the end of each semester. Figure 9 is a summary of these data for the 16 semesters I have taught this course. This figure presents the percent of the respondents who agreed or strongly agreed with the following statements: "The instructor appeared to be thoroughly competent in his/her area," (competence) and "In general, the instructor was an effective teacher" (effectiveness). It is apparent that on "competence" and "effectiveness," there is substantial autocorrelation, but the overall trend is positive, though not spectacularly so. The rate of improvement may be slowing through time.

Additional Measures of Course Quality

Since one of my main reasons for volunteering to teach this course was to increase the fraction of students leaving the course who think that statistics is useful and who are confident that they can successfully use statistical tools, I have developed my own course evaluation questionnaire (CEQ) to measure these variables. Students

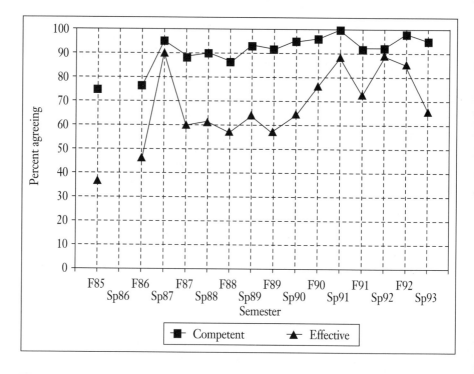

Figure 9. Competence and effectiveness as measured by SIRS: Fall 1985 to spring 1993.

receive it the last day of lecture and turn it in at the final examination, receiving 10 extra credit points (total points possible is 1000). The response rate is 90 percent to 99 percent.

Figure 10 summarizes student responses to the items.

- *Recognize:* I can recognize where statistical thinking and procedures can help address a managerial question.

- *Can do:* I can do a basic statistical study and interpret the results.

- *Uses:* As of now, I can see potential uses of statistics in my career.

- *Got it:* Considering the course as a whole, did you get what you came for?

The available responses for the first three questions ranged from "strongly agree" to "strongly disagree," with "strongly agree" and "agree" being collapsed in the results represented in Figure 10. The percent graphed in Figure 10 for "got it" is the percent answering "yes."

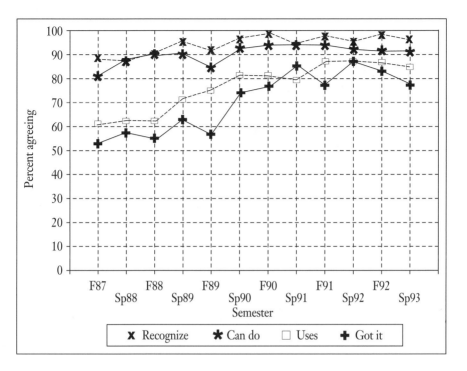

Figure 10. CEQ results for fall 1987 to spring 1993.

All four measures suggest autocorrelated, positive trends, with a hint of decreasing rate of improvement over time. The most conspicuous improvements are in the percents reporting that they can see uses for statistics and that they did get what they came for in taking the course. Some improvement may be due to the introduction of an extensive handout on process improvement in Fall 1989.

Figure 11 shows the percent of students agreeing that they were satisfied with the project (satisfied) and that the project was a valuable learning experience for them (learn). The percent satisfied with the project has been stable at a level of about 75 percent, while the percent regarding it as a valuable learning experience has slowly increased from a level of roughly 55 percent to a level in the 70s. I attribute the latter to the fact that the TAs and I have gradually learned how to present a project assignment to a class of 250, clarifying the instructions each succeeding semester.

Figure 12 shows the percent of students reporting that they are satisfied with various aspects of the course: the course as a whole (course), the lectures (lecture), and the recitation sections (recitation). Satisfaction dipped in fall 1989, when I had

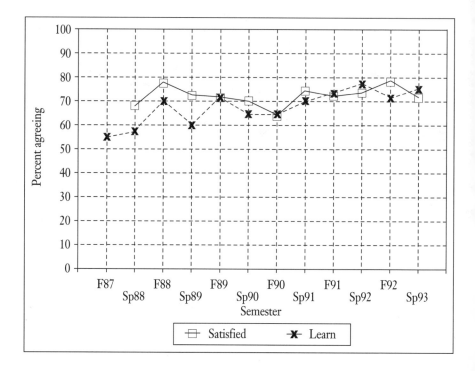

Figure 11. CEQ results for project satisfaction fall 1987 to spring 1993.

an entirely new team of three TAs, and then returned to previous levels in spring 1990, when all three had by then worked with me at least one semester. All three measures have shown modest improvement since that time. It is interesting that satisfaction with the recitations tends to be the highest of the four measures, since the TAs are in charge of these and TAs are often regarded as the weakest link in large lecture courses.

The general improvement in these measures starting in 1990, which followed relatively flat performance from 1987–1989, may be attributable to the introduction of material on quality and productivity improvement, which began in 1989.

Data from Observing the TAs

Initially, the TAs strenuously resisted my attendance at their classes to gather data for coaching. Videotaping was also resisted. I found that a way to really destroy the all-on-one-team attitude was to show up at a recitation unannounced with the camcorder. Another way was to speak up in a recitation when I was observing. I really

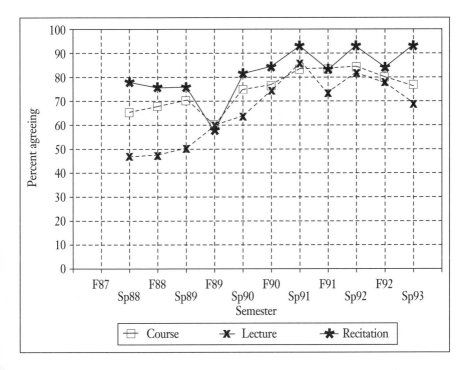

Figure 12. CEQ results for satisfaction levels fall 1987 to spring 1993.

knew better than this, but it was surprisingly difficult to manage myself when I saw a TA making a mistake while I was watching. It took a while to mend the damage.

Here are some observations about coaching using videotape.

• Coaching using videotape is tougher than teaching itself because it requires watching both the TA and the class, learning how to identify critical aspects of effective and ineffective instruction on the tape, and learning how to deliver the coaching to the TA in a constructive way.

• TAs resist being observed and being videotaped, though the resistance is lower now than it used to be, perhaps because they know that this is what is required of my TAs. Their resistance, coupled with my discomfort in holding people accountable, can produce an unproductive "racket": I don't coach and neither of us holds the other accountable for our failed commitment to doing supervision, coaching, and quality improvement.

The following are some common quality problems that arise with TAs. Many of these quality problems also show up in the videotapes of my own lectures!

- Giving the class before getting mentally prepared and centered, often because of rushing from another class

- Answering a question before being certain what the question is

- Not making sure that the rest of the class knows what the question is before answering it

- Not checking whether the answer given answered the question asked

- Speaking to the board

- Not checking to see if they are being understood

- Not handling talking in class effectively

- Not being aware of when they are "making students wrong," blatantly or subtly

- Getting defensive

- Not waiting at least five seconds for an answer after they asked a question

Sources of Variation in Grades

The relative stability of the course and final exam grades from term to term led me to investigate whether the variation within a semester is related to various performance or background variables. My regression studies along these lines were limited and inconclusive. However, one small experiment is worth reporting. In spring 1990 I collected names of students present in lecture on three consecutive days about two-thirds of the way through the semester. This is the point in the semester when regularly only about two-thirds of the students are attending lectures. The groups that were present more days had a higher grade distribution both for the course and the final examination.

Quality Improvement Actions: Fall 1989 to Spring 1990

In part because of my disappointment with slow quality improvement in Statistics 3014, I decided to implement additional steps. In December 1989, I asked all students in the lecture one week before the end of the semester to write down the two highest and the two lowest quality aspects of the course. A week later I also asked them to name these aspects in the free response section of the Student Instructional Rating System form. The results indicated that in the students' view, the highest quality aspects of the course were the project, the course organization, and the applications they saw of statistics to business. The lowest quality aspects were that there was too much material in the course, the project was too much work, the class was too large, no quizzes were dropped, there was no midterm, and lecture time was wasted on activities like reporting on the minute papers or doing crowd management.

In December 1989 I also met with a group of eight students to construct cause-and-effect diagrams for two persistent problems: the drop in quiz scores and attendance as the semester progresses. As a result, I decided to implement the following changes in spring 1990.

• Assign daily homework to be done in notebooks to be collected three times in the semester.

• Get into the more difficult material quicker.

• Make the earlier quizzes harder.

• Have a midterm exam.

• Reduce the amount of lecture time spent on announcements, the minute paper report, and working homework problems from prior lectures.

• Pay two points extra credit for the 10 percent sample chosen each lecture to do minute papers.

Following are the results from spring 1990.

• Quiz scores dipped earlier, recovered, and then dipped again at the end of the semester.

• Lecture attendance was about the same, perhaps a bit lower after the midterm.

• The minute paper response rate improved; the "got it" percent steadily improved during the semester, while the "no mud" percent proved to be difficult to get above 60 percent.

• Complaints about the lack of homework and exams were drastically reduced.

• The final exam average was similar to previous semesters.

The Student Instructional Rating System free responses indicated that for the 98 students who responded, the aspects of the course students liked best were the course structure, the commitment to improving the course, the project, the use of realistic examples, and management of the course as though it were a business. The aspects of the course students liked least were the time demands of the project, the amount of lecture time spent on managing the quality of the lecture, doing the project in teams, and rushing through the tougher material at the end of the semester.

Quality improvement is a never ending process!

In the semesters since spring 1990 I have continued to develop the course, at times feeling like I am walking a fine line between tampering with the course and making improvements in it. I have dropped the homework notebooks because my TAs did not have enough grading time available to do the quality of grading job that they wanted to do.

Perhaps the biggest addition I have made since 1990 is the Outstanding Project Program. I created this program to have a way to acknowledge the 5 to 10 project teams each semester that did a superb job. To be eligible for the program a student team must do a project with a business. Someone at the business is the team's contact. This person helps the team come up with a project that matters to the business and writes an assessment of the team's work and its contribution to the business that is included in the written final report. Awards range from 5 to 40 extra credit points, where there are 1000 points possible in the course.

Unknown and Unknowable Variables

W. Edwards Deming discusses the dangers of managing on the basis of numbers alone, asserting that the most important numbers relating to a company's survival are unknown and unknowable. I think this is also true in higher education. What are the losses to us, to future classes, to the business school, to future employers, or to society when

- A student leaves the course convinced that the rumors were right? Statistics is useless; the course serves only to filter students for the business school.

- A student leaves the course thinking he or she does not know how to use statistical tools, or a student is treated with disrespect by a TA or lecturer?

On the other hand, what are the benefits when

- Energy is spent by a team working on its project and talking about statistics late at night over soda and popcorn?

- Students are talking to each other before and after class, rather than arriving and leaving silently in the typical anonymity of a large class?

- Students come to office hours to discuss project ideas?

- The syllabus reflects topics thought to be useful by practitioners?

- The class has adopted the all-on-one-team concept so that it is silent in lecture, people are in their seats on time, and stay to the end?

- The steady flow of questions and ideas from the students' work on their projects helps the instructor feel fresh, rather than stagnant after teaching this course 16 times in the past nine years?

The benefits of the quality improvement efforts that are the most difficult to quantify are also the ones that most provide me with energy and inspiration to continue. These are reflected in comments on the minute papers, CEQs, and the Student Instructional Rating System forms.

One percent to 3 percent of these comments are negative, sometimes strongly negative. For example, "Fire the instructor! He can't relate to students!" But the percent of comments that are positive has grown steadily over the years. I find this growth, as well as the specific things said, to be encouraging. Here are six recent comments.

"At first, I didn't understand why a course project was required, but as we moved along in the semester as well as in our project, I started to realize the practical aspects of the statistics I learned, and I enjoyed putting what I had learned to use so quickly."

"I saw many, many ways in which the material I learned can be applied to real-life, everyday situations. Statistics 3014 truly has been a personal asset."

"When I took this course last fall under a different instructor, at the end of the course I had no idea how you incorporated statistics to a business. Thanks to doing a project, I now understand."

"I came to statistics to learn formulas and that I did, but I learned a lot more. . . . I learned how to apply it to my career and just basic everyday things."

"I learned what stats was all about and became aware of just how it can be used in the field of business. Before this class I did not know what it involved and now I can see its usefulness."

"I got an overview of just how important statistics are in everyday life, and especially their importance to businesses and their processes. This is what I expected to learn, and I did, especially with the project."

Students do not often encounter improvement efforts in the courses they take. When they do, they generally appreciate them; many will become part of a team to help improve the course.

Most Improved Aspects of the Course

My goal is to encourage those who are considering the introduction of systematic quality improvement into their teaching. That these results have been achieved is due to a combination of the power of the quality improvement strategies; the quality of the staff, TAs, and students who have worked with me; and my commitment and persistence.

From my perspective the most improved aspects of the course over the last nine years are these.

• The management of my anxiety before, during, and after the semester: preparing for the first day of class, handling grade complaints during and after the semester, dealing with the thought, "I should have covered more this term."

• The distinctions I am beginning to make as to what I am and am not accountable for, and what I do and do not have control over.

• The crowd management aspects of lectures to large classes.

• The use of lecture time.

• The system for working with the TAs.

• The project oral presentation days.

• The TA job description.

• The term project instructions and the overall quality of the projects.

• The general information handout.

• The course content.

Toughest Challenges to Continued Course Quality Improvement
For me, the toughest current challenges to continued improvement of the quality of Statistics 3014 are these.

• Assessment (I yearn for more authentic assessments than my quizzes and exams, though I feel pretty good about the authenticity of the project grades).

• The lecture attendance drop.

• The late semester quiz score drop.

• The low average score on the final.

• Those students who interpret comments about "quality improvement" and "all on one team" as evidence that I am being totally unrealistic in my approach to the course.

• The lack of routine use of computers in the course.

• Variation in input: my TAs and students come from many suppliers; I do not hire them.

• Managing the course so that those who are committed to learning are not impeded by those who are not.

- How to create the project teams and how to facilitate them to manage themselves so that the freeloader problem is handled.

- How to bridge the gaps between the many points of view that the faculty in my department have toward this course so that quality improvement of all courses taught may become a departmental theme.

Conclusion: The Next-Generation Course

I propose that the defining characteristic of the next generation of large lecture, introductory statistics course be that it contain both on- and off-line quality improvement activities. Admittedly, quality improvement is not easy in this environment: relationships are adversarial, fear is rampant, breakdowns are not seen as opportunities, collecting data on how well you are doing is potentially embarrassing, and resources are limited.

In spite of all this, I propose that statisticians have only two choices: systematically improve the quality of the large lecture course or offer excuses for not doing so. If statisticians continue to make excuses for the poor quality of our introductory course and if statistics is really as useful as we say it is, then I predict that nonstatisticians will learn how to teach large lecture, introductory statistics courses effectively and efficiently. Statisticians will then lose all of this business.

Do statisticians have the courage to take on the task of improving the quality of the large lecture, introductory statistics course? If not us, who? If not now, when?*

Making a Difference

All it takes to make a difference is the courage to stop proving I was right in being unable to make a difference—to stop assigning cause for my inability to the circumstances outside myself and to be willing to have been this way, and to see that the fear of being a failure is a lot less important than the unique opportunity I have to make a difference (author unknown).

As Dan Boroto has said, it takes courage to maintain commitment in the face of uncertainty.

---

*__Editor's note:__ The problems of teaching large classes are encountered by faculty in many disciplines, and it is reasonable to assume that Zahn's remarks about the usefulness of quality improvement in the classroom would apply to them too. Statisticians can be singled out only because of the generally bad reputation they have created for statistics, as discussed earlier in this paper.

An Invitation

I am looking for coaches and partners. Coaches will help me consider the questions, "What is missing from the system? How can this work be done better?" Partners are individuals who are willing to collaborate in some way in the task of systematically improving the quality of these types of service course. Please let me know if you are interested in either of these activities.

Networking is an essential part of quality improvement. One aspect of it that has been especially valuable to me has been the series of conferences, Making Statistics More Effective in Schools of Business. Individuals from that conference have made valuable contributions to my efforts over the years. This brings me to my final purpose in writing this paper: to offer support and encouragement to anyone thinking of starting an effort such as this.

Finally, I have several papers and handouts my colleagues and I have produced over the years that I'd be happy to send to you for the price of copying and postage.

Acknowledgments

I gratefully acknowledge the support I have received over the years in this project in so many ways from my wife, Andrea Zahn. Several colleagues have also provided valuable input: Harry V. Roberts, Lawrence A. Sherr, P. George Benson, Robert Miller, Blan Godfrey, Dan Boroto, Duane Meeter, and Ron Polland. All my teaching assistants have been helpful in improving the course. Three especially stand out for special thanks for their contributions: Karen Kinard, V. Ramakrishnan, and Heather S. Smith. Last, but by no means least, I am grateful to the over 3000 students with whom I have worked in Statistics 3014 over the past nine years for all they have taught me about teaching, learning, statistics, quality improvement, commitment, life, and myself.

This paper is an update and extension of Zahn, Doug, *Communications in Statistics—Theory & Methods*, Marcel Dekker, Inc., N.Y., 1990, pgs. 4383–4418, from which substantial material has been drawn; by courtesy of Marcel Dekker, Inc.

Notes

1. C. McCulloch, D. R. Boroto, D. Meeter, R. Polland, and D. A. Zahn, "An Expanded Approach to Educating Statistical Consultants," *The American Statistician* 39 (1985): 159–167.

2. B. L. Joiner, "The Key Role of Statisticians in the Transformation of North American Industry," *The American Statistician* 39 (1985): 224–227.

3. D. R. Boroto, "On Being Valued and Utilized: The Problem of Assessing What Is Wanted and Needed" (paper presented at the 1990 Winter Conference of the American Statistical Association, Orlando, Fla., January 1990).

4. Ibid; D. R. Boroto and D. A. Zahn, "The Wanted-and-Needed Conversation: A Tool to Enhance Consulting Effectiveness," *1989 Proceedings of the Section on Statistical Education of the American Statistical Association* (Alexandria, Va.: American Statistical Association, 1989).

5. D. A. Zahn, "Student Projects in a Large Lecture Introductory Business Statistics Course," 1992 Proceedings of the Business and Economic Statistics Section of the American Statistical Association (Alexandria, Va.: American Statistical Association, 1992).

6. K. Ishikawa, *Guide to Quality Control* (Tokyo: Asian Productivity Organization, 1976); H. Gitlow, S. Gitlow, A. Oppenheim, and R. Oppenheim, *Tools and Methods for the Improvement of Quality* (Homewood, Ill.: Irwin, 1989).

7. W. E. Deming, *Out of the Crisis* (Cambridge, Mass.: Center for Advanced Engineering Technology, 1985), x.

Bibliography

Boroto, D. R., and D. A. Zahn. "Promoting Statistics: On Becoming Valued and Utilized." *The American Statistician* 43 (1989): 71–72.

Zahn, D. A. "Quality Breakdowns: An Opportunity in Disguise." *42nd Annual Quality Congress Transactions* (Milwaukee, Wis.: American Society for Quality Control, 1988): 56–62.

———. "Experiences with a Course Project in a Large Lecture Course." Paper presented at the Fourth Conference on Making Statistics More Effective in Schools of Business, Ann Arbor, Mich., June 1989.

———. "Current Challenges in Statistics: Large Lecture Courses." *Communications in Statistics: Theory and Methods* 19 (1990): 4348–4418.

Zahn, D., G. Benson, B. Godfrey, R. Miller, and L. Sherr. "Improving the Quality of Business Statistics: A Process Approach." *1987 Proceedings of the Section on Statistical Education of the American Statistical Association* (Alexandria, Va.: American Statistical Association, 1987).

Zahn, D. A., and L. A. Sherr. "Systematically Improving the Quality of Statistics Courses: An Invitation." *1988 Proceedings of the Business and Economic Statistics Section of the American Statistical Association* (Alexandria, Va.: American Statistical Association, 1988).

Appendix: Executive Summaries of Two Term Projects

Executive Summary, Project 1

1. Our group of three studied the waiting time in the reception area for scheduled patients prior to seeing the dentist, Dr. Glenn Beck, Jr. The quality improvement question we studied is a beneficial factor in aiding the doctor and his staff in keeping an efficient schedule, thus keeping patients satisfied.

2. Our study was conducted by sampling 16 hours, which is 40 percent of the 40-hour work week. We randomly selected the hours form the random numbers table to determine which hours we would time the patients' waiting period. The team member doing the timing was given a daily schedule and was seated in the reception room. The stopwatch was started when the patient went to the window and stated his or her name. We stopped timing when the patient's name was called and was then seated in an operatory.

3. Variable A—Our findings indicate that the average waiting time is longer than the 1200 seconds we had estimated.

   Variable B—We found that, on the average, a patient waits longer on Wednesday then followed by Thursday, Tuesday, Monday, and then Friday.

   Variable C—Our statistics have shown conclusively that first-time scheduled patients have a shorter waiting time than other patients.

4. We recommend that the doctor and his staff work together to produce a more efficient schedule that runs more smoothly and keeps the patients waiting less time.

O GLENN BECK, JR., D.M.D.
MARCI MARANO BECK, D.M.D., M.S.
1728 NORTH MAGNOLIA DRIVE
TALLAHASSEE, FLORIDA 32303
—
TELEPHONE 677-7112

April 11, 1989

Dr. Zahn
Florida State University
Tallahassee, FL

Dear Dr. Zahn:

I have recently been informed of the findings in the statistical study made by a group of your students involving the average time a patient spends in our office waiting to see the dentist.

I find these figures to be very accurate according to my own personal observations since becoming the office manager for this office.

By being able to determine the average waiting time of a patient, I will be able to better schedule the dentist's time according to the procedure he will be performing on said patient. It will also allow me to give the patient a more accurate accounting of the total time he or she will spend in our office. The time that is allotted by the dentist involves his work only.

I have also pointed out that a new patient is seen faster than a regular patient and this study concurs with my own observations. By being able to present this to the dentist, I will be able to encourage them to work on their time management in regards to their regular patients.

I sincerely would like to thank the students involved with this project. It has been informative and will help me bring better time management to our office.

Sincerely yours,

Judy H. Adams
Office Manager

Executive Summary, Project 2

1. The quality improvement question we studied was the length of time taken for a client's bill to be processed, a check to be received at Oven Park, and that check to be deposited into the park's bank account.

2. We studied 25 consecutive weeks of operation at the park between Sunday, April 9 and Saturday, September 30, 1989. We studied all of the functions during a given week unless there were six or more, in which case we chose five functions at random. We measured the time, in days, from the date of the function to the date an invoice was written; the time, in days, from the date of invoice to the date the client's check was received; the time, in days, from the date the check was received to the date the check was deposited; and the time, in days, from the date of the function to the date the check was deposited.

3. Our first finding is that the majority of the functions do not follow the normal billing process as described in part II, section 1. In most of the cases this was to the park's benefit because the deviant functions' processes were generally less time-consuming than the normal process and, thus, brought money into the park much faster than the normal process functions. However, it was found that 25 percent of the deviant functions were delinquent accounts. That corresponds to an overall delinquency rate of 13 percent for the sample we studied. Other statistics of interest include an average time of 11 days from the date of the function to the date of invoice, an average time of nearly 35 days for the check to be received after invoice, an average time of 10 days from the date the check is received to the date of deposit, and an overall average of 56 days for the process to complete itself. Although these figures are based only on the functions we studied that followed the normal process, they are not very far from what we expected to find. The average for writing the invoice is one day more than we had anticipated, the average for collecting the account is 10 days less than what we expected, the average for depositing the check is three days more than what we expected, and the average for the whole process is nine days less than what we had anticipated it being. We feel that these statistics are extremely representative of all the functions at Oven Park because out of the possible 101 billed functions that took place at the park during the 25 weeks we studied, 97 were chosen for our sample.

4. Based on our findings, we would like to recommend the following changes. First, a full-time bookkeeper should be added to the staff at Oven Park. Second, we suggest that the trips to Meyer's Park and City Hall be eliminated. This could be accomplished if Oven Park had its own typewriter, mail meter, and mailbox. Third, we suggest that the center supervisor be instructed in the procedures for

reporting delinquent accounts to the city's legal department for purposes of collection. Finally, in the spirit of ongoing process improvement, we recommend that a follow-up study be performed so that the effects of changes made can be noted as well as to explore new areas in need of improvement.

November 29, 1989

Dr. Zahn
Department of Statistics
Florida State University
Tallahassee, FL 32306

Dear Dr. Zahn,

On behalf of the City of Tallahassee Parks & Recreation Department, I would like to thank you and your students, particularly Cyndi Barnes, for the recently completed accounting study.

I will be using the information gathered in this study as support data for my upcoming budget request for more staff at the Oven Park facility. I feel positive this information will add credence to my request.

Your students were very polite and caused no interruptions in our operations.

Thank you again for allowing this study. If there is any follow-up information needed, please feel free to contact me.

Sincerely yours,

Debbie Pullen, Center Supervisor
Dorothy B. Oven Park and House
(904) 422-1507

DP/jr

Real-World Total Quality Projects for Statistics Courses

George R. Bateman and Harry V. Roberts

A Special Role for Total Quality in Statistics Courses

One interesting route to total quality in the curriculum is available in any statistics course—elementary, intermediate, or advanced—that includes practical data analysis within its scope. The instructor can guide students in the application of statistical tools to quality improvement projects in real organizations, business or other, including their own college or university.

Only minimal background in total quality is required of either instructor or student, and this paper outlines that background. Instructors who start with minimal background will find that the experience in guiding students very rapidly enhances their capability. Beyond statistical tools, the key to success is a very simple total quality idea: waste reduction guided by customer requirements. Elements of waste reduction are presented in this paper.

We now have several years of experience in guiding students along the lines explained in this paper. We have found that students have surprisingly little trouble in locating good quality improvement projects on their own initiative and that they can do a good job once they become engaged in a project. The projects can be done by individual students or by small teams. When we have permitted students to choose between individual and team projects, we have found that most of them prefer individual projects. This may reflect the fact that at our business school, students get plenty of experience in team projects in other courses.

The quality improvement projects in our courses usually are completed within a few weeks during the term the statistics course is offered, so elaborate formal methodology and protracted efforts are not possible. But most students aim at, and often achieve, substantial improvements during those few weeks. In view of the fact that many organizations have substantial difficulties in making quality improvement projects succeed and that some critics say that total quality does not work or works too slowly, the success of students on these class projects is gratifying.

Our experience has been largely with business students, but limited experience with students from other fields suggests that lack of detailed knowledge of quality tools or of business functions and terminology is not critical. Most of the improvement comes from waste reduction. Once students are briefed on the kinds of wastes to look for, they will find them easily. A little instruction in waste recognition and elimination can go a long way, and this paper outlines the needed instruction.

A paper by Professor Zangwill in this volume, "Fast Quality for Fast Results," reports on a similar approach to improvement projects that places lesser emphasis on statistics. In Zangwill's variation, students have just two weeks to make changes based on their quality investigations. Zangwill not only requires that his students get permission to work within organizations, but that they get the organization to commit to making changes indicated by the students' analyses. John Flueck's and Doug Zahn's papers also report on experiences with student projects.

We do not claim that all quality improvements can be made by small-scale projects of the kind we describe. Indeed, many of these projects are successful because they attack the most obvious short-term opportunities, the "low-hanging fruit." Some contend that it is short-sighted to harvest low-hanging fruit, that a better strategy is to aim at more thoroughgoing, systematic improvements, improvements that may never be made if we rest on our initial short-term improvements. Our position is that most of these short-term improvements not only bring tangible immediate benefits, but valuable training and experience for later improvements when there is no longer low-hanging fruit to be picked. Moreover, we argue that no harm can be done in the long term by short-term waste elimination.

The purpose of this paper is twofold.

- To give guidance for teachers who would like to have their students do similar quality improvement projects in real time and in real organizations

- To suggest how surprisingly easy it is to achieve quick quality improvement with simple improvement strategies based on ideas of waste reduction and elementary statistics, and to show which statistical tools are especially suitable for these projects

We provide a few typical applications to illustrate concretely the kinds of projects that are possible.

The Role of Data and Data Analysis in Total Quality

The road to improvement via total quality is seldom smooth. For example, there may be lack of top-management support or there may be only nominal management support for total quality as just another program rather than a fundamentally different approach to management. But even if some progress is being made, two related problems often remain to hinder further progress.

- A poor organizational culture: rigid, top-down leadership with resulting fear, pessimism, and apathy in the ranks. No technique of total quality by itself can offset a poor organizational culture.

- Overreliance on opinion, judgment, and authority to the near exclusion of data collection, display, and analysis. The word *data* is to be construed in the broadest sense. Defect counts are data, but so are flowcharts, process maps, and even anecdotal information ("anecdata") and casual observations. It is essential to base action on reasoned analysis of data, not to shoot in the dark or tamper aimlessly, hoping thereby to improve quality.

Data analysis and statistics do not offer direct mitigation of fear, pessimism, and apathy, but by bringing facts into the picture, they introduce an external restraint on the unchallenged exercise of management authority that is often the source of fear, pessimism, and apathy. Moreover, data analysis and statistics offer a dependable route to consistent improvement because they tie improvement efforts to reality rather than personal fancy.

The Interplay Between Data Analysis and Action

We are concerned with the use of data to improve quality, a broad objective that can include any of the following:

- Direct improvement in the sense of a decrease in cycle times or defect rates or an increase in customer satisfaction

- Holding the gains from past improvements by standardization of the improved process

- Monitoring or controlling a process to detect possible setbacks or apparently spontaneous improvements (both subsumed under the term *special cause*)

- Adapting improvements from a study of one process to other, similar processes

- *Benchmarking:* studying someone else's process with the aim of evaluating its good features and, if sufficiently promising, adapting them to one's own use

- Planning for future quality improvement

We are concerned with ongoing operational processes such as production or order filling, and also with metaprocesses like strategic planning and new product development and innovation.

We assume that pertinent process data are being collected on a continuing basis through time and that there is provision for collection of special additional data from time to time as need suggests. In collecting and analyzing data, we always have two questions in mind.

1. What action on the process, if any, is indicated in the light of current data?

2. What additional data, if any, will cast light on the wisdom of further action?

We repeatedly follow the alternating sequence of steps: action, analyze data, action, analyze data, action, analyze data, and so on. *Action* includes

- Process adjustments and improvements that seem promising in the light of current data

- Gathering more data as the need is perceived

Analyze data includes

- Judgmental evaluation of all available data

- Intuitive graphical analysis

- Numerical analysis, including elementary regression tools

The aim is to make continual improvement, or at least to refrain from doing harm, at each action step.

Juran has stressed two broad aspects of data gathering and analysis.

- *Diagnostic journey:* Search for root causes of quality shortcomings.

- *Remedial journey:* Search for remedies, countermeasures, and, more broadly, better ways of doing things.

Simple tools of statistical experimentation, which are or can be introduced in most statistics courses, sometimes make it possible to combine diagnosis and remedy by experimental alteration of the causes (for example, process inputs, such as raw materials, or environmental conditions, such as temperature) that may affect the process.

Some Key Uses of Data Analysis for Quality Improvement

Many implementations of total quality stress extensive initial training in quality, which is followed by deployment of temporary, part-time cross-functional teams working on major organizational problems, following lengthy problem-solving sequences and looking for substantial improvements, often in the relatively distant future. This is one viable strategy, but it is not easy to implement successfully when the organization has not had much experience with quality improvement or does not have sufficient commitment of leadership or resources. Also, this strategy tends to make total quality seem distinct from ordinary daily work.

An alternative, though not exclusive, strategy is to do simple statistical studies of the kind discussed in this paper. These statistical studies can be done either by individuals or by small, natural, local teams. They can also be done by students coming into the organization to do projects for their statistics courses, which is the central focus of the paper.

Simple statistical studies—whether done by students, employees, or both—offer good prospects of improvement, often fast improvement. They can stand alone or be part of a larger quality improvement project, perhaps carried on by a cross-functional team. We base these claims mainly on our own experience in supervising hundreds of improvement projects in MBA courses by students working with real organizations for relatively short periods of time (typically a few weeks). Some students, working part-time in our evening, weekend, or executive MBA programs, do the projects in their own organizations; full-time MBA students, sometimes assisted by us, make arrangements with outside organizations to work on these projects. Most projects have led to modest, but useful, improvements; a few have led to very large improvements, measured by cost savings in six and even seven digits. Only a few student projects have drawn blanks, and these have often resulted from difficulties in convincing an organization to collect needed data or to implement indicated improvements, rather than failure to find opportunities for improvement.

The statistical tools needed for these projects can be classified into two groups.

- Very elementary total quality tools, such as cause-and-effect charts (fishbone charts), run charts, Pareto diagrams, affinity analysis, and flowcharts, described in *The Memory Jogger II*, an inexpensive, compact publication that can be used as an inexpensive supplementary text for any statistics course in which quality improvement projects are to be used.[1]

- Tools covered in statistics courses, including regression and elementary time-series analysis, implemented by ordinary regression. One text that covers these tools at an elementary level and emphasizes practical data analysis is *Data Analysis for Managers with Minitab*, 2nd edition.[2]

Types of Statistical Studies That Have Proven Useful

Here is a suggestive listing of the types of simple statistical studies that can be pursued.

1. Surveys of external and internal customers can suggest processes that need improvement and specific ways to go about improving them, and these suggestions can be quickly implemented.

Customer satisfaction surveys should be sound methodologically and, for purpose of course projects, should normally be kept very simple: short questionnaires; scientific sampling; serious efforts to keep nonresponse rates low. For examples of short, simple, but useful customer-satisfaction questionnaires, see "Total Quality for Professors and Students" in this volume.

Even informal conversations with customers can help. In the early 1980s, when Motorola was beginning its quality improvement efforts that culminated in the Baldrige award of 1988, chairman of the board Bob Galvin talked with many users of Motorola products. He found that Motorola hardware was highly regarded, but that service support—instructions, installation, invoicing, after-sales servicing, answering requests for information—was often not highly regarded. Galvin's information pointed the way to many improvements, and his leadership position helped to assure that the improvements were achieved.

Focus groups can be useful. They don't have to be fancy. Just get customers together to talk informally about their experiences with and preferences for the product or service of interest. Be relatively nondirective in the questioning. For example, don't pose leading questions. Remember to record and summarize the ideas that come out of the discussion.

Employee attitude surveys can also be useful, especially at the early stages of total quality implementation. For example, employee surveys often show that employee attitudes toward an organization-wide total quality initiative are much less favorable than top management had expected. This discovery can be the first step toward putting the quality improvement on a secure human foundation. Similarly, surveys of suppliers can be valuable as a first step in establishing effective supplier partnerships.

2. Map key processes to bring out obvious waste that can be quickly eliminated. Often process mapping alone will show obvious opportunities for improvement by the elimination of unnecessary process steps or running some steps in parallel rather than in series in order to reduce cycle time. For example, in service processes, steps that require a signature of approval from an executive may serve no real purpose and simply inject an unnecessary delay. Examples of process mapping are

• Flowcharting, simple and sophisticated.

• Manuals and other descriptive text needed to flesh out flowcharts.

- Photographs, drawings, videotapes, also to flesh out flowcharts.

- "As-is" mapping and "should-be" mapping.

- Involvement of work associates in as-is mapping. Different people involved in implementing a process may have different knowledge and perspective on the process.

3. Gather, display, study, and act upon the information provided by process metrics for processes that are important to customers. The process metrics include defect rates, cycle times, output rates, customer satisfaction, and, possibly, costs. As a simple example, an executive MBA student, who was also president of a manufacturing company, had an operator gather dimensional measurements from a grinder that was not holding tolerances, resulting in defective output. The run chart showed that the operator was frequently changing machine settings, and this was greatly increasing the variability of output and therefore producing large numbers of defectives. The president explained to the operator that the changing of settings constituted a form of tampering that was actually harmful. The operator realized that benign neglect was appropriate; he was henceforth able to make the grinder meet tolerances.

Simple statistical analyses of process data provide a background for all quality improvement activities, and often, as illustrated by the grinder example, suggest immediate opportunities for improvement by providing perspective on how the process has been performing. For example, favorable or unfavorable trends, which are otherwise easy to miss, may become obvious, and appropriate action—especially search for root causes—can be initiated.

Whatever process you are trying to improve, whatever metric you are using, you should continually be doing these statistical analyses. In getting started, you should try to dig up available historical data so that you can obtain better perspective on the current behavior of the process and better assess the effectiveness of any improvements that you attempt.

The key display tool is the run chart and its extension, the control chart. These charts should be displayed conspicuously and kept up-to-date.

Intuitive analysis of run charts and control charts is valuable in distinguishing systematic trends from random fluctuations in process behavior. Formal numerical and graphical analysis is sometimes required. Then the tools of the statistics course, mainly regression analysis, are needed.

Stretch goals—ambitious improvement goals—for process metrics of all key processes provide a simple way to drive improvement efforts throughout an organization without micromanagement or even without formal quality improvement projects. Examples of stretch goals are "cut cycle time by a factor of 10 every five years," or "cut defect rates by a factor of 10 every two years."

Other Useful Statistical Tools

The first two tools listed here can be developed, as needed, from the background instruction of any statistics course that covers regression. The remaining tools are elementary; all are explained in detail in *The Memory Jogger II.*

1. *Intervention analysis:* how did the behavior of the run chart or control chart change when a process improvement was implemented?

2. *Experimental designs:* combining the diagnostic journey and the remedial journey by trying out a process modification based on a hypothesis about root causes.

3. *Cause-and-effect diagrams:* organizing thinking and knowledge about root causes. Can be used effectively either by individuals or teams.

4. *Pareto analysis:* setting priorities as to the most important quality problems to be dealt with: for example, which customers or products or territories account for the bulk of the complaints or product returns? Improvement efforts can then be better focused.

5. *Benchmarking,* local or global: steal and improve anything that isn't proprietary. Benchmarking is not strictly a statistical tool, but it relies heavily on seeking out, and getting data on, best—or at least better—processes, whether in our own organization, in similar organizations, or in the world at large.

The Key Role of Waste and Waste Reduction

An article by Roberts in this book, "A Primer on Personal Quality," also contains a discussion on waste and waste reduction. This section is included to make the present paper self-contained.

The pervasiveness of waste can make it possible to make quick and substantial improvements in quality simply by spotting and reducing the most obvious wastes. In a word, stop doing the dumb things. After these quick improvements, there will still be plenty of room for continuing improvement by reducing the less obvious wastes that then become apparent.

Waste is failure to add value commensurate with cost, either in an individual instance or on the average. Complete failure to add any value at all is a special case of this definition. There are four important species of waste.

- Waste of poor quality
- Waste of unnecessary work

- Waste of missed opportunities
- Waste revealed by redesign

This fourfold classification of species of waste helps to sensitize us to the kinds of waste that we should be looking for, so that we can better identify specific wastes that can be removed.

The classification serves another important purpose. By bringing all four types of waste into the picture, we can better understand the potential gains from removal of all forms of waste. The total of cost and/or loss of customer satisfaction attributable to all four wastes can be much greater than one would expect from looking at any single type.

It is useful to define different sources or species of waste, starting with the waste of poor quality.

Waste of Poor Quality

One important source of waste stems from not doing something right the first time because of process flaws and breakdowns that lead to process outcomes different than those intended. Poor quality increases costs by comparison to what they would have been with perfect process execution. The need for inspection and rework is the most obvious example.

This does not mean that inspection and rework are themselves wasteful; given that defects are being produced, they may add value. If inspection and rework do not add value, we should not be doing them. The failure to add value occurred when the defectives were first produced. Thus the waste of poor quality stems from the fact that the original process failed to add as much value as expected, perhaps did not add any value at all, perhaps added negative value (for example, an oil spill). The work was not done right the first time.

The ultimate effects of poor quality are not confined to the costs of inspection and rework. If defects reach customers, there are costs associated with returns, warranty obligations, claims, dealing with complaints, recalls, lawsuits, loss of credibility of company advertising, and the like. Moreover the resulting customer dissatisfaction may cause reduced future sales to these customers, or to others who hear of their dissatisfaction.

The waste of poor quality has been the traditional concern of quality control and quality management, but it is only a part of the overall waste picture.

Waste of Unnecessary (or Even Counterproductive) Work

Even with perfect quality—even if the processes never have undesired outcomes—there could still be unnecessary work. Examples include a report that no one reads or pays attention to or that adds less value than the cost of its preparation; or special efforts to improve delivery time when customers are completely satisfied with current delivery time.

Another, very important example is the production of output for which there is no immediate demand at the current price so it goes into inventory to be sold, if at all, at a reduced price. This has been called the *waste of overproduction*. (Production for inventory to meet predicted seasonal demand peaks is not regarded as overproduction.) Avoidance of the waste of overproduction has been strongly emphasized by leading Japanese companies such as Toyota.

In the extreme, unnecessary work can actually subtract from value rather than add to it. For example, a medical treatment might do more harm than good.

Waste of Missed Opportunities

Another important species of waste is the waste of missed opportunities, which could include failure to benchmark on better processes in other organizations, failure to recover useful by-product from scrap, failure to prevent or remove environmental hazards, failure to buy supplies and raw materials at the most favorable price, or failure to draw effectively on skills and knowledge of the workforce. Perhaps the most important example of the waste of missed opportunities is failure to take advantage of opportunities to add value. This can happen, for example, when the product is waiting for value to be added, simply marking time, when resources could economically be made available to add value. A service example would be a document waiting in an in-basket for someone's approval. A worker waiting, doing nothing, while tending machines is a manufacturing example. Another example would be a patient waiting for diagnosis and treatment at a medical clinic.

Waste Revealed by Redesign

It is useful to distinguish still another species of waste: work that is currently necessary but becomes unnecessary by improved process or product design; or opportunities for improvement that can be exploited only by improved process or product design. We call this *waste revealed by redesign*. Waste revealed by redesign is a major concern of reengineering. (Reengineering is the side of quality management that deals with discontinuous improvement or breakthrough, as opposed to continuous improvement or kaizen. See the paper in this volume by Richard T. Greene, "Reengineering: How to Do It with Quality in Academia and Elsewhere.")

Example of Waste Reduction: Order Filling

As an example of unnecessary work, consider a pervasive and important service process that is found in almost all organizations: filling orders. For organizations that have not systematically tried to improve the order-filling process, there is typically a great deal of waste. During most of the time of filling, nothing is happening to the order; opportunities to add value are missed while the order sits around waiting to be processed. Simple flowcharting and mapping of the order-filling process is often rewarded by discovery of unnecessary waiting, unnecessary or redundant steps, or steps that can be economically combined or farmed out. Elimination, simplification, or combination of such steps often leads to substantial reduction in the cycle time and a reduction in the rate of error in order filling. Cost is reduced and customer satisfaction is enhanced, often substantially and quickly.

The flowchart is used to clarify the process, both as it actually works (as-is flowchart) and as it could work after improvement (should-be flowchart). Major differences between the two charts come from removal of waste of unnecessary work. The should-be chart is typically simpler and cleaner than the as-is chart.

For another simple example of waste removal, see the shaving example in Roberts, "A Primer on Personal Quality," in this volume.

Examples of Student Projects

In each of the following cases, the students were enrolled in a basic course in quality management at the Graduate School of Business, University of Chicago, or in a special section of that course especially aimed at health care applications. The course emphasizes both statistical tools and the management and leadership issues relevant to quality improvement and reengineering of individual processes or whole organizations. Each student is required to complete two projects, one aimed at improvement of an organizational process; the other, improvement of a personal process. (For discussion of personal improvement projects, see Roberts, "A Primer for Personal Quality," in this volume.)

For the organizational project students are advised to select a project that is of clear interest and manageable within the few weeks of the course and limitations of student time. Students are encouraged, but not required, to form small teams. The teams can include other students in the class, but also other MBA students and employees of the client organizations. There is typically about five or six weeks to do the work and draw conclusions. The final status report includes

- A statement of progress that addresses difficulties faced and lessons learned
- A cogent plan for completing the improvement project

The following four examples were well done, but they were chosen simply to convey the flavor of what students can accomplish and the kinds of projects that they can undertake, not to single out prize winners. From applications provided by our students, we could produce a book of equally interesting examples, and we may do so in the future.

Example 1: Operating Room Efficiency

A team of four campus students and an off-campus student (who was a physician and director of operating rooms) attempted to increase the efficiency of operating rooms at Central DuPage Hospital, a 300-bed community hospital in the Chicago suburbs. The principal measure of efficiency was the turnover time between cases: the time between the exit of one patient from the operating room to the entrance of the next patient. The team also tried to measure the satisfaction of the internal customers—surgeons—and external customers—patients.

The team members began by interviewing a cross-section of medical staff and patients. Then they employed an affinity process with the medical staff to brainstorm root causes of problems and potential solutions. The results of the brainstorming were organized into a fishbone diagram that provided the basis for further discussion with medical and administrative staff. Extensive flowcharting of relevant processes helped to identify waste. In parallel with these steps, they observed the operating room processes over time and used run charts and regression to gain insights into the behavior of delays through time. All this hands-on analysis was supplemented by benchmarking against two area hospitals, Northwest Community and Lutheran General.

The statistical analysis of operating room delays suggested that the process was in control, but the interviews and flowcharts pointed to complexity in the process that created waste or unnecessarily long cycle times. The team's recommendations focused on improving the process of patient and information flow, both before and during the day of surgery. The team made recommendations on block scheduling and on salaries of operating room nurses and technicians who appeared to play a critical role in the flow of patients.

Customer satisfaction was addressed by a survey of surgeons and a "one-stop-shopping" system for patients, which enables patients to take care of all paperwork, lab tests, and so on at one place. To relieve patients of the burden of providing the same information over and over, the team recommended a common patient database available over a hospital network.

The team's final report included a plan for implementation of recommendations, including a checksheet for monitoring the relevant processes.

Example 2: Student Participation in Quality Improvement

Two students in the university's graduate program in health administration and policy developed a process to improve graduate student participation in quality improvement projects at the University of Chicago Hospitals and Clinics (UCHC). They conducted numerous in-depth interviews of UCHC staff, university faculty, and graduate students, and carefully reviewed documentation of UCHC and information on graduate programs curriculum. For the benefit of UCHC, they constructed a simple model for predicting the number of graduate students available in a given academic year to participate in their improvement projects. They led brainstorming sessions that were summarized by fishbone diagrams, and they employed force field analysis and informal process mapping to determine how most effectively to identify, launch, and manage relevant projects. The force field analysis allowed them to identify and articulate driving factors and restraining factors in successful engagement of students in UCHC improvement projects.

In addition to sorting out the complexities associated with addressing the real requirements of a major medical center, of graduate faculty and programs, and of students in various graduate programs, the final report offered clear and sensible recommendations on how to move forward—including insight into how the Pew Foundation might be approached. The report also included simple forms for launching projects, instruments to enable students to evaluate their UCHC project experience, and a short manual for university faculty and UCHC staff to facilitate identification, launching, and management of UCHC projects.

Example 3: Improving Safety at PVS Chemicals

PVS Chemicals had an injury rate twice the average of the industry. Discussions with PVS management and personnel and preliminary data analysis suggested that strains, particularly back strains, were frequent and serious problems.

Four MBA students formed a team. The students first introduced PVS personnel to total quality problem-solving tools, and then engaged them as a part of an expanded team from the university and the company in the process of problem resolution. The expanded team began by flowcharting a process improvement plan to ensure that all members agreed on how to proceed. Then they brainstormed possible sources of worker safety problems, which they summarized in a fishbone diagram. This diagram guided further discussion of and search for root causes.

Data on type and seriousness of injuries over the past 11 years were summarized in a Pareto diagram in an attempt to focus on the vital few root causes. Using a nominal group technique, the team decided to focus on back strains. (Another good choice would have been acid burns.) The team went through a similar problem-solving process—brainstorm, fishbone diagram, data gathering, and Pareto diagram—to identify three primary root causes: poor lifting technique, new loading valves, and awkward placement of equipment. Repeating the problem-solving process to identify promising remedies, team members decided to design and install a modified valve handle for the loading valves, which allowed the drivers to avoid the original awkward position. They also acquired safety training materials and videos from the National Safety Council for use in a new safety training program.

The implementation plan presented in the final report includes monitoring of injuries, implementation of the training program, and benchmarking on an industry leader in safety that they had identified. PVS personnel who worked with the students on this project have now become a PVS safety quality improvement team with responsibilities for carrying out the implementation plan. They anticipate at least a 50 percent reduction in injuries during the first year.

Example 4: Reducing Seal Ring Defects

A manufacturer of engines and earth-moving equipment had a serious problem with a product called seal rings. Historically, 70 percent of the product was defective and had to be scrapped. The annual cost of scrap was about a quarter of a million dollars. In addition, it was estimated that lost sales due to insufficient supply of seal rings was over $1 million.

An off-campus, weekend MBA student employed Juran's breakthrough-study approach: show proof of need; identify the vital few problems; organize for improvement; study the symptoms; theorize about causes; analyze data; implement a solution based on the analysis; test to validate the solution; provide recommendations for further experimentation; and hold the gains.

Two simple run charts of the number of good seal rings per month for two different molds showed a clear alternating effect from month to month: one month the number of good seal rings was up, the next month it was down, and so on. This finding prompted a review of the production records, which revealed that the company had been alternating two operators on a monthly rotation. A subsequent regression analysis verified this operator effect and also revealed that three or four chemicals were being overdosed and should be reduced. Based on this information, the better operator was studied to find out how he did it, and the mix of chemicals was altered. With the revised process and chemical mix, a test run of 80 seal rings was produced. At the time of the final report, 43 seal rings had been produced with only 3 defects, which suggested the potential for substantial improvement. The student and the company are continuing to monitor the process and have designed an experiment to measure the effect of other variables and design parameters.

Other Student Projects

The four projects just described give an idea of what most student team projects are like. Individual projects are able to achieve comparable results, particularly in the Executive MBA program, where students are often in a position to command considerable company resources and have a head start on problems because of their previous experience in the organization. We are consistently impressed by student willingness to take the initiative, and by how much students accomplish in so short a time with only limited time for coaching and guidance from us. We are also pleased by student feedback on lessons learned about data analysis, problem solving, and organizational dynamics and change.

When we relied mainly on examinations, before we used projects in our teaching of quality management and statistics, we were discouraged by what seemed to be mediocre performance of students, who often seemed unable to pin down the theoretical subtleties that we were trying to convey. Now, the ability of students to do good, often outstanding, projects has made us realize that not the students, but our old system was at fault. When the only challenge was that posed by examinations—even the most realistic examinations we were able to devise—students simply did not have an opportunity to show what they really knew and were capable of doing.

To convey the types of opportunities that students find, we now report on an exercise conducted by one of the authors. During the first class, he facilitates an affinity exercise in which students are instructed to write a simple sentence about their prospective project or projects on a Post-It note. Students also provide their name and names of any prospective team members along with phone numbers. During the class break, the notes are stuck on flip chart panels that have been taped to the wall. Students can then move the notes around until they feel that they have established useful groupings of projects. The exercise stimulates students to think about potential projects and team members. (The author encourages metateams, in which individuals and teams working on similar problems occasionally meet to share experiences.)

The students are allowed to edit the affinity diagram over the next two or three weeks, and the author provides updated printed versions for the students as they define or redefine their organizational projects. What follows is a modestly edited version of ideas that have been generated in recent classes. This listing shows both the variety of projects and the relatively general nature of students' early thoughts by comparison with what they typically achieve on their final reports at the end of the course.

Health Care

- Reduce antibiotic turnaround time at UCHC (University of Chicago Hospitals and Clinics) Pediatrics—"Would you wait four hours for a hamburger?"

- Make recommendations for improvement of a small, private sports medicine and physical therapy center. Design, implement, and analyze results of a customer (patient) satisfaction survey.

- Improve the organizational excellence of the American Academy of Pediatrics.

- Review quality improvement in patient care in ambulatory/outpatient clinic. Improve process of transporting patients.

- New UCHC project attempting to improve the administration of narcotic drugs.

- Establish benchmarks in the practice of physical therapy for diagnostic groups (for example, back strain, anterior cruciate ligament injuries, rotator cuff tears) to control variations in cost, duration, and treatments and further establish a range of predictable outcomes for these diagnostic groups.

- Reduce waste and complexity and improve processes in the health care setting. Overall goal: Improve life safety in two million square foot academic medical center. Project: reduce complexity and waste in identifying and correcting fire code violations.

- Improve multisite physical therapy rehabilitation sites, specifically with regard to record tracking and discharge processes.

- Review the process of how Ancor HMO does its physician referrals to specialist. In this case, it would be gastrointestinal specialists.

Manufacturing Industry and Processes

- Eliminate overtime in the assembly department of a manufacturing company.

- Redesign the way sales leads are generated, the way leads are qualified, how they are distributed to the field, and what process will be used to follow up and pursue "good" leads.

- Improve information availability and flow in a manufacturing environment (petroleum industry). Process evaluation and redesign targeting elimination of redundancy and waste.

- Analyze existing process in marketing/manufacturing firm where trade show promotion programs are designed, implemented, and monitored for effectiveness. Develop new tools and modify existing processes to improve effectiveness of trade promotion spending.

- Improve/modify GE Motor's Simulated Customer Acceptance Test (SCAT). SCAT is a quality audit of finished product built in a manufacturing plant.

- Improve welding process at a manufacturing company (using design of experiments).

- Investigate location of pilot hole in side bars at A.O. Smith, an automobile component manufacturing firm.

- Improve the efficiency of the Crystal Light "Club Store" Line and also reduce packaging-related quality defects of the product.

- Reduce down time for the corrugation process. This process is a human managing the machine to manufacture corrugated board, which is used to produce corrugated board boxes that are sold to external customers. Problem may be mechanical or operator related.

- Cycle time improvement in the delivery of developmental materials from a specialty chemical pilot plant facility to customer. Date order placed until ship date constitutes cycle time. Inventory position is not an option.

- Analyze why and reduce the number of overtime schedules and premium shipments resulting from a high-volume product-line component manufacturing mismanagement.

- Meet customer's schedule needs by reducing cycle time associated with the delivery of spare parts.

- Understand raw material acquisition, supplier selection, supplier partnership, and so on in a chemical company. The activities will be benchmarked against widely accepted standards for their execution.

Chemical Industry

- Minimize customer complaints at PVS Chemicals. Determine the reasons for complaints, investigate the main causes, and recommend appropriate corrective actions.

- Improve the timing of shipment of Specialty Chemical Inc. (SCI) goods to customers.

Improving Work Processes

- Improve the accuracy of a project status (P&L) report for a medium-sized construction company. Notes: This is a key report for profit analysis, project management, catching costly errors, catching changes in scope (entitlement to more money), and so on. Several departments provide input for this report.

- Construct a quality plan to facilitate quality client service and continuous improvement on a business process reengineering consulting engagement.

- Improve the efficiency of engineering department. I run a small (8-person) engineering department that exists for the sole purpose of supporting manufacturing operations through application of new technology, equipment installation, process improvement, and technical maintenance assistance. The problem is manufacturing complexity and size are growing while the department is shrinking. The way we do work must be improved through eliminating waste. I will be using the project engineer in my department as a team member.

- Improve cycle time in processing customs entries in a customs brokerage operation.

Information and Work Flow

- Improve information flow from remote sales reps to internal customers.

- Improve the information-gathering process in my department.

- Improve work-flow process within the recruiting center at the University of Chicago Graduate School of Business (GSB).

- Analyze and improve GSB admissions process. Key problem areas include joint-program applications and personal interview evaluations.

- Investigate whether the GSB alumni can be better utilized in the recruiting process such that the GSB on-campus placement percentage (internships and full-time positions) increases significantly.

- Process improvement of information flow during a significant incident (such as an oil spill) from the field to their management and corporate management.

- Reduce cycle time for a clerical process in a publishing company by improving efficiency of work flow and reducing errors in mail processing.

Information Technology and Systems

- Improve a software product that combines internal data and external data into trade promotion analysis. Intend to improve internal and external data and program control. The current processes are unreliable and labor intensive.

- Develop process/methodology to plan, manage, and execute the upgrade process for major manufacturing software system upgrades. The intent is to apply this standard approach to several manufacturing locations within our organizations.

- Incoming requests for service and support at information center of Tribune Information Systems are not being addressed and resolved in a timely manner (as indicated by customer complaints and an independent survey). Examine the process and try to improve so customers are satisfied with the level of service.

- Reduce the number of nondelivered mail messages in the corporatewide Motorola E-mail system.

- Improve the effectiveness of test planning documents in finding software defects.

- Improve the new software product development at a small sales management consulting firm.

Financial Systems and Services

- General quality improvement project to identify customer needs and correct criticized processes in a support department of a bank office.

- Improve the effectiveness of the first-time/start-up fundraising effort at the Joint Commission on Accreditation of Healthcare Organizations by promoting board and staff understanding; improving information flow regarding prospects and projects; and improving the process for stewarding prospects.

- A study of inner city currency exchanges—processes and potential for improvement. Specifically, means of improving services and learning about services needed by communities (working with First Chicago Bank).

- Improve the targeting, tracking, and follow-up process in an investment banking regional office.

Marketing and Business Development

- Improve and possibly automate process for gathering suggestions and maintaining *Best Practices and Resource Guide* for marketing department while providing a means for the facilitation and support for the implementation of suggestions.

- "How to build quality into all processes (one step at a time)." From start-up proceeding through QFD, customer needs analysis, customer involvement, and other. Key issues addressed: mission statement, vision statement, product attributes, customer expectations, marketing strategy, brandedness, product name definition. This is a consumer product(s).

Sales and Professional Services

- Improve the process of Andersen Consulting to staff consultants on projects. Our goal is to improve the process to serve our clients and consultants better.

- Analyze the current sales/service process with a goal of thoroughly understanding the present process and recommending areas for improvement.

- The team will analyze the selling process of the direct sales business unit by characterizing the current business environment and identifying high potential market segments in order to formulate an effective sales strategy to penetrate accounts and secure profitable business.

- Revise an existing process for delivering a computing-related professional service to a customer. Delivery process involves contract processing, subcontracting, billing, resource tracking, and so on. Create plan for measuring effectiveness of process and incorporating constant improvement.

- Reduce cycle time, costs (both time and system money), and improve the accuracy of Client Logistics Benchmarking Reports.

- Develop a system to measure and enhance quality and productivity in a service group in R&D.

- National Opinion Research Center (NORC) NELS Survey Process—telephone survey center. Shorten cycle time to achieve target response level (92 percent).

Human Resources

- Make improvements to our department's reward systems. This would include career paths, compensation, and information systems.

- Develop an ongoing process that measures customer satisfaction. Additionally develop process that forwards information uncovered in step one to the responsible organizations within the company.

- Customer satisfaction survey process. Eastman has an elaborate survey process; some people are concerned that sales reps and customers are becoming disenchanted with the process. How can we improve it?

Food Services

- Improve food quality at International House.

- Evaluate the present food service at the cafe of Stuart Hall on campus. Offer possible process improvements and consider benefits of vendor change.

Theater

- Improve the process of set design, construction, and demolition at the University Theater (student theater).

Summary and Conclusions

We started from the conviction that statistics students cannot learn statistics without doing data analysis: we had found that only by having students do statistics could we motivate most of them to learn about underlying statistical theory. We learned that data analysis is more meaningful when it is directed to applications that students can relate to, which means that the data are collected by the students themselves, who are encouraged to focus on something that is of genuine interest to them.

As we introduced total quality ideas into our statistics courses, we found it natural to guide students toward quality improvement projects, personal or organizational. It was a pleasant surprise to discover that these projects not only served to provide good learning experiences in data analysis, but that they often led to improvements in quality, sometimes substantial improvements, within just a few weeks of an academic term. The key ideas from total quality centered on the theme of waste reduction, including fewer errors or flaws in carrying out work processes and fewer unnecessary steps in the processes themselves. Reduction of waste was facilitated by simple quality tools such as process mapping and customer satisfaction questionnaires. Students could then collect relevant data, analyze it, make constructive recommendations for improvement, and, in many instances, get further data to demonstrate that improvement had, in fact, been achieved.

By pursuing the idea of teaching statistics by practical data analysis and by focusing data analysis on quality improvement, we learned some important things.

- The same students who do only mediocre work on statistics course examinations that stress statistical theory can do outstanding work on applied data analysis in projects of their own choosing.

- The applied student projects can be focused on quality improvement, and real-world quality improvement can be achieved as a by-product of a statistics course.

- As stressed elsewhere in this volume by Professor Zangwill in "Fast Quality for Fast Results," the success of students has a lesson for those in organizations who are working on quality improvement: it need not take a lot of time or elaborate training, just do it!

Notes

1. Michael Brassard, *The Memory Jogger*™ *II* (Methuen, Mass.: GOAL/QPC, 1994).

2. Harry V. Roberts, *Data Analysis for Managers with Minitab*, 2d ed. (Danvers, Mass.: Boyd & Fraser, 1991).

The Laboratory Class in Quality Management

Selwyn W. Becker
University of Chicago Graduate School of Business

Background

During the 1980s, several elective courses in total quality were introduced into the MBA curriculum at the Graduate School of Business, University of Chicago. (Officially, the school uses the phrase *quality management*, but in keeping with the terminology of this book I use *total quality*.) These total quality courses were mostly listed either as courses in statistics or operations management. Faculty members felt that a worthwhile addition to these courses would be one that included material on culture, culture change, small group dynamics, and other psychological and sociological topics.

As a behavioral scientist with an interest in total quality that had been kindled by practical work with manufacturing organizations, I had the opportunity to coteach a course in total quality with William A. Golomski, a distinguished quality consultant who was also a senior lecturer at Chicago. Our charge was very general: deal with topics relating to culture and culture change. Little else was specified.

Golomski and I recognized that the existing courses presented the principles of total quality fairly well and that all of them provided practice in using the tools of total quality through individual projects requiring data collection and analysis in real-life applications, mainly in business organizations. It seemed natural to us to focus on the organizational problems associated with total quality programs. Such a course could build on the existing total quality courses as well as on an introductory behavioral science course in which organization structures, group and individual behavior, and motives were studied.

We decided the focus should be on how to implement total quality in existing organizations. This would require consideration of an organization's structure, its culture, the people and their tasks, and how total quality would affect all these factors and how to go about effecting the necessary changes. Before describing how we jointly undertook to teach these ideas, some personal history of mine is relevant.

The Small Group Course

For some years, I had been teaching a course on small-group dynamics. I began teaching it in a most traditional way: lecture format with some discussion, formal examinations, and then assignment of grades. In the years prior to student ratings of courses, which started at Chicago in the late 1960s, I made few changes in the course. When student ratings became available, it was unpleasantly clear that the course as I presented it was not highly valued. I introduced more discussion and reduced formal lectures. The ratings changed little. The in-class discussions, however, provided a few clues as to what might be done.

I noticed that the discussions became much livelier and that student interest was most aroused when questions arose about how to deal with specific situations that students encountered in their organizations or in their daily lives. I began to elicit, in writing, descriptions of situations encountered by the students in their workplaces. I then introduced these situations into the discussions when they were appropriate to the topics being covered. In-class participation increased, and the student ratings improved slightly. Although I didn't know it at the time, I was applying total quality principles in an effort to improve my product.

I continued using this technique for a while until persistent questions arose about the veracity of an empirically based decision-making phenomenon that had been reported in the literature. The students found it difficult to believe that if a decision alternative accumulated 15 net positive valence points—that is, the total of positive endorsements minus negative endorsements by group members was at least 15—that decision alternative almost always is adopted by group consensus. Although I couldn't explain why the phenomenon occurred, I decided to at least show them that it was genuine.

So I held a decision-making exercise in class. It was an artificial problem, but was similar to problems faced by supervisors and personnel managers involved in selecting or rejecting people for promotion. Several student groups participated in the exercise, while others observed and scored the decision process based on predetermined criteria that I set. The phenomenon was demonstrated to exist. Now the student participants and observers used the discussion time not to further question the veracity of the phenomenon, but to speculate on why the phenomenon occurred, and, more importantly, how they could apply this new knowledge in their own work. Oral student feedback about the exercise was very positive, so I decided to use the same exercise again in succeeding classes. Eventually, I introduced another phenomenon that elicited similar skepticism: I had discussed the role of language in conflict resolution and how the parent–child approach escalated rather than resolved conflict. Again, the students couldn't believe that such a simple change in language could make such a difference. So I repeated the previous strategy. I devised another in-class exercise. The result was similar. The principles deduced from the exercise were easily accepted by the previously skeptical students, and the discussion centered on why and how to use the newly gained information. Positive student feedback convinced me to retain this exercise as well in future classes.

At this point, I was faced with a decision. Should I use more class time on similar exercises? The problem was time. With a class exercise I could demonstrate and discuss one or two principles in an hour or an hour and a half. In the same amount of time, however, I could cover many more principles in a lecture–discussion format.

I talked with some ex-students to determine how much of the material they remembered and used. It became clear that even if they remembered the ideas, they had difficulty applying them to specific situations. The class exercises presented specific situations. To the degree that I could introduce real situations, the exercises would be more instructive.

I decided to make the entire course experiential, to build real situations into as many of the exercises as possible. I asked the students for descriptions of actual decisions faced by them. I used those situations as in-class exercises in decision making, with observers and decision makers alternating roles. Now the course had a mixture of role playing and real exercises.

The students rated the course more highly than ever. Class discussions centered on how ideas from previous weeks were actually applied at work or at home. I had made a trade-off: instead of lecturing on a large number of ideas, I covered a smaller number of ideas that could be internalized and thus made useful to the student. I decided that the trade-off was worth making. (An approach to softening the trade-off would be to try to get students to read more effectively outside of class, since readings can include a large number of ideas.) I continue to teach the course in that manner. In addition, in recent years I have applied total quality principles to grading, empowering the students to work out the procedures by which grades would be arrived at.

Application to the New Course on Total Quality

The experiences with the small-group course colored my discussion with Golomski about how to teach implementation of total quality principles. I argued that if we talked and discussed culture and culture change, we would teach students how to talk about culture and culture change, but not how to do anything about it. Golomski agreed. We decided it would be best if the students could experience the problems of inducing cultural change.

The Graduate School of Business already had developed and used the concept of the laboratory class in the New Product Laboratory developed by Harry Davis. For this laboratory, outside sponsoring organizations (usually companies) made a $75,000 donation to the school for necessary expenses. Students who elected the course were formed into teams that worked directly with executives of the sponsoring organizations. Students and executives jointly established general specifications for a new product or service. Then the student team was charged with actually developing a new product or service within those specifications. The faculty functioned as coaches rather than professors, asking questions and discussing team relationships, guiding behavior in an indirect fashion. The students were encouraged to take risks; errors and mistakes occurred and were discussed. The executives of the company also served, in part, as coaches.

The product of the new product laboratory class was a report, detailing the new product, the research that supported the idea, and recommendations for actual implementation. Actual implementation was left to the sponsoring organization. (For further background on laboratory courses, see Roberts, "Grassroots Total Quality in Higher Education: Some Lessons from Chicago," in this book.)

Given this history and background, Golomski and I considered how best to provide students with experience in changing organization culture in order to implement total quality. We quickly came to the laboratory class as a general model. We called the course Laboratory in Organizational Excellence.

We agreed almost immediately that the outcome or output of the laboratory would not be a paper report on what to do or how to do. There might be such a report, but the payoff would be the outcomes of an actual intervention. *The students were actually to effect change in an organization.*

We further decided that a two-quarter sequence would be appropriate in order to give the students a 22- to 23-week period to have an impact on the organization. Some of our colleagues pointed out that this was a very short period. They mentioned organizations that actually took years just to decide whether or not they would attempt implementation of total quality; and then, having decided to go ahead, devoted a year to mass training of all employees before any substantial quality improvement was attempted.

Our goals for the students were that they

- Learn how to implement total quality in an organization.

- Have a positive impact on the sponsoring organization and leave a legacy—the ability to continue total quality without additional outside help.

- Learn to function more effectively with and through peer groups.

- Learn to function more effectively with and through groups in the sponsoring organization.

We solicited organizations to become sponsors of the laboratory, and over the years we have had some modest successes in that area. I will later highlight examples from two organizations to convey some elements of the educational process. First, however, I sketch the typical lab process.

How the Lab Course Has Worked

The basic process that has emerged is as follows. The representatives of the sponsoring organizations, typically a president and a vice president, or a division head and a relevant assistant, appear at the first class meeting, describe their organization, and give their perception of the problems and opportunities faced by the student team.

Typically, there are two sponsors, each of which makes such a presentation. The students then sort themselves into two teams, one for each sponsor. (Sometimes we specify criteria, like minimum numbers for each team, or even discuss desired capabilities relevant to a sponsor's situation.) The student teams then visit the company, tour the facilities—plant, office, or laboratory—and meet with the upper-level managers, who give their views of the opportunities in their areas of responsibility.

The students then meet to determine their strategy. Usually they collect some financial and other relevant performance data about the company. Then they usually ask: What do we look for now?

As coaches, Golomski and I never answer such a question directly. Rather, we ask another question, like: "Let's start at the beginning with raw materials; what could go wrong there?" The students eventually come up with a list of things to look for, such as

- Materials are late in delivery.

- Incorrect materials are delivered.

- There are material shortages.

- There are machinery breakdowns with no backups; downtime occurs because of die changes.

- There is employee lateness and absenteeism.
- Employees are inexperienced or inadequately trained.
- There are late shipments.
- The company must make callbacks or return goods.
- The company has high scrap rates.
- Payments are withheld.
- There are avoidable accidents.
- There are misbills, overbills, and late bills.
- Payroll data are incorrect or not timely.
- Work report forms contain errors.
- Inventory adjustments are frequent or large.
- There are arbitrary assignments of overhead costs.
- A small fraction of quotes results in sales; 4–5 calls are required on average to close a sale.

The students then interview company personnel who might be able to provide information about any of these or additional problems. Next they review their data, decide on a strategy, and negotiate with management to get endorsement or a revision of the proposed strategy.

A usual sequence would find the student team establishing a steering committee. Membership varies depending on student perceptions of the situation, sometimes the team includes the CEO, sometimes not. Students then meet with the steering committee to explain the basics and the whys of total quality. The students emphasize that

- The product or service delivered will be of high quality 100 percent of the time.
- High quality is defined by customer needs and wants.
- Customers are internal as well as external.
- The organization should strive to make employees feel the company is a desirable, safe place to work where the long-term employment outlook is stable with career enhancement possible.
- Employees should be committed to the organization and to customer satisfaction to the point that they continually think of ways to reduce waste and improve methods of satisfying customers.

- Decisions must be based on fact. Company employees and executives learn the seven elementary tools of total quality and provide data for practice in use of the tools.

The steering committee then establishes priorities from among the situations found by the students and those based on their own knowledge. The steering committee may itself function as a problem-solving team, or it may identify areas for separate problem-solving teams. In either case, a problem-solving team is assembled, usually including one or two from the steering committee.

The students meet with that team, teach the tools and provide practice, and then facilitate the team meetings as the team defines problems, identifies causes, collects data, proposes solutions, tests solutions, and then makes final recommendations.

This team, upon achieving success, is dispersed to new teams where the old problem-solving team members function as teachers of tools and facilitators to the new teams, with members of the student team functioning as monitors and coaches.

The typical sequence also includes identifying external customers' definition of quality. The students select and engage a market research firm to help them design the questionnaires and collect the appropriate data. The steering committee usually participates in this process. The students also engage other subcontractors as necessary.

In one company a simulation of the factory operation minus one key machine was required before a decision could be made about assigning that machine to one particular manufacturing cell. A software company was engaged to do the simulation. Subcontractors such as market research firms and software companies are paid with the funds donated to the school by the sponsor.

Problems of Implementation: A Manufacturing Company

All this reads like it is easy to accomplish, but, typically, the students run into substantial difficulties. In one company, for example, the students developed a plan that included four alternative possibilities for the initial project. They presented their plan to the president and his vice presidents, whose enthusiasm was immediate and unrestrained. Rather than set priorities and choose one of the four projects, they opted for all four.

Somewhat taken aback, the students debated, and then decided they could manage all four projects. They committed themselves to do so.

The students' next step was to present the proposal to the level of management reporting to the vice presidents. The same presentation was given and was expected to result in specific suggestions relative to the proposed projects as well as any other concrete suggestions the group (about 15) may have had. These lower-level managers responded with silence until a few decided to speak up.

"You guys are full of crap, just like all the other consultants that come through here every month or so," said one.

"Yah, your program sounds good, but as soon as you leave, the ball will be dropped and nothing will happen," said another.

"All you guys do is create more work for us and waste time in meetings like this," finished the last manager.

The students were no longer riding high. Their learning experience had begun in earnest. They returned to campus, not to lick their wounds, but to discuss how to get the buy-in and to effect cultural change. They also discussed whether the real problem was with the upper management quartet or the 15 who reported to them.

Again, the faculty coaches provided no answers. The course is designed to provide students a (reasonably safe) opportunity to take risks, make errors, and fail; of course, success is preferred by all. The faculty coaches listened to the various student plans, asking questions only while the team was settling on some alternatives.

The basic student strategy was to form a continuous improvement and communication team from among the 15 lower-level managers. The focus of this team would be to devise and establish a framework that would guarantee continuation of the programs and ensure progress after the proposed projects were completed. Further, the team's function was to structure the communication program, including the president's role, in introducing the program to the rest of the factory and office.

Approval of this plan was sought from upper management. When approval was given it was introduced to the 15 managers. Endorsement, but not enthusiasm, was obtained, and the rest of the projects were launched under the guidance of the continuous improvement team.

One of the first projects undertaken by the continuous improvement team was to survey employees about a variety of attitudes and in-plant situations that might affect quality of product and quality of continuous improvement efforts. The survey covered the usual quality-of-life issues, but it also included questions about issues that could be considered sensitive, such as sexual discrimination or harassment as well as behavior toward minorities. The continuous improvement team recommended that the data be made available to everyone. Upper management met and considered every conceivable (and some that seemed inconceivable) risk in so doing. The president finally said, "If we're going after quality, we have to take a few risks and go all the way." The survey results were arrayed on large posters that lined the walls of the hall between the factory and the employee locker rooms. They were there for everyone to see: no questions or results were eliminated or edited. That's when the members of the continuous improvement team became believers. It was the beginning of real culture change.

This breakthrough, however, didn't prevent other problems from arising. A variety of communication errors occurred: between the team and vendors, the vendors and company management, the team and the company. All had to be overcome before all four projects could be brought to successful conclusions. The work of one team—a manufacturing cell assembly team—in solving a parts identification and misassembly problem saved enough money to pay for all the projects' costs, including management time.

At the time of the team's final presentation, the company was about to appoint a total quality director to continue the work begun by the laboratory class.

Application to a Police Department

Different problems of culture and cultural change were encountered by a student team initiating total quality into a suburban police department. Not only was the culture attuned to a hierarchical, rather authoritarian system, but survival depended on suspicion rather than trust. The department was predominately male and all white. Our students were all female, one was black. (I was certain our laissez-faire method of team selection had done us in. I seriously underestimated the intellectual quality and personal courage of our students.)

The students recognized their problem after interviewing the chief and deputy chief of police. How the chief defined the problems provided the clue to the culture. The team's strategy, in retrospect, may seem obvious; given the actual situation, it was brilliant. The three women students decided to split up, and each would ride with patrolmen as they went about their duties. This meant riding all shifts. The students sat in patrol cars all night long—talking with the police officers; listening to their stories about the department; and watching them chase automobiles, investigate break-ins, and so on.

The student team gained the confidence of the patrolmen. When the team taught problem solving to a group of policemen and facilitated problem-solving groups, they were among friends. They were trusted. The team developed a procedure for reporting arrests that promised to virtually eliminate cases thrown out of court because of inadequate or inaccurate information given by the police to the prosecutors office.

Conclusions

I have sketched two concrete examples among about 10 in our four years of experience with the Laboratory in Organizational Excellence. Not all the other projects have been this successful, but several have been. In one instance I have good reason to believe that the laboratory was instrumental to organizational survival. A few have presented frustrations and disappointment, but even in these there was considerable progress, and the students learned a great deal. What can we conclude from these experiences?

• Students learn more about total quality from the experience of implementing it than they could in any classroom. I don't have a great deal of data to substantiate this very strong impression, but several of our graduates have begun successful independent consulting careers while others function in larger management consulting firms as associates. Several have told us the lab class was their most valuable experience in the MBA program.

Students learn about group behavior. They learn that there are problems with recalcitrant members or those less diligent than others. They learn about communication problems. They learn about the power of the group in moving toward a goal; the power to engage a less than enthusiastic member or to circumvent that person and manage goal achievement under trying circumstances.

Students learn that cultural change can be managed, but that doing so is more difficult than it first appears. Some unanticipated barriers exist or something negative always happens and must be confronted and accounted for.

In a recent effort, the group had encountered little difficulty for virtually two quarters. Everything they did yielded success. Company problem-solving teams were finding success, one after another. As the students were beginning to think about the final presentation two weeks before the end of the course, the president fired the plant manager, a total quality champion. The students managed that situation, too.

Students learn that the kinds of achievement I have described require time and effort. The students report spending an average of 18 hours per week on the course, well over twice the average for MBA courses.

• From the sponsoring organization's point of view, we have learned that it is possible to get total quality solidly established in an organization in 22 weeks. In that time, the rudiments of total quality can be taught and problem-solving groups can achieve sufficient success to more than offset the costs of implementation.

Initial success is very important in driving total quality forward. If the first team fails, the naysayers have ammunition. We have learned that all kinds of resistance can be overcome, save that of indifference in top management. If the president or CEO or division head does not demonstrate that quality is high on his or her list of priorities, it won't be high on anyone else's list for long.

• The coaches have learned a few things as well. To begin, it's not easy to get sponsoring organizations. (Even the New Product Laboratory, which has been highly successful for over 15 years, has to invest a lot of effort each year in finding new client organizations.) Large companies that readily spend large amounts for studies by major consulting firms have to be persuaded that "mere MBA students" can deliver value and do so economically.

Coaching is not easy when you're accustomed to professing. It takes patience and discipline to not answer a question directly, so that the students can work through the issue themselves, either individually or with the student team. Sometimes this results in meetings with the various student groups on Saturday nights and/or Sunday mornings. The faculty coach has to be willing to meet whenever the students can find time to get together.

There is no formula for managing culture change. Although some general principles can be drawn upon, every single case presents a new challenge and requires an individually tailored approach.

Even old coaches can learn new tricks. In some instances, the students were able to accomplish tasks that would have stumped us.

• Finally, our experience reinforces that reported in other papers in this volume. Namely, students can learn about total quality by actually doing it, in real time and in real organizations. A good start on organizational implementation of total quality can be achieved in a few months. Years of feasibility study and mass training are not necessary.

Appendix: A Simple Model of Total Quality Implementation

In the light of our experiences with the Laboratory for Organizational Excellence, I have formulated a very simple outline for implementation of total quality. The outline contains nothing new, but it has the essentials in a condensed form that I have found useful. Harry Roberts, the editor of this volume, thought that some readers also might find it useful.

   I. Establish quality priorities

      A. High-quality product 100 percent of the time

      B. Quality defined by the customer

   II. Identify and satisfy internal customers

   III. Employee satisfaction

      A. Employee commitment

      B. Customer satisfaction

      C. Stockholder satisfaction

IV. Trust and respect employees

    A. Invest in human resources

        1. Training

        2. Time

    B. Responsibility for problem solving

V. Steering committee

    A. Establish problem-solving priorities

    B. Designate problem-solving teams

VI. Celebrate victories

    A. Serve as model for others

    B. Provide positive reinforcement

VII. Continuous improvement

    A. Permanent work teams

    B. Temporary problem-solving teams

VIII. Include everyone

    A. Start at the top

    B. Define the culture of quality

        1. Delegation

        2. Direct action

A Company-Based Pedagogy for Teaching Process Improvement Within an MBA Program

Scott Dawson, Associate Professor
Richard Sapp, Professor
School of Business
Portland State University

Introduction

This chapter describes the three-year evolution of an MBA course in process improvement. The sections that follow provide background relevant to the course; describe its first two years briefly and the most recent in detail; and report data collected to evaluate the course. The final section discusses several steps for continuous improvement of the course.

Portland State University is located in Oregon's major metropolitan area, comprising about 1.2 million people. Between serving primarily working students, interacting in professional associations, and engaging in consulting activities, the faculty within the School of Business have close ties to the concerns and questions of Portland's business community. In general, faculty performance at Portland State is weighted more heavily in the directions of teaching and service than it is at typical research universities. However, many Portland State faculty continue to focus on research and publication in traditional research journals.

Portland State operates on 10-week quarters, rather than 15-week semesters. Its business school is accredited by the American Assembly of Collegiate Schools of Business and has about 1500 undergraduate and 600 graduate students.

In 1990 a number of events occurred that substantively changed what the business school teaches, how it is taught, and how the school operates. First, representatives from a group of local electronics firms offered the school seed money and assistance to develop a masters degree in quality management. Second, a state fiscal crisis caused the school to face a 10 percent budget cutback. Third, in part to answer this budget cutback, the faculty in the School of Business voted by a huge margin to eliminate functional departments. Finally, one faculty member, H. Thomas Johnson, challenged the faculty to consider proposals for changing the direction of business education in his book *Relevance Regained: From Top-Down Control to Bottom-Up Empowerment*, which has since become well-known internationally.

These factors, along with support from the dean of the School of Business and resolute determination by the associate dean of graduate studies, combined to create a fertile environment for change that catalyzed a desire among a surprisingly large number of faculty to learn more about quality management. During the summer of 1992, faculty listened to presentations by several international authorities on quality such as Richard Schonberger, Robert Hall, Noriaki Kano, and Jinichiso Nakone, and to executives from local exemplars of quality such as Xerox and the Oregon Cutting Systems division of Blount. The business school also received funds from a national bank and a local utility to release the authors from half our normal teaching responsibilities so that we could become involved for one year in the quality efforts of these two companies. We also attended several conferences and read widely in the existing quality literature.

By late 1992 the school had a core group of faculty convinced that, at a minimum, elements of quality management belonged in our MBA curriculum. The faculty decided early on to reject the idea of offering a master's degree in quality management, largely because of budget constraints. Since the business school's flagship product is the MBA program, our initial efforts were directed at integrating quality concepts into existing courses within that program and at developing the dedicated course on process improvement that is described here.

The next section provides a brief summary of the first two years in the evolution of teaching the new process improvement course. The subsequent section will provide a much more specific look at the most recent offering of this course.

The First Two Years

Integrating quality into the MBA program has been a three-year journey that began in 1991. To date this integration has taken place within the daytime MBA program, since most of our daytime students enroll full-time and thus face fewer scheduling constraints for working off campus with local organizations.

During the winter quarter of 1992 we cotaught a one-term elective in quality management. In class we covered material on team behavior and tools for process improvement in *The Team Handbook*, a Xerox-like process improvement model, and a few of the management planning tools. Philosophically, we felt that the most effective learning would occur when students worked as teams on real process improvement projects within organizations. Teams of four to five students were formed; two teams worked on processes at local companies and two on administrative processes within the university.

A course assessment using brainstorming and affinity diagramming at the end of the first term revealed that the greatest opportunity for improvement was to extend the course to two terms. After a two- to three-week start-up time with their sponsoring organizations, teams had just eight to nine weeks to complete their improvement projects. While both of us had previously placed student teams with organizations to work on functionally oriented projects, this was our first realization that process-improvement projects necessitated students having to learn much more from people and to work much harder to generate data. Trying to identify processes (perceive a process where none may explicitly exist) in an organization with which the student is totally unfamiliar is a daunting, frustrating, and time-consuming process.

During the second year, more comprehensive changes ensued with the launching of an experimental daytime MBA program, which included lockstepping students into the same classes during the first year. The first term included courses on effective team behavior, marketing management, and business statistics, and a course taught by Tom Johnson that used his own book and Deming's *Out of the Crisis* to provide students with an understanding of the roots of our present-day concern with quality management. The now two-term process-improvement course started during the second term, alongside an operations management course that included material on statistical process control and just-in-time material ordering.

The experimental approach was seen as a way to quickly offer a program of courses integrated around quality. At the same time, a curriculum committee began the arduous task of designing a permanent program. In order to assess the effectiveness of the experiment, students were recruited during the fall term to serve on a year-long customer assessment team. One of the coauthors served as the initial leader and facilitator of this group. Ian Hau's work on quality improvement in teaching at the University of Wisconsin-Madison played an important role in shaping the team's work.[1] First, the team conducted focus groups and brown bag meetings with students, which led to making several immediate changes in administration of the experimental program. It also developed and administered a survey to track satisfaction during each of the three terms. This information proved invaluable in designing and obtaining faculty approval for an entirely new MBA program that commenced in the fall 1994.

Extending the length of the process improvement course to two terms allowed expanding the scope of the processes studied and more than doubled the depth of analysis produced by student teams. Whereas the one-term course had resulted in four-page quality storyboards, the teams were now completing 20-page documents that included extensive analysis using many different quality tools. The additional class time from the second term was used in four ways. First, we conducted three field trips to local quality-focused manufacturing firms. Second, we spent class time discussing the problems encountered by student teams in analyzing their processes. Third, we designated a number of class periods as time for students to conduct analyses at their sponsoring firms. Finally, in addition to *The Team Handbook*, students read the *Memory Jogger Plus*, *The Fifth Discipline*, and *The Goal*.

The most significant learning from the second course was that teams could too easily focus on detail complexity, thereby losing sight of the dynamics in the entire process. Teams too often focused their efforts on improving relatively inconsequential pieces of a larger process. Additionally, we learned that field trips can be a valuable tool for both visualizing and validating quality concepts. We now turn to a full description of the most recent course.

Full Description of the Course

Before beginning the process improvement course, students received training in team behavior. Then, in a concurrent course, they studied statistical process control and just-in-time material ordering. Also, students were introduced to organizational learning and operations management from *The Fifth Discipline* and the *Soul of the Enterprise*.

The authors team taught the two-term process-improvement course from winter quarter 1994 through spring quarter 1994. We made a number of changes in the course based on our prior experiences and comments from previous students and sponsoring companies. While the syllabus for this two-term course is included in the appendix, elaboration on several points should be helpful.

Sponsoring Companies

A significant aspect of this sequence of courses was to give students practical, real-company experience with the tools and techniques that were discussed in class. To this end, we arranged with several local companies to sponsor a student process-improvement team. The objective of this effort was to have the students involved in a process-improvement effort from idea to implementation. During the fall quarter we met with the sponsoring companies and discussed the nature of the course, the purpose of the projects, and our expectations of the students and sponsoring companies. We asked each company to appoint a sponsor to be the primary contact person for the student team. In most cases, the company appointed a member of senior management.

The company then selected a project for the students to work on. The criteria we provided to the companies included the following:

- The project should entail a real problem with a formal or informal cross-functional process that the students could meaningfully work on improving.

- The results should be important to the company.

- The scope of the project must be such that the team could realistically expect to complete it in approximately 18 to 20 weeks.

Other issues we discussed with the sponsoring companies included

- Ideally, the team should have the support of the key managers and should be shielded from excessive internal politics.

- The students could either be a self-contained team or could be integrated into a larger process-improvement team that would include sponsoring company employees.

- Sponsors should expect periodic presentations from the team members and would be expected to present their organization's project in class to students at the beginning of the course.

- We, as instructors, would respect any confidentiality issues with respect to the students' presentations as identified by the sponsor.

- Sponsors could expect a team of five graduate students to spend approximately 270 hours working on projects on-site (in other words, 5 students × 3 hours per week × 18 weeks).

- The student teams would make regular progress reports in class and share their experiences with other teams.

The following companies sponsored teams to work on the processes noted.

- Northwest Natural Gas (gas utility—service process for commercial accounts)

- Hoody's (peanut and snack food packaging—reorder process for one packaging line)

- U.S. Bancorp (national bank—two teams working on mail delivery and automobile fleet reimbursement processes)

- PacifiCare (health maintenance organization—physician expansion process)

- In Focus (manufacturer of LCD projector systems—corrective action process)

- ADC Kentrox (telecommunication switching device manufacturer—vendor corrective action process)

- Coast Distributors (wholesaler—order fulfillment process)
- McLean Clinic (medical clinic—lab order process)
- Blount (chain saw manufacturer—engineering change orders)

Statistical and Management Planning Tools

As all experienced faculty know, teaching forces the instructor to develop a deeper understanding of a subject than gained through the typical student role. We applied this insight to our teaching of the process improvement tools. Our objective was for students to gain a working knowledge of six of the statistical tools (statistical process control was covered in a parallel course) and all seven of the management planning tools. Outside of statistical process control, we feel that these tools are not complex enough for MBA students to require spoon-feeding by instructors.

The assignment required student teams to not only lecture to the class on the basics of the tool, but also to involve the whole class in an exercise based on that tool. Each team was allowed approximately 90 minutes for its presentation and exercise. The instructors and a designated student team (a suggestion made by the students) provided comments at the end of the period. We attempted to schedule the tool presentations within the two academic terms to coincide with the teams' likely need for each tool in completing their company projects.

Student comments about this approach varied considerably. In general, students found it easy to develop the lecture, but challenging to develop the exercise. Peer pressure made each team take the assignment seriously. While some found this to be a valuable learning experience, others felt that such training was the instructors' responsibility.

System Archetypes

While middle- and upper-level managers must have sufficient knowledge to support and participate in process-improvement projects, familiarity with detail complexity is not the primary responsibility for these individuals. Many process improvement activities in organizations are localized in scope, allowing subordinates to focus on specific details (for example, using statistical process control to bring a process under control). However, managers must understand the dynamic complexity that exists "when an action has one set of consequences locally and a very different set of consequences in another part of the system." Moreover, "the real leverage in most management situations lies in understanding dynamic complexity, not detail complexity."[2] Dynamic complexity is typified by such management tasks as balancing growth and capacity, designing and implementing product line strategy, and improving total quality in order to satisfy customers.

The most frequent and apparent dynamics that exist within a system are captured by a number of basic archetypes, which describe the relationships that exist between elements of structure within an organization such as capacities, measurement systems, control mechanisms, norms and values, delays, and mental models. We went over five archetypes including "short-term fix" (also known as "fixes that fail"), "shifting the burden," "limits to growth," "tragedy of the commons," and "accidental adversaries."

In brief, "short-term fix" maps the unintended long-term consequences that occur as the result of short-term interventions. An all too frequent example is using price promotions to combat falling sales. "Shifting the burden" is similar but more extensive, reflecting how a quick fix in reaction to a symptom can make accomplishing the fundamental solution even more difficult. This archetype is pervasive; a classic example is hiring a consultant (quick fix) to solve quality problems rather than integrating quality practices into organizational culture.

"Limits to growth" maps the engine for growth in a system (for example, quality product) and forces participants to anticipate what factors might eventually work in opposition to that engine (for example, manufacturing capacity). "Tragedy of the commons" occurs when individual actions produce an undesirable collective result, such as the depletion of a shared resource. This archetype is named after the collapse of grassy commons areas that occurred in late medieval times as the result of individuals each grazing more and more sheep. Finally, "accidental adversaries" is a complex system in which a mutually beneficial relationship between organizations is threatened as the result of the unintended consequences of each other's behaviors. Perhaps the best example of "accidental adversaries" is the peaks and valleys in all aspects of production that occur as the result of using trade promotions to entice retailers to buy more products during limited but predictable periods of time. Mapping this dynamic is very much responsible for Procter & Gamble's strategy of eliminating trade promotions.

The archetypes mentioned were discussed in class late in the second term, after the students had become deeply submerged in the structure of their sponsoring organizations. We felt that the archetypes would help students develop a broader systems perspective, since many students in the previous year's course had a narrow outlook. An assignment called for each team to construct at least two archetypes they felt captured some of the dynamics within their sponsoring organizations. Four teams presented their archetypes in class, which, in each case, were accompanied by powerful discussion. All teams used the archetypes in their final reports and presentations.

Students found using the archetypes to be highly valuable. The archetypes forced students to consider their mental models and to organize their thoughts about what they were seeing, hearing, and feeling in a way that they had previously been unable to articulate. In turn, sponsors were able to see dynamics in new and valuable ways.

We also included in the course *Reengineering the Corporation* and lectures on reengineering in order to encourage a systemic perspective. Here too is an area of thought that may challenge participants to consider whether a subprocess or process has merit for existence before spending resources on its improvement. Moreover, the magnitude of change needed for this kind of improvement requires the leadership of management for which MBAs are being trained.

Survey Results

A course assessment survey beyond the required standardized course evaluation was constructed and administered to both students and sponsors. Questions were both open-ended (for example, "What could the instructors have done to most improve the success of this project?") and close-ended (for example, Likert-type scales). Sponsor and student surveys shared several common measures. The majority of sponsors (8) and students (28) responded to the questionnaire.

Student and Sponsor Satisfaction

As shown in Table 1, the majority of students were "very satisfied" with the concept of company-based projects, though overall satisfaction with implementation of the project for this class was somewhat less. All sponsors responding to the survey felt that the project was "successful" and had "met expectations." Most students rated their sponsoring organization's implementation of total quality as "more than average" when compared to other organizations. A notable finding is that student satisfaction with projects is higher when sponsoring organizations have progressed further in implementing total quality ($r = .61, p < .001$).

Student–Sponsor Relationship

In a course such as this, it is very difficult to integrate student teams into an organization's ongoing quality efforts. While three student teams were made part of sponsors' process-improvement teams, the remaining student groups essentially acted as consultants. The degree of integration within existing teams and independence are crucial determinants of how both students and sponsors describe their relationship.

Table 1 indicates that the relationship between teams and sponsors was generally perceived as high in trust, flexibility, and accessibility. Degree of control exerted by sponsors was also quite high and varied significantly across relationships.

Table 1. General perceptions and evaluations by students.*

Measure	Scale	Mean	Standard Dev.	Mode
Student satisfaction				
Satisfaction with concept of company-based projects	Very dissatisfied (1) to Very satisfied (5)	4.6	.56	5
Satisfaction with this project	Very dissatisfied (1) to Very satisfied (5)	3.9	.77	4
Sponsor criteria				
Sponsoring organization's implementation of quality	At the bottom (1) to Exemplary (5)	3.50	.79	4
What sponsor would say about project	Completely unsuccessful (1) to Completely successful (5)	4.18	.56	4
Relationship with sponsor				
Trust	No trust (1) to High level of trust (10)	8.11	1.71	8
Flexibility	Not at all flexible (1) to Flexible (10)	8.11	1.77	10
Accessibility	Not at all accessible (1) to Accessible (10)	8.36	1.83	10
Control by sponsor	Low control (1) to High control (10)	6.46	2.85	8

*$n = 28$

Interestingly, five of the eight sponsors responding to the survey felt that the relationship had featured a markedly lower level of control that what students had perceived. Also, three sponsors perceived that trust was at a lower level than the level characterized by students.

Team folded into sponsor teams were initially the most frustrated and in the end felt the most controlled. While in a consultant setting, one sponsor reflected that, "I had to work hard to keep my hands out of the students' project to allow them to attempt, fail, and learn." Student teams that were folded into sponsor teams were initially not allowed to conduct interviews or collect data outside of regularly scheduled sponsor team meetings.

The lowest levels of trust, flexibility, and access, and highest level of control existed for a student team that was folded into a process team at a medical clinic. A significant problem became finding meeting times. This project's sponsor reflected that "in a clinic environment it is hard to work around staffing schedules and patient load." A student in this setting complained, "We were not given an option to do what we felt was necessary. . . . We struggled with the clinic team members for their support and help in obtaining data for our project." Eventually, this team did obtain the data needed to conduct statistical process control and was able to administer a survey to physicians, ultimately providing a number of on-target recommendations.

Correlational analysis suggests that student satisfaction with a particular process improvement project is significantly related to the perceived levels of trust ($r = .46$, $p < .01$) and accessibility ($r = .44$, $p < .01$) characterizing the relationship with the sponsor company. Also, flexibility in the relationship strongly affected students' overall assessment of company-based projects ($r = .45$, $p < .01$).

Time will tell whether integrated or independent teams are more successful. The problem with the consultant (independent) style is that student recommendations may be less likely to be adopted because individuals from different functions within the sponsor have not come together as a team to collectively improve their process. After the student consultants present their recommendations, the individuals from the sponsor can all go back to work and hope that nobody bothers them anymore. In the short run, the consultant role may be more pleasurable and inspiring to students, but in the long run a sponsor may benefit more from including students within an actual process team.

Helpfulness of Tools/Activities

Testimony to the power of system archetypes to add clarity to thinking is that students rated archetypes as the most helpful tool of all (see Table 2). This is not surprising when we reflect on the intensity of conversation that ensued when groups struggled to construct and describe archetypes.

In general, students found the statistical tools more helpful than the management planning tools. For instance, process flow diagrams were evaluated as the second most helpful tool. Constructing and following a process improvement model was also seen as very helpful . Finally, 50 percent of students considered plant tours to be very helpful in completing their projects.

We had numerous open class discussions concerning the progress made and problems faced by teams, sessions that were considered very helpful by 46 percent of

Table 2. Helpfulness of tools/activities in completing projects.

Tool/Activity	Percent saying "very helpful"*
System archetypes	79%
Process flow diagram	68
Plant tours	50
Improvement model	50
Cause-and-effect diagram	46
Team problem discussions in class	46
Pareto chart	43
Affinity diagram	39
Interrelationship digraph	18
Matrix diagram	11
Activity network	7
Tree diagram	7

*Three-point scale, ranging from "very helpful" to "not al all helpful." *n* = 28

the students. In order to avoid the perception of checking on or attempting to control teams, we had encouraged teams to invite us to their meetings when the team wanted an advisor. The most frequent comments regarding what the instructors could have done to improve the course touched on this issue. Teams who did invite us (the minority) were very happy with this approach, while a frequent theme from groups that did not invite us was that they would have liked more one-on-one discussion with and guidance from the instructors. Perhaps a blend of these two approaches would satisfy the needs of more students. Instructors could start by scheduling individual group meetings every two to three weeks, leaving the team to schedule meetings after a period of time.

Conclusions

We remain committed to a company- and team-based pedagogy for teaching process improvement in an MBA program. Starting in the fall of 1994, Portland State will be launching a new MBA program in which the course described here will be folded into two four-hour courses integrated together during one term. These courses —Performance Measurement and Integrated Process Management—will bring together process improvement tools with concepts from operations management, activity-based costing, information technology, and measurement. A company-based project will be the central activity for learning.

In the spirit of continuous improvement, we still have ample opportunity for improving the approach described in this chapter. Student evaluations of this course were below normal with an above normal level of variation. Beyond issues of personality, we attribute this outcome to three factors identified in the data reported earlier. First, some unhappiness can be traced to students involved in projects characterized by a poor sponsor–team relationship and a not-so-significant process. We clearly need to increase the amount of time spent screening and defining sponsor projects. Previously, we have settled for a vague sense about the project and its importance, letting students and sponsors define it more clearly as their work progressed. In many cases this approach works fine, but when it does not, a team's morale can suffer.

A second step for improvement is to require teams to meet individually with instructors every two weeks for at least half the term, if not the entire term. As noted earlier, the most satisfied students were those working in teams who asked for our involvement. Teams often do not know they can ask, or they are unwilling to ask for help. Regular meetings with teams can help clarify direction and use of tools, monitor the relationship with sponsors, and observe the degree to which teams follow their stated ground rules.

Finally, greater hands-on involvement with teams is needed to help those students who have a very difficult time dealing with ambiguity. Most have become conditioned to expect courses to be a predictable instructor-knows-all-lecture-test-paper format. We feel strongly that schools do a disservice to students by continuing to reinforce this expectation. However, those students feeling the most uncomfortable with the ambiguity of entering a new firm to improve a nonvisible process would benefit from closer instructor contact.

In short, while we have spent an unusually large amount of time preparing and delivering this course, a more successful outcome will require instructors to spend more one-on-one time with student teams and more time carefully recruiting and selecting project settings. This is not a trivial consideration, as in recent years many business schools like Portland State have increased faculty teaching loads while still demanding high levels of research and publication. Properly teaching a course in process improvement requires more time away from the classroom than typical course loads. That time must come from somewhere, possibly from continual improvement of teaching and facilitation methods, which can remove much of the waste that has been built into traditional teaching approaches.

Appendix

Course Syllabus
Process Improvement—Management 507
Winter–Spring 1994

Scott Dawson   Richard Sapp
Office: 260d SBA   260a SBA
Phone: 725-3757   725-3732

Prerequisites

An interest in quality and continuous improvement! You must also be committed to *completing both terms* of this class.

Required texts (for both terms)

Reengineering the Corporation, Hammer and Champy
The Memory Jogger Plus, Michael Brassard
The Team Handbook, Peter Scholtes
Readings packet (various articles)

Supplemental text

The Fifth Discipline, Peter Senge

Course objectives

To learn through hands-on experience the tools and techniques for process improvement

To build an awareness of the need to balance detail and dynamic (system) complexity in improving process performance

To further the skills needed to effectively participate in a group

To gain familiarity with a process in a business setting

To have fun!

Grading

Class participation	20 percent
Improvement model	10 percent
Tool presentations	20 percent
Team charter, project plan, and team-building exercise	10 percent
Project write-up	40 percent

Class participation

This course relies heavily on student participation, whether through discussion or presentation of exercises. Traditional lecturing will be held to a minimum in favor of the instructor leading an active discussion. Ultimately, your learning will be determined by how actively you participate and by the contributions of others. Participation will be graded on how well your comments address the question offered, build on the previous speaker's thoughts, show command of the reading material, and reflect a strong belief that is put forth with a passion.

Key to participation is carefully reading the assigned material, integrating that material with previous readings and class discussions, and, perhaps most importantly, listening to your cohorts' comments. Do not try to fill a quota of air time, rather listen and offer your thoughts when they will add to the discussion. Often the most effective contributors in class are those students who carefully choose their opportunities to participate.

Improvement model

Many models exist for guiding process improvement work. These tend to share a common logic surrounded by an author's or firm's need for customization. Your group should construct its own improvement model by examining those developed by Scholtes (chapter 5, Appendix 2), Brassard (Appendices A and B), and Xerox (see readings). You will share these with the class and turn in your model with a one- to two-page single-spaced narrative.

Tool presentation

Project groups will demonstrate tools once during each of the two terms. You should develop an example that involves the class in one or more phases of using the tool. For example, your group could facilitate a brainstorming session with the class, which in turn would provide the data for having smaller groups from class sequentially perform an affinity diagram. The goal here is to effectively involve the class in learning a new tool. While you do not have to hand in any material for this assignment, you probably will want to use handouts during the demonstration.

Team charter, project management plan, and team-building exercise

These three items are due on February 15. The charter should clearly delineate your team's mission and objectives and specifically describe the beginning and the end of the process. The project management plan should present the staging of steps you will complete by specific weeks over the duration of the entire two-term project. Choose one of the team-building exercises described at the back of Scholtes (or some other favored exercise). Use this exercise and hand in your results. This last exercise is the only of the three that may require some narrative. Suggested readings for these exercises: Scholtes, chapters 2 (2-37–2-46), 3, 4, 6, 7 and Appendix 3; Brassard, chapter 8 and Appendices A and B.

Archetype assignment

During the second term you will illustrate three different systems archetypes among those illustrated in Senge ("shifting the burden," "limits to growth," "tragedy of the commons," "quick fixes that fail," "escalation") that exist within your project context. You will be asked to present these in class and hand in the archetypes with a short narrative.

Team project

The major activity in this two-term class is a process-improvement project you will perform as a team with a local company or department at PSU. If you work in a firm where process improvement is valued, please discuss with us the prospects of using a process at your firm for the project. Otherwise, we will supply the projects. Sponsors for each will visit with class on January 13 and 18 to briefly describe their projects. During the January 20 class meeting we will choose who will work on which projects in the fairest manner possible.

The goal of the project is to make recommendations that could significantly improve the process you will be working on over the two terms. Key to your success will be balancing your perspective between dynamic complexity (using the systems archetypes, seven management planning tools, and reengineering) and detail complexity (using the seven statistical tools, mental models). Several basic questions include: (1) What is the theory *implicit* in the process (rarely mentioned but often there)? (2) What is the managerial interpretation of the theory (mental models)? (3) Does this managerial interpretation match its administrated interpretation? (4) What is the value added in each step of the process? (5) Who are the customers, and what are their requirements? (6) What can we do to ensure that our project sponsor implements our recommendations?

The vast majority of work will be done in teams. At the end of each term you will present the team's progress to date in process improvement. Your team's presentation during the first term should also include a plan of activities for the second term. You probably will also be requested to present your final work at the sponsor's location.

Key to the quality of the projects will be *documented* use of quality and team improvement tools (keep a notebook). For example, many of Scholtes' exercises beginning on page 7 might be used throughout the duration of the project. Each of the seven management planning and statistical tools may be used at different stages of your projects. Carefully document each of these and include it with your write-up. Examples of finished products from previous classes are available.

Your team will receive a single grade for its project work.

Schedule

Term 1

Week	Date	Assignment/Activity
1 Jan	4	Course overview and introductions Scholtes, chapters 1 and 2 (2-1 to 2-16)
	6	Reengineering Hammer and Champy, chapters 1–3
2	11	Reengineering Hammer and Champy, chapters 4–5, 7
	13	Sponsor presentations
3	18	Sponsor presentations
	20	Select projects, choose teams
4	8	Improvement models Scholtes, chapter 5, Appendix 2 Brassard, Appendices A and B
	10	Teams present improvement models; hand in description; "The Quality Interview"
5 Feb	1	Guest speaker—Project management
	3	Work day
6	8	Pareto demonstration (qualitative)
	10	Affinity demonstration
7	15	Team problem discussion Hand in team charter, project management plan, and a team-building exercise
	17	Team problem discussion
8	22	Flow diagram demonstration
	24	Cause-and-effect diagram demonstration
9 Mar	1	Field trip
	3	Discussion
10	8	Work day
	10	In-class project discussions
11	11	In-class project discussions

Schedule
Term 2

Week	Date	Assignment/Activity
1 Mar	29	Reengineering (Hammer, chapters 8–9, 14)
	31	Reengineering cases
		Taco Bell, capital holdings (chapters 11, 12)
		"Staple Yourself to an Order"
2 Apr	5	David Howitz, Claremont Technology
		Reengineering and information technology
	7	Facilitation skills, benchmarking
3	12	Pareto chart demonstration (quantitative)
	14	Interrelationship digraph demonstration
4	19	Tree diagram demonstration
	21	Matrix diagram demonstration
5	26	Quality days—no class
	28	Warn Industries tour
6 May	3	Rhoda Ryba, Systems Approach to Quality
	5	Systems Thinking, Senge, chapters 4–7
7	10	Systems thinking
		Kauffman, "Complex systems," "Appendix" in readings
	12	Archetype write-up and presentation
8	17	Prepare St. Mary's continuous quality improvement case
	19	Project work
9	24	Project work
	26	Speaker—effective presentations
10	31	Project work
June 2–10		Project presentations (in-class and on-site)

Notes

1. Ian Hau, "Teaching Quality Improvement by Quality Improvement in Teaching," Report No. 59, Center for Quality and Productivity Improvement (Madison, Wis.: University of Wisconsin, February 1991).

2. Peter Senge, *The Fifth Discipline*, 71–72.

Bibliography

Brassard, Michael. *The Memory Jogger Plus*™. Methuen, Mass.: GOAL/QPC, 1989.

Deming, W. Edwards. *Out of the Crisis*. Cambridge, Mass.: MIT Center for Advanced Engineering, 1986.

Goldratt, Eliyahu. *The Goal*. Croton-on-Hudson, N.Y.: North River Press, 1992.

Hall, Robert. *Soul of the Enterprise*. New York: HarperBusiness, 1993.

Hammer, Michael, and James Champy. *Reengineering the Corporation*. New York: HarperBusiness, 1993.

Johnson, H. Thomas. *Relevance Regained: From Top-Down Control to Bottom-Up Empowerment*. New York: Free Press, 1992.

Scholtes, Peter. *The Team Handbook*. Madison, Wis.: Joiner Associates, 1988.

Senge, Peter. *The Fifth Discipline*. New York: Doubleday Currency, 1990.

Continuous Improvement in Education: The Process of Learning in an Introductory Statistics Class

Lawrence A. Sherr
Catherine E. Schwoerer
The University of Kansas
School of Business

Introduction: Improving the Educational Process by Taking a Total Quality Management Approach

In this paper, we describe ongoing experiences in teaching introductory statistics in a spirit and manner consistent with total quality. The spirit reflects a central proposition that teaching is both art and craft with room for continual development. We believe that total quality offers a unique and valuable manner or approach to improvement in teaching. Central to this approach is a view that the focus should be on facilitating student learning rather than improving the performance of a teacher. We believe that this distinction is important because it highlights the active, rather than passive, nature of learning.

In order to illustrate how a total quality approach can improve the process of learning, this paper briefly discusses a central tenet of total quality: continuous improvement of work process driven by data gathering, which improves quality, and a complementary view of learning as a process. We use an introductory statistics course to illustrate and demonstrate improvements that facilitate learning. Our discussion is intentionally specific to this course, although we are confident that the process and some of the details are widely relevant.

Continuous improvement is driven by a cycle of investigation, implementation, and evaluation. Although our discussion reflects experience over a fairly lengthy time period, neither this course nor the process of applying total quality to education is complete. They never will be!

Continuous Improvement

While definitions of quality are varied and often vague, we focus here on the concept of a quality process. Quality improvement itself involves a process of systematically evaluating the steps that are involved in completing work. This requires what is referred to as the Shewhart or plan-do-check-act (PDCA) cycle.[1]

- *Planning* requires (1) collecting data in order to understand the process to be improved and (2) developing a theory to guide improvement. In teaching, this means moving beyond typical measurements of progress, which are often limited to exams and end-of-course evaluations, to a much more active and ongoing data-collection process. Gathering and interpreting data drives the cycle; we cannot overemphasize the importance of data as a driving force in improving the process of learning. Data are the foundation for understanding this process and for planning and developing changes—the "doing."

- *Doing* refers to trying out a solution suggested by the data and related theory. We must generate alternatives that make sense given the data and conditions, and choose a solution or combination of solutions that fit the analysis.

- *Checking* is the step in which support for the solution or change is gathered and evaluated. Here again, data are central. Data relevant to outcomes are collected and evaluated. The evaluation may lead to revisions or adjustments to a preliminary solution or solutions.

- In the *acting* stage, an effective solution is permanently implemented wherever it is relevant. The cycle continues; continuous improvement involves repeated cycling through these steps.

Learning As a Process

Postsecondary education is commonly organized into courses. We view a course as a process in which the work to be accomplished is student learning. This is in contrast to a focus on presenting or covering material.

Learning is a process that involves repetitive steps and some rework or scrap. Learning is sometimes encumbered by unnecessary complexity. So, continuously improving a course requires identifying steps that will minimize rework, scrap, and complexity and help students to learn effectively and efficiently. We continuously improve within a single administration of a course, for example, within a semester, and also across semesters.

Some Background Information

In this paper, we describe experiences in improving the learning process for students in an introductory statistics class. Successful completion of the course is necessary for admission to the school of business undergraduate program, and 75 percent to 85 percent of those who enroll are future business school students. Two semesters of calculus for the social sciences are prerequisites for the course.

The format of the course is a large lecture; enrollment varies between 200 and 425 students per semester. The course meets two times a week for two hours at a time. The content includes data collection and analysis, probability theory, statistical inference, and quality control.

The process of improvement that we will describe and its rationale, as well as other specific aspects of the changes discussed, are offered for consideration in other courses, including courses that have a nonquantitative focus. As mentioned earlier, we believe that the process is relevant to learning processes other than statistics, but that relevance should be established through the PDCA cycle that was previously described.

Sherr teaches statistics, while Schwoerer teaches organizational behavior, a field with roots in psychology, sociology, and other social science disciplines. In the process of writing this paper, we discovered commonalities not previously suspected. These perceived common elements can help in planning, and the organizational behavior course is then the focus for additional steps in the cycle. We believe that increased communication among faculty can foster a quality orientation across disciplines that will significantly benefit students.

Data-Driven Continuous Improvement over Time

In subsequent sections, we describe changes or developments that reflect the application of the PDCA cycle to the statistics course. First, we would like to share some general observations that have proved relevant to moving through the cycle. These observations focus on teachers, students, roles, and the assumptions that we bring to the educational setting of a statistics class. These observations are derived from experience in teaching the statistics class and also from knowledge of total quality efforts in settings in and beyond educational contexts. They reflect an informal theory of learning relevant to this class. They thus reflect assumptions about important variables or issues that are key to adopting a quality approach and evaluating and improving processes. They include necessary starting points or skills for teaching, contrasting views of students, the process of preparation for teaching, and goals in teaching.

• Knowing the material (in this case, statistics) and being able to be present it is necessary, but not sufficient. Speaking skills count, just as spelling and grammar count in writing a paper. Traditionally, these skills were perhaps seen as end points rather than beginning points in postsecondary education. Improving teaching was largely focused on improving these teacher-related factors.

• Since we are shifting our perspective to facilitating student learning, we recognize the key role that students play in determining the success of a class. We want students to come and to be prepared, and we want to get their minds actively involved, alone or with others. We recognize, however, that the concept of "what we want students to do" is somewhat inconsistent with a quality approach. Our focus will be on providing conditions that increase the likelihood that students will also want these same things.

• Considerable practice is involved in mastering statistical material. Over time, the set of assumptions just outlined has been enlarged as we have realized that what is most important is to encourage students to work outside the classroom. While homework is clearly a common part of coursework, we propose that homework should be seen as central, rather than supplemental, to improving learning.

Given that we are trying to improve the learning process for students, how do students fit into a quality model, or, what role do they play? Various possible roles for students have different implications for improving the process of learning. Some possible roles for students are raw material, customers, products, and coworkers. Each of these brings valuable perspective to improving the learning process.

• *Raw material.* A view of students as raw material suggests that we must understand students' backgrounds, attitudes, and perhaps variation in their preparation. This does not suggest that students are passive recipients of the teaching process. Rather, understanding students, including their differences, can increase our sensitivity to their participation in the learning process. For example, if we assume that completion of the calculus prerequisites means that students are comfortable at the prospect of studying statistics, we may be badly mistaken. We can find out whether some students are anxious because they feel uncomfortable about studying quantitative material. If they are, we can encourage them and build their confidence by clarifying what the class requires.

• *Products.* Viewing students as products has some commonalities with viewing them as raw materials, but the focus is on the end of our contact with them. Again, we do not mean to suggest that students are passive or acted upon, the results or the outcomes of our teaching methods. We view students as products in the sense that we can identify relevant skills and information that they will have upon completing the process of a course. This can help us develop a better match between course content and activity and the desirable outcomes.

• *Customers.* Viewing students as customers can be controversial. We propose that they are indeed appropriately viewed as customers in the sense of being beneficiaries, suggesting the importance of meeting their needs. While we would stop short of viewing students as customers in the commercial sense of being ultimate arbiters of quality, they are well-equipped to evaluate a delivery system, if not to choose its content.

• *Coworkers.* If we view students as coworkers, we begin to view the course we teach as a collaborative undertaking. We are responsive to student input and consider it when designing and redesigning the process of the course.

Each of these perspectives of students has proved to be useful in improving the learning process in the statistics class. All can be seen in the significant changes that have been made in the course over time and in the changes that occur in the form of adjustment within a given semester. All are relevant, and all enrich the process of improving learning.

In teaching the introductory statistics course, we have viewed students from these different perspectives, gathered data, employed the theoretical elements discussed earlier, and used these interactive pieces to engage in many iterations of the PDCA cycle. This cycle is applied to improving the process of teaching or helping students to learn. Next, we describe the steps that comprise the process of teaching. We then discuss six areas in which significant changes have been made that reflect the process of continuous improvement. We then discuss how these areas constitute an interrelated system.

The Process of Preparing to Teach

We'd like to briefly review the steps involved in preparing to teach a course and actually teaching it. We envision the process as one of continual preparation consisting of seven steps.

1. Know the material. This should not be surprising. We emphasize the ongoing need to actively maintain your knowledge of your field of expertise. It can be relevant to adapting even an introductory course, and it also allows you to share excitement about your specialty with your students. (This will be discussed more later.)

2. Know your students. As discussed in the material on different possible views of students, this refers to your students' backgrounds, attitudes, and, perhaps, variation in their preparation. It also refers to knowing what's going on with

your students during the semester. What are they experiencing? How well have they learned recent material? It does not mean that you will always know your students as individuals or on a personal level, but it does mean that you will know them in the ways that are most relevant to facilitating their learning.

3. Know your goals. There are specific goals for each course in terms of the skills and knowledge that students will acquire. It is also useful to think about common sets of goals. We have the following for every course we teach with process improvement in mind.

- Challenge students. Do not trivialize your subject.

- Move students to learn themselves. Sometimes we must teach students how to do this.

- Work on verbal and written skills of communication.

- Communicate why the subject matter is important.

- Convey why you love the subject. Help the student to understand why you are excited to be teaching the material.

- Help the student to move along the continuum of learning, on which one end is grappling with the process of learning in general, and the other is self-teaching. Students on one end can benefit from learning study habits—how to learn. On the other end of the continuum are students who are able to apply methods of inquiry, pointed ultimately toward adding to knowledge. Students are at many different points along this continuum; it is a worthy goal to move a student toward being capable of inquiry.

- Help students to develop a love for learning as well as increasing their capacity.

Steps two and three, knowing your students and your goals, allow a teacher to begin thinking about how the connection can best be made between the material and the students. What are we trying to do, and how can we best do it given current conditions?

4. Develop the concrete, specific plan or outline for class based on making these connections.

5. Prepare for and actually give the class.

6. Provide for individual attention to ensure that learning is complete.

7. Evaluate the previous six steps.

The steps become a continuous loop or process. Conscious attention to them helps put one's teaching in the context of a class as it develops, rather than focusing primarily on delivering a course. By applying the PDCA cycle to this process, we are continually improving the introductory statistics class. A description of some changes that have been implemented follow. We emphasize that they do not represent ends, but improvements in the process.

Changes in the Statistics Course

Technology Changes

Technology changes are important because the physical environment has a significant influence on learning and motivation. Underestimating the effect of physical conditions that impede or enhance learning can result in undermining the effects of other changes. In this particular example, the large class and nature of the room used could make hearing and note taking very difficult. This suggests the appropriateness of evaluating and improving the technology used.

Although technology can be enticing, we believe that its use should be based on student needs. All of the adjustments described here were driven by data and technological development, although they certainly evolved as technology became feasible. Student surveys were conducted that asked about practical issues, such as the ability to hear and see as well as to understand.

Originally, lectures were supported through the use of blackboards. Surveys of students led to use of 35 millimeter slides and slide projectors. Currently, computer presentation technology is used. We did adopt computer presentation technology early, very soon after it became available. It allows for easy changes and adjustment in the material presented. It also allows the students to absorb material incrementally and to take notes at a comfortable speed as the instructor adds points to the discussion.

Changes in delivery method are key in using class time effectively. However, we view the classroom technology as less central than we did in earlier stages of teaching the class. Over time, we have realized that most of the significant learning does take place outside of the classroom. Sherr is fond of saying, "I do my best teaching at night while asleep." The following areas of changes in the course specifically address facilitating the process of learning beyond the classroom.

The Purpose of Class Meetings

When the primary goal of the course is to facilitate learning outside the formal meeting period, what is the purpose of the class meeting? It does not become irrelevant by any means. The class meeting serves as a gathering point to provide a framework that will move the students to learn themselves, reflecting an assumption that students will benefit from (some of them need) a galvanizing force. The class meeting can be designed and delivered with this effect in mind. Design and delivery include communicating the importance of the subject matter and why the professor is excited to be teaching the material, and avoiding trivialization of the subject, goals which were identified earlier.

The class meeting also helps students understand how learning will take place. Here is where understanding students as raw material is relevant. At one end of the continuum, a student may need to learn study habits. At the other end, a student is poised to develop his or her own skills in methods of inquiry. The point of the class meeting is to help all students develop along this continuum.

Teaching Assistants' Roles

While teaching assistants are commonly used in support of large lecture format classes, they are most often assigned to recitation or lab sections in which they work problems. In this statistics class, this seemed to add little value beyond the primary lecture meeting. Thus, a challenge existed to use teaching assistants in new ways.

We have done this by expanding the role of teaching assistants and improving student access to them. Teaching assistants serve as providers of highly personalized, detailed help. We have hired more of them. They are undergraduate students who have successfully completed the course, never graduate students. We have found that they are able to communicate with and empathize with students currently enrolled far better than graduate students. We do as much as we can to ensure that they are diverse in gender, race, background, physical abilities, personality, and any other variation that may occur in an applicant pool. And we have them coach and work with students in an open hours help session. The hours have been extended over time so that students can get help whenever they are working. Often some current students begin to develop into informal teaching assistants by helping others in class. Although certain students can develop this type of learning structure on an ad hoc basis, this approach to studying and working in the statistics class makes it easily available to all students.

Teaching assistants are paid to attend class, and some are compensated to take official notes that are available in notebooks in the help sessions to all students. New teaching assistants are encouraged to review the material through taking notes that will serve as resources for others and responsibility and care are encouraged.

Since all of the teaching assistants are former students, they help the instructor to restructure the class in a continuous fashion: feedback from earlier semesters as well as current semesters plays a role. The perspectives of instructor, students who have previously experienced the class, and current students can be applied to evaluating and using feedback. When the instructor takes feedback from students and acts on it in a way that stresses its importance and relevance, the message conveyed is that feedback matters, which encourages thoughtful feedback.

The teaching assistants serve an additional, extremely significant function: they are a source of constant feedback to the instructor about how students are doing and how learning is proceeding. Thus they are a continual source of data about what was clear or unclear in a lecture meeting or an assignment. This information is a necessity, not a luxury.

These assistants provide relevant data on both statistics-related issues and the temper of the class. In fact, they are an effective substitute for minute papers or minute essays and serve as a continuous process improvement team. They also serve as a teaching equivalent of managing by walking around.

Homework Assignments

Homework assignments become central to learning in this model. In the class, we have moved toward structuring homework to build and maintain knowledge as students develop their statistical skills. Further, interaction with teaching assistants serves as a check on the class members' progress. Feedback from teaching assistants regarding areas of most perceived difficulty or trouble with understanding is used to guide lecture material and shape future assignments. There is no mechanical, straightforward set of problems that are worked through as the class proceeds. Instead, the homework assignments serve as the primary process through which learning occurs.

Tailored to the progress of a class, the homework is generally designed to build and maintain knowledge. There is continual overlap of material covered. Repetition and building are used to consolidate knowledge and to connect earlier material as new concepts are added. The intent is to improve student understanding of how material is related and to increase the period in which a student works actively with a body of material, increasing mastery. This is accomplished by providing a sequence that builds continually with overlap.

Reading assignments are specifically designed to connect with the need to learn. The instructor is likely to find that more time is required to prepare assignments than to prepare the class meeting itself. Assignments and class serve as the mechanisms for constructing a staircase for learning statistics. A good staircase has consistent risers and helps the user to move easily without tripping.

Students are given prompt, consistent, and accurate feedback. This is crucial to facilitating the learning that is happening by correcting and reinforcing as appropriate. It also communicates the way that students are perceived by the instructor. They are significant customers, and their learning is important.

Information Provided to Students

As the statistics class has evolved, it has increasingly asked students to change some assumptions and to operate in some ways that might contrast with their experience in other courses. In particular, it is not sufficient to attend class or to get notes from those who do; deeper involvement is needed. It becomes crucial to communicate to students that statistics requires them to do things beyond what has been necessary for success in other courses in the past.

This message is not conveyed by haranguing, even gentle haranguing. It is conveyed by documenting and sharing the relationship between how students approach the class and their outcomes. Evaluation—a grade—affects the motivation of students. We try to provide information that motivates students to work in a way that will help them to learn statistics effectively.

This information includes the structure of the grading system. This is commonly provided to students in material provided early in a class, often in a syllabus or course description. This information is somewhat abstract and impersonal, however, and does not communicate how learning best occurs in the class.

The more crucial element, then, is to share with students documentation of the relationship between homework and course outcomes. This provides students with a clear understanding of the process of work and learning that will best serve them in the class. We will illustrate how this is done in some detail, using representative illustrations from the actual computer-based presentation.

First, the grading system is communicated (Figure 1). In the statistics class, 100 points are allotted for homework, three exams are worth 100 points each, and a final exam is worth 200 points, for a total of 600 points. Students glancing at this structure may conclude that homework is relatively inconsequential and that doing well on exams is most important. In order to be motivated to engage effectively in the learning process that must happen outside of the class, the students must understand that the homework is the most effective preparation for success in exams. Further motivation comes from feedback that is rapid, consistent, and of high quality. This feedback effectively demonstrates commitment to and caring for students, and it completes the loop of learning that begins in tackling the homework problems.

Figure 2 depicts the distribution of homework grades in a spring semester. This information serves as a basis for building a picture of the connections between

Grading system	
	Points
Homework	100
3 exams at 100	300
Final exam	200
Total	600

Figure 1. Grading system.

homework and course outcomes. A bar graph in the upper portion provides a picture of the frequency of different grades. The lower portion provides a box and whisker plot summary of this distribution. The box and whisker plot is an effective graphic technique for summarizing information about a distribution of some data. In this figure, the information is presented horizontally. The rectangle indicates the 25th (left side) and 75th percentile (right side) limits of the distribution. The line in

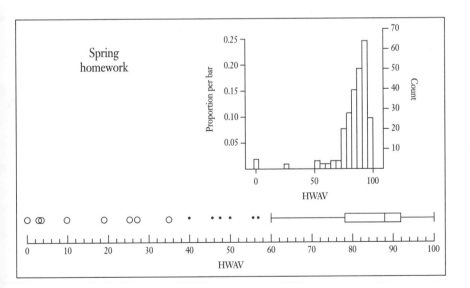

Figure 2. Distribution of homework grades.

the interior of the rectangle is the median, the homework score that represents the point at which half of the scores are higher and half lower. The whiskers, or lines extending beyond the rectangle, indicate the broader range of scores. The circles and asterisks or stars indicate outlier homework scores.

Figure 3 provides a summary of the relationship between these homework grades and grades in the course. The vertical box and whisker plot shows the distribution of homework scores for those who earned each grade (A through F) in the course. In general, the figure provides evidence that students with higher homework grades tend to receive higher grades in the course. Note, for example, that the median homework grade decreases for each category of class grade, and the distribution of grades moves toward lower scores for each successively lower course grade.

Figures 4, 5, and 6 are used to build a basis for generalizing this relationship beyond this single spring semester. Figure 4 depicts the actual class results for the spring semester and a fall semester. Students can note easily that the spring class did much better than the fall. But to emphasize that the relationship between an individual's class grade and the homework score is constant, Figure 5 shows that the relationship between homework scores and course grade was identical in both semesters, regardless of the semester or the overall pattern of performance in the class. Figure 6 provides quantitative information on the distribution of homework scores in the two semesters. The distributions of homework scores, then, are key to understanding grades.

The message for students? "Don't worry about how you're doing relative to other people in the class; it will not help or hurt you. There is no fixed structure or

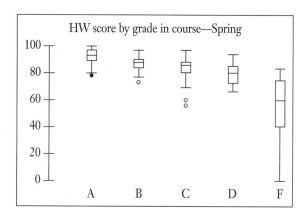

Figure 3. Relationship between homework grades and course grades.

	Spring		Fall	
Grade	Count	%	Count	%
A	63	21.9	25	11.6
B	97	33.7	66	30.7
C	63	21.9	54	25.1
D	40	13.9	37	17.2
F	25	8.7	33	15.3
Total	288	100.1	215	99.9

Figure 4. Actual class results for two semesters.

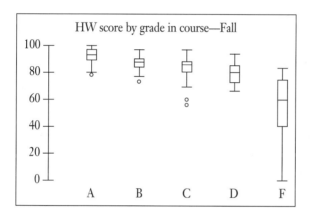

Figure 5. Consistent relationship between homework grades and course grades over semesters. See Figure 3.

Why?	Homework score	
	Effort	
	Spring	Fall
Median	88	85
25th percentile	80	78
75th percentile	93	92
Percent over 74	85.1	80.9

Figure 6. Distribution of homework scores in two semesters.

quota system for grades. What *will* help you is within your control, and it is to work on your homework." Homework scores reflect individual effort to learn in the class, and they are associated with learning and outcomes.

In this process of information sharing, students are also asked about their expected or planned effort for the course. Students respond to the question, "How many hours per week do you expect to spend studying for this course?" The responses vary greatly, as one might expect. Students are also asked about what they expect to earn as a grade. These responses are used to calculate an expected class GPA, for example, one semester it was 3.41/4.00. This contrasts with the actual class GPA of 2.06/4.00. The intention is not to shock or discourage students, but to encourage realistic thinking about how they will achieve their goals. In effect, a total quality process designed to facilitate learning for the class can affect the quality of individual learning processes.

Student feelings as they begin the course, particularly comfort and confidence, are also recognized and explored. We consider the relationship between student attitudes toward studying statistics (ranging from very comfortable to terrified) and hours of expected study. This suggests that plans for effort do not correlate well with feelings. That is, student anxiety level is not associated with student plans to spend time on the course each week. At the start of the course, students do not feel that they can control their performance through their own actions. The provision of information about the relationship between homework grade (clearly controlled by students) and the final grade is a beginning step in encouraging student responsibility for learning and performance in the course.

Changes in the Statistics Class As a System

We have discussed areas of change: technology changes, the purpose of the class meeting, teaching assistants' roles, homework assignments, and the information provided to students. These areas are interrelated and interdependent. The changes occur in a system that is dynamic and changing. It takes thought to implement positive changes. We hope that the description of how we are continually improving the process of teaching introductory statistics will be helpful to others who are interested in commitment to continuous improvement in education.

How Did the Transition to Continuous Improvement Occur?

In discussions about how the course in introductory statistics evolved, Schwoerer was curious about how the process of change had begun. Sherr identified an "ahaa! experience" that can help us understand.

He described the continuous improvement approach as 180 degrees opposed in direction from his initial efforts in teaching. When he started, he wrote notes on the board and worked problems, and students copied them. There was little need for students to read the book or to invest significant effort outside the classroom. Interestingly, Schwoerer thinks that this describes many beginning teaching careers: you hope that things are going well, you try to improve your presentation style and convey the material effectively, and your primary focus is on feedback after the class, which you may use to try to change some elements in your course in some way.

We do not mean to criticize this approach harshly; with enthusiasm, it can work. Goodwill and hard work and caring are important in good teaching. However, we are struck by how the total quality cycle we have discussed can direct these elements and result in systematic, data-driven, effective changes.

The ahaa! experience was the time that Sherr became very ill with a terrible flu and was out for a little over a week. At that point, the school was low on statisticians and unable to provide a substitute lecturer. When teaching assistants asked what to do, Sherr directed them to give them some homework assignments related to the planned topic and to let it go; they would adjust later as necessary.

The lectures would have been on confidence interval theory, which at that time involved working examples for several days. The students were told that the homework would be collected, and they would be helped later with any difficulties. The expectation, natural at that point, was that students might not have learned this material well.

When the next exam was given, student performance for this area of the material was checked carefully, and contrary to expectations, found to be very strong! These data were used as a beginning step for rethinking the approach to learning in the class as it was structured at that point. The message is not that the instructor is superfluous, but that there are some alternatives that encourage more active student learning.

Beyond the Introductory Statistics Course: Improving the System of Teaching

We have described some experiences in teaching introductory statistics in a business school. We would like to note that a process of continuous improvement has implications beyond a single course or a single professor. Sherr, for example, is sharing his ideas and experiences in the school and beyond. He has a significant impact through providing seminars for graduate students who teach while in the Ph.D. program and soon will begin their own teaching careers.

We believe that creating a method of sharing teaching improvements based on total quality principles could improve teaching throughout our school. Earlier, we mentioned that in collaborating on this paper we discovered greater commonalities between teaching in our subject areas than we had suspected. While the primary purpose of this paper is to describe and illustrate a total quality approach to continuous improvement in the introductory statistics class, we would like to briefly discuss some of the key, common principles that are relevant regardless of subject matter or teaching conditions.

• *A shift of emphasis from teacher performance to the process of learning.* While we emphasize that an instructor's skills are an important foundation for promoting learning, we consider them to be a beginning point. Instructors teach best in a way that is individually expressive and comfortable. The additional step is to focus on the process of student learning and how it can best be accomplished.

• *Preparing to teach.* We identified these steps: knowing the material, your students, and your goals; developing a plan for class; teaching the class; providing for individual attention; and evaluating the process, including timely, detailed feedback for students and instructor. These steps obviously span disciplines. When coupled with a total quality approach as accomplished through the completion of a PDCA cycle, they provide a structure for undertaking continuous improvement.

• *Documenting and communicating to students requirements for doing well.* This process challenges instructors to examine the consistency between intentions for the class and what the class actually rewards. For example, in organizational behavior, Schwoerer is learning to balance rewards for mastering conceptual material with the ability to apply related skills in live situations. This step makes learning a more collaborative, interactive process.

• *The roles of class meetings, homework, and teaching assistants.* Sherr described the purpose of class meeting to be a galvanizing force, facilitating learning outside the formal meeting. Homework, teaching assistant support, and feedback are key to learning. While Schwoerer's situation is not identical, the discussions about where and how learning occurs helped to identify how the purposes of class and homework in organizational behavior vary. For example, some class sessions involve experiential exercises that provide active practice and learning in simulated conditions. Follow-up assignments and prompt, detailed feedback may be used to further develop learning and encourage reflection. While the organizational behavior class has no teaching assistants, a team structure used for a major course assignment can be adapted to help students learn and provide feedback to the instructor throughout the semester. The key, common element is to understand how learning occurs and to structure the elements of the course in a supportive way.

- *Continuous improvement means just that.* A total quality approach to improvement is never finished. Updating and improving course content is a familiar idea; continually improving the process of learning that occurs in a class is just as important. It is necessary to address student capacity and readiness as well as instructor expectations. If this is done only at the individual course or instructor level, it is less effective than if the entire system of the school, college, or university is investing in total quality.

Throughout these common threads we recognized a shared interest in developing and improving our teaching in a way that encourages active learning, responsibility, and excitement in students. A total quality approach provides data-driven alternatives to exhorting and haranguing. The latter are generally most effective at frustrating the exhorter and alienating and boring the harangued. In contrast, a total quality approach, with its data-driven PDCA cycle, provides a constructive process for involving students significantly in teaching improvements, regardless of the subject matter. It provides a structure for coming up with answers that fit, rather than relying on decisions that may have worked in the past. It encourages instructors and students to define learning as a development process that is self-managed, rather than a process of transfer and storage.

We believe that teaching in higher education is generally good and that there is a high level of caring; much energy is devoted to teaching. However, we also think that increasing the level and quality of communication about the process of teaching (in and outside of class) and how it can be improved could help many instructors be more effective. We believe the key lesson to be extracted from this discussion is the value of moving beyond a view of the instructor as a somewhat isolated figure, often a performer, hoping that teaching is going well, to a view of an instructor as a catalyst for learning, investing energy in collecting relevant data and using that data to inform a process of continuous improvement. We believe these shifts in perspective and role will benefit both current and future students.

Note

1. W. E. Deming, *Out of the Crisis* (Cambridge, Mass.: MIT Center for Advanced Engineering Study, 1986), 88.

Fast Quality for Fast Results

Willard I. Zangwill
University of Chicago

About a year ago in my Operations Management and Strategy course for MBA students I dramatically changed the course. I decided that the students should see for themselves what happens, so I started requiring the students to go into actual organizations and implement the concepts taught. Due to other course requirements, the students often had to accomplish this implementation in only two or three weeks. Because two or three weeks is very brief (traditional quality improvement projects often take many months or even years), I had to develop and teach to the students what I call "fast quality," a new improvement approach with very rapid implementation. So far, the results using fast quality have turned out to be impressive: no student team has failed to produce some improvement, and most teams obtained substantial improvements, often boosting performance measures 50 percent to 90 percent.

Because fast quality is so different from traditional approaches, in order to develop it, I had to completely revise and reorient my thinking about total quality and quality improvement. What precisely is this different and quite rapid approach? Indeed, what was it about traditional quality that spurred me to this radical change, and what does fast quality imply, not just for students, but for quality techniques, throughout business and industry? To consider these matters adequately, we must examine what happened at the beginning.

About 15 years ago I introduced the Operations Management and Strategy course as one of the first two total quality elective courses to be taught in the Graduate School of Business, University of Chicago. (See Roberts, "Grassroots Total Quality in Higher Education: Some Lessons from Chicago," in this volume.)

The course design was influenced by ideas from the United States and Europe, as well as by what I had learned in Japan, where I had been a visiting professor at Tokyo Science University. Student interest in the course grew, and soon there was sufficient demand for three or four sections each academic year.

The course presents some of the major concepts for running an operation efficiently. Since the power and value of teams is one of these concepts, the course has always required the students to do all of their work in teams. On the first day of class the students were divided into teams, and for the entire quarter the students on any one team would work together on their case presentations, homework, and other assignments. (See Zangwill, "Tips for Student Teams," also in this volume.)

As principal course requirement, each student team had to do a term paper project about a particular real organization (business, governmental, or educational), a different organization for each team. The project, at least prior to the change I made in the course, was to analyze how the concepts taught might be applied to improve that organization. In a final report, the team presented its analysis and recommended what the organization should do differently.

A few years ago, however, I started to have some doubts and second thoughts. Total quality was one of the foundations of the course, yet it was coming under increasingly critical scrutiny. Stories in leading business magazines and newspapers, such as the *Wall Street Journal*, were pointing out that in many firms total quality was failing. A firm that won a Baldrige award, soon after winning that award, went bankrupt, and, indeed, total quality, its philosophy and practice, was being attacked.

Also, I was becoming increasingly concerned about the claim by many gurus that enormous patience was needed and that substantial payoff from quality might require years. After all, the gurus asserted, entire workforces must be trained and organizational cultures must be changed. Somehow this did not make sense to me, and I felt that quicker results could and should be possible.

My concern and impatience were by no means personal quirks, as I knew several CEOs, strong believers in and supporters of total quality, who were also uneasy. They were willing to give total quality strong backing and more than a fair chance, but they also knew that the training and restructuring necessary to implement total quality was costly. After a reasonable period of time, they had to see their investment returned, but too often there was little tangible payback. Their frustration was apparent and mounting.

For instance, to train its employees, one large bank spent over $250,000 in one year. The bank did everything that the gurus recommended: teams tackling problems, a quality council, and strong leadership from the top. But after only a few successes and with no real beachhead established, the program's continuing negative cash flow discouraged and disappointed top management, derailing the entire quality effort.

Because I taught and believed in total quality and had a personal investment in its success, these developments were disturbing to me. Moreover, my background in total quality suggested to me that the failures and unfortunate events I kept hearing about were not inevitable. From both my teaching and my direct experiences, I was convinced of the soundness of concepts underpinning quality—such as just-in-time, process analysis, new product development,[1] incentives, and organizational structure.

What is more, I knew of organizations where these concepts did work, of organizations that had deployed total quality concepts and obtained substantial results fast. Interestingly, it was my probing of how those organizations implemented quality so successfully and swiftly that led me to change my own thinking and to make the turnaround in my teaching.

Examples of Fast Results

One such organization is General Electric with its work-out technique. The typical work-out consists of a three-day weekend retreat, during which the employees in a unit, perhaps 30 to 100 of them, meet to discuss problems and how to improve their operation. The employees, being very knowledgeable about details of the operation, usually have many ideas about how to obtain improvements. Over the long weekend the work-out uses a structured process of identifying problems and then suggesting solutions, many of which lead to specific recommendations.

The coup de grace, however, happens near the end of the retreat when the employees present their recommendations to the head of the unit. By the rules of the work-out process, the head has to make a decision on the recommendation there and then: either accept, reject, or return for further analysis. Also, the unit heads are under great pressure from upper management to implement as many ideas as possible, because upper management knows the potential for listening to the worker. In fact, of the recommendations proposed, typically 90 percent are accepted and implemented. Top management also insists that the implementation has to be done immediately or as fast as possible. The net result is that GE usually gets many good ideas from the people most knowledgeable in the process, and by implementing them right away, sees the improvement fast.

Given the success of GE's work-out, I wondered if students in my course could emulate it and, in a similar manner, obtain definite improvements quickly.

Another influential input came from my experience when I attended a four-day kaizen course at the University of Dayton. The purpose of the course was to teach how to get improvements fast, and, in fact, before the four days were over, the students taking that course had actually made those improvements in a real plant. All students in this course were experienced in methods of production and quality, most being plant managers or process engineers; I was the only academic. Despite the high level of knowledge of most participants, something special was taught that none of the participants had previously understood: how to apply the quality methods fast and get results fast.

The course took place in an actual plant, a Copeland site that made compressors. My team, one of several at the site for those four days, attacked a compressor block machining line. Under the direction of a Japanese master, we, indeed, learned how to make improvements fast. In just a couple of days we cut the number of people on the line from seven to four, while also improving output and quality. The three other teams participating in the course tackled other parts of the Copeland plant, and all of them also made improvement in efficiency of about 40 percent to 50 percent in the four days.

In my mind, what made this approach so successful was similar to what drives the success of the GE work-out: most processes have an enormous potential for improvement. By direct observation and/or by seeking worker input, one can identify many of those areas for improvement. Then, as long as management is willing to implement the changes quickly, it is possible to make improvements fast, often in a matter of days. And, as the Copeland example illustrated and GE has repeatedly demonstrated, the gains can be substantial.

Implications of These Examples

The GE and Copeland examples may sound like traditional total quality applied fast with some added excitement and enthusiasm. However, there are also some key differences from traditional quality as conventionally set forth by gurus, differences that led me to fast quality and the change in my MBA course. In particular, traditional quality suggests that careful problem-solving procedures be followed, usually in the plan-do-check-act framework. Often these are embodied in 5-step or 7-step procedures (or 9-step or 11-step) that the teams are supposed to follow in order to solve a problem. Typical steps might include identifying possible causes of the problem; collecting and analyzing data; trying solutions; and so on. Also, the steps themselves generally require use of a number of basic quality tools, such as cause-and-effect diagrams, histograms, run charts, control charts, customer analysis, and other data analysis techniques.

Certainly, these problem-solving procedures can be very helpful. The difficulty is that to follow them completely, utilizing the steps and tools the way one is supposed to, can take a very long time, in practice, many months. This is especially true when problem solving is implemented by part-time improvement teams whose members are devoting only a fraction of their time to the problem.

The GE and Copeland examples suggest, however, that the entire problem-solving apparatus may not always be necessary. Conventional total quality wisdom stresses not jumping to quick solutions. But does that really mean problems must be studied for months and months? Instead, a high fraction of problems may be due to wastes that to a trained person are relatively obvious. Indeed, the 80-20 rule (Pareto principle) may apply here, specifically, that a very substantial percent of improvement opportunities are of this obvious kind and can be implemented quickly. Perhaps in only a small percent of the cases is a detailed and careful analysis needed to identify and make the improvement.

This application of the Pareto principle is consistent with the GE work-out, my kaizen experience at Copeland, and other experiences as well. Very frequently, the way to solve or at least significantly remedy a problem is easily identified. So, why go through a lengthy problem-solving approach when it is not cost-effective and not needed for a large number of problems?[2]

What we arrive at is the following two-step approach to total quality.

Step 1. Attack the easy problems, that is, the wastes in the process that are obvious and easily remedied. For these, quick analysis may be enough. The lengthy problem-solving approach may be unreasonable and extravagant.

Step 2. After tackling the easy problems, attack the tough problems. For these more careful analysis and detailed effort likely will be needed.

If the analogy with the Pareto principle is correct, a high percentage of potential improvements can be accomplished using step 1. Moreover, for step 1, since only brief training is needed, the cost of the extensive training in the quality techniques can be avoided, at least initially.

Once several of the easy, step 1, problems have been solved, then step 2 can be implemented. Of course more training is needed for step 2, but by that time, step 1 should already be producing results, justifying the value of total quality to top management and encouraging its approval of the additional training .

A Crucial Experiment in My Class

I summarized these observations as the following fundamental conjecture: some problems are difficult to solve, but many problems, including some large ones, are easy to solve. Consequently by attacking the easy problems first, there is no need for the usual long delays, and no reason not to expect big improvements fast.

Given that conjecture, the challenge for me was to test it in my class. I changed the requirements of the term paper project for the students in my class. No longer were the student teams merely to write a final report with recommendations. No longer were they to be passive observers standing on the sidelines. Instead, they would be required to actually implement a technique they had learned in class in a real operation and observe the results. Moreover, I required that they employ a metric (quantitative performance measure) and show the change in the metric due to their implementation, before and after.

To prepare students for this challenge, I used the first three to four weeks of the class to cover some fundamental concepts valuable for improving processes. These included just-in-time, cycle time reduction, defect and error reduction, and process analysis. I also strongly emphasized the notion of waste, where waste is anything that happens in a process that is not needed in order to sell the product and satisfy the customer. Examples of waste include unnecessary work, rework, delays, incorrect information, late information, schedule changes, machinery breakdowns, extra steps, late parts, wrong parts, defective parts, software bugs, inventory, any product that does not sell, and failure to take advantage of opportunities for improvement, for example, buying parts at a lower price or drawing on knowledge and ability of the workforce.

There are two reasons for placing high emphasis on waste.

- Most processes have a great deal of waste. Numerous chunks of waste are lying around.

- Many of those chunks of waste can be identified and eliminated fast, thereby yielding improvements fast.

Examples of Waste

To illustrate how rampant waste is, here are some examples.

- At a factory one women had the keys to the equipment locker. If a worker needed a tool, he or she had to go to that woman to get that tool. Having a single person be responsible for the locker made sense for security reasons. The problem was that the woman was on the edge of the plant, so people had to walk a long distance to get to her. In addition, the equipment locker itself was about 150 feet from where she worked. So, after wasting time walking to the woman, the worker and she had to walk an additional 150 feet to get the tools.

- A given firm was asked by its customers to submit proposals for jobs. Usually there was deadline when the bid was due to the customer. Unfortunately, the firm had difficulty meeting the deadlines, often requiring overtime to get the bid out.

The proposals were about 10 pages long and to prepare them three managers had to complete different sections. Previously, the proposal was routed to the three people sequentially. This meant that the proposal spent considerable time sitting on someone's desk or being routed to the next person. The solution was to have each of the three managers work on their aspect of the proposal simultaneously. This was done by making three copies of the customer's request and sending a copy to each of the three managers at the same time.

- A major telecommunications firm has several laboratories to develop new products. At one of the labs there is a group of top researchers that decides whether or not to fund new projects. A marketer or engineer has to get approval from this group. The problem is that this group meets once a year. Thus, a person typically has to wait many months to obtain approval and funding. (To the author's knowledge, this cumbersome process remains in effect today.)

These examples illustrate not only that wastes comprise a vast epidemic, but that many of them can be easily identified and eliminated. Thus, I thought that my conjecture was reasonable and that students, after some training in the key concepts, should be able to go into firms and achieve substantial improvements in a matter of weeks.

Some readers may question the assumption that MBA students, occupied with other courses and other responsibilities, could be the catalysts for such improvements in outside organizations. My own earlier experience and that of my colleagues (see the papers in this volume by Bateman and Roberts; Becker and Golomski; Dawson and Sapp; and Flueck) suggests that empowered students, once unleashed, can create impressive results. All these considerations gave me the courage to go ahead.

The Actual Test

The students in my classes were given the challenge of testing my conjecture about a year ago. They were almost always successful. Here are examples of the actual improvements the students obtained, as stated in the executive summary of the reports they submitted.

Kraft USA's Accounting Group

- Plant cost accounting variances reported in same month, before 0 percent, after 80 percent.
- Cycle time to record variances dropped from four to five weeks to one day.

Chicago Mercantile Exchange

• Time to order a personal computer cut from three to eight weeks before, to one to two weeks after.

ORIGA Corp (pneumatics device manufacturer, Elmhurst, Illinois)

• Work-in-progress reduced from 280 units to 203.

• Manufacturing cycle time cut from six days to two days.

• Assembly productivity increased over 80 percent.

Northern Telecom

• Credit request processing times dropped from an average of 27 days to 8 days, a reduction of 70 percent.

Admiral Tool (metal stamping, Chicago)

• Time to respond to a quote cut from 18 days to 6 days, a 67 percent reduction.

Precision Scientific (medical instruments, Chicago)

• Cycle time to process engineering change notices cut from seven days to one day.

Steel Pro (slit and edge steel, Hammond, Indiana)

• Time to process a truckload of steel cut from 72 hours to 32 hours.

• Defects of 1.5 percent cut to essentially zero.

• Equipment downtime due to defects and poor equipment location cut from 3 hours and 35 minutes per shipment to 2 minutes.

Moore Medical (distribution operation, Lemont, Illinois)

• For the picking and packing process, cycle time cut 26 percent and work time to total time ratio improved 37.5 percent.

Obviously, the success of this classroom experiment may have implications for a wide range of courses in business and engineering schools, and possibly elsewhere.

Note that the students usually have an interest in improving personal quality, the application of quality to oneself, and that personal quality improvement projects can play the same role as the organizational improvement projects that I am describing. (My colleagues Harry Roberts and George Bateman have been requiring their students to do such projects since 1992.)

Fast Quality: A New Philosophy of Quality?

This success seems applicable not just to the classroom, but to business and other organizations. If students can do it in actual firms, management and employees in these firms should also be able to do it.

In particular, a firm might consider implementing quality employing the following approach that I call fast quality. After brief training emphasizing the topics just mentioned and especially the recognition of waste, the various work groups can start making improvements. Unlike the current models for implementation of total quality, however, fast quality work groups are expected to get the initial improvement fast, in a month or less.

In addition, fast quality adds the requirement, necessarily untested by my students, that in each and every month (or other relatively short time interval) thereafter, the work groups are to get an additional improvement. The purpose of requiring an improvement every month is to make continued improvements routine—simply part of the job. Moreover, because improvements are to be made frequently, there is no need to seek large improvements each time. Even small improvements are acceptable since fast quality emphasizes not the size of the improvement, but getting some improvement, even small, monthly and routinely.

It seems reasonable that over time some improvements will be small, others moderate, and some very substantial. Judging from the experience of my students, many of the improvements will be large. The important point, however, is to get employees used to making at least some improvement at frequent intervals. This aim has been a distinctive feature of Toyota's approach to quality over several decades.

After improvement experience increases and successes appear, additional training seems appropriate. This could include training in traditional total quality improvement teams, complete with sophisticated tools and systematic, multistep improvement projects. Fast quality does not obviate the value of traditional quality; it simply suggests that for a wide range of problems and opportunities, a faster and more flexible strategy might help.

Also after a half a year or so when monthly improvements become routine and standard operating procedure, then deviations from the monthly routine can be attempted and more complex problems tackled.

Fast quality may also appeal to management. Even a skeptical manager begins to get convinced when he or she sees an improvement month after month. Also, the approach is self-supporting, as the gains made should more than pay for additional training. Moreover, considering that from the students' experiences, the typical improvement is likely to be sizable, and that the improvements will accumulate over time, the total improvement achieved by the fast quality approach may well be impressive.

A Potential Problem with Fast Quality?

One possible argument against fast quality would run along the following lines. Fast quality is simply exploiting the fact, well-recognized by total quality gurus, that most organizations have many easy opportunities for major quality improvements, opportunities sometimes called the low-hanging fruit.

Therefore fast quality may bring quick successes at the expense of gaining insight into deeper, more persistent problems. These deeper problems may not be amenable to quick resolution, but may require disciplined, long-term improvement efforts. Fixing the easy problems may delay attention to these deeper problems.

Although this argument has superficial plausibility, it is not cogent. To justify why this argument is not valid, I offer the following reasons.

• Fast quality does not avoid attacking the difficult problems. Rather, as steps 1 and 2 on page 475 suggest, the concept is to tackle the easy problems first and then, when that is proceeding well, to tackle the more difficult problems. Thus the tough problems do indeed get solved, but by attacking the easy ones quickly, the gains occur faster. Also, easy problems are not necessarily small problems, which implies that when easy problems are solved, at least some of the gains are likely to be sizable. In fact, as the students' results showed, most of the gains are likely to be quite reasonable in size.

• An organization that has no experience with resolution of easy problems is likely to be hampered when it attempts to solve hard problems. Practice on easy problems is good training for hard ones. That is the usual pattern of learning.

• There are reports on organizations who have gained virtually nothing from their attempts to implement total quality (or, in the currently popular term, business process reengineering). By obtaining some successes quickly, fast quality may help to avoid despair and disillusionment.

• A key reason for the success of fast quality is waste removal. It is hard to see how removal of waste can do harm. It seems more reasonable that removal of waste would make other opportunities for improvement more visible.

• The success of GE's work-out, which still continues, is evidence of the staying power of fast quality.

Summary

Obtaining improvements in actual organizations need not take months or years; some substantial improvements may take only days or weeks. Fast quality is an approach to quality based on fast repeated improvements, with the goal of obtaining an improvement frequently and regularly, say monthly. Fast quality seeks to get employees used to making improvements and changes routinely, an important objective in and of itself. Also, under fast quality the emphasis is not on the size of the improvement, as even tiny improvements are acceptable, but on regularity and frequency. Still, some improvements will likely be large, and the many large and small improvements will add up to a large aggregate improvement. In addition, when improvement becomes routine, more complex problems can be attacked and obtaining large improvements should also become more routine.

Conceptually, the key to this approach is that the fast, monthly repetition produces fast-cycle learning. The fast cycles mean that the organization should be on a steep improvement curve, with the organization itself getting better and better at making improvements and, particularly, at making quite large improvements. Indeed, the experience of my students doing improvement projects suggests that fast quality may be widely feasible, both in the classroom and in industry.

Notes

1. Willard I. Zangwill, *Lightning Strategies for Innovation* (New York: Lexington, 1993).

2. Perhaps this is another example of nonobvious wastes. See Richard J. Schonberger, *Building a Chain of Customers* (New York: Free Press, 1990).

Reengineering: How to Do It with Quality in Academia and Elsewhere

Richard T. Greene

The Reengineering Challenge to Total Quality

Total quality, reengineering, and downsizing are three bodies of knowledge that claim attention in business today. Unfortunately, it is hard to say precisely what each embraces. They share many principles, but it is not clear where total quality ends and reengineering begins, or whether reengineering is anything other than a euphemism for downsizing. We have here a question of definition and boundaries and a need for empirical support.

For those in schools of business who have struggled to inject quality principles into MBA curricula, there is a further problem. During the 1980s, both leading corporations and the big 12 general consulting companies complained that MBA students had no exposure to the principles and methods of total quality and severely criticized schools of business for this omission from their curricula. During the 1990s this criticism was partly reversed. In 1993, for the first time, I noticed that the big 12 general consulting companies (but not yet most big corporations or smaller companies seriously engaged in total quality) were rejecting total quality. The consulting companies were telling MBA students that reengineering is where the action and leverage are to be found; reengineering is what the business schools should be teaching.

This switch of signals coming from industry poses a problem for those universities and business schools who are gearing up to teach total quality. At Chicago, where many MBA students seek employment with consulting firms, enrollments in quality management courses have declined during the 1993–1994 year, and student feedback suggests that recruiters have actively discouraged them from pursuing courses in total quality. Clearly schools of business risk failure to incorporate total quality into their curricula if enrollments in total quality–related courses become problematic.

Schools that wish to make total quality a permanent body of knowledge in their curricula can preserve the integrity of what they are trying to do in these areas by one or both of the following responses.

• Repackage quality courses by explicitly introducing reengineering and making it clear that reengineering and total quality draw on the same body of principles. We can keep nearly all the content of our total quality courses while repackaging those courses as reengineering-related courses. The advantage of this response is immediate. Enrollments are restored, intellectual integrity is maintained, and students and employers are well served. The disadvantage is a switch in packaging and labeling dictated by what may turn out to be a passing fad of reengineering.

• Rethink traditional business fields—policy, marketing, accounting, finance, and so on—from the perspective of total quality, and expose students to total quality principles as they take core courses in these areas. This response is difficult because it requires that professors in these areas rethink their courses from a total quality perspective. I am not sanguine that this will happen soon enough or thoroughly enough to help us with quality enrollment problems in the near future.

As a total quality instructor in a business school, my own approach has been to make sense of the interrelations of total quality, downsizing, and reengineering in the various courses that I teach. To that end I have developed two models of how these areas are related. These have worked well for me and for my students thus far.

Total Quality Reengineering

Figure 1 shows a triangle wherein the areas are defined as follows:

• Total quality is "defining and improving what is essential" in business.

• Downsizing is "eliminating the nonessential" in business.

• Reengineering is "building the essential out of new materials" in business.

All three concepts share the same principles or body of knowledge but each applies it differently. Total quality defines what is essential and how to continually improve it; downsizing uses that definition to eliminate nonessentials; and reengineering builds on total quality to come up with new ways of organizing work.

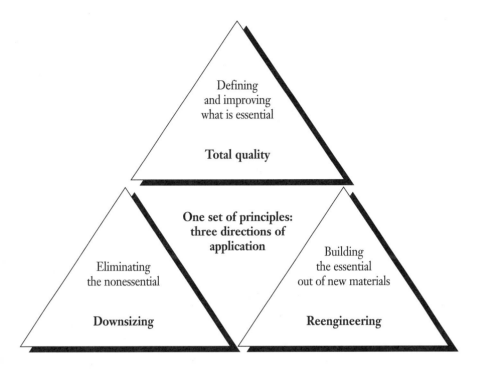

Figure 1. Total quality reengineering.

Reengineering and Total Quality in One Integrated Model

Figure 2 shows a model of 24 approaches to total quality used around the world. It is the result of research in a number of Japanese, U.S., Swedish, German, French, and British companies. In particular, notice these approaches.

- *Process architecting,* approach 13 in the figure, is what the current vendors and literature refer to as reengineering.

- *Process improvement,* approach 14, is what total quality calls continuous improvement plus the discontinuous stretch goals: the leap improvements sought by policy deployment and other programs in total quality.

- *Process deployment automation,* approach 15, is a more advanced extension of reengineering than currently offered by any reengineering vendor, but it is being done by two corporations.

- *Process execution automation,* approach 16, is the automation of approaches 13–15 (as contrasted with simple automation of direct work processes).

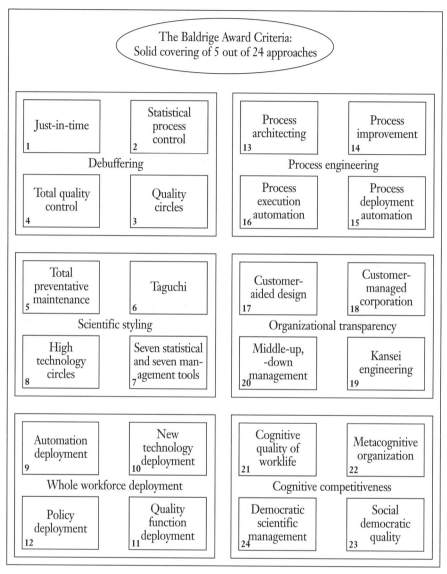

Figure 2 presents the 24 quality approaches of the global quality model. The Baldrige Award covers 5 of the 24 approaches with some degree of thoroughness. Again, this is very much because the Baldrige Award was designed to assess companies beginning their quality journeys; no one pretended that the Baldrige Award would be a good assessment instrument of companies in Japan with a 30-year track record since winning the Deming Prize, for example.

From the book *Global Quality* published by ASQC Quality Press and Irwin Professional Publishing.

Figure 2. Reengineering and TQM in one integrated model.

I like the perspective of Figure 2 because it joins total quality and reengineering in one overall model showing both the distinct differences and distinct contributions of each. I also like it because it correctly locates reengineering work as fitting in after a sequence of total quality initiatives that are necessary if reengineering is to succeed. This is supported by research by Kim Cameron and others that I refer to in more detail later. Figure 2 is further elaborated in *Global Quality*, published in 1993 by ASQC Quality Press and Business One Irwin.[1]

I like also the perspective of Figure 1 because it shows how one body of principles can underlie techniques so apparently distinct—at least in the minds of advocates—as downsizing, reengineering, and total quality.[2]

Students find Figures 1 and 2 to be powerful road maps for understanding and organizing thinking about management.

A Tale of Three Companies

To test our understanding of reengineering, let's consider three actual company scenarios and ask which of the three scenarios corresponds to reengineering and which is best.

• Company M asked a purchasing manager to do the same work better, allowed her to organize her staff into problem-solving teams, watched as over a two-year period the teams came up with and implemented 3310 improvements in purchasing operations, and found as a result that work formerly done by 250 people was now done by 5, with the surfeit employees reassigned elsewhere in the company.

• Company F benchmarked its purchasing functions with that of a competitor (Company M), found it was using 250 people to do what 5 people did in the competitor, asked its purchasing manager to do something about this gap, allowed the purchasing manager to arrange detailed benchmarking visits with that competitor, found the new purchasing system did with 5 people what was formerly done with 250, with the surfeit employees reassigned.

• Company V hired a consultant to reengineer core processes, observed the consultant suggesting the purchasing process be reengineered, assisted as the consultant formed a team of consultants with company workers to reengineer that process, watched as key assumptions about doing business were undone in the analysis done by that reengineering team, found as a result that what was formerly done by 250 employees was done by 5 in the new design, with the surfeit employees reassigned.

Which of these three approaches is reengineering? The first is clearly total quality, in that quality improvement teams worked in the standard way to achieve the result. The second is also clearly total quality, in that benchmarking was used to achieve the result. Only the third is clearly reengineering. Why?

It is interesting and revealing that we reach this judgment because of the involvement of an outside consultant. I shall return to this point later.

Which of these three approaches is best? When I pose the question to students, I get ferocious arguments. Some insist that the first, Company M, approach is better because it empowers much of the workforce and it self-generates major change. Others insist that the third approach, Company V, is better because it identifies past assumptions and breaks them. Others insist that the middle approach, Company F, is best because it opens the narcissistic company culture to outside models and learning.

My view is that the first approach produces as a by-product a workforce competent at improving itself; the second approach, a willingness to learn from outsiders; the third approach, an intellectual model of assumptions worth breaking.

In my view, good reengineering, then, is reengineering that preserves all three of these by-products: a self-improving workforce, capability for learning from outsiders, and increasing clarity about outmoded past assumptions.

Reengineering that leaves out any one of these three is weaker than reengineering that combines all three. The lesson: *only total quality forms of reengineering are worth doing.*

You may be interested in noting that Company M is Mazda, Company F is Ford Motor Co., and Company V is Volvo. Two of these three achieved the same end point using quality circles and benchmarking that the third achieved using reengineering. (I used the same set of numbers in all three examples in order to focus on the main question. In reality Ford has far more employees involved than Mazda, which in turn had more than Volvo.)

Origins of Reengineering

The word *reengineering* provides an important clue to the origin of reengineering. The *re* is the clue. Something had to have been engineered in the first place. The first conference proceeding with reengineering in its title that I could find was produced in 1983. The *re* in that conference's title referred to reengineering software applications. People within the software community were combining three or four software applications from related sections of a business and reengineering them as one overall application. System integration companies did this kind of reengineering until 1989 without attracting attention or interest from business at large.

Why, then, was reengineering as software integration so little noticed, while reengineering of business processes today attracts such wide attention? All through the 1980s chief information officers (CIOs) in Fortune 200 companies annually traipsed across the hall to visit chief executive officers (CEOs) and apologize for the $70 million or so a year that the corporation spent on computing that had done nothing discernible to improve productivity. Each year the CEOs demanded an explanation, and each year the CIOs said the same thing: meeting tens of thousands of small requests for enhanced information capabilities was expensive, but it could not be expected to produce much bang-for-the-buck. CEOs listened to this without really hearing, understanding, or believing it.

Then, somewhere around 1989, CEOs began to grasp the meaning. When the usual annual excuse was offered, suddenly and unaccountably, the CEO understood the excuse, patted the CIO on the back, and made available $100 million with which to reengineer major processes across departmental and organization chart boundaries. The CIOs were astonished. What had happened?

What had happened is total quality thinking had reached the CEOs and convinced them of a process view of the business that allowed them, for the first time, to make sense of the annual CIO excuse about why major investments in computation were producing no productivity results. So total quality saved the CIOs and allowed reengineering to emerge from their previous frustrations with information management functions.

Unfortunately, the technical biases of CIOs caused 80 percent or more of initial reengineering projects to fail. System integration companies, also strongly technically biased, failed in reengineering for the same reason.

Development of Reengineering

With this background about the origins of reengineering we can examine its roots. Its intellectual roots include

- Total quality, which defines what process management is about.

- Sociotechnical systems stemming from the Tavistock Institute's 1948 work in redesigning coal mining in Britain. Autonomous work teams developed there and later a technique—variance analysis—of looking at how upstream errors generated downstream further errors in processes was created.

- Information systems and, in particular, the 1991 development of organizational computing. This is a subspecies of computational sociality—a systematic examination of how organizations can be treated as computers with arrays of parallel processors who happen to be human beings.

Organizational learning and culture are also given some lip service by vendors of reengineering vendors, but they have played a minor role.

Several business practices have contributed to reengineering.

• Total quality changed businesses into processes to be managed and improved. This began long before reengineering came along and was independent of it.

• Application integration by system-integrator companies that attempted to view larger components of the business than those shown as boxes on organization charts and to create applications that supported these larger components.

• The decrease of the cost of computation until nearly all products and processes could include computational support. Further, the cellular telecommunications industry lowered the cost of coordination so that much more coordination could be done at the same cost. (Without low-cost coordination, autonomous work groups create more initiatives than people can coordinate, thus placing limits on what they can accomplish.)

• Global competition exposed many complacent managements to lean foreign firm competitors, creating an incentive to reexamine work practices throughout the business.

Failures and Successes

Press observations about reengineering produce a paradoxical picture. The following observations were all made in the June 20, 1994 issue of *Information Week*.

> Nearly 2/3s of re-engineering efforts will fail; only 16 percent of those doing re-engineering say at the end they are satisfied with their efforts; 68 percent of executives reported that re-engineering created new problems instead of solving old ones; total US spending on re-engineering will grow 20 percent a year for the next 3 years; of the $50 billion spent on re-engineering in the next 3 years, $40 billion will be spent on information systems; 42 percent of companies claiming to be doing re-engineering are actually tweaking existing processes; in spite of all this failure and risk, re-engineering will grow yearly for the next 3 years.[3]

The obvious question is why a method that fails the vast majority of the time, as does reengineering, is increasing in popularity? One explanation is the self-interest of two consulting industries.

• Management consultants have found reengineering easier to market and implement than total quality was; it fits American biases better (more on this later).

- System houses have found reengineering an excellent way to get companies to pay for major new information systems without seeing that that is what they are paying for.

Consulting companies can make money even when techniques they promote fail. Their marketing power apparently suffices to sell products with an 80 percent failure rate.

Implementation of Reengineering

Another recent study of reengineering is one I conducted the last year and a half, in which I looked at the processes of doing reengineering used by 46 consultants in reengineering services.[4] I found six subprocesses of the reengineering process itself. Most consultants offer four of these; only two consultants offered all six. These subprocesses were

- Launching reengineering

- Designing the new process

- Transitioning to the new process arrangements

- Doing work the new designed way

- Initiating reengineering regularly or when certain events occur

- Renewing the new process at regular intervals

Key success factors in doing the reengineering process included

- Putting experienced product development team leaders as heads of the reengineering effort.

- Applying product development phase gates to the reengineering product design process. Product development bounds risks by requiring that particular criteria be met before moving from concept phase to design phase to pilot phase (hence the term *phase gate*), and so forth. This prevents the mindset that any problem that crops up can be handled later in the process, a disaster for both product development and reengineering.

- Using quality metrics for each subprocess of the reengineering process.

- Using the design subprocess and transition subprocess to incrementally embody the values and tools of the new process design (while expanding team membership to include many future employees of the new process being designed). "Incrementally embodying values and tools" of the intended outcome means refers to the process of designing new ways of doing things and the process of transitioning the workforce to learning and doing them. Both processes are managed so that gradually, as it becomes clear that such and such a tool will be used in the new design and such and such a social arrangement will be used, these new tools and arrangements are embodied to do the rest of the design and transitioning process.

A recent article by T. Davenport has lamented that failure in reengineering to involve all the new workforce in the design of the new work arrangements leads to training lapses, design flaws, and the failure to properly implement the new processes.[5]

The idea of elites planning a new work way for the masses may itself be an error. It may indeed be possible for the masses to plan a new work way for themselves, applying two new materials (*materials* includes, but is not limited to, technologies) of reengineering itself: design workshops using management by events and workflow computing.

Six key decisions of doing reengineering were found, each of which needs a reasoned basis.

• When to initiate reengineering.

• What performance the new process should shoot for.

• Which new arrangements of work are best for going beyond past performance.

• Which new materials (again, including but not limited to technologies) to use to realize core process functions.

• Which aspects of each new material to use.

• The priority among alternative ways that any one new material is used. For example, one new material might be electronic meeting mediation groupware software. Such software can provide tools to facilitate typical meeting processes, such as brainstorming or weighted voting; it can also provide automatic workflow execution of action items from meetings. Which of these two—meeting processes or workflow execution—has higher priority in the new process design?

Why Is Reengineering Needed?

The proponents of reengineering say all businesses need reengineering. Their fundamental argument is as follows: the organizational form of nearly all businesses is based on assumptions about the division of labor in workforces that come from the scientific management tradition started by Frederick Winslow Taylor,* assumptions that are now out of date. Since the assumptions are out of date, all businesses need the same solution.

––––––––––
*Principles of scientific management.

What are these assumptions? Writers on reengineering agree on the following.

• Organize work into separate departments each specializing in a certain type of knowledge. This kept businesses simple for the founders to manage, but blocked response to changes in customer wants.

• Make jobs small and narrow. This permitted illiterate workforces to master tasks quickly, but current workers have higher capabilities.

• Centralize control. This was needed when jobs are narrow and workers uneducated, but it leads to a communication process that seems slow today.

• Reward primarily those at the top of the organization. Employees were thought of as machinery; only owners were persons, but today's knowledgeable workers do not accept this proposition.

If these assumptions are true of your business or your process, it is argued that you need to reengineer it on a foundation of different assumptions. The different assumptions amount to something very similar to the assumptions of advanced total quality work in Japan. Professor Kawase at Keio University, has suggested an end point vision toward which all total quality tends—the line-centered organization ideal—that amounts very much to reversing the four assumptions just given.

Kawase says that sales, service, and product development make money for corporations, while executives, line management, and staff are costs, though they get preferential salaries, perks, facilities, and deference. In other words, current organizations reward those who do not add value to customers more than they reward those who do. Kawase defines the line-centered organization as one that plots out a 40-year transition of the functions of the three non-value-adding groups to the new line, which embraces sales, service, and product development.[6] Each group—sales, service, and product development—internally performs the needed functions of executives, line management, and staff.

Much of the confusion about the relation of reengineering to total quality comes from a fallacious argument made by reengineering proponents trying to differentiate reengineering from total quality. Hammer and Champy make the following three statements.

• Re-engineering does what total quality cannot.

• Quality programs work within the framework of the company's existing processes.

• Re-engineering seeks break throughs by discarding existing processes and replacing them.[7]

The last statement is partially true; the first two are false. The experience of advanced quality programs around the world supports my position. In the book cited above, Hammer and Champy point to the purchasing functions of Mazda and Ford (discussed earlier) as examples of reengineering. They do not point out that Mazda's astonishingly effective purchasing function was the result of a quality circle effort that went beyond the framework of current processes and that Ford's was the result of quality benchmarking. In other words, Hammer and Champy's examples of reengineered processes include the results of two common total quality approaches. These two reengineering-via-quality approaches provide fast and powerful routes to radical productivity improvement today. Mazda's approach deepens standard quality problem solving with good root-cause analysis and does so in an effort that focuses on problems shared across three or more departments. Ford's approach relies heavily on the benchmarking approach that is credited with much of Xerox's revival in the 1980s.

At present, there is little evidence that reengineering (taken through implementation) is faster than these two quality approaches, but there is much evidence that the quality approaches have a smaller failure rate than reengineering (total quality suffering a 50 percent failure rate in common citations, while reengineering is cited as suffering a 75 percent to 80 percent failure rate).

So there are two routes to fast major leaps in productivity and quality: several of the quality approaches (when using deeper problem solving and causal analysis) and reengineering.

Why do reengineering proponents denigrate total quality in favor of reengineering? I offer two explanations.

• In some companies, as time goes on, there are smaller and smaller paybacks from quality improvement teams. This happens because, as quality improvement spreads across a company, root-cause analyses get beyond low-hanging fruit harvested from the removal of obvious waste and start dealing with problems of major processes. These problems are more deep-seated. They reflect conflicts between quality improvement and the career dynamics of upper middle management, which ultimately are threatened by total quality. Many quality programs come to a stop when they begin to confront the realities of upper–middle management career systems.

The cure is to deepen problem solving, to ally executives with middle management, and to reengineer. Deepening problem solving involves Deming's original 1950 insights into how the workplace was a system, not a bunch of jobs. Deming's principle of distribution of causes asserted that local symptoms of a problem are often far from root causes, which are diffused widely in the system that management is responsible for.[8] For example, an unlubricated bolt in a machine is caused by poor training of newly hired employees, wrong incentives for upper–middle management, and misspecification of machine tool control systems with vendors.

Deming also offered a principle of distribution of solutions. Solutions should not necessarily be applied at the location at which a particular root cause is spotted. Real solutions should be widely distributed throughout the workplace and various dimensions of work itself. Deming's two principles of distribution help define what I mean by "deepening problem solving" for making the total quality improvement framework match reengineering in scope and depth.

In addition to deepening of causal analysis in quality improvement teams, there are at least two other quality approaches that achieve leap improvements toward stretch objectives, such as tripling patents in a year or doubling international sales in a year. One is policy deployment (sometimes referred to as *hoshin kanri*), which tries to deploy stretch goals through a whole workforce in a one-year planning cycle. The other is metacognitive corporation work, which achieves the same-sized increments in the cognitive process capabilities of a corporation in one-, three-, or five-year efforts.

• The second force denigrating total quality in favor of reengineering comes from what appears to be an eight-year life cycle of new ideas in the management consulting industry. A study of 41 new management approaches promoted by the management consulting industry over the last 20 years by A. Huczynski confirmed this eight-year life cycle.[9] The first two years are spent in educating the market: the middle four years, in selling the idea to the Fortune 200 at substantial profit; and the last two years, in winding down the idea in favor of a successor idea.

Total quality fits this pattern. It was picked up in 1985 by the major general consulting firms, and by 1992 they were about finished profiting from it, so they were anxious to change to reengineering. By 1993, after years of actively promoting total quality for industry, they switched sides. They began to say that total quality is over the hill and that reengineering is what to do instead.

I believe that this history reflects a paradox in general management consulting. Only the clients who take up a new idea during the first three years of its eight-year life cycle achieve competitive advantage over other Fortune 200 competitors; it amounts to a three- to five-year head start. But in the remaining years of the eight-year cycle, the other competitors do apply the idea and catch up. There is no longer a competitive advantage in application of the idea.

It is not true that total quality is over the hill; it is true that consulting companies must make you believe that it is over the hill in order to sell newer services. It is not true that reengineering is better than total quality; it is true that consulting companies must make companies believe that it is true in order to sell you reengineering as a new service.

There are two other related factors: (1) Total quality has apparently become unpopular in many organizations; and (2) reengineering minimizes the need for long-term constancy of purpose, which is Deming's very first point. It appeals to what I call American national neuroses, and will be discussed further.

Many in the total quality community have been puzzled by an apparent loss of momentum from the developments of the 1980s. What has happened? Are the quality principles no longer valid? Not at all! What has happened is a result of the free advertising, first provided, then taken away, by the management consulting industry. From 1985 until 1992 the capabilities of total quality were exaggerated (and the demands it imposed for successful implementation were understated) as the management consulting industry built up total quality consulting practices. Abruptly in 1993 the management consulting industry dropped promotion of total quality and switched to promotion of reengineering.

Practitioners in industry and professors in business schools alike have been confused and have even come to doubt the worth and efficacy of total quality. They need not do so; quality endures; its best practitioners defeat competitors. The only change is the free advertising that quality got from consulting companies is now gone, replaced by counterquality advertising for reengineering.

This leads us to a deeper understanding of reengineering and of why it is being ballyhooed. Reengineering can be interpreted as the revenge of our national neuroses on our economic productivity. Throughout the 1980s the traditional organizational design consultants in the United States lost consulting jobs to crusty old statisticians and quality practitioners (gurus) and their many disciples—quality professionals within companies and independent, usually small, consultants.

Robert Cole in a recent *California Management Review* article explained why the total quality statisticians succeeded in implementing many participatory management practices, which the organizational design consultants had promoted for 40 years with little success. The key was that the statisticians offered precise measures and methods that were not offered by the organizational design consultants.[10]

Total quality challenged what I call our national neuroses. The emphasis on incremental continuous improvement challenged our preference for home run solutions. The emphasis on mobilization of the whole workforce for problem solving challenged our elitism. The emphasis on reward for implementations that are carefully monitored and managed by fact challenged our conceptual bias for rewarding great ideas. The emphasis on sustained careful measurements of the effects of innovations challenged our bias for spectacular launches that are not carefully evaluated afterwards.

Reengineering reverses all this. Reengineering is elitist, assigning the major role to outside elite consultants. Reengineering is home run–oriented, redesigning from scratch, totally and quickly. Reengineering is conceptually biased, valuing brilliant process analyses more highly than hard fought battles in the trenches of implementation. Reengineering is launch biased, the leading reengineering project managers and consultants receiving promotions long before the success or failure of the newly launched process is clear.

Total quality calls for blood, toil, tears, and sweat, that is, for remedying our national weaknesses. Reengineering appeals to our national weaknesses and deepens them. Reengineering consultants readily admit that reengineering markets easily and well compared to total quality. They say things like, "Quality was a pain to implement—mobilizing whole workforces and that sort of thing; reengineering is much neater," and "Americans got bored with quality—all that incremental small stuff, whereas reengineering is a big-risk-and-bold-change effort."

What Reengineering Offers Higher Education

The primary approaches to reengineering (I count 15 overall) all work with organizational architecture. Think of the Chicago skyline. At first buildings were built of stone and could at most reach six or eight stories with thick bulky walls. Then reinforced concrete became available. Suddenly buildings became taller and leaner: 10 stories with thin walls. Then elevators appeared and skyscrapers were built, 80 and 100 stories tall. With each new material or technology, old well-known human needs could better met, and new human needs appeared, some that were met and some not.

In the same way, we can examine a process and its key functions and suggest ways of doing those functions (ways of building them out of new materials) that produce new organizational designs. This is what I call the organizational architecture approach to reengineering. Before new materials are suggested, however, reengineering systematically breaks past assumptions about how and for what processes are done. Earlier in this paper I described briefly this assumption breaking.

The idea of assumption breaking is simple: list the assumptions of the current form of a process and systematically break them, coming up with new designs of the organization for each assumption broken. Let's examine how assumption breaking might be applied to the reengineering of three higher education processes: software education, business education of MBAs, and getting doctorates in business.

Software Education

Here are some assumptions and ways in which they might be broken, replaced by new approaches.

- *Assumption:* Higher education is nonprofit.

  New approach: Design the combined homework/classwork of the course so it is a sellable product and include market work as valid course content of all software courses.

- *Assumption:* Software creation is an art.

  New approach: Structure each software class as a software factory of 20 two-student teams using a total quality software construction process.

- *Assumption:* Work and talent are individual.

  New approach: Assign students to software factory teams specializing in aspects of the final product such as interface, object library, and data/knowledge base.

- *Assumption:* Software construction is a separate domain from marketing, finance, and other traditional business areas.

  New approach: Use a total quality process for software production, including total quality methods of specification development, software production, and application delivery.

- *Assumption:* Classrooms are physical entities.

  New approach: Design an electronic and video-enabled classroom that supports students at remote sites who electronically share a single class, with simultaneous video/audio. Thus, for example, local government offices, corporation labs, and university classrooms could participate in a single such class.

- *Assumption:* Syllabi and teaching plans are paper documents.

  New approach: Develop software that coaches students in class through particular analysis procedures and that coordinates between-class subgroup work by students, finally selling this software after it is perfected by use in a number of courses.

The instructional process in software as found in computer science departments treats software in a narrow technical way that cripples student business abilities and ignores customer requirements for actual software functioning in favor of abstract technical developments in software. As with reinforced concrete and elevators, we have new materials and technology to draw upon.

One of the new materials out of which we can build course processes is some workflow software available as groupware. It can be used to coordinate many student teams working on one overall project/product, including coordination of subgroup meetings outside of class, research visits off-site at companies, and library work. This allows all the students to work on different assignments while staying tightly coordinated. And, for the most part, there is no need for intervention by the professor. This was not possible in the past without heavy professorial involvements that were not forthcoming.

MBA Education

- *Assumption:* A particular course must be taught in a particular city at any one time.

   New approach: One course taught simultaneously in six cities around the globe, so that the course is within two hours plane travel of all company locations around the world, something no university can now do.

- *Assumption:* Faculty members teach courses in their own individual ways.

   New approach: An international team of faculty codesign courses for simultaneous teaching around the world in six cities using common measures of course process and output quality.

- *Assumption:* Companies send employees to a university for training.

   New approach: Large companies train their own employees, worldwide.

- *Assumption:* Normally, people go to college in the decade following high school graduation.

   New approach: The decade-college concept of education, the equivalent of a full master's degree of education every decade (at the boundary between decades, ages 18–22, 28–32, 38–42, and so on) through one's career, with curricula tailored to the career needs of each decade.

The global Internet is a new technology out of which processes of course construction can be codesigned by a distributed faculty without the need for much face-to-face meeting. Motorola University has a vision of such a global faculty, putting the universities of the world gradually out of business because of the refusal of universities to respond to corporate customer requirements for globally delivered, consistent education.

Getting Doctorates in Business

- *Assumption:* Doctoral students can research only problems small enough for individuals to tackle.

  New approach: Large groups of doctoral students tackle major problems and do one dissertation on a major problem together, combining people from several departments and universities.

- *Assumption:* Individuals do scientific research.

  New approach: Groups combining students from several different fields and universities do one dissertation together.

- *Assumption:* Research results are judged by peer review.

  New approach: Dissertations are examined by two committees: one of academics, and one of practitioners.

- *Assumption:* Doctoral research is funded largely by universities and government grants.

  New approach: Dissertations are funded by the practitioner committee members' corporations.

- *Assumption:* Each student gets a doctorate in one field or discipline at a time.

  New approach: Dissertation coauthors are examined on the contribution of their own field to the group dissertation, but also on the contributions of the other fields involved. One new material for coordinating group doctoral projects is workflow software available as groupware. This allows people at five or more sites to work as if together at one site, if a few actual face-to-face meetings are included.

Discussion

These three examples provide simple applications of a few reengineering principles to higher education. They emphasize the importance of articulating the working assumptions that lie behind current education practice. When the assumption is out in the open, new approaches—a few of which will turn out to be useful—spring into view. Many possible innovations in education can result when the full panoply of reengineering materials and technology and assumption-breaking exercises are applied.

Reengineering in higher education must be clear about the organizational level at which processes are to be worked on and redesigned. I distinguish seven such levels for reengineering of higher education.

- The overall societal process for handling knowledge; for example, the school-to-work transition program of the U.S. Department of Labor.

- The process of tertiary education; for example, Motorola University creating a global faculty and university structure to replace traditional universities.

- The core processes of our universities; for example, just-in-time textbook composition of custom textbooks by professors from their desktop computers with software automatically charging out copyright fees and permissions through E-mail.

- The core processes of our disciplines of knowledge; for example, electronic journals on the Internet replacing slow-to-compose paper journals.

- The process of getting a Ph.D.; for example, group doctorates supported by workflow software across multiple disciplines and universities.

- The process of going to undergraduate school; for example, teaching doctoral-level research skills to college freshmen and developing publishable under-graduate theses.

- The process of classes; for example, groupware sharing of one class by remote sites in government, industry, and academia. At each of these levels waste reduction, root-cause analysis, assumption breaking, and new material replacement analysis can be done.

Although it may not at first appear obvious, higher education has some advantages for doing reengineering. Many of the drivers of change in delivery of education are being developed and researched in universities. Scholars who switch to electronic development and delivery of research put competitive pressure on traditional scholars. Scholars dislike the bureaucracy that they have, but the new materials of reengineering promise even less bureaucracy in the future. Scholars are beginning to study reengineering of other societal institutions. A few pioneer universities have applied total quality to improving research, teaching, community service, and administration, thereby preparing the way for reengineering. The collaborative nature of scholarly work across national and institutional boundaries, united by disciplinary concerns, fits well the emerging groupware collaborative technologies.

In sum, reengineering is not so much hard for academia to do as it is hard for academia to imagine. There is an academic tradition of ignoring facts about academics. Consider the following:

- Such research as has been done on the subject shows at best weak correlation of grades with career outcomes, yet we award grades and employers take them seriously. Why do we maintain a signal system that manifestly is not related to outcomes we seek?

• More extensive research shows that nearly no one except other scholars read the leading academic journals in business, yet tenure decisions are based heavily on peer review of publications in academic journals. Why do we treat our peers as our principal customer, at the risk of loss of respect and trust by society at large?

• Research shows well-articulated macrostructures make lecture content better retained at three- and five-year intervals, yet practically no professors know what a macrostructure is and optimize it for student retention. Walter Kintsch and Teun A. Van Dijk at the University of Colorado Center for Research on Intellectual Behavior documented this in a series of studies over a 20-year period.

The knowledge modeling chapter of *Global Quality* presents this use of macrostructures. *Macrostructures* are inferred themes common to references in language—they are the "what is being talked about" that unites clauses in a sentence or sentences in a paragraph.

• Why do we develop research on better knowledge transmission and then entirely ignore it in our teaching?

These contradictions are not unlike the paradoxes of ineffective business processes: for example, purchasing operations that ensure highest prices from suppliers through low nominal prices accompanied by quality defects that vastly increase costs of using the supplies. Academia's need for reengineering is urgent.

That is, however, not the same as saying that current consultants in reengineering services will actually help if they are hired by academia. With a self-announced 80 percent failure rate, reengineering consultant vendors are hardly a sure bet. I interviewed consultants in 46 firms and found that fewer than 2 percent of them could name the major steps in their own company's announced reengineering process. Fewer than 5 percent of company employees on reengineering teams could agree very roughly on names for the major steps of the reengineering process they had just been through. No consulting firm had a method of getting beyond past process capabilities other than to break assumptions, and only two firms out of 46 had serious methods for development of new materials and technology.

I did find a few startling reengineering successes, however. In one company, seven employees saved $100 million a year in one process by making one fundamental change—inserting one new material at a key step, at a total cost of less than $1.5 million and one year of work. Kim Cameron is one of the first academics to do serious research of reengineering, downsizing, and total quality. He found that only companies that established a total quality culture well before downsizing or reengineering succeeded with their downsizing or reengineering projects.[11]

In one sentence: only total-quality reengineering is likely to succeed. In my doctoral dissertation, I found several factors that predict faculty reaction (support or resistance) to total quality and reengineering: faculty leadership, faculty mission, faculty polity, faculty professionalism, faculty method, and faculty mode of work.[12] All of these served as barriers to implementation of quality and reengineering, and only two of them served as enablers. Any attempt to implement total quality or reengineering on campus that does not articulate and plan for their interaction with these factors will either marginalize by omitting faculty concerns or produce revolts by directly attacking key faculty values.

Although new information technologies are the leading new material mentioned for reengineering, in part because of commercial self-interests of systems companies using reengineering as a banner to sell complex software applications that people would not otherwise buy, there are other materials and technologies just as radical and even more powerful. Some of these are social, some organizational learning systems, and so forth.

Management by events is one such learning system. Management by events is having large numbers of people in mass workshop events do work that formerly was done by a few or by elites across long spans of time. Research shows that, after all, processes are not a good replacement for departments, even though nearly all reengineering vendors assume departments are bad and processes are the answer. It turns out departments were not the problem, but turfism was. Suboptimizing territoriality and empire building diverted departments from customer concerns.

Much evidence for this comes from companies having long experience with process management systems. Examination of companies with process management systems more than 10 years old shows that processes become little empires every bit as disruptive to customer service as departments ever were. The solution is to counteract territoriality and empire building, whether in departments or processes. There should not be blind dependence on processes as the one right way to organize business forever, as reengineering consultants and some quality consultants tend to advocate.

Similarly, there should not be blind dependence on two other widely-advocated cure-alls.

- *Self-managing work teams.* There is not one form of human polity that is right for every function and for all time.

- *Advanced information systems.* These exchange largely concepts, not beliefs and commitments. It is beliefs and commitments that get implementations done well.

Some Positive Guidelines

I offer some suggested guidelines for successful reengineering and a set of criteria for measuring the quality with which an organization does reengineering. Here are the guidelines.

- Establish a total quality culture before attempting reengineering, or reengineering will almost surely fail.

- Establish a total quality process of doing reengineering including metrics of the quality with which you do each of the six subprocesses.

- When launching reengineering, measure and counteract specific national neuroses pandered to by the reengineering idea.

- In doing reengineering, counteract the turfism that makes departments harmful rather than depending blindly on processes as a right answer.

- Replace departments with processes, and processes with events wherever possible.

Here are some of the 19 metrics for measuring the quality of a reengineering project presented in *Competent Reengineering*.

- Are all six subprocesses of the reengineering process designed on total quality grounds with good process management applied to them during reengineering?

- Are there formal approaches to six key decisions of reengineering?

- Are the new types of material for building businesses examined for each key process step?

- Are total quality ways of improving processes—I list 40 of them in the book—being applied before assumption breaking is applied?

- Are the design and transition subprocesses of reengineering managed so as to create incrementally the new tools and culture of the new version of the process?

- Are total quality principles of good process management followed in the management of each of the six subprocesses of reengineering?

Satisfying these metrics could provide a good start in moving from an 80 percent failure rate to an 80 percent success rate for reengineering.

Notes

1. R. T. Greene, *Global Quality: A Synthesis of the World's Best Management Methods* (Milwaukee, Wis.: ASQC Quality Press; Homewood, Ill.: Business One Irwin, 1993).

2. R. T. Greene, *Competent Reengineering: Advice, Warnings, and Recipes from Eye Witnesses*, Addison-Wesley Series on Organizational Design (Reading, Mass.: Addison-Wesley, 1995).

3. "Who Should Actually Do the Re-Engineering?", *Information Week*, 20 June 1994, pp. 20–23.

4. Greene, *Competent Reengineering*.

5. T. Davenport, "Don't Forget the Workers," *Information Week*, 8 August 1994, p. 70.

6. T. Kawase, *The Line Centered Organization* (Methuen, Mass.: GOAL/QPC, 1992).

7. M. Hammer and J. Champy, *Reengineering the Corporation* (New York: HarperBusiness, 1993), 50–51.

8. W. E. Deming, *Out of the Crisis* (Cambridge, Mass.: MIT Center for Advanced Engineering Research, 1986).

9. A. Huczynski, *Management Gurus* (London: Routledge, 1993).

10. R. Cole, P. Bacdayan, and J. White, "Quality, Participation, and Competitiveness," *California Management Review* 35, no. 3 (1993).

11. K. Cameron, S. Freeman, and A. Mishra, "Downsizing and Redesigning Organizations," in *Organizational Change and Redesign*, ed. G. Huber and P. Glick (New York: Oxford, 1993).

12. R. T. Greene, "Predictors of Adoption of TQM by Research Faculty: The Collision of Professionalization of Knowledge in the Academy with TQM's Concept of Deprofessionalizing Knowledge" Ph.D. diss., University of Michigan, 1994), 98.

Grassroots Total Quality in Higher Education: Some Lessons from Chicago

Harry V. Roberts
University of Chicago Graduate School of Business

Grassroots Versus Top-Down Total Quality

For implementation of total quality in any organization, it is usually recommended that there be strong leadership from the top. The idea is that the CEO (or other very senior manager) grasps the essentials of total quality; sees the desirability of applying them; has the technical knowledge and leadership skills needed to guide the deployment of total quality throughout the organization; and spends a substantial fraction of his or her own time on total quality implementation. In the 1980s, two CEOs in the business sector who exemplified this top-down approach were Robert Galvin of Motorola and David Kearns of Xerox.

A variation of this top-down approach comes to much the same thing. The total quality initiative begins in middle levels of the organization, then reaches the attention of the CEO or other very senior manager, who then exercises leadership from the top for subsequent deployment of total quality. Something like this happened at Procter & Gamble in the 1980s.

Even in the business sector, top-down quality is not commonplace, and it is certainly not widespread in higher education. A few of the applications of total quality to higher education in this book did start at or near the top, but many were initiated by that small scattering of faculty and staff quality champions who seem to be found on almost all campuses. I call these latter applications grassroots total quality. Grassroots applications often are not encouraged or even supported by top leaders; indeed the top leaders may even be unaware of them.

This paper argues that while top-down total quality is highly desirable for grass-roots quality, grassroots quality efforts can move ahead under less-favorable circumstances, including benign neglect by top leadership. Active encouragement, as illustrated in this paper, is, of course, better. Only active opposition from the top poses a fatal obstacle to grassroots total quality champions.

If top-down total quality is present, grassroots total quality is a valuable complement to the top-level efforts. Typically these efforts include extensive training, a quality council, and the deployment of quality improvement teams. The need for such a complement is suggested by the fact that leading total quality Japanese companies actively encourage and support top-down quality by two types of grassroots efforts.

- Quality control circles, or local teams, dedicated to quality improvement and improvement of the working environment

- Massive suggestion systems, in which large numbers of employee suggestions are implemented each year

Hence there is no need for quality champions to roll over and give up if the president or other academic leader does not directly command a college or university quality initiative. I shall report an educational case history in which much was accomplished when the dean of the Graduate School of Business at the University of Chicago felt that he had little time for personal involvement in total quality, but gave total and enthusiastic support to a series of local, grassroots, initiatives within the school.

I do not present the Chicago case history as a unique accomplishment, nor am I trying to vaunt the school at which I have taught for several decades. But the Chicago story suggests the range of innovations that can be achieved by grassroots initiatives in education and the ultimate limitations on how far grassroots initiatives can carry.

On Academic Organizational Culture

At Chicago, as well as in much of academia, there are two especially relevant aspects of the organizational culture, one unfavorable to total quality, and the other, favorable.

- *Unfavorable:* there is strong faculty commitment to academic research and teaching in specialized disciplines. Some specialization is necessary for research, and research is the new-product engine of higher education, but specialization makes cross-functional cooperation more difficult.

- *Favorable:* for the faculty and high-level administrators there is substantial freedom to make changes and considerable self-interest in making them.

Freedom to make changes is key to grassroots quality improvement. The organization must permit at least some degree of freedom in how individuals perform their own jobs and how small work groups function. The organizational culture must welcome, or at least not automatically oppose, experimentation and change. Fulfillment of this requirement can, by itself, permit substantial implementation of total quality because it can free up the enormous potential energy and reservoir of knowledge that exists at the grassroots level of any organization.

Self-interest also enters in. If employees—faculty or staff—can modify the way they work, they can hope to make their jobs less stressful and more satisfying. The prospects for success of total quality are greatest when all or most employees perceive total quality as something more than tears, toil, and sweat to be endured for the sake of organizational success.

The Chicago Story

Much of my story is concerned with the period 1983–1993, when John P. Gould was dean of the Graduate School of Business, but many of the important incidents occurred even earlier. Gould was in large measure carrying on a tradition set by deans who had preceded him.

Gould understood total quality very well, but there were cogent reasons that militated against his active personal leadership.

- There were no clear organization-endangering crises. The one serious challenge was met largely by a grassroots effort—the LEAD Program—by Deputy Dean Harry L. Davis, an effort that had Gould's full support.

- Fund-raising was an overriding organizational goal that absorbed an enormous share of Gould's time and effort during this period.

- Gould understood that in any university unit dedicated to research and scholarship, the academic CEO—dean or president—has less clout than the CEO of a business. A dean is more like the managing partner of a professional firm than the CEO of a company that makes and sells things for profit. It is even possible that intensive involvement by the dean could be counterproductive to the cause of total quality in the school.

- Gould made a major effort to convince the senior faculty that the school's academic excellence—research and teaching in the basic disciplines and functional areas—could actually be strengthened if simultaneous efforts were made to strengthen what he called the school's "business leadership." This effort complemented the grassroots total quality initiatives reported below.

The paper by Zangwill and Roberts in this volume, "Academic Leadership from the Top: Total Quality for Higher Education," shows that in some circumstances, some college and university leaders can assume active leadership in total quality. I do not know how often these circumstances prevail or how many leaders there are who can take advantage of them. My present purpose is only to show that top-level support and encouragement of grassroots quality can help enormously even in the absence of active involvement by those at the top.

Total quality has not bypassed higher education. Many colleges and universities, or units thereof, have attempted its implementation. The most common emphasis has been on the improvement of administrative rather than academic functioning. Professors are felt to be more resistant than administrators to improvement ideas coming from the business world, so it is often hoped that professors can be involved in total quality at some time in the indefinite future after administrative successes have illustrated the value of total quality. Three observations about this strategy are germane.

- Administrative improvement is not necessarily easy. University bureaucracies can be rigid. University career administrators (the contrast is with faculty who become involved in administration) are often treated as second-class citizens. They are much less free than are faculty to initiate improvements.

- If total quality succeeds in improving administrative support but does not touch the central academic functions, its contribution, though helpful, will have been marginal.

- As noted, professors have a strong self-interest in improving teaching and research, and individual professors often have substantial freedom to act on their own in doing so.

Professorial freedom is most apparent in research, in which innovation is highly esteemed and must largely come from individual innovations, large and small. (Later I will comment on possible contributions of total quality to research.) The business school at Chicago has long had a strong record of research innovation, dating back at least to the revolution in academic finance in the 1960s. The main academic focus in this paper, however, is on innovation in teaching and curriculum.

In the last 10 years Chicago, like many other business schools, has had several total quality champions who applied total quality ideas to teaching and, to a lesser degree, to curriculum design and administrative procedures. As I look back over a much longer period of time, it is now apparent to me that the total quality champions of recent years were preceded by innovative faculty members who, before the term *total quality* had been coined, were total quality champions in their own time.

For all these quality champions, present and past, the primary motivation was self-interest in more satisfying work.

The school's organizational culture had traditionally been highly favorable for grassroots efforts at improvement. Change and innovation had been considered as intrinsically desirable in research, and this carried over into teaching and curriculum. Finally, as explained earlier, Gould, following a long-established tradition, was invariably supportive of grassroots innovations.

Grassroots Improvements of Individual Courses

At Chicago, as at many business schools, there has been continuous improvement of teaching and curriculum even when there were no changes of course titles or descriptions. Professors want their courses to reflect the latest developments in their fields. As one colleague recently put it, "75 percent of the readings on my current reading list were not on my list three years ago." Professors also change teaching methodology. The case method is now used very widely at Chicago, even though Chicago has had an anticase reputation. The use of individual and group course projects has grown rapidly in almost all areas of the curriculum; examples are given in papers by Zangwill, Bateman and Roberts, and Becker in this volume.

Coordination of individual teaching innovations has been spotty. When it has occurred, it has been within individual fields, such as accounting, finance, or statistics, not between the different fields. Uncoordinated individual teaching innovations are not unmixed blessings because there is tension between individual teaching improvements in sections of courses and the desirability of standardization of curriculum. For example,

- If individual professors are continually but independently changing their own courses, the current best teaching practices will not automatically be diffused.

- The de facto curriculum that emerges from these individual changes may not be as well unified and coordinated as might be desirable.

My view is that, in the individualistic organizational culture of Chicago, formal coordination of individual faculty improvements would be very hard and there is much to be said for encouraging individual improvements and hoping that a good deal of informal coordination will occur.

Consider, for example, the question of course prerequisites. I think the desirability of careful alignment of prerequisites is often exaggerated. Even if one's current students have been exposed to a desired prerequisite at a propitious time, the effect has usually faded so much that one has to start nearly from scratch when that prerequisite is actually needed. (For example, in my statistics teaching, I have found that concepts like confidence intervals and statistical significance always have to be thoroughly reviewed, almost regardless of depth or intensity of previous exposure.) Student motivation for learning a prerequisite concept may be higher when it is seen that the concept is now going to be applied in a serious way. (Just-in-time training—introducing a topic when it is needed for application—has become thoroughly established in total quality implementation in the business world.)

New Elective Courses

At Chicago, the freedom to make changes extends beyond the freedom to modify existing courses. There has also been freedom to introduce new elective courses. (As shown later, it has also been easy to introduce new educational programs and even new administrative processes.)

For innovation through new elective courses to be possible, a high ratio of student elective courses to required core courses is essential. At Chicago, that ratio is greater than 1/1. Thus, as an example, from 1983 to 1993 over a dozen MBA elective courses in quality management were introduced, all the result of initiatives by individual faculty members or teams of two faculty. All proposed elective courses—quality or other—were approved by the Deans' office during those years.

Broader Innovations

Over the years, freedom and encouragement of change have led to many innovations that are broader than revisions of current courses or introduction of new elective courses using the same teaching modalities as existing courses. The following list provides illustrations. Several of the innovations on this list predate the 1983–1993 period in which conscious total quality activities began. No coverage of research innovations is included on the list.

- The first executive MBA program (1943)
- Avoidance of formal departments by disciplines (1956)
- Introduction of the meeting format of alternating Friday/Saturday all-day class meetings for the executive MBA program (early 1960s)
- Public course evaluations for all courses (1968)
- "Curriculum Guide" with up-to-date, detailed course descriptions of each section of each course, written by the instructor of that section (as contrasted with the "Announcements" with its short, uninformative, and seldom-changing official course descriptions) (1970)

- Computerized competitive bidding for sections of courses and employment interviews (1970s)

- Widespread use of interactive computing in courses, including the development of educational software (1971)

- The New Product Laboratory course, in which teams of students, coached by faculty, work with companies to develop new product ideas for commercial application (1978)

- The Weekend MBA program, a Saturday MBA program staffed by regular faculty, appealing to students from a broad area of the United States, who fly to Chicago once a week to take two classes a term (early 1980s)

- The research and teaching supplement (RATS), in which all faculty members are given budgets to be used at their own discretion for secretarial help, computers, professional dues, books, journals, professional travel, and the like (1984)

- The LEAD program—a major exercise of student empowerment to strengthen student action skills, as opposed to the intellectual skills stressed in the regular curriculum (1989)

- Systematic student involvement in improvement of administrative quality within the school, both in improvement projects in MBA courses to a Continuous Improvement Committee of students, an extra-curricular activity (1990)

- Laboratory course in management processes (1990)

- Training for faculty in presentation skills based on techniques developed in the business world by Bob Savard and Dick Beach (1990)

- Training for faculty in teaching based on a theater metaphor developed by Barbara Lane Brown in which the teacher plays three separate roles: playwright, director, and actor (1990)

- Senior scholar program for the Ph.D. program (1990)

- Laboratory course in organizational excellence, stressing total quality implementation in companies and nonbusiness organizations (1991)

- Laboratory course in application of TQM to teaching, curriculum development, and research (1991)

- Administrative staff training in total quality (1991)

- A suggestion system for students, faculty, and staff (1991)

Many individuals have contributed to these innovations. None of the innovations was seriously contested when introduced. Administrative approval was usually informal and casual. People just went ahead and acted. And all the innovations are consistent with the total quality theme of continual improvement.

Discussion

We now examine in more detail some of the innovations just listed as well as some other more specifically quality-related innovations.

Executive MBA Program

This was the creation of a single individual, Professor Willard Graham. It was successful from the start: there was a ready market and students found the program valuable for their careers. It was not imitated for two decades. It is the direct ancestor of the many executive MBA programs offered by business schools today, including Chicago.

Avoidance of Formal Departments by Disciplines

When W. Allen Wallis became dean in 1956, he and his associate dean, James H. Lorie, made a long-term plan for the school. One of the constraints they imposed was that the faculty should not become so large that formal departments by disciplines would become necessary. Although the faculty size has grown beyond what they envisaged, departments have never even been contemplated. The really essential functions of departments are performed informally. The purely bureaucratic functions have never appeared.

The Curriculum Guide

The "Curriculum Guide" is an interesting example of the ease of innovation. It resulted from a recommendation of a tentative draft of the Curriculum Review Committee of 1970. Long before the final committee report was prepared and approved, the deans of the school went ahead to implement this recommendation, because it seemed like, and has proven to be, a good idea.

RATS Program

The RATS program is also interesting. An administrative innovation, it was introduced by faculty during their service in the dean's office. RATS resulted in substantial reduction in overhead costs and a sharp alteration of the pattern of use of support resources for faculty. Most younger faculty, for example, opted for personal computers or workstations, often state-of-the-art, rather than secretaries. Bureaucratic procedures for authorization of faculty travel were eliminated.

RATS is also interesting because it has not been widely implemented elsewhere, even though faculty members from other schools are usually strongly attracted to the concept. This experience reinforces my earlier observation about the importance of freedom to experiment and to make changes as a prerequisite for grassroots total quality.

Public Course Evaluations and Improvement of Teaching

Since the late 1960s, the school has used student course evaluations with systematic public reporting of results. Just as examinations can make students uncomfortable, course evaluations can make professors uncomfortable. But faculty accept the course evaluations as the best generally available information about teaching effectiveness. Further, although I cannot prove it, I believe that teaching at Chicago is much better than it would have been in the absence of public course evaluations. Public evaluations encourage the faculty to treat students as if they are customers, whether or not the word *customer* is used. Also, faculty are competitive, so if their teaching ratings are going to be made public, they will try hard to get better ratings.

Introducing Total Quality into the Curriculum

We have seen that the introduction of total quality in elective courses at Chicago was made possible by the wide freedom of students to elect courses and by the minimal red tape for faculty who want to introduce new elective courses. As quality concepts became commonplace, there was some osmosis of total quality from quality electives into core courses, but the core curriculum has not been affected in any major way by the elective courses in total quality.

Another strategy for introducing total quality into the curriculum, represented by at least two other papers in this volume, is to work toward a unified core curriculum for all students, with total quality concepts appearing wherever they can effectively contribute. This unified core might even be team taught, as at the University of Tennessee, thus bringing in the cross-functional emphasis that is so much a part of modern total quality. For better or worse, however, the unified core would probably not be feasible in the organizational culture of Chicago where faculty specialization is so strong.

A third strategy, also consistent with total quality philosophy, would be an entirely elective curriculum from which students, aided by written and oral counseling, could assemble academic programs that seemed best to fit their own needs. This interesting suggestion, made informally by Stuart Greenbaum of Northwestern University, has not been implemented, so far as I know.

Students As Instruments of Change

All the Chicago quality elective courses mentioned earlier require at least one organizational quality improvement project of the student's choice. Some of these projects are team projects, some are individual. The project approach is another application of the principle of just-in-time education because students apply total quality ideas and methods as they learn them. Usually, students are able to make the necessary contacts and arrangements with the organizations where the projects are carried out. Included among these organizations have been units of the University of Chicago itself. We have found that MBA students can do surprisingly good practical work on quality improvement when they are given the responsibility for it.

Further discussion of quality improvement projects in courses is given in papers in this volume by Bateman and Roberts, Zangwill, and Becker. Other student improvement activities are illustrated in the next discussion.

Laboratory Courses and the LEAD Program

Former Deputy Dean Harry L. Davis started two major educational innovations—laboratory courses and the LEAD Program—that have strengthened the school's orientation toward total quality. The following descriptions were written by Davis.

Laboratory courses

> There has been rapid growth of laboratory courses in new product development, quality, and organizational consulting that involve teams of 10–12 students working on a broad general management assignment funded by a real client over a period of six months. The laboratories fundamentally shift the role of faculty from one of knowledge expert to one of learning design engineer and coach—and who, in these roles, support students' work at both an intellectual and emotional level. Working with students is the essence of the role.

LEAD

> [There] has been the introduction of a highly experiential, required leadership course for all 500 entering first year campus students that is created anew each spring by a group of 48 first year students and then facilitated by these same students during

the fall quarter. The LEAD Program, as it is known, is a major exercise of student empowerment to help them take personal responsibility for developing their action skills. All first year students work in cohorts of about 50 students each during the first quarter of their academic studies. Each cohort is assigned a team of four second-year students who facilitate activities and discussions around such topics as leadership, communication skills, and so forth. A faculty and staff member are assigned to each cohort and participate along with the first-year students.

Laboratory courses and LEAD harmonize well with total quality.

- They emphasize team effort.
- They represent student empowerment.
- Students are no longer passive recipients of wisdom.
- Students become responsible for applying what they know or are learning.
- Students have to accomplish things in the real world.

As Davis puts it in an internal document,

> Both . . . LEAD . . . and the management laboratories represent a very different model of education. . . . The objective of both initiatives is to get students to become self-sufficient learners in order to achieve higher levels of personal performance. . . .

One offshoot of LEAD was a suggestion forum that provides a mechanism to elicit and to act on student suggestions. Another was the student continuous improvement committee mentioned earlier.

Two-Way Fast Feedback

End-of-course evaluation questionnaires are useful, but they are general and the information is provided too late to benefit the class that fills them in. As a result of experimentation in the laboratory course for teaching, curriculum development, and research, it was discovered that a simple tool for grassroots improvement in teaching is the fast-feedback questionnaire, a way of systematically finding out what is and is not working in the classroom.

Using fast feedback, an instructor can make corrections as a course proceeds. The feedback questionnaires are short, simple, and easily tabulated. A number of faculty members use them frequently, some after every class meeting. As the faculty member gives feedback to students on the student feedback just received, a new channel of communication opens up, hence two-way fast feedback. There is no presumption that students can give faculty informed advice about what should be taught, but it has been learned that students are very capable of reporting when they are confused, bored, or skeptical. Further discussion of two-way fast feedback is given in Bateman and Roberts in this volume. Several other papers provide discussions of fast feedback.

Personal Quality

Bernard F. Sergesketter, formerly vice president of the central region of AT&T, has developed a simple tool called a personal quality checklist to apply total quality principles at the level of the individual job. I and other faculty members at Chicago have helped him during the last three years. The idea of the personal quality checklist is that one makes simple defect counts of failures to perform certain personal work processes in the way one desires. Analysis of past defect counts—usually intuitive graphical analysis based on a run chart—suggests ways of improving quality so that the defects are less likely to occur in the future. An overview of personal quality checklists and other total quality tools applied at the individual level is given in Harry V. Roberts and Bernard F. Sergesketter, *Quality Is Personal: A Foundation for Total Quality Management.*[1] A summary is provided in Roberts, "A Primer on Personal Quality" in this volume.

Personal quality has become an important part of several of the Chicago statistics and quality courses, in which personal improvement projects are sometimes required in addition to organizational improvement projects.

Quality Office

Although total quality efforts at Chicago have emphasized academic quality more than administrative quality, in late 1990 Deputy Dean Harry Davis set up an administrative quality office headed by then assistant dean for management, Bill Kooser. Kooser was also made executive secretary of a steering group called the Quality Executive Council, which was chaired by Davis until he stepped down from his administrative assignment in July 1993. In spring 1993, the Quality Executive Council included four faculty interested in quality (Bateman, Becker, Greene, and Roberts) and a student, Robert Kenmore. Whenever Davis could attend, he presided; when Davis could not attend, Kooser chaired the meeting.

The Quality Executive Council worked on all aspects of quality, academic and administrative, but placed especially high priority on problems faced by MBA students. Kooser's office oversaw extensive staff training in quality (some of it provided by Bateman and Roberts of the faculty, much by Kooser himself). Kooser's office supported the dozen or more student/staff teams that worked regularly working on improvement projects in the areas of student and alumni services, and carried out a quarterly exit survey of all graduating students. This office also established procedures for following up and reporting on the more than 250 suggestions that were received each year from students, staff, and faculty.

The activity of Kooser's office within the business school has thus far had relatively small effect on the rest of the University of Chicago. The school has opened up its staff training courses to employees from other parts of the university. Many staff members have taken these courses, and a few have become grassroots quality champions in their own departments.

Effects on Organizational Culture of the Business School

Although grassroots efforts already described have had a great impact on the school, their success has come largely because of their consistency with the school's traditional organizational culture, which, in turn, has many points in common with total quality. But a total quality culture has not emerged in the school, and is not likely to emerge. The faculty involved with total quality electives, laboratory courses, and LEAD are relatively few in number. Many are not on tenure track.

Aside from the small number of total quality champions, most faculty are absorbed in their own specialized work. They are relatively unaffected by total quality and have relatively little awareness of it or interest in it. The total quality activities described in this paper almost constitute a school within a school.

In retrospect, this should not be surprising. As pointed out earlier, the organizational culture is strongly oriented toward specialized research in the various academic disciplines to which most faculty members look for recognition and approval. This recognition and approval, in turn, translate directly into promotion and salary increases. The culture is not likely to change unless there is an external challenge.

Is an External Challenge Likely?

1. The most obvious challenge would come from companies and other organizations that are succeeding in total quality and would demand students who were competent in total quality. It is not clear whether or not there are enough such organizations to make a substantial impact. It is also possible that these organizations would prefer to do their own training in total quality, in-house. It is interesting to note that Motorola University plans to become accredited. Although this is primarily for Motorola employees, the capability is there for direct competition with traditional universities. See the article by Brenda Sumberg elsewhere in this volume.

2. Economic austerity for higher education might be a source: total quality does offer ways to do more with less.

3. MBA bashing, which has become popular in recent years, is another source. The core of this bashing is the argument that much of specialized academic research has little immediate relevance for professional training in business. Some large organizations take this position sufficiently seriously that they have begun to offer their own management education programs, some in direct competition with academic schools of business. Also, at least in three of the business schools for which there are reports in this book, alternative curricula with a strong emphasis on total quality have been developed, and these schools are in obvious contention for increased market penetration.

Is Total Quality Itself a Cogent Response to MBA Bashing?

If there is any substance in MBA bashing—and I think that there is some—total quality has something to offer to counter it. Total quality draws on and integrates useful concepts from academic research and puts them to work in improving organizations. It has become clear that total quality aspires to include much more than what has traditionally been regarded as quality; indeed, it aspires to become a new management paradigm, a paradigm that has much in common with the current paradigm, but also many sharp and significant departures from it.

Potential Uses for Personal Quality in Improvement of Research

Here are reasons to think that grassroots efforts can stimulate improvement in research as well as teaching.

• Improvement of teaching and curriculum may eventually free more time for research, even though the short-term effects are likely to mean less free time. Remember, though, elimination of student rework saves time both for student and professor.

• Total quality offers ideas and tools for improvement of processes that apply to research. For example, personal quality checklists and other applications of total quality at the personal level can be used to improve research. There is good reason to believe that the amount of unnecessary rework and waste in research is as high as it is for other human activities. Personal quality can thus help faculty research by showing how to find more time to do research.

• One specific potential improvement centers on the possibility that professors can substantially reduce task-switching (changeover) costs. In manufacturing, for example, it has often been possible to reduce die changes from hours to minutes. In higher education, little thought has been given to reducing changeover costs, it being assumed that interruptions are very costly and must be avoided whenever possible. It may be, however, that the researcher's attitude toward interruptions is the real problem. If interruptions are accepted as inevitable (as is often true), their effects become less disruptive.

For example, E. C. Olson, formerly of Geophysical Sciences at the University of Chicago, was able to keep up his research even when he was on administrative assignments. How did he do it? "It's easy. I do my research between phone calls," he said. Olson was extraordinary, because research typically demands sustained concentration. Most small tasks arising in administration do not require sustained concentration. Rather, they require a tolerance for changing mental focus, a tolerance that can be cultivated. Once cultivated, it can lead to progress on research in small increments, so that the overall momentum of the research effort can be maintained under less-than-ideal circumstances.

• The array of ideas, techniques, methodologies, and small-group cooperation subsumed under total quality is designed to improve processes. Improving processes entails a diagnostic journey that in essence is the scientific method so central to research. The total quality diagnostic journey, however, usually does not entail highly sophisticated statistical analysis or advanced mathematics; rather it stresses simple, commonsense tools, such as flowcharting, brainstorming, cause-and-effect charts, run charts, scatter plots, Pareto analysis, affinity analysis, and the like. Many researchers are unaware of the value of such simple tools in attacking problems, whether they be everyday operational problems or the problems pursued in academic research. This reflects the strong emphasis that academic researchers place on cleverness, sophisticated mathematics, and advanced statistics. It is easy therefore to overlook the obvious.

• In one special way, total quality reasoning is specially suited for academic research: total quality is impatient with constraints of all kinds. Total quality tries to visualize radical solutions in which current constraints are assumed away, under the assumption that most constraints can be eliminated if it is sufficiently desirable to do so. Hence I suspect that even mature scholars would find that practical lessons from total quality problem solving carry over to their own research interests.

Strategic Planning of Research

One large company has greatly simplified its strategic planning process by aligning its most important customer requirements with the processes that fall farthest short of meeting these requirements, thus defining gaps. By the Pareto principle, there are only a few really major gaps. These can be summarized in a strategic plan of just a few pages and subsequently given high-priority attention. Detailed schedules and timetables may not be essential so long as these gaps are kept clearly in view.

Much the same idea can be applied to research strategies. Thus one can, like Olson, always have in mind the most important research that needs to be pursued between the phone calls as well as in occasional periods when large blocks of time become available.

Conclusion

The story of grassroots total quality efforts at Chicago contains two important lessons for total quality in higher education.

Grassroots total quality initiatives in an educational institution can bring about many good results, even in absence of a strong top-down quality effort. So long as the educational organization is tolerant of change—and preferably, encourages it— many educational innovations can be achieved. Total quality champions should not despair if the top administration is not leading the quality charge or even if most faculty members are not interested in total quality ideas. (It helps, however, to have quiet encouragement both from the top administrators and from faculty in areas outside quality management.)

For full realization of the potential of total quality, however, grassroots efforts alone are not likely to carry the day. Here more active leadership from the top is clearly needed. But there also has to be some moderation of the fragmentation of academic culture by highly specialized research disciplines. More cross-disciplinary cooperation is needed to restructure curriculum and research in the direction of total quality.

Note

1. Harry V. Roberts and Bernard F. Sergesketter, *Quality Is Personal: A Foundation for Total Quality Management* (New York: Free Press, 1993).

A Primer on Personal Quality

Harry V. Roberts
University of Chicago Graduate School of Business

Quality Management: A Quick Overview

A good short definition of quality management is doing the right things right the first time. But that definition doesn't tell you what the right things are or how you should go about doing them right. Consider then this more explicit and only slightly longer definition. *Continually serve customers better and more economically, using scientific method and teamwork, and focusing on removal of all forms of waste.*

The term *process* is key to quality management: a process is a well-defined series of steps by which inputs are converted to outputs (either goods or services). Continual improvement of work processes (by small or large increments) is guided by the two simple goals implicit in the phrase "serve customers better and more economically."

"Serving customers better" means adding more value, increasing customer satisfaction. This serves as an implicit definition of the word *quality* itself: anything that serves customers better, as customers see it, is an improvement of quality. "Serving customers more economically" means reducing cost to provide any given customer service.

"Scientific method and teamwork" are the two main strategies for serving customers better and more economically. Scientific method entails the application of ideas of systematic learning—mainly the domain of statistics. Teamwork entails the processes by which people can cooperate in doing their work—mainly the domain of behavioral sciences.

"Focusing on removal of all forms of waste" gives an idea as to how improvement efforts are achieved. Waste and waste removal are key. The meaning of waste is clear intuitively, but there is more to waste than is apparent at first glance. Some waste is obvious, but even in well-managed organizations, waste—even substantial waste—can be pervasive without making its presence obvious.

Opportunities for rapid improvement come from the pervasiveness of waste. Key types of waste are

- Waste caused by mistakes, errors, and defects.

- The waste of doing things that are unnecessary or counter-productive, even if there are no defects.

- The waste of missed opportunities.

- Waste that can be eliminated by redesign or reengineering: "assumption breaking."

Later, we will discuss these different kinds of waste at some length.

The working assumptions of quality management are

- Further improvement—increased customer satisfaction, lower costs—is always possible, no matter how long and hard you have been working to improve.

- Never ending and substantial improvement is necessary for long-term survival of most organizations.

The Just-in-Time Principle

Finally, the pursuit of waste reduction often leads to what can be called the just-in-time principle, which was developed in manufacturing by Toyota and has revolutionized production worldwide. From an individual's perspective, the two key points of this principle are

- If tasks come to you in more or less a steady stream, it is usually better to do each one promptly as it arrives, rather than waiting to form a batch of tasks before starting to work.

- It is advantageous to try to arrange the system so that tasks arrive in a steady stream.

We can illustrate the just-in-time principle by the following example of replying to telephone or voice mail messages. You could follow two strategies.

- Answer each message as you receive it, as promptly as possible. This is just-in-time or immediate response.

- Save messages until you have a substantial batch, then work through the entire batch consecutively. This is the batch approach. Many people find batching natural.

Suppose that the successful return of a message takes you about the same length of time in either the just-in-time or the batch mode. In many situations, just-in-time is better than batch because

- Your customer—the person who called you—gets prompter and better service on average.

- You save the wastes entailed by the batch approach: keeping track of your inventory of unanswered messages and playing phone tag with the person who called you.

In manufacturing, the improvements of customer satisfaction and the reductions of waste achieved by just-in-time production can be enormous. Similar improvements and waste reductions are often achievable in service applications. See Appendix C for an example.

The just-in-time principle works best when there is little cost of changeover from one process to another. For example, fast changes of die on an assembly line can make it possible to switch quickly from one model of motorcycle to another. The analogue for services is the ability to make quick mental transitions from one task to another, even when the need for transition is caused by an irritating interruption.

Personal Quality

Personal quality is the application of quality ideas to your own individual job (and even to your own personal life). Personal quality does not directly tell you how to do your job better. Rather, it offers a philosophy and methodology for learning how to do it better.

Personal quality helps people to perceive, and remove, waste in their own jobs. As a result they can achieve both continuous improvement—repeated small gains that add up to substantial gains over time—and breakthrough—substantial gains in short periods of time. They can do this whether or not their organizations are trying to implement quality management.

There are three potential gains to the individual.

- Increased job satisfaction

- Education in quality management concepts and tools

- Assessment of the usefulness of quality management concepts and tools based on direct experience rather than claims of others

The only prerequisite for these gains is a degree of individual freedom in how jobs are carried out.

Personal quality differs from traditional time management, although it may help to make better use of time-management tools. Nor is personal quality just another self-improvement program, like speed reading, public speaking, or memory development, although these skills also can lead to improvement of personal quality.

To help to understand what personal quality is about, begin by counting the number of *yes* responses you would make to the questions on the following two brief surveys. (The questions are predicated on the assumption that you are currently holding a job; if you are not, answer in terms of your best recollection about your most recent job or, if you are a full-time student, answer only those that translate in an obvious way to your student activities.)

Quick Survey 1

In the last week, have you (yes or no)

- Been late to an appointment or meeting, or not adequately prepared for one?
- Lost or misplaced something, with resulting delay and frustration?
- Worked on a report that no one is likely to read?
- Failed to reply to phone message/E-mail/voice mail/fax within 24 hours?
- Repeatedly started work on a small task, but set it aside before finishing it?
- Worked on a task that could advantageously have been delegated?
- Experienced so many interruptions that you felt you were not getting anything done, you were just spinning your wheels?
- Put off starting something that you should have begun to work on?
- Lost your temper or showed frustration or impatience when it was counterproductive to do so?
- Arrived at work in the morning later than you should?
- Forgotten to work on a high-priority task?
- Caused extra work for your associates because of a mistake you made?
- Failed to listen carefully to what an associate or customer was telling you?
- Done something that was work-related, but totally unnecessary?
- Spent too much time in meetings where your presence wasn't essential?

- Complained about something you can't control, and complaining didn't make you feel better?
- Agreed to do something against your better judgement?
- Continued working when you were too tired to work efficiently?
- Watched more television than you intended to?
- Overeaten?
- Gone to bed later than you intended?

I have tried out these questions on a variety of audiences and have so far encountered only one person who claimed zero yeses; most report somewhere between 3 and 10. Each yes suggests waste in the way you are doing your job (or leading your personal life). Quality management, recall, aims at "elimination of all forms of waste."

Quick Survey 2

In the last week, have you (yes or no)

- Felt that you have not been spending as much time as you should on the most important things you have to do?
- Spent too little time with your direct reports?
- Spent too little time with your organization's customers?
- Spent too little time in networking; that is, in developing and maintaining contacts with people who are important to you?
- Spent less time on business/professional reading than you think you should?
- Felt that you had too little time for quality improvement activities in your organization?
- Spent too little time in keeping your office in good order or your computer files up to date?
- Failed to avail yourself of opportunities for job or professional training?
- Got less exercise than you really need?
- Get less rest than you really need?
- Had less time for recreation than you would like?
- Spent too little time with your family?
- Didn't take enough time to eat properly?

The last five questions relate to personal activities, not your job; quality ideas apply to your personal life as well as your job. Again, yes answers to these questions are frequent, suggesting that many people do not find enough time to do all the things that they think are important.

If ways can be found to reduce the waste—save the time—suggested by yes answers to the questions in survey 1, the questions in survey 2 point the way to putting this time to good use. We now explore personal quality checklists can contribute to this goal.

A Key Tool of Personal Quality: The Personal Quality Checklist

A precursor to the personal quality checklist was pioneered over two centuries ago by Benjamin Franklin. In his *Autobiography*, written late in life, Franklin described how he had pursued the "bold and arduous project of arriving at moral perfection."[1]

Franklin defined 13 virtues: temperance, silence, order, resolution, frugality, industry, sincerity, justice, moderation, cleanliness, tranquillity, venery, and humility. Over several decades he kept a checklist of his shortcomings on each of these.

As Franklin looked back on the experience, he was, overall, satisfied with the improvements achieved by working to remove the root causes of his failings. ". . . on the whole, tho' I never arrived at the perfection I had been so ambitious of obtaining, but fell far short of it, yet I was, by the endeavor, a better and happier man than I otherwise should have been if I had not attempted it. . . ."

One interesting failure was under "Humility: Imitate Jesus and Socrates:" ". . . even if I could conceive that I had completely overcome [my pride], I should probably be proud of my humility."

All of Franklin's virtues are important; his list is indeed reminiscent of Steven Covey's approach!

Three of Franklin's virtues are closely related to modern quality management and to the idea of waste elimination.

- *Order:* Let all your things have their places; let each part of your business have its time.

- *Frugality:* Make no expense but to do good to others or yourself; that is, waste nothing.

- *Industry:* Lose no time; be always employ'd in something useful; cut off all unnecessary actions.

Aside from humility, one of Franklin's failures occurred in order, the first of the three quality-related standards. His experience is instructive for users of personal quality checklists today.

> Order, . . . with regard to places for things, papers, etc., I found extreamly difficult to acquire. I had not been early accustomed to it, and, having an exceedingly good memory, I was not so sensible of the inconvenience attending want of method. This . . . therefore cost me so much painful attention and my faults in it vexed me so much, and I made so little progress in amendment, and had such frequent relapses that I was almost ready to give up the attempt. . . .
> . . . In truth, I found myself incorrigible with respect to order; and now that I am grown old and my memory bad, I feel very sensibly the want of it.

Franklin's good youthful memory compensated for order—keeping your working materials where you know you can find them when you need them. When Franklin's memory began to fail him in old age, he experienced the frustrations of trying to find things that were lost or misplaced, a major source of waste in job performance. A broader message is that being systematic is at least as important in improving quality as innate abilities, high intelligence, and the capacity to work hard. You may not have as good a memory as Franklin, and old age may start earlier than you think!

Bob Galvin's First "New Truth"

The bridge from Benjamin Franklin to the modern personal quality checklist was made by Bob Galvin, former chairman of the board of Motorola. In Galvin's "Welcome Heresies of Quality," he (like W. Edwards Deming) offers 14 points, but each of Galvin's points comes in two versions: ot: old testament and NT: NEW TRUTH. For example,

> ot: Better quality costs more.

> NT: YOU CANNOT RAISE COST BY RAISING QUALITY.

All 14 points are instructive, but Point 1 is particularly germane to our story:

> ot: Quality control is an ordinary company and department responsibility.

> NT: QUALITY IMPROVEMENT IS NOT JUST AN INSTITUTIONAL ASSIGNMENT, IT IS A DAILY PERSONAL PRIORITY OBLIGATION.

Bernie Sergesketter

The next step in the story involves Bernie Sergesketter, formerly vice president of the central region of AT&T. In the late 1980s Sergesketter was trying to find ways of adapting quality management ideas from manufacturing to the service organization (network sales) for which he was responsible. Sergesketter went to a training session at Motorola where he heard Galvin's first new truth and decided that he himself had to do something about it. He conceived the idea of making a personal quality checklist to apply quality principles to his own work.

Initially, Sergesketter was trying only to set a good example in collecting quality-related data. He thought that his work performance was very efficient and that there was only modest room for improvement. (We shall see that this assumption proved incorrect!)

Franklin's broad concepts had to be translated into specific standards for specific work processes. Sergesketter's rationale for this translation had four key steps.

1. All work is part of a process. That is, do not think in terms of the outputs of work, but of the steps by which inputs to a process are converted into the outputs of the process. (Keep your eye on the ball, not on the scoreboard!)

2. Set standards for specific work processes based on customer requirements. Remember that quality is defined by customer requirements.

3. Count defects against those standards. As they occur, defects for each standard are tallied by days, weeks, or months, and defect counts on individual standards are added up to obtain total defects by days, weeks, or months.

4. Keep it simple. This is essential! The key to simplicity is the simple stroke tally for defects for the key standards. There are many other ways to measure quality shortcomings, and they have their place; but the simplicity of defect counts is a major element in success of personal quality checklists. This concept was particularly revealing for me. As a statistician interested in quality improvement, I had for years been trying to figure out how my students and I could improve personal quality by relatively sophisticated statistical studies. It never occurred to me that such a simple approach as tallying defects could be so useful.

Some feel that the word *defect* has a negative ring and say that they would rather keep track of the things done right. One problem with this argument is that, fortunately, we do many more things right than wrong. Hence recording all the good things we do would entail a lot more record keeping, and unnecessary record keeping is itself wasteful. Moreover, it is sometimes hard or even impossible to count the number of times we do things right. For example, if avoidance of accidents is a standard on our list, we can easily count accidents, but it is difficult or impossible to keep track of the accidents that we avoid.

Moreover, the word *defect* need not have a negative connotation once we, like Benjamin Franklin, learn to exploit defects to improve quality. Defects are friends: they teach us how to improve by giving hints about root causes. Habitual search for root causes of defects brings continuing insight into potential improvements, large and small, by removing or moderating these root causes. Thus potential improvements are actually realized, and, as improvements are realized, more opportunities for improvement become apparent. Fortunately, there appears to be no end to the improvement process.

Finally, in some instances it is well to use measures other than defects. We may want to use these measures for some standards and keep track of these standards separately from those standards for which defects are tallied. For example, for some processes, executing the process faster is cheaper and leads to higher quality. Hence cycle time may be the key measure: this is the time from beginning to end of one execution of the process.

In other processes, positive measures are easy and natural. Thus for a sales representative, it may be desirable to keep track of total time spent with customers than of defects defined by failure to reach some target number of sales calls. Or, for personal fitness, one may keep track of miles run, biked, skied, or swum, or of total time spent on fitness activities rather than assigning defects to failure to meet workout objectives, such as "at least one hour a day, five days a week." ("I don't have a full hour for a workout today, so I might as well skip it, since I'll get a defect anyway.")

Whether you measure defects, cycle times, or positive achievements, the aim is to use the measurements to guide improvement efforts. A saying often heard at outstanding companies is, "Measured processes are the best processes."

Sergesketter's First Checklist

As Sergesketter analyzed his own work processes, he saw that three activities—meetings, telephone, and correspondence—were central to carrying out his work. A high fraction of a typical day was taken up with these three processes. He set very simple standards for each.

- Be on time to meetings.

- Answer the phone no later than the second ring or reply to phone messages within a day.

- Reply to all correspondence within five working days.

He also set standards for such things as "clean desk" and "only same day's work on credenza," and purely personal standards for such things as regular exercise, weight control, and personal appearance.

The usefulness of such simple standards may at first be hard to appreciate. Prompt phone answering or getting back to phone messages, for example, sounds like a minor thing to be fussy about. But if customers have trouble in making telephone contact, sales may suffer. Also, quick reply to phone messages can save long periods of wasteful phone tag. This is the just-in-time principle discussed earlier.

At the end of the first month he used the checklist, Sergesketter was astonished to find that he had accumulated 100 total defects! He *thought* that he had been getting to meetings on time, he *thought* that he had been getting back promptly on phone messages, and he *thought* that he had been replying quickly to correspondence. *The data showed otherwise.*

But Sergesketter learned quickly from the defects. (Franklin had the same experience: "I was surpris'd to find myself so much fuller of faults than I had imagined; but I had the satisfaction of seeing them diminish.") He reduced the defects rapidly at first, then more slowly, and within 18 months, his monthly defect total was running in the low single digits. He had achieved more than a tenfold (not 10 percent) reduction in defects. See Figure 1 for a time-series chart or run chart, in which defects are plotted in time order of the first 18 monthly totals.

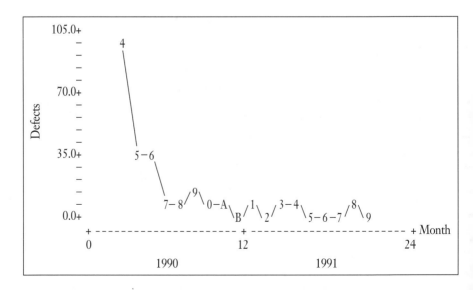

Figure 1. Number of defects per month against months.

No refined statistical analysis is needed to see the substantial drop in the number of defects, rapid at first, slowing more toward the end.

A statistical lesson is important here. Perhaps the most important single tool in quality management is to display your progress on a simple run chart like the one in Figure 1. Control charts and control limits are also useful, but they require more background and are harder to use correctly. Also, they work really well only when the process is close to what is called "a state of statistical control."

Sergesketter wisely did not mandate personal quality checklists in his organization. Such a mandate would have appeared intrusive to many of his associates. But his example encouraged a number of his associates to try checklists. Of those who did, most incorporated the on-time-to-meetings standard into their own checklists, and there were enough of them to influence the character of meetings generally. Whereas late meeting starts had been chronic at AT&T (as in most other organizations), meetings now began to start on time, and on-time starts became typical. Moreover, it was found that meetings that started on time finished on average one-third faster, a gratifying reduction in waste. (Many people now add to the on-time standard, "on-time *and prepared.*")

At the purely personal level, the gains were noticeable. Sergesketter estimates that his personal time saving amounted to about two hours a day. Such a saving opens up time for the kinds of activity-expanding activities mentioned in the second quick survey earlier in this paper and can make time for improvement activities introduced by an organization's quality management initiative.

Experience suggests that by using personal quality checklists and other personal quality approaches to be discussed, many people may achieve substantial time savings very quickly.

How Checklists Work

A checklist cannot and need not explicitly include standards that cover all aspects of all personal work processes. Successes on standards on a checklist can drive other improvements. For example, a "clean-desk" standard at work may call attention to the desirability of cleaning up the desk in your home office. An "on-time-to-meetings" standard may also lead to being on time for appointments or even for meals at home. It may also make you more aware of the need to be prepared for meetings. Returning phone messages quickly may suggest answering E-mail promptly, even immediately after reading messages that require a response.

As a checklist user gains experience, new opportunities for improvement keep suggesting themselves. They can be exploited in a revised checklist: the original checklist can itself be improved. For example, work associates can suggest useful new standards. Sergesketter's secretary, Mary McGrail, often composed first drafts of letters for him. She suggested that a single edit by him should suffice, so he added a standard "no second edit" to his list.

Experience with checklists suggests that personal improvement can be sustained long after the initial period of rapid improvement. As time goes on, you can retain all old standards on the list, since, for most of them defects are rare, recording is minimal, and it's just a question of "holding the gains." Alternatively, you can drop standards that have become internalized and simply list them for reminder on the back of the revised list.

Finally, you can supplement the checklist approach by personal quality improvement projects, to be discussed later.

My First Checklist

Although I had long known of Benjamin Franklin's checklist, I did not see its applicability to my own work until I learned about Sergesketter's checklist. My experience was equally gratifying. One key standard from my first checklist was, "Putting a small task on a temporary hold pile." I had been doing this chronically, and this bad habit resulted in a badly cluttered desk.

In the very first week of my checklist, there was an immediate and unanticipated effect: my desk went from badly cluttered to clean. It has remained that way ever since. The psychological spur of the checklist was enough to keep me from setting aside small tasks with the intent of doing them later. The "small-task" standard caused me to eliminate the root cause of desk clutter: the hidden waste of paper shuffling. I achieved other important gains from my checklist, but this immediate improvement was by far the most important.

Again, this is an application of the just-in-time principle, and many other people have since tried similar standards with gratifying results. A simple general principle has emerged from their experiences: *If you are going to do a small task eventually, you will eliminate substantial waste by doing it when it first presents itself.* There is one danger: you may find yourself keeping up on the small tasks, but falling behind on the bigger ones. If so, there are three main options: get additional support, delegate, and/or decide that some small tasks will not be done at all.

Whenever possible—it's not always possible—try to touch paper no more than once, so that you immediately dispose of the small tasks, as well as your junk mail.

My miracle of the clean desk also illustrates another quality principle: checklist standards should deal with root causes of poor quality, not superficial symptoms. The simple "clean-desk" standard worked for Sergesketter because his desk had been reasonably clean before he started his first checklist. For him, it served as a reminder not to backslide.

However, the same clean-desk standard worked badly for another checklist user who found himself painfully clearing off working materials at the end of the day, so that his desk would indeed be clean once a day. Then, the next morning, he had to bring these same materials out of the filing cabinets in order to work on them. He quickly realized that the clean-desk standard was itself wasteful, and that he had to deal with the paper shuffling process that led to the cluttered desk in the first place.

Purely Personal Standards

Like Sergesketter, I included some purely personal standards on my checklist: for example, griping, unpleasantness, driving lapses. (I discuss driving lapses briefly in Appendix B.) To my surprise, the presence of such standards on my list had an immediate, substantial, and favorable effect on my actual behavior.

The most common personal standard for checklist users has been exercise/fitness; many users feel that they need more exercise than they are getting and use the checklist to correct this shortcoming. But since additional exercise requires more time and most people are already pretty busy, the discouraging result is often defect after defect, day after day. But gradually the accumulation of defects teaches checklist users that, to maintain fitness, they are either going to have to find the needed time by other, time-saving checklist standards, or to modify their exercise programs, or both. Appendix A includes some of the lessons they have learned.

Improving the Initial Checklist

Like Sergesketter, I found that additional standards kept suggesting themselves as I gained experience with the initial checklist. For example, I adopted a standard that had been used effectively by a colleague, Wayne Baker: *On every working day, make some improvement in the organization or functioning of your office.* The most obvious improvement is to throw out things you don't need, but as you keep thinking about how you are going to improve, more and more opportunities for improvement come to mind. For me, this standard has been invaluable in disposing of most of the working materials that I had been hoarding for decades against possible need. Beyond that, however, the standard has led to the discovery of additional forms of waste—obvious and hidden—in all aspects of personal job performance, and, once discovered, these wastes can be eliminated. For example, I realized that I had habitually tried to file away too much material in archival files, with the result that these files had become almost totally disorganized, yet I had not worked out efficient ways of finding what I needed for current projects.

The "Baker standard" can be adapted to any continuing project that can be advanced by small increments, but that is easy to give up on completely if you don't keep at it. Examples: housecleaning, yard maintenance, networking, giving deserved recognition to work associates, and keeping up on background professional reading. The exact amount of time you spend each day is not critical, and I recommend that you not set a minimum time. What matters is that you make some improvement each day and, in so doing, are prompted to think about desirable next steps, so that you continue to make steady progress.

Two Mechanisms for Improvement

Experience suggests that checklists achieve improvement by two distinct mechanisms.

1. By helping you to find and deal with root causes of waste. This is the analytical route to quality improvement.

2. Behavior modification achieved by the psychological spur of having the checklist in your pocket. This is the behavioral route to improvement.

The analytical route is usually associated with continuing small improvements (kaizen) that cumulate over time to big improvements. The behavioral route is often associated with breakthroughs (personal reengineering). It is desirable to aim both at continuing small improvements and frequent breakthroughs. And it is desirable to try to exploit both mechanisms—analytical and behavioral—on your own checklist.

Behavioral modification doesn't work for everyone as it has for me. (A psychiatrist in the audience at a recent presentation suggested to me that obsessive personality tendencies, which he thought I displayed, help one to get more value out of checklists.) But it does work for many people (I suppose they, too, are obsessive) and when it does work, it means instant, though unmeasured improvement. I say unmeasured because, of course, you cannot know exactly how many defects you would have incurred before you started your checklist, but you may be quite confident that there were many more defects than the numbers you record after you start the checklist, especially when your defects go to zero the moment you start your checklist!

Similarly, some people have trouble with the analytical approach, in which you learn from your "friendly" defects and remove their root causes. For these people, their defects are reduced slowly or not at all. I suppose that these people have non-analytical personalities; but analysis can be taught and learned.

A Sample Current Checklist

As a concrete illustration of how a checklist might be laid out, my own current checklist is shown on the next two pages. In actual use it is printed on the two sides of a single sheet of paper. It is more elaborate than a starting checklist needs to be. A shorter list—even a list with only one standard—may be better to start with. (The "Baker standard" was the only standard on Baker's checklist.)

I keep my tallies by days and aggregate to weekly totals for measuring progress. Others may prefer to tally by weeks; Sergesketter tallies by month. From time to time I enter the data into a computer file for statistical analysis, but since defects are now infrequent, detailed analysis is less essential than at earlier times. The main thing is to keep recording defects, removing their root causes, and improving the checklist.

The space for comments on the second page can be used for keeping track of special personal quality improvement projects, a topic covered at length later in this paper. One example is a temporary standard that I called "rushing"—ill-advised attempts to get more work done by rushing or hurrying—which result in mistakes and costly rework. I discuss this small, but successful project later.

Harry Roberts' revised personal quality checklist: week of _____

Defect standard	Mon	Tue	Wed	Thu	Fri	Sat	Sun	Total
Late for meeting or appointment								
Search for something misplaced or lost								
Failure to improve office when I work there								
Failure to improve home office when I work there								
Loss of concentration								
Working when I should be doing something else								
Failure to have a major project in background								
Overeating								
Late to bed								
Aimless TV browsing								
Driving lapses								
Total								

Comments:

Definitions and Explanations

Late for meeting or appointment: Late by even one second. I always carry background reading or work materials in case others are late.

Search for something misplaced or lost: More than momentary confusion as to location of important document, book, address, working materials, and so on. Forgetting a task or working material is included here.

Failure to improve office when I work there: Failure to get rid of junk, better organize files, and so on.

Failure to improve home office when I work there: Same for work location at home.

Loss of concentration: Realization that I have not been paying attention to what I was doing or listening carefully to someone who was talking directly to me. This may be a hard standard to keep score on, but it's worth a try because it's very important.

Working when I should be doing something else: I think that I can recognize when I get to this stage. "Something else" could include resting or relaxing.

Failure to have a major project in background: Some important project that I can make progress on, even in short time slots.

Overeating: Eating when not really enjoying food. I have a bad habit of thinking I must finish my plate to avoid wasting food.

Late to bed: To bed after 10:30 P.M. or more than 45 minutes after first opportunity after 10:30 P.M.

Aimless TV browsing: Mindless channel hopping, not aimed at finding something I really want to watch.

Driving lapses: Mental lapses, usually minor (forgetting to make a turn) but worrisome, even though they have thus far never resulted in an accident.

Reminder: Hold the Gains

Delayed return of phone call or reply to letter
Putting a small task on a hold pile
Failure to discard incoming junk promptly
Flustering
Griping
Unpleasantness
Worry
Defeatism
Unkind humor

Tips on Effective Use of Checklists

Most checklist users make at least some progress within a short period of time and obtain considerable insight into the nature of their work. Almost all feel that the experience is helpful. A substantial minority have experienced truly major personal breakthroughs: "I feel that I'm finally on top of my job, rather than the other way around." I have evidence that my own checklist has led to a substantial expansion in my work output during a period when demands on my time were increasing substantially.

Some users are satisfied with short-term improvements and discontinue their checklists after a few weeks or months. A small number just don't get a good start and give up before realizing any substantial benefits. My son was one of the latter: he lost his checklist after a week and decided not to continue! For people who have trouble in getting started on checklists, a quick and productive personal improvement project may be helpful. A list of ideas appears later in this chapter. Still other people are simply not much motivated to improve!

Here are useful practical tips for increasing the effectiveness of checklist use.

• Even though the checklist may sound at first like an entertaining parlor game or an onerous additional chore, take it seriously. Don't be misled by its simplicity: give it a real chance. (Some of the most successful checklist users have told me, "I was skeptical at first" or, "I never liked the idea of checklists.")

• It's easy, and you don't have to develop an elaborate list to get started: just start. You can improve your list with experience.

• A checklist with just one good standard can make a big difference.

• Waste reduction is key: you must be sensitized to the ubiquitous presence of waste, obvious and hidden. (Conscientious use of the checklist provides excellent training in the nature of waste and a blueprint for waging a never ending war on waste.) A more detailed discussion of waste will be given later in this paper.

• It is essential to have clean, operational definitions of checklist standards. The test is whether you can recognize unambiguously when a defect occurs. For example, "procrastination" can lead to serious waste, but procrastination is hard to define. Right this minute, as you read these lines, you may be aware that you are procrastinating on a number of tasks. But you did not begin to procrastinate today. Rather, you began at some time in the past, and probably did not even think consciously about it. To make procrastination a checklist standard, you have to be able to define when you started to procrastinate so that you will know when a defect occurs. To do that, you have to have a system for setting starting dates for important tasks. (Such a system can be helpful whether or not you are keeping a checklist.)

There are instances in which a standard may be ambiguous, but helpful. For example, with my standard of "driving lapses," I am often in doubt as to whether a particular incident should be called a lapse. But reflecting on the question has led me to think more carefully about my driving and thereby to improve it. This point is also discussed in Appendix B. Again, even when it is hard to keep score on a standard such as "loss of concentration," the presence of the standard on the checklist serves as a continuing reminder to keep trying to keep one's concentration.

• Relate checklist standards to root causes, not to symptoms (remember "clean desk").

• Don't set up a socially acceptable standard if your heart isn't in it. For example, for one friend, "no more smoking" is in that category. He made it into a standard; it didn't work. He then realized that he really didn't want to stop smoking! But checklists have been used by others to kick the smoking habit. One near-alcoholic brought his drinking into statistical control at a low "social-drinking" level. Again, perhaps people with obsessive personalities have an advantage!

• Checklist standards should not be new year's resolutions for which you hope that by trying harder, you will somehow manage to find time for all the good things you should be doing, but aren't (see Quick Survey 2 at the start of this paper). It isn't for want of trying hard that most people fail to find time for all the things they want to do.

In particular, you should use standards that are primarily waste reducers/time savers, not activity expanders. Activity expanders should be used sparingly, if at all. Sometimes, however, an initial activity expander may bring fast time savings. A plant manager put frequent plant visits on his checklist, and, as a consequence, realized many quick improvements that simplified his office activities. As you begin to save time from the waste-reducing standards, however, you will be freeing up time that can be used to your own best advantage.

• Don't try to change everything at once. You have a lifetime for continuous improvement and breakthrough.

• Similarly, don't delay starting a checklist until your life becomes less stressful. Just find one or a few easy, time-saving standards, and you are likely to notice an immediate reduction in stress. (On the other hand, if you start with activity expanders, the checklist itself will contribute to increased stress.)

• Keep it simple! Don't, for example, set up elaborate weighting schemes for major and minor defects.

- Tips for useful, tried-and-true, performance standards for your first checklist follow.

    —Be on time to appointments and meetings; promptly reply to phone, fax, E-mail, and so on.

    —If you are going to do a small task eventually, do it when it first presents itself.

    —Every day you work in your office, make some improvement in its organization or functioning.

    —Don't let interruptions throw you off stride. After each interruption, switch back smoothly to what you had been doing.

    —Don't ever put anything down other than in the place it belongs: if necessary, think where it belongs before putting it down.

    —Plan a realistic, congenial fitness program and count defects on failure to conform; or alternatively, keep track of positive efforts in the program.

Improvement Projects in Personal Quality

The personal quality checklist is a simple and practical example of the application of quality management ideas to improve personal quality, but quality ideas and tools other than checklists are also available. For example, improvement can often be achieved by a special effort, or project, directed to a perceived improvement opportunity.

For a simple example, I recount a little project that I undertook to speed up shaving. When shaving one morning during the late fall of 1992, it occurred to me that my shaving process might be wasting a lot of time: simply doing something for a long time is no guarantee that you are doing it well. This thought had occurred to me in the past, and I had tried to shave faster, but with little success and increased incidence of razor nicks.

But in 1992, for the first time, I thought of applying quality principles to improve the shaving process by identifying and removing waste. I launched a special improvement project for shaving. (This was an activity distinct from, or supplementary to, my continuing personal quality checklist.)

Here is an outline of my shaving process as it had existed from 1939 to 1992.

- Lather haphazardly, with lots of redundancy.

- Rinse (time-consuming because a lot of soap must be removed).

- Lather again, haphazardly.

- Many repeated, overlapping, short razor strokes, progressing slowly but erratically over the entire shaving area, with each stroke backtracking over part of the area covered by the previous one, as in mowing tall grass with an old-fashioned hand mower. Lots of unsystematic jumping around.

- Rinse again, haphazardly.

- Haphazard touchup of spots that had not been closely shaved. Lots of inspection to find where they were.

Instead of measuring defects (say, razor nicks or patches of missed whiskers), I measured cycle time, the time from beginning to end of one execution of the shaving process. Often, though not always, it's well to focus improvement projects on reduction of cycle time, which is a good objective in itself and often drives improvement in defect rates as well.

For about a week, I timed how long it took to shave using the existing process. The mean time was six minutes, with very little variation from day to day. During that week I was thinking of possible ways to simplify the process, cut out waste, and thus save time without trying simply to hurry up, with consequent increased risk of razor nicks and consequent rework with a septic stick. One helpful model was the way people cut their lawns with a power mower.

I came up with the following alternative process, which, I hoped, would be an improvement.

- Lather as before, but systematically so as to save waste motion and use less shaving soap.

- A few long, smooth strokes, without backtracking, to quickly cover the entire face. Minimal sideways overlapping between long strokes.

- Rinse systematically, with less waste motion (for example, don't wring out washrag at the end; just hang it up wet since it will dry of its own accord).

- Systematic touchup of hard-to-reach spots that had not been closely shaved on the long, smooth strokes. (Take advantage of the fact that these spots tend to be in the same place, so little time is needed to search for them. Also, for further improvement, try to modify the long strokes so as to get these spots the first time.)

The major changes were these.

- One lathering step instead of two.

- One rinse step instead of two.

- Long, purposeful razor strokes, no back and forth fidgeting over the same small areas.

- Touchup only as needed, in places suggested by experience.

I tried out the new process for the next week. My mean shaving time was only three minutes, again with very little variation from day to day.

By relatively casual analysis of the process in just a short time, I had cut the cycle time in half! I suspect that a time-and-motion study expert could have told me how to achieve this much or even greater improvement. But experts can be expensive, they never seem to be around when you really need them, and the idea of an expert consultant on shaving seems like overkill.

What impressed me was that, following a systematic improvement methodology, I could do so well on my own in just a few days. I simply figured out how the current process worked and then looked for improvement opportunities; that is, I took two key steps.

- Map the existing (1939–1992) process.

- Modify the map by cutting out waste.

Note that I did not attempt to shave faster. Rather, I eliminated some steps, introduced the idea of long razor strokes, and cut out waste of multiple razor passes over the same skin area.

When I tell this story to others, people find it amusing and mildly impressive, but some also wonder whether saving a mere three minutes a day amounted to much. One response to this reaction is this; if, when I first began shaving, I had known what I learned in this little quality-improvement experiment, I would have saved about 900 hours—nearly half a work year! Or, if lifetime savings seem nebulous, I saved three working days in 1994! (This latter estimate includes additional time savings to be reported.)

There is another response to those who felt the saving was trivial. If it is possible so easily to cut cycle time on shaving by 50 percent, how many other repetitive personal activities might there be for which comparable savings would be possible. How much aggregated saving might be possible? This suggests the possibility of a series of personal projects—say one a month—targeted at potentially wasteful personal processes. We'll come back to this.

In shaving, there remained the possibility of further improvements. The long strokes might be modified to a more systematic pattern, the sideways overlap of the long strokes might have been reduced, and execution of the long strokes might be improved so as to better cover the hard-to-shave spots on the first pass.

Indeed, continuing small improvements along these lines have reduced my mean shaving time from 3 minutes to less than 2 minutes—more than a two-thirds reduction from the original start. This improvement is a reduction of cycle time obtained by greater efficiency of execution of the actual process steps. Cycle time can also be improved by better organization of a process—say by going from large batches to small batch size, possibly a batch size of one—without changing the actual processing steps.

How much further improvement is possible or worth taking the time to seek? It is probable that future improvements will be small, individually and even cumulatively. But studying the process is costless because I have to shave anyway. I have even come to regard it as entertaining: each morning shave is an adventure in incremental improvement! Further, continued attention to improvement possibilities may help me to hold the gains I have already made. Also, as suggested earlier, I am seeking further improvement by looking at other personal processes for which small personal improvement projects might bring substantial improvement with relatively little effort.

People ask about cuts and nicks. I have not kept data, but I now typically go for days or weeks without needing to use a septic stick. My best recollection of the 1939–1992 process is that I rarely shaved without at least a small nick. The emphasis on low cycle time causes me to pay close attention to avoidance of cuts, because each cut increases cycle time. It appears that the danger of cuts is greatest with a new blade, so I take extra precautions and my times are a few seconds slower.

When dullness of a blade begins to slow shaving time, I change blades. I have discovered that I can efficiently use the same blade for longer than I had thought: usually three weeks or more.

People also ask about closeness of shave. Again, I have not kept data, but by paying close attention to the touchup at the end, I believe that I am doing at least as well as with the 1939–1992 process.

For the shaving process, I should also mention the possibility of radical redesign—reengineering. For example, one friend claims that shaving while showering can reduce shaving time. Another friend reports reducing shaving time to zero by growing a beard. (However, he does not provide an estimate of the average time of beard trimming or the extra time needed to wash the beard.) Still another possibility would entail investment in an electric shaver, as has been done by a friend who shaves with a cordless razor while driving. Whenever we take into account the possibility of radical process redesign—personal reengineering—the potential for improvement by waste reduction is bounded only by zero cycle time.

How much further improvement is possible or worth seeking? It is probable that future improvements will be small, individually and even cumulatively. But studying the process is costless because I have to shave anyway. Further, continued attention to improvement possibilities may help me to hold the gains I have already made. So I am still seeking further improvement. Also, I am beginning to work on other personal processes— for example, getting dressed in the morning, showering, loading the dishwasher, and various chores around the house. We consider this possibility in the next section.

Waste Elimination by Simple Personal Improvement Projects

In organizational quality improvement, one useful strategy is to pursue a series of quality-improvement projects conducted by cross-functional teams. The aim is to make steady improvement that cumulates over time to large aggregate improvement.

The shaving project suggests the possibility, just mentioned, of a series of personal improvement projects, perhaps aiming at one a month. But since these projects are primarily aimed at reducing waste, it is often possible to get both quick and substantial improvement without the application of elaborate problem-solving processes and tools. Possible examples include

- Dressing and undressing
- Bathing
- Putting on makeup
- Hair drying
- Cooking
- Dishwashing
- Housecleaning
- Yard work
- Opening mail (especially in families with more than one adult mail recipient)
- Laundry
- Ironing
- Typing
- Reading newspapers and magazines
- Personal filing
- Proofreading

- Organizing the disk on your personal computer
- Improving the organization of storage in your pockets
- Improving the organization of storage in your purse
- Organizing attaché case or backpack for commuting
- Choice of commuting modes and routes
- Exercising and fitness activities
- Losing weight
- Controlling blood pressure (I know a physician who has her patients monitor their own blood pressure, including making run charts on the readings.)
- Television viewing
- Studying

It is easy to combine improvement miniprojects with a personal quality checklist. One simply inserts a temporary standard in which responses—cycle times, defects, output measures, and so on—can be recorded. For example, a few days ago I noticed that in my desire to get more work done, I was rushing my activities in an obviously wasteful way. For example, I would try to write comments on student papers as fast as I could, and I found myself constantly making mistakes, scratching out, and starting over. I created a temporary standard, rushing. Availing myself of the behavioral power of the checklist as a psychological spur for obsessive personality types, I have now had 12 defect-free days on rushing. The desired behavior is now so internalized that I no longer feel the need to keep score. I have decided to return to a miniproject that had been successful two years earlier, though it had not been nearly as easy: stopping a bad habit of clenching my teeth. I suspect that I have not been holding the gains, so I will look at that situation again.

A reasonable objective might be to always have one ongoing personal improvement project, keeping the necessary records on the personal quality checklist.

In 1995 for the first time I assigned personal quality improvement projects (in addition to checklist projects) to students in my Executive MBA class at the University of Chicago, and the results were spectacularly good. Here is a report I made to the class on their work.

To give an idea of specifics, here were projects for which I invited students to make presentations to the entire class. Most projects were highly successful! Most focused on reduction of cycle time.

- Define and obtain measures, often some measures prior to intervention.

- Map as-is process.
- Devise one or more interventions to simplify process, cut out waste. (Move toward a should-be process.)
- Carry out interventions.
- (All projects focused on cycle time reduced it, often very substantially.) Use data analysis to show whether improvement is statistically significant. (The course emphasized statistics and data analysis.)
- Improvements are large: 10- to 45-minute gains per day are typical. This makes for simple analysis: comparing mean cycle time, before and after, or graphical interpretation of a run chart.
- Significance of a 20 minute per day improvement: frees up about three full workweeks a year. The saving can be used to do more work, or, maybe, take a good vacation!

Other types of projects

- Fitness improvements
- Skill acquisitions

On these projects, too, success was typical.

- Fast morning start
- Efficient packing for trips
- Faster, cheaper, more productive commuting
- Improving efficiency of weekly meetings with boss
- Major changes in life, including "virtual office"
- Mathematical typing to speed up technical reports
- Surveying opportunities to save time
- Reexamination of all major activities
- Learning to touch type
- Learning Spanish
- Time saving, weight loss, fitness improvement
- Exercise, weight loss
- Processing expense accounts

Projects Focused Directly on Saving or Making Better Use of Time

Time-saving projects are often rapidly and dramatically successful. "Getting ready for work" or "getting out of the house in the morning" often produce quick gains of 15–30 minutes, which dwarf the 3- to 4-minute improvement from my shaving project. For example, one woman with long hair got a major gain from cutting hair-drying time after her morning shower. Two other women did the same thing, not by reduced drying time directly but by going to shorter haircuts!

A student recently cut 24 minutes a day from the time needed to walk the family dog. He went from three daily walks to two, and he increased the benefits to both dog and student by mixing in a little jogging and fast walking.

When I told a colleague of these examples, he asked, "What did they do with the time they saved?" This made me realize that, with the aid of inexpensive digital watches with stopwatch capability, it is now very easy to measure daily total time for any important activity. Consider, for example, study time by students. I suspect that most students think that they are studying more than they actually are. With the aid of a digital watch, it would be easy to measure cumulative study time per day, just as people measure the time needed to get ready for work in the morning: you just press a button each time you start to study and press it again when you stop. I suspect that even without process mapping and other formal methods, the process of making and recording measurements of actual time studying would tend to drive improvements both in finding more time for studying and in making good use of the time actually spent. Similar projects could be directed to professional or recreational reading, self-improvement activities, relaxation, and the like.

This simple methodology could be extended to many other activities, one by one. For example, routine housecleaning chores, television viewing, commuting, meetings, phone conversations are all possible projects.

On an even more ambitious scale, one could easily measure total daily time that is spent in what you regard as real work. Do you do as much real work as you think you do? If you discover that you do not, you will have a substantial motivation for locating easy ways to increase work time.

Here are other examples in which such time measurement might be helpful.

- Time spent on what you regard as highest-priority activities

- Time spent on fitness activities, any and all kinds

- Time spent on work you regard as value-added (Don't be shocked if you are spending less than you thought you were.)

You could also measure time on wasteful activities, such as time spent as a consequence of mistakes that you have made previously, or mistakes that other people have made previously (for example, fixing bugs in computer programs). Also, by timing all activities that appear to be wasteful, you could get a quick idea of important specific wasteful activities for which you could then design an improvement project.

My rough guess is that by combining the techniques we have studied—checklists and improvement projects—most people ought to be able to free up at least 2 hours a day for higher and better use, including having more fun.

Further Discussion of the Nature of Waste

Waste of Unnecessary Work

Personal quality checklists aim at the reduction in the frequency of process flaws or failures—defects. But defects are only one source of waste. Another major source is unnecessary work, as illustrated by the shaving example.

Unnecessary work includes also tasks that are completely unnecessary, that add no value whatever. Detailed process mapping and analysis is unnecessary. Once you realize that a process step adds no value, you just stop doing it. A homely example is rinsing dishes and glasses before putting them into an automatic dishwasher. If you have been doing this, just try not doing it, and then check to see if the dishwasher is getting everything clean.

A task that you can advantageously delegate is unnecessary for you to do. *Advantageously* means that there is an available person who is able to do the job and may benefit from doing it.

How can we decide what is unnecessary? Suppose that you are using a photocopier to make copies of an article. You may wait by the machine for five minutes while it does its work. Unless you have to fix a stoppage, you are apparently accomplishing nothing. But waiting seems necessary if you are going to complete your mission. It is only if you find some way to use part or all your waiting time for a value-adding purpose that waiting becomes unnecessary. For example, you may inspect the pages as they go through the machine to be sure they are in the correct order (an inspection that seems often to be rewarded by the discovery of a problem), or you may read an important, work-related memorandum.

Here is another example of unnecessary work. Consider an operator who is working on two machines and has to walk back and forth to do so. The walking is necessary to the operator's job. If, however, the two machines are moved closer together, less walking is needed; less walking is now necessary, so some of the previous walking can now be seen to have been unnecessary.

Waste of Missed Opportunities

As an example of this type of waste, consider changing your commuting from personal automobile to public transportation. In some instances the public transportation may be cheaper and faster, and, even more important, you may be able to do additional work or, for that matter, just relax.

Another example is the substitution of word processing for typing. During the 1980s I worked as an expert witness with several law firms that repeatedly retyped boilerplate materials each time they were needed in a new document.

Some book publishers still do typesetting by hand even though authors furnish electronic source. By contrast, in June 1994, when there was a strong market incentive to do so, a biography of O. J. Simpson was written, copy edited, typeset, printed, and distributed within two weeks. This is not intended to suggest that all books could or should be done with a cycle time of two weeks, but examples like this tend to raise our sights. For example, the Pentagon was built in less than a year in World War II, while a station rebuilding on the commuter line I use has already taken nearly twice that time.

Redesign Waste

Consider a man who irons his own cotton shirts and applies quality improvement methods to reduce ironing time. Suppose then he decides that polyester shirts, which require no ironing, are satisfactory for him. In effect, he has redesigned his process so that ironing is unnecessary. So long as he wore cotton shirts, ironing was a necessary activity that entailed waste of unnecessary work of the kind I reduced in my shaving project. With the process redesign, all the ironing can be seen in retrospect as having been wasteful.

A Simple Strategy for Personal Improvement Projects

The shaving example combined with the previous discussion of personal quality checklists suggests the beginnings of simple but systematic strategies for continuous improvement of quality for any process, not only personal but organizational. As suggested earlier, a reasonable goal might be always to have at least one active improvement project going at all times. The strategy of rapid elimination of obvious waste has been discussed. For less obvious waste, however, a more systematic approach is needed. I offer a simple strategy for doing this through personal quality improvement projects. Determine a process that is important to your personal customers and that appears to be wasteful: the cycle time is long or the defect rate is high. Launch an improvement project.

Here are detailed steps.

1. Identify processes that are important to customers by finding out customer preferences for process outcomes.

   - At the personal level, we are, for the most part, our own customers. For my shaving process, I knew that I wanted to shave faster.

   - For our jobs, we have internal customers within the organization and external customers outside, and it is well to seek out their preferences to find out which processes, and which aspects of these processes, are important to them. For example, a product may be defect free, but it may be hard for customers to obtain needed information about it or how to install and use it.

   - Direct conversation and simple questionnaires are two ways to find out about customer preferences.

2. Map the existing process, remove unnecessary process steps, and simplify necessary ones.

   - Study the current process carefully and in some detail, as I did above for my shaving process. My listing of steps in shaving is a simple illustration of the quality tool of process mapping.

   - Remove wasteful steps, simplify, combine, run steps in parallel, and change order of steps, all as needed.

   - Look for possibilities to add more value while carrying out the process. For example, it may be possible to reduce or eliminate waiting time by a better setup or by better arrangement of tools (the tools could be a computer, a printer, desk layout, the telephone, and so on).

   - Measure and keep track of process cycle time, say by plotting a run chart of cycle times. A run chart plots quality measures—for example, defects or cycle times—on the vertical axis; time periods (for example, days) on the horizontal axis. Sergesketter's run chart for the first 19 months of his checklist was shown in Figure 1.

   - Keep on eliminating, rearranging, and simplifying steps.

   - Keep on evaluating success by analysis of the continuing run chart of cycle times.

3. Remove root causes of defects: mistake proof the process.

- Identify, count, and keep track of defects, say by plotting a run chart of defects.

- Use defects as signals to learn about root causes of defects.

- Keep removing or palliating root causes of defects: mistake proof the process. In manufacturing, small process modifications can make certain kinds of defects impossible. An everyday example of mistake proofing: in the early days of unleaded gasoline, if you had absentmindedly tried to pump leaded gas into the tank of a car designed to run only on nonleaded gas, as I once did, you would have found that the nozzle was too large to fit.

- Mistake-proofing is harder for service processes than for manufacturing processes because inattention is a major source of error, but simple devices can do a lot. For example, on telephone charge-card orders, repeating the customer's charge card number can greatly reduce errors.

- Use self-inspection when appropriate: check over the form you have just filled out before mailing it or passing it on to the next step for processing.

- Finally, process redesign may lead to further improvements.

4. Evaluate success by analysis of the continuing run chart of defects.

5. Make provisions for holding all gains thus achieved and for communicating your successes to those who can benefit.

Conclusion

This approach to personal quality improvement is good preparation for organizational quality improvement projects using teams. If team members have tried out waste removal at the personal level, they will be well prepared for rooting out organizational waste as well! And they will understand that organizational quality improvement need not be slow and tedious, and need not aim only at small improvements, at least for projects at the grassroots level.

Appendix A: Fitness

I include this short appendix on fitness because I have learned a lot about the subject both from my own experience and the experience of checklist users, and because the subject is so difficult yet so important to so many.

The commonest personal standard for checklist users has been exercise/fitness; many users feel that they need more exercise and use the checklist to correct this shortcoming. But since additional exercise requires more time and most people are already pretty busy, the discouraging result is often defect after defect, day after day. But gradually the accumulation of defects teaches checklist users that, to maintain fitness, they are either going to have to find the needed time by other, time-saving checklist standards, or to modify their exercise programs, or both. Here are some of their modifications.

- Cross train. Diversify the types of exercise that count as satisfying the fitness standard, so that under almost any circumstance, say when traveling or when the weather is inclement, there will be a convenient and congenial fitness activity. (Cross training also tends to prevent overuse injuries caused by concentration on a single activity such as running or tennis.)

- Reassess the logistics of exercise. If you are spending an hour traveling in order to use an exercise machine for 30 minutes at a health club, consider buying a similar machine for home use.

- Find ways of exercising that take little, if any, extra time beyond what you would have spent anyway: take stairs rather than elevators, walk rather than drive to the commuter train, or combine TV viewing with some form of indoor exercise.

For some people, the exercise problem reflects lack of willpower. The checklist may help this problem, but try to find some kind of exercise that you genuinely enjoy. Failing that, combine exercise with something you enjoy: for example, read the morning paper while using a stationary cycle or a stepper.

Finally, quick and noticeable improvement can be a powerful motivator for fitness. One of my executive program students included this fitness standard on his checklist: "Take the stairs rather than the elevator." He noticed within a week that he was no longer getting winded climbing the stairs. Within a month, he had more than halved the time it took to reach the top! Similar improvements for upper body fitness can be obtained by a mixture of bent-knee situps, pushups, and stretches that takes about three minutes.

My father kept remarkably fit for 9 months of the year by maintaining a large and spectacular garden. He didn't think much of my running: he regarded it as nonproductive because I ended up where I started without any output of value to others. Perhaps a few readers who are unmotivated by any of the workout strategies suggested above will be able to find an absorbing hobby that is both agreeable and productive.

Appendix B: Quality Is Personal for Leaders

This appendix is drawn from a working paper by Paul Batalden, M.D., of the Dartmouth Medical School. Batalden develops a framework that leads to many specific checklist standards that bear on the job of top leaders. I will not attempt to recapitulate the framework, but I will set forth a few standards to illustrate. As a leader, do you

- Fail to see another's point of view?

- Fail to listen before talking, thus preventing actual clarification?

- Fail to understand system dynamics?

- Fail to understand historical evidence, including past data?

- Fail to document assumptions and beliefs for later checking?

- Fail to write a statement of focus?

- Fail to resist distractions?

- Fail to use ceremonies?

Each standard relates to a capability that is important for leadership. From the standpoint of a personal quality checklist, however, there are two problems: there are too many standards for a single checklist, and many of the standards are difficult to define. But there are ways of getting around such problems. Some ideas include

- One or two leadership standards at a time can be added to a basic personal checklist that also includes more general checklist standards like those I have illustrated.

- The leadership standards can be rotated through time. (Actually, Benjamin Franklin concentrated each week on only one of his 13 standards.) In time, you can cover all or most of them, and also add some of your own.

- The difficulty of definition can be a strength. For example, although it may be hard to define "failure to see another's point of view," a consistent attempt to do so may sensitize you to what is entailed in seeing another's point of view.

- The "driving lapses" standard on my own personal quality checklist brings out the same point: in trying to define a lapse, I have become much more aware of my own driving. I believe that the effort has made me a better driver. Where before I would have blamed the other driver for an uneasy driving encounter ("he was driving too fast") or my wife ("your backseat driving distracted me"), I now can be detached in examining my own performance, thinking of how I could have driven differently, and asking how I might modify my behavior for future driving. Scoring of defects may be subjective, but the learning and improving is more important than rigorous bookkeeping. Further, the checklist standard is a continual reminder of the need to avoid inattention in driving, regardless of past success. A recent driving lapse defect reminded me that, had the lapse been only a bit more egregious, my checklist would have stopped permanently.

Appendix C: Illustration of the Just-in-Time Principle

A particularly vivid example of the just-in-time principle is given by three of the four standards on the personal quality checklist of my student in the Executive MBA program, Cheryl Lynn Walker, M.D.

Complete charts: Complete all notations in patients charts by the end of the day.

Complete dictations: Complete all dictations by the end of the day.

Answer phone calls: Return all calls by the end of the day.

(Cheryl's final standard was *"Academic responsibilities:* Do not accept additional responsibilities while in the executive program.")

Here are some of Cheryl's comments.

Complete charts: I examine up to 20 patients and answer up to 40 patient calls per day and would often have a few charts at the end of the day that required detailed notes. Sometimes, I would leave them until the next day. Charts were building up on my desk and overflowing onto the floor. It seemed that the pile was only growing, no matter how much I worked on it. I was anxious to include this on my checklist because I knew that my life would be better if I were able to improve my recordkeeping habits. It was not long before I began to complete the charts. I no longer have a pile on the floor. The charts on my desk are waiting for lab results.

Complete dictation: Health care reform has resulted in an amazing increase in the percentage of patients who are managed care and, thus, the number of referrals. Each referral requires a letter, and sometimes a follow-up letter. I would usually wait until the end of my day to dictate; now I dictate right after I see the patient. This has made my life a lot better, and I am sure that the charts are not accidentally filed before dictation. I am sure my colleagues appreciate the quicker follow-up. I have decided to improve further and am investigating ways to decrease the amount of time it takes to get a letter typed and mailed in my office. This will save my time and the time of my assistant.

Answer phone calls: Phone calls have been overwhelming on some days. I used to wait until the end of the day before I returned the calls because I needed to devote my attention to the patients in the office. I also had the problem of not being able to reach patients because of voice mail. Needless to say, voice mail only complicates my life because of the need for confidentiality. The checklist focused my attention on answering calls efficiently. I have improved the return-call time by

- Having my secretary ask for the number at which the patient can be reached.
- Returning calls at set times so patients can be available.
- Leaving times during the day when the patient can call back and be put through (when I am not seeing patients). Although I am still working on how to improve the phone call answering system, it is better. I am thinking about getting a new phone system that would allow patients to leave refill requests on voice mail.

Cheryl's defects total per day, Monday through Friday for four weeks was

6 9 4 4 3   3 3 0 2 0   4 0 0 2 0   1 0 0 2 0

If you are statistically minded, you can check that her reduction in defects was highly significant statistically.

Note

1. Benjamin Franklin, *Autobiography* (New York: Grosset & Dunlap, 1935), 109–122; Another early application of personal quality to moral improvement is to be found in Louis J. Puhl, S. J., trans., "Daily Particular Examination of Conscience," *The Spiritual Exercises of St. Ignatius* (Westminster, Md.: The Newman Press, 1951), 15–17.

Bibliography

Further information about personal quality can be found in Roberts, Harry V., and Bernard F. Sergesketter. *Quality Is Personal: A Foundation for Total Quality Management*. New York: Free Press, 1993.

Tips for Student Teams

Willard I. Zangwill
University of Chicago

Several of the papers in this volume, including my "Fast Quality for Fast Results," make references to quality improvement projects using student teams. Although the total quality literature has volumes of material on team functioning, it is far too vast to easily wade through. Instructors unfamiliar with how to train teams may find the following guidelines useful. I review and discuss these with my students on the first day of class. Some of these guidelines were contributed by Harry Roberts when we jointly taught a course on best practices in total quality some years ago. Also, further ideas are included in the discussion of the PACER system, explained briefly in Zangwill and Roberts, "Academic Leadership from the Top: Total Quality for Higher Education."

In achieving a well-functioning team, perhaps the most crucial issue is to have clear and strong rewards for the group as a whole. Stated another way, if an individual on a team perceives that he or she will be rewarded for accomplishments different from the others, then trouble is highly likely. For that reason, unless there are compelling reasons otherwise, I generally give each member of the team the same grade.

One compelling reason a person may not receive the same grade as the others on the team is lack of contribution to the team. Since I am not aware of the team's detailed functioning and of exactly what any member contributed, however, I obtain feedback on that from the team members. At weeks 5 and 10 (of an 11-week quarter) each student team member grades the other members of the team as inadequate, good, or excellent. They confidentially submit that information to me.

It turns out that in well-functioning teams, most people rate each other as excellent. Occasionally, however, there will be a problem because a team member is reported by others to be uncooperative. My first response is to give the team members every encouragement and help to work out the problem. If the problem turns out to be intractable, I will reluctantly downgrade the uncooperative team member. Fortunately that seems to occur only about 2 or 3 percent of the time.

Excellent team functioning is also promoted if the team members understand the following concept: When the team members act as individuals, each person has no one except himself or herself as support. But when each team member helps the others and is supportive of all needs and ideas, then each team member has all the other team members for support. Indeed, it is when the team members are mutually supportive and interactive that the group takes on its unique power, energizing the team members and making them more creative and productive.

Consider the following specific suggestions for the team members to follow.

Group Management Suggestions

1. If you have an objection to a person's idea, do not bring it up as an objection. Instead raise it as a question, "How do we solve . . . ?

Bad: "That won't work due to the low profits."

Better: "In view of the low profits, how can we do that?"

Bad: "The union there will kill it."

Better: "The union there is tough; is there a way to gain its support on this issue?"

2a. Great ideas were born dumb. It is easy to criticize a new idea because it is not yet well-formulated. Resist the urge to criticize, instead, help the person to develop it.

2b. Listen. If a person wants to develop an idea, give him or her 10 minutes. Also help to explore it. Listening to others is very powerful, as this brief story demonstrates.

One team was in the midst of the final paper with three days to go, and one team member had an idea for a totally different approach. The other members groaned, but gave him 10 minutes to explain it. Then they helped him think how it could be accomplished. It took about 15 minutes, but the fractious team member became convinced that his new approach was impossible to do in three days. He then gave full effort to the project. The team members were convinced if they had not given him the full opportunity and support to explore his idea, he would never have changed his mind and become fully committed to the original approach.

3. Help another person when he or she needs help, even if you do not want to help. If each team member helps any other member when that member needs help, then everyone gets help and support when they need it. The result is exceptional group esprit and synergy.

4. The team will come up with much better and deeper ideas than you would by yourself. Team members helping each other will accomplish far more than the individuals would by themselves. Remember: you may be smarter and more able than any other member of the team, but you can't do as well as the team if it works effectively. This is especially true when it comes to brainstorming for new ideas.

5. Always debate and discuss ideas at length because in doing so deeper ideas will emerge. Never disparage, ridicule, reject, or not listen to another person's idea, as this behavior kills idea development.

6. If you feel a team member is not contributing properly or is shirking work, do not speak to him or her yourself. First confirm your perceptions with a third team member. Perhaps you are wrong. If your perceptions are confirmed, then two or three team members should speak to the noncontributor about correcting the problem. The impact will be greatly enhanced if two or three members express the view. When speaking to the person, be helpful and supportive, not critical.

The feedback to the instructor in weeks 5 and 10 on your teammates also helps to reign in an errant team member.

7. Written goals are very helpful. There are two main kinds.

Long-term general plan: When you begin work on a project, write down your plans for accomplishing the steps in the project with times and responsibilities.

Short-term detailed plan: At the end of each meeting, pass around a sheet of paper on which each person jots down what he or she is going to do prior to the next meeting.

8. Do not expect to get your way 100 percent of the time. Be persistent in your viewpoint to ensure it is well heard and considered. Thorough analysis of ideas helps, but do not be bull-headed. In well-functioning groups, you can get your way 95 percent of the time on the issues that you feel to be most important.

9. Successful teams generally require a group goal. One cannot have a successful group if the team members are pulled in different directions due to a perverse incentive system. That is why all members of the team, with minor exceptions, receive the same grade in this course.

People have mentioned that in other courses or in companies, teams often fail because the rewards are primarily individual. The team members then vie to get attention from the boss or instructor for doing a good job individually, and this destroys the group cooperation.

10. Continually reinforce the value of group work and the need to cooperate and listen to your teammates. During class I will frequently try to emphasize this point.

11. Group cooperation is fostered by the knowledge that you will have to work with your team members for a while, so you had better learn to get along. That is one reason to start working together immediately and to start working out group disagreements quickly.

Further Suggestions for Effective Team Performance

• Useful guidance on the functioning of effective teams can be found in *The Team Handbook: How to Use Teams to Improve Quality.*[1]

• Brainstorming techniques—expression of ideas without discussion or criticism—are often useful, especially in the early stages when the project is being defined.

• Brainstorming—and other team discussion—can be facilitated by the designation of one member (possibly rotating) as scribe. The scribe's duty is to summarize all discussion, as it proceeds, by summary statements on a flip chart. As flip chart sheets are filled, they are taped, in sequence, to the wall or blackboard. This permits viewing and reviewing of salient features of the discussion as it proceeds; it also greatly facilitates writing up a summary of the discussion afterwards or presentation of the team's thinking to others.

• The scribe should be as nondirective as possible, contributing to the discussion only when he or she thinks that a salient point is being overlooked by the team.

• It is possible to combine the role of scribe and team leader. (It keeps the leader from trying to dominate the team). The leader/scribe, however, should formulate in advance the questions to be discussed.

• All discussion should be aimed at clarification and suggestions before attempting persuasion.

• Disagreements should be resolved by appeal to data rather than by debates and appeals to authority.

• If the data aren't available, the team should arrange to get some. Don't try to jump from problem to solution without studying causation; study of causation is facilitated by data.

• Teams often benefit by having short meetings at regular intervals, with assignments to team members for tasks to be accomplished before the next meeting.

• The leader of the team should be responsible for a written agenda in advance of each meeting.

• One member of the team can be designated as secretary, with the task of preparing compact and timely minutes of meetings.

• At each meeting, one member can be designated as timekeeper with the responsibility of declaring that the discussion has become repetitious or contentious, so that the subject should be switched to what the team should do next. For example, the team might summarize agreements reached and tasks assigned, and then adjourn; or it might switch to the next item on the agenda.

• Scheduling of team meetings may pose a problem, especially as many other courses in the school of business require team projects, with a consequent preemption of many potential meeting times. One good time for most teams is the time immediately before and after class.

Note

1. Peter R. Scholtes, *The Team Handbook: How to Use Teams to Improve Quality* (Madison, Wis.: Joiner Associates, 1988).

Academic Leadership from the Top: Total Quality for Higher Education

Willard I. Zangwill and Harry V. Roberts
University of Chicago Graduate School of Business

Introduction

Suppose that you are a university president, provost, or dean and are confronting a difficult decision. Are there principles of quality management that might help you make that decision better? To explore this question, we conducted an informal benchmarking study of a small group of presidents, provosts, and deans. Benchmarking means a study of best practices in a given field. As applied to educational leaders, the first step is to identify leaders who are considered to be outstanding. The next step is to identify practices or techniques that make them excellent. The final step is to disseminate information on those practices to others who potentially can benefit from them. What we discovered is that these top academic leaders followed quality management principles, but often instinctively, not consciously aware that they were indeed practicing these principles. This paper outlines some of the principles of quality management our study uncovered, key principles that these leaders employed to reap superior results and attain excellence.

In conducting our study, however, we were aware of the conventional wisdom that presidents and deans can shape administration and external activities, yet can have only limited impact on the intellectual and academic mission of their institutions. Faculties are too independent, too powerful, and too resistant, many people feel, to heed attempts at academic leadership from the top. Any serious effort by a leader to do so can make the faculty bristle with resentment and distrust. As a president of the University of Chicago (Lawrence A. Kimpton) once put it, "When I put aside the beggar's cup I use in fund-raising and begin to twirl my Phi Beta Kappa key, there is general alarm."

Today resistance to the twirling of the Phi Beta Kappa key remains as firm as it was in Kimpton's time, but it is not totally unyielding. This paper will present some management principles the outstanding leaders employed to gain faculty support and to enhance the academic excellence of their institutions.

Of all the principles, one served as a foundation for many of the others and was clearly the most crucial: *strive to become the best by using innovation.* In other words, an institution should pursue becoming best in its market, area, or niche—best-in-class—and do so in innovative ways. These leaders perceived that pursuit of best-in-class reaps exceptional rewards. Indeed, even if the pinnacle of being best is not reached, as long the institution makes clear and noteworthy improvement, major benefits should accrue, as the recruitment of faculty and students and fund-raising should become more fruitful and easier.

As these top leaders also perceived, however, attempting to become best by going down the same old pathways followed by others is likely futile. Rather, to overcome the innumerable obstacles to becoming best, the institution has to blaze new paths, create new ideas, and innovate.[1]

Striving to become best through innovation is by no means a new theme. Throughout the history of higher education a standard way institutions upgraded themselves was through significant innovation. Johns Hopkins revolutionized medical education. Cincinnati instituted cooperative education. Antioch capitalized on having campuses around the world. Elliot transformed Harvard from a largely theological school to a modern university. The University of Chicago, Graduate School of Business, instituted the first executive MBA program. The Kent College of Law at Illinois Institute of Technology introduced exciting new programs and transformed itself from second-rate to highly regarded. The Kellogg Management School at Northwestern University moved rapidly from research mediocrity to research excellence. Fox Valley Technical College pioneered in total quality, thus sparking similar innovations at other technical and community colleges.

The process of striving to be best through innovation can be quite interesting. Consider when the University of Chicago decided in the mid-1980s to create a computer science department. By that time it was rather late to start such a department, since many other universities already had well-established computer science departments. As a result, for Chicago to attract top faculty from these places would be very difficult and very expensive, vastly more costly than possible within the budget. Hence, the dilemma—the same dilemma faced by nearly all university leaders trying to upgrade their institutions: how does one strive to become distinguished when the budget is inadequate and meager? The answer is that innovation is needed, a creative idea that allows the institution to pursue excellence inexpensively.

For the computer science department an innovative solution did emerge. It was decided to have a steady stream of visitors, some for a few days and others for much longer, luminaries from academia and industry who would conduct seminars and interact with the students and local faculty. Moreover, the visitors would not just be put in an office and forgotten, but interaction with the visitors would be a featured and major part of the program. In this way the computer science department almost instantly created a highly stimulating and exciting intellectual environment, without the huge expense of hiring a large number of faculty.

This theme of using innovation, new and creative ideas, to overcome monetary limitations is fundamental and will be seen repeatedly in the examples that follow. To put this theme into a more general perspective, we start with some key total quality principles for leadership.

Key Total Quality Leadership Principles

The leadership principles discovered in our informal benchmarking study harmonize well with total quality, even though most of the leaders did not explicitly have total quality in mind. We learned that their pursuit of becoming best through innovation was guided by several important total quality principles: goals, criteria, quick hits, and structured decisions.

Goals. Goals should be developed that spell out what best-in-class means for the particular institution, since best-in-class for a small college is different than for a large university. The selected goals should benefit the organization itself and those associated with it; should have the support of the key individuals needed to implement them; and should promote innovative, pathbreaking ideas. Also, if striving to become best-in-class is totally unrealistic for a given institution, then a goal of impressive, dramatic improvement should be pursued instead.

Criteria for evaluating programs. Goals are often stated abstractly, for instance, the goal of a chemistry department might be to become distinguished. That abstract goal should be fleshed out by having the developers of the program answer questions that define what the word *distinguished* means and how that goal will be achieved. For example,

How will the proposed program

—Attract top students?

—Attract top faculty?

—Attract funding?

—Become known as distinguished by key constituencies (other academics, the public, business and industry leaders, government leaders, and so on)?

How will the program accomplish these objectives on the inadequate budget allotted?

Often it is the provost or dean who should pose these types of questions. Moreover, it is important to pose these questions at the very beginning when the program is being conceptualized, since they help the developers of the program think through the key issues carefully and creatively.

Get a quick hit, get people moving. The planning of the program to become best can take a long time, perhaps a year or two. Many administrators make the mistake of waiting until the planning is virtually completed before taking any action. During that delay, however, criticism and opposition to the program likely will increasingly mount. Instead, get some quick hits; that is, even while the more comprehensive planning is going on, undertake some small projects virtually certain to be successful. The quick hits demonstrate tangible, definite progress, which helps counter criticism and gets people moving in the new direction.

Chris Galvin, president of Motorola, has noted that rational discussions rarely change opinion, but that experiences are what change opinion. The quick hits provide that experience and helps to convince people that becoming one of the best is well worth the effort.

Structured decision processes. Becoming best-in-class is almost impossible if there is significant dissension, yet in academia, decision making is frequently harmed by faculty disagreement and conflict. The cause of this conflict is typically the poor structure of most common decision processes, a loose structure that gives emotionalism almost free reign and allows it to easily overwhelm and defeat reason. A well-structured decision process, however, can help reason and rationality triumph, thereby ensuring a superior decision.

Often participants need to try a well-structured process two or three times before getting used to it, but then many people actually voice their pleasant surprise, sometimes amazement, at how much it helped. A well-structured decision process will thoroughly ferret out facts, clarify the criteria for making a decision, and foster a thorough and creative analysis. Structured processes should be employed for decisions from small to highly complex.

In the following sections we will see how these basic principles can foster innovation and help the institution become best in class. First, we look more closely at the goal principle.

Goals, Being Best, and Benchmarking

Systematically thinking about how to become best-in-class almost automatically promotes innovative thinking because it focuses attention on the possibility of radical change and major improvement. Further, as noted, institutions that strive to be best seem to reap a disproportionate amount of the benefits: they attract students, faculty, and funding.

Don Jacobs, dean of the Kellogg School at Northwestern, articulated that type of goal in his mission, "Be the number one business school in the United States." When Jacobs formulated that mission in the 1970s, the Kellogg School was a distinct also-ran. Jacobs recalls that when he announced his goal of being number one, he was openly laughed at and ridiculed, even by colleagues at Northwestern. But Jacobs refused to be discouraged, and, as we describe, instituted a number of innovative programs. As reflected in ratings by *Business Week*, Jacobs has met substantial success: in the biennial surveys of graduate business schools conducted in 1988, 1990, and 1992, Kellogg was ranked number one.

As another example, Joe White, dean of business, University of Michigan has (much more recently than Dean Jacobs) enunciated the goal of making his business school number one. Having that goal was very important, he states, since it provoked him to undertake a particularly risky and novel program, a program he would never have undertaken without that goal. Under the program all first-year MBA students, during the last seven weeks of the year, undertake a project in industry. Each student team is overseen by a cross-functional group of faculty members. The students are actively involved in a real project, but are still under the tutelage of the faculty. The program has been an outstanding success, not only helping the students, but helping to recruit new students and in finding jobs for the students.

The University of Minnesota Carlson School of Management wants to create the best program in total quality management. Pursuit of being best has promoted it to create interdisciplinary activities with other departments and to actively involve industry in cooperative activities.

The be-best principle may sound like empty exhortation—a slogan of the kind deplored by W. Edwards Deming. When taken seriously, however, what sounds like a slogan can help an organization target what is most important. For example, programs should be sufficiently focused to make a clear impact. When Stanford started its march to greatness a generation ago, provost Fred Terman called this the Pillars of Excellence strategy. He knew that one outstanding program is better than 10 mediocre ones, since that one outstanding program could act as an attraction to bring in students, faculty, and money, not just to itself but to the other, less-distinguished programs.

Money and Funding

Because money is so important, the point that outstanding programs attract funds is worthy of considerable attention. Even though becoming distinctive or best-in-class usually requires money, excellence attracts money. Indeed, institutions that are best or striving to be best-in-class have an advantage in fund-raising. Ted Marchese notes how, because they greatly improved themselves, Northeast Missouri State, James Madison, and Miami Dade Community College were able to boost their funding. Northeast Missouri, Marchese reports, has a more select student body than the University of Missouri and became designated as the state's liberal arts college, which brought in additional funds. Similarly, notes Richard Chait, the Weatherhead School of Business at Case Western Reserve University upgraded itself and thereby garnered additional contributions.

One of the most impressive examples was George Rupp during his eight-year tenure as president of Rice (he has since been installed as president of Columbia). At Rice he spearheaded a revamping of the undergraduate curriculum featuring new interdisciplinary centers that cut across traditional disciplines. In the lively educational environment that innovation created, funding for faculty research rose sharply. Moreover, this innovation helped him more than double the endowment from $500 million to $1.25 billion.[2]

If done adeptly, pursuit of being the best through innovation tends to bring in funds and to more than pay for itself. In our interviews with academic leaders, we had expected to hear that fund-raising was an all-consuming challenge. What we heard was that they felt successful fund-raising to be a by-product of educational innovations. For example, at the Kellogg Management School, a very small staff is devoted to development (the academic term for fund-raising), but fund-raising is going very well. Jacobs feels the best way to raise funds is to tell people stories about what exciting things are going on in the institution today and to tell them about plans for the future that will create an institution even greater than today. Arnold Weber, former president of Northwestern, also followed this approach and strongly emphasized its importance, pointing out the limited value of the approach in which a president seeks out and tries to charm an individual into donating.

Mission/Vision Statement

To apply the best-in-class concept, an excellent place to start is the institution's mission or vision statement, a declaration that describes what best-in-class means for a particular institution. Interestingly, as Ted Marchese has stressed, it is not important to have a written mission statement. What is important, however, is that the key individuals should agree with it and thus be guided in working together toward a common, understood goal.

This observation was confirmed by Chait, Holland, and Taylor in their pathbreaking study of what made trustees of universities successful or unsuccessful. The most important predictor they found was: Having a clearly defined mission and ensuring that the board's actions and decisions support that mission.[3]

As an example, consider how a trustee of a small college articulated his college's mission, adapted from Chait, Holland, and Taylor.

> This college is unique in this state. It is a top-quality, small, private liberal-arts college that provides individualized teaching and stresses excellence in all aspects of scholarship. The curriculum is varied but generally we combine pre-professional studies with a strong liberal arts foundation. We do have an athletics program, but it plays a supportive role, not dominating the campus as you see at some places.[4]

This statement clearly enunciates what this college means by being best-in-class, namely, top quality in liberal arts and unique in its state. By contrast, at the unsuccessful boards, Chait, Holland, and Taylor found that the trustees' notions of the mission were often bland generalities, such as "provide a good education," or "help the students develop into adults." Clearly, these statements contain little concept of pursuing best-in-class.

In short, a mission statement should express the institution's overall goals for becoming best-in-class. But even the most eloquent mission statement means little unless the key decision makers wholeheartedly agree with and vigorously pursue that mission.

Benchmarking

In the implementation of the mission, one of the most crucial pillars for becoming best-in-class is benchmarking. Benchmarking forces the institution's leadership to see what programs other institutions are undertaking, programs that are often more surprising and ingenious than had been realized. The thorough benchmarking study of other institutions by John White, dean of engineering at Georgia Tech, led him to make important revisions in funding of programs. John Brighton of Penn State and Robert Mehrabian of Carnegie–Mellon declare that benchmarking identified many opportunities for improvement of their institutions. This paper is itself an example of the information and insights a benchmarking study can obtain.

Complacency

Despite the value of the best-in-class principle, it is often resisted because nearly all faculties and trustees believe, honestly but mistakenly, that their institution is better and more renowned than it really is. Such complacency not only impairs motivation for improvement, but keeps people unaware of new and exciting ideas that are being pioneered elsewhere. The quality principle of management by fact directly addresses this issue, and proclaims that complacency should be fought by vigorously seeking facts. (Management by fact also can serve as a counter to another, equally debilitating attitude, namely that nothing can be done to improve our institution.)

As noted, benchmarking can very effectively obtain the facts about what other institutions are doing. Helpful also is to seek the knowledge and viewpoints of outside independent experts. One way to do this is a program review by outside experts, a powerful approach that will be described later. Surveys and focus groups of students, alumni, and even the general public can be beneficial, especially in unearthing opportunities that most faculty and administrators are unaware of.

For example, the Graduate School of Business, University of Chicago, employed surveys and focus groups to get the reaction of current students, prospective students, alumni, businesses who hire its students, faculty from other universities, and so on. The facts learned were contrary to what many faculty believed, yet they were enlightening and led to the establishment of new programs. It was discovered, for example, that students and alumni were appreciative of outstanding intellectual components of the MBA curriculum, but they keenly felt the need for more training in action skills, such as making presentations, working on teams, networking, and formulation of career strategies. This finding led in 1989 to the development of the LEAD program, an innovation that received considerable attention.

One might also compare different institutions, using data such as acceptance rate of students, percent of faculty members in national academies, placement of graduates, graduation rates, and so on. In this regard, time-series comparisons can be invaluable. For example, in the early 1950s the University of Chicago experienced a rapid enrollment decline. Tedious but simple statistical studies showed that this decline was unique to the University of Chicago: not a single college or university had experienced such a strong decline, either from the last pre–World War II year or from the peak of enrollment created by returning veterans in the late 1940s.

Further statistical detective work showed that the decline was almost surely attributable to the fact that a radical reorganization of the undergraduate college in the 1940s had not been successful, and that this failure had led to a massive loss of enrollment in the traditional junior and senior years, a loss that was disguised by the way in which enrollment statistics were kept. Chancellor Lawrence A. Kimpton launched a lengthy rollback of the college to normalcy. He was later credited with having saved the University of Chicago.

Creating a Sense of Urgency for Change

While facts can fight complacency, facts alone are rarely enough to make people change. A useful way to overcome complacency and resistance is to create a sense of urgency. At the Wharton School, University of Pennsylvania, Jerry Wind helped convince the faculty to adopt a major restructuring of the curriculum by convincing them that the school could not survive as it was presently constituted. He underscored that the time for change was then, while the school was still strong. That approach helped ignite the fires under people and convince them to support the new curriculum.

Marilyn McCoy, vice president of Northwestern, concurs with this approach and suggests presenting specific examples of how the present system does not work properly. The specific examples seem to bring home and make personal the fact that change is needed. In short, although change is difficult, it is useful to stress that continuing in the present way will soon cause even greater difficulties, so that change is really the easier path.

Comparative Advantage

Selecting the particular path to be best is very important. To do that, a leader can draw on a powerful concept from economics, the principle of comparative advantage. The idea is to emphasize not just activities that the institution can do well in an absolute sense, but activities that it can do well relative to competitive institutions.

To implement the principle of comparative advantage, leaders should examine the current or easily acquired capabilities of their own institutions in order to find niches that can be exploited to achieve distinction.

The following steps can help in the process of finding where the comparative advantages may lie.

- Determine the strengths and weaknesses of the institution or unit.

- Evaluate the competition, their strengths and weaknesses, and what they are likely to do.

- Assess future trends in students, research, funding, and other relevant areas. Apparently obvious sources of information such as demographic data on age groups in the population can be useful, but they are sometimes overlooked. Analysis of demographic trends was key to changes in the geographical emphasis in student recruitment at Carnegie-Mellon during the presidency of Richard Cyert.

- Speak to and gather information from key constituencies such as students, faculty, alumni, parents, business and government leaders, other educators, and funding agencies.

- Consider the costs of various approaches.

Richard Cyert at Carnegie–Mellon applied the principle of comparative advantage not only to the entire university, but to subunits right down to the departmental level. English, for instance, was a weak department when Cyert became president in 1972. It was a service department in a university that placed primary emphasis on engineering and science. Analysis showed that it would be virtually impossible to become one of the top departments in literature and literary criticism. Other schools had extensive libraries and other formidable advantages.

It was felt, however, that Carnegie–Mellon University could become one of the very best in rhetoric, defined as written communication. Also many of the engineering departments wanted the English department to help their students to write better. Thus rhetoric was determined as the area in which the English department could have a comparative advantage. Carnegie–Mellon then took the steps that placed it among the best two or three departments of rhetoric. Then it undertook to leverage its strength in rhetoric to improve its capabilities in literature.

Another example at Carnegie–Mellon was the mathematics department. Although some in the department aspired to emulate Harvard in pure mathematics, this goal was not easily reconcilable with the broader goals of the university in engineering and applied science. Led by George Fix, who said that he was "not taking the job to balance the budget," they were able to develop strength in applied mathematics, where they could and did rise to distinction.

Cyert required every department to do an analysis of comparative advantage and to develop a strategic plan that set forth their comparative advantage and how the department planned to become best-in-class. Such a plan was a prerequisite for an increase in departmental funding. Nearly always this plan required a great deal of creativity and innovation, and it included consideration of how the plan would contribute to bringing in more funding.

The pursuit of comparative advantage requires relentless dedication to the maintenance of standards. As we have seen, Cyert used his office and the power of the budget to goad departments to improve and seek distinction. His approach helped Carnegie–Mellon to become one of the outstanding schools in fields relating to computers and information.

Arnold Weber, when president of Northwestern, adopted a similar approach and strongly emphasized that the standards must be uncompromising. If a department suggested a program that did not exploit a comparative advantage, was not sufficiently innovative, was not cost-effective, or did not have support of key people, Cyert and Weber would not approve it. Instead they would work with the department to develop an appropriate plan.*

Measurement of Success

Ambitious goals and pursuit of comparative advantage are important, but we also need to evaluate progress toward the goals and to help in making policy decisions. One way is to ask "how would we know if" questions. For example, suppose the institution's goal were to become tops in engineering. Then the following questions can be posed.

- How would we know if we were tops in engineering?
- How would we know if we were making progress toward that goal?
- How would we know if we had the leading faculty?
- How would we know if we were attracting the best students?

The answers to these questions should provide criteria (measures, standards, guidelines) that should help in policy decisions and in moving the institution toward its goal. Further, having to answer these questions often promotes creativity and innovation.

Suppose, for example, that a small liberal arts college wants its biology department to become the best in the state. To evaluate progress toward that goal, the question might be posed: "How would we know if we had the best biology department

---

*The principle of comparative advantage may seem to suggest that some departments are hopeless and should be left to stagnate because a college or university cannot hope to be outstanding in everything. We once heard an administrative department admit and accept mediocrity on this ground. An important total quality theme, however, argues against defeatism, as with a little ingenuity and innovation almost any organization can make enormous improvement. See Zangwill, "Fast Quality for Fast Results," in this volume.

in the state?" The college might decide that, compared with any other college in the state, it would want

- To have a higher percent of all undergraduate students who select biology as a major
- To produce biology majors who obtain higher paying jobs or go to better graduate schools
- To have better laboratories and facilities in biology

For an application at the departmental level, consider the mission statement of Bruce Gewertz, chief of surgery of the University of Chicago Hospitals: "Deliver the highest quality patient care while fostering exceptional academic achievement by trainees and faculty." To evaluate progress toward this goal the following measures are being employed.

- Clinical measures: the number of regionally and nationally multidisciplinary programs, improvements in patient outcomes by complex measures, and increased clinical activity.
- Academic measures: the number of externally supported research grants, the number of peer-reviewed publications, the quality of residency applications, and the number of trainees choosing full-time academic careers.

Measures like these help Gewertz evaluate if his department is making progress toward its goals, and they are major inputs into the departmental decision process. These measures thus help to evaluate the department's progress toward being best-in-class.

Creating Alignment: Structured Decision Processes

We noted the need for the key constituencies to agree on the important goals and directions of the institution. In practice, however, there is almost universal difficulty of obtaining that agreement. A decision made to emphasize one faculty group generally means that other faculty groups will receive less emphasis. The English faculty who teach literature might not be delighted to learn that rhetoric will be emphasized over literature. And trouble is clearly ahead at a university where one strong group wants to stress adult education, another wants engineering, and a third wants a basketball championship. Richard Spies, vice president of Princeton observes, "It is remarkable how much progress can be made when administration and faculty cooperate. And how deadly and debilitating it can be when the administration and faculty conflict."

What is worse, as Mike Dolence of UCLA has stressed, many of the usual processes for deciding goals and making decisions actually foster disagreement. Even the formulation of the overall mission can lead to a sharp divergence of views with resulting dispute and dissension that can be paralyzing. "I think we ought to be more elite." "I think we should be more oriented to undergrads." "I think adult education should be stressed."

The principle of structured decision process addresses this problem directly, since obtaining general agreement on the plans and directions is perhaps the greatest challenge for the leadership. As Bill Bowen, former president of Princeton, expressed it, unless the major constituencies are of like mind about the general directions, "Rancor will follow all of your days."

Bowen instituted a structured decision process by establishing a Priorities Committee. The committee, founded in the late 1960s when Bowen was provost, set the funding priorities for the university. The committee included the financial vice president (Richard Spies for the first 15 years), had elected faculty members, and was chaired by the provost. The president was ex-officio and attended when his schedule permitted. There were frequent meetings at which deans and others made presentations. To make sure the committee operated with good facts and data, it had strong staff support, headed by the controller, to provide detailed financial and other analyses.

An example of the committee's work in the 1980s was its recommendation to make a major thrust in molecular biology, which was highly successful. One of the prime reasons for the committee's success, Bowen believes, was that the faculty members were elected, indicating that the university community held them in high regard. The Priorities Committee served excellently and still functions.

The Miller Model

For another example of a structured decision process, consider an intriguing example of budget allocation used in the 1970s at Stanford by Provost William Miller.[5] Miller's model starts with an explicit statement of the four criteria he used for evaluating proposals.

- Academic importance
- Student interest
- Possibility for excellence in the program
- Funding potential

Each year the various deans submitted proposals that Miller evaluated using these four criteria. Each proposal was supposed to address how well it satisfied the criteria and, if possible, to provide any data or documentation that might be helpful. Finally, Miller selected the proposals that he felt best met the criteria, and this set of proposals formed the budget.

The explicit statement of the four criteria promoted funding of those proposals that assisted Stanford to attain its goals. Also, the use of a formal approach reduced the importance of political clout or of emotional rhetoric. (The approach was administered flexibly with some exceptions permitted, since some proposals that rated poorly on the goal criteria will still be meritorious and deserve funding.)

The Miller model, by having explicit criteria, differs from most approaches to decision. Most people (including academics) tend to approach an issue by giving an opinion, hoping thereby to convince others that theirs is the most reasonable approach. That generates conflict. By contrast, total quality suggests that opinions should be given last. First the criteria on which to base a decision should be decided, as with Miller. Then data are collected and analyzed. Indeed, if the decision-making process is well designed, the final decision should arise out of the analysis, as a virtually obvious conclusion. What this suggests is the following approach in which the criteria for making a decision are decided first, then facts are gathered, brainstorming is carried on, and, finally, the decision is made. Specifically,

• *Decide the criteria for evaluating the options and making a decision.* The criteria for evaluating options and alternatives should be developed before everything else. We do not want people to determine the decision criteria after they make up their minds, as that will severely distort the decision. Rather the criteria should be decided first. Miller did this when he announced the criteria for evaluating budget requests ahead of time. As noted, that helped focus the budget proposals in the desired direction and simplified the decisions. And the same notion applies to almost any major decision. To formulate the criteria for evaluating the options, one key is to ask questions of the form, "how we would know" if we had achieved our goals.

• *Determine the facts, starting with the external environment and working in.* As mentioned, opinions are not acceptable; instead it is helpful to ask, "How do we know that?" And remembering the danger of complacency, start with the external environment. That might entail benchmarking, program review, and seeking opinions from outsiders.

• *Brainstorm and prioritize the ideas and options.* These approaches are well known in decision making and are essential tools of total quality. Like many other decision-making techniques, they are useful and effective, but often not used.

• *Make a decision by evaluating the options using the criteria developed in the first step.* This is perhaps the most difficult step for most participants, as it forces them to systematically examine their own ideas using criteria they previously agreed to. The emphasis on advance determination of decision criteria forces all participants to agree beforehand about how the various options or proposals will be evaluated, thereby reducing conflict and frustration later. In this way, the decision evolves as the reasonable conclusion of the steps taken.

Running Meetings

In implementing almost any decision-making approach, many individual meetings may be needed, and meetings also require structure. Most implementations of total quality provide simple ground rules for meeting structure and conduct, and we present a technique employed by a business organization, UOP. The technique is identified by the acronym PACER.

*P*urpose:	The purpose of the meeting should be clearly stated.
*A*genda:	An agenda is decided ahead of time with time allotments for discussion of each topic.
*C*ode of Conduct:	No put downs, no negativity, no side conversations, and all issues raised must pertain to the topic. If an important issue is raised not related to the topic under discussion, it is tabled for discussion later.
*E*xpectations:	Make the expectations of the meeting clear. Obtain agreement on what structured decision process will be used and what criteria will be employed for making decisions.
*R*oles:	Certain participants are given roles to help run the meeting. For example, a timekeeper tracks the time consumed discussing a topic. If that discussion exceeds the time allotted, the question is posed, "Is this topic important enough to continue, and if so, what topic do we delete from the agenda?"
	A facilitator helps keep the meeting on topic and ensures that everyone shows each other respect with absolutely no personal criticisms, put-downs, or negativism. Also he or she steps in when the participants get involved in a heated discussion and seeks to resolve the dispute.

Structured approaches to run meetings, like PACER, are often initially greeted with skepticism, but participants soon perceive that they are very effective. Meetings do not need to be frustrating and wasteful.

Minimizing Contention

Although running meetings more productively can help reduce dissension and gain support, much more important is a leader who is involved in extensive conversations and discussion. Many presidents, provosts, and deans continually interact and speak with students, alumni, and the faculty. Richard Cyert, however, went a step further. On a regular basis he met with the faculty of each different department for an extensive discussion. He used these sessions both to get across what his views were as well as to learn about the faculty's issues. He especially wanted to get the faculty thinking about how to make the department distinguished.

In particular, he usually asked questions such as, "Why would a student come to this department to study? What is special about this department and/or what is being done to make it special?" He used these sessions to foster consensus and agreement on goals and directions. Moreover, what he heard in these sessions often influenced his thinking about the funding and directions for the department. In this manner, Cyert prompted the faculty of a department to generate it own goals, thereby providing a decision process that is credible to those affected.

Support the Faculty

Although structured decision processes will likely help, nothing will bring harmony if the faculty is basically distrustful or resentful. Apparently minor issues like secretaries, classrooms, travel money, and small projects can cause irritation if not handled well. Lew Collens, when he was dean of the Kent College of Law at Illinois Institute of Technology, was delighted to assist faculty with their projects and requests. He wanted to encourage the faculty to explore new avenues and move ahead, so he made it easy for the faculty to do so.

The Graduate School of Business, University of Chicago, in an effort to simplify approvals, gave each faculty member a special individual budget to be used at the faculty member's discretion for books, travel, professional dues, secretarial support, or computers. One early effect was a sharp reduction in secretarial staff and a corresponding increase in individual computing equipment. Moreover, faculty made minor administrative decisions themselves, without the intrusion of administrators, with consequent saving of time that would otherwise be wasted by bureaucratic procedures.

Faculty, like other employees, appreciate considerate treatment by leaders. We stumbled across one simple example in which leaders are sometimes lax: the return of faculty phone calls. As Joe White, dean of business at Michigan, puts it, the faculty must be respected.

Program Review

We next consider a structured decision process that gathers the facts necessary for systematic strengthening of academic and administrative units and programs: program review. Arnold Weber, former president of Northwestern University, employed a program review because it minimized distortions and thereby helped to make better decisions. Although Weber has stepped down, his approach continues and a second cycle of reviewing all departments is well underway.

Program review is not a new concept, but the Northwestern approach has some appealing features. As program review is usually practiced, a group of reviewers analyze an academic department (or administrative unit) and report their findings. Quite different is the Northwestern approach, as it reviews a department using not one, but three separate groups of reviewers. First, the department reviews itself. Second, a team of three faculty members from other departments at Northwestern reviews the department. Third, a group from outside the university reviews the department. By conducting three separate examinations, Weber's approach obtains a more balanced view of the department.

To facilitate their investigation, the reviewers are provided considerable quantitative data, such as, quality of student, external funding, graduation rates, where graduates get jobs, and faculty research grants and publications.

The outsider reviewers, usually two of them, are selected to be as distinguished and knowledgeable as possible: Nobel prize winners, National Academy members, and so on. Weber especially stressed the importance of having excellent outside reviewers. The president cannot tell the physics department what it should do, Weber noted, because the physicists would retort, "You are not a physicist. What do you know?" But Weber can tell the physicists, "This Nobel prize winner from Columbia said you should do X."

The Northwestern review is targeted on upgrading and improving quality. Administrative as well as academic units are reviewed. Over the years the review process has exposed units that were weak and required reorganization or even closing, but those instances were few. In nearly all instances the reviews have helped to improve the unit reviewed, and, over time, faculty and staff have learned that the review process benefits them.

The Northwestern reviews help to improve quality, which contrasts sharply with many other program reviews. At many universities, performance reviews (whether explicitly stated or not) are designed to ferret out the "weak sisters" for cutting or to provide ammunition to justify budget reductions. But when the review is to help to wield the budget hatchet, people, fearful of the consequences, will not cooperate. Reviews designed to cut are likely to fail even to maintain quality, and they spawn resentment and distrust.

To further gain faculty support and commitment at Northwestern, a campuswide faculty committee directs the entire effort. The committee coordinates with the central administration, but faculty control strengthens the real objective, enhancing university quality.

Finally, the Northwestern reviews do not end up becoming just another unread report. Rather the president and provost carefully study the reviews, which not only underpin the planning for the future of the unit reviewed, but play a pivotal role in the upgrading of the university. In a study of program reviews, Lisa Mets, University of Michigan, determined that a program review activity will soon disintegrate if the faculty feel that all the effort they put into doing the reviews is disregarded or not being usefully applied to improve the program.[6]

Carnegie–Mellon Review Process

The Northwestern process, by using three reviews, provides excellent accuracy and strongly buttressed conclusions. Carnegie–Mellon University has a process that forgoes some of the precision and comprehensive scope of the Northwestern approach, but is simpler. According to its current president, Robert Mehrabian, instead of three separate reviews, Carnegie–Mellon employs only one. The review committee comprises approximately equal numbers of experts from outside the university and of faculty from other departments or schools at Carnegie–Mellon. The committee takes three days to conduct the review. Reviews are undertaken about every two and a half years. As at Northwestern, the Carnegie–Mellon reviews play a very important role because the president scrutinizes them and uses them to help allocate budgets.

Further Examples of Improvement by Top Leadership

To further illustrate the development of innovative new programs, we present several examples. Sometimes these programs can be exceptionally bold and novel such as Stanford University's decision to become one of the world's preeminent universities, and, in the process, to hire 150 star professors, develop an industrial park, and raise hundreds of millions of dollars. Most program efforts, however, will be on a much less grandiose scale. For example, consider the experiences of Lew Collens, when he was dean of Kent College of Law at the Illinois Institute of Technology.

Kent College of Law

When he became dean, Collens recalls, "We were very mediocre, and really could not come up with a reason why students should come here." He then developed a vision to be preeminent in some areas (the best-in-class principle), with those areas helping to gain attention and prestige for Kent as a whole. To obtain the necessary background facts, Collens spoke to numerous law firms, students, faculty, alumni, deans, and faculty from other law schools. Based on this information, Collens and his colleagues conceived and launched three programs.

Through his discussions, Collens learned that almost all law firms had the same complaint: law school graduates cannot write or research the law competently. To remedy that, Kent required that students take three full years of research and writing, which is more than any other law school.

Collens knew that the computer and information processing were going to dramatically change the practice of law. Also, Kent faculty already had one of the leading experts in that field. So, Collens decided to build on that strength to become a world center in that field.

Finally, Kent did something unique among law schools. It started a law firm within the college itself. Faculty would handle actual law cases and students would assist, thereby providing the students with experience with real cases under expert tutelage.

To get all three of these programs fully underway took years, but in this manner Kent launched three programs, each of which was unique and designed to be preeminent in its area. As these program were launched and grew, they attracted attention for Kent and helped bring in not only better students and faculty, but more funds. The programs were thus a fulcrum, helping to lever up the rest of the school. Moreover, since most of the faculty had interest in at least one of these three programs, nearly all of the faculty perceived a personal benefit from Collens's effort, and thus supported the programs.

QCEL at Illinois Institute of Technology

When he later became president of Illinois Institute of Technology, Collens designed an innovation based on the proposition that there are four fundamentals that all students should learn, quite apart from the specific intellectual content of the curriculum.

- Quality (essentially, concepts of total quality)
- Creativity and innovation
- Ethics
- Leadership

The acronym for these fundamentals is QCEL. The idea is that learning these fundamentals should help students to cope with the future challenges and uncertainties of life and work. What is special about QCEL is that, as much as possible, it works these four fundamentals into every course. For example, in a thermodynamics course, students will learn, in addition to the usual technical concepts, what thermodynamics has to do with quality, creativity, ethics, and leadership. Similarly, a literature course will devote at least some of the time to these issues. Presumably, by the time the student graduates, he or she will have approached these four issues from many perspectives and should understand them deeply.

Under QCEL, a few crucial themes are taught throughout an entire curriculum. Illinois Institute of Technology uses this approach as a selling point to prospective students, emphasizing how students are thoroughly exposed to concepts that should greatly foster their future well-being and success.

Kellogg School of Management

Many of the same patterns can be seen in the improvement of Northwestern's Kellogg Graduate School of Management, under Dean Don Jacobs. When Jacobs proclaimed the mission of making Kellogg the number one business school, nearly everyone else laughed. As we pointed out earlier, now Jacobs is doing the chuckling as Kellogg has moved into the ranks of the top business schools in the closely watched rankings.

Jacobs more or less single-handedly inculcated the goal of high-quality scholarly research. Jacobs was able to do this by exercising close personal control over the early faculty appointments of his administration. Funds were not available to hire top senior researchers, so Kellogg decided to hire promising youngsters and nurture them. Moreover, Jacobs personally oversaw the hiring and promotion to ensure standards were high.

The other essential component of Jacobs's strategy was to emphasize management and, thus (in Jacobs's view), to distinguish Kellogg from all other leading business schools. He felt that these schools emphasized research in specialized disciplines such as economics, finance, accounting, and management science, disciplines that were of greater interest to business school professors than to practicing managers.

In order to get the faculty interested in the management approach, Jacobs stressed relatively short courses—a week to a month—devoted to topics of management education of special interest to senior executives (those with much more substantial experience than the younger students found in the usual executive MBA programs). In that way the faculty would teach and interact with senior executives, learn about the problems they faced, and become more interested in management issues.

Jacobs also provided two financial incentives to the faculty: the extra compensation for teaching in these special short courses, and the plowback of revenues into the disciplines within the school that contributed these teachers. Thus, the incentive to learn more about managers and management was clear.

The emphasis on management permeated the MBA program as well, since Kellogg, under Jacobs, stressed teamwork in the classroom, the empowerment of students, and education in managerial skills as well as technical skills.

To attain his goal, Jacobs also needed to upgrade the student level, so he tried a novel tack. He made sure that all applicants were personally interviewed, often by Kellogg alumni, even though no other business school did that. At Kellogg, however, the interview was to serve two purposes. It not only evaluated the potential of the applicant; it also was a marketing tool aimed at selling the applicant on attending Kellogg. Kellogg wanted to be sure the applicant got an exciting description of the school, not just from a brochure, but from a person personally knowledgeable about the place. This extra sales effort increased the yield of accepted applicants who matriculated at Kellogg.

The LEAD Program

The LEAD program at the Graduate School of Business, University of Chicago, is designed to teach action and leadership skills to first-year MBA students. Although nongraded, LEAD is required and functions largely independently of the regular curriculum. The program is facilitated by faculty and administrators, but the central planning and execution is done by a team of second-year MBA students.

LEAD was conceived by then Deputy Dean Harry Davis to provide balance between intellectual training and action skills. Under his facilitation it was developed in only three months in the spring of 1989 and was implemented full-scale (not in a test version) for the new MBA class of 600 students in the fall of that year. LEAD has attracted national attention, and it has observably improved student satisfaction as measured on attitude surveys both inside and outside the Graduate School of Business. It has also apparently helped to raise the school's ranking in the *Business Week* survey: in 1992 Chicago was ranked second to the Kellogg School.[7]

3M Model

One approach worth mentioning comes from industry rather than academia. The 3M model captures the mode of operation of a famous and highly successful firm, 3M. At 3M innovation is the mission. Since the 1920s, employees have been encouraged to spend up to 15 percent of their time in developing new ideas on their own initiative. At any instant, a substantial fraction of company's sales comes from products that did not exist five years earlier. Division managers have goals for the numbers and sales of new product innovations, and innovative employees are rewarded and promoted. The organizational culture has been shaped to promote innovation, with the objective of speeding the development of successful innovative products. According to the 3M philosophy, if the right incentives and culture are provided, employees will burst forth with innovation after innovation and propel the company to success.

The 3M model is well suited for academic institutions, especially given the rapid changes of markets, competition, and technology that are affecting higher education today. Many of the top educational institutions follow it closely. The model is appropriate because faculty are ordinarily in a better position to innovate than are the administrators. The administrator's role is to develop the environment and incentives that stimulate faculty innovation. Thus energized and supported, the faculty themselves will create the new programs, develop the fascinating courses, and conduct the excellent research. In particular, it is important that the administrators make innovation easy; as an example, they should eliminate cumbersome and lengthy approval processes. (For other examples of administrative encouragement of innovation, see Roberts, "Grassroots Total Quality in Higher Education: Some Lessons from Chicago," in this volume.)

A Checklist for Innovative Academic Programs

From the framework and examples developed in earlier sections, we now formulate a suggested checklist. Rarely can a program satisfy all the points on the checklist, but successful programs seem to embody many of the points.

• *Does the program strive to be best-in-class?* The program should aspire to making the institution (or subunit) preeminent, at least in certain important areas. Pursuit of preeminence enhances creativity and innovation, as well as enthusiasm.

• *Will the program likely attract external funding and money?* One of the virtues of innovative programs, particularly in difficult financial times, is that they can attract money. More funds will likely flow to innovative programs than to retreads.

• *Will the program likely attract faculty or students?* If the program is really unique and special, it will probably attract faculty and students.

• *What is in it for the faculty?* Faculty support is essential so the incentives to enhance faculty interest in the program should be clear. The professional school initiatives by Collens and Jacobs that we described earlier included incentives to interest faculty and thereby to reduce dissension and gain support. Typical incentives include more money, more facilities or equipment, a more exciting and stimulating environment, and so on.

• *Is the program exciting?* The program should create excitement and fun, and be highly stimulating for the participants. Excitement and fun are often overlooked, hidden ingredients, yet few innovations are successful without them.

• *Will a vigorous champion spearhead the program?* The program should have a champion who will not readily accept failure. The champion will shepherd the program through difficult times and maintain the standards. (Any compromise of standards makes it harder to become known as unique and preeminent, and to reap the benefits of being so). Both Weber at Northwestern and Hanna Gray at the University of Chicago spoke of the difficulty of obtaining effective faculty champions for new programs. Gray spoke tongue-in-cheek of faculty members who wanted to be "entrepreneurs in a welfare state," that is, to suggest bold new ideas, while expecting administrators to raise funds and bring the ideas to realization.

• *Will the program generate good publicity for the institution?* Exemplary programs will be more valuable if people hear about them.

• *Will the key target groups perceive the program as special, unique, and worthy of their support or involvement?* Very often the people who develop a program believe it is special and unique. But others may not agree. In developing a program, it is therefore important to obtain input from the relevant target groups (prospective students, funding sources, faculty at other institutions) to check if they share the belief that the program will be special, unique, and best-in-class.

Downsizing

This paper has been written at a time of near-universal reductions in funding of colleges and universities. Nevertheless, of the leaders we have studied, a number were able to innovate even in the midst of economic austerity, cutbacks, and budget crises. Their experience runs counter to the common belief that times of crisis are not times to pioneer new strategies, that survival must come first. This belief seems especially compelling during a period when many leading colleges and universities are having their budgets slashed, sometimes 10 percent to 20 percent, and the future looks foreboding and bleak.

But innovation can be an appropriate response even to hard times. Many of our top leaders realized that excellent educational innovations and initiatives can make it easier to cope with financial problems. As Richard Cyert repeatedly stressed to his administrators, "We cannot use an economic downturn as an excuse." Cyert assumed leadership at Carnegie–Mellon in the early 1970s when three consecutive deficits had been incurred. The trustees were very much concerned about the deficit. He told them that the deficit could be easily controlled (he did so in his first year), but that the real challenges lay elsewhere, in improving the institution. Cyert understood that during cutbacks people can get discouraged, and a vicious downward cycle of discouragement and disappointment can be set spinning. Rather, the best way out of a crisis is to inspire and excite people with new concepts, new strategies, and new programs. In balancing the budget, Cyert cut some areas a bit more than absolutely necessary, to provide funds for innovation. The innovative new programs renewed hope, and they often attracted new funds, thus helping to ease the budget crisis for all programs.

Innovation and Austerity

Financial austerity poses obstacles to innovative leadership, but there is often a potential for surmounting them. Given thoughtfulness in defining goals—vision and mission—budget reduction is less likely to be needed; if unavoidable, it can be done more effectively.

- An institution that is innovative and moving ahead will generally suffer less severe budget problems because, as we have mentioned, individuals and funding agencies like to invest where something special is happening.

- Having a clear mission and direction will help focus and promote innovative ideas that can alleviate the budget problems.

- When budget cutting is necessary, clear mission and direction should make the budget reduction, however difficult, a bit easier.

Relative to cost reduction, an additional lesson of total quality is the existence of enormous, though often nonobvious, wastes in nearly all processes in nearly all organizations. Colleges and universities are no exceptions. George Keller, University of Pennsylvania, notes that there are many ways to achieve budget reductions that have little impact on the academic functioning, teaching and research. This claim seems counterintuitive, but there is ample precedent in the business sector, where companies like Xerox and Motorola had to cut out large amounts of waste to cope with Japanese competition.

Institutions of higher education probably have, on balance, more waste than Xerox or Motorola in the early 1980s when the full force of the Japanese threat was being felt. Many colleges and universities have begun to use total quality to reduce waste in administrative processes; similar opportunities exist in academic processes. We now explore some of them.

Greater Efficiency in Teaching

Nearly five years ago, a challenge was issued to academia that is beginning to evoke a response. At the Xerox Total Quality Forum of 1989, attending deans and professors from business schools were urged to introduce total quality courses into MBA programs. There was agreement on the desirability of the goal, but the academics saw formidable obstacles: MBA curricula were already packed full, they said. Several other new areas were contending for inclusion: international business, business ethics, environment, diversity, regulation, and so on. How could they possibly make room for TQM? What would they have to give up? Bob Galvin, then chairman of the board of Motorola, challenged the group to teach 50 percent more in a year (see Bateman and Roberts, "Total Quality for Professors and Students," in this book.)

In 1994, five years after Galvin's challenge, there is serious discussion of achieving academic objectives in shorter time: one-year MBA programs instead of two, and four-year engineering programs instead of the de facto five. Moreover, there has been an upsurge in efforts to apply tools of total quality to the improvement of teaching, and there is interest in using the same tools for the improvement of research. (See Bateman and Roberts, "Total Quality for Professors and Students," and Roberts, "Grassroots Total Quality in Higher Education: Some Lessons from Chicago," in this volume.) Such innovations may not only greatly improve the efficiency and effectiveness of teaching and research, they may provide new opportunities for handling meager budgets.

Involve the Faculty

Keller of Pennsylvania also highlights another powerful means of budget reduction, that of involving the faculty and exposing them to the reality of the budget numbers. The faculty, being bright and creative, often suggest ingenious ways to cut the budget.

Keller also mentions that this approach of mobilizing the faculty to ease budget problems, while often very successful, may require that the faculty receive some education in financial matters beforehand. For example, it is important for the faculty to understand that the endowment is not something that should be employed to solve routine deficits. Also, there is a danger that some faculty might want to reduce certain vital administrative services, such as admissions, student housing, or student aid, before they cut activities related to their own teaching or research.

An even more important faculty contribution may be in helping to raise funds. Bill Nowlin of Rochester Institute of Technology notes that in one department the faculty was made aware that 25 percent of their revenue came from service courses taught for other departments. Armed with that information, the faculty started to visit other departments, learn their needs, and develop even more service courses.

But the potential of the faculty is perhaps most promising in raising funds from external sources. Obtaining research grants from foundations and government agencies has long been regarded as part of faculty job specifications, and most research faculty acquire considerable skill at this tedious process. But faculty are much less frequently involved in more general fund-raising efforts—especially those aimed at unrestricted funds, funds that can be used for any purpose deemed important, not just a specific department, research proposal, or building. At large research universities, fund-raising is the province of professional fund-raisers and the most senior administrative leadership. But more teamwork between professional fund-raisers and faculty is certainly worth exploring. This kind of fund-raising by faculty might be seen as equally important with seeking research grants, which is now felt to be a major faculty responsibility.

Catastrophic Reductions

If your college or university has undergone a really severe budget cut, you might be reading this section with a bit of cynicism. No amount of innovation or striving to be best-in-class can immediately compensate for such a massive slashing of funds. We, ourselves, have not had major administrative responsibilities in higher education. We do not minimize the difficulties posed by downsizing, nor deny that a sufficiently large downsizing program can virtually decimate an institution. We are also mindful that many, though not all of our illustrations, are drawn from private universities. Our discussion with Tom Wallace, president of Illinois State University at Normal, suggested that a total quality initiative by a public institution faces more serious obstacles than a similar initiative at a private institution. Boards of public colleges and universities have to reconcile broad and conflicting political pressures, and they cannot always give strong support to policies advocated by presidents and faculties, as, say, Arnold Weber's board when he was president of Northwestern. John Heilbron of the University of California at Berkeley has suggested that we would find something like nuclear destruction if we look at public higher education in California.

Severe budget slashing might even force entire departments to be closed. It should emphasized, however, that it is easy to make serious errors when cutting back academic departments. Princeton decided to eliminate its East European studies department because it was very costly, requiring the teaching of many languages and a specialized library. Soon thereafter, however, the Berlin wall came done, and Princeton was bereft in one of the hottest and most important international areas.

What we have observed, however, is that innovation can not only ease the pain and difficulty of enormous cuts, but prevent some of it. Suppose, for instance, the state legislature cuts the state's contribution massively. Even in that case, as mentioned, institutions striving to be best generally have an easier time raising funds, so can more easily cushion the cuts. Further, innovation often suggests novel means to raise funds. Curt Tompkins, president of Michigan Technological University, notes that he got deans and department heads involved in fund-raising. Soon thereafter someone suggested that trustees get involved with individual departments, to assist in the fund-raising. Each trustee chose the department he or she preferred. Never before had trustees coordinated with individual department heads and faculty about how to jointly raise money.

Finally, total quality principles suggest that cost reductions can be obtained without catastrophe. If an organization downsizes by focusing on workforce reduction, performance is indeed almost sure to suffer. But if downsizing is sought through applying quality principles to reduce cycle time and error rates, costs will be reduced and performance will be improved. These principles are supported by empirical studies.[8]

Summary

Our informal benchmarking study suggests that outstanding top academic leaders, often intuitively, draw on principles and ideas of total quality in seeking educational leadership. Perhaps the most important of those principles is that of striving to be best through innovation. Attempts to become best tend to lead to innovation, since new ideas and new programs are often the fastest and least costly way to elevate an institution. Indeed, the potential for improvement exists even—perhaps especially—in times of financial austerity. Striving to be best, even if it is not fully attained, does more than just improve an institution, it adds life, excitement, and intellectual stimulation—all essential requirements of an outstanding educational environment.

Notes

1. Willard I. Zangwill, *Lightning Strategies for Innovation* (New York: Macmillan, Lexington Press, 1993).

2. "The Making of Columbia's Eighteenth President," *Columbia: The Magazine of Columbia University* (winter 1994): 23.

3. Richard Chait, Thomas P. Holland, and Barbara E. Taylor, *The Effective Board of Trustees* (New York: American Council on Education; New York: Macmillan, 1991).

4. Ibid., 15.

5. Ellen Earle Chaffee, "The Role of Rationality in University Budgeting," *Research in Higher Education* 19, no. 4 (1983): 387–406.

6. Lisa A. Mets, "Departmental Responses to Program Review Recommendations: Planning Strategies and Quality Improvement Efforts" (paper presented at SCUP-28, Boston, Mass., July 1993.)

7. John A. Byrne, "The Best B-Schools," *Business Week*, 26 October 1992, 60.

8. Kim S. Cameron, Sarah J. Freeman, and Aneil K. Mishra, "Downsizing and Redesigning Organizations," in *Organizational Change and Redesign*, ed. George P. Huber and William H. Glick (New York: Oxford University Press, 1993), 19–63.

Index